MANAGEMENT SCIENCE:
QUANTITATIVE METHODS IN CONTEXT

The Wiley Series
in Management

MANAGEMENT SCIENCE:
QUANTITATIVE METHODS IN CONTEXT

Lee J. Krajewski
Ohio State University

Howard E. Thompson
University of Wisconsin—Madison

John Wiley & Sons

New York   Chichester   Brisbane   Toronto

Library of Congress Cataloging in Publication Data:

Krajewski, Lee J
  Management, science.

  Includes bibliographical references and indexes.
    1. Decision-making—Mathematical models.
2. Operations research.   I. Thompson, Howard Elliott,
1934–   II. Title.
HD30.23.K7   658.4′034   80-17103
ISBN 0471-06109-3

Printed in the United States of America

10 9 8 7 6 5 4 3 2 1

ABOUT THE AUTHORS

Lee J. Krajewski is chairman of the Quantitative Methods Coordinating Committee and professor of management sciences in the College of Administrative Science at the Ohio State University. He is also director of the Executive MBA Program. Krajewski received his Ph.D. in business, M.S. in production, and B.S. in mathematics at the University of Wisconsin—Madison. He has developed and taught graduate and undergraduate courses in quantitative methods, production and operations management, and statistics. Krajewski is an active member of the American Institute of Decision Sciences, the Institute of Management Sciences, and the American Production and Inventory Control Society and has reviewed numerous articles for their journals. He is editor of the *Journal of Operations Management*. A frequent contributor to research journals, he received the Ohio State University Alumni Distinguished Teaching Award.

Howard E. Thompson is professor of business at the University of Wisconsin—Madison. He has B.S. and M.S. degrees in mathematics from the University of Wisconsin and a Ph.D. in business from the same institution. Thompson is the author or coauthor of two previous books on the application of mathematics to business problems and over 40 articles in professional journals. His papers have appeared in *Management Science*, *Operations Research*, the *Bell Journal of Economics*, *Naval Research Logistics Quarterly*, *Decision Sciences*, as well as the *Journal of Business*, *The Journal of Finance*, the *Journal of Financial and Quantitative Analysis*, the *Journal of Risk and Insurance* and others. He reviews papers for eleven scholarly journals and is a member of eight professional associations. He has extensive consulting experience and has provided expert testimony before federal courts and regulatory bodies and before state regulatory commissions. He has served as mathematician and operations research analyst at A. O. Smith Corporation and was visiting professor of management science at Ohio State University. He was elected a full member in the Operations Research Society of America in 1968.

PREFACE

Management Science: Quantitative Methods in Context is designed for students who aspire to be managers in the private or public sectors or for staff consultants to those managers. Emphasis is given to the *application* of the various quantitative techniques most often practiced today as opposed to a theoretical development. The chapters typically begin with the statement of a decision problem followed by an analysis of the problem using quantitative techniques. The theory is introduced as needed within the context of the decision-making process. Although all of the necessary theory for each quantitative technique is presented as generally as possible, the text emphasizes the rigor of the decision-making process and provides a liberal amount of intuition relating to the theoretical development.

As instructors of management students, our philosophy is that quantitative techniques can provide both useful and invaluable inputs to the decision-making process; if a quantitative technique cannot be shown to be useful in practice, it has only marginal benefits in a curriculum designed for pragmatic students. This text conveys our philosophy and incorporates our experiences with management students and practicing managers in all fields of interest. The text starts slowly, laying a solid foundation in the fundamentals and process of decision making, ensuring that the nature of the problem is clearly understood before the methods are applied. Part I, consisting of the first three chapters, provides an overview and framework for the material to follow. Chapter 1 introduces the decision-making process within the context of a decision problem faced by a small manufacturer engaged in prefinishing doors, door and window moldings, wainscoting strips, and other decorative wood for building-material suppliers. Through an analysis of the financial statements of the firm, several alternatives aimed at increasing profits are enumerated and evaluated. By means of this example the essential elements of the decision-making process (problem recognition; specification of objectives, performance measures, and constraints; model construction; enumeration of alternatives; prediction of outcomes; alternative selection) are demonstrated.

Chapters 2 and 3 are also philosophical in nature. Chapter 2 discusses the formulation of the measures of effectiveness for a decision problem, again by use of simple examples. The role of uncertainty in this phase of the decision-making process is also demonstrated and discussed. Chapter 3 addresses the model-building process, emphasizing the importance of identifying the proper model form to use in a decision problem and stressing the iterative nature of model building. By the end of Part I the student has the proper foundation to begin the study of quantitative techniques. All too often this important material is de-emphasized in management science texts, unfortunately leading to many mis-applications of the quantitative techniques and to undesirable consequences.

Parts II and III of the text are concerned with building models for common decision problems and with the techniques used to solve the problems. Part II is confined to deterministic models applicable to decision problems in which risk is of minor importance and can be ignored. Part III covers stochastic models or decision problems in which it is unreasonable to ignore risk. In Parts II and III the optimization techniques implicitly enumerate the alternatives and select the one considered best.

The purpose of the layout for Parts II and III is to begin with the deterministic techniques and finish with the stochastic techniques, thus permitting a continuity of flow for the material and allowing the student to study a group of techniques under a unifying set of assumptions. Although the chapters do not have to be presented in any particular order, each chapter provides incentive to study the next. The chapters motivate the study of the techniques by presenting them in the context of realistic decision problems and by demonstrating the usefulness of sensitivity analysis in providing important information for decision making.

The last chapter emphasizes the role of quantitative methods in the total decision-making process. Although they are an important element in the analysis of the problem, the quantitative inputs must be reconciled with the inputs of other sources before a final decision is made. The feedback and control process is also discussed in this concluding chapter.

Management Science: Quantitative Methods in Context is intended for students interested in learning the most commonly used management-science techniques within the context of realistic decision problems. The text exists at several levels, depending on the mathematical background and maturity of the student. For those students with little or no background in calculus we recommend skipping Chapter 9 (Classic Optimization) and Section 12.5 of Chapter 12 (Dynamic Programming). In addition, Section 2.3 of Chapter 2 (Objectives, Performance Measures, and Constraints) and parts of Section 13.1 of Chapter 13 (Decisions Under Risk, Dynamic Decision Problems, and Dynamic Programming) contain some calculus, but these parts can be skimmed. In general, Chapters 12, 13, and 14 require some calculus but this poses no difficulty with appropriate help from the instructor. There is no loss in continuity with the omission of the recommended chapters and sections.

Students with a modest background in differential and integral calculus should not be uncomfortable with any of the chapters in this text. Although Chapter 9 and Section 12.5 of Chapter 12 are the most demanding parts of the text, they were designed with these students in mind.

Students with substantial background in mathematics should also find the text useful because it emphasizes the *applications* of methods in management decision making. We have taken care to introduce each area within the context of a realistic problem and to provide insights into how the mathematical technique meshes with the characteristics of the problem itself.

The text is designed for students with varying degrees of mathematical maturity. It is appropriate for introduction to operations-research courses at the junior, senior, and master's levels. It should be used by business-administration, public-administration, and engineering students where the emphasis is on the application of management-science techniques within the context of the decision-making process.

Finally, we wish to thank the many people who have provided help and encouragement to us in this undertaking. In particular, the detailed reviews and suggestions provided by John P. Evans of the University of North Carolina and Richard M. Soland of the University of Montreal were a constant source of encouragement and enlightenment throughout this project. We also thank several people who reviewed the manuscript: Robert Abrams, University of Illinois; J. B. Anderson, Seattle University; Barry Pasternack, Boston University; Kenneth Ramsing, University of Oregon; Annie Thomas, New York University; Ed Wasil, University of Maryland. Of course, the masterful job that Valerie Hamre and Linda Tkac did transforming illegible handwriting into readable manuscript cannot be overstated. Last, but certainly not least, we express our loving appreciation to Judy Thompson and Judie Krajewski for their patience and understanding during our prolonged sequestration. Even with all of this help we, as authors, must take full responsibility for the content of this manuscript.

Lee Krajewski
Howard E. Thompson

CONTENTS

PART I RATIONALE AND OVERVIEW   **xxii**

CHAPTER 1 THE DECISION PROCESS AND DECISION MAKING   **2**

1.1 PREFINISHING CORPORATION   **3**

1.2 THE DECISION-MAKING PROCESS   **5**

Problem Recognition   6

Specification of Objectives, Performance Measures,
and Constraints   7

Model Construction   8

Enumeration of Alternatives   8

Prediction of Outcomes   9

Alternative Selection   9

Data Collection   10

1.3 THE DECISION-MAKING PROCESS APPLIED TO PREFINISHING   **12**

Problem Recognition   12

Specification of Objectives, Performance Measures,
and Constraints   12

Model Construction   12

Enumeration of Alternatives   13

Prediction of Outcomes   14

Alternative Selection   16

1.4 THE CONTINUING PROCESS OF DECISION MAKING   **17**

References   18

Review Questions   18

CHAPTER 2   **OBJECTIVES, PERFORMANCE MEASURES, AND CONSTRAINTS**   **20**

2.1   **WHAT IS A GOOD DECISION?**   **21**

2.2   **MEASURES OF EFFECTIVENESS**   **26**

Measures of Effectiveness for Low-Level Decisions   26

Measures of Effectiveness for Intermediate-Level Decisions   27

Measures of Effectiveness and Constraints   30

Measures of Effectiveness for Top-Level Decisions   31

2.3   **THE CONCEPT OF UTILITY AND MEASURES OF EFFECTIVENESS**   **31**

Utility of Wealth and Decisions Involving Uncertainty   31

Measures of Effectiveness in Business Decision Making   36

2.4   **SUMMARY**   **37**

References   38

Review Questions   38

Problems   39

CHAPTER 3   **MODELS AND MODEL BUILDING**   **42**

3.1   **WHAT IS A MODEL?**   **43**

Model Components   43

Why Build Models?   44

3.2   **A CLASSIFICATION OF MODELS**   **45**

Verbal Models   45

Physical Models   46

Mathematical Models   46

3.3   **A CLASSIFICATION OF MATHEMATICAL MODELS**   **47**

Deductive Consequences   47

Time Dimension   48

Degree of Uncertainty   49

3.4   **THE MODEL-BUILDING PROCESS**   **51**

Problem Recognition   51

Specification of Objectives, Measures of Effectiveness, and Constraints   52

Formulating the Model   52

Validating the Model   56

3.5   SUMMARY   **58**

References   59

Review Questions   60

Problems   61

PART II   DETERMINISTIC MODELS   **64**

CHAPTER 4   INTRODUCTION TO LINEAR OPTIMIZATION   **66**

4.1   LINEAR PROGRAMMING MODELS   **67**

The General Linear Programming Model   67

A Portfolio-Investment Problem   68

Assumptions of Linear Programming   70

Applications of Linear Programming   71

4.2   BASIC CONCEPTS IN LINEAR PROGRAMMING   **73**

Maximization Problems   74

Minimization Problems   84

4.3   SHADOW PRICES   **88**

Calculation of Shadow Prices   88

Use of Shadow Prices   93

4.4   SUMMARY   **96**

References   97

Review Questions   98

Problems   99

CHAPTER 5   LINEAR PROGRAMMING: THE SIMPLEX METHOD, DUALITY, AND THE DECISION PROCESS   **106**

5.1   THE SIMPLEX METHOD   **107**

Maximization Problems   108

Minimization Problems   119

Review of the Simplex Method   123

5.2	**DUALITY**	**125**
	The Primal-Dual Relationship	125
	Economic Interpretation of the Dual Surplus Variable	127
	Duality Theorems	127
	Computational Advantages of the Dual	130
5.3	**MODELING CONSIDERATIONS**	**133**
	No Feasible Solution	134
	Unbounded Solution	136
	Degeneracy	138
	Multiple Optima	140
5.4	**POSTOPTIMALITY ANALYSIS**	**141**
	Objective Coefficients of Nonbasic Variables	141
	Objective Coefficients of Basic Variables	143
	Right-Hand Sides	144
	Technical Coefficients	149
5.5	**MULTIPLE OBJECTIVES**	**150**
	Generating Noninferior Solutions	150
	Incorporating Preferences	152
5.6	**SUMMARY**	**155**
	References	157
	Review Questions	158
	Problems	159
CHAPTER 6	**THE TRANSPORTATION MODEL**	**166**
6.1	**THE PROPERTIES OF THE TRANSPORTATION MODEL**	**167**
6.2	**THE STEPPING-STONE AND MODI METHODS**	**170**
	Problem Identification, Data Gathering, and Specification of Objectives	170
	The Linear Programming Model	172
	The Stepping-Stone Method	173
	The Modified-Distribution (MODI) Method	189
	Review of the Stepping-Stone and MODI Methods	195
	Special Modeling Considerations	196

6.3	**SUMMARY**	**201**
	References	202
	Review Questions	203
	Problems	203

CHAPTER 7	**INTEGER PROGRAMMING METHODS**	**212**
7.1	**EXAMPLES OF INTEGER PROGRAMMING MODELS**	**214**
	Capital Budgeting	214
	Plant Location	215
	Production Scheduling	216
7.2	**CUTTING-PLANE METHOD**	**218**
	Steps in the Cutting-Plane Method	219
	Summary of the Cutting-Plane Method	226
	Practical Considerations of Cutting-Plane Methods	227
7.3	**BRANCH-AND-BOUND**	**228**
	Steps in the Branch-and-Bound Method	228
	Finding the Optimal Solution	233
	Summary of the Branch-and-Bound Method	237
	Practical Considerations of Branch-and-Bound Methods	239
7.4	**SUMMARY**	**240**
	References	240
	Review Questions	241
	Problems	242

CHAPTER 8	**METHODS OF NETWORK ANALYSIS**	**248**
8.1	**NETWORK MODELS**	**249**
	Network Terminology	249
	Applications of Network Models	250
8.2	**SIMPLE NETWORK-OPTIMIZATION METHODS**	**251**
	Shortest-Route Problem	251
	Maximal-Flow Problem	258
8.3	**PROJECT PLANNING AND CONTROL METHODS**	**264**
	The Critical-Path Method	264
	The Program Evaluation and Review Technique	273
	Review of Project Network Methods	277

8.4   SUMMARY   **277**
    References   278
    Review Questions   279
    Problems   279

CHAPTER 9   CLASSIC OPTIMIZATION   **290**

**9.1   OPTIMIZING FUNCTIONS OF ONE DECISION
    VARIABLE**   **291**
    Some Examples of Optimization Using Single-Variable
    Calculus   291
    First and Second Derivatives and Optimization   300
    Convex and Concave Functions   302
    An Additional Comment   303

**9.2   UNCONSTRAINED OPTIMA FOR FUNCTIONS OF
    MANY VARIABLES**   **304**
    Partial Derivatives, Total Differentials, and Maximization   304
    Maximizing Functions of Many Variables   310

**9.3   CONSTRAINED OPTIMIZATION: EQUALITY
    CONSTRAINTS**   **311**
    The Lot-Size Model With Equality Constraints   311
    The Stock-and-Bond Investment Problem with Equality
    Constraints   317

**9.4   CONSTRAINED OPTIMIZATION:
    INEQUALITY CONSTRAINTS**   **319**

9.5   REVIEW AND SUMMARY   **320**
    References   321
    Review Questions   322
    Problems   322

PART III   STOCHASTIC MODELS   **326**

CHAPTER 10   QUEUING THEORY   **328**

10.1   STRUCTURE OF QUEUING PROBLEMS   **329**
    Input Source   330
    Queue   335
    Service Facilities   335

Decision Variables 338

Outcomes 339

10.2 THE EXPONENTIAL DISTRIBUTION AND THE BIRTH AND DEATH PROCESS **339**

Characteristics of the Exponential Distribution 340

The Birth and Death Process 341

10.3 QUEUING MODELS BASED ON THE SIMPLE BIRTH AND DEATH PROCESS **344**

Case 1: Single Server 345

Case 2: Multiple Servers 346

10.4 MODIFICATIONS TO THE ASSUMPTIONS OF THE SINGLE-SERVER MODEL **348**

Unspecified Service-Time Distribution 348

Finite Input Source 350

10.5 THE ROLE OF QUEUING MODELS IN THE DECISION-MAKING PROCESS **351**

The Design of a Banking System Using Queuing Theory 351

Objectives, Performance Measures, and Constraints 351

Model Construction 351

Prediction of Outcomes 354

Analysis of Outcomes 355

Analysis of a Work-Methods Proposal 359

10.6 SUMMARY **360**

References 361

Review Questions 361

Problems 361

Appendixes 366

CHAPTER 11 SIMULATION **370**

11.1 SIMULATION AS A TOOL FOR PREDICTING OUTCOMES **371**

What is Simulation? 371

Why Use Simulation? 371

11.2 SIMULATION AND QUEUING **372**

The Design of a Banking System Using Simulation 373

Monte Carlo Simulation 374

Estimating Outcomes Using Monte Carlo Simulation 378

Simulating a Job Shop 381

11.3 HEURISTIC PROBLEM SOLVING **384**

The Mail-Processing System 384

Problem Statement and Objectives 386

The Heuristic Procedure 387

11.4 ESTIMATING PROBABILITY DISTRIBUTIONS WITH SIMULATION **388**

A Capital-Budgeting Example 389

Simulation and the Probability Distribution of RR 390

Managerial Use of the Probability Distribution for RR 391

11.5 DESIGN OF SIMULATION EXPERIMENTS **393**

Initial System Conditions 393

Sample-Size Considerations 394

Design Considerations 398

11.6 SUMMARY **399**

References 400

Review Questions 401

Problems 402

CHAPTER 12 DYNAMIC PROGRAMMING: INTRODUCTION **410**

12.1 DYNAMIC DECISION PROBLEMS **411**

12.2 TERMINOLOGY AND BASIC CONCEPTS **412**

12.3 AN INVENTORY PROBLEM **413**

Specifications and Solution of the Problem 413

Some Comments on the Problem Formulation and Solution 422

12.4 A CAPITAL-BUDGETING PROBLEM **428**

12.5 AN EQUIPMENT-REPLACEMENT PROBLEM **432**

Problem Formulation and Solution 432

An Alternative Method of Solution 435

Discussion 436

12.6 SUMMARY **437**

References 439

Review Questions 439

Problems   440

Appendix 12.1 Newton's Method for Solving Equations of
a Single Variable   442

CHAPTER 13   DECISIONS UNDER RISK, DYNAMIC DECISION PROBLEMS, AND DYNAMIC PROGRAMMING   444

13.1   **STATIC-DECISION PROBLEM**   **445**

An Inventory-Stocking Problem   445

The Value of Perfect Information   450

Evaluating a Forecasting System   450

Generalization and Discussion   454

13.2   **DYNAMIC DECISION PROBLEMS**   **457**

Building a Generating Plant   457

Establishing an Inventory Policy   464

Midwest Book Stores   475

13.3   **SUMMARY AND DISCUSSION**   **478**

References   481

Review Questions   481

Problems   482

CHAPTER 14   PROGRAMMING UNDER UNCERTAINTY   486

14.1   **A TWO-STAGE PROBLEM USING DYNAMIC PROGRAMMING**   **487**

Formulation and Solution of the Model   487

Discussion of the Solution   490

14.2   **TWO-STAGE LINEAR PROGRAMMING**   **490**

A Production Problem   492

Linear Programming Formulation and Solution   493

Model Modifications   494

Expected Value of Perfect Information   498

Generalization   499

14.3   **CHANCE-CONSTRAINED PROGRAMMING**   **500**

Problem Statement and Formulation   500

Equivalent Linear Program   502

Discussion of the Solution   504

14.4   SUMMARY   **506**
References   507
Review Questions   508
Problems   508

**CHAPTER 15   EPILOGUE: QUANTITATIVE METHODS IN
CONTEXT**   **512**

**15.1   QUANTITATIVE ASPECTS OF THE DECISION
PROCESS**   **513**
Choice of Measures of Effectiveness   513
Integration of Quantitative Methods   513
An Iterative Process   514
Problem Complexity   515
Problem Size   515
Functional Area Interaction   516
Informational Aspects   516

**15.2   PROCESSING INFORMATION FOR FINAL
ALTERNATIVE SELECTION**   **516**
Quantitative Model Inputs   517
External Inputs   518
Peer-Group and Superior Group Inputs   519
Personal Inputs   519
Making a Decision   519

15.3   FEEDBACK AND CONTROL   **519**
Elements of Control Problems   520
Dynamic Programming and Control Problems   520
Classifying Decision Problems   521
The Importance of Feedback and Control   523

15.4   A FINAL WORD   **523**
References   524
Review Questions   524

APPENDIX   EXPONENTIAL FUNCTIONS   **527**
APPENDIX   NORMAL DISTRIBUTION   **530**
GLOSSARY   **531**
APPLICATION INDEX   **537**
GENERAL INDEX   **539**

Part I
RATIONALE AND OVERVIEW

There are essentially two polar points of view regarding quantitative methods in management science: (1) if used properly the methods will give the one "correct" answer to a decision problem and will prescribe the course of action for an executive to take; or (2) the methods are naive and essentially useless, the proverbial "will o' the wisp," and therefore "practical" people should not waste time studying them. The truth, as always, lies somewhere between this blind and naive acceptance and total rejection. Quantitative methods can be useful if their proper place in the analysis of decision problems is clearly seen.

In Part I we make more than the usual effort to discuss the role of quantitative methods in decision making. The goal of Part I is to prevent the reader from taking a polar position from the start. Readers who like neat ribbons and bows tied around methods may feel uneasy reading through Chapters 1 and 2. These chapters leave open the question of where alternatives come from and how measures of effectiveness are constructed. They discuss aspects of decision problems with lots of loose ends. But that is more like the real world than problems that are neatly packaged. Chapter 3 discusses models and model building. It emphasizes that a model is not the real world but is instead a convenient representation of it. This means that a model can never be used unthinkingly by the decision maker but must be looked at as a device that provides information that is helpful in decision making. The methods are indeed useful when looked at from this point of view.

In Chapter 1, the decision process is discussed and the general theory and framework for thinking about decision problems are presented. A simple example of decision making is developed. In it a manufacturer seeks ways to improve his profit position. His primary source of information is the accounting statements for his firm and his knowledge of how the business operates. From these sources of information, the manufacturer develops alternative solutions to a decision problem. We do not know whether he has thought of the best alternative but, nonetheless, he has thought of some that need analysis. The quantitative (mathematical) methods that he uses to analyze the alternatives are unsophisticated, but they do the job of organizing and processing the information at hand into something useful for his decision problem. The example illustrates the framework for analyzing decision problems and the fact that the analysis should have as its goal the processing of useful information. If the accomplishment of the goal can be done with simple mathematical and statistical tools, so be it!

Chapter 2 discusses the formation of measures of effectiveness. Sometimes such measures can be formed easily in an unambiguous way. But this is not always the case. The higher the level at which the decision problem arises in the organization, the more difficult the formation of the measure of effectiveness becomes. Uncertainty and lingering effects play more important roles at higher levels. The chapter discusses the effects of these concepts in detail. Finally, it introduces the idea of a certainty equivalent, which basically permits a certainty problem to be solved in place of a problem involving uncertainty.

Chapter 3 is also a "philosophical" chapter. Since a model is an abstraction of reality that we hope to use to understand reality, it must delicately weigh and balance the features of reality that are important in a decision situation. Oversimplifying can lead to poor decisions. Making a model too complex can lead to untimely decisions as well as decision recommendations that are really not understood by anyone. A well-balanced model can provide important and useful information at low cost. Chapter 3 discusses the fact that models do not simply appear; model building is a trial-and-error process. It is hard work. A model must be solved. Here mathematical methods play the predominant role. Finally, a model must be validated so that confidence can be achieved in the usefulness of the information it provides.

1

THE DECISION PROCESS
AND DECISION MAKING

1.1 PREFINISHING CORPORATION

1.2 THE DECISION-MAKING PROCESS

Problem Recognition
Specification of Objectives, Performance Measures, and Constraints
Model Construction
Enumeration of Alternatives
Prediction of Outcomes
Alternative Selection
Data Collection

1.3 THE DECISION-MAKING PROCESS APPLIED TO PREFINISHING

Problem Recognition
Specification of Objectives, Performance Measures, and Constraints
Model Construction
Enumeration of Alternatives
Prediction of Outcomes
Alternative Selection

1.4 THE CONTINUING PROCESS OF DECISION MAKING
References
Review Questions

Decision making is a function that pervades all organizational levels in any business enterprise. Anyone acting in a managerial capacity must at various times make choices among various alternatives to the solutions of problems. In a rapidly changing economic environment, the careful evaluation of decision alternatives is mandatory not only to provide a competitive edge, but also to survive. For example, the mid-1970s presented difficult decision problems to most businesses in the United States. Increasing labor, material, and energy costs had serious effects on the profits of firms that did not take timely counteractive measures. Raw-material shortages also contributed to cost increases and triggered reevaluations of many firms' product mixes. In addition, changes in government regulations drastically altered the business environment. Because of the severity of the economic situation, judgment, intuition, and experience alone could no longer resolve complex issues. Careful calculations were the basis for decision making in successful firms.

Today, a number of quantitative techniques can be used to solve problems that were too complex to analyze quantitatively in the past. This text will present a variety of these techniques and will examine them in the context of the role they play in the total decision-making process. Since decision making is the unifying theme throughout this text, the total decision-making process is examined in this initial chapter and the role of quantitative methods in the decision process is illustrated. Perhaps the best way to demonstrate the decision-making process is to apply it to a simple illustrative example. The next section provides a short case scenario of the Prefinishing Corporation, an organization facing a problem of declining profits. Following the scenario, the steps of the decision-making process are discussed in general terms. In Section 4, the decision-making process is applied to the Prefinishing Corporation problem. Finally, the last section discusses the issue of control.

1.1   PREFINISHING CORPORATION

The Prefinishing Corporation is engaged in prefinishing doors, door and window moldings, wainscoting strips, and other decorative wood for builders and building-material suppliers in a five-state Midwestern region. The builders or building suppliers either ship their own unfinished materials to Prefinishing to finish and return, or they place orders with Prefinishing to supply the raw materials and the finished products.

Historically, Prefinishing has been a profitable business. Ray Yef started the business on a "shoestring" backed up by enthusiasm, energy, and a penetrating engineering and entrepreneurial mind. In the eighth year of operation the production facilities of Prefinishing were completely destroyed by fire, and a new physical plant was built. Since that time, the business has not been as profitable as it previously had been. Mr. Yef initially attributed this to "getting the bugs out" of the new plant. But as time passed, he became extremely concerned with the profit situation at Prefinishing. It had fallen to unacceptably low levels. Furthermore, a chronic shortage of cash was causing delays in production.

Table 1.1 shows the income statement for June. The net income of $364 caused Mr. Yef to become concerned with his profit situation. Projecting the monthly profit to an annual rate of $4368 ($364 × 12) and dividing by the net worth of $600,000 shown on the balance sheet in Table 1.2 yields a rate of return on equity of 0.728%. Mr. Yef considers such a rate of return totally unacceptable.

Table 1.1   Prefinishing Corporation Income Statement, June

Sales	$110,000
Cost of goods sold	55,000
Gross margin	$ 55,000
Deduct	
Light and power	$ 600
Advertising	2,000
Selling expense	4,000
Purchase discounts foregone	5,000
Depreciation	21,160
Interest ($4,875 short term; $16,666 long term)	21,541
Income before income taxes	699
Income taxes	335
Net income	$ 364

Further reference to Table 1.2 reveals a shortage of working capital and cash. About 80% of Prefinishing's cost of goods sold is material cost and 20% is labor cost. Consequently, it takes about $11,000 of labor costs to produce sales of $110,000 per month ($55,000 × 0.20). Since these expenses must be met before the sales can be made, it seems that Prefinishing, with only $5000 in cash, cannot produce and sell at the current rate with its present cash position. After reviewing this information, Mr. Yef realized that he must make a *decision* that would enable Prefinishing to return to a more acceptable financial position.

Table 1.2 Prefinishing Corporation Balance Sheet, June

Assets		
Current assets		
Cash		$ 5,000
Accounts receivable		220,000
Finished-goods inventory		30,000
Raw-materials inventory		500,000
Total current assets		$ 755,000
Long-life assets		
Building	$2,000,000	
Less allowance for depreciation	190,000	$1,810,000
Equipment	1,500,000	
Less allowance for depreciation	300,000	1,200,000
Total assets		$3,765,000
Liabilities		
Current liabilities		
Accounts payable		$ 80,000
Notes payable		585,000
Total current liabilities		$ 655,000
Long-term debt		$2,500,000
Net worth		
Capital stock		$ 500,000
Retained earnings		100,000
Total net worth		$ 600,000
Total claims		$3,765,000

1.2 THE DECISION-MAKING PROCESS

A decision can be defined as the selection of a particular alternative from a set of two or more feasible alternative courses of action for resolving a particular problem. This activity is only the last step in a series of interrelated activities that can be called the decision-making process. This process is diagrammed in Figure 1.1. Because the decision-making process is the integrating theme in this text, it is beneficial at this point to discuss briefly each step in this process.

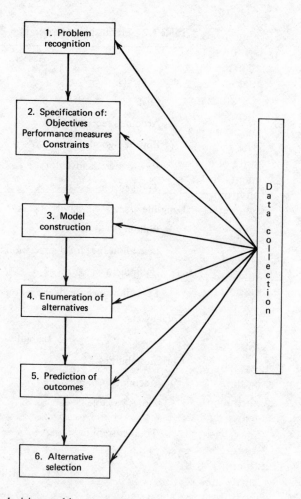

Figure 1.1 The decision-making process.

Problem Recognition

Before any decision can be made, a problem must be present. Thus, problem recognition provides the first step in the decision-making process. This task may not be as simple as it first appears. Very often problem symptoms are interpreted as the problem itself. For example, consider a financial manager who sees that the organization desperately needs more working capital and defines the problem as one of determining the appropriate mix of fundings from the money market. In reality, the real problem might be a grossly inefficient inventory-control system that requires large amounts of working capital to finance unneeded inventories. Alternatively, consider the vice president of marketing who sees that sales are slipping and defines the problem as one of determining the appropriate advertising budget and media mix, when a better assignment of the sales force to market regions could bring sales back up for little or no expense. Although recognizing symptoms is the usual way of detecting problems, care must be taken to ensure that the correct problem is being addressed because the success of the decision-making process depends on an accurate assessment of the problem.

Perhaps a better way to proceed is to anticipate problems before they manifest themselves in poor performance. One way to accomplish this is to develop an observing attitude and study the environment for conditions calling for change. The economic, political, technological, and social environments are in a constant state of flux, and the astute manager will monitor the condition of these environments to see if new problems will present themselves in the near future. These environmental conditions, which will affect the goodness of a decision, but over which the decision maker has little or no control, are called *states of nature* in the language of decision theory. Factors such as weather conditions, competitive behavior, economic conditions, or government policies are examples of conditions that are not under the control of the typical manager, but they could certainly affect a decision that may have to be made. Recognizing which states of nature are important for a particular decision problem is an essential part of recognizing the problem itself.

Specification of Objectives, Performance Measures, and Constraints

Even though recognizing the problem is an important prerequisite to decision making, no decision can be made without specifying the objective to be achieved through the decision process. The objectives selected for any given decision problem are dictated by the circumstances of the situation. For example, a post office may wish to maximize customer service, whereas an industrial goods manufacturer may wish to maximize profits. If the objectives are ambiguous or difficult to quantify, surrogates for the objectives may be used instead, and the choice of these surrogates may depend in part on the organizational level of the decision maker. For example, a tour supervisor at a post office may translate the objective of maximizing customer service to that of minimizing employee idle time. Alternatively, the director of mail processing may attempt to minimize the work-in-process inventory of mail when making decisions relating to process design. Both surrogates conceivably contribute to the organizational objective of maximizing customer service but are easier to measure. However, caution must be used. There is a danger in substituting one objective for another. We must be sure that the surrogate objective accurately reflects the true objective.

Having the appropriate performance measures only enables us to evaluate alternatives when we generate them. We must be sure that the alternatives are "feasible." As such, all the constraints on the choice of alternatives must be specified before proceeding with the next step in the decision process. As discussed in Chapter 2, whether these constraints are economic or technical, their basic purpose is to refine the set of alternatives to a smaller set of "feasible" ones. In addition, if a problem has more than one objective, secondary objectives might be used as constraints on the decision problem. If the superintendent of mails in the foregoing example saw a decision problem in terms of selecting an appropriate process design for minimizing average mail-transit time, a reasonable constraint on the whole process would be a budgetary limitation, thus embodying a sub-objective of cost control. If it were not for a constraint such as this in the example, an alternative may be chosen that would be too expensive for the benefit received as given by the measures of performance. Of course, when reflecting multiple objectives in the constraints, there is always the problem of deciding which objective should be dominant and which should be subobjectives. That in itself is a decision problem.

Model Construction

The third step in the decision process depicted in Figure 1.1 is that of model construction. In the context of decision making, a model relates alternatives with certain constraints to objectives for various states of nature. When the number of alternatives is large and there are numerous constraints, states of nature, or both, a decision model is a most useful decision-making aid. In this step quantitative techniques formally enter into the decision-making process, since the formal process of model building includes a consideration of the solution technique to be used. Since Chapter 3 goes into this concept in more detail, it is sufficient to say here that, for ease of selection, the solution techniques can be categorized according to their properties, and that the choice of technique depends on the specific problem characteristics.

Enumeration of Alternatives

Of all the steps of the decision-making process, perhaps enumerating alternatives highlights the ingenuity of the decision maker. If the best alternative is overlooked, the best decision cannot be made, and the decision-making process is compromised. Unfortunately, there is no way to ensure that such a thing will not happen. This possibility emphasizes an important point about the decision-making process—the human decision maker is very much an integral part of the whole process. The success or failure of the process depends on the person using it and not on the process itself.

Of course, there is sometimes virtually an infinite number of alternatives to a problem, and it would seem an unwise use of time to ask our decision maker to enumerate them completely. Such would be the case in the problem of determining the product mix for an oil-refining company. Over a given period, decisions must be made about what products to produce and how much of each one. Producing more of one product means that less of another product can be produced because of raw materials and capacity constraints. When faced with such a problem, it is most comforting to know that, under certain conditions, there are quantitative techniques that "implicitly enumerate" all of the alternatives and even select the best one for the stated objective of the decision problem. More will be said about these techniques in other chapters; however, if the problem conditions violate the assumptions of these decision aids, the only other possible approach is to enumerate a partial list of feasible alternatives and to suppress the nagging feeling that the best alternative was omitted.

Prediction of Outcomes

Given the alternatives to be evaluated and the future potential states of nature, the model developed in Step 3 is used to project the outcomes to be expected for each alternative under each state of nature. Table 1.3 conceptualizes the elements of the decision-making problem and demonstrates the relationship of the outcomes (O_{ij}) to the alternatives (A_i) and the states of nature (N_j). For each alternative state-of-nature pairing, there is an outcome measured in terms of the

Table 1.3 Symbolic Representation of the Elements of a Decision Problem

Alternative	N_1	N_2	$\cdots$	N_m
A_1	O_{11}	O_{12}	$\cdots$	O_{1m}
A_2	O_{21}	O_{22}	$\cdots$	O_{2m}
$\vdots$	$\cdot$	$\cdot$	$\cdot$	$\cdot$
$\vdots$	$\cdot$	$\cdot$	$\vdots$	$\vdots$
$\vdots$	$\cdot$	$\cdot$	$\cdot$	$\cdot$
$\vdots$				
A_n	O_{n1}	O_{n2}	$\cdots$	O_{nm}

Table 1.4 Decision Problem under Conditions of Certainty

Alternatives	N^*
A_1	O_1
A_2	O_2
A_3	O_3
$\vdots$	$\vdots$
$\vdots$	$\vdots$
$\vdots$	$\vdots$
A_n	O_n

objectives or their surrogates. Although this conceptual framework seems simple, remember that determining the outcomes may not be an easy task. Decision models and quantitative techniques are useful in this context. We will use this framework throughout the remainder of the text so that the quantitative techniques can be discussed in their proper perspective. For example, some of the techniques assume that the state of nature that will prevail is known with certainty, thus reducing the previous decision matrix to the one in Table 1.4. We will see that even this problem, which seems overly simple on the surface, can be challenging when the number of alternatives is infinite, the outcomes are the result of complex inter-actions among alternatives, constraints, and objectives, or both.

Alternative Selection

At this point in the process, the decision matrix in Table 1.3 (or Table 1.4) has been at least conceptually filled in. The last step of the decision process is con-cerned with selecting the best alternative. As one might expect, it is a rare occurrence when one alternative dominates all the rest by producing the best outcome for each state of nature (except for the case of certainty, mentioned earlier). Thus each alternative is ranked using the measure of performance. The one alternative that does best in this sense is chosen as the solution to the decision problem. Thus, at this point, the decision maker culminates the decision-making process by selecting an alternative.

Some quantitative techniques combine the steps of outcome prediction and alternative selection and arrive at a suggested alternative in one step. These techniques will be presented in subsequent chapters.

Data Collection

An activity that pervades the entire decision-making process and impinges on each of the steps is data collection. Throughout the entire decision-making process, data inputs are necessary. Without meaningful data or informational inputs at each step, it would be difficult, if not impossible, to complete the decision-making process. Because of the importance of data input to all steps in the process, data collection does not appear as a single step in the sequence illustrated in Figure 1.1. Instead, it is a supporting function that provides inputs to each of the steps in the decision-making process.

There are five ways in which data can be collected: (1) sampling; (2) survey; (3) observation; (4) experimentation; and (5) historical search.

Sampling Statistical sampling procedures allow one to sample a portion of the total universe to make inferences about certain aspects of it. For example, a city traffic manager may be interested in knowing the average number of vehicles per hour that pass through a certain intersection on weekdays between the hours of

4 P.M. and 6 P.M. A random sample of weekday dates could be selected and the actual number of vehicles passing through that intersection on the selected days could be recorded. Based on the sample, the average number of vehicles per hour could then be computed. Such data could be useful in determining whether or not traffic lights should replace the present arterial stop signs at the intersection, for example.

Of course, if the cost of sampling is small compared to the cost of inaccurate data, complete, 100% sampling of the universe could be appropriate. Such would be the case of the quality-control checks of equipment on piloted space flights. The point, however, is that there is a trade-off between more accurate data and the added cost of sampling. The implications of the trade-off cannot be realized until the entire decision-making process has been expended, since the real issue is the effect of data inaccuracy on the ultimate decision.

Survey   The survey is actually a special form of sampling; however, the method is one of asking individuals to respond to a number of questions pertinent to some decision problem at hand. Marketing-research groups, political-opinion pollsters, and governmental agencies are perhaps the biggest users of surveys for decision-making purposes. These surveys could consist of questionnaires mailed to a representative random sample of the target universe or a series of questions and answers conducted by telephone. In either case, the survey must be skillfully developed so that the response rate is high and the data that are generated are accurate and useful for decision-making purposes.

Observation   In this procedure, the system in question is observed and the data pertinent to the decision problem are recorded as they appear, supplying up-to-the-minute information for decision makers. Real-time data systems come under this heading. A real-time data system is one in which the needed data come to the decision maker promptly enough to permit reaction to the circumstances surrounding a continuing stream of events. Computerized airline-reservation systems and bank-accounting systems are examples of real-time data systems. This type of data collection is usually used for repetitive decision problems as opposed to the one-time, "once-and-for-all," decision problem.

Historical search   Perhaps the method used most often for gathering data important for decision-making purposes is an historical search of available records. The data could be extracted from diverse sources such as newspapers and governmental reports and from publications generated internal to the organization such as accounting reports, inventory records, and market-research reports. When using historical data, care must be taken to ensure that the data are representative of present conditions. If they are not, one of the other methods for gathering data must be used. Of course, if the decision problem is such that none of the aforementioned methods is appropriate, opinions or subjective estimates can be used in lieu of hard data as a last resort.

1.3   THE DECISION-MAKING PROCESS APPLIED TO PREFINISHING

With the steps of the decision-making process in mind, let us return to the Prefinishing Corporation and attempt to apply these steps to Mr. Yef's problem. We will assume that the data inputs to the decision steps that follow will, for the most part, come from a search of existing historical financial information by Mr. Yef.

Problem Recognition

According to the steps in the total decision process, the first step with which Mr. Yef had to contend was that of identifying a problem. Analysis of the income statement and balance sheet for June indicated to Mr. Yef that the performance of his company was not as good as the performance prior to the fire. Specifically, he noted that cash and working capital were currently at inadequate levels, as was the return on equity. His desire was to return Prefinishing to a more acceptable financial position. One way to achieve a better financial position was to increase profits, so the problem could be stated as follows: How can profits and return on equity be increased by the end of the year? Finally, Mr. Yef assumed that the economic, social, and technological factors that might affect the goodness of his solution would remain unchanged for the year. Thus, the decision problem can be said to have one state of nature, as shown in Table 1.4.

Specification of Objectives, Performance Measure, and Constraints

The specification of an objective in the case of Prefinishing is relatively straightforward. Mr. Yef has expressed a desire to increase the amount of profit that the firm realizes. Assuming conditions of certainty, the objective can be stated as maximizing profits, and the performance measure for each alternative would simply be the profit it generates. Instead of listing constraints at this point, we will discuss constraints on the choice of alternatives as we generate the alternatives. In this way, the difference between generating alternatives and generating *feasible* alternatives will be emphasized.

Model Construction

The next step in the decision-making process just presented is that of model construction. Since a model relates alternatives to objectives, the construction of specific models will be performed in conjunction with the enumeration and evaluation of alternatives generated next in order to simplify their understanding at this early point in the text. Also, because models and the modeling process are covered in depth in a later chapter, the models employed in conjunction with the alternatives discussed here will be relatively simple mathematical models. Because of the profit objective, for example, we will employ a simple mathematical model consisting merely of defining the profit objective in terms of the entities that go together to make profits. That is,

$$\pi = S - C - OH - AX - SX - D - I - T$$

where

π = profit
S = sales
C = cost of goods sold
OH = overhead
AX = advertising expense
SX = sales expense
D = depreciation
I = interest
T = taxes

The effects on profit of various alternatives can be predicted by estimating their effects on the factors comprising profit. To do this, it may be necessary to conduct additional analysis to predict the effects of the alternatives on the factors comprising profit. Such auxiliary analysis will be evident in the enumeration and evaluation of alternatives.

Enumeration of Alternatives

At this point, a listing of alternatives must be made. This is the step at which the ingenuity of the decision maker is put to its most stringent test. The decision maker must attempt to enumerate alternatives that are feasible, practical to implement, and reasonably likely to result in acceptable performance. Although Mr. Yef saw that something was wrong at Prefinishing and that profits had to be increased, there was no obvious solution to the problem.

Mr. Yef realized that increased profits could come from increasing revenue more than costs or from decreasing costs more than revenue. Consequently, he began by studying the income statement for June. After considering the manner in which revenues could be increased, Mr. Yef determined that, at the present time, his two salespeople each cost $2000 per month in salary and expenses and were able to generate $110,000 of business each month. An additional salesperson could be expected to increase sales about 30%, or $33,000 per month, and would add costs of $2000 per month. On the surface, it seems that an additional salesperson would be an alternative worth further consideration. The alternative "additional salesperson" was designated as A_1 by Mr. Yef.

While examining the income statement in search of further alternatives, Mr. Yef felt that the production operations of his plant were about as efficient as they could be. Therefore, there was no feasible alternative associated with trying to reduce the cost of goods sold. Furthermore, he felt that there was nothing that could be done to reduce light and power, advertising expense, or depreciation. The purchase-discounts foregone and the interest expense caught his eye as potential savings, however.

The purchase-discounts foregone of $5000 indicate that because Prefinishing was not paying its bills for materials purchased from suppliers within 30 days, it was not taking advantage of the 10% discount. Therefore, the second alternative presented itself. Paying bills on time should save approximately $5000 in expenses. Alternative A_2 was so defined.

The next major item is the interest charges. Reduction of interest charges could conceivably be a major source of savings. The balance sheet revealed more information on the potential of this source of savings. The long-term debt of $2,500,000 carried an interest rate of 8% and could not be reduced. Thus, $16,667 (0.08/12 × $2,500,000) of the interest charge is fixed. The remainder results from the 10% annual rate on the short-term notes of $585,000. These short-term notes could be renewed when due; however, the bank informed Prefinishing that the amount outstanding could not be increased. The only way interest could be reduced was to reduce short-term notes. To generate alternatives for doing this, Mr. Yef looked to the asset portion of the balance sheet and noted two possibilities. Accounts receivable consisted of about 2 months' sales. If these receivables could be reduced and the funds generated used to pay off some of the short-term debt, there would be a reduction in interest expenses. This became Mr. Yef's third alternative, A_3.

A fourth alternative presented itself when Mr. Yef looked at raw-materials inventories. These inventories seemed to be excessive; therefore, a reduction to a lower level would allow a reduction in notes payable. This formed the basis of alternative A_4.

From the generation of the first four alternatives, Mr. Yef began to get some ideas about another alternative. Suppose that (1) the receivables were reduced to approximately 1 month's sales, implying a collection period of 30 days; (2) the raw-materials inventory was reduced to approximately a 2-month supply (which Mr. Yef felt would be viable); (3) the funds generated by the reductions were used to take advantage of discounts on raw-materials purchases; and (4) the remainder of the funds generated were used to finance more sales and production, requiring an additional salesperson. This complex alternative forms the fifth alternative, A_5.

Although these alternatives may not exhaust all of the possible alternatives for this problem, Mr. Yef felt that he had generated a reasonable set of alternatives that had potential for increasing profit. These alternatives are summarized in Table 1.5.

Prediction of Outcomes

After having enumerated his alternatives, Mr. Yef was in a position to begin evaluating these alternatives and to predict the outcome of each. The analysis that Mr. Yef performed on each of these alternatives now follows.

Alternative A_1 Some of the expenses associated with A_1 were easy to determine, whereas others posed more difficulty. For example, it was assumed that light and power would remain unchanged, as would the advertising and depreciation

Table 1.5 Decision Alternatives for Prefinishing Corporation

Alternative	Description
A_1	Additional salesperson
A_2	Take advantage of purchase discounts
A_3	Decrease receivables collection time
A_4	Reduce raw-materials inventory
A_5	"Complex alternative"

expenses. The selling expense would increase to $6000. The purchase-discounts foregone would rise to $6500 ($71,500 × 5000/55,000), assuming that the ratio between purchase-discounts foregone and cost of goods sold remained constant.

When trying to calculate the interest cost for A_1, Mr. Yef determined that this alternative was actually infeasible. The receivables amounted to 2 months' sales. If sales increased to $143,000, receivables would increase by $66,000, to $286,000. This would mean that short-term debt would also have to increase by $66,000. Because the bank had indicated that the short-term debt could not be increased, however, this alternative was infeasible.

This occurrence points out a circumstance that can happen while evaluating alternatives. Even though the constraint on increasing short-term debt could have been stated before enumerating alternatives, there was no way of telling at that time that alternative A_1 would be infeasible. In this example, further analysis was required to determine the infeasibility.

Alternative A_2 Knowing the results of the analysis for alternative A_1, Mr. Yef began to suspect that alternative A_2 was likely to be infeasible. To take advantage of the discounts, Prefinishing would have to reduce accounts payable to about one-half of its existing level. Barring any reductions in cash, receivables, or inventories (which were not part of alternative A_2), this would mean that notes payable would have to be increased. This was not possible, and alternative A_2 was thus also infeasible.

Alternative A_3 Alternative A_3 called for a reduction in the receivables from approximately 2 months' sales to 1 month's sales. Speedier collection would cause a reduction of receivables by $110,000 and an increase in cash of $110,000. Cash was needed to meet wage payments for production, which amounted to 20% of the cost of goods sold. Mr. Yef felt that $11,000 in cash was required to maintain current production; therefore, $104,000 of the total cash ($5,000 + $110,000 − $11,000) would be available to repay short-term notes. The reduction in interest charges of $867 per month ($104,000 × 0.10/12) would result in an increase in the net income. At a tax rate of 48%, the result of alternative A_3 would be a net income of $814, as evaluated by the model for profits.

Alternative A_4   Alternative A_4 advocated a reduction in the raw-materials inventory. Mr. Yef had determined that he could reduce the raw-materials inventory to about 2 months' supply without reducing the efficiency of his production operation. Since 80% of the cost of goods sold consisted of materials, it follows that 2 months' supply of raw-materials inventory would be $88,000. Thus, a reduction of $412,000 ($500,000 − $88,000) would be possible. Subtracting the $11,000 needed to finance wages during the production cycle, the remainder of $401,000 ($412,000 − $11,000) could be used to reduce notes payable to $184,000 ($585,000 − $401,000). Interest would thereby be reduced by $3342 ($401,000 × 0.10/12). This would produce an after-tax net income of $2101 for alternative A_4.

Alternative A_5   Alternative A_5 represented a complex alternative that essentially combined the first four alternatives. To evaluate this, Mr. Yef began with the addition of a salesperson. This would increase sales by $33,000 per month, to $143,000, and the cost of goods sold would increase by $16,500, to $71,500. The gross margin would also increase, by $16,500, to $71,500.

If, at the same time that a salesperson was added, the receivables were cut to 1 month's sales and raw-materials inventory was cut to 2 months' supply, these changes would reduce receivables to $143,000 and raw-materials inventory to $114,400. If cash was held at 1 month's wages, the new level of cash would have to be $14,300 ($71,500 × 0.20). Thus, receivables would decrease by $77,000, raw-materials inventory would decrease by $385,600, and needed cash would increase by $9300. The net effect would be an increase in excess cash of $453,300. With this $453,300 in available cash, Prefinishing could take advantage of discounts on purchases and retire some short-term debt.

The new level of payables, reduced to 1 month of materials, would be $57,200 (0.8 × $71,500). This amounted to a decrease of $22,800 for June. Short-term notes could then be reduced by $430,500 ($453,300 − $22,800). The reduction of short-term debt by $430,500 resulted in a monthly reduction in interest charges of $3587 ($453,300 × 0.10/12). In summary, alternative A_5 produced the following changes in the income statement: (1) an increase in gross margin of $16,500; (2) an increase in selling expense of $2000; (3) a reduction in purchase-discounts foregone of $5000; and (4) a reduction of $3587 in interest. The net effect of these changes was an increase in income before taxes of $23,087 and an after-tax profit increase of $12,005, to $12,369. These alternatives and their outcomes are summarized in Table 1.6.

Alternative Selection

At this point, the final step of the decision-making process can be performed. It can now be seen that selecting an alternative, which is often interpreted as decision making, is simply the culminating step in a more complex process. In the case of Prefinishing, Mr. Yef had to select one of the alternatives summarized in Table 1.6. In this instance, alternative selection did not pose much difficulty because he could quickly reject the two infeasible alternatives and consider only

Table 1.6 Summary of Alternatives and Their Outcomes

Alternative	Description	Monthly Profit
A_1	Additional salesperson	Infeasible
A_2	Take advantage of purchase discounts	Infeasible
A_3	Decrease receivables collection time	$814
A_4	Reduce raw-materials inventory	$2101
A_5	Complex alternative	$12,369

the three that were feasible. From these three, alternative A_5 clearly dominates, since it yields the highest profit. Selection of alternative A_5 was made by Mr. Yef in accordance with his objective of profit maximization. It should be emphasized that other complex alternatives may exist that could have been considered, but Mr. Yef chose not to expend any more resources searching for them.

1.4 THE CONTINUING PROCESS OF DECISION MAKING

It is important to recognize that the process of decision making should not end with the selection of an alternative. If this were the case, there would be no awareness by the decision maker of whether the alternative selected proved to be an appropriate one. To avoid such a situation, after the desired alternative has been implemented, there must be some monitoring of the system to determine whether or not the resulting performance is acceptable. This continued monitoring of the system is the process of *control*. A lengthy discussion of the control process will not be presented here. However, it can easily be seen that the control process is simply an extension of the decision-making process.

In its very basics, control would require that actual performance be compared with desired performance. If actual performance is not acceptable, some corrective action must be taken. If actual performance is acceptable, nothing need be done. In either event, the system must be rechecked periodically to ensure that performance is acceptable.

We can see that much that is inherent in the control process relates back to the decision-making process. The notion of determining whether performance is acceptable requires that we specify a set of objectives, performance measures, and performance standards. This was required in the decision-making process described earlier, since such functions comprise the second step. When performance proves unacceptable, some corrective action must be taken. This implies that some alternative course of action must be implemented. But, because this is the culmination of the decision-making process, we must perform the steps leading up to this culminating step in order to do this. Since we now have our objectives and performance measures (with which we determined performance to be inadequate), we must go through the steps of model construction, enumeration of alternatives, prediction of alternatives, prediction of outcomes, and alternative selection before we can undertake corrective action. We can see that the control process that follows the decision-making process may require that we go through many of the steps in the decision-making process again. And because the control process requires that we periodically check the performance of the system, we may continually have to make corrections. Consequently, we may need to implement continually the steps in the decision-making process.

Throughout this continual process of decision making, the decision maker may make behavioral adjustments based on past performance. If objectives or performance standards are continually not met and corrective action does not remedy the situation, the decision maker may feel that the stated objectives are inappropriate or the performance standards too high. In such a case, the decision maker might attempt to revise these objectives or lower the performance standards based on these experiences. On the other hand, if performance standards are continually being met, the decision maker might interpret this to mean that aspiration levels and performance standards are simply too low and, consequently, too easy to achieve. In such cases, standards might be raised or higher aspiration levels determined. Both of these situations represent cases in which the decision maker, when continually confronted with a situation, adjusts his or her behavior based on experience gained and past performance.

A final observation should be made regarding the steps in the decision process. Although they were presented in a straightforward manner, the actual application of these steps may not be quite so simple. A strict, sequential, step-by-step application of the process may not always be possible. For example, the initial step, problem recognition, is one that is usually peculiar to a given situation and is best handled by a decision maker familiar with the situation. This is because it is difficult to recognize a problem without at least some feeling for (if not direct knowledge of) objectives to be achieved in a situation. Consequently, the effort to define the problem often necessitates at least a partial clarification or identification of the objectives. Then, as the problem is gradually structured, the objectives may be continually modified and firmed up. In such cases, the decision maker is essentially moving back and forth between the problem-recognition and objective-determination steps in the decision-making process.

Similar shifting might also occur between the second and third steps. Upon tackling the model construction in the third step, the decision maker might find it necessary to return to the second step to review, add, or delete constraints or performance measures. Such steps might be necessary if the initial model is overly simple and virtually useless as a predictor of the real situation. Alternatively, such steps might be necessary if the model is too rich and complex to be workable. These two situations are further examples that the decision-making process can be slightly more complex than the steps might imply.

References   Ackoff, R.L., *Scientific Method: Optimizing Applied Research Decisions*, New York: John Wiley & Sons, 1962, Chapters 2 and 3.

Archer, S.H., "The Structure of Management Decision Theory," *Academy of Management Journal*, Vol. 7 (1964), pp. 269–287.

Bross, I.D.J., *Design for Decision*, New York: Macmillan, 1953, Chapters 1–3.

Grayson, C.J., Jr., "Management Science and Business Practice," *Harvard Business Review*, Vol. 51 (1973), pp. 41–48.

Harrison, E.F., *The Managerial Decision Making Process*, Boston: Houghton-Mifflin, 1975.

Hovey, R.W., and Wagner, H.M., "A Sample Survey of Industrial Operations Research Activities," *Operations Research*, Vol. 6 (1958), pp. 878–881.

Morris, W.T., *Management Science in Action*, Homewood, Ill.: Richard D. Irwin, 1963.

Morris, W.T., *Management Science*, Englewood Cliffs, N.J., Prentice-Hall, 1968.

Newell, A., and Simon, H.A., *Human Problem Solving*, Englewood Cliffs, N.J.: Prentice-Hall, 1972.

Schumacher, C.C., and Smith B.E., "A Sample Survey of Industrial Operations Research Activities II," *Operations Research*, Vol. 13 (1965), pp. 1023–1027.

Simon, H., *The New Science of Management Decision*, New York: Harper & Row, 1960.

Review Questions

1. Using as examples some decision situations with which you are familiar distinguish between problems and problem symptoms.

2. Give some examples of states of nature in decision situations with which you are familiar.

3. Distinguish between goals and surrogates by using examples of decision situations with which you are familiar.

4. Within the context of the Prefinishing Corporation, develop an alternative that you feel might be worthwhile evaluating.

5. For a decision situation with which you are familiar, describe a constraint and discuss how it limits the solution. Does the constraint express a secondary goal or a "physical" limitation on the solution?

6. For a decision situation with which you are familiar, describe the types of data collection that would be important to the solution of the decision problem.

7. Evaluate the alternative you developed for Question 4.

8. Explain how control enters the decision process.

9. Explain, within the context of Tables 1.3 and 1.4, why decisions under certainty could be considered easier to analyze than decisions under uncertainty.

10. In an uncertain situation, why might two decision makers with the same set of "facts" *logically* make different decisions?

2

OBJECTIVES, PERFORMANCE MEASURES, AND CONSTRAINTS

2.1 WHAT IS A GOOD DECISION?

2.2 MEASURES OF EFFECTIVENESS

Measures of Effectiveness for Low-Level Decisions
Measures of Effectiveness for Intermediate-Level Decisions
Measures of Effectiveness and Constraints
Measures of Effectiveness for Top-Level Decisions

2.3 THE CONCEPT OF UTILITY AND MEASURES OF EFFECTIVENESS

Utility of Wealth and Decisions Involving Uncertainty
Measures of Effectiveness in Business Decision Making

2.4 SUMMARY

References
Review Questions
Problems

Decision makers are frequently doubtful about the quality of the decisions they make. This is not unusual or peculiar, since not all decisions are easily judged with respect to their quality. In this chapter we will discuss setting measures of effectiveness in decision problems. The discussion is largely nontechnical; its purpose is to portray some of the fundamental difficulties associated with setting these measures for a real-life problem.

2.1   WHAT IS A GOOD DECISION?

The ability to distinguish a good from a bad decision, or to isolate the best decision, depends heavily on the context of the decision-making situation. This section will be devoted to two extreme examples of decision problems. The first will be the choice of job sequencing by a printer and will illustrate a case in which we can clearly tell a good decision from a bad one. The second will be a price decision by a steel producer in which the quality of the decision will be in doubt.

The printer does specialty printing using three colors. Each day the printer makes three production runs. One production run requires black and green inks, another requires green and red inks, and the third requires only black ink. When changing from one production run to the next, the printer must do some cleanup and must change inks. The amount of time spent on the change depends on its nature. Table 2.1 shows the amount of time necessary for each possible change.

There are six possible sequences for the production runs:

A: black, green and black, green and red.
B: black, green and red, green and black.
C: green and black, black, green and red.
D: green and black, green and red, black.
E: green and red, black, green and black.
F: green and red, green and black, black.

Table 2.1   Change Time for Production Runs (hours)

From \ To	Black	Green and Black	Green and Red
Black	—	0.5	1.0
Green and black	0.5	—	0.5
Green and red	1.0	0.5	—

From Table 2.1 it can be seen that the time required for the change will be 1.5 hours for sequences B, C, D, and E, and 1.0 hours for A and F. Clearly, the printer will choose either sequence A or F.

Completing the change in the shortest time will be consistent with completing the total production for the lowest cost and the largest profit and maximizing the output per hour. Furthermore, even if sequence C were selected, for example, there are no important lingering effects of the choice. The effects will not carry beyond the time for which the decision is made. The decision situation is clearly closely contained in both time and space. It is for this reason that the "shortest-time" objective is consistent with least cost, maximum profit per job, and maximum number of jobs.

There are other aspects of the sequencing problem worth noting. The length of the change time required to complete any sequence is forecast by the printer in preparing bids for printing jobs. Uncertainties in forecasting—or the inability to forecast accurately—will have effects on the bidding strategies. Although the use of an inefficient sequence will mean that predicted change times will be longer, the *ability to so predict* will not differ noticeably from that where an efficient sequence is used. Thus, the choice of sequence will not affect the uncertainties with which the printer must deal. The printer can accurately calculate the time of change with any sequence.

The economic situation, or level of printing activity, will have little effect on the efficiency of using any sequence. If business is good, it is likely that it will take just as long to change with sequence A as it would when business is slow. The same statement can be made regarding any other sequence. We can make analogous arguments relating good and bad weather or happy and unhappy workers. In other words, the choice of which sequence to use will be unaffected by the state of nature.

Finally, note that if the printer made a bad decision on the first day by choosing sequence B, this can easily be recovered on the second day by selecting sequence A. There are only relatively minor carry-over effects from day to day. The efficiency of using sequence A on the second day will be unrelated to the particular sequence used on the first day. This means that the printer need look only to the completion of the first day to make a decision. Only a short time horizon is necessary.

The sequence selection is a good example of being able to distinguish a good from a bad decision easily. Whether we were looking *prospectively*, toward making the decision, or *retrospectively*, subsequent to the decision, we can tell the good from the bad decision. It is easy to formulate decision situations in which this is not the case. Consider a *steel company* making a pricing decision. Suppose the choice is simply between no increase and an increase of 5%. The decision situation is drastically different from that described for the *printer*. First, the objective sought by the steel company is not clear. Presumably, the objective is related to the welfare of the company's owners. But is welfare maximized by maximizing expected short-term profits, "long-run" profits, or the market value of a share of stock? Maximizing expected short-term profits may be inconsistent with the maximizing of expected long-run profits. Furthermore, neither measure may be consistent with maximizing the market value of a share of stock. In other words, whereas a price increase may maximize expected short-term profits, a no-increase decision may maximize long-run profits. Thus, depending on which criteria you select, either decision may be judged good or bad.

One of the main reasons for the steel company decision being more difficult to deal with than the printing-sequence decision is that the ramifications of the price decision are extensive and far reaching. Increasing the current price may bring forth from competitors reactions with lasting effects on profits. Current-price increases could bring from government a reaction that would severely limit the company's future profit potential. Furthermore, price increases could spur the search for new technologies not using steel. All of these reactions to the price increase will have delayed effects, thus leading to a potential conflict between objectives that, by themselves, seem reasonable and consistent.

In addition to noting that the steel-price problem produces far-reaching and extensive ramifications that are absent in the sequence-selection problem, we must add that the mere *quantification* of these effects is an uncertain task. If a competitor enters the market, by what magnitude will the profits of the steel company be affected? How long will it take to produce competing technologies? These are important questions to the steel company but are very difficult to quantify. That is, there is uncertainty associated with merely predicting outcomes for the decisions. Moreover, the difficulty in prediction is magnified if the decision choice is a bold new move. For example, if a no-increase strategy had been the policy of the steel company (and the steel industry) for many years, it would probably be relatively easy to predict the results of a no-increase decision. But to predict the results of the increase decision would be difficult. No history would be available from which to make predictions.

The quantitative prediction of the outcome of a decision is further complicated by the state of nature. In the printer's problem, the time to change was independent of the state of the economy. But in the steel-price problem, the effect of a particular decision on profits—short-term or long-run—is clearly dependent on the state of the economy. Moreover, it depends not only on the immediate state of the economy, but on the state of the economy over an extended period. A no-increase strategy may be the better decision if economic activity is falling and continues to deteriorate, but it may be the inferior decision if the economy suddenly recovers. Thus, in the steel problem, the state of nature has an important bearing on what, in retrospect, was a good or bad decision.

The sequence decision and the price decision also differ in a more fundamental way. We can look at the sequence decision as one that can be repeated many times. It is also a reversible decision. If you choose the wrong sequence the first time, the correct sequence can be selected the next time the decision is faced, without concern about the lingering effect of your first decision. Thus, the first and subsequent decision problems are independent. This is not the case with the price-decision problem. Making either decision on price sets the steel company on an irreversible course and, to a large extent, circumscribes the future decision alternatives available to the company. Clearly the current decision on price de-

Table 2.2a Decision Matrix for Sequence Example Outcomes in Total Daily Change Time

	N_1	N_2	N_3
A_1	1.5	1.5	1.5
A_2	1	1	1

where

A_1 = use sequences B, C, D, or E

A_2 = use sequences A or F

N_1 = economic decline

N_2 = normal economic activity

N_3 = rapid economic expansion

O_{1j} = 1.5 hours ($j = 1, 2, 3$) of change time

O_{2j} = 1.0 hours ($j = 1, 2, 3$) of change time

pends on how the company can recover from unforeseen events brought by the future for each alternative to the current decision.

Thus, while some decision problems can be analyzed easily, there will always be room for doubt about whether a decision is good when a complicated decision problem, such as the steel company price decision, presents itself. But whether there is an easily analyzable decision problem or whether the context of the problem presents numerous ambiguities, we have a better prospect for distinguishing good from bad decisions if we systematically analyze a decision problem. A framework for such an analysis was discussed in Chapter 1 and can be used to analyze the two decision problems presented here.

Table 2.2a shows the decision matrix for the sequence problem. Selecting the best alternative is easy. We could also state outcomes for the decision problem

Table 2.2b Decision Matrix for Sequence Example Outcomes in Change Costs per Day

	N_1	N_2	N_3
A_1	$88	$88	$132
A_2	$22	$22	$33

where

O_{ij} is the cost of change time

Table 2.3a Decision Matrix for Steel Company Example Outcomes in Profit for Next Year

	N_1	N_2	N_3
A_1	-3	2	5
A_2	-8	4	7

where

A_1 = no price increase

A_2 = 5% price increase

N_1 = economic decline next year

N_2 = normal economic activity next year

N_3 = rapid economic expansion next year

O_{ij} = reported short-term profit in millions of dollars

in terms of the cost of idle time. This is done in Table 2.2b. Note that in the case of an economic expansion, the cost is larger. This results from an assumption that wages would increase by 50% in a period of rapid economic expansion. Notice that even though the costs are different under N_3, the relative advantage of sequences A and F remains.

Table 2.3a and 2.3b show hypothetical decision matrices for the steel company problem. Table 2.3a indicates the short-term profit in the body of the matrix, whereas Table 2.3b indicates the long-term profit. Consider first Table 2.3a. The choice of an alternative is not clear from this decision matrix. Although the choice of A_2 seems the best for N_2 and N_3, alternative A_1 is better if the economy should decline (N_1 occurs). We do not know which alternative to select. Next consider Table 2.3b. Here the numbers in the table represent the average profit over a

Table 2.3b Decision Matrix for Steel Company Example Outcomes in Average Profit Over Next 5 Years

	N_1	N_2	N_3
A_1	2	6	4
A_2	-1	3	5

where

O_{ij} = average profits over the next 5 years

5-year interval. Again, the choice between A_1 and A_2 is not clear. A no-price increase decision would be better if the economy declined or continued normally, whereas a price increase would be better if there were rapid economic expansion.

In reflecting these two examples, it is clear that in some decision problems, almost any "reasonable" criteria will suffice to produce a good decision. Furthermore, almost any reasonable criteria will produce the *same* decision. The sequence-choice problem was such a decision problem. It did not require much thought about criteria for choice or (what amounts to the same thing) specification of the objectives of the decision problem. The criterion (or objectives) in the steel company problem is a major source of consternation. Not only do we have the conflict between short- and long-term profit objectives but, since profit depends on the state of nature, we have the problem of obtaining a single *measure of effectiveness* that is an indicator of a complex of profit situations for each alternative.

In discussing general decision problems such as those pictorially represented in Table 1.3, the basic elements are: (1) alternatives A_i; (2) states of nature N_j; (3) outcomes O_{ij}; and (4) measures of effectiveness $e_i = f(A_i)$. Note that the measures of effectiveness are independent of the states of nature, N_j. This is more apparent than real. The function f contains all aspects of the relevant states of nature. The emphasis of this chapter will be on ways of establishing measures of effectiveness. Our discussions of the remaining elements will depend heavily on knowledge of the issues in developing these measures of effectiveness.

2.2   MEASURES OF EFFECTIVENESS

Measures of Effectiveness for Low-Level Decisions

As mentioned in the previous sections, some problems facing decision makers lend themselves to easy establishment of measures of effectiveness. These decisions, like the sequence decision, are usually technical in nature, have little carry-over into or interaction with other decision-making situations and are contained in a limited time frame. These are the types of decisions generally faced by the lowest level of management in an organization. Ordinarily the objective the decision maker faces is specified by a higher-level decision-making authority—middle management—and the measure of effectiveness is clear. For example, an assignment is given to the shop supervisor to produce 1000 units of output this week and to do it at the lowest cost. The supervisor will then assign the individual tasks in such a way that the given (usually fixed) work force produces the 1000 units with a minimum of cost. This usually implies that the measure of effectiveness is the minimization of overtime cost. The same objective could be accomplished by the supervisor assigning the workers in a way that maximizes the average productivity of each worker.

One characteristic of the decision problem we described in the previous paragraph is that it is likely that the measure of effectiveness would be equally good for one supervisor as for another. As we discuss measures of effectiveness for decision problems arising at higher positions in the decision-making hierarchy of an organization, we will find that a measure of effectiveness selected by one decision maker may differ significantly from a measure of effectiveness selected by another decision maker, even though both face apparently similar situations.

Measures of Effectiveness for Intermediate-Level Decisions

Suppose we move up the organization hierarchy. The division manager will find less exactitude in translating an objective into a measure of effectiveness. Suppose the president of the company calls the division manager in, charging that the return on investment is too low in the manager's division and that "something must be done to improve the profit situation of the division." In general terms, the division manager has an objective. But translating this objective into a measure of effectiveness by which to judge an alternative course of action may be a problem for the division manager.

Since the profitability of the division depends on many unpredictable or only imperfectly predictable factors, the division manager faces a problem in which uncertainty plays an important role. Some alternative courses of action to "improve the profit situation" will have more uncertainty with respect to outcomes than other alternatives. For example, consider the case of an appliance-manufacturing division of a large conglomerate corporation facing an impending recession. Simplifying the decision problem, suppose the division manager faces three alternatives: (1) embark on a price-cutting campaign in the hope of stimulating sales and increasing profits; (2) institute a cost-reduction program requiring only methods improvements suggested by a study made by the division industrial engineers; (3) reduce the capacity of the division by selling all general-purpose machinery not now in use, thereby eliminating a substantial portion of fixed charges.

Each of the foregoing alternatives has different effects on the profitability of the enterprise; each also has a substantial difference in the uncertainties with which it is associated. The profitability of the price-cutting alternative depends on the increased demand that the price cutting will induce. In the jargon of the economist, its profitability depends on the elasticity of demand. This cannot be known exactly, and some degree of uncertainty thus exists with the policy.

The program of cost reduction is assumed to be associated with a reduction of the variable cost of manufacturing the product. Since no price change is contemplated, no changes in demand will result from this policy. Although there is some doubt about the magnitude of the change that would result in variable costs, the uncertainty with respect to this policy is far less than that with the first alternative.

The third alternative—selling some of the division's productive equipment—will have very predictable effects in terms of reducing fixed costs. Uncertainties about the attainable profits are minor.

Now let us examine the uncertainty more carefully, through some break-even charts (Figures 2.1*a*, 2.1*b*, and 2.1*c*). In each curve, the current profit-output

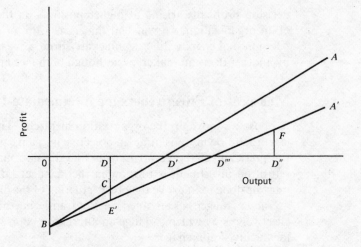

Figure 2.1a Analysis of price-cutting campaign.

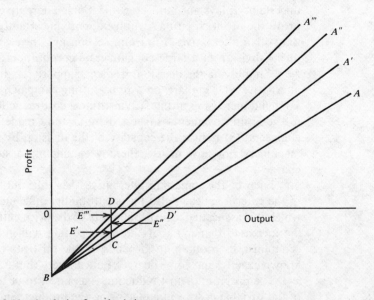

Figure 2.1b Analysis of methods improvement.

relationship before any alternative is adopted is denoted by the line *BA*. The company is assumed to be operating at output *D* and a resulting (negative) profit of *C*.

Figure 2.1a can be used to analyze the price-cutting decision. Since a price reduction would reduce the operating margin—price less variable costs—we would find the resulting profit-output relationship to be *BA'*. Now, if the price reduction does not induce an increased demand (demand is inelastic), the losses

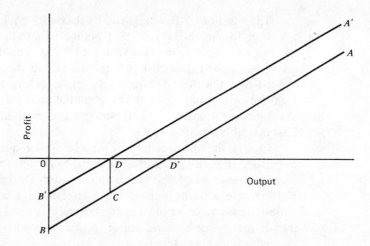

Figure 2.1c Analysis of capacity reduction.

will increase from C to E' as a result of the move. The situation would worsen. Suppose, however, that the demand increases substantially, to D'', because of the price cut. In this case, profits would be F. Let us assume a substantial probability that demand will be D and also a good chance that demand will be D'' such that the *expected* demand is D'''. Thus, the price-reduction alternative has an expected profit of zero, but a substantial range of possible profits from E' to F.

Next consider alternative 2, shown in Figure 2.1b. The methods improvement will not affect demand (or output), but will increase the operating profit. Therefore, it will cause the profit-output function to increase in slope. Since the effect on variable costs is not certain, we cannot be sure of the exact increase. BA', BA'', and BA''' represent three possible changes due to methods improvement. Let us assume that they can be characterized as least favorable, expected, and most favorable. The losses produced would be uncertain, ranging from E''' in the most favorable case to E' in the least favorable case. In all cases, the profit would be negative, and the uncertainty with respect to the magnitude of the losses would be substantially less than for alternative 1.

Figure 2.1c considers the third alternative—selling some equipment. We will assume that there is no uncertainty with respect to the effects on profit of this alternative. When the profit-output function changes to $B'A'$, the profits will increase to the break-even profit.

Which alternative should be selected? Let us see if we can make some comparisons. First, limit the comparison to alternatives 1 and 2. Alternative 1 has an expected profit of 0, whereas alternative 2 has an expected profit that is negative. By this measure of effectiveness, alternative 1 seems preferable to alternative 2. On the other hand, if our worst predictions were to materialize, alternative 1 would produce a loss even greater than that obtained without any change, whereas alternative 2 will assure at least some improvement in the profit position. By this analysis, alternative 2 increases in desirability.

The selection of the alternative by the division manager depends on his or her tolerance for accepting risk. Acceptance of alternative 2 would ensure some improvement. At the end of the year, the manager could point to reduced losses as a reflection of good stewardship of the assets that the top management let him or her manage. On the other hand, the manager can accept alternative 1 and be regarded by top management as a potential board chairperson if the most favorable outcome is achieved—and perhaps as a candidate for unemployment if the least desirable outcome arises.

Clearly, the tolerance for risk is an individual quality that varies from person to person. Thus, because of their differing tolerances for risk, two different division managers may make different decisions when facing the identical decision situation. Furthermore, whereas both the lower-level manager and his or her supervisor will almost always agree on the decision criterion selected by the lower-level manager, the top management may disagree substantially with the measure of effectiveness the division manager selects.

Measures of Effectiveness and Constraints

We have deliberately avoided discussion of alternative 3 in order to focus on the two important factors in a decision problem—uncertainty and tolerance for uncertainty—and to illustrate how these factors affect decision making.

Let us now turn to alternative 3. If one compares alternative 3 to alternative 2, it is hard to imagine a decision maker preferring 2 to 3. The expected profit with 3 is larger than that with 2; furthermore, no uncertainty exists with alternative 3, whereas a substantial amount exists with alternative 2. Even in its most favorable outcome, alternative 2 will yield a smaller profit than alternative 3. Can't we rule out alternative 2 as unreasonable and *dominated* by alternative 3?

Alternative 3 is clearly preferable to alternative 2 *if one considers only the measure of effectiveness that we have used*. That measure of effectiveness is expected short-term profit. But, as in the case of the steel company problem, perhaps one should be looking at long-term profits. Alternative 3 is severely lacking when one considers long-term profits. If the capacity of the plant is reduced, the division manager will be unable to take advantage of the economic recovery predicted to follow the recession without severe cost consequences. Notice that each of the other two alternatives would leave the division manager in a flexible position to deal with the future.

Expected short-term profits seem to be a reasonable measure of effectiveness for alternatives 1 and 2 because the long-term profit will be unaffected by either decision. Thus, short-term and long-term profit maximizations seem to be consistent objectives for these alternatives. This is definitely not the case for alternative 3. Therefore, the decision maker is likely to rule it out of consideration. There is a *constraint* that rules this alternative out of the decision problem. There are two reasons for constraints that rule out alternatives—technical and economic. If an alternative cannot be accomplished because of legal barriers, lack of resources, or similar reasons, we will call the constraint technical. Examples of technical constraints would, for example, be (1) fair-trade laws that prevent a manufacturer from reducing price; (2) union agreements that rule out reducing manpower and, therefore, variable production costs; and (3) the lack of a resale market for equipment. Economic constraints rule out alternatives because of *undesirable economic effects that are not incorporated in the measure of effectiveness*. Thus, economic constraints help in formulating the measure of effectiveness.

Measures of Effectiveness for Top-Level Decisions

In our discussions of intermediate-level decisions, we discussed the important roles of uncertainty, risk tolerance, and constraints in formulating measures of effectiveness. These factors also play an important role in establishing measures of effectiveness for top-level decision making. We have nothing new to add in this section. Suffice it to say that we can distinguish levels of decision making in an organization by indicating that with movement up the hierarchical structure, uncertainty, risk tolerance, and constraints play a much more evident role. Furthermore, because of this, with upward movement in the structure, differences in individual's risk tolerance at the same management level are likely to lead to differences of opinion about appropriate measures of effectiveness and, therefore, differences in the quality of decision making.

2.3 THE CONCEPT OF UTILITY AND MEASURES OF EFFECTIVENESS

Anyone who has taken an elementary economics course has an intuitive grasp of the concept of utility. The utility function for an individual is a measure of effectiveness that allows that individual to choose which goods are to be consumed. The function is a theoretical concept that permits analysis of the degree of satisfaction obtained from a consumption choice. This concept of utility can be taken and applied to decision making in general.

In this section, the concept of utility will be used to develop some reasonable measures of effectiveness for decision-making problems involving uncertainty. However, before getting to the main task of this section, it will be necessary to discuss some recent developments in utility theory and decision making.

Utility of Wealth and Decisions Involving Uncertainty

Even though we ordinarily think of utility as derived from consumption, we can abstract from the choice of goods and indicate that utility would obviously be a function of income. In turn, since income is clearly related to wealth, it is convenient and traditional to express utility as a function of wealth.

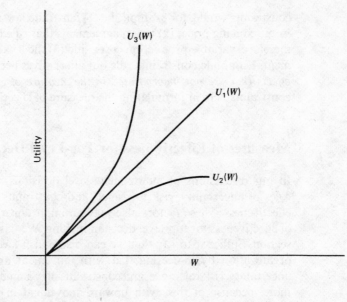

Figure 2.2 Some hypothetical functions.

Furthermore, we will characterize utility as a nondecreasing function of ending wealth, W. That is, utility will be characterized by a function somewhat resembling those shown in Figure 2.2. Consider an individual with $U_2(W)$ as a utility function. As wealth increases, so does utility. However, with more and more wealth, the increase in utility per unit increase in wealth decreases. (Mathematically, the function is concave.) Thus, the function indicates diminishing marginal utility. The utility function, $U_1(W)$, shows constant marginal utility. Each incremental unit of wealth produces the same incremental utility. An increasing marginal utility of wealth is characterized by the curve $U_3(W)$.

The curvature of the utility function has an important relationship with the concept of risk tolerance that we discussed in the previous section. An individual who is indifferent to risk can be considered as having a utility function of the $U_1(W)$ type, whereas an individual who is *risk averse* will have a utility function with the curvature shown in $U_2(W)$. Individuals who *like* risk are associated with a utility function of the $U_3(W)$ type. Most analyses of business decision making ignore utility functions such as $U_3(W)$ as unreasonable descriptions of the majority of decision makers and concentrate on decision makers who are risk indifferent or risk averse. We will follow this practice. To illustrate the difference between $U_1(W)$ and $U_2(W)$, we will consider two individuals with these type of utility functions. The $U_1(W)$ and $U_2(W)$ functions are characterized by $U_1'(W) > 0$ and $U_2'(W) > 0$ for all $W \geq 0$, and $U_1''(W) = 0$ and $U_2''(W) < 0$ for all $W \geq 0$. There are, of course, many mathematical functions with these properties. To illustrate

Table 2.4 Realized Ending Wealth

	N_1 $P_1 = \frac{1}{2}$	N_2 $P_2 = \frac{1}{2}$
A_1	1100	1200
A_2	800	1600

how each affects the choice between risky alternatives, suppose we choose two specific mathematical forms, such as[1]

$$U_1(W) = aW \qquad a > 0 \tag{2.1}$$

and

$$U_2(W) = W - aW^2 \qquad 0 < a < \frac{1}{2W^*} \qquad \text{where} \qquad W^* \geq \text{Max } W \tag{2.2}$$

Assume analysis has shown that $a = 0.002$ for (2.1), and that $a = 0.0003125$ for (2.2). Suppose that each individual must choose between two uncertain alternatives A_1 and A_2. Table 2.4 describes the characteristics of the two alternatives in the form of a decision table. The body of the table gives the ending wealth for each alternative and each state of nature. The probabilities of the states of nature are shown.

It has been established, and is well accepted, that maximizing the expected utility of ending wealth is the appropriate measure of effectiveness for problems with uncertain alternatives. Then, if we define W_i as the ending wealth if alternative A_i is adopted and recognize it as a random variable, alternative A_1 should be accepted over alternative 2 if

$$E[U(W_1)] > E[U(W_2)]$$

That is, A_1 should be accepted if

$$(\tfrac{1}{2})U(1100) + (\tfrac{1}{2})U(1200) > (\tfrac{1}{2})U(800) + (\tfrac{1}{2})U(1600) \tag{2.3}$$

Now consider the linear utility function in (2.1). Expected utility for alternative A_1 becomes

$$E(U_1(W_1)] = (\tfrac{1}{2})a(1100) + (\tfrac{1}{2})a(1200) = 1150a$$

and for A_2 it is

$$E[U_1(W_2)] = (\tfrac{1}{2})a(800) + (\tfrac{1}{2})a(1600) = 1200a$$

---

[1] The conditions placed on (2.2) guarantee that for all possible values of ending wealth, $U_2'(W) \geq 0$. This condition merely states that if we use a quadratic function to describe utility, we must make sure it does not decrease in the range of possible values of W.

Clearly, since $1200a > 1150a$, alternative A_2 would be selected. Since $E(W_1) = 1150$ and $E(W_2) = 1200$ and since $a > 0$, it follows that the criterion of maximizing expected utility can be accomplished by merely picking the alternative with the largest expected ending wealth. The fact that $a = 0.002$ was not useful.

The criterion developed in the previous paragraph for the example is more general that it seems at first glance. It holds for *all* linear utility functions. That is, we may state the general rule that if the utility function is linear, expected utility is maximized by selecting the alternative with the largest expected ending wealth.

Next, consider the quadratic utility function (2.2). In this case, the expected utilities of alternatives A_1 and A_2 are

$$E[U_2(W_1)] = (\tfrac{1}{2})[1100 - a(1100)^2] + (\tfrac{1}{2})[1200 - a(1200)^2]$$

and

$$E[U_2(W_2)] = (\tfrac{1}{2})[800 - a(800)^2] + (\tfrac{1}{2})[1600 - a(1600)^2]$$

respectively.

Now with $a = 0.0003125$, $E(U_2(W_1)] = 735.9375$ and $E[U_2(W_2)] = 700.0000$. Clearly, alternative A_1 is more desirable, even though alternative A_2 has a larger expected value of ending wealth. The reason for this result was that the variability of alternative A_2 was much greater than the variability of A_1, and the greater expected ending wealth of A_2 was insufficient to offset its greater variability.

In general, we can say that a linear utility function describes indifference to risk, or *risk neutrality*, on the part of the decision maker. A utility function that is strictly concave $[U''(W) < 0]$ exhibits an attitude of *risk aversion* on the part of the decision maker. Risk aversion is the case in which the shape matters. Risk neutrality can be described intuitively as a case in which the shape of the probability distribution is of no concern to the decision maker. Only the mean matters.

It is difficult to generalize regarding choice procedures under risk. The mathematical form of the utility function and the mathematical form of the probability distribution affect the choice of an alternative. The following statements summarize some facts about utility functions; these facts are developed in more detail in more advanced works.

1. If the utility function is linear, the only characteristic of the probability distributions that affects choice is the expected value of ending wealth. The alternative with the greatest expected value of ending wealth will produce the greatest expected utility.

2. (a) If the utility function is quadratic [with $U''(W) < 0$], only the expected value and standard deviation of terminal wealth affect the choice. Defining $E(W_1) = \mu_1$ and $E(W_2) = \mu_2$ as the expected ending wealths of alternatives A_1 and A_2, respectively, and $\sigma_1{}^2$ and $\sigma_2{}^2$ as the variances of ending wealth, alternative A_1 is preferred to alternative A_2 if $\mu_1 > \mu_2$ *and* $\sigma_1{}^2 \le \sigma_2{}^2$. If $\mu_1 > \mu_2$ and $\sigma_1{}^2 > \sigma_2{}^2$, no statement on preference can be made without examining the specific utility function.

    (b) If the utility function is concave and nonlinear (but not necessarily quadratic) *and the probability distribution of ending wealth is normal*, only the expected value and standard deviation of ending wealth affect the choice. As in case a, A_1 is preferred to A_2 if $\mu_1 \geq \mu_2$ and $\sigma_1^2 \leq \sigma_2^2$. If $\mu_1 > \mu_2$ and $\sigma_1^2 > \sigma_2^2$, no statement on preference can be made without examining the specific utility function.

3. If the utility function is concave (but not quadratic), and the probability distribution is nonnormal, little can be said about the choice between prospects without knowing the mathematical forms of the probability distribution and the utility function.

Much decision-making theory has developed around the assumptions underlying point 2. They allow decisions to be made on the basis of only means and standard deviations of ending wealth for alternatives. It is easy to extend the analysis into what has been called *mean-variance space*. In Figure 2.3, we have plotted the (μ_i, σ_i^2) combinations for a set of alternatives. Using the assumptions of point 2, we can conclude that A_1 is preferred to A_6, since $\mu_1 > \mu_6$ and $\sigma_1^2 < \sigma_6^2$. Furthermore, A_2 is preferred to A_3 for the same reason. Thus, we can conclude that A_3 and A_6 are dominated by other prospects and need be given no further consideration. Note, however, that we cannot make similar statements concerning A_1, A_2, A_4, and A_5. For example, $\mu_4 > \mu_2$, but $\sigma_4 > \sigma_2$, and thus no clear preference between A_2 and A_4 can be established. The set of points (A_1, A_2, A_4, A_5) is frequently called the *efficient set*. One of these points is the optimal choice. The choice however, depends on the specific utility function.

It should be obvious that each of the aforementioned four points will be the optimal choice for some utility function. For example, if the utility function is

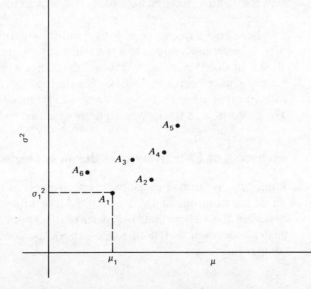

Figure 2.3 Mean-variance plot at alternatives.

linear—that is, the decision maker is risk neutral—point A_5 will be selected. On the other hand, if the decision maker is "extremely" risk averse, he or she would choose A_1, since it has the smallest standard deviation. The most likely cases would be A_2 or A_4, in which the decision maker is not risk neutral and not "extremely" risk averse. The final selection would, of course, depend on the specific nature of the utility function.

The conclusion of the previous paragraph leaves us still undecided. We can make the final choice by evaluating the expected utility function. But whereas utility functions are very useful for theoretical analysis, they are difficult to specify in practical situations. Utility is an abstract concept difficult for practical persons to grasp. Therefore, most methods that attempt to specify utility functions as measures of effectiveness proceed by indirect methods that involve the decision maker in a series of personal questions about the choice of specific hypothetical prospects. The utility function must then be derived from the decision maker's responses.

Another approach for incorporating risk tolerance in the decision-making process that has been proposed has the advantage of specifying a simple measure of effectiveness that will behave like a utility function and has some intuitively appealing properties. Suppose we form a function

$$F(\mu_i, \sigma_i) = \mu_i - k\sigma_i^2 \qquad k \geq 0$$

and describe the choice procedure as selecting that prospect for which $F(\mu_i, \sigma_i)$ is a maximum.

Note that if $k = 0$, the optimal choice for our example is A_5. On the other hand, if $k = k_L$ is sufficiently large, the choice will be A_1. Then there exist values of k between 0 and k_L for which A_2 or A_4 will be selected. Thus, by specifying k, we act as if we were specifying the utility function.[2]

Note that $F(\mu_i, \sigma_i) = \mu_i - k\sigma_i^2$ can be interpreted as a *certainty equivalent* of μ_i. The certainty equivalent is an amount assigned to uncertain prospects that allows the decision maker to act as if the choice were between certain alternatives instead of uncertain ones. That is, when the prospect is risky, we subtract an amount from its expected ending wealth—$k\sigma_i^2$—to get an *adjusted* expected ending wealth. The prospect with the highest adjusted expected ending wealth is then selected.

Measures of Effectiveness in Business Decision Making

What help in forming measures of effectiveness in business decision making can we derive from our analysis of utility? The idea of a certainty equivalent, discussed in the last section, is a particularly appealing one to carry over into a business decision situation. Let us apply the concept to the printer and steel company problems.

---

[2] See J. Pratt, "Risk Aversion in the Small and in the Large," *Econometrica*, *32* (1964), pp. 122–136, for a justification of the formula $F(\mu_i, \sigma_i) = \mu_i - k\sigma_1^2$.

For the printer we could argue that the value of k should be close to zero, and we would therefore merely select the alternative that maximized the expected value of productivity (minimized change-over time). This could be justified on two grounds. First, since the variabilities present in the alternatives are presumably about equal, the choice would be made only on the expected value of productivity. Second, since the decision could be thought of as being repeated many times over the long run, the *average* productivity of each sequence would have a negligible standard error, thus essentially removing uncertainty from the problem. This would mean that we could treat the utility function as if it were linear.

In the steel company problem we have alternatives that do not have equal variance. It is thus impossible to rule out consideration of variance in favor of the expected profit alone. Furthermore, the variance will not be reduced by repeated consideration of the same problem. The decision is isolated and will not be repeated. It also has lasting long-run consequences that are serious. Thus, one can reason that k will not be zero but will take on some positive value.

A modification of the certainty equivalent principle, while less secure theoretically, has a certain intuitive appeal. Suppose we replace $F(\mu_i, \sigma_i) = \mu_i - k\sigma_i^2$ by $F^*(\mu_i, \sigma_i) = \mu_i - k^*\sigma_i$. In choosing k^*, we could reason intuitively about F^* in a manner similar to our reasoning about F with respect to k; for example, $k^* = 0$ implies ignoring risk and $k^* > 0$ implies taking some cognizance of risk. If, however, we let $k^* = 3$ (and our assumption of a normal distribution was reasonably accurate), it would follow that the adjusted expected profits would be $F^*(\mu_i, \sigma_i) = \mu_i - 3\sigma_i$. With $k^* = 3$, $F^*(\mu_i, \sigma_i)$ would be the practical minimum value of profits that would be obtained from prospect i. Maximizing $F^*(\mu_i, \sigma_i)$ would amount to choosing the alternative with the "maximum-minimum" value of profit. This measure of effectiveness, called maxi-min, has been frequently described as the pessimist's criterion.

2.4 SUMMARY

There is no magic formula that, if followed, will lead to good decision making in a business organization. Some decision-making situations are obvious and easily and unambiguously analyzed. Other situations have an irreducible element of ambiguity. The amgibuity arises because of lingering effects of the decision, occurring far beyond the immediate time frame, because of inherent uncertainties in the situation that cannot be removed and because of the risk tolerance of the decision maker.

The factors previously cited—lingering effects, uncertainties, and risk tolerance—appear with greater intensity at higher organizational levels. The decisions to be made by the shop supervisor are clearer and more easily analyzable than those the company president faces. It is almost always possible to look back on the shop supervisor's decision-making history and determine whether he or she had made good or bad decisions. It is much more difficult to judge the decision-making performance of the company president.

At higher organizational levels, the tolerance for risk is an important element in decision problems. The concept of utility helps in abstract discussion of decision problems and in showing how the inherent uncertainty in the problem interacts with the risk tolerance of the decision maker. We used these ideas to develop the concept of a certainty equivalent as a measure of effectiveness for business decision problems. Although the certainty equivalent does not obviate the need to specify the relevant outcomes of a decision problem, it does help in handling uncertainty once the relevant outcomes have been specified.

References

Chernoff, H., and L.E. Moser, *Elementary Decision Theory*, New York: John Wiley & Sons, 1959.

Friedman, M., and L.J. Savage, "The Utility Analysis of Choices Involving Risk," *Journal of Political Economy*, Vol. 56 (1948), pp. 279–304.

Jedamus, P., and R. Frame. *Business Decision Theory*, New York: McGraw-Hill, 1969. Chapters 1 and 2.

Markowitz, H.M., "The Utility of Wealth," *Journal of Political Economy*, Vol. 60 (1952), p. 155.

Miller, D.W., and M.K. Starr, *Executive Decisions and Operations Research*, Englewood Cliffs, N.J.: Prentice-Hall, 1963.

Pratt, J.W., "Risk Aversion in the Small and in the Large," *Econometrica*, Vol. 32 (1964), pp. 122–136.

Raiffa, H., *Decision Analysis*, Reading, Mass: Addison-Wesley, 1968, Chapters 1–4.

Schlaifer, R., *Probability and Statistics for Business Decisions*, New York: McGraw-Hill, 1959.

Schlaifer, R., *Analysis of Decisions Under Uncertainty*, New York: McGraw-Hill, 1969. Chapter 5.

Review Questions

1. (a) Describe one decision problem with which you are familiar in which uncertainties are important to the choice and describe one decision problem in which uncertainties are relatively unimportant. (b) Describe one decision problem with which you are familiar in which "lingering effects" are important and one in which they are not.

2. Distinguish between outcomes and measures of effectiveness.

3. Using as an example a decision problem with which you are familiar, show how measures of effectiveness within an organization may differ depending on the level within the organization where the decision is made.

4. Distinguish between technological constraints and economic constraints. Describe the function of each. Give examples in decision problems familiar to you.

5. Explain how the tolerance for risk is related to the curvature of the utility function.

6. Explain the reason for the conditions placed on the quadratic utility function in Equation 2.2.

7. Explain the meanings of the terms risk neutrality and risk aversion.

8. Explain and discuss the significance of (a) mean-variance analysis, and (b) the efficient set.

9. Explain the concept of certainty equivalent.

Problems
1. For each of the following decision problems, describe two potential measures of effectiveness. In which problems are the two measures likely to produce different decisions?

(a) A manufacturer must choose one of three potential clamps for attaching hoses to fittings in an automatic washer. The clamps have different purchase prices and require different times to install. The quality can be considered comparable.

(b) A trucking company must deliver goods to seven different locations in a midwestern city. Looking at the problem from a purely mechanistic point of view, there are 7 different routings of a truck. The company must select one route.

(c) A computer-services company has five systems analysts who must be assigned to five contracts that the company has signed. The analysts' salaries and productivities on the five contracts are different. An assignment must be made.

(d) A small plastics firm can sell any quantity of laminated desk tops or decorative counter tops that it can produce. The two product classes share the same production facilities, which consist of a chemical department, a forming department, and a trimming and finishing department. Each product class requires time in each department. The difference between selling prices and variable costs is known for each product.

(e) The demand for Christmas trees at the Boy Scout lot is known only in terms of its probability distribution. The scouts must purchase trees well in advance of the season to meet the uncertain demand. Any trees left over at the close of the season must be scrapped. The selling price for a tree is set by competition and is beyond the control of the scouts. They must decide how many trees to purchase.

(f) An investor wants to determine the proportion of bonds and stocks to include in an investment portfolio.

(g) An automobile manufacturer is considering producing a new, low-pollution car. The production would require drastic changes in the production process. If the car is successful, the company will have a 2-year "jump" on competitors for the market. If the car is unsuccessful, it will suffer disastrous economic consequences. The manufacturer must decide whether to go ahead with the new car or continue producing the old one.

2. Which of the decision problems described in Problem 1 are reversible?

3. For each of the decision problems in Problem 1, describe the potential constraints on the solution to the decision problem. Which of the constraints that you described rule out undesirable economic effects and which are purely technical?

4. Suppose you had a choice between two alternatives, A_1 and A_2. Alternative A_1 would increase your wealth by $100,000, with a probability of $\frac{1}{2}$, or *decrease* your wealth by $10,000, with a probability of $\frac{1}{2}$. Alternative A_2 offers an increase of $120,000, with a probability of $\frac{1}{2}$, and a decrease of $20,000, with a probability of $\frac{1}{2}$.

    (a) If your present wealth is $100,000 and your utility function is $U(W) = \sqrt{W}$, which would you select?

    (b) If your present wealth is $25,000, would your choice be different? Given an explanation of your answer.

    (c) How would your answers to parts a and b differ if $U(W) = W$?

5. Suppose your utility function were $U(W) = 5\sqrt{W} + 3$; would you make the same decisions on parts a and b of Problem 4 as with $U(W) = \sqrt{W}$?

6. An investor must choose one of 10 portfolios with the following expected rate-of-return and variance-of-rate-of-return combinations. A_1: (0.04, 0); A_2: (0.03, 0.01); A_3: (0.05, 0.01); A_4: (0.08, 0.03); A_5: (0.10, 0.02); A_6: (0.12, 0.04); A_7: (0.05, 0.02); A_8: (0.13, 0.07); A_9: (0.09, 0.04); A_{10}: (0.11, 0.06).

    (a) Plot the alternatives in mean-variance space.

    (b) Which portfolios form the efficient set?

    (c) If the measure of effectiveness for choice is $\mu_i - 5\sigma_i^2$, which portfolio maximizes the measure of effectiveness?

    (d) If the measure of effectiveness is $\mu_i - 0.05\sigma_i^2$, which portfolio would be chosen?

7. Prefinishing Corporation is considering increasing the mechanization of finishing door moldings. Three machines are being considered. Although the machines have different initial costs and different operating costs, it is possible to summarize their economic characteristics with the expected uniform annual profit and the variance of that profit. Machine 1 has $(\mu_1, \sigma_1^2) = (5000, 500)$, machine 2 has $(\mu_2, \sigma_2^2) = (7500, 300)$, and machine 3 has $(\mu_3, \sigma_3^2) = (8000, 400)$. If the profits are normally distributed and you know only that the utility function is concave, can you determine the alternative that maximizes utility? (*Hint.* Plot the three probability distributions on a single graph. Plot several "likely" utility functions on the same graph.)

8. Suppose a decision maker has a utility function $U(W) = \sqrt{W}$ and faces an uncertain alternative that promises to yield a *change* in wealth that is normal with mean $100 and variance $49.

    (a) Determine the certainty equivalent for this alternative if the decision maker's wealth is $100,000.

      (b) Determine the certainty equivalent if the decision maker's wealth is $25,000.

9. Solve the previous problem if the decision maker's utility function is $U(W) = W - 0.0003125W^2$.

10. Carefully examine the results of Problems 8 and 9. How is the certainty equivalent related to wealth in each case? Based on your instinct on how the certainty equivalent should be related to wealth, determine which utility function you think is more plausible (or realistic as describing the behavior of decision makers).

3

MODELS AND MODEL BUILDING

3.1 WHAT IS A MODEL?

Model Components
Why Build Models?

3.2 A CLASSIFICATION OF MODELS

Verbal Models
Physical Models
Mathematical Models

3.3 A CLASSIFICATION OF MATHEMATICAL MODELS

Deductive Consequences
Time Dimension
Degree of Uncertainty

3.4 THE MODEL-BUILDING PROCESS

Problem Recognition
Specification of Objectives, Measures of Effectiveness, and
  Constraints
Formulating the Model
Validating the Model

3.5 SUMMARY

References
Review Questions
Problems

Thus far we have suggested the relationship among alternatives, states of nature, and outcomes shown in Table 1.3. However, this simple relationship belies the complexity of the problem. Part of this complexity arises because the decision maker is immersed in the day-to-day activities of the organization and can see the far-reaching and immediate realities of any decision he or she must make. In order to make an effective decision, the unimportant complexities of the real world must be ignored.

3.1 WHAT IS A MODEL?

Models can make the decision problem more tractable. A *model* is an abstraction of reality that maintains only the essential elements of a problem. A model should be as simple as possible *and still give the desired results*. Of course, oversimplifying the problem can lead to poor decisions. For example, a model designed to determine an appropriate marketing-campaign strategy in a manufacturing organization should include at least some consideration for productive capacity and financial condition; otherwise, the organization could find itself in the untenable situation of generating a large demand for items that it cannot produce or finance. Selecting the important problem elements for the model is a part of the process of model building that we will defer until later. For now, let us concentrate on the concept of "model."

Model Components

Just as the components of a television set work together to generate a good picture, so does a decision-making model have a number of components that, when correctly assembled, produce good decision-making information. Each decision-making model has the following four components: (1) dependent variables (outcomes or measures of effectiveness); (2) independent variables (alternatives and states of nature); (3) constants and parameters; and (4) relationships between the variables.

The *dependent variables* of a decision model can be the outcomes resulting from the pairing of a particular alternative and state of nature or the measures of effectiveness that combine two or more possible outcomes into one decision criterion. Thus, the values of the dependent variables are affected by the alternatives and state of nature or, more specifically, by the *independent variables*. The decision alternatives are called controllable independent variables, whereas the states of nature are uncontrollable independent variables.

Two other important components of decision models are the constants and the parameters, and the relationships between the variables. A *constant* is an entity that does not change with time and whose value is known. For instance,

$\pi \doteq 3.1415927$ is a constant used frequently in mathematics. A *parameter*, however, varies with the particular application and, in most instances, must be estimated or determined by the decision maker. An example would be the percent change in demand per 1 % change in price. The value of this parameter, referred to by economists as elasticity, varies with the product being considered.

Frequently, constants and parameters help specify the *relationships* between the variables. In some models, such as verbal or physical models, the relationships may not be well defined or very explicit. On the other hand, the relationships in mathematical models are explicit expressions that define or constrain the dependent and independent variables. In such models, constants and parameters become identifiable elements in the relationships, whereas in the former model types, the role of the constants and parameters in the relationship is not always clear. As an example of a mathematical relationship, consider the following expression, which relates sales, S, for a particular product to the advertising expenditure, A, and disposable personal income, I.

$$S = a + bA + cI \tag{3.1}$$

In this expression, S is a dependent variable, A represents the decision alternatives, and I is an exogeneous variable. The factors a, b, and c are parameters that must be estimated. Thus, once the values of the parameters have been determined, the decision maker can adjust the values of A for given values of I to see what impact advertising has on sales. Of course, this relationship may be only a small part of a much larger system of relationships defining and constraining the dependent and independent variables in the problem. The entire system of relationships is called a model.

Why Build Models?

Before we classify the various types of models of particular interest and discuss the principles of modeling, we must provide some insight about why the concept of models is so important. In the first place, modeling forces the decision maker to consider all aspects of the problem and to identify all the important relationships between the variables. It also forces the problem solver to abstract from the complexities of the real situation and focus attention on the few important variables and relationships. This, in itself, is a good reason to study models.

Another reason for building models is that, in many cases, it is very costly to experiment in the real world. Consider the airport manager who, after considering several alternative designs for a new airport, tells the construction contractor, "Build design A. If that doesn't work out, we can always try design B later." Experimentation of this kind is extremely costly. No managers in their right mind would suggest such procedures. It is much less expensive to build a model and then use that model for experimentation. Since models relate decision alternatives to objectives, the airport manager, for example, could try the various different designs to see the effects of each on the objectives.

A third reason for using models is that managers in this dynamic world continually face changing environmental conditions. With such change, it is of great help to have decision models available that take into account the environmental factors of importance. Then, when significant changes are apparent, they can be incorporated into the model and the decision problem can be reanalyzed quickly and efficiently.

3.2 A CLASSIFICATION OF MODELS

A decision maker must identify which type of model best suits the decision problem. This is why we will discuss a classification of models before getting into the principles of model building. Although we will concentrate on mathematical models in the remainder of this text, we will first discuss two other model types because of their prevalence in practice.

Verbal Models

A verbal model expresses all of the functional relationships between the variables in a word passage. For example, consider the advertising manager of a company that manufactures breakfast cereal who makes the following statement concerning television commercials on Saturday mornings: "A 20-second spot has much more impact on our target audience than a 15-second spot." In this example, the different time durations of the commercial are the decision alternatives; its "impact" which, we could infer, relates to the propensity of the viewers' parents to purchase the company's cereal, is the dependent variable. Thus, we have a relationship between decision alternatives and a dependent variable that relates to company objectives. Such models are used extensively in the business world and have the advantage of being easy to understand. Often they are an outcropping of many years of managerial experience and are useful for summarizing this experience in understandable language.

Verbal models, however, have a number of shortcomings. The decision maker cannot experiment with them, nor do they indicate specifically how the outcomes or measures of effectiveness change with the decision alternatives. In the preceding verbal model, we do not know how *much* more impact a 20-second commercial has over a 15-second commercial.

A second drawback is that it is not easy to show how the *relationships* change with the decision alternative. We infer that a 20-second spot has more impact than a 15-second spot. However, does a 30-second spot have more impact than a 20-second spot? What is the relationship between a 30-second spot and a 15-second spot? We cannot answer these questions with the verbal model. If we constructed a verbal model that answered such questions for all possible commercial lengths, we would have a very lengthy verbal model that would be difficult to understand and not useful for experimentation.

Nevertheless, verbal models can play an important role in the decision process. They can be used to verbalize decision strategies from more sophisticated models.

Physical Models

A model that takes on the physical appearance of the object it is to portray is called a physical model. This type of model is used to display or test the design of items ranging from new buildings to new products. In the aircraft industry scale models of new aircraft are built and tested in wind tunnels to record the aerodynamics of the design. An automobile-parts manufacturer may have a three-dimensional scale model of the plant floor, complete with miniature machines and equipment, so that a new layout of the plant can be analyzed. The machines in the model can be rearranged and new layouts studied in order to improve the material flow.

Physical models have the advantage of being usable for experimentation. In the aircraft example, the testing of a different design may mean that a completely new model must be built. In addition to offering the advantage of experimentation, physical models lucidly describe the problem or system under study; this is helpful in generating innovative design alternatives for solving the decision problem.

Nevertheless, only a relatively small class of problems can be solved with physical models. Problems such as portfolio selection, media selection, and production scheduling are examples of problems that cannot be analyzed with a physical model. Basically, physical models are useful only in design problems, and even some of these can be analyzed more efficiently and completely with mathematical models and a computer. Besides this, physical models do not contain explicit relationships between the decision alternatives and dependent variables or objectives and, thus, trial-and-error methods of problem solving must be used. Although this in itself is not a major drawback, the trial-and-error process, coupled with a need to rebuild the model for each design change, can lead to a very time-consuming and costly process in some cases.

Mathematical Models

A mathematical model is one whose relationships are expressed in the rigorous language of mathematics. In this way, a mathematical model is abstract because one cannot visualize the system it is supposed to portray by merely looking at it.

Before mentioning some of the advantages of mathematical models, let us see what some of the disadvantages are. The degree of abstraction, already mentioned, is a definite impediment to the managerial acceptance of such models. It is not surprising to get resistance to their use from managers who have not had sufficient training in and exposure to these models—and also from managers who have training but do not have the time to pay close attention to the model.

Another shortcoming of mathematical models is that the symbolic language of mathematics has its own limitations. Some models may be too complex to solve efficiently, requiring gross oversimplifications of the real problem in order to get a solution of some kind. Under these circumstances, the problem that is "solved" no longer resembles the original problem and, if the solution is implemented, disastrous organizational effects could result. Proper selection of model type and solution technique, discussed later in this chapter, should minimize this type of mistake.

On the positive side, mathematical models facilitate experimentation because all dependent variables, independent variables, constants, and parameters are explicitly related through the language of mathematics. The decision maker can test the effects of different decision alternatives, constants, and parameter values on the dependent variables much more easily than with any other type of model. Furthermore, mathematical models can represent many complex problems efficiently and concisely and, in many cases, provide the cheapest way to analyze these problems. It is for these reasons that we address the various mathematical models and solution techniques most often used in practice.

3.3 A CLASSIFICATION OF MATHEMATICAL MODELS

Mathematical models can be classified according to: (1) the deductive consequences the decision maker desires; (2) the inclusion of the time dimension in the model components; and (3) the degree of uncertainty associated with the model components.

Deductive Consequences

There are two types of deductive consequences relating to model output: *normative* and *descriptive*. Normative models select the best decision alternatives for the problem. They incorporate a measure of effectiveness so that a *choice* between decision alternatives can be made in solving the model.

For example, consider a manufacturer who must choose the appropriate production quantities for two types of chemicals, A and B. Each gallon of A sold yields $15 in profit, whereas each gallon of B sold yields $20 in profit. The total production of A and B must be at least 40 gallons to satisfy customer demands. However, each gallon of A requires 3 hours of production time, whereas each gallon of B requires 5 hours. There are only 150 hours of production capacity available.

Let X represent the gallons of A and Y the gallons of B produced. Given the preceding information, the normative model may have the following form.

$$\text{Max } Z = 15X + 20Y$$

subject to

$$X + Y \geq 40 \quad \text{(Demand)}$$
$$3X + 5Y \leq 150 \quad \text{(Capacity)} \tag{3.2}$$
$$X \geq 0$$
$$Y \geq 0$$

Notice that the objective is to maximize total profits subject to restrictions on demand, capacity, and nonnegativity of the decision variables. The model is formulated so that a choice between alternative production quantities of X and Y can be made. This model is called a linear program. We will discuss this class of models in more detail in subsequent chapters.

Descriptive models, on the other hand, merely describe the system or problem area and thus, by themselves, cannot prescribe what should be done about the problem. They can be used to estimate the outcomes that would be generated by a given set of decision alternatives for the problem or to predict the values of certain dependent variables that would occur with changes in various exogenous variables. Descriptive models do not have an objective function as a part of the model.

For example, a model describing the operation of a checkout counter at a grocery store may consist of the following relationships:

$$Wq = \frac{\lambda}{\mu(\mu - \lambda)}$$

$$Lq = \frac{\lambda^2}{\mu(\mu - \lambda)} \tag{3.3}$$

where Wq is the average waiting time per customer, Lq is the average length of the waiting line at the checkout counter, λ is the average number of customer arrivals per hour, and μ is the average number of customers served per hour. The model describes only the waiting time and queue length for given values of λ and μ. It does not tell us what should be done to resolve any problems at the checkout counter.

All decision models are by definition normative models. Because the measure of effectiveness can be a function of a number of different outcomes, however, descriptive models can be embedded in normative models. In some instances, it may be virtually impossible to specify the measure of effectiveness in terms of outcomes and therefore impossible to build a normative model. Factors such as the number of variables and constraints, the nature of the relationships (linear versus nonlinear), and whether or not the objective function can be simply stated in mathematical terms usually determine whether or not a useful normative model can be formulated. If it cannot, a descriptive model relating the alternatives to outcomes becomes paramount.

Time Dimension

Mathematical models can be further classified with respect to the importance of time in the decision problem. In a *static* model the dependent and independent variables, constants, and parameters are unaffected by time. In other words, a static model represents a snapshot of the problem or system at some specified instant. Alternatively, a *dynamic* model incorporates dependent and independent variables, constants, and parameters that may be affected by time. In addition, time lags may be a part of a dynamic model. For example, if D_t is the demand for furniture in month t, I_t is the disposable income in month t, and H_t is the new-housing starts in month t, a relationship for D_t, which could be a part of a dynamic model, might resemble

$$D_t = a + bI_t + cH_{t-6} \qquad (3.4)$$

where a, b, and c are parameters and new-housing starts lag by 6 months. This simply implies that new-housing starts of 6 months ago are an important determinant of the present demand for furniture.

The nature of the problem will dictate whether a static or dynamic model should be used. Static models are typically easier to construct and understand. In some cases, if the problem has a time dimension, a normative-static model can be repeatedly solved over time—in each instance changing the values of the parameters affected by time—to approximate the solution of a normative-dynamic model. However, even though static models are easier to construct and solve, one must be careful not to overlook or ignore important dynamic relationships. To do so could result in a poor decision, which is a bad trade-off for model simplicity.

Degree of Uncertainty

If there is one trait that characterizes most managerial-decision problems, it must be uncertainty. Although virtually all managerial problems possess some degree of uncertainty, mathematical models can be classified as to the *assumptions* one makes regarding the elements of the environment. A deterministic model is one in which the values of all parameters and constants are known (or are assumed to be known) with certainty when the decision is made.

For example, suppose that a manager wants to determine the number of machines of a certain type that should be in the manager's department over the next year.[1] Let

$T_{ij} =$ performance time for operation i on product j, measured in hours per unit of product
$D_j =$ demand for product j measured in units per year
$E =$ effectiveness factor; a fraction taking into account such things as personal allowances, machine downtime, material shortages, and scrapped production
$H =$ number of working hours in a year

Even though T_{ij}, D_j, and E are in reality random exogeneous variables, in a deterministic model they are assumed to have the value of their averages over the next year. H is a constant in this example. Under these assumptions, a deterministic model that prescribes the number of machines required in this department can be written as

$$\overline{M} = \sum_j \sum_i \frac{\overline{T}_{ij}\overline{D}_j}{\overline{E}\,\overline{H}} \qquad (3.5)$$

[1] William T. Morris, *The Capacity Decision System*, Irwin Series in Operations Management, H.L. Timms, Coordinating Editor, Homewood, Ill.: Richard D. Irwin, Inc., 1967. p. 87.

where $\overline{M}$ is the average number of machines needed. The numerator gives the average total number of productive hours required, whereas the denominator gives the average number of productive hours available from each machine.

This model could be used for the decision problem if the uncertainty in performance, demand, and effectiveness is insignificant when compared to the average value of these variables. If this is not the case, problems involving uncertainty should be represented with a stochastic model.

A *stochastic* model is one in which at least one parameter or exogenous variable is assumed to be a *random variable*. The frequency at which any particular value of a random variable is observed is determined by its probability distribution, which must be defined in a stochastic model. In addition, at least one dependent variable will be a random variable in a stochastic model because dependent variables are functions of the independent variables, parameters, and constants.

For example, consider again the manager who must determine the optimal number of machines of a certain type to have in his or her department over the next year.[2] A simple stochastic model can be developed that can be used to minimize the expected operating cost of providing the machines. Let $C(M)$ (a dependent variable) be the expected cost of providing M machines. The criterion function can be written as

$$\text{Min } C(M) = C_1 M + C_2 \sum_{m=M}^{\infty} (m - M) f(m) \tag{3.6}$$

where

$f(m)$ = the probability distribution of the actual number of machines required over the next year
C_1 = fixed charges per machine per year
C_2 = cost penalty (excess over regular time) per machine per year of overtime production

In this stochastic model, M is an independent variable (decision alternative), and m, the actual number of machines required over the year, is a *random* dependent variable whose value depends on the *random* exogenous variables, T_{ij}, D_j, and E. The parameters C_1 and C_2 are averages and are assumed to remain unchanged throughout the next year. Even though the mathematical form of $f(m)$ can be complex in practice, the model can be easily solved. The optimal number of machines, M^*, can be shown to satisfy the following relationships:

$$F(M^* - 1) \le \frac{C_2 - C_1}{C_2} \le F(M^*) \tag{3.7}$$

where

$$F(M) = \sum_{m=0}^{M} f(m)$$

[2] *Ibid.* pp. 87–95.

In general, it is difficult to say *a priori* whether a deterministic model or stochastic model should be used to solve a given problem. Stochastic models offer more realism but, as the number of random variables increases, it is less likely that such a model can be easily solved. On the other hand, deterministic models can be easier to solve, but one runs the risk that model elements assumed to be known with certainty actually have important stochastic variations. In our aforementioned examples, the deterministic model could give a good solution if the variation of each of the random exogenous variables is very small. In that way, the average values used in the model would be fairly accurate estimates of actual experience. If the variation is significant, the stochastic model would be the better choice.

In this section, we have seen that mathematical models can be classified as normative or descriptive, static or dynamic, and deterministic or stochastic. If we keep in mind that normative models may have descriptive models embedded within them, we may classify a given model in any one of eight possible ways. Thus, the model may be a normative-static-deterministic model or perhaps a descriptive-dynamic-stochastic model. Since the model builder in decision situations will always be concerned with a normative model, which may have a descriptive model embedded within it, the real choices the model builder has are static or dynamic and deterministic or stochastic. How the model builder finally arrives at a useful model for the decision problem is the subject of the next section.

3.4 THE MODEL-BUILDING PROCESS

Identifying the appropriate model type—static or dynamic, deterministic or stochastic—for a given situation is only part of the process of constructing a useful model. In particular, the model-building process actually consists of the first three steps in the decision-making process described in Figure 1.1. The entire model-building process, with the model construction step expanded, is shown in Figure 3.1. Since the first two steps have been generally discussed in Chapters 1 and 2, only the relationship of these steps to the model-building process will be discussed here.

Problem Recognition

The problem-recognition step would include classifying the nature of the independent variables. Thus, the exogenous variables or states of nature that must be acknowledged should be identified.

The degree of uncertainty necessary for an adequate model should also be assessed at this time. The choice of the appropriate model-solution technique will depend on the existence of stochastic elements in the problem. In addition, an initial assessment of the dynamic properties of the problem can be made here. The final assessment of the need for stochastic elements or dynamic properties may have to be made after initial model formulations are attempted.

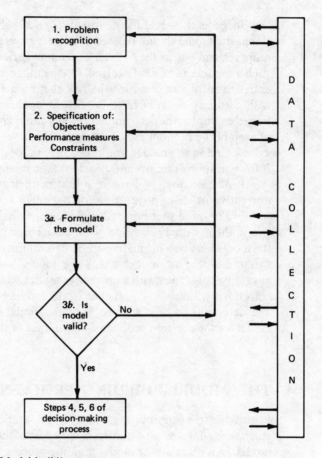

Figure 3.1   Model-building process.

Specification of Objectives, Measures of Effectiveness, and Constraints

Much has already been said about this step in Chapter 2, so it will not be necessary to repeat that discussion here. However, it should be emphasized that the nature of the objectives, measures of effectiveness, and constraints should be defined. Questions such as, "Are the relationships linear or nonlinear?" and "Are the relationships static or dynamic?" should be answered.

Formulation of the Model

Given the problem definition, the next step is to formulate the model. This entails two activities that are often inextricably enmeshed: (1) translation of the problem into mathematical relationships and (2) solution-technique selection. Unfortunately, in some cases, the form of the mathematical relationships depends on the choice of solution technique. There is little point in formulating a model, no matter how accurate, if solution procedures are unavailable. This is why the statement of mathematical relationships and choice of selection technique are so interrelated. We will treat the modeling of the mathematical relationships first, keeping in mind this interrelatedness.

Even though developing the relationships can be a very time-consuming activity, not much can be said about how to do it generally. However, there are a few guidelines. At the outset, a symbolic variable name must be assigned to each parameter and variable in the problem. As far as possible, the symbol should suggest the item it represents. Thus, W_t could represent the quantity of workers on hand in period t and S_t could be the predicted sales for period t. Sometimes Greek letters are used to represent parameters so as to differentiate them from dependent and independent variables. The point to remember is that the parameters and variables should be named in such a way that the model is as easy to under-stand as possible. Mathematical models are sufficiently abstract without the use of confusing notation.

The task of modeling the relationships among the variables, constraints, and parameters can sometimes be eased by conducting some research into the models that have already been proposed for problems similar to the one at hand. Trade journals, some research-oriented journals, and textbooks report models that can be used as a basis for developing the relationships for the problem being modeled. It is always worthwhile to review the literature prior to approaching model building, even though a model that fits the problem *exactly* will not usually be found. Sometimes a model close to that needed can be modified to fit the situation. In addition, the literature search could provide a basis for selecting the appropriate solution technique when there are several from which to choose.

Finally, one must take care that all relationships are specified and that every variable identified in the problem-recognition step as having an impact on the objectives is put in the objective function. In other words, the model must be complete and all the relationships specified correctly. It may not be possible to determine whether or not the relationships are "correct" until the model-validation step; however, the relationships should reflect the present problem definition and, if the problem definition turns out to be inadequate, a new model may be required (see Figure 3.1).

The information generated in the first two steps is sufficient to generate a number of alternative solution techniques for the model that has been developed. Table 3.1, which provides a cross-classification of the various model types with the quantitative methods presented in this text, can be used to generate the potential candidates for a solution methodology. For example, if the desired model is to be of the normative-static-deterministic type, techniques such as integer program-ming, dynamic programming, calculus, or one of the linear programming methods could be used as a solution methodology for the model.

The list of potential solution techniques for a particular problem might be further reduced by considering some of the other aspects of the decision problem. Table 3.2 shows the decision characteristics of the quantitative methods presented

Table 3.1 Model Types and the Quantitative Methods Most Useful for Solution

| | Quantitative Methods Presented in This Text | | | | | | | | | | |
| | Chapter | | | | | | | | | | |
Model Type	4–5 Linear Programming	6 Transportation Linear Programming	7 Integer Programming	8 Network Methods	9 Calculus	10 Queuing Theory	11 Monte Carlo Simulation	12 Dynamic Programming	13 Markov Chains	13 Decision Trees	14 Stochastic Programming
Deductive consequences											
Normative	×	×	×	×	×			×		×	×
Descriptive				×	×	×	×		×		
Time dimension											
Static	×	×	×	×	×	×	×	×		×	×
Dynamic	×	×	×	×	×		×	×	×	×	×
Degree of uncertainty											
Deterministic	×	×	×	×	×			×			
Stochastic				×	×	×	×	×	×	×	×

Table 3.2 Solution Characteristics of the Quantitative Methods Presented in this Text

	Quantitative Methods Presented in This Text										
	Chapter										
Solution characteristics	4-5	6	7	8	9	10	11	12	13	13	14
	Linear Programming	Transportation Linear Programming	Integer Programming	Network Methods	Calculus	Queuing Theory	Monte Carlo Simulation	Dynamic Programming	Markov Chains	Decision Trees	Stochastic Programming
Procedure											
Single pass					×						
Iterative	×	×	×	×		×	×	×	×	×	×
Decision alternatives											
Continuous	×				×						
Discrete		×	×	×		×	×	×	×	×	×
Solution quality											
Optimal	×	×	×	×	×			×		×	×
Satisfactory				×		×	×		×		

in this text. Solution procedures can be either *single pass* or *iterative*. A single-pass solution procedure is one in which the final values of *all* the decision variables are determined simultaneously according to some well-defined procedure. An iterative solution technique, on the other hand, is one in which a number of steps are required to arrive at a final solution and where partial or complete solutions are entertained at each step. Discrete or continuous variables are frequently necessary for a particular problem. Finally, an *optimal* solution is one that can be shown to be at least as good as any other given the assumptions of the model, whereas a *satisfactory* solution is one that is considered "good" with respect to the objectives and constraints, yet cannot be shown to be the best. Thus, if in our previous example of the normative-static-deterministic model the decision variables are continuous, the relationships linear, and an optimal solution is desired, the list of potential solution techniques for the model can be reduced to just one—linear programming. In this way, one or more viable alternatives for the solution methodology can be identified, and the formulation of the model can begin.

Several words of caution are in order. First, Tables 3.1 and 3.2 do not contain all of the solution techniques that can be found in the literature. Many techniques have not yet found the practical prominence that those in this text have, but may enjoy wide use in the future. This should be kept in mind when using Tables 3.1 and 3.2. Second, one must avoid the temptation of looking for a problem that can be solved with a "pet" solution technique. That is, it is unwise to try to fit a problem to a certain technique. Instead, as just indicated, a technique should be chosen that fits the characteristics of the problem. The analysis of the first two steps of the model-building process should not be bypassed. Finally, the result of this step is a model. In some cases, there is the danger that the model builder actually believes that the model is *reality*. A model is an abstraction of reality, involving a number of assumptions and simplifications. Even though the model may pass the validation step, it should only be used as a guide and help in decision making and not as a replacement for the decision maker.

Validating the Model

The model-validation step is given the least attention by novice model builders. In this step the assumptions and the logic in the relationships are tested to see if they conform to reality. Model validation is a two-step process. The first step is to determine whether the model is internally correct in a logical sense. Even though tests for this would depend on the type of model being validated, several suggestions can be made.[3]

1. Compute some outcomes with the model that can be verified with hand calculations when computers must be used to solve the model.

---

[3] Robert Meier, William T. Newell, and Harold L. Pazer, *Simulation in Business and Economics*, Englewood Cliffs, N.J.: Prentice-Hall, 1969. The first and third suggestions are modified somewhat to make them more general in scope.

2. Run separate segments of complicated models alone so that the results can be verified.
3. Eliminate random elements from stochastic models to ease verification of essential logic.
4. Replace complex probability functions with elementary ones so that results are more easily verified.
5. Construct simple test situations that test as many combinations of circumstances in the model as feasible.

The second step in the model validation phase is to compare the model outputs against actual data from the real situation. If the model outputs are in the form of a time series, Cohen and Cyert[4] suggest three tests that can be made.

1. Distribution-free statistical tests to see whether actual-time series and generated-time series have the same timing and amplitude.
2. Regression of generated-time series on the actual-time series to see whether the regression equation has slope and intercept not significantly different from 1 and 0.
3. Factor analysis on the two time series to see whether factor loadings are significantly different.

When the output is in the form of mean values, variances, proportions, or probability distributions, various statistical tests can be used to test the hypothesis that these output elements differ significantly from the actual mean values, variances, proportions, or probability distributions. However, when the model has been constructed for a problem in which there are no past data with which to compare, the model builder must rely on a thorough, logical check and a careful study of the model results for any discrepancies or unusual circumstances. This approach to model validation is used, for example, when a normative model is being validated or when a model has been built to propose a solution to a problem never before faced by the decision maker. In addition to checking the logic and studying the results, there are several questions that could help in assessing the validity of a model in this case.[5]

1. Relatedness. How many previously known theorems or results does the model bring to bear on the problem?
2. Transparency. How obvious is the interpretation of the model? How immediate is its intuitive confirmation?
3. Robustness. How sensitive is the model to changes in the assumptions that characterize it?

If the model contains some previously known theorems or results, or if the model has much intuitive appeal, the model builder can be more confident in the

---

[4] Kalman J. Cohen and Richard M. Cyert, "Computer Models in Dynamic Economics," *The Quarterly Journal of Economics*, Vol. 75, No. 1, (February 1961), pp. 120–121.
[5] William T. Morris, "On the Art of Modelling," *Management Science*, Vol. 13 (August 1967), pp. 707–717.

model. However, a model whose outcomes are quite sensitive to changes in the assumptions should be studied further with regard to the nature of the assumptions made in the problem-definition step.

There could be a number of reasons why a model would fail the validation step. Sometimes the model is intractable or too complex to work with and thus cannot be adequately verified. Morris provides some suggestions for simplifying complex models.[6]

1. Make some variables into constants.
2. Eliminate some variables entirely.
3. Use linear relationships in lieu of nonlinear relationships.
4. Add stronger assumptions and restrictions.
5. Suppress randomness.

Another reason for a model's failing the validation step is that it is too simple. Morris's suggestions can be applied in the reverse in this case. No matter what the reason is for failing this step, the model builder must return to an earlier phase in the model-building process (see Figure 3.1). In this way, the model-building process is iterative.

Of course, once a valid model has been obtained, the model is put to work as an aid to decision making. Although this task may sound easy, it should not be taken for granted. A model builder may arrive at a model that can be shown to save thousands of dollars per year, yet it is worth nothing if the person who is to use it does not accept it. This can happen because the decision maker does not understand the model or the techniques used to solve it or, as Churchman[7] believes, the model builder does not understand the manager and the *coalition* with which the manager associates. A coalition is made up of the persons, books, journals, and other communication devices in the manager's environment. They are the sources the manager consults; the basis of the language he or she uses; and the sources of criteria for what is and is not important. This emphasizes that if the model builder and the decision maker are not the same person, the model builder is well advised to include the decision maker in every step of the model-building process. In this way, the chances of having a successful model implemented are greatly increased. More will be said about this in Chapter 15.

3.5 SUMMARY

This chapter has discussed the nature of models and the process of model building. It is extremely important to understand the concepts and philosophy in this chapter before embarking on the remainder of this book. If models are to play a useful role in business decision making, we must know what to expect from a model and

---

[6] *Ibid.*, p. 715.

[7] C. West Churchman, "Managerial Acceptance of Scientific Recommendations," *California Management Review*, Vol. 7, No. 1, (Fall 1964), pp. 31–38.

from the process of model building. To understand the significance of the techniques used in solving problems in the remainder of the book, the reader must have a firm grasp of the role of a model and the process of model building.

A key to success in modeling is the recognition that the model is an abstraction. Models are not constructed to provide the only answer to a decision problem. Instead, they provide information that is helpful in decision making. A model should not have all the complexities of reality. If it did, it would be extremely difficult to solve and would probably provide the decision maker with little insight or, indeed, information. Conversely, the model should not be so much of an oversimplification that it bears little resemblance to the real world. A good model strikes a balance.

All models—verbal, physical, and mathematical—contain independent variables, dependent variables, parameters, and constants. In verbal models, these elements are put together in a loose and often intuitive fashion, making understanding apparent and communication easy. As one moves from verbal to physical to mathematical models, the relationships between the variables and parameters become more specific. The degree of specificity needed determines the type of model that will be used in a specific situation.

There are a variety of model types within the classification of mathematical models. Classification of mathematical models as descriptive or normative, static or dynamic, deterministic or stochastic is not idle taxonomy. Since the decision model must be formulated to provide useful information in such a way that the model can be expeditiously solved, it is important for both decision makers and model builders to be aware of the existing models and their essential features.

The process of model building is described as an iterative process. No one, even the most experienced model builder, develops a usable model in a single, straightforward development. Instead, there is a process of tentative formulation and validation, followed by reformulation and revalidation until a degree of confidence in the usefulness of the model is developed.

In the following chapters, the model-building process will be put to work in a number of different problem settings. Periodically, we will return to the important issues discussed in Chapters 1, 2, and 3 to emphasize that there is no such thing as a "grab bag" of models from which to choose, but only a number of quantitative methods available to solve properly formulated models.

References   Ackoff, R.L. *Scientific Method: Optimizing Applied Research Decisions*. New York: John Wiley & Sons, 1962.

Camp, G.D. "Approximation and Bounding in Operations Research." *Operations Research*, Vol. 2, Record of the 1957–1958 Seminar in Operations Research, University of Michigan, Ann Arbor.

Cohen, K.J., and R.M. Cyert. "Computer Models in Dynamic Economics." *The Quarterly Journal of Economics*, Vol. 75 (1961), pp. 120–121.

Churchman, C.W. "Management Science—Fact or Theory?" *Management Science*, Vol. 2 (1956), p. 185.

Churchman, C.W. "Managerial Acceptance of Scientific Recommendations." *California Management Review*, Vol. 7 (1964), pp. 31–38.

Greenhut, M.L. "Mathematics, Realism, and Management Sciences." *Management Science*, Vol. 4 (1958), pp. 314–320.

Good, I.J. "How Rational Should a Manager Be?" *Management Science*, Vol. 8 (1962), pp. 383–393.

Helmer, O., and N. Rescher. "On the Epistemology of the Inexact Sciences." *Management Sciences*, Vol. 6 (1959), pp. 25–52.

Huysmans, J.H.B. *The Implementation of Operations Research*. New York: John Wiley & Sons, 1970.

Miller, D.W., and M. K. Starr. *Executive Decisions and Operations Research*. 2nd ed., Englewood Cliffs, N.J.: Prentice-Hall, 1969.

Meier, R., W.T. Newell, and H.L. Pazer. *Simulation in Business and Economics*. Englewood Cliffs, N.J.: Prentice-Hall, 1969.

Morris, W.T. *Management Science in Action*. Homewood, Ill.: Richard D. Irwin, 1963.

Morris, W.T. *The Capacity Decision System*. Homewood, Ill.: Richard D. Irwin, 1967.

Morris, W.T. "On the Art of Modelling." *Management Science*, Vol. 13 (1967), pp. 707–717.

Schuckman, A. *Scientific Decision Making in Business*. New York: Holt, Rinehart & Winston, 1963.

Review Questions

1. The intersection of the demand curve and supply curve for a particular product is an important model in economic theory and applied economics. Discuss the manner in which this model is an abstraction from reality, and how, although the model is as simple as possible, it gives the desired results.

2. Distinguish between controllable and noncontrollable variables in decision problems. Give an example of each for a decision problem with which you are familiar.

3. Distinguish between a parameter and a constant. Describe a decision situation with which you are familiar and identify parameters and constraints.

4. Explain why it may be advantageous to build models to help solve a decision problem.

5. Give an example of verbal and physical models with which you are familiar that are not discussed in this text.

6. How does the solution technique influence the selection of a model?

7. Discuss how you would go about deciding whether it is explicitly necessary to incorporate uncertainty into a decision model.

8. With reference to the discussion of measures of effectiveness in Chapter 2, can you suggest the type and organizational level of decisions that would most likely need to be treated as uncertainty problems?

9. Explain the meaning and purpose of validation.

10. What is a coalition within the context of decision models? Why is the concept important?

Problems 1. You are manager of a small woodworking shop that employs full-time and part-time employees. Each full-time employee can produce 25 units of product per week, and each part-time employee can produce only 10 units per week.
   (a) Develop a model that specifies the total weekly output of the shop, given the number of full-time and part-time employees, respectively. Describe your model from the standpoint of deductive consequences, time dimension, and degree of uncertainty.
   (b) Suppose there is a policy that the number of full-time employees must be twice as large as the number of part-time employees. Use your model to determine the number of full-time and part-time employees needed to achieve 600 units of output per week.

2. A manufacturer would like to maximize total revenues from the sale of a particular product X. However, because of competitive pressures, the *per-unit* revenue decreases as the level of sales increases. In particular, the *per-unit* revenue is estimated to be $50 - X$. Finally, it takes 10 hours to produce a unit of X and there are only 300 hours of capacity available.
   (a) To help the manufacturer decide on the quantity of X to produce, develop a normative model that maximizes total revenue subject to the capacity restriction.
   (b) Using a graphical approach or calculus, find the optimum production quantity. What is the total revenue?
   (c) Suppose that the number of hours of capacity was reduced to 200. Will this change your recommendation in part b? How sensitive is your model to changes in the capacity?

3. The management of a retail outlet would like to develop a cost model for the inventory control of a certain item. The total costs consist of annual ordering costs plus annual inventory-holding costs. The model is to determine the order quantity that minimizes total costs. Management is willing to assume that the average annual inventory *level* is equal to one-half the order quantity. The following parameters have been identified

   D = annual demand for the item
   Q = quantity ordered each time an order is placed with the supplier (decision variable)
   C_o = cost to place one order
   C_h = cost to hold one unit of the item in inventory for 1 year

   (a) Develop the cost model desired by management.

(b) Suppose $D = 1000$ and $C_O = \$10$. Plot the annual ordering costs as a function of Q.

(c) Suppose $C_h = \$2$. Plot the annual inventory-holding costs as a function of Q on the same graph used in part b.

(d) Using the graph you developed in parts b and c, identify the order quantity that minimizes total costs. (You could have solved for the optimal quantity using calculus).

4. Consider the model given in Equations 3.6 and 3.7. Suppose that the probability distribution for the number of machines required is:

m	$f(m)$
1	0.1
2	0.3
3	0.2
4	0.2
5	0.15
6	0.05

Thus, for example, $F(2) = 0.1 + 0.3 = 0.4$, and $F(3) = 0.1 + 0.3 + 0.2 = 0.6$.

(a) Suppose the annual fixed charge per machine is $600 and the overtime cost per machine on an annual basis is $4000. Determine the optimal number of machines.

(b) What is the expected cost of providing the optimal number of machines?

5. A financial analyst at the Hometown Bank wants to determine how much to invest in each of two possible portfolios. Portfolio 1 consists of stocks that yield $0.12 per dollar invested, whereas portfolio 2 consists of bonds that yield $0.08 per dollar invested. The bank has a total of $1000 to invest. In addition, the bank has a policy that the total amount invested in portfolio 1 must not exceed three times the amount invested in portfolio 2.

(a) Specify the objective and constraints appropriate for the analyst's problem.

(b) Formulate a model.

(c) Describe your model from the standpoint of deductive consequences, time dimension, and degree of certainty. Using Table 3.1, which quantitative techniques would be most appropriate for your model?

(d) Discuss how you would validate your model.

Part II
DETERMINISTIC MODELS: RATIONALE AND OVERVIEW

In Part I we discussed laying out the framework for decision making and specifying the role of mathematical models in the decision process. In Parts II and III we will discuss selecting the best alternative from a set of feasible alternatives. The main concern of these sections is with techniques of optimization, which are the standard "bill of fare" of operations research and management science. But it is too easy to be deceived by the apparent exactness of mathematical optimization techniques; to be lulled into thinking that optimization is the "end all" to management science; and to feel that communicating the "best" alternative to a decision problem ends the job of the analyst. We want to dispel this notion before you study the techniques of optimization, and we want to remind you of this as you study what follows. To this end, we have done two things throughout Parts II and III. We have developed the techniques around business-decision problems. Also, we have discussed these problems both in terms of how the solution would change if parameter values changed and of how management would use the results. In this way, the choices of the model builder that affect solutions and the way in which management would use the results of the analysis should promote respect for, and not worship of, the utility of the techniques.

The chapters that follow describe a variety of optimization techniques. Chapters 4 to 9 are about deterministic models and solution techniques. It is easy to mistake the role of deterministic models. From a managerial viewpoint, we can regard deterministic models as applicable either when risk has a minor role in decision making, or as simplified approaches to decision problems in which risk plays a more important role.

In order to develop an efficient computing procedure, the techniques introduced in Chapters 4 to 9 almost always take advantage of a special problem structure. Chapters 4 and 5 discuss linear programming and its applications. The mathematical structure that consists of a linear objective function and linear constraints allows the development of a specialized algorithm for computing solutions. Chapter 6 discusses a class of linear programming problems whose structure allows further efficiencies. Furthermore, this class of problem has a wide variety of applications.

Chapter 7 develops solutions to programming problems for which the decision variables are constrained to integers. Capital budgeting, plant location, and production-scheduling problems are among the many problems in which integer solutions are frequently necessary. Integer-programming problems are very difficult to solve, and the chapter makes this point clear. Chapter 8 is concerned with network analysis. Shortest-route problems have obvious applications in business, and PERT and CPM have been used extensively.

We end Part II with a chapter on classical optimization—based on calculus. Whereas Chapters 4 to 8 are concerned with linear models, Chapter 9 extends our analysis to nonlinear models. Although Chapter 9 is based on the concepts of calculus, it is not a review of one-variable calculus; it describes methods of optimization for many-variable problems and optimization with constraints. Some parts of Chapter 9 are "heavy" on mathematics, but the bulk of the chapter is built around two common business problems; inventory decision making and the investment-portfolio problem.

4

INTRODUCTION TO LINEAR OPTIMIZATION

4.1 LINEAR PROGRAMMING MODELS

The General Linear Programming Model
A Portfolio-Investment Problem
Assumptions of Linear Programming
Applications of Linear Programming

4.2 BASIC CONCEPTS IN LINEAR PROGRAMMING

Maximization Problems
Minimization Problems

4.3 SHADOW PRICES

Calculation of Shadow Prices
Use of Shadow Prices

4.4 SUMMARY

References
Review Questions
Problems

The decision-making paradigm presented in Figure 1.1 indicated that once a model has been constructed, the next steps in the decision-making process are the enumeration of alternatives, the prediction of outcomes, and the selection of alternatives. In the case in which deterministic models make sense, only one state of nature is assumed to exist. Seemingly, the enumeration of alternatives, followed by the prediction of outcomes and the selection of the best alternatives, would be a simple task. This is not generally true because the number of alternatives may be extremely large. Explicitly enumerating each alternative and predicting its outcome with respect to the objective would be too time consuming. However, techniques have been developed that *implicitly* enumerate alternatives, predict their outcomes, and select the best alternative in such a way that only a fraction of the total number of possible alternatives is evaluated. This chapter is the first of five chapters that treat linear-optimization models. Chapter 9 will discuss nonlinear-optimization models.

4.1　LINEAR PROGRAMMING MODELS

Linear programming models represent a class of optimization models useful for linear-optimization problems. A *linear program* is a mathematical model consisting of a linear objective function and linear constraints. The techniques for solving linear programming models are members of a more general class of techniques, called mathematical programming techniques, that address nonlinear- as well as linear programming problems.

The General Linear Programming Problem

The general linear programming problem involves maximizing or minimizing an objective function

$$Z = c_1 X_1 + c_2 X_2 + c_3 X_3 + \cdots + c_n X_n \tag{4.1}$$

subject to a set of m constraints

$$a_{i1} X_1 + a_{i2} X_2 + a_{i3} X_3 + \cdots + a_{in} X_n \leq b_i \quad i = 1, 2, \ldots, k$$

$$a_{i1} X_1 + a_{i2} X_2 + a_{i3} X_3 + \cdots + a_{in} X_n = b_i \quad i = k + 1, k + 2, \ldots, k + r \tag{4.2}$$

$$a_{i1} X_1 + a_{i2} X_2 + a_{i3} X_3 + \cdots + a_{in} X_n \geq b_i \quad i = k + r + 1, \ldots, m$$

The general problem has n decision variables and m constraints, of which k are *upper-bound* constraints ($\leq$), r are *equality* constraints ($=$), and the rest are *lower-bound* constraints ($\geq$). Of course, any specific problem may contain only one or two of the different types of constraints.

The c_js in (4.1) are coefficients representing the per-unit contribution of variable X_j to the value of the objective function. The a_{ij}s in (4.2), called the technological coefficients, represent the amount of resource i that is "consumed" by one unit of variable X_j. In any given constraint, the a_{ij}s can be positive, negative, or zero. The b_is in (4.2) represent the total availability of the resources. The term resource is used in a very general sense here to include any numerical value associated with the right-hand side of a constraint. Without loss of generality, we can assume $b_i \geq 0$ for all i since, if a given $b_i < 0$, we could multiply both sides of constraint i by -1 and reverse the inequality of the constraint. For example, (4.3) is equivalent to (4.4).

$$3X_1 - 7X_2 \geq -10 \tag{4.3}$$

$$-3X_1 + 7X_2 \leq 10 \tag{4.4}$$

Of course, if the constraint was originally an equality constraint, it would remain an equality constraint after the multiplication of both sides by -1.

Finally, we require that all variables are nonnegative; that is:

$$X_j \geq 0 \qquad j = 1, 2, \ldots, n \tag{4.5}$$

Thus, (4.5) represents the *nonnegativity restrictions* for the general linear programming problem. It is actually possible to relax the nonnegativity restrictions on a decision variable by a simple modification. Suppose X_j could actually take on negative values in a particular decision problem. We could replace X_j in (4.1) and (4.2) with the following transformation.

$$X_j = (X_{j1} - X_{j2}) \tag{4.6}$$

We require both X_{j1} and X_{j2} to be nonnegative as before but, if $X_{j2} > X_{j1}$ in the final solution, we have the equivalent of a negative value for X_j. Similarly, a positive value of X_j is indicated when $X_{j1} > X_{j2}$.

In this chapter, we will present the assumptions and the basic terminology and concepts of linear programming. Thus we do not need to address large problems here, since we can easily present these ideas in the context of a small-example problem. We defer the presentation of a methodology for solving larger problems until the next chapter. For now, consider the following problem.

A Portfolio-Investment Problem

An investor desires to determine the amount of money to invest in each of two stock portfolios such that the total return is maximized. Each dollar spent on portfolio 1 yields an expected 6 cents (0.06 dollars) annual return, while each dollar spent on portfolio 2 yields an expected 8 cents (0.08 dollars). The total amount of funds available for investment is $400; however, no more than $250 should be invested in portfolio 2 to insure diversity in the investment. Finally, the investor recognizes that portfolio 2 is more risky than portfolio 1. Based on the past variance of annual returns for each portfolio, a subjective measure of riskiness, called a "risk unit," was devised. Assigning a risk of 5 to each dollar invested in portfolio 1 and a risk of 10 to each dollar invested in portfolio 2, the investor requires that the total investment not exceed 3000 risk units.

Let us now formulate this problem as a linear program. First, we define the decision variables. Let

$$X_1 = \text{number of dollars invested in portfolio 1}$$
$$X_2 = \text{number of dollars invested in portfolio 2}$$

Since the objective is to maximize total return, the objective function becomes

$$\text{Max } Z = 0.06X_1 + 0.08X_2 \tag{4.7}$$

Next, we must specify the constraints. Since a maximum of \$400 can be invested, we have

$$X_1 + X_2 \leq 400 \tag{4.8}$$

In addition, no more than \$250 can be invested in portfolio 2.

$$X_2 \leq 250 \tag{4.9}$$

Finally, we cannot exceed 3000 risk units, which can be written

$$5X_1 + 10X_2 \leq 3000 \tag{4.10}$$

Of course, it would not make sense to have negative expenditures; we thus impose the nonnegativity restrictions

$$X_1 \geq 0; \quad X_2 \geq 0 \tag{4.11}$$

Summarizing the linear-programming formulation for this problem, we have

$$\text{Max } Z = 0.06X_1 + 0.08X_2$$

subject to

$$
\begin{array}{llll}
X_1 + X_2 & \leq 400 & \text{Investment limit} & \\
X_2 & \leq 250 & \text{Portfolio 2 limit} & (4.12) \\
5X_1 + 10X_2 & \leq 3000 & \text{Risk limit} & \\
X_1 & \geq 0 & & \\
X_2 & \geq 0 & &
\end{array}
$$

Comparing this formulation to the general linear programming problem, it is obvious that we have only *upper-bound* constraints and nonnegativity restrictions. It is also apparent that in formulating the linear program, we have actually developed a *model* for evaluating the alternatives for the problem. The model relates each alternative (specific value of X_1 and X_2) to the objective in the problem and specifies the restrictions on the alternatives (in this example, the upper-bound constraints and nonnegativity restrictions).

Assumptions of Linear Programming

A series of important assumptions is implicit in linear programming models. These assumptions should be kept in mind during the model-building stage in the decision process to ensure that the resulting model is valid.

Additivity   Let $(\hat{X}_1, \hat{X}_2, \ldots, \hat{X}_n)$ be a vector of values for each of the n decision variables in a linear programming problem. Each value can be thought of as an "activity level" for that decision variable. The assumption of additivity requires that the total value of the objective function for a given vector of activity levels equals the sum of the contributions of each activity level considered independently of all of the other levels. Similarly, given a vector of activity levels, the total amount of a resource consumed is equal to the sum of the resource consumption of each activity level considered independently of the other activity levels. In other words, there are no nonlinear interaction effects.

With respect to our investor's problem, we assume that if, for example, we invest in portfolio 2, the return per dollar experienced by investment in portfolio 1 will not be affected. The return of 6 cents for portfolio 1 will remain valid, no matter how much we invest in portfolio 2. Also, investment in portfolio 2 will not increase the riskiness of portfolio 1, and thus each dollar investment in portfolio 1 will increase the total risk units by 5, no matter what the level of investment in portfolio 2.

Proportionality   The assumption of proportionality goes hand in hand with that of additivity to define the concept of linearity. Consider any given activity j. Proportionality requires that the contribution of activity j to the objective function, $c_j X_j$, and the resource usage of activity j for any resource i, $a_{ij} X_j$, be directly proportional to the activity level X_j. For example, we assume that the contribution *per dollar invested* in portfolio 1 remains the same, no matter how much we invest in portfolio 1. Also, the number of dollars invested in portfolio 1 decreases the total amount to be invested on a one-for-one basis. In particular, there are *no* fixed charges. Such a cost, for example, might comprise a broker's fee, which is a fixed amount charged for handling an investment transaction but is not dependent on the *size* of the investment. If fixed charges were part of this problem, we would have to use a mixed-integer programming model. Such a model requires that a subset of the decision variables take on only integer values. Chapter 7 will present a technique called branch-and-bound, which can be used for solving mixed-integer programming models.

Certainty   Linear programming models require that the parameters c_j, a_{ij}, and b_i be constants known with certainty. For example, the expected return of 6 cents per dollar invested in portfolio 1 is assumed to be exactly 6 cents. We know its value. Rarely does the assumption of certainty actually hold in practice. Most parameter estimates have a degree of uncertainty associated with them. The model can be checked with regard to the criticality of this assumption by performing a *sensitivity analysis.* Each parameter suspected of violating the certainty assumption can be systematically modified in value in order to see how the optimal solution to the problem is affected. More will be said about sensitivity analysis later. Also, more direct methods of dealing with uncertainty in linear programming will be discussed in Chapter 14.

Divisibility Finally, we must assume that the activities, or decision variables, can take on fractional values. In the investor's problem, there is no conflict with this assumption because the decision variables are expressed in dollars. However, in some applications, the activities should be only integer valued (e.g., employees, chairs, and trucks). In many cases linear programming can still be applied and, if the activities turn out to be noninteger, the activity levels can be rounded to the closest integer value, provided no constraints are violated in the process. This remedy works well as long as the activity *levels* are reasonably large. For example, if a linear programming analysis results in a recommendation of 100.2 employees, rounding it to 100 employees would probably not affect the problem very much. On the other hand, if the recommendation is for 0.2 employees, rounding it to zero may violate the spirit of the problem, and an integer programming approach must be used. Sometimes, however, the problem structure (relationship of the constraints) is such that the application of linear programming automatically results in integer solutions. We will explore some of these problem structures in Chapter 6.

Applications of Linear Programming

Linear programming is a powerful tool for selecting alternatives in a decision problem and, consequently, has been applied in a wide variety of problem settings. The number of applications is so extensive that we cannot list them all here; however, we will indicate a few applications covering the major functional areas of a business organization.

Finance The problem of the investor that we introduced earlier is an example of a *portfolio-mix* problem. In general, the number of different portfolios can be much larger than the example indicates, and more and different kinds of constraints can be added.

Another decision problem involves determining the mix of funding for a number of products when more than one method of financing is available. The objective may be to maximize total profits where the profit for a given product depends on the method of financing. For example, funding may be done with internal funds, short-term debt, or intermediate financing (amortized loans). There may be limits on the availability of each of the funding options as well as financial constraints requiring certain relationships between the funding options so as to satisfy the terms of bank loans or intermediate financing. There may also be limits on the production capacity for the products. The decision variables would be the number of units of each product to be financed by each funding option.

Production and Operations Management Quite often in the process industries a given raw material can be made into a wide variety of products. For example, in the oil industry, crude oil is refined into gasoline, kerosene, home-heating oil, and various grades of engine oil. Given the present profit margin on each product, the problem is to determine the quantities of each product that should be produced subject to numerous restrictions such as limits on the capacities of various refining operations, raw-material availability, demands for each product, and any government-imposed policies on the output of certain products. Similar problems also exist in the chemical and food-processing industries.

Personnel planning problems can also be analyzed with linear programming. For example, in the telephone industry, demands for the services of installer-repair personnel and line-repair personnel are seasonal. The problem is to determine the number of installer-repair personnel and line-repair personnel to have on the work force for each month of the planning horizon such that the total costs of hiring, layoff, overtime, and regular-time wages are minimized. The constraint set includes restrictions on the service demands that must be satisfied, overtime usage, union agreements, and the availability of skilled people for hire. This example runs contrary to the assumption of divisibility; however, the work-force levels for each month would normally be large enough that rounding to the closest integer in each case would not be detrimental, provided the constraints are not violated.

Marketing Linear programming can be used to determine the proper mix of media to use in an advertising campaign. Suppose that the available media are radio, television, and newspapers. The problem is to determine how many advertisements to place in each medium. Of course, the cost of placing an advertisement depends on the medium chosen. We wish to minimize the total cost of the advertising campaign, subject to a series of constraints. Since each medium may provide a different degree of *exposure* of the target population, there may be a lower bound on the total exposure from the campaign. Also, each medium may have a different *efficiency* rating in producing desirable results; there may thus be a lower bound on efficiency. In addition, there may be limits on the availability of each medium for advertising.

Another example of an application of linear programming is in the area of distribution. Consider a case in which there are *m* factories that must ship goods to *n* warehouses. A given factory could make shipments to any number of warehouses. Given the cost to ship one unit of product from each factory to each warehouse, the problem is to determine the shipping pattern (number of units that each factory ships to each warehouse) that minimizes total costs, subject to the restrictions that demand at each warehouse be satisfied, and that each factory cannot ship more product than it has the capacity to produce. Figure 4.1 shows a distribution pattern for four factories shipping goods to seven warehouses located in various U.S. cities. Although it is theoretically possible for any given factory to ship to any given warehouse, notice that each factory ships only to a subset of all the warehouses in this example. Linear programming can help determine the

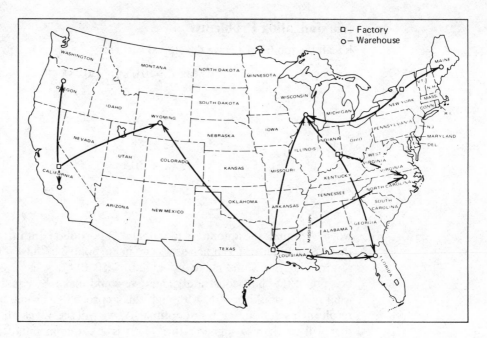

Figure 4.1   Factory-warehouse distribution pattern showing how the outputs of four factories are allocated to the demands at seven warehouses.

minimum cost allocation for factory output-to-warehouse distribution. This problem has a special structure that ensures that the optimal solution (units of product shipped from each factory to each warehouse it serves) will always have an integer value. We will explore this problem in more depth in Chapter 6.

As we can see from these examples, linear programming can be applied in a number of varied ways. Nonetheless, each application has a point in common with the others. In each case, we attempt to *allocate* scarce resources to *competing* demands so as to achieve some objective. The constraint set specifies the availability of the resources and, for any given resource, increasing one activity level means that there are fewer resources to allocate to some other activity. We must find the mix of activities that optimizes our objective. In so doing, we must make trade-offs between the activities competing for the resources. The nature of the objective function determines which activities are to get the resources.

4.2   BASIC CONCEPTS IN LINEAR PROGRAMMING

So far in this chapter we have not discussed how to *solve* linear programming problems. In this section we will present the basic concepts and terminology of linear programming as it applies to simple, two-variable problems. This will enable us to display graphically the geometry and ease the presentation of the solution logic. We will begin with the investor's portfolio-mix problem.

Maximization Problems

Recall the model (4.12) we developed earlier:

$$\text{Max } Z = 0.06X_1 + 0.08X_2$$

subject to

$$X_1 + X_2 \leq 400$$
$$X_2 \leq 250$$
$$5X_1 + 10X_2 \leq 3000$$
$$X_1 \geq 0$$
$$X_2 \geq 0$$

where X_j equals the amount of investment in portfolio j. Intuitively, it would seem that we should invest as much as we can in portfolio 2 because it yields the greatest return. Thus, we would make X_2 equal to $250. But this leaves only 500 risk units because of the third constraint. Thus, we could make X_1 equal to $100, and our total return would be $26. Although this approach has some intuitive appeal, it results in a solution that is not optimal. As we will see, we can find a portfolio mix that will result in a higher return. This is a common pitfall awaiting decision makers who approach problems "intuitively." The trouble is that we have not considered the relationship between the region of feasible solutions (defined by the constraints) and the objective function. Let us see why this is so important.

The Feasible Region Each constraint helps to define the region of feasible solutions. Examine (4.8), the constraint on the funds available for investment.

$$X_1 + X_2 \leq 400$$

This constraint says that any combination of X_1 and X_2 that does not exceed 400 is acceptable. The *maximum* allowed, however, is some combination *equal to* 400. We can represent this constraint graphically by plotting the straight line,

$$X_1 + X_2 = 400$$

Solving for X_1, we get

$$X_1 = 400 - X_2 \qquad (4.13)$$

Since we need only two points to graph a straight line, the simplest method is to find the points at which the line intersects the X_1, X_2 axes. Thus, if $X_2 = 0$, X_1 must equal 400. Similarly, since

$$X_2 = 400 - X_1 \qquad (4.14)$$

$X_2 = 400$ if $X_1 = 0$. This line is shown on Figure 4.2. Any point (combination of X_1 and X_2) that falls in the shaded areas or *on* the line is acceptable with respect to this constraint. Although we seem to have eliminated many alternative combinations of X_1 and X_2 (those for which $X_1 + X_2 > 400$), we still have an infinite number of combinations to consider. Notice that we have already imposed the

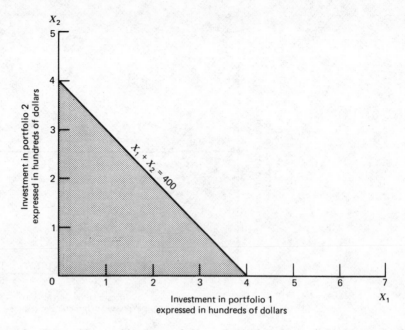

Figure 4.2 Acceptable combinations of X_1 and X_2 for the available-investment-funds constraint.

nonnegativity restrictions. The region of acceptable values for X_1 and X_2, considering only this constraint, is merely a triangle defined by the two axes and the straight line segment connecting the points $X_1 = 400$, $X_2 = 0$ and $X_1 = 0$, $X_2 = 400$.

Of course, we must satisfy more constraints than the one limiting the total funds available for investment. In particular, (4.9) states that the total investment in portfolio 2 must not exceed \$250, or

$$X_2 \leq 250$$

By plotting the maximum value allowed, $X_2 = 250$, the region of feasible values of X_1 and X_2 relative to the two constraints changes to the four-sided polygon shown in Figure 4.3. The shaded area of the polygon represents all combinations of X_1 and X_2 that satisfy both constraints.

Finally, we can graph the risk constraint (4.10) in the same way as the others. Using the equality portion of the constraint and solving for X_1, we have

$$X_1 = \frac{3000 - 10X_2}{5} = 600 - 2X_2 \tag{4.15}$$

If $X_2 = 0$, X_1 must be 600. Similarly, from (4.15),

$$X_2 = \frac{3000 - 5X_1}{10} = 300 - 0.5X_1 \tag{4.16}$$

and, if $X_1 = 0$, $X_2 = 300$.

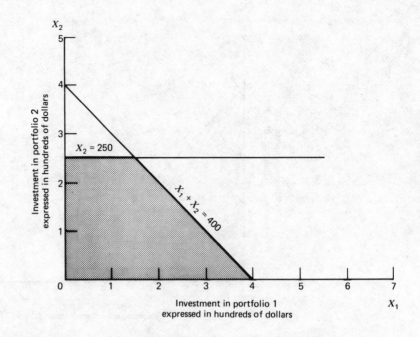

Figure 4.3 Acceptable combinations of X_1 and X_2 for the upper limit on investment in portfolio 2 and the available-investment-funds constraint.

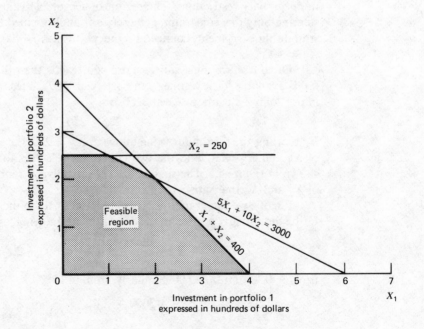

Figure 4.4 Feasible region for the investor's portfolio-mix problem.

Figure 4.4 shows the effect of imposing this constraint on the region of acceptable values for X_1 and X_2. The region of acceptable values of the decision variables relative to all the constraints in a linear programming model is called the *feasible region*. Notice how the constraints have combined to give the *shape* of the feasible region. In this example we have a five-sided polygon because each constraint, including each nonnegativity restriction, has provided one face of the polygon. If a constraint in a linear programming problem does not form a boundary of the feasible region, it is called *redundant*. Such a constraint for the present problem would be

$$2X_1 + 3X_2 \leq 1200 \qquad\qquad (4.17)$$

which is less restrictive than (4.8):

$$X_1 + X_2 \leq 400$$

Any combination of X_1 and X_2 that does not exceed 400 will certainly satisfy the other constraint. When solving for the optimal solution to the problem, we can disregard redundant constraints, provided we can identify them. This may not be easy for problems involving more than two decision variables.

Although the constraints in the model define the feasible region, that region must have a special property if linear programming is to be used to solve the problem. The feasible region must constitute a *convex set*. This property of convexity can be easily demonstrated in a two-variable problem. Select any two points in the feasible region. If the straight line segment connecting these two points also lies completely within the feasible region (or on its boundary), the feasible region is convex. Consider Figure 4.5. The feasible region is *not* convex because two points lying in the region can be found such that the straight line segment connecting these points is not completely contained in the feasible region. Notice that the feasible region in Figure 4.4 *is* convex.

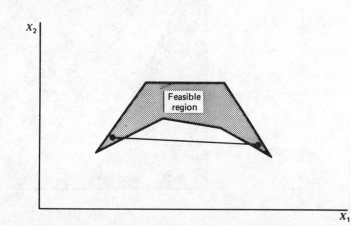

Figure 4.5 Example of a feasible region that is not convex.

The linear constraints in a linear programming model will always define a convex feasible region provided they are consistent. If a set of constraints is *inconsistent* no feasible region exists because there are no values that the decision variables can assume that will satisfy all constraints. For example, consider the following constraint set

$$2X_1 + X_2 \leq 10$$
$$3X_1 + 2X_2 \geq 24 \qquad (4.18)$$

There are no values of X_1 and X_2 that satisfy (4.18), as shown in Figure 4.6. The shaded areas represent the acceptable points for each constraint. In such a situation we say that the problem is *infeasible*. No solution can be found that satisfies the constraints.

Finding an Optimal Solution   Consider Figure 4.7. Any combination of values for X_1 and X_2 that is contained in the feasible region is an acceptable solution to the investor's portfolio-mix problem. It is obvious that there are an infinite number of alternatives to consider. Fortunately, we do not have to evaluate each one. We only want the alternative that maximizes the objective function. Figure 4.7 demonstrates that the optimal solution to a linear model is found on the boundary of the feasible region. Suppose we plot the objective function (4.7) for our model.

$$Z = 0.06X_1 + 0.08X_2$$

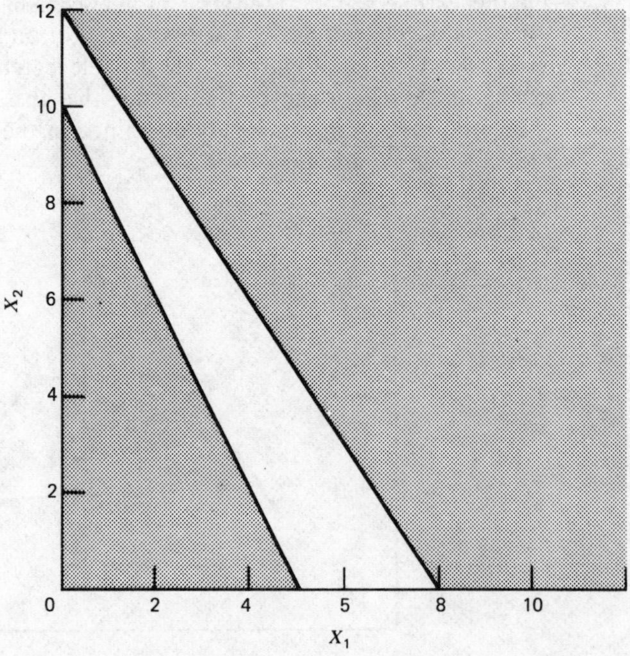

Figure 4.6   Example of a constraint set that is inconsistent.

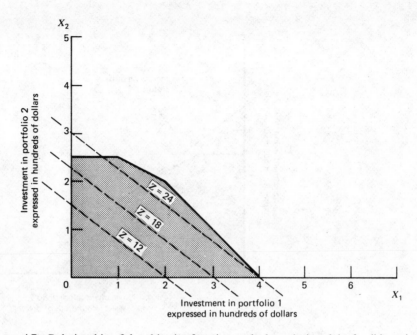

Figure 4.7 Relationship of the objective function to the boundaries of the feasible region.

We can accomplish this by specifying a value for Z and plotting the resulting equation. Suppose we arbitrarily pick $Z = 12$. We then plot

$$0.06X_1 + 0.08X_2 = 12$$

This equation is called an *iso-profit* line because it specifies all combinations of X_1 and X_2 that yield a profit (or return) of \$12. Notice what happens as the profits *increase*. The iso-profit lines move closer to the outer boundaries of the feasible region. Thus, since we want to find the combination of X_1 and X_2 that maximizes the objective function, that combination must be on the boundary of the feasible region.

Figure 4.8 indicates the optimal solution to the problem. Profits (or returns) increase as the iso-profit line moves farther away from the origin and closer to the outer boundaries of the feasible region. Consequently, the optimal solution must be the point that is still feasible but allows the objective function to attain its largest value.

Although we could read the optimal solution from the graph itself, let us derive the solution algebraically. Notice from the graph that the optimal solution is determined by the intersection of the risk constraint and the budget constraint. Since both of these constraints must be satisfied as equalities (that was how we were able to plot them originally), we must find the values of X_1 and X_2 such that

$$X_1 + \quad X_2 = 400 \qquad \text{Budget constraint}$$

$$5X_1 + 10X_2 = 3000 \qquad \text{Risk constraint}$$

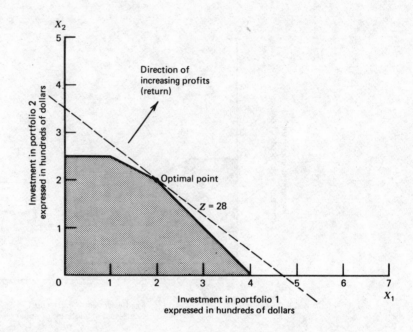

Figure 4.8 Point of maximum returns for the investor's portfolio-mix problem.

If we can *transform* these equations into an *equivalent* set of the form

$$1X_1 + 0X_2 = k_1$$

$$0X_1 + 1X_2 = k_2 \qquad (4.19)$$

where k_1 and k_2 are constants, we will have an easy solution to the problem: $X_1 = k_1$ and $X_2 = k_2$. Begin with the last constraint in the original set and the variable farthest to the right, X_2 in this example. Divide both sides of the equation by the coefficient multiplying X_2. This results in a new (but equivalent) equation for the risk constraint.

$$X_1 + X_2 = 400 \qquad \text{Budget constraint} \qquad (4.20)$$

$$0.5X_1 + X_2 = 300 \qquad \text{Risk constraint} \qquad (4.21)$$

Next, eliminate X_2 from (4.20) by multiplying (4.21) by a constant such that when (4.21) is *added* to (4.20), the coefficient of X_2 in the newly formed equation is zero. In our case, that constant would be -1.

$$
\begin{array}{ll}
X_1 + X_2 = 400 & \text{Budget constraint} \\
\underline{-0.5X_1 - X_2 = -300} & \text{Risk constraint} \\
0.5X_1 + 0X_2 = 100 &
\end{array}
$$

The new equation is

$$X_1 + 0X_2 = 200$$

which is obtained by multiplying both sides of the new equation by 2. We then have a new (but equivalent) set of equations to solve.

$$1X_1 + 0X_2 = 200 \qquad\qquad (4.22)$$

$$0.5X_1 + 1X_2 = 300 \qquad\qquad (4.23)$$

To eliminate X_1 from (4.23), we work in reverse. Multiply (4.22) by -0.5 and add the transformed equation to (4.23) to give the desired result.

$$
\begin{array}{r}
-0.5X_1 - 0X_2 = -100 \\
\underline{0.5X_1 + 1X_2 = 300} \\
0X_1 + 1X_2 = 200
\end{array}
$$

We then have the following set of equations in the form of (4.19):

$$
\begin{aligned}
1X_1 + 0X_2 &= 200 \\
0X_1 + 1X_2 &= 200
\end{aligned}
\qquad\qquad (4.24)
$$

which indicates that we should invest $200 in portfolio 1 and $200 in portfolio 2. The total return is given by

$$Z = 0.06(\$200) + 0.08(\$200) = \$28$$

A quick check indicates that $X_1 = \$200$, $X_2 = \$200$ satisfies all of the constraints. Thus, we have found the optimal solution. Notice that this solution results in a return larger than the one we got earlier using intuitive notions.

At this point, it would seem that our approach to solving the system of equations is too sophisticated for the problem. It is true that, once we found $X_1 = 200$ after the first operation on the budget equation, the value of X_2 could be determined by putting $X_1 = 200$ into the risk equation and solving for X_2. However, the procedure we used (called *Gaussian elimination*) is useful for solving linear programming problems involving more constraints and variables than are involved in our simple example problem. A more formal statement of the method is found in the references at the end of this chapter.

The Uniqueness of the Solution The solution to our problem was found at the intersection of the risk and budget equations. The intersection of two such constraints in a two-variable problem is called an *extreme point* of the feasible region. Figure 4.9 shows the five extreme points in the investor's portfolio-mix problem. As long as the slope of the iso-profit line differs from the slopes of the constraint equations, the solution will be at *one* extreme point of the feasible region and hence will be unique. This is the case in our example problem, where the point (200, 200) is optimal and unique.

It is not always the case that the optimal solution is unique. Suppose we change the objective function in our example problem to

$$Z = 0.04X_1 + 0.08X_2$$

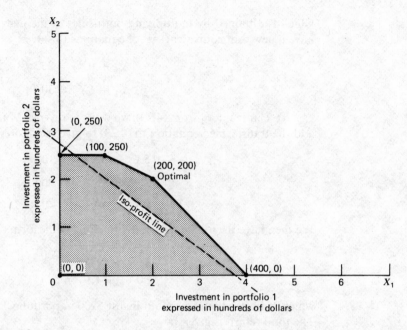

Figure 4.9   Extreme points in the investor's portfolio-mix problem.

The new situation is shown in Figure 4.10. The iso-profit line is parallel to the risk equation and, as the iso-profit line moves farther from the origin, it ultimately coincides with that portion of the risk equation that forms the boundary of the feasible region. The conclusion is that there are an infinite number of optimal solutions to the problem: (100, 250), (200, 200), *and* all points lying on the line segment connecting these two points. Any of these points, when put into the objective function, will yield the same optimal total return of $24.

Although it may be discouraging to learn that a linear programming analysis may result in an infinite number of optimal solutions, it should be recognized that the *extreme points*, (100, 250) and (200, 200), are included in this infinite number of solutions and also yield the optimal value of the objective function. Thus, there is no need to consider all the solutions lying on the line segment connecting the extreme points. It is sufficient to consider only the extreme points of the feasible region. This leads us to the following conclusion regarding linear programming problems: *The optimal solution to any linear programming problem will always be at an extreme point of the feasible region.* With regard to the present example, either of the points (100, 250) or (200, 200) can be chosen as the solution to the problem. We can disregard all the points on the line segment connecting these two extreme points.

The fact that we need only consider extreme points limits the number of alternatives worthy of consideration to a finite number. Even though every point in the feasible region is acceptable, we know that some extreme point will provide an optimal solution. In the investor's portfolio-mix problem, we need only consider

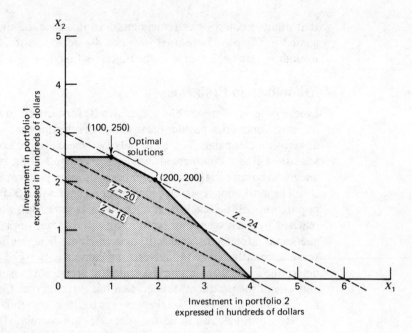

Figure 4.10 Example of multiple optimal solutions.

the alternatives shown in Table 4.1 (see Figure 4.9). Obviously, some alternatives can be eliminated immediately.

Table 4.1 Alternatives in the Investor's Portfolio-mix Problem

Alternative	Investment in Portfolio 1	Investment in Portfolio 2
1	$0	$0
2	$0	$250
3	$100	$250
4	$200	$200
5	$400	$0

Alternative 1 is not reasonable, and alternative 2 is dominated by alternative 3. The rest of the alternatives could be evaluated in the objective function, and the one (or more) alternative(s) providing the largest return would be optimal. This is easy to do for a two-variable problem; however, as the number of variables and constraints increases, the difficulty in determining the alternatives (extreme points) also increases. Even though there are only a finite number of extreme points, that number could be extremely large. In this case techniques such as those presented in Chapter 5 are used to select the optimal alternative without explicitly evaluating each alternative in the objective function.

Minimization Problems

Linear programming problems can also be formulated to *minimize* some suitable objective function. Consider the problem of selecting the optimal media mix for an advertising campaign. There are only two media under consideration: radio and television. Radio commercials are each 10 seconds long and cost $2000, whereas television commercials are 15 seconds in duration but cost $3500 apiece.

The marketing research department estimates that 50,000 persons in the target population will be reached by each radio commercial, while only 30,000 will be reached by each television commercial. The target population consists of teenagers and adolescents who will most likely be listening to the radio during the summer months, when the advertising campaign is to be conducted. It has been determined that there is a high correlation between exposures to an advertisement and sale of the product. Management has directed that the advertising campaign must result in at least 900,000 exposures to the commercials.

Research has also indicated that sales are correlated with the total *time* the target population is exposed to the product. In this respect, television commercials are 1.5 times as long as radio commercials. Management has decided that the campaign should result in a minimum of 300 seconds of prime-time coverage in the media. Finally, the radio station indicates that there are only 22 commercial "spots" left, whereas the television station has 25 spots left during the time period to be covered in the campaign.

Suppose management would like to minimize the cost of the campaign, subject to the restrictions just discussed. If we are willing to accept the assumptions of linear programming, a linear programming model can be designed that will help us select the optimal alternative. The objective function can be written

$$\text{Min } Z = 2000X_1 + 3500X_2 \tag{4.25}$$

where

X_1 = the number of 10-second radio commercials to be used in the campaign

X_2 = the number of 15-second television commercials to be used in the campaign

The constraints are

$$
\begin{array}{lll}
50{,}000X_1 + 30{,}000X_2 \geq 900{,}000 & \text{Target population exposures} & \\
10X_1 + 15X_2 \geq 300 & \text{Prime-time coverage} & (4.26) \\
X_1 \leq 22 & \text{Availability of radio commercials} & \\
X_2 \leq 25 & \text{Availability of television commercials} & \\
X_1 \geq 0 & \text{Nonnegativity} & \\
X_2 \geq 0 & \text{Restrictions} &
\end{array}
$$

The first constraint of (4.26) says that the total exposures from radio commercials plus the total exposures from television commercials must result in *at least* 900,000 total exposures of the target population. The second constraint requires that the total time spent in radio commercials plus the total time spent in television commercials must total at least 300 seconds of coverage. These two constraints are examples of *lower-bound* constraints.

The remaining constraints of (4.26) are examples of upper-bound constraints. The number of radio spots cannot exceed 22, and the number of television spots cannot exceed 25. The nonnegativity restrictions complete the model formulation.

The Feasible Region   The feasible region can be easily identified graphically. Let us begin with the lower-bound constraints and the nonnegativity restrictions of (4.26). As before, we plot the equality portion of the constraints and identify all points acceptable to both constraints. In this case the equations are easy to plot, as shown in Figure 4.11.

$$X_1 \qquad = 22 \qquad \text{Radio-availability equation}$$

$$X_2 = 25 \qquad \text{Television-availability equation}$$

Notice that if these were the *only* constraints in the problem, the solution would be simple (and ridiculous). The solution would be to have no radio or television commercials at all! The objective function would have attained its

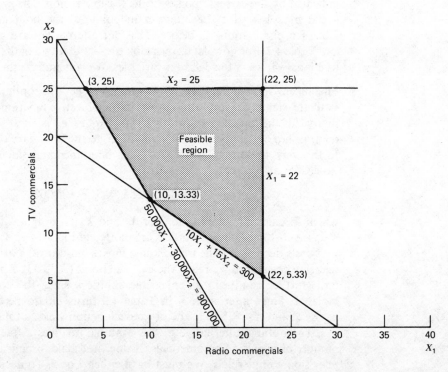

Figure 4.11   Feasible region for the media-mix problem indicating the four extreme points.

lowest possible value: zero. The reason for this is that the origin is a feasible alternative. Since all of the objective-function coefficients in our model are positive and the point $(0, 0)$ is not an acceptable solution, there must be *at least* one constraint that renders the origin infeasible. This constraint must be a *lower-bound* constraint or an *equality* constraint. Fortunately, in our example problem, we have two lower-bound constraints that will make point $(0, 0)$ infeasible.

Let us now superimpose the population-exposure constraint on the upper-bound constraints. The equality portion of the constraint is

$$50,000X_1 + 30,000X_2 = 900,000$$

or

$$X_1 = \frac{900,000 - 30,000X_2}{50,000} = 18 - 0.6X_2 \qquad (4.27)$$

Thus, if $X_2 = 0$, $X_1 = 18$ and if $X_2 = 30$, $X_1 = 0$. The straight line connecting these points is shown in Figure 4.11. Notice that any combination of X_1 and X_2 in this constraint that results in a value greater than or equal to 900,000 is acceptable. Notice also that the origin has now been rendered infeasible.

Similarly, the restriction on prime-time coverage can be superimposed on the rest of the constraints to form the feasible region for the problem, as shown in Figure 4.11. Notice that there are only four alternatives that need be evaluated, as indicated by the extreme points of the feasible region. The extreme points can be found by solving for the intersection points of the boundary equations using Gaussian elimination, as before. The four alternatives are given in Figure 4.11 and Table 4.2. For now, let us overlook the fact that two of the alternatives involve fractional values in the decision variables. We will address this issue later.

Finding an Optimal Solution   One way to select the optimal alternative is to evaluate each of the four alternatives in the objective function and choose the one that yields the lowest cost. Another way is to use an *iso-cost* line to determine the relationship of the objective function (4.25) to the boundary of the feasible region. In this way, the optimal alternative can be immediately identified. Consider the iso-cost line

$$2000X_1 + 3500X_2 = 105,000$$

which specifies all combinations of X_1 and X_2 yielding a total cost of \$105,000. This iso-cost line and a few others are plotted in Figure 4.12. It is immediately seen that costs decrease as the iso-cost line moves closer to the origin. We continue to decrease costs until we reach the extreme point (22, 5.33). Any attempt to reduce costs further results in an infeasible solution, since the constraints would be violated. Thus, alternative 4 in Table 4.2 turns out to be optimal. Evaluating $X_1 = 22$ and $X_2 = 5.33$ in the objective function yields a total cost of \$62,666.67.

The optimal alternative in this example involves a fractional value for the number of television commercials. It does not make practical sense to have 5.33 television commercials. We must have either 5 or 6. To decide which of these is

Table 4.2 Alternatives in the Media-Mix Problem

Alternative	Radio Commercials X_1	TV Commercials X_2
1	22	25
2	3	25
3	10	13.33
4	22	5.33

best, we must refer to the constraint set. Suppose we evaluate $X_1 = 22$ and $X_2 = 5$. We see that this combination satisfies the population-exposure constraint, since

$$50,000(22) + 30,000(5) = 1,250,000$$

which is greater than the specified lower bound of 900,000. However, this combination does not satisfy the prime-time coverage constraint, since

$$10(22) + 15(5) = 295 \text{ seconds}$$

which is less than the lower bound of 300 seconds. If management is not willing to

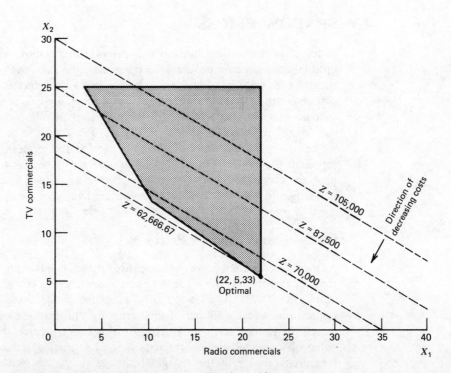

Figure 4.12 Optimal solution to the media-mix problem.

change the lower bound on prime-time coverage to 295 seconds, we must discard this solution to the problem.

The other possibility is the combination $X_1 = 22$ and $X_2 = 6$. Certainly, the population exposure constraint will be satisfied with this, since we had more than enough when $X_2 = 5$. The prime-time constraint is also satisfied, since

$$10(22) + 15(6) = 310 \text{ seconds}$$

which exceeds the lower bound. Since the two upper-bound constraints on commercial availability are also satisfied, this combination would be the final recommendation. The total cost would be $65,000. If we had been able to accept the combination $X_1 = 22$, $X_2 = 5$, the cost would have been only $61,500. Herein lies the trade-off between costs and the lower bound on prime-time coverage. For an additional 5 seconds of coverage to meet the restriction, we must pay $3500. Management must evaluate the consequences of this trade-off. Nonetheless, linear programming has helped narrow the search for a practical solution to the area around the extreme point (22, 5.33). Nevertheless, merely "rounding off" to get integer values for the decision variables will not necessarily yield feasible solutions. In Chapter 7 we will present techniques that ensure integer solutions to problems of this type.

4.3 SHADOW PRICES

A linear programming analysis can provide much more information than the optimal solution to a problem. In particular, the net benefit (or cost) of adjustments to the right-hand quantities, b_i, can be easily determined. This information can be useful in making policy decisions if the b_i quantities are under the control of management. Alternatively, if these quantities must be forecast, the information can be used to determine the consequences of inaccurate estimation. In this section we will discuss the concept of *shadow prices* (or dual prices). These shadow prices represent the relative "value" of each resource with respect to the objective in the problem. Once the shadow prices have been determined, we can assess the impact of changes to the b_i quantities on the optimal value of the objective function.

Calculation of Shadow Prices

As mentioned earlier, the b_i quantities are referred to as resource levels, even though these quantities may not all refer to actual resources in any given problem. For example, the 900,000 target-population exposures in the media-mix problem do not relate to any real resource of the company but, for ease of discussion, we will attach the general term "resource" to it. A shadow price, then, is defined as the value of an added (or subtracted) unit of a particular resource. The value is measured relative to the marginal change in the objective function when the resource is adjusted by one unit. This value is also called a *dual price*. The rationale behind this second name will be made clear when we discuss the economics of duality in Chapter 5.

Let us use the media-mix model (4.25) and (4.26) to illustrate the computation of the shadow price for each resource. Assume that fractional values of X_1 and X_2 are permissible. Recall that the model is

$$\text{Min } Z = 2000X_1 + 3500X_2$$

subject to

$$50{,}000X_1 + 30{,}000X_2 \geq 900{,}000$$
$$10X_1 + 15X_2 \geq 300$$
$$X_1 \leq 22$$
$$X_2 \leq 25$$
$$X_1, X_2 \geq 0$$

We begin by *augmenting* this model to make all of the constraints *equalities*. To do this, we must add some variables to the model. Consider the first constraint of (4.26). We require that $50{,}000X_1 + 30{,}000X_2$ be equal to *or* greater than 900,000. To make an equality relationship, we must include a *surplus* variable that will pick up the difference between $50{,}000X_1 + 30{,}000X_2$ and 900,000 when the former *exceeds* 900,000. The equation would then be

$$50{,}000X_1 + 30{,}000X_2 - S_1 = 900{,}000 \tag{4.28}$$

where $S_1 \geq 0$. Thus, if $X_1 = 20$ and $X_2 = 6$, S_1 must equal 280,000. Since there is no cost or benefit for exceeding 900,000, the cost coefficient for S_1 is zero in the objective function.

Similarly, we can add surplus variable S_2 to the next constraint, which results in

$$10X_1 + 15X_2 - S_2 = 300 \tag{4.29}$$

Notice that we only use surplus variables for lower-bound constraints. The surplus variables measure how much the resource quantities b_i (lower bounds) are exceeded.

Now consider the third constraint. This is an upper-bound constraint. To make an equality relationship, we include a *slack* variable, which measures the amount of resource that is not consumed.

$$X_1 + S_3 = 22 \tag{4.30}$$

As before, $S_3 \geq 0$. If $X_1 = 20$, $S_3 = 2$. Since there is no cost or benefit for not consuming all of the radio-commercial spots available in this problem, the cost coefficient of S_3 in the objective function is zero. Similarly, we can include slack variable S_4 to the fourth constraint to yield

$$X_2 + S_4 = 25 \tag{4.31}$$

The complete, augmented model is given here.

$$\text{Min } Z = 2000X_1 + 3500X_2 + 0S_1 + 0S_2 + 0S_3 + 0S_4$$

subject to

$$
\begin{aligned}
50{,}000X_1 + 30{,}000X_2 - 1S_1 &= 900{,}000 \\
10X_1 + 15X_2 - 1S_2 &= 300 \\
X_1 + 1S_3 &= 22 \qquad (4.32) \\
X_2 + 1S_4 &= 25 \\
X_1, X_2, S_1, S_2, S_3, S_4 &\geq 0
\end{aligned}
$$

Notice that we have added four new variables to the model. The surplus variables are always subtracted whereas the slack variables are always added. Neither slack nor surplus variables make a contribution to the objective function.

In the previous section, we found the optimal solution to be $X_1 = 22$ and $X_2 = 5.33$, or $\frac{16}{3}$. With respect to the augmented model, this implies the solution

$$
\begin{aligned}
X_1 &= 22 & S_2 &= 0 \\
X_2 &= \tfrac{16}{3} & S_3 &= 0 \\
S_1 &= 360{,}000 & S_4 &= \tfrac{59}{3}
\end{aligned}
$$

which can be verified by putting $X_1 = 22$ and $X_2 = \frac{16}{3}$ into each equation and computing the values of the slack and surplus variables. In particular, notice that there are four variables that have nonzero values, and there are four equations in the model. Thus, if we had known *a priori* that $X_1, X_2, S_1,$ and S_4 would be nonzero in the optimal solution, we could have solved the system of four equations in (4.32) for these variables in terms of constants and the variables that are not in the solution. This algebraic solution would enable us to evaluate the shadow prices of the resources.

To see how this is so, rewrite the equations in the following way, where S_2 and S_3 are treated as if they were constants.

$$50{,}000X_1 + 30{,}000X_2 - 1S_1 + 0S_4 = 900{,}000 \qquad (4.33)$$

$$10X_1 + 15X_2 + 0S_1 + 0S_4 = 300 + S_2 \qquad (4.34)$$

$$1X_1 + 0X_2 + 0S_1 + 0S_4 = 22 - S_3 \qquad (4.35)$$

$$0X_1 + 1X_2 + 0S_1 + 1S_4 = 25 \qquad (4.36)$$

We now have four equations with four unknowns; these can be solved using Gaussian elimination. Let us first reorder the equations to ease the task of solution. Equations 4.37 to 4.40 are the rearranged equations. Notice that we multiplied

(4.33) by -1 and exchanged it with (4.35). In addition, all variables with zero coefficients have been dropped from each equation.

$$X_1 \qquad\qquad\qquad = 22 - S_3 \qquad\qquad (4.37)$$

$$10X_1 + \quad 15X_2 \qquad\qquad = 300 + S_2 \qquad\qquad (4.38)$$

$$-50,000X_1 - 30,000X_2 + S_1 \qquad = -900,000 \qquad\qquad (4.39)$$

$$X_2 \qquad + S_4 = 25 \qquad\qquad (4.40)$$

Notice that S_1 and S_4 are already in the proper form. We now concentrate on eliminating X_2 from (4.39) and (4.40). Dividing both sides of (4.39) by 15 results in the following system of equations.

$$X_1 \qquad\qquad\qquad = 22 - S_3 \qquad\qquad (4.41)$$

$$\tfrac{2}{3}X_1 + \qquad X_2 \qquad\qquad = 20 + (\tfrac{1}{15})S_2 \qquad\qquad (4.42)$$

$$-50,000X_1 - 30,000X_2 + S_1 \qquad = -900,000 \qquad\qquad (4.43)$$

$$X_2 \qquad + S_4 = 25 \qquad\qquad (4.44)$$

Variable X_2 can be eliminated from (4.43) by multiplying (4.42) by 30,000 and adding the result to (4.43). Similarly, multiplying (4.42) by -1 and adding the result to (4.44) yields the desired form for X_2, as shown.

$$X_1 \qquad\qquad\qquad = 22 - S_3 \qquad\qquad (4.45)$$

$$(\tfrac{2}{3})X_1 + X_2 \qquad\qquad = 20 + (\tfrac{1}{15})S_2 \qquad\qquad (4.46)$$

$$-30,000X_1 \qquad + S_1 \qquad = -300,000 + 2000S_2 \qquad\qquad (4.47)$$

$$-(\tfrac{2}{3})X_1 \qquad\qquad + S_4 = 5 - (\tfrac{1}{15})S_2 \qquad\qquad (4.48)$$

Variable X_1 can be put in the proper form by (1) multiplying (4.45) by $-\tfrac{2}{3}$ and adding the result to (4.46), (2) multiplying (4.45) by 30,000 and adding the result to (4.49), and (3) multiplying (4.45) by $\tfrac{2}{3}$ and adding the result to (4.48). The final solution is now shown.

$$X_1 \qquad\qquad = 22 - S_3$$

$$X_2 \qquad = \tfrac{16}{3} + (\tfrac{1}{15})S_2 + (\tfrac{2}{3})S_3$$

$$S_1 \qquad = 360,000 + 2000S_2 - 30,000S_3 \qquad\qquad (4.49)$$

$$S_4 = \tfrac{59}{3} - (\tfrac{1}{15})S_2 - (\tfrac{2}{3})S_3$$

Since we know that S_2 and S_3 are zero, we have the same solution as before.

The algebraic solution gives the values of X_1, X_2, S_1, and S_4 in terms of constants and the variables S_2 and S_3. This enables us to analyze the effects of changes in the original b_i values on total costs. For example, recall that S_3 is a slack variable associated with the availability of radio commercials. Suppose that we want to determine the effect of a decrease of 1 in the availability of radio commercials.

That is, we would like to compute the shadow price of the radio-commercial availability. The augmented constraint from (4.32) is

$$X_1 + S_3 = 22$$

or

$$X_1 \qquad = 22 - S_3$$

If $S_3 = 1$, the net effect would be to limit X_1 to be 21. Thus, an increase of 1 unit in a slack variable has the effect of *reducing* the resource availability by one unit.

Now let us return to the optimal algebraic solution. If we hypothetically set S_3 equal to 1, we see that X_1 must be *reduced* by 1 to a value of 21. Since X_1 has a cost coefficient of $2000, this results in a net *savings* of $2000 compared to the optimal solution of before. However, if $S_3 = 1$, X_2 must *increase* by $\frac{2}{3}$ and, since X_2 has a cost coefficient of $3500, costs will *increase* by $\frac{2}{3}(\$3500)$, or $2333.33. In like manner, S_1 and S_4 must *reduce* by 30,000 and $\frac{2}{3}$, respectively. Since there is no cost associated with these variables, total costs will not be affected. The net effect on total costs, then, is an increase of $333.33. Thus, the shadow price is $333.33 for radio-commercial availability because a restriction of the availability of one "spot" will result in an increase in costs of $333.33.

Consider the constraint on prime-time coverage, an example of a policy constraint under the control of management. Suppose we would like to evaluate the effects of requiring 1 second more of coverage (i.e., require 301 seconds of coverage). The augmented equation from (4.32) is

$$10X_1 + 15X_2 - S_2 = 300$$

or

$$10X_1 + 15X_2 \qquad = 300 + S_2$$

Setting S_2 equal to 1 has the effect of *increasing* the lower bound to 301. Returning to the optimal algebraic solution, where S_3 is now back to a zero level, we see that increasing S_2 by 1 increases X_2 by $\frac{1}{15}$ for a net *increase* in costs of $233.33 ($3500/15). Also, S_1 increases by 2000 and S_4 declines by $\frac{1}{15}$, but total costs are not affected. There is no change in X_1. Thus, the shadow price on prime-time coverage is $233.33. Management now has a measure of the consequences of adjusting the policy on prime-time coverage. As it turns out, the shadow price also holds for a *reduction* of the lower bound to 299 seconds, except that we would expect total costs to *decrease* by $233.33. The same thing can be said for the shadow price on radio-commercial availability. In that case, we would expect total costs to *decrease* by $333.33 if availability is *increased* to 23.

Notice that the surplus variable corresponding to the population-coverage constraint is in the optimal solution at a value of 360,000. Since we already have a surplus, the shadow price on population coverage would be zero, because a 1-unit change in the target value of 900,000 would have no effect on total costs.

In a similar fashion, a 1-unit change in the availability of TV commercials would not alter the optimal solution to the problem because we are not using all of that resource as it is. The slack variable, S_4, has a value of $\frac{50}{3}$ in the optimal solution. Since costs would not be affected, the shadow price is zero for TV commercial availability.

Use of Shadow Prices

Shadow prices can be used to estimate the effects of changes of more than 1 unit of resource i on objectives. Let V_i be the shadow price of resource i. Then, for a change in b_i of Δb_i, we might expect that the objective function, Z, would change in *absolute value* by the amount

$$\Delta Z = V_i |\Delta b_i| \qquad (4.50)$$

However, there is only a limited range of values Δb_i for which V_i is a valid measure of the effect on Z. For example, we will see that the shadow price of \$333.33 on radio-commercial availability is valid only for values of Δb_i from zero to -12. That is, if availability were 10 instead of 22, the absolute value of the change in total costs would be

$$\Delta Z = \$333.33 |-12| = \$3999.96$$

From our previous discussion, we know that this is an increase in costs. Thus, the new value of the objective function would be

$$Z' = Z + \Delta Z = \$62,666.67 + \$3999.96 = \$66,666.63$$

If, however, availability were only 9, the shadow price of \$333.33 would no longer be a valid measure of the increase in total costs.

Consider Figure 4.13. The surplus relative to the population-coverage constraint is shown as the horizontal difference between the population-coverage boundary equation and the optimal-solution point. The slack in the TV commercial availability constraint is indicated by the vertical difference between the optimal-solution point and the corresponding boundary equation. As we restrict the availability of radio commercials, the vertical boundary equation representing this constraint moves to the left in the diagram. The optimal-solution point, then, would move along the boundary equation

$$10X_1 + 15X_2 = 300$$

Eventually, the corner point (10, 13.33) is reached, and $S_1 = 0$. Further restriction of radio-commercial availability would cause the optimal-solution point to move along the boundary equation

$$50,000X_1 + 30,000X_2 = 900,000$$

Notice that the slope is different, and hence the rate of increase in the objective function is different than before.

This can be seen in Figure 4.14. With the availability of radio commercials at 14, the optimal total cost is \$65,333.33. If the availability is only 10, the optimal cost is \$66,666.63, or an increase of \$1333.30. This implies a cost per unit reduction

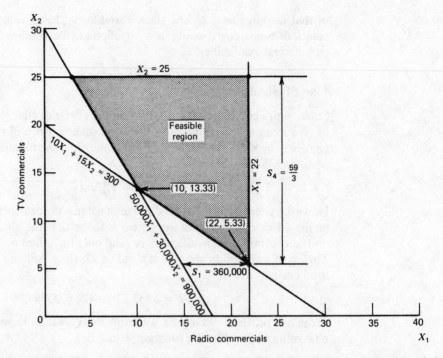

Figure 4.13 Feasible region for the media-mix problem showing the relationship of the surplus variable S_1 and the slack variable S_4 to the optimal solution point.

of \$333.33, the computed shadow price. However, if the availability is further reduced to a value of 6, total cost becomes \$82,000, or an additional increase of \$15,333.37 over the total cost when availability was 10. Since the reduction in radio commercials is four, this implies that the shadow price is now \$3833.34 for radio-commercial availability over this range.

The range over which the shadow price of \$333.33 is valid can be easily obtained from the optimal algebraic solution to the original problem. Recall (4.49)

$$X_1 \qquad\qquad = 22 - S_3$$

$$X_2 \qquad\qquad = \tfrac{16}{3} + (\tfrac{1}{15}) S_2 + (\tfrac{2}{3}) S_3$$

$$S_1 \qquad\qquad = 360{,}000 + 2000 S_2 - 30{,}000 S_3$$

$$S_4 = \tfrac{59}{3} - (\tfrac{1}{15}) S_2 - (\tfrac{2}{3}) S_3$$

An increase in S_3 has the effect of reducing radio-commercial availability. How much can we increase S_3 before one of the variables in the present solution is reduced to zero? With respect to X_1, this is obviously 22. However, any *increase* in S_3 would only increase X_2, and X_2 will thus never be reduced to zero by restricting the availability of radio commercials. With respect to X_2, S_3 could (theoretically) be infinite.

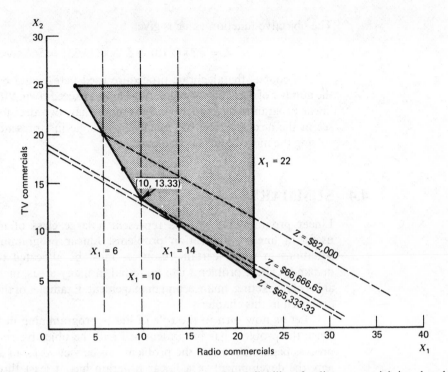

Figure 4.14 Pattern of optimal solutions as the availability of radio commercials is reduced.

The surplus variable, S_1, is affected differently. Each unit increase in S_3 results in a 30,000-unit decrease in S_1. Since S_1 currently has a value of 360,000, the maximum increase in S_3 is 12 ($= 360,000/30,000$). Any further increase in S_3 would make S_1 negative. Similarly, the maximum increase in S_3 is $29.5 (= \frac{59}{3}/\frac{2}{3})$ for S_4.

The maximum amount by which we can increase S_3, then, is the *minimum* of these maximums just calculated; otherwise, one or more of the variables in the model would be driven to a negative value, which would violate the nonnegativity restrictions. Thus,

$$S_3 = \text{Min}(22, \infty, 12, 29.5) = 12$$

This implies that radio-commercial availability could be reduced anywhere in the range from 22 to 10, and the shadow price of \$333.33 would be representative of the increase in total costs for a reduction in the availability of one commercial. Substituting this value of S_3 into the algebraic solution and recognizing that $S_2 = 0$ yields

$$
\begin{aligned}
X_1 &= 22 - 12 & &= 10 \\
X_2 &= \tfrac{16}{3} + \tfrac{2}{3}(12) + \tfrac{1}{15}S_2 & &= \tfrac{40}{3} + \tfrac{1}{15}S_2 \\
S_1 &= 360{,}000 - 30{,}000(12) + 2000S_2 &&= 2000S_2 \\
S_4 &= \tfrac{59}{3} - \tfrac{2}{3}(12) - \tfrac{1}{15}S_2 & &= \tfrac{35}{3} - \tfrac{1}{15}S_2 \quad (4.51)
\end{aligned}
$$

The objective-function value is given by

$$Z = \$2000(10) + \$3500(13.33) = \$66,666.63$$

Of course, the algebraic procedure used here would be necessary any time the number of decision variables in the model exceeds two. Virtually every practical linear programming model involves more than two decision variables. We will see in the next chapter that much of the logic just presented will be useful for solving the more complex problems.

4.4 SUMMARY

Linear programming models represent a large class of mathematical models useful in linear-optimization problems. Linear programming is applicable in situations in which certain resources must be allocated to certain competing demands. These problems can be found in many areas, including the functional areas of marketing, finance, and management. Examples of these applications were discussed in this chapter.

Let us now turn to the role of linear programming in the decision process. Once the problem has been identified and the objective specified, the modeling process begins. Provided the problem can be viewed as an allocation-type problem, the development of a linear program has at least three advantages. First, it forces the model builder to identify all of the relevant decision variables and constraints and the assumptions that must be made. On many occasions, the mere act of modeling the problem provides decision makers with greater insight into the problem, particularly as it relates to the nature of the constraints considered important for the decision and the assumptions inherent in a linear program. The assumptions of additivity, proportionality, certainty, and divisibility are made clear when a linear program is developed. Sometimes the decision problem, when modeled as a linear program, is not representative of the real decision problem. In such cases, other optimization models discussed in this text may be more appropriate. Nonetheless, the modeling process will help in deciding on the appropriate model to use.

If the assumptions of linear programming are appropriate for the decision problem, the second advantage of linear programming is that the techniques used for solving a linear programming model determine the optimal alternative for the problem. In this chapter we presented the graphical method for solving linear programming models. Although the graphical method is useful only for solving linear programs with two decision variables, it enabled us to present the basic concepts of linear programming. The procedure is outlined here for maximization (minimization) problems.

1. Prepare a graph of the equality portion of the constraints in the linear program. Identify the points that satisfy all of the constraints. This is the feasible region.

2. Identify the extreme points of the feasible region. These are the points at which two or more boundary equations intersect. The extreme points represent the alternatives in the problem.

3. Draw an iso-profit (iso-cost) line for a particular value of the objective function.

4. Move parallel iso-profit (iso-cost) lines in the direction of increasing (decreasing) objective-function values. This direction is typically away from (toward) the origin.

5. The feasible extreme point for which the value of the iso-profit (iso-cost) line is largest (smallest) is the optimal alternative.

6. Determine the exact solution by solving the two simultaneous equations representing the boundary equations that intersect to form the optimal extreme point. Use the method of Gaussian elimination. If more than two boundary equations form the optimal extreme point, select any two to find the solution.

A technique for solving linear programs with more than two decision variables will be presented in the next chapter.

The third advantage of linear programming is the information it provides over and above the specification of the optimal alternative. Given the optimal solution, we can determine the net benefit or cost of adjustments to the resources, b_i. These net benefits or costs are called shadow prices and represent the relative value of each resource with respect to the stated objective in the problem. These shadow prices are useful for assessing the impact of changing policies or resources under managerial control. For example, in the media-selection problem we found that increasing the prime-time coverage policy by only 1 second would cost an additional $233.33. We can also assess the impact of changes in the availability of some resources outside the direct control of management. In the media-selection problem, one less radio commercial spot would cost an additional $333.33. Information such as this can be useful in assessing the economic impact of changes in the current environment.

Shadow prices can be easily determined once the model has been augmented for slack and artificial variables with the help of Gaussian elimination, as we have shown in Section 4.3. Of course, we had to know the optimal solution before we could proceed since, in our example, we had six variables and only four equations. Nonetheless, we showed that the algebraic procedure was very useful, not only in determining the shadow prices, but also in determining, in each resource, the range of changes over which each shadow price is valid. The procedures presented in this chapter will be expanded in the next chapter to develop a procedure useful for analyzing larger linear programs.

References   Dantzig, G.B. *Linear Programming and Extensions*. Princeton, N.J.: Princeton University Press, 1963.

Gass, S.I. *Linear Programming: Methods and Applications*. 4th ed., New York: McGraw-Hill, 1975.

Hadley, G. *Linear Programming*. Reading, Mass.: Addison-Wesley, 1962.

Hillier, F.S., and Lieberman, G.J. *Introduction to Operations Research*. 2nd ed., San Francisco: Holden Day, 1974.

Hughes, A.J., and Graiwog, D.E. *Linear Programming: An Emphasis on Decision Making*. Reading, Mass.: Addison-Wesley, 1973.

Levin, R.I., and Lamone, R.P. *Linear Programming for Management Decisions*. Homewood, Ill.: Richard D. Irwin, 1969.

Spivey, W.A., and Thrall, R.M. *Linear Optimization*. New York: Holt, Rinehart and Winston, 1970.

Strum, J.E. *Introduction to Linear Programming*. San Francisco: Holden Day, 1972.

Wagner, H.M. *Principles of Operations Research*. 2nd ed., Englewood Cliffs, N.J.: Prentice-Hall, 1975.

Review Questions

1. Chapter 1 presented the steps in the decision-making process. Discuss the role of techniques such as linear programming in this process.

2. Compare and contrast the method of calculus with that of linear programming as techniques for solving models. What are the assumptions that must be made in each approach? When is linear programming the appropriate technique to use? What are the limitations of each method?

3. What is meant by the term "feasible region"? Why must there be a well-defined boundary for maximization problems?

4. Why is it necessary to render the origin infeasible in a minimization problem? Is it necessary to have upper-bound constraints in a minimization problem? Explain.

5. Define the concept of *convexity*. Why must the feasible region exhibit the property of convexity in linear programming problems?

6. Consider the following constraints in a linear programming model.

$$8X_1 + 3X_2 \le 240$$
$$3X_1 + X_2 \le 12$$

Describe the nature of the feasible region defined by this constraint set. Are any of the constraints redundant? Why?

7. Consider the following constraints in a linear programming model.

$$4X_1 + 10X_2 \le 100$$
$$X_1 - X_2 \le 15$$
$$2X_1 + X_2 \ge 60$$
$$X_1, X_2 \ge 0$$

Describe the nature of the feasible region defined by this constraint set.

8. What is an *extreme point*? Why can the extreme points in a linear programming problem be considered "alternatives" in the decision-making process?

9. What is a *shadow price*? How can this information be useful in making decisions?

10. How can linear programming be used to study managerial policies regarding a specific problem? What information can a linear programming analysis supply that is useful in assessing the economic impact of changing these policies?

11. What is a *slack* variable? How does it differ from a *surplus* variable? Of what use are these variables?

Problems

1. Using graphic methods, solve the following problem.

$$\text{Max } Z = 4X + 8Y$$

subject to

$$2X + 8Y \leq 24$$

$$X + 9Y \leq 18$$

$$X + Y \leq 10$$

$$X, Y \geq 0$$

2. Using graphic methods, solve the following problem.

$$\text{Max } Z = 4X + 2Y$$

subject to

$$2X + 2Y \leq 5 \qquad \text{Resource 1}$$

$$7X + 6Y \leq 42 \qquad \text{Resource 2}$$

$$12X + 3Y \leq 24 \qquad \text{Resource 3}$$

$$X, Y \geq 0$$

Is there a redundant constraint in this model? Why?

3. Solve the following problem using graphical methods.

$$\text{Min } Z = 3X + 2Y$$

subject to

$$7X + 3Y \geq 42$$

$$5X + 6Y \geq 60$$

$$12X + 8Y \geq 96$$

$$X, Y \geq 0$$

4. Using graphic methods, solve the following problem.

$$\text{Min } Z = 10X + 12Y$$

subject to

$X + Y \geq 8$	Resource 1
$12X + 6Y \geq 72$	Resource 2
$X + 2Y \geq 12$	Resource 3
$X + 8Y \geq 16$	Resource 4
$X, Y \geq 0$	

5. Consider the following linear programming model.

$$\text{Max } Z = 60X + 40Y$$

subject to

$$8X + 6Y \leq 48$$
$$X \leq 3Y$$
$$6X + 12Y \leq 72$$
$$X, Y \geq 0$$

Determine the alternative that minimizes total costs. (*Note.* The constraint $X \leq 3Y$ can be graphed by plotting two points satisfying the equation $X - 3Y = 0$. The equation passes through the origin.)

6. Find the optimal solution to the following model.

$$\text{Min } 7X + 11Y$$

subject to

$$X + Y \geq 10$$
$$4X - 2Y \geq 20$$
$$4X + 14Y \geq 56$$
$$X \leq 9$$
$$X, Y \geq 0$$

7. Consider Problem 1. Suppose the objective function were

$$\text{Min } Z = -4X - 5Y$$

Would the solution change? Why?

8. Consider Problem 2. What are the shadow prices of resources 1, 2, and 3? How much can we increase resource 1 before the shadow price is no longer valid? Verify your conclusions graphically as well as algebraically.

9. Consider Problem 4. Compute the shadow prices for *reductions* in resources 1, 2, and 3. How much can each resource be reduced before the shadow price is no longer valid? Base your conclusions on a graphical analysis and explain the results.

10. Consider the investor's portfolio-mix model.

$$\text{Max } Z = 0.06X_1 + 0.08X_2$$

subject to

$$
\begin{array}{llll}
X_1 + & X_2 \le & 400 & \text{Availability of funds} \\
& X_2 \le & 250 & \text{Upper bound on portfolio 2} \\
5X_1 + & 10X_2 \le & 3000 & \text{Investment risk upper bound} \\
X_1, X_2 & \ge & 0 &
\end{array}
$$

(a) Augment the model to include the slack variables. Use S_1 for the first constraint, S_2 for the second, and S_3 for the third.

(b) Using the optimal solution of $X_1 = \$200$ and $X_2 = \$200$, determine the values of the slack variables.

(c) Using the equations of the augmented model, use Gaussian elimination to solve for X_1, X_2, and S_2 in terms of constants, S_1 and S_3.

(d) Using the solution from part c, compute the shadow price of the availability of funds. How much can we increase the available funds and still expect the shadow price to be valid? Explain, using graphical methods.

11. Consider the media-mix problem of Section 4.2. Recall that the optimal solution was $X_1 = 22$ and $X_2 = 5.33$, where X_1 is the number of radio commercials and X_2 is the number of TV commercials to use in the advertising campaign. (Assume that fractional commercials represent the possibility of extending one commercial beyond the standard time. Thus, 5.33 means that we have four commercials of 10 seconds and one of about 13 seconds.) The firm has just found out that the price of a standard radio commercial has just been increased to $2500. Management is concerned that the best media mix may now be different from the preceding solution. The model is given next.

$$\text{Min } Z = \$2500X_1 + 3500X_2$$

subject to

$$
\begin{array}{rrr}
50{,}000X_1 + 30{,}000X_2 \ge & 900{,}000 \\
10X_1 + 15X_2 \ge & 300 \\
X_1 \le & 22 \\
X_2 \le & 25 \\
X_1, X_2 \ge & 0
\end{array}
$$

(a) Does the optimal media mix change? Use graphic methods to show the effects of the change in radio-commercial costs. Compute the new solution.

(b) Compute the shadow price on population coverage (first constraint). Use the procedure presented in Section 4.3.

(c) Compute the shadow price on prime-time coverage.

(d) Suppose that management is willing to relax (make less restrictive) either the population coverage constraint *or* the prime-time coverage constraint to reduce total costs. Which of these two would you recommend? Why?

12. A certain paint manufacturer must decide on how to finance paint production over the next 6 months. One possibility is to use internally generated funds. There is currently $200,000 in cash. The other possibility is to get a short-term bank loan. The firm has an unlimited line of credit from the bank; however, there is a liquidity condition on all loans. Cash (net of the amount used for financing production with internal funds) plus the accounts receivable must be at least as large as three times the loan quantity. The accounts receivable is merely $10 times the total production in gallons of paint, regardless of how the production is financed. In addition, the firm has a production processing limit of 60,000 gallons for a 6-month period. Finally, it costs $5 per gallon to produce paint with internal funds, whereas it costs $6 per unit to produce it on short-term loan because of interest charges. As such, the contribution to profits and overhead is $5 and $4, respectively.

(a) Let X be the number of gallons produced with internal funds and Y the number of gallons produced with the short-term loan. Write down the linear programming model for this problem. (*Hint.* Assume that the amount of the loan equals $6Y$.)

(b) Find the optimal funding mix for this problem.

(c) The production manager says that processing capacity can be increased by overtime. What is the shadow price on processing capacity? What is the maximum amount that capacity can increase before the net benefit of an additional capacity increase of 1 gallon is zero?

13. A small furniture manufacturer produces wooden chairs and rockers. The manufacturer wants to determine the product mix that maximizes profits. Each chair generates $15 in profits, whereas each rocker generates $30 in profits. There are two bottleneck operations in the production process: finishing and assembly. Each chair requires 4 hours of finishing and 2 hours of assembly. Each rocker requires 5 hours of finishing and 4 hours of assembly. There is a capacity of 200 hours in finishing and of 240 hours in assembly. Finally, forecasts indicate a demand potential of 40 chairs and 28 rockers. Management considers these forecasts as upper bounds on production.

(a) Specify the linear programming model for this problem.

(b) Graph the feasible region. What are the alternatives for this problem?

(c) Determine the optimal product mix.

(d) What is the shadow price on finishing capacity? Assembly capacity?

    (e) Suppose the *updated* forecasts indicate a potential demand of 30 chairs and 35 rockers. Does this change the optimal product mix? Why?

14. The plant manager of a plastic-pipe manufacturer has the opportunity to use two different routings for a particular type of plastic pipe. Routing 1 uses extruder process A and routing 2 uses extruder process B. No matter which routing is used, the raw material for the pipe must pass through a melting process. The table below gives the hours per 100 feet of pipe required in each process.

	Hours Per 100 Feet		
Process	Routing 1	Routing 2	Maximum Hours Available
Melting	2	2	100
Extruder A	10		400
Extruder B		8	360

In addition, 100 feet of pipe produced on routing 1 require 30 pounds of plastic, whereas 100 feet of pipe only require 25 pounds on routing 2 because of the higher production quality. There is a total of only 1350 pounds of raw plastic material available. Also, the minimum production quantity is 3000 feet of pipe to ensure that existing production orders are fulfilled. Finally, it costs more to use routing 1; thus the profit per hundred feet is $50 for routing 1 and $80 for routing 2.

    (a) Specify the linear programming model for this problem.

    (b) Determine with graphical methods the solution that maximizes profits.

    (c) How much would the profit per 100 feet of pipe produced on routing 1 have to increase before it would pay to increase production on that routing?

    (d) With reference to the solution in part b, management can buy an addition to the melting process that costs $500 but increases the capacity by 50 hours. It is worth it? Why?

15. The postmaster of a sectional-center post office in Sandstone, Kentucky, must make a decision regarding the mix of transportation modes to use in transporting mail from Sandstone to Charwood, Kentucky. There are two possible modes: star routes (trucks) and air taxis (small private air carriers). A local trucking firm has offered to make *at most* 5 trips per day at a cost of $150 per trip. There are several air taxi services in Sandstone that collectively can supply *at most* 12 trips per day at a cost of $200 per trip. Each truck can carry 4 tons of mail per trip, whereas each air taxi can carry only 2 tons per trip. Capacity should be planned such that at least 24 tons of mail per day can be transported to Charwood. Although the postmaster wishes to minimize costs, service must also be considered. Because of mechanical failures and weather conditions, only 80% of the trucks arrive at Charwood on time to make dispatches for local delivery. However, air taxis are much more reliable, with 95% of the trips arriving on time. The standard for service states that no matter what mix of modes is chosen, at least 90% of the *total trips* must arrive on time for dispatch.

(a) Let X be the number of star route trips per day and Y the number of air taxi trips per day. Set up the linear programming model to minimize costs. (*Hint*. The service constraint reduces to a simple relationship between X and Y of the form $Y \geq KX$.)

(b) Determine the modal mix that minimizes costs.

(c) Augment the model to include the slack and surplus variables. Determine the shadow price on the transport capacity constraint (e.g., the constraint stating that at least 24 tons must be transported). How much more would it cost if that lower bound were 32 tons? How would the optimal modal mix change? Show this graphically.

5

LINEAR PROGRAMMING: THE SIMPLEX METHOD, DUALITY, AND THE DECISION PROCESS

5.1 **THE SIMPLEX METHOD**
Maximization Problems
Minimization Problems
Review of the Simplex Method

5.2 **DUALITY**
The Primal-Dual Relationship
Economic Interpretation of the Dual Surplus Variable
Duality Theorems
Computational Advantages of the Dual

5.3 **MODELING CONSIDERATIONS**
No Feasible Solution
Unbounded Solution
Degeneracy
Multiple Optima

5.4 **POSTOPTIMALITY ANALYSIS**
Objective Coefficients of Nonbasic Variables
Objective Coefficients of Basic Variables
Right-Hand Sides
Technical Coefficients

5.5 **MULTIPLE OBJECTIVES**
Generating Noninferior Solutions
Incorporating Preferences

5.6 **SUMMARY**
References
Review Questions
Problems

Linear programming is a powerful technique for selecting alternatives in situations in which the objective function and constraints are linear and the decision variables are continuous. We have seen how the optimal alternative can be chosen when there are only two decision variables. Unfortunately, real-world problems invariably involve more than two decision variables. Graphic methods are useful for displaying the logic of linear programming solution methods; however, more general procedures are needed if practical problems are to be solved. The *simplex method* is one such procedure. It is an algebraic procedure that systematically evaluates extreme points of the feasible region. Section 5.1 of this chapter discusses the application of this technique to maximization and minimization problems.

The solution of linear programming models provides more information than the optimal alternative for a decision problem. Economic information regarding the value of the firm's resources is a by-product of the linear programming analysis. Although this information, which we have called shadow price, is immediately available upon solution of the original model, or *primal* problem, using the simplex method, a more intuitive interpretation of the economic consequences of linear programming can be achieved by analyzing a related problem called the *dual*. The dual problem has the *shadow prices* as decision variables. Solving the dual problem is equivalent to solving the primal problem. As we will see in Section 5.2, there may even be a computational advantage to solving the dual problem instead of the primal problem.

Chapter 3 emphasized the importance of constructing a valid model for the decision problem. Section 5.3 discusses some of the common pitfalls encountered in linear programming modeling as well as some of the technical aspects of the solutions to certain problems.

A fundamental understanding of the available economic information from a linear programming model is critical to effective managerial use of such models. Section 5.4 presents an activity called *postoptimality analysis*, in which various "what-if" questions can be asked about the assumed values of the parameters in the model. It was obvious in Chapter 4 that the shadow prices play an important role in such an analysis.

Finally, Section 5.5 expands the technique of linear programming to incorporate more than one objective. A technique called *goal programming* is used to demonstrate the nature of the information that can be generated with a linear programming model that incorporates the preferences of the decision maker for various conflicting objectives.

5.1 THE SIMPLEX METHOD

The simplex method is an iterative algebraic procedure for solving linear programming models. Starting with an initial feasible solution, the procedure systematically modifies the solution such that at each iteration, the objective criterion improves or, at worst, stays the same. As we saw in Chapter 4, an optimal solution to a linear programming model occurs at least at one extreme point of the feasible region. Thus, the simplex method is a procedure for systematic evaluation of extreme points. In this section we first demonstrate the technique for maximization problems and then show the slight modifications that must be made for minimization problems.

Maximization Problems

The simplex method consists of a series of well-defined steps. Although the method is applicable to larger problems, we apply these steps to a simple two-variable problem so the logic of the method can be demonstrated graphically.

Step 1.   Augment the Model   Consider the investor's portfolio-mix problem presented in Chapter 4. The original model (Equation 4.12) was

$$\text{Max } Z = 0.06X_1 + 0.08X_2$$

subject to

$$X_1 + X_2 \leq 400$$
$$X_2 \leq 250$$
$$5X_1 + 10X_2 \leq 3000$$
$$X_1, X_2 \geq 0$$

Since the model consists solely of upper-bound constraints, only slack variables are required to augment the model; that is,

$$\text{Max } Z = 0.06X_1 + 0.08X_2 + 0S_1 + 0S_2 + 0S_3$$

subject to

$$
\begin{aligned}
X_1 + X_2 + S_1 &= 400 \\
X_2 + S_2 &= 250 \\
5X_1 + 10X_2 + S_3 &= 3000 \\
X_1, X_2, S_1, S_2, S_3 &\geq 0
\end{aligned}
$$

(5.1)

Notice that the parameters to the right of the equality signs are all nonnegative. This is a requirement for any linear programming model.

The augmented model (Equation 5.1) consists of five variables and three equations. Because the simplex method automatically ensures the nonnegativity of the variables, there is no need to augment these restrictions.

Step 2.   Set Up the Initial Tableau   The extreme points of the feasible region are defined by the intersection of linear boundary equations and the simplex method is thus actually a procedure for solving linear equations. Unfortunately, the augmented model presents a situation where the number of variables exceeds

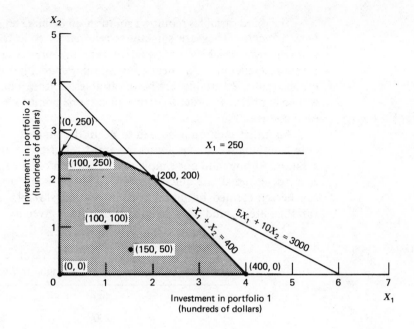

Figure 5.1 Feasible region of the investor's portfolio-mix problem showing the extreme points and two other feasible points.

the number of equations and, hence, there may be an infinite number of solutions to such a system. To see why this is so, consider Figure 5.1, in which the feasible region of the investors' portfolio mix is displayed. Every point in the feasible region represents a solution to the system of equations in the augmented portfolio-mix model. For example, setting $X_1 = 100$ and $X_2 = 100$ implies that $S_1 = 200$, $S_2 = 150$, and $S_3 = 1500$. This constitutes a solution to the three-equation system. Similarly, $X_1 = 150$, $X_2 = 50$, $X_1 = 250$, $S_3 = 200$, and $S_3 = 1750$ is also a solution. Because an infinite number of combinations of X_1 and X_2 are feasible, there is an infinite number of solutions to the system of equations.

It should not be too upsetting, however, that there are an infinite number of solutions. In Chapter 4 we learned that an optimal solution to any linear programming problem occurs at an extreme point of the feasible region. In Figure 5.1, each of the extreme points can be determined by solving for the point of intersection of two boundary equations. But since we have three equations in the augmented model, each extreme point can be represented by only three of the five variables. In this example, three variables will have nonzero values and the other two will have zero values. For example, consider the extreme point (100, 250). This point is represented by $X_1 = 100$, $X_2 = 250$, and $S_1 = 50$, while $S_2 = S_3 = 0$. Similarly, (200, 200) can be represented by $X_1 = 200$, $X_2 = 200$, and $S_2 = 50$, while $S_1 = S_3 = 0$. Thus, solving for extreme points amounts to choosing the three variables for which to solve in terms of the other two variables. This is analogous to the algebraic manipulation done at the end of Chapter 4, using Gaussian elimination.

The three variables requiring solutions in defining an extreme point are called *basic variables*. They are sometimes referred to collectively as a *basis*. The remaining two variables, set equal to zero in our example, are called *nonbasic variables*. Generally, if a linear programming model has n decision variables and m constraints, m variables are basic variables, or form a basis, and $n - m$ variables will be nonbasic. In order to define an extreme point,[1] we require one variable for each constraint.

An initial solution is needed to begin the simplex method. Because we want only to evaluate extreme points, we must select one extreme point as an initial solution. Although in our simple two-variable problem any extreme point can be easily determined, the quickest point to obtain is the origin. This extreme point can be represented by taking the three slack variables as basic. The nonbasic variables are X_1 and X_2. The initial solution is given by

Basis		R	Nonbasic Variables
S_1	$=$	400	$-X_1 - X_2$
S_2	$=$	250	$-X_2$
S_3	$=$	3000	$-5X_1 - 10X_2$

Note that augmenting the model for this problem with slack variables has performed two functions: (1) transforming all inequalities into equalities, and (2) providing for a simple determination of the initial set of basic variables.[2]

For computational purposes, it is much easier to represent the problem in a tableau format. A partial simplex tableau (we will add to it later) for the portfolio-mix problem is given by

c_j	Basis	0.06 X_1	0.08 X_2	0 S_1	0 S_2	0 S_3	R
0	S_1	1	1	1	0	0	400
0	S_2	0	1	0	1	0	250
0	S_3	5	10	0	0	1	3000

---

[1] Under certain circumstances, some basic variables may have zero values. This condition, called degeneracy, will be discussed later.

[2] The initial solution may not be feasible for models with equality or lower-bound constraints, or both, because it includes fictitious variables called artificial variables. It may take several iterations of the simplex method to get a feasible solution to the original problem. We discuss this in more depth later.

All of the information regarding the problem is contained in the tableau. The top row gives the objective-function coefficient for each variable, whereas the column on the far left gives the objective-function coefficients for the basic variables shown in the second column. The columns headed by each variable give the technical coefficients (a_{ij}) of that variable in each constraint. These columns are called *vectors* and each entry in a vector represents the coefficients of that variable in a constraint in the problem. The last column specifies the resource levels b_i for each constraint.

The initial solution to the problem can be identified easily from the tableau. The basic variables can be represented by a special type of column vector called a *unit vector*. A unit vector has one element equal to one and all other elements equal to zero. For example, the following vectors are unit vectors:

$$\begin{pmatrix} 1 \\ 0 \\ 0 \\ 0 \end{pmatrix} \begin{pmatrix} 0 \\ 0 \\ 0 \\ 1 \\ 0 \\ 0 \\ 0 \end{pmatrix} \begin{pmatrix} 0 \\ 1 \end{pmatrix}$$

In general, vector ε_r is a unit vector of dimension m if it consists of m elements, $\delta_i, i = 1, 2, \ldots, m$ such that

$$\delta_i = \begin{cases} 1 & \text{if } i = r \\ 0 & \text{if } i \neq r \end{cases}$$

In the portfolio-mix problem, the unit vectors ε_1, ε_2, and ε_3 have dimension 3 because there are three constraints in the problem. The basis is a collection of *independent* unit vectors of dimension m. Unit vector ε_j is independent of unit vector ε_k if δ_j in vector ε_j is not equal to δ_k in vector ε_k. In other words, the vectors are independent unless $j = k$. For example, the system below does *not* represent a basis because vector 1 is not independent of vector 3.

$$\begin{bmatrix} (1) & (2) & (3) \\ \begin{pmatrix} 1 \\ 0 \\ 0 \end{pmatrix} & \begin{pmatrix} 0 \\ 1 \\ 0 \end{pmatrix} & \begin{pmatrix} 1 \\ 0 \\ 0 \end{pmatrix} \end{bmatrix}$$

The initial basis of the portfolio-mix problem is easily seen to consist of S_1, S_2, and S_3 because each of these is represented by independent unit vectors of dimension 3. The initial solution is determined by assigning each basic variable the value of b_i in the row $i, i = 1, 2, \ldots, m$, for which its unit vector has $\delta_i = 1$. Thus, $S_1 = 400$, $S_2 = 250$, and $S_3 = 3000$. Notice that this solution satisfies the nonnegativity restrictions. We would have violated these restrictions if we originally had a model with negative b_i.

Step 3.   Select the Pivot Variable   The initial solution to the portfolio-mix problem is not very interesting. Because $X_1 = X_2 = 0$, it specifies an alternative that instructs us to do nothing. Obviously, a better alternative can be found. This amounts to changing the basis in such a way that the objective function is increased. The easiest way to do this is to work with one variable at a time. Two questions must then be answered in this and the following step:

1.   Which nonbasic variable is to enter into the basis?
2.   Which basic variable is to leave the basis and become a nonbasic variable?

To answer the first question, it is best to return to the algebraic solution of the initial basis for an intuitive understanding of the logic. To this end consider

$$S_1 \qquad\quad = 400 - X_1 - X_2 \qquad\qquad (5.2)$$

$$S_2 \quad = 250 \qquad\quad - X_2 \qquad\qquad (5.3)$$

$$S_3 = 3000 - 5X_1 - 10X_2 \qquad\qquad (5.4)$$

There are two nonbasic variables. The choice of which one to enter into the basis should be made with respect to the *net contribution* of each to the objective function. The net contribution is the difference between the profits gained from including the variable in the basis and the profits given up because of a change in the present solution. The nonbasic variable that provides the largest net contribution per unit is chosen to enter into the basis. Consider variable X_1. According to (5.2), an increase of one unit in X_1 causes a one unit reduction in S_1. Since S_1 has a coefficient of zero in the objective function, the reduction of S_1 by one unit has no effect on the objective function. Equation 5.3 indicates that X_1 can increase by any amount with no effect on S_2 because $a_{21} = 0$. In (5.4), an increase of one unit in X_1 reduces S_3 by 5 units; however, this has no effect on the objective function because in that function S_3 has a zero coefficient. The total *decrease* in profits (or return) per unit increase in X_1 is given by

$$0(1) + 0(0) + 0(5) = 0$$

This quantity can be called the *opportunity cost* of including one unit of X_1 in the solution. It is a measure of how much we have to surrender in profits relative to the existing solution to the problem if we introduce one unit of X_1. In this case, the opportunity cost is zero for X_1.

The net contribution per unit of X_1 introduced is the difference between the per-unit profit (or return) and the per-unit opportunity cost. This amounts to

$$0.06 - 0 = 0.06$$

In more general terms, if z_j is the opportunity cost for introducing one unit of variable j into the solution, the net contribution of variable j is given by $c_j - z_j$. In this case, $c_1 - z_1 = 0.06$.

The computation of the net contribution of X_2 is similarly obtained. A one-unit increase in X_2 results in a one-unit decrease in each of S_1 and S_2 and a 10-unit reduction in S_3. Each of these basic variables contributes nothing to the objective function, and the opportunity cost of introducing one unit of X_2 into the solution z_2 is zero. Because the contribution of X_2 is 0.08, the net contribution

$$c_2 - z_2 = 0.08 - 0 = 0.08$$

This entire analysis can be easily performed with the tableau presented earlier by adding two rows—one for z_j and one for $c_j - z_j$.

c_j	Basis	0.06 X_1	0.08 X_2	0 S_1	0 S_2	0 S_3	R
0	S_1	1	1	1	0	0	400
0	S_2	0	1	0	1	0	250
0	S_3	5	10	0	0	1	3000
	z_j	0	0	0	0	0	0
	$c_j - z_j$	0.06	0.08	0	0	0	

The opportunity cost associated with the introduction of any variable j is easily computed by multiplying each *element* in the column vector a_{ij} by the corresponding *objective function coefficient* in the far left column and summing the results. For X_2, this amounts to $0(1) + 0(1) + 0(10) = 0$. The value in the z_j row in the R column is the current value of the objective function. This is computed in the same way as the opportunity cost for any variable. The net contribution row is computed by subtracting each z_j value from the c_j value at the top of each column j.

We can now answer the first question. The nonbasic variable that should enter into the basis is the one with the largest net contribution per unit to the objective function. This variable is called the *pivot variable*. In this case, the pivot variable is X_2.

Step 4. Select the Pivot Row The answer to the second question is still not apparent, however. We must return to the algebraic representation of the initial solution.

Basis		R	Nonbasic Variables
S_1	$=$	400	$-X_1 - X_2$
S_2	$=$	250	$-X_2$
S_3	$=$	3000	$-5X_1 - 10X_2$

We would like to make X_2 as large as possible, since it has the largest per-unit contribution to the objective function. Only one thing limits the increase of X_2:

the nonnegativity restrictions. X_2 can be increased until one of the basic variables is driven to zero. Any increase beyond this point would make at least one basic variable negative. From the algebraic representation, we see that as far as S_1 is concerned, the largest X_2 can become is 400. If X_2 is set equal to 401, S_1 would have to be -1 to balance the equation. With respect to S_2, X_2 must not exceed 250. Finally, S_3 is driven to zero when X_2 is $300(= 3000/10)$. Therefore, the maximum increase allowed for X_2 is given by the minimum of the ratios (b_i/a_{i2}) for all $a_{i2} > 0$

$$X_2 = \text{Min}\left(\frac{b_1}{a_{12}}, \frac{b_2}{a_{22}}, \frac{b_3}{a_{32}}\right)$$

or

$$X_2 = \text{Min}\left(\frac{400}{1}, \frac{250}{1}, \frac{3000}{10}\right) = 250 \tag{5.5}$$

If X_2 is increased to a value of 250, the basic variable that is driven to zero is S_2. Thus, we have answered the second question. The variable that leaves the basis is S_2. Since S_2 is associated with the second equation, row 2 is called the *pivot row*.

Returning to the tableau format, the pivot variable and pivot row are easily determined. The tableau shown below has a new column at the far right, labeled Ratio. The row corresponding to the minimum value of the ratio is the pivot row. The ratios are given by (b_i/a_{ik}), where variable k is the pivot variable. If $a_{ik} \leq 0$ for a given i, the ratio is assigned a value of $+\infty$, since the pivot variable could be increased indefinitely without causing the basic variable associated with row i to go negative. Since row 2 is the pivot row—denoted by * in the ratio column—the element in the second row of the X_2 column, a_{22}, is called the *pivot element*. It is circled in the tableau below.

	c_j	Basis	0.06 X_1	0.08 X_2	0 S_1	0 S_2	0 S_3	R	Ratio
	0	S_1	1	1	1	0	0	400	$\frac{400}{1} = 400$
Pivot row $\rightarrow$	0	S_2	0	①	0	1	0	250	$\frac{250}{1} = 250*$
	0	S_3	5	10	0	0	1	3000	$\frac{3000}{10} = 300$
	z_j		0	0	0	0	0	0	
	$c_j - z_j$		0.06	0.08	0	0	0		

$\uparrow$
Pivot
variable

Step 5. **Generate the New Basis** Basic variables are represented by unit vectors, so the column vector representing X_2 must be transformed into a unit vector. We must create a new unit vector in which $\delta_2 = 1$ corresponds to the row in which the pivot element resides, and $\delta_1 = \delta_3 = 0$. Notice that this amounts to transforming the X_2 column into a unit vector identical to the one representing S_2.

The transformation can be done with Gaussian elimination. We know that S_1, X_2, and S_3 are the basic variables, and we can solve for these variables in terms of constants and the nonbasic variables X_1 and S_2. The system of equations from (5.1) is

$$S_1 + \quad X_2 \quad = \quad 400 - \quad X_1 \tag{5.6}$$

$$X_2 \quad = \quad 250 \quad\quad - S_2 \tag{5.7}$$

$$10X_2 + S_3 = 3000 - 5X_1 \tag{5.8}$$

Since (5.7) is the pivot row, X_2 must be eliminated from (5.6) and (5.8). We begin by converting the pivot row to standard form by multiplying (5.7) by the inverse of the pivot element, or $1/a_{22}$ in this case. Since $a_{22} = 1$, (5.7) is already in standard form.

Using the standardized form of the pivot row, X_2 can be eliminated from (5.6) by multiplying the pivot row by $-a_{12}$ and adding the result to (5.6). Since $a_{12} = 1$, the new equation is

$$S_1 = (400 - 250) - X_1 + S_2$$

Similarly, X_2 can be eliminated from Equation (5.8) by multiplying the standardized pivot row (5.7) by $-a_{32}$, or -10, and adding the result to Equation 5.8. The new solution is

$$S_1 \quad\quad = 150 - X_1 + \quad S_2$$

$$X_2 \quad\quad = 250 \quad\quad - S_2$$

$$S_3 = 500 - 5X_1 + 10S_2 \tag{5.9}$$

which can be written in tableau form as

c_j	Basis	0.06 X_1	0.08 X_2	0 S_1	0 S_2	0 S_3	R	Ratio
0	S_1	1	0	1	−1	0	150	
0.08	X_2	0	1	0	1	0	250	
0	S_3	5	0	0	−10	1	500	
	z_j						20	
	$c_j - z_j$							

The new tableau indicates that the basis now consists of S_1, X_2, and S_3, and the solution is $S_1 = 150$, $X_2 = 250$, and $S_3 = 500$. The body of the tableau contains new technical coefficients, a'_{ij}, which are the result of the algebraic manipulations of Gaussian elimination. From now on, a'_{ij} will be the technical coefficient in row i, column j, in a particular simplex tableau and will not necessarily equal the a_{ij} in the original constraint.

Step 6. Test for Optimality   The test for optimality in the simplex method amounts to determining the desirability of including a nonbasic variable in the basis. If it is not desirable to do so, the present basis must constitute an optimal solution. Let us complete the last tableau by filling in the z_j and $c_j - z_j$ rows.

c_j	Basis	0.06 X_1	0.08 X_2	0 S_1	0 S_2	0 S_3	R	Ratio
0	S_1	1	0	1	−1	0	150	
0.08	X_2	0	1	0	1	0	250	
0	S_3	5	0	0	−10	1	500	
	z_j	0	0.08	0	0.08	0	20	
	$c_j - z_j$	0.06	0	0	−0.08	0		

The $c_j - z_j$ row indicates that bringing in X_1 will contribute \$0.06 for each dollar that can be invested in portfolio 1. Because inclusion of X_1 in the basis will improve the objective function, the present solution cannot be optimal.

How many iterations must we perform before we get the optimal solution? That question is difficult to answer in general; even for the largest of linear programming problems, there are only a finite number of extreme points. Even if we had to evaluate each of these points (the simplex method is much more efficient than this), we would eventually solve the problem. Nonetheless, the simplex method has a *stopping rule* that indicates when we have found the optimal solution in *maximization* problems

> *If every entry in the $c_j - z_j$ row is zero or negative, the current solution is optimal. If at least one entry is positive, the solution can be improved and the present solution is not optimal.*

Obviously, we cannot pass the test for optimality in our problem at this iteration; thus, we must return to Step 3 and continue. Using the methods of Steps 3, 4, 5, and 6, let us start with the results of the first iteration and proceed to the optimal solution.

Iteration 1

c_j	Basis	0.06 X_1	0.08 X_2	0 S_1	0 S_2	0 S_3	R	Ratio
0	S_1	1	0	1	-1	0	150	150
0.08	X_2	0	1	0	1	0	250	$+\infty$
0	S_3	5	0	0	-10	1	500	100*
	z_j	0	0.08	0	0.08	0	20	
	$c_j - z_j$	0.06	0	0	-0.08	0		

The pivot variable is X_1 (why?) and the pivot row is row 3. The pivot row cannot be row 1 because X_1 would have to be 150 before S_1 would be zero. If X_1 were 150, S_3 would have to be negative to balance row 3, as indicated in the Ratio column. The pivot element is 5. In the next iteration, X_1 will enter the basis at a value of 100, and S_3 will leave the basis.

Iteration 2

c_j	Basis	0.06 X_1	0.08 X_2	0 S_1	0 S_2	0 S_3	R	Ratio
0	S_1	0	0	1	①	$-\frac{1}{5}$	50	50*
0.08	X_2	0	1	0	1	0	250	250
0.06	X_1	1	0	0	-2	$\frac{1}{5}$	100	∞
	z_j	0.06	0.08	0	-0.04	0.012	26	
	$c_j - z_j$	0	0	0	0.04	-0.012		

The pivot variable is S_2 and the pivot row is row 1. Notice that S_2 was the variable that left the basis in the first iteration. This situation frequently occurs in linear programming problems and should not be confused with a phenomenon called *cycling*, in which a variable repeatedly enters and leaves the basis without increasing the value of the objective function. Cycling rarely occurs in practice; it is associated with a condition called *degeneracy*, which we will discuss later. In this case, the objective function will be increased (a positive $c_j - z_j$ value) and S_2 will enter the basis at a positive level (ratio is greater than zero). Variable S_1 will leave the basis in the next iteration.

The criterion for optimality has been met at iteration 3. All entries in the $c_j - z_j$ row are zero or negative; thus, no further improvement in the objective function is possible. The optimal solution is $X_1 = 200$, $X_2 = 200$, $S_2 = 50$, and the maximum return is $28.

Iteration 3

c_j	Basic	0.06 X_1	0.08 X_2	0 S_1	0 S_2	0 S_3	R	Ratio
0	S_2	0	0	1	1	$-\frac{1}{5}$	50	
0.08	X_2	0	1	-1	0	$\frac{1}{5}$	200	
0.06	X_1	1	0	2	0	$-\frac{1}{5}$	200	
	z_j	0.06	0.08	0.04	0	0.004	28	
	$c_j - z_j$	0	0	-0.04	0	-0.004		

Figure 5.2 shows the extreme points evaluated by the simplex method at each iteration. The initial solution was $(0, 0)$. We then proceeded to $(0,250)$ for the first iteration, followed by $(50,250)$, and finally $(200,200)$ for the second and third iterations, respectively. Although we had to evaluate four of the five possible extreme points in our simple problem, the simplex method is much more efficient for larger problems. A problem with n variables (including slacks) and m constraints will have $\binom{n}{m} = n!/m!(n-m)!$ different ways to form a basis of m variables. Some of these combinations may not be feasible because of the constraints.

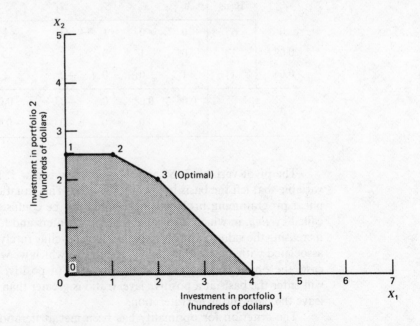

Figure 5.2 Pattern simplex method followed in evaluating extreme points in portfolio-mix problem.

Nonetheless, in practice, it usually requires from m to $3m$ iterations to solve a problem. For example, if our problem had 10 variables and only 3 constraints, there could be as many as 120 bases to evaluate. We would expect only to have to evaluate, at most, 9 of them to find the optimal solution.

Minimization Problems

The solution procedure for minimization problems is very similar to the procedure just described for maximization problems. The major difference lies in the stopping rule. We will demonstrate the solution procedure by solving a problem involving four decision variables subject to upper-bound, lower-bound, and equality constraints. In this way, the problem is more complex than the two-variable problems we solved previously, and it enables us to introduce the principle of model augmentation for lower-bound and equality constraints.

Consider the problem of a production manager who must determine the weekly production schedule for each of two plants. The company produces two types of plastic pipe. Each plant can manufacture both types of pipe. The Hometown plant can produce 1000 feet of type 1 pipe for $50 and 1000 feet of type 2 pipe for $75. Owing to differences in raw-material costs, labor rates, and plant conditions, the Bakersfield plant can produce the same quantities of type 1 and type 2 pipe for $60 and $70, respectively.

Although there are a number of production processes involved in the manufacture of plastic pipe, the extrusion process is the bottleneck in both plants. In the Hometown plant, this requires 5 hours per 1000 feet of type 1 pipe and 8 hours per 1000 feet of type 2 pipe. At that plant, only 100 hours per week of extrusion time can be expected. In the Bakersfield plant, it takes 6 hours for type 1 and 7 hours for type 2 pipe of the same length. A maximum of 80 hours per week is available at Bakersfield.

The sales department feels it can sell as much type 1 pipe as the company can produce; however, a *minimum* of 12,000 feet must be produced weekly to cover known commitments. Type 2 pipe, however, is a special product and does not have the same universal demand as type 1 pipe. Thus, the present plan must produce *exactly* 16,000 feet of type 2 pipe per week to satisfy a contract with a construction company. An overrun of type 2 pipe can be very costly because it may be a long time before another customer will demand it.

There are four decision variables in this problem (all expressed in thousands of feet of pipe)

X_1 = quantity of type 1 pipe manufactured at Hometown

X_2 = quantity of type 2 pipe manufactured at Hometown

X_3 = quantity of type 1 pipe manufactured at Bakersfield

X_4 = quantity of type 2 pipe manufactured at Bakersfield

The model for this problem is given as

$$\text{Min } Z = 50X_1 + 75X_2 + 60X_3 + 70X_4$$

subject to

$$5X_1 + 8X_2 \qquad\qquad\qquad \le 100$$
$$6X_3 + 7X_4 \le\ 80 \qquad\qquad (5.10)$$
$$X_1 \qquad + X_3 \qquad\qquad \ge\ 12$$
$$X_2 \qquad + X_4 =\ 16$$
$$X_1, \quad X_2, \quad X_3, \quad X_4 \ge\ 0$$

Step 1. Augment the Model One purpose of augmentation is to transform the constraints in the model to equalities. In the present problem, this amounts to including some slack and surplus variables in the model. The result is shown by (5.11), in which S_1 and S_2 are slack variables and S_3 is a surplus variable. The slack and surplus variables do not contribute to the objective function and thus have coefficients of zero in this function.

$$\text{Min } Z = 50X_1 + 75X_2 + 60X_3 + 70X_4 + 0S_1 + 0S_2 + 0S_3$$

subject to

$$5X_1 + 8X_2 \qquad\qquad + S_1 \qquad\qquad = 100$$
$$6X_3 + 7X_4 \qquad + S_2 \qquad = 80 \qquad (5.11)$$
$$X_1 \qquad + X_3 \qquad\qquad - S_3 =\ 12$$
$$X_2 \qquad + X_4 \qquad\qquad\qquad = 16$$
$$X_1, X_2, X_3, X_4, S_1, S_2, S_3 \qquad\qquad \ge\ 0$$

The other purpose of augmentation is to provide an initial solution for the simplex method. Unfortunately, merely transforming the constraints into equalities does not provide us with an initial basis in this case. Because there are four constraints in the model, the basis must consist of four independent unit vectors. So far, the augmentation has only provided us with two unit vectors, S_1 and S_2. The column vector for S_3 is not a unit vector because of the -1. Merely multiplying the third equation of (5.11) by -1 will not help because it would imply that $S_3 = -12$ in the initial solution. This would obviously violate the nonnegativity restrictions. Also, notice that no unit vector is associated with the fourth equation.

In order to provide an initial solution, we can add *artificial* variables to the model. Unlike slack or surplus variables, artificial variables have no tangible relationship to the decision problem. Their only purpose is to provide an initial solution to any problem (maximization or minimization) in which lower-bound or equality constraints are present. Because these artificial variables become a part of the initial basis, the initial solution to the augmented problem is not *feasible* in the original problem. An artificial variable with a nonzero value means we have not yet found a feasible solution to the original model. Thus, we try to drive the artificial variables out of the basis, through the usual simplex method, as soon as possible. In minimization problems, this is accomplished by attaching an arbitrary, but extremely large, *cost* to each artificial variable in the objective function. To avoid making this cost explicit relative to other costs in the problem, we designate this large cost as M and proceed as if it were larger than any finite number. This procedure for handling artificial variables in linear programming problems is called the "big M" method.[3] The normal simplex process for selecting variables that are to leave the basis will eventually drive the artificial variables out of the basis. Once the basis consists solely of decision variables, slack, or surplus variables, the solution is feasible. It may then take more iterations to arrive at an optimal solution.

The model, augmented with artificial variables, is given by

$$\text{Min } Z = 50X_1 + 75X_2 + 60X_3 + 70X_4 + 0S_1 + 0S_2 + 0S_3 + MA_1 + MA_2$$

subject to

$$
\begin{aligned}
5X_1 + 8X_2 \quad\quad\quad\quad\quad + S_1 \quad\quad\quad\quad\quad &= 100 \\
6X_3 + 7X_4 \quad\quad + S_2 \quad\quad\quad\quad &= 80 \quad\quad (5.12)\\
X_1 + \quad\quad X_3 \quad\quad\quad\quad\quad - S_3 + A_1 \quad\quad &= 12 \\
X_2 \quad\quad + X_4 \quad\quad\quad\quad\quad\quad + A_2 &= 16 \\
X_1, X_2, X_3, X_4, S_1, S_2, S_3, A_1, A_2 \quad\quad\quad\quad\quad &\geq \quad 0
\end{aligned}
$$

Step 2. Set Up the Initial Tableau Once the model has been augmented with slack, surplus, and artificial variables, the initial tableau can easily be written. We have included the z_j and $c_j - z_j$ rows to facilitate the next step.

c_j	Basis	50 X_1	75 X_2	60 X_3	70 X_4	0 S_1	0 S_2	0 S_3	M A_1	M A_2	R
0	S_1	5	8	0	0	1	0	0	0	0	100
0	S_2	0	0	6	7	0	1	0	0	0	80
M	A_1	1	0	1	0	0	0	-1	1	0	12
M	A_2	0	1	0	1	0	0	0	0	1	16
	z_j	M	M	M	M	0	0	$-M$	M	M	$28M$
	$c_j - z_j$	$50 - M$	$75 - M$	$60 - M$	$70 - M$	0	0	M	0	0	

---

[3] The big M method for maximization problems works in a similar manner. Since we do not want artificial variables in the final solution, we set the coefficient of each artificial variable in the objective function equal to $-M$.

Notice that the basis consists of two slack variables and two artificial variables. In particular, since $A_1 = 12$ and $A_2 = 16$, we do not have a feasible solution at this stage.

Step 3.   Select the Pivot Variable   Recall that the net contribution $c_j - z_j$ indicates the effect on the objective function for an increase of one unit of variable j in the solution. We are minimizing the objective function, so it makes sense to select, as the pivot variable, the variable that causes the largest *reduction* in the objective function. Thus, we must find the $c_j - z_j$ value that is most *negative*. (This logic is analogous to that for a maximization problem.) In this case, variable X_1 is chosen as the pivot variable because $50 - M$ is the most negative entry in the $c_j - z_j$ row.

Step 4.   Select the Pivot Row   The pivot row is selected in precisely the same manner as before. The maximum increase in X_1 is given by the minimum of the ratios (b_i/a_{i1}) for all $a_{i1} > 0$.

$$X_1 = \text{Min}\left(\frac{100}{5}, \infty, \frac{12}{1}, \infty\right) = 12 \tag{5.13}$$

Since the minimum in (5.13) occurred at (b_3/a_{31}), row 3 is the pivot row and A_1 leaves the basis.

Step 5.   Generate the New Basis   The usual Gaussian elimination results in the following tableau for the first iteration:

c_j	Basis	50 X_1	75 X_2	60 X_3	70 X_4	0 S_1	0 S_2	0 S_3	M A_1	M A_2	R
0	S_1	0	8	-5	0	1	0	5	-5	0	40
0	S_2	0	0	6	7	0	1	0	0	0	80
50	X_1	1	0	1	0	0	0	-1	1	0	12
M	A_2	0	1	0	1	0	0	0	0	1	16
	z_j	50	M	50	M	0	0	-50	50	M	$600 + 16M$
	$c_j - z_j$	0	$75 - M$	10	$70 - M$	0	0	50	$M - 50$	0	

Step 6.   Test for Optimality   Is the present solution optimal? Obviously it is not, since there are still negative entries in the $c_j - z_j$ row. More formally, the stopping rule for *minimization* problems is the following

If every entry in the $c_j - z_j$ row is zero or positive, the current solution is optimal. If at least one entry is negative, the solution can be improved and the present solution is not optimal.

We do not have the optimal solution after the first iteration; therefore, we must continue until the stopping rule indicates that the optimal solution has been found.

The remaining iterations are shown in Table 5.1. Notice how the objective function has decreased at each iteration, from $28M$ for the initial solution to $12,200/7$ or $1742.86 for the optimal solution. Also, it took three iterations to drive the two artificial variables out of the basis. In this example, the first feasible solution to the problem was found at the third iteration and turned out to be the optimal solution. In general, in order to achieve optimality, more iterations may be required after the first feasible solution. The optimal schedule calls for no production of type 1 pipe at Bakersfield.

$$X_1 = 12, \text{ or } 12,000 \text{ feet at Hometown}$$

$$X_2 = \tfrac{32}{7}, \text{ or } 4571 \text{ feet at Hometown}$$

$$X_3 = 0$$

$$X_4 = \tfrac{80}{7}, \text{ or } 11,429 \text{ feet at Bakersfield}$$

The Hometown plant will have $S_1 = \tfrac{24}{7}$ or 3.43 hours of slack in the extrusion process. The Bakersfield plant will be used to full capacity.

Review of the Simplex Method

The procedure for solving linear programming models with the simplex method is as follows:

Step 1. Augment the Model Add a slack variable to each upper-bound constraint and a surplus and an artificial variable to each lower-bound constraint. Only an artificial variable need be added to equality constraints. Slack and surplus variables have a coefficient of zero in the objective function, whereas artificial variables have a coefficient of big M.

Step 2. Set up the Initial Tableau Summarize the augmented model in the tableau format, in which an initial solution to the problem is represented.

Step 3. Select the Pivot Variable In maximization problems, choose the non-basic variable with the largest positive value of $c_j - z_j$ as the pivot variable. In minimization problems, choose the one with the most negative value of $c_j - z_j$.

Step 4. Select the Pivot Row The row with $\text{Min}_i (b_i/a_{ij})$ in which X_j is the pivot variable is the pivot row. The variable in the basis corresponding to the pivot row leaves the basis.

Step 5. Generate the New Basis Use Gaussian elimination to transform the column vector associated with the pivot variable to a unit vector.

Step 6. Test for Optimality In maximization problems, if all $c_j - z_j \leq 0$, the current solution is optimal. In minimization problems, the criterion for optimality is all $c_j - z_j \geq 0$. If the criterion for optimality is not satisfied, return to Step 3.

Table 5.1 Successive Iterations for the Production Planning Problem

Iteration 1

c_j	Basis	50 X_1	75 X_2	60 X_3	70 X_4	0 S_1	0 S_2	0 S_3	M A_1	M A_2	R	Ratio
0	S_1	0	8	-5	0	1	0	5	-5	0	40	∞
0	S_2	0	0	6	⑦	0	1	0	0	0	80	$\frac{80}{7}$*
50	X_1	1	0	1	0	0	0	-1	1	0	12	∞
M	A_2	0	1	0	1	0	0	0	0	1	16	16
	z_j	50	M	50	M	0	0	-50	50	M	$600 + 16M$	
	$c_j - z_j$	0	$75 - M$	10	$70 - M$	0	0	50	$M - 50$	0		

Pivot Variable $= X_4$ Pivot Row $=$ Row 2

Iteration 2

c_j	Basis	50 X_1	75 X_2	60 X_3	70 X_4	0 S_1	0 S_2	0 S_3	M A_1	M A_2	R	Ratio
0	S_1	0	8	-5	0	1	0	5	-5	0	40	5
70	X_4	0	0	$\frac{6}{7}$	1	0	$\frac{1}{7}$	0	0	0	$\frac{80}{7}$	∞
50	X_1	1	0	1	0	0	0	-1	1	0	12	∞
M	A_2	0	①	$-\frac{6}{7}$	0	0	$-\frac{1}{7}$	0	0	1	$\frac{32}{7}$	$\frac{32}{7}$*
	z_j	50	M	$110 - \dfrac{6M}{7}$	70	0	$10 - \dfrac{M}{7}$	-50	50	M	$1400 + \dfrac{32M}{7}$	
	$c_j - z_j$	0	$75 - M$	$\dfrac{6M}{7} - 50$	0	0	$\dfrac{M}{7} - 10$	50	$M - 50$	0		

Pivot Variable $= X_2$ Pivot Row $=$ Row 4

Iteration 3

c_j	Basis	50 X_1	75 X_2	60 X_3	70 X_4	0 S_1	0 S_2	0 S_3	M A_1	M A_2	R
0	S_1	0	0	$\frac{13}{7}$	0	1	$\frac{8}{7}$	5	-5	-8	$\frac{24}{7}$
70	X_4	0	0	$\frac{6}{7}$	1	0	$\frac{1}{7}$	0	0	0	$\frac{80}{7}$
50	X_1	1	0	1	0	0	0	-1	1	0	12
75	X_2	0	1	$-\frac{6}{7}$	0	0	$-\frac{1}{7}$	0	0	1	$\frac{32}{7}$
	z_j	50	75	$\frac{220}{7}$	70	0	$-\frac{5}{7}$	-50	50	75	$\frac{12,200}{7}$
	$c_j - z_j$	0	0	$\frac{200}{7}$	0	0	$\frac{5}{7}$	50	$M - 50$	$M - 75$	

Optimal

5.2 DUALITY

The use of the term *dual* in the general sense implies *two* or *double*. With respect to linear programming, it implies that there are two ways of analyzing each problem. Each linear programming maximization problem has a corresponding minimization problem as a dual. By the same reasoning, each minimization problem has as its dual a maximization problem. Solving one type of problem is equivalent to solving the other. An understanding of the dual concept enables one to generate the desired solution by solving the original (primal) problem or its corresponding dual problem. In some cases, considerable computing time can be saved by solving the dual. In addition, the fundamentals of duality highlight the economic implications of linear programming analysis, which is so important for the effective managerial use of linear programming models.

The Primal-Dual Relationship

Consider the portfolio-mix problem (4.12). We will call this formulation, repeated below, the *primal* problem.

Primal problem

$$\text{Max } Z = 0.06X_1 + 0.08X_2$$

subject to

$$X_1 + X_2 \leq 400$$
$$X_2 \leq 250$$
$$5X_1 + 10X_2 \leq 3000$$
$$X_1, X_2 \geq 0$$

In the primal problem, the dollars invested in portfolios 1 and 2, (X_1 and X_2), were subject to three constraints, which we called (generically) resource limitations. The first resource was the budget, 400. The second resource was a limitation of 250 put on portfolio 2, and the third resource was 3000 risk units. The primal problem picked X_1 and X_2 subject to these resources.

To motivate the concept of the dual problem, suppose that the decision maker wanted to know the value of the resources available. Clearly, the value would be the sum of the amount of each resource times the value of a unit of that resource; that is,

$$400V_1 + 250V_2 + 3000V_3$$

where V_1, V_2, and V_3 are the unit values or *shadow prices* for the three resources.

The value of a unit of resource is, in economic terms, the amount that resource would command in the market or the amount the owner of the resource could command for its use. Suppose the investor of our problem decided to reduce the investment in portfolio 1 by one dollar. This would release some of each of the three resources for an alternative use. One unit of budget and 5 units of risk resource would become available. Suppose these resources could be sold in the marketplace. How much would the investor need to sell these resources for in order to be at least as well off as before? If V_1 and V_3 are thought of as selling prices for budget and risk resources, then V_1 and V_3 must be such that

$$V_1 + 5V_3 \geq 0.06 \tag{5.14}$$

where 0.06 is the profit foregone and $V_1 + 5V_3$ is the sale price of the resources.

The same argument can be developed for reducing investment in portfolio 2 by one unit. This would release 1, 1, and 10 units of the three resources, respectively. Thus, V_1, V_2, and V_3 must satisfy

$$V_1 + V_2 + 10V_3 \geq 0.08 \tag{5.15}$$

to make the release of the resources worthwhile.

Now it can be seen that an infinite number of very large values of V_1, V_2, and V_3 would satisfy (5.14) and (5.15). We are not concerned with these large values. Rather, we seek a set of values satisfying (5.14) and (5.15) that allocate the return from the purchase of portfolio 1 and portfolio 2 to the resources. This is accomplished by choosing V_1, V_2, and V_3 in order to

$$\text{Min } Z' = 400V_1 + 250V_2 + 3000V_3 \tag{5.16}$$

Equation (5.16) states that we wish to minimize the total value of the resources used in acquiring portfolios 1 and 2. In this way we can determine, in terms of our profit, the shadow prices of the resources consumed by these purchases. Suppose we chose some values of V_1, V_2, and V_3 that did not minimize (5.16). For example, let $V_1 = V_2 = V_3 = 100$. The total value of the resources at these prices is \$36,500. Is this a useful measure of the value of the resources in generating profits? A quick check of (5.14) and (5.15) indicates that the value of the resources consumed *exeeds* the profit per unit of portfolios 1 and 2, respectively. In this case the investor would be wise to sell the resources in the marketplace and forget about portfolios 1 and 2. Obviously we have grossly *overstated* the value of the resources for generating profits, because there would be no profit from portfolios 1 and 2 at these prices. The investor will want to utilize resources to purchase a portfolio only if the value of the resources consumed equals the profit to be generated by the transaction. We can determine these values by minimizing (5.16) subject to (5.14) and (5.15). Thus, the dual problem becomes

Dual problem

$$\text{Min } Z' = 400V_1 + 250V_2 + 3000V_3$$

subject to

$$
\begin{aligned}
V_1 \qquad\quad + \;\; 5V_3 &\geq 0.06 \\
V_1 + V_2 + 10V_3 &\geq 0.08 \\
V_1,\, V_2,\, V_3 \qquad\quad &\geq 0
\end{aligned}
\tag{5.17}
$$

Notice that the dual problem (5.17) has one variable for each primal constraint and one constraint for each primal variable.[4]

Economic Interpretation of the Dual Surplus Variable

Define L_j to be the dual surplus variable associated with dual constraint j. Then the augmented dual problem becomes

$$\text{Min } Z' = 400V_1 + 250V_2 + 3000V_3 + 0L_1 + 0L_2$$

subject to

$$
\begin{aligned}
V_1 \qquad + 5V_3 - L_1 \qquad &= 0.06 \qquad (5.18) \\
V_1 + V_2 + 10V_3 \qquad - L_2 &= 0.08 \\
V_1, V_2, V_3, L_1, L_2 \qquad &\geq 0
\end{aligned}
$$

Consider the first constraint of (5.18), which can be rewritten in the following way:

$$L_1 = \underbrace{V_1 + 5V_3}_{\substack{\text{Value of} \\ \text{resources} \\ \text{consumed} \\ \text{by } X_1}} - \underbrace{0.06}_{\substack{\text{Return} \\ \text{from} \\ X_1}} \qquad (5.19)$$

This constraint was derived from analysis of portfolio 1—that is, X_1. If the value of the resources consumed by the investment of \$1.00 in portfolio 1 exceeds the return from that investment, the dual surplus variable L_1 will be positive. In particular, L_1 measures the disparity in portfolio 1 between the value of the resources and the return that can be realized from consuming them. Thus, L_1 is the *opportunity cost* for investing \$1.00 in portfolio 1. If L_1 is positive, we would not want to invest in portfolio 1 because there is a better use for the resources. If L_1 is zero, the resources are being used to their greatest advantage and investment in portfolio 1 is desirable. A similar logic applies to L_2 and investment in portfolio 2.

Duality Theorems

The relationship between the primal and dual problems is easily demonstrated for our example. Expanding (5.18) to include artificial variables results in the following model:

$$\text{Min } Z' = 400V_1 + 250V_2 + 3000V_3 + 0L_1 + 0L_2 + MA_1 + MA_2$$

subject to

$$
\begin{aligned}
V_1 + \qquad 5V_3 - L_1 \qquad + A_1 \qquad &= 0.06 \qquad (5.20) \\
V_1 + V_2 + 10V_3 \qquad - L_2 \qquad + A_2 &= 0.08 \\
V_1, V_2, V_3, L_1, L_2, A_1, A_2 \qquad &\geq 0
\end{aligned}
$$

---

[4] The dual problem may have more than one variable for each constraint when equality constraints are in the primal problem. This will be explained when we discuss the computational advantages of the dual.

Table 5.2 contains the iterations required to reach optimality. Comparison of the optimal dual tableau in Table 5.2 to the optimal primal tableau reveals some interesting relationships between the dual and primal problems.

The solutions for the two problems are summarized by

Primal	Dual
$X_1 = 200$	$L_1 = 0$
$X_2 = 200$	$L_2 = 0$
$S_1 = 0$	$V_1 = 0.04$
$S_2 = 50$	$V_2 = 0$
$S_3 = 0$	$V_3 = 0.004$

Look at the $c_j - z_j$ row in both optimal tableaus. The solution to the dual problem is found in the $c_j - z_j$ row of the optimal primal tableau, disregarding the minus signs. The values for L_j are found in the X_j columns, and the values for V_i are found in the S_i columns. Similarly, the solution to the primal problem is found in the $c_j - z_j$ row of the optimal dual tableau, disregarding the entries for the artificial variables. The values for X_j are found in the L_j columns, and the values for S_i are found in the V_i columns. Thus, the optimal primal tableau contains the optimal solution of the dual (and vice versa).

Another interesting point is that if X_j is positive, L_j is zero. This follows from the previous discussion of the economic implications of the dual surplus variables. In addition, if S_i is positive, V_i is zero, whereas if S_i is zero, V_i is positive. This implies that if resource i is a limiting resource (no slack in the optimal solution), it must have an imputed valued V_i, which measures the benefit to the objective function for increasing that resource by one unit. If there is slack in resource i, there is no potential for affecting the primal objective function by adjusting that resource by one unit. Thus, in summary, we can say that the following holds true for the optimal solution

$$X_j \cdot L_j = 0 \qquad j = 1, 2 \tag{5.21}$$

$$S_i \cdot V_i = 0 \qquad i = 1, 2, 3 \tag{5.22}$$

The relationships in (5.21) and (5.22) are known as the property of *complementary slackness*. Either the primary decision variable or its complementary dual surplus variable (and possibly both) must be zero. Similarly, either the dual shadow price or its complementary primal slack variable (and possibly both) must be zero.

Finally, note that the optimal value of the primal objective function is *equal* to the optimal value of the dual objective function. That is, $0.06X_1 + 0.08X_2 = 400V_1 + 250V_2 + 3000V_3 = \$28$. This implies that we have imputed all of the profits from the purchase of \$200 of portfolio 1 and \$200 of portfolio 2 to each of the resources in such a way that only the fully utilized resources have value. In particular, we have used up all of the available cash resources, and because $V_1 = 0.04$, an additional dollar authorized for investment will generate \$0.04 of profit. The reason for such a low profit increase is that one of the policy constraints is binding.

Table 5.2 Successive Iterations for the Dual Problem

Initial Tableau

c_j	Basis	400 V_1	250 V_2	3000 V_3	0 L_1	0 L_2	M A_1	M A_2	R	Ratio
M	A_1	1	0	5	-1	0	1	0	0.06	0.012
M	A_2	1	1	10	0	-1	0	1	0.08	0.008
	z_j	$2M$	M	$15M$	$-M$	$-M$	M	M	$0.14M$	
	$c_j - z_j$	$400 - 2M$	$250 - M$	$3000 - 15M$	M	M	0	0		

Pivot Variable $= V_3$ Pivot Row $=$ Row 2

Iteration 1

c_j	Basis	400 V_1	250 V_2	3000 V_3	0 L_1	0 L_2	M A_1	M A_2	R	Ratio
M	A_1	$\frac{1}{2}$	$-\frac{1}{2}$	0	-1	$\frac{1}{2}$	1	$-\frac{1}{2}$	0.02	0.04
3000	V_3	$\frac{1}{10}$	$\frac{1}{10}$	1	0	$-\frac{1}{10}$	0	$\frac{1}{10}$	0.008	0.08
	z_j	$300 + \frac{M}{2}$	$300 - \frac{M}{2}$	3000	$-M$	$\frac{M}{2} - 300$	M	$300 - \frac{M}{2}$	$240 + 0.02M$	
	$c_j - z_j$	$100 - \frac{M}{2}$	$-50 + \frac{M}{2}$	0	M	$300 - \frac{M}{2}$	0	$\frac{3M}{2} - 300$		

Pivot variable $= V_1$ Pivot row $=$ Row 1

Iteration 2

c_j	Basis	400 V_1	250 V_2	3000 V_3	0 L_1	0 L_2	M A_1	M A_2	R
400	V_1	1	-1	0	-2	1	2	-1	0.04
3000	V_3	0	$\frac{2}{10}$	1	$\frac{2}{10}$	$-\frac{2}{10}$	$-\frac{2}{10}$	$\frac{2}{10}$	0.004
	z_j	400	200	3000	-200	-200	200	200	28
	$c_j - z_j$	0	50	0	200	200	$M - 200$	$M - 200$	

Optimal

Optimal Primal Tableau

c_j	Basis	0.06 X_1	0.08 X_2	0 S_1	0 S_2	0 S_3	R
0	S_2	0	0	1	1	$-\frac{1}{5}$	50
0.08	X_2	0	1	-1	0	$-\frac{1}{5}$	200
0.06	X_1	1	0	2	0	$\frac{1}{5}$	200
	z_j	0.06	0.08	0.04	0	0.004	28
	$c_j - z_j$	0	0	-0.04	0	-0.004	

The optimal portfolio mix uses up all of the allowed risk. If management is inclined to accept more risk, profits will increase by $0.004 per additional risk unit allowed because $V_3 = 0.004$. The policy of portfolio diversity, which places an upper bound of $250 on portfolio 2, does not affect the optimal mix; thus, no value is imputed to that resource and $V_2 = 0$. Minor adjustments in this policy will have no effect on total profits.

The duality theorems can now be stated more concisely.

1. The optimal value of the primal objective function always equals the optimal value of the dual objective function. In particular,

$$\sum_j c_j X_j = \sum_i b_i V_i$$

2. The property of complementary slackness holds for corresponding optimal primal and dual solutions; that is,

$$X_j L_j = 0 \quad \text{for all } j$$
$$V_i S_i = 0 \quad \text{for all } i$$

Computational Advantages of the Dual

Formulating a primal problem in its dual form may result in some computational advantages. In this section, we demonstrate the formulation of the dual problem for a primal minimization problem that will result in some potential computational advantages.

Consider the following primal problem:

Primal problem

$$\text{Min } Z = 60X_1 + 25X_2 + 190X_3$$

subject to

$$
\begin{aligned}
2X_1 + X_2 + X_3 &\le 80 \\
5X_1 + 9X_2 + 10X_3 &\ge 150 \\
55X_1 + 16X_2 + 9X_3 &\ge 600 \\
9X_1 + 7X_2 + 3X_3 &\le 400 \\
X_1 + 3X_2 + X_3 &= 100 \\
X_1, X_2, X_3 &\ge 0
\end{aligned}
\tag{5.23}
$$

The primal problem has three decision variables and five constraints, one of which is an equality. The first step is to transform all of the constraints into *lower-bound* constraints because the primal problem is a minimization problem. If the primal were a maximization problem, we would transform the constraints into upper-bound constraints. In our minimization problem, this can be accomplished by multiplying both the upper-bound constraints by -1. Notice that this will make some b_i quantities negative, but these quantities will appear in the objective function of the dual, so the nonnegativity restrictions on the *dual* will not be violated. This results in the following transformation:

$$\text{Min } Z = 60X_1 + 25X_2 + 190X_3$$

subject to

$$
\begin{aligned}
-2X_1 - X_2 - X_3 &\geq -80 \\
5X_1 + 9X_2 + 10X_3 &\geq 150 \\
55X_1 + 16X_2 + 9X_3 &\geq 600 \\
-9X_1 - 7X_2 - 3X_3 &\geq -400 \\
X_1 + 3X_2 + X_3 &= 100 \\
X_1, X_2, X_3 &\geq 0
\end{aligned}
\tag{5.24}
$$

The first lower-bound constraint in (5.24) is equivalent to the first upper-bound constraint in (5.23). The same is true for the fourth constraint in (5.24) and (5.23).

The equality constraint in (5.24) can be written in the desired form by recognizing that it can be replaced with an upper-bound and a lower-bound constraint, both of which must be satisfied—that is, by

$$X_1 + 3X_2 + X_3 \leq 100 \tag{5.25}$$

$$X_1 + 3X_2 + X_3 \geq 100 \tag{5.26}$$

Multiplying (5.25) by -1 and including *both* constraints in the formulation, we have the primal problem in the standard form

$$\text{Min } Z = 60X_1 + 25X_2 + 190X_3$$

subject to

$$
\begin{aligned}
-2X_1 - X_2 - X_3 &\geq -80 \\
5X_1 + 9X_2 + 10X_3 &\geq 150 \\
55X_1 + 16X_2 + 9X_3 &\geq 600 \\
-9X_1 - 7X_2 - 3X_3 &\geq -400 \\
-X_1 - 3X_2 - X_3 &\geq -100 \\
X_1 + 3X_2 + X_3 &\geq 100 \\
X_1, X_2, X_3 &\geq 0
\end{aligned}
\tag{5.27}
$$

The next step is to model the dual problem. The dual has a decision variable for each row in the revised primal problem. In addition, each column vector of coefficients in the revised primal problem becomes a row vector of coefficients in the dual problem. Since each constraint is a lower-bound constraint in the revised primal, each constraint in the dual is an upper-bound constraint. The primal objective-function coefficients become right-hand-side entries in the dual problem, and the b_i values appear in the objective function.

In general, if the primal problem is a minimization problem stated in the standard form, with all lower-bound constraints (some b_is may be negative),

$$\text{Min } Z = C_1 X_1 + C_2 X_2 + \cdots + C_n X_n$$

subject to

$$a_{11} X_1 + a_{12} X_2 + \cdots + a_{1n} X_n \geq b_1$$
$$a_{21} X_1 + a_{22} X_2 + \cdots + a_{2n} X_n \geq b_2$$
$$\vdots \qquad \vdots \qquad\qquad \vdots \qquad \vdots \tag{5.28}$$
$$a_{k1} X_1 + a_{k2} X_2 + \cdots + a_{kn} X_n \geq b_k$$
$$\vdots \qquad \vdots \qquad\qquad \vdots \qquad \vdots$$
$$a_{m1} X_1 + a_{m2} X_2 + \cdots + a_{mn} X_n \geq b_m$$
$$X_1, X_2, \ldots, X_n \qquad\qquad \geq 0$$

the dual problem is given by

$$\text{Max } Z' = b_1 V_1 + b_2 V_2 + \cdots + b_k V_k + \cdots + b_m V_m$$

subject to

$$a_{11} V_1 + a_{21} V_2 + \cdots + a_{k1} V_k + \cdots + a_{m1} V_m \leq C_1$$
$$a_{12} V_1 + a_{22} V_2 + \cdots + a_{k2} V_k + \cdots + a_{m2} V_m \leq C_2 \tag{5.29}$$
$$\vdots \qquad \vdots \qquad\qquad \vdots \qquad\qquad \vdots$$
$$a_{1n} V_1 + a_{2n} V_2 + \cdots + a_{kn} V_k + \cdots + a_{mn} V_m \leq C_n$$
$$V_1, V_2, \ldots, V_k, \ldots, V_m \qquad\qquad \geq 0$$

Alternatively, if the primal problem is a maximization problem stated in the standard form, with all upper-bound constraints (some b_is may be negative),

$$\text{Max } Z = C_1 X_1 + C_2 X_2 + \cdots + C_n X_n$$

subject to

$$a_{11} X_1 + a_{12} X_2 + \cdots + a_{1n} X_n \leq b_1$$
$$a_{21} X_1 + a_{22} X_2 + \cdots + a_{2n} X_n \leq b_2$$
$$\vdots \qquad \vdots \qquad\qquad \vdots \qquad \vdots \tag{5.30}$$
$$a_{k1} X_1 + a_{k2} X_2 + \cdots + a_{kn} X_n \leq b_k$$
$$\vdots \qquad \vdots \qquad\qquad \vdots \qquad \vdots$$
$$a_{m1} X_1 + a_{m2} X_2 + \cdots + a_{mn} X_n \leq b_m$$
$$X_1, X_2, \ldots, X_n \qquad\qquad \geq 0$$

the dual problem is given by

$$\text{Min } Z' = b_1 V_1 + b_2 V_2 + \cdots + b_k V_k + \cdots + b_m V_m$$

subject to

$$a_{11} V_1 + a_{21} V_2 + \cdots + a_{k1} V_k + \cdots + a_{m1} V_m \geq C_1$$
$$a_{12} V_1 + a_{22} V_2 + \cdots + a_{k2} V_k + \cdots + a_{m2} V_m \geq C_2 \qquad (5.31)$$
$$\vdots \qquad \vdots \qquad \qquad \vdots \qquad \qquad \vdots \qquad \vdots$$
$$a_{1n} V_1 + a_{2n} V_2 + \cdots + a_{kn} V_k + \cdots + a_{mn} V_m \geq C_n$$
$$V_1, V_2, \ldots, V_k, \ldots, V_m \qquad \qquad \geq 0$$

The dual problem for the specific example (5.27)

$$\text{Max } Z = -80 V_1 + 150 V_2 + 600 V_3 - 400 V_4 - 100 V_5 + 100 V_6$$

subject to

$$-2 V_1 + 5 V_2 + 55 V_3 - 9 V_4 - 1 V_5 + 1 V_6 \leq 60$$
$$-1 V_1 + 9 V_2 + 16 V_3 - 7 V_4 - 3 V_5 + 3 V_6 \leq 25 \qquad (5.32)$$
$$-1 V_1 + 10 V_2 + 9 V_3 - 3 V_4 - 1 V_5 + 1 V_6 \leq 190$$
$$V_1, V_2, V_3, V_4, V_5, V_6 \qquad \qquad \geq 0$$

The potential computational advantages are now apparent. Although the dual problem (5.32) has six decision variables compared to only three in the primal problem (5.23), there are only three constraints in the dual problem as opposed to five in the primal problem. Because the number of iterations required for optimality is closely related to the number of constraints, the dual problem has the potential of requiring less computational effort to find the optimal solution. In general, if the number of constraints exceeds the number of decision variables in the primal problem, the dual problem should require less effort to solve.

5.3 MODELING CONSIDERATIONS

The third step in the decision-making process, given in Figure 1.3 of Chapter 1, is model construction. Once a linear programming model has been constructed, the simplex procedure implicitly performs the subsequent steps of enumeration of alternatives, prediction of outcomes, and alternative selection. The simplex method cannot select the optimal alternative if the model has not been properly constructed. Many times it is very difficult to determine if a model has been improperly constructed (incorrect c_j, a_{ij}, or b_i values, or incorrect constraints), especially if the model involves many decision variables and constraints. In general, checking the final solution to see if it satisfies the constraints, as well as judging the *reasonableness* of the solution, will in many cases help uncover model deficiencies.

It may be necessary to check each c_j, a_{ij}, and b_i parameter as well as all the constraint relationships to validate the model; however, this can be a long and arduous task for large-scale problems. In some cases, the simplex procedure will itself pinpoint model deficiencies. We will discuss the situations in which the model has no feasible solution or has an unbounded solution.

No Feasible Solution

Consider the media-mix problems (4.25) and (4.26) introduced in Chapter 4. Suppose that the availability of television commercials is limited to 5, as opposed to 25 in the original model. The model, with the new constraint, now becomes

$$\text{Min } Z = 2000X_1 + 3500X_2$$

subject to

$$50{,}000X_1 + 30{,}000X_2 \geq 900{,}000 \qquad \text{Target-population exposure}$$

$$10X_1 + 15X_2 \geq 300 \qquad \text{Prime-time coverage}$$

$$X_1 \leq 22 \qquad \text{Availability of radio commercials} \qquad (5.33)$$

$$X_2 \leq 5 \qquad \text{Availability of TV commercials}$$

$$X_1, X_2 \geq 0$$

Figure 5.3 shows that there is no feasible region in which all constraints can be satisfied simultaneously. Of course, with our simple two-variable problem, it is easy to see that no feasible solution exists. Problems involving more than two variables cannot be graphed, and it may not be obvious at the time the model is constructed that no feasible solution exists. The simplex method can provide information indicating where the infeasibility lies.

Augmenting (5.33) to include slack, surplus, and artificial variables gives us the following model:

$$\text{Min } Z = 2000X_1 + 3500X_2 + 0S_1 + 0S_2 + 0S_3 + 0S_4 + MA_1 + MA_2$$

subject to

$$50{,}000X_1 + 30{,}000X_2 - S_1 \qquad\qquad\quad + A_1 \qquad\quad = 900{,}000$$

$$10X_1 + 15X_2 \quad - S_2 \qquad\qquad + A_2 = \quad 300$$

$$X_1 \qquad\qquad\qquad\quad + S_3 \qquad\qquad = \quad 22 \qquad (5.34)$$

$$X_2 \qquad\qquad\qquad\qquad + S_4 \qquad = \quad 5$$

$$X_1, X_2, S_1, S_2, S_3, A_1, A_2 \qquad\qquad\qquad\qquad \geq \qquad 0$$

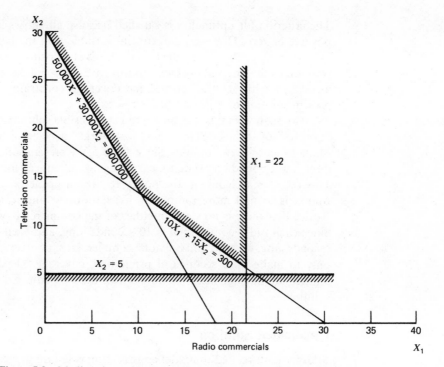

Figure 5.3 Media-mix problem showing that no feasible region exists.

After three iterations, we get the following simplex tableau:

c_j	Basis	2000 X_1	3500 X_2	0 S_1	0 S_2	0 S_3	0 S_4	M A_1	M A_2	R
2000	X_1	1	0	0	0	1	$\frac{3}{5}$	$\dfrac{1}{50{,}000}$	0	22
M	A_2	0	0	0	-1	-10	-15	$\dfrac{-10}{50{,}000}$	1	5
0	S_1	0	0	1	0	50,000	30,000	0	0	350,000
3500	X_2	0	1	0	0	0	1	0	0	5
	z_j	2000	3500	0	$-M$	$2000 - 10M$	$4700 - 15M$	$\dfrac{2000 - 10M}{50{,}000}$	M	$61{,}000 + 5M$
	$c_j - z_j$	0	0	0	M	$10M - 2000$	$15M - 4700$	$\dfrac{49{,}990M - 2000}{50{,}000}$	0	

The criterion for optimality is satisfied because all entries in the $c_j - z_j$ row are positive or zero. However, an artificial variable is in the basis at a positive level. Whenever an artificial variable is in the basis at a positive level, there is no feasible solution to the original problem. In this case, $A_2 = 5$ indicates that the constraint associated with A_2 (the prime-time coverage constraint) is violated with the present solution of $X_1 = 22$ and $X_2 = 5$.

How can we adjust the model to get a feasible solution? This requires getting "outside" of the model into the "real-world" aspects of the decision problem. Management has two options. Since $A_2 = 5$, the present solution would be feasible if the lower bound on prime-time coverage were reduced from 300 to 295 seconds. This requires a change in the policy regarding prime-time coverage. The other option is to find more radio and TV stations willing to sell commercial time. Notice that there is no slack in either of the commercial-availability constraints. Since each radio commercial is 10 seconds long, and each TV commercial is 15 seconds long, we need find only one commercial spot of any kind because we have only to make up 5 seconds of prime-time coverage. Depending on the option selected by management, the model can then be adjusted to provide a feasible solution.

Unbounded Solution

Another fault related to model construction is failure to ensure that the objective function is bounded over the feasible region. When this occurs, the result is that

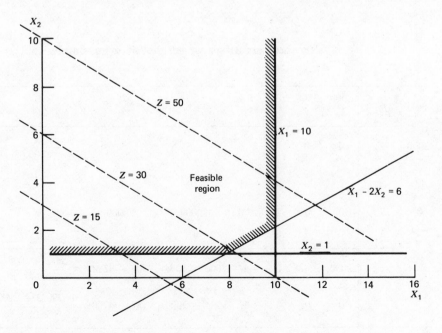

Figure 5.4   Unbounded feasible region.

one or more decision variables can be increased indefinitely without violating any constraints. For example, consider the following model:

$$\text{Max } Z = 3X_1 + 5X_2$$

subject to

$$X_1 - 2X_2 \le 6$$
$$X_1 \le 10 \tag{5.35}$$
$$X_2 \ge 1$$
$$X_1, X_2 \ge 0$$

Figure 5.4 shows that X_2 can be made indefinitely large, increasing the objective function without bound. The iso-profit line can be moved upward indefinitely without violating any constraints.

The simplex method will also indicate that this problem has an unbounded solution. The augmented model requires slack, surplus, and artificial variables. It is

$$\text{Max } Z = 3X_1 + 5X_2 + 0S_1 + 0S_2 + 0S_3 - MA_1$$

subject to

$$X_1 - 2X_2 + S_1 = 6$$
$$X_1 + S_2 = 10$$
$$X_2 - S_3 + A_1 = 1 \tag{5.36}$$
$$X_1, X_2, S_1, S_2, S_3, A_1 \ge 0$$

After the first iteration, we have the following simplex tableau.

c_j	Basis	3 X_1	5 X_2	0 S_1	0 S_2	0 S_3	$-M$ A_1	R	Ratio
0	S_1	1	0	1	0	-2	2	8	∞
0	S_2	1	0	0	1	0	0	10	∞
5	X_2	0	1	0	0	-1	1	1	∞
	z_j	0	5	0	0	-5	5	5	
	$c_j - z_j$	3	0	0	0	5	$5 - M$		

We do not have an optimal solution because two entries in the $c_j - z_j$ row are positive. In particular, the pivot variable should be S_3, since $c_5 - z_5$ is the largest value. Note that the a'_{i5} coefficients are all negative or zero. This implies that S_3 can be increased indefinitely without driving one of the basis variables to zero.

Since S_3 is associated with X_2 in the third constraint, X_2 will also become indefinitely large. This can be seen by rewriting the third row of the tableau in algebraic form.

$$X_2 = 1 + S_3 - A_1 \tag{5.37}$$

In this example, it is easy to identify the unbounded decision variable. In more complex models this may not be so easy. Many decision variables related to each other in a multitude of constraints complicate the search for unbounded variables. In this example, a constraint is needed to provide an upper bound on X_2. In practice, an unbounded solution in a decision problem is an absurdity; therefore, a formulation with such a solution indicates that the original model is incomplete and that at least one constraint is missing.

Degeneracy

Degeneracy occurs when one or more basis variables has a value of zero. As an example of a model that causes degeneracy, consider the portfolio-mix model (4.14). The upper bound on risk has been changed to 2500. The problem becomes

$$\text{Max } Z = 0.06X_1 + 0.08X_2 + 0S_1 + 0S_2 + 0S_3$$

subject to

$$
\begin{aligned}
X_1 + X_2 + S_1 &= 400 \\
X_2 + S_2 &= 250 \\
5X_1 + 10X_2 + S_3 &= 2500 \\
X_1, X_2, S_1, S_2, S_3 &\geq 0
\end{aligned}
\tag{5.38}
$$

Table 5.3 contains the iterations required for optimality. Variable X_2 is the first pivot variable, but there is a tie for the pivot row. This is a sign that we have

Table 5.3   Degeneracy in the Portfolio Mix Problem

Initial Tableau

c_j	Basis	0.06 X_1	0.08 X_2	0 S_1	0 S_2	0 S_3	R	Ratio
0	S_1	1	1	1			400	400
0	S_2		①		1		250	250 *TIE
0	S_3	5	10			1	2500	250 *TIE
	z_j	0	0	0	0	0	0	
	$c_j - z_j$	0.06	0.08	0	0	0		

Pivot Variable $= X_2$ Pivot Row (Arbitrary) $=$ Row 2

Iteration 1

c_j	Basis	0.06 X_1	0.08 X_2	0 S_1	0 S_2	0 S_3	R	Ratio
0	S_1	1		1	-1		150	150
0.08	X_2		1		1		250	∞
0	S_3	5			-10	1	0	0*
	z_j	0	0.08	0	0.08	0	20	
	$c_j - z_j$	0.06	0	0	-0.08	0		

Pivot Variable $= X_1$ Pivot Row $=$ Row 3

Iteration 2

c_j	Basis	0.06 X_1	0.08 X_2	0 S_1	0 S_2	0 S_3	R	Ratio
0	S_1			1	1	$-\frac{1}{5}$	150	150*
0.08	X_2		1		1		250	250
0.06	X_1	1			-2	$\frac{1}{5}$	0	∞
	z_j	0.06	0.08	0	-0.04	0.012	20	
	$c_j - z_j$	0	0	0	0.04	-0.012		

Pivot Variable $= S_2$ Pivot Row $=$ Row 1

Iteration 3

c_j	Basis	0.06 X_1	0.08 X_2	0 S_1	0 S_2	0 S_3	R
0	S_2			1	1	$-\frac{1}{5}$	150
0.08	X_2		1	-1		$\frac{1}{5}$	100
0.06	X_1	1		2		$-\frac{1}{5}$	300
	z_j	0.06	0.08	0.04	0	0.004	26
	$c_j - z_j$	0	0	-0.04	0	-0.004	

Optimal

degeneracy, because no matter which row is selected, two basic variables will be driven to zero. We arbitrarily selected the second row as the pivot row. After the first iteration, the pivot variable is X_1 but the minimum ratio (b_3/a'_{31}) equals zero. Thus, S_3 leaves the basis and X_1 enters at a zero level. The value of the objective function remains at \$20 through the second iteration. Eventually, S_2 is chosen to enter the basis at a positive level and the objective function is increased to \$26. The final solution has each basic variable at a positive level, although in general this need not be the case.

Degeneracy does not pose a problem in practice. Theoretically, there is a chance that *cycling* can occur when degeneracy is present. The minimum ratio for some row is zero; therefore, it is possible that the same row will be constantly chosen for the pivot row. This means that some variable may enter, leave, then reenter the basis in a repetitive cycle. Although there are sophisticated rules for selecting the pivot row to avoid cycling when there is a tie in the (b_i/a'_{ij}) ratio, they are beyond the scope of this text. In most cases, *arbitrarily* choosing the pivot row is sufficient.

Multiple Optima

The solution to a linear programming model may not always be unique. Refer to Figure 4.10 in Chapter 4, where the objective function for the portfolio-mix problem was changed to Max $Z = 0.04X_1 + 0.08X_2$. Note that the iso-profit line is parallel to one of the boundaries of the feasible region, thus allowing two extreme points to become optimal—(100, 250) and (200, 200). This same information is contained in the optimal simplex tableau. Consider the model (5.39).

$$\text{Max } Z = 0.04X_1 + 0.08X_2 + 0S_1 + 0S_2 + 0S_3$$

subject to

$$
\begin{aligned}
X_1 + X_2 + S_1 & = 400 \\
X_2 + S_2 & = 250 \\
5X_1 + 10X_2 + S_3 & = 3000 \\
X_1, X_2, S_1, S_2, S_3 & \geq 0
\end{aligned}
\tag{5.39}
$$

The optimal simplex tableau is as follows:

c_j	Basis	0.04 X_1	0.08 X_2	0 S_1	0 S_2	0 S_3	R	Ratio
0	S_1	0	0	1	1	$-\frac{1}{5}$	50	50
0.08	X_2	0	1	0	1	0	250	250
0.04	X_1	1	0	0	-2	$\frac{1}{5}$	100	∞
	z_j	0.04	0.08	0	0	0.008	24	
	$c_j - z_j$	0	0	0	0	-0.008		

The solution is $X_1 = 100$, $X_2 = 250$; one of the alternative optima. Note that the $c_j - z_j$ row satisfies the condition for optimality; however, one nonbasic variable, S_2, has a zero net contribution. This means that S_2 could be made a basic variable without changing the optimal value of the objective function. Suppose we perform another iteration with S_2 as the pivot variable. The maximum level that S_2 can attain is 50, as indicated by the minimum ratio. Row 1 is the pivot row. The new tableau follows.

c_j	Basis	$\begin{matrix}0.04\\X_1\end{matrix}$	$\begin{matrix}0.08\\X_2\end{matrix}$	$\begin{matrix}0\\S_1\end{matrix}$	$\begin{matrix}0\\S_2\end{matrix}$	$\begin{matrix}0\\S_3\end{matrix}$	R
0	S_2	0	0	1	1	$-\frac{1}{5}$	50
0.08	X_2	0	1	-1	0	$\frac{1}{5}$	200
0.04	X_1	1	0	2	0	$-\frac{1}{5}$	200
	z_j	0.04	0.08	0	0	0.008	24
	$c_j - z_j$	0	0	0	0	-0.008	

The solution in the new tableau is the other extreme point, $X_1 = 200$, $X_2 = 200$. The value of the objective function is still \$24. Thus, more than one alternative will maximize profits. In practice, certain nonquantitative criteria may be applied to provide a choice between the two solutions. Be that as it may, the optimal simplex tableau will identify situations where multiple optima are present.

5.4   POSTOPTIMALITY ANALYSIS

Perhaps more important than the optimal solution to a linear programming model is the answer to the question: how will the optimal solution change if the c_j, a_{ij}, or b_i parameters change? The answer to this question can be found through *postoptimality analysis* or, as it is sometimes called, *sensitivity analysis*. Obviously, one could systematically adjust a particular parameter of interest, each time resolving the linear program, to answer the question of how the solution changes as a function of the parameter values. But it would save a lot of work if we could find, directly from the final, optimal simplex tableau, the range of values a particular parameter can take before the optimal basis changes. This is the purpose of postoptimality analysis.

Objective Coefficients of Nonbasic Variables

Consider the production-planning problem introduced in Section 5.1 of this chapter. The model is reproduced below.

$$\text{Min } Z = 50X_1 + 75X_2 + 60X_3 + 70X_4 + 0S_1 + 0S_2 + 0S_3 + MA_1 + MA_2$$

subject to

$$5X_1 + 8X_2 \qquad\qquad + S_1 \qquad\qquad\qquad\qquad\qquad = 100 \qquad \text{Hometown capacity}$$

$$6X_3 + 7X_4 \quad + S_2 \qquad\qquad\qquad\qquad = 80 \qquad \text{Bakersfield capacity}$$

$$X_1 + \qquad X_3 \qquad\qquad - S_3 + A_1 \qquad = 12 \qquad \text{Demand for Type 1 pipe}$$

$$X_2 \quad + \quad X_4 \qquad\qquad\qquad + A_2 = 16 \qquad \text{Demand for Type 2 pipe}$$

$$X_1, X_2, X_3, X_4, S_1, S_2, S_3, A_1, A_2 \qquad\qquad\qquad \geq 0 \qquad\qquad (5.40)$$

The optimal simplex tableau indicates that Hometown produces both types of pipe ($X_1 = 12$, $X_2 = \frac{32}{7}$), whereas Bakersfield produces only type 2 pipe ($X_4 = \frac{80}{7}$). There is slack capacity at the Hometown plant.

c_j	Basis	50 X_1	75 X_2	60 X_3	70 X_4	0 S_1	0 S_2	0 S_3	M A_1	M A_2	R
0	S_1	0	0	$\frac{13}{7}$	0	1	$\frac{8}{7}$	5	-5	-8	$\frac{24}{7}$
70	X_4	0	0	$\frac{6}{7}$	1	0	$\frac{1}{7}$	0	0	0	$\frac{80}{7}$
50	X_1	1	0	1	0	0	0	-1	1	0	12
75	X_2	0	1	$-\frac{6}{7}$	0	0	$-\frac{1}{7}$	0	0	1	$\frac{32}{7}$
	z_j	50	75	$\frac{320}{7}$	70	0	$-\frac{5}{7}$	-50	50	75	$\frac{12{,}200}{7}$
	$c_j - z_j$	0	0	$\frac{100}{7}$	0	0	$\frac{5}{7}$	50	$M - 50$	$M - 75$	

Currently, the Bakersfield plant is not producing any type 1 pipe. Suppose that the engineers at the plant have devised a more efficient way to produce type 1 pipe at Bakersfield such that the cost per 1000 feet will be reduced to $50. Management must determine if this will affect the schedule at the two plants, and also whether the new procedures should be implemented at all.

Since X_3 is a *nonbasic* variable, the answer to these questions is straightforward. The optimal solution will not be affected so long as the $c_j - z_j$ row still contains only zero or positive entries in a minimization problem. If c_3' is the new cost per thousand feet of X_3, the following condition must hold for the present solution to remain optimal

$$c_3' - z_3 \geq 0$$

or

$$c_3' - \tfrac{320}{7} \geq 0 \qquad\qquad (5.41)$$

Thus, if the new cost is at least $\tfrac{320}{7} = \$45.71$, the present solution is unaffected. The new cost is estimated to be \$50, and management should not consider funding the new method because it would continue to be cheaper to produce all of the type 1 pipe at the Hometown plant.

In general, for minimization problems, if X_j is a nonbasic variable, the cost coefficient c_j can vary to as low as z_j without affecting the current solution. Because X_j is not in the basis, c_j can be made indefinitely large without affecting the optimal solution.

Objective Coefficients of Basic Variables

The analysis for basic variables is slightly more complicated. A change in the objective function value of a basic variable can affect the z_j values for a number of nonbasic variables. Suppose the cost of X_1 is adjusted by an amount δ_1, making the total cost per unit $\$50 + \delta_1$. What is the range of values that δ_1 can take on while keeping the present solution optimal?

The revised tableau is as follows.

c_j	Basis	$50 + \delta_1$ X_1	75 X_2	60 X_3	70 X_4	0 S_1	0 S_2	0 S_3	M A_1	M A_2	R
0	S_1	0	0	$\tfrac{13}{7}$	0	1	$\tfrac{8}{7}$	5	-5	-8	$\tfrac{27}{7}$
70	X_4	0	0	$\tfrac{6}{7}$	1	0	$\tfrac{1}{7}$	0	0	0	$\tfrac{80}{7}$
$50 + \delta_1$	X_1	1	0	1	0	0	0	-1	1	0	12
75	X_2	0	1	$-\tfrac{6}{7}$	0	0	$-\tfrac{1}{7}$	0	0	1	$\tfrac{32}{7}$
	z_j	$50 + \delta_1$	75	$\tfrac{320}{7} + \delta_1$	70	0	$-\tfrac{5}{7}$	$-50 - \delta_1$	$50 + \delta_1$	75	$\tfrac{12{,}200}{7} + 12\delta_1$
	$c_j - z_j$	0	0	$\tfrac{100}{7} - \delta_1$	0	0	$\tfrac{5}{7}$	$50 + \delta_1$	$M - 50 - \delta_1$	$M - 75$	

The present solution will be optimal so long as each $c_j - z_j \geq 0$. In particular, we must have

$$\tfrac{100}{7} - \delta_1 \geq 0 \qquad\qquad (5.42)$$

$$50 + \delta_1 \geq 0 \qquad\qquad (5.43)$$

(We disregard the artificial variables in this analysis because M is made much larger than the largest possible cost coefficient for any variable in the problem.

Thus, the $c_j - z_j$ value for any artificial variable will always be positive once the variable has been driven out of the basis.)

The relationships above imply an upper and a lower bound for δ_1.

$$-50 \leq \delta_1 \leq \tfrac{100}{7} \tag{5.44}$$

Let $c_1' = 50 + \delta_1$, or $\delta_1 = c_1' - 50$. Then

$$-50 \leq c_1' - 50 \leq \tfrac{100}{7}$$

or

$$0 \leq c_1' \leq \$64.29 \tag{5.45}$$

Equation (5.45) implies that the cost of producing X_1 can range from zero to \$64.29 without affecting the present production schedule. If the price of raw materials or labor were to force the cost of producing type 1 pipe at the Hometown plant to become in excess of \$64.29, the schedule would call for production of type 1 pipe at the Bakersfield plant, because $c_3 - z_3$ would be negative.

The analysis of X_2 is slightly different. The conditions on δ_2 become

$$\tfrac{100}{7} + (\tfrac{6}{7})\delta_2 \geq 0 \tag{5.46}$$

$$\tfrac{5}{7} + (\tfrac{1}{7})\delta_2 \geq 0 \tag{5.47}$$

Rewriting these relationships, we find that there are two lower bounds on δ_2

$$\delta_2 \geq -\tfrac{100}{6} \tag{5.48}$$

$$\delta_2 \geq -5 \tag{5.49}$$

Because we must satisfy both inequalities, $\delta_2 \geq -5$ is the effective lower bound. Thus, c_2' must not get lower than \$75 − \$5 = \$70 to keep the current solution optimal. It is interesting to note that there is no upper bound on c_2'. Any increase in the cost of producing type 2 pipe at the Hometown plant will not affect the present optimal schedule.

In general, if X_j is a basic variable associated with column j and row i of the optimal simplex tableau, we must find the range of values for δ_j that satisfy

$$(c_k - z_k) - a_{ik}'\delta_j \geq 0 \tag{5.50}$$

for each nonbasic variable k where a_{ik}' is the technical coefficient in row i associated with nonbasic variable k. The most restrictive upper and lower bounds on δ_j define the range of values for δ_j that maintain the present optimal solution.

Right-Hand Sides

The right-hand-side quantities b_i in a linear programming model often represent resource capacities or managerial policies considered critical to the selection of the optimal alternative in a decision problem. If the resources are fully consumed, or the managerial policies strictly satisfied in the optimal solution, a nonzero shadow price V_i will be associated with these constraints because of the condition of complementary slackness, as we discussed earlier. The question naturally arises: over what range of values for b_i will the shadow price V_i be valid? This analysis is sometimes called *right-hand-side ranging*.

Consider the optimal tableau for our plastic-pipe example. The artificial variables have been excluded for convenience.

c_j	Basis	50 X_1	75 X_2	60 X_3	70 X_4	0 S_1	0 S_2	0 S_3	R
0	S_1	0	0	$\frac{13}{7}$	0	1	$\frac{8}{7}$	5	$\frac{24}{7}$
70	X_4	0	0	$\frac{6}{7}$	1	0	$\frac{1}{7}$	0	$\frac{80}{7}$
50	X_1	1	0	1	0	0	0	-1	12
75	X_2	0	1	$-\frac{6}{7}$	0	0	$-\frac{1}{7}$	0	$\frac{32}{7}$
	z_j	50	75	$\frac{320}{7}$	70	0	$-\frac{5}{7}$	-50	$\frac{12{,}200}{7}$
	$c_j - z_j$	0	0	$\frac{100}{7}$	0	0	$\frac{5}{7}$	50	

Since S_2 is not in the basis, we must be utilizing all of the extrusion capacity at the Bakersfield plant. The shadow price on extrusion capacity at Bakersfield is found in the $c_j - z_j$ row, in the S_2 column. It indicates that if we had one *less* hour of capacity, costs would *rise* by $\frac{5}{7}$ dollars. Suppose that instead of the original 80 hours of capacity, we had only 79 hours. The new solution would be the following.

c_j	Basis	50 X_1	75 X_2	60 X_3	70 X_4	0 S_1	0 S_2	0 S_3	R
0	S_1	0	0	$\frac{13}{7}$	0	1	$\frac{8}{7}$	5	$\frac{16}{7}$
70	X_4	0	0	$\frac{6}{7}$	1	0	$\frac{1}{7}$	0	$\frac{79}{7}$
50	X_1	1	0	1	0	0	0	-1	12
75	X_2	0	1	$-\frac{6}{7}$	0	0	$-\frac{1}{7}$	0	$\frac{33}{7}$
	z_j	50	75	$\frac{320}{7}$	70	0	$-\frac{5}{7}$	-50	$\frac{12{,}205}{7}$
	$c_j - z_j$	0	0	$\frac{100}{7}$	0	0	$\frac{5}{7}$	50	

The objective function has *increased* by $\frac{5}{7}$, as expected. In addition, the values of the basic variables have been adjusted by subtracting the value of the corresponding technical coefficient found in the S_2 column. This is summarized as follows:

$$
\begin{pmatrix} S_1 \\ X_4 \\ X_1 \\ X_2 \end{pmatrix} = \begin{pmatrix} \frac{24}{7} \\ \frac{80}{7} \\ 12 \\ \frac{32}{7} \end{pmatrix} - 1 \begin{pmatrix} \frac{8}{7} \\ \frac{1}{7} \\ 0 \\ -\frac{1}{7} \end{pmatrix} = \begin{pmatrix} \frac{16}{7} \\ \frac{79}{7} \\ 12 \\ \frac{33}{7} \end{pmatrix} \tag{5.51}
$$

Thus, we did not have to go through all of the simplex calculations to arrive at the new solution. The coefficients in the S_2 column indicate how the values of the basic variables will change. The logic is analogous to the logic discussed in Chapter 4 with respect to the two-variable media-mix problem. Increasing S_2 by 1 hour has the equivalent effect of reducing extrusion capacity by 1 hour.

What about *increasing* extrusion capacity by 1 hour? From the preceding discussion, we would expect the opposite effect on the basic variables. If capacity were increased to 81 hours, the following solution would be optimal:

c_j	Basis	50 X_1	75 X_2	60 X_3	70 X_4	0 S_1	0 S_2	0 S_3	R
0	S_1	0	0	$\frac{13}{7}$	0	1	$\frac{8}{7}$	5	$\frac{32}{7}$
70	X_4	0	0	$\frac{6}{7}$	1	0	$\frac{1}{7}$	0	$\frac{81}{7}$
50	X_1	1	0	1	0	0	0	-1	12
75	X_2	0	1	$-\frac{6}{7}$	0	0	$-\frac{1}{7}$	0	$\frac{31}{7}$
	z_j	50	75	$\frac{320}{7}$	70	0	$-\frac{5}{7}$	-50	$\frac{12,195}{7}$
	$c_j - z_j$	0	0	$\frac{100}{7}$	0	0	$\frac{5}{7}$	50	

The objective function has been *reduced* by $\frac{5}{7}$. The optimal values of the basic variables have been adjusted by the values of the technical coefficients in the S_2 column in the following way.

$$
\begin{pmatrix} S_1 \\ X_4 \\ X_1 \\ X_2 \end{pmatrix} = \begin{pmatrix} \frac{24}{7} \\ \frac{80}{7} \\ 12 \\ \frac{32}{7} \end{pmatrix} + 1 \begin{pmatrix} \frac{8}{7} \\ \frac{1}{7} \\ 0 \\ -\frac{1}{7} \end{pmatrix} = \begin{pmatrix} \frac{32}{7} \\ \frac{81}{7} \\ 12 \\ \frac{31}{7} \end{pmatrix} \tag{5.52}
$$

In this case, we simply added the technical coefficients to the right-hand sides to get the new values for the basic variables.

How much can we adjust b_2, the extrusion capacity at Bakersfield, before the basis changes? As capacity is decreased, S_1 is the basic variable that will be driven to zero first. If we increase capacity, X_2 is the basic variable that will leave the basis first. Let δ_2 be the *change* in extrusion capacity at Bakersfield,

$$\delta_2 = b_2' - b_2$$

where b_2' is the new capacity level. Keep in mind that δ_2 can be positive or negative. In order to maintain the present basis, the following conditions must hold:

$$\begin{pmatrix} S_1 \\ X_4 \\ X_1 \\ X_2 \end{pmatrix} = \begin{pmatrix} \frac{24}{7} \\ \frac{80}{7} \\ 12 \\ \frac{32}{7} \end{pmatrix} + \delta_2 \begin{pmatrix} \frac{8}{7} \\ \frac{1}{7} \\ 0 \\ -\frac{1}{7} \end{pmatrix} = \begin{pmatrix} \frac{24}{7} + \frac{8}{7}\delta_2 \\ \frac{80}{7} + \frac{1}{7}\delta_2 \\ 12 + 0\delta_2 \\ \frac{32}{7} - \frac{1}{7}\delta_2 \end{pmatrix} \geq \begin{pmatrix} 0 \\ 0 \\ 0 \\ 0 \end{pmatrix} \quad (5.53)$$

These conditions imply upper and lower bounds on b_2. In particular,

$$\delta_2 \geq -3$$

$$\delta_2 \geq -80$$

$$\delta_2 \geq -\infty \qquad (5.54)$$

$$\delta_2 \leq 32$$

The effective bounds are those that are most restrictive. Thus, from (5.54) we have

$$-3 \leq \delta_2 \leq 32 \qquad (5.55)$$

Since $\delta_2 = b_2' - b_2$, and $b_2 = 80$, we get

$$-3 \leq b_2' - 80 \leq 32$$

or

$$77 \leq b_2' \leq 112 \qquad (5.56)$$

If the extrusion capacity at Bakersfield stays within these limits, the decision as to which products are to be produced at each plant remains the same, although the production quantities will be changed. Whenever the capacity of a limiting resource is changed, the values of the basic variables will change.

This information is useful for decision making. For example, management can evaluate a proposal to increase extrusion capacity to a total of 100 hours at Bakersfield. Because 100 hours is within the range for maintaining the present basis, the shadow price on extrusion capacity is a valid estimator of the impact on total costs. The extra 20 hours of capacity can be expected to *reduce* total costs by $20(\frac{5}{7}) = \$14.29$. This benefit can now be compared to the cost for acquiring the added capacity. If the proposal called for an increase to 130 hours, however, a new simplex tableau would have to be computed because the basis would change. The shadow price of $\$\frac{5}{7}$ is not valid for capacity levels in excess of 112 hours.

In general, right-hand-side ranging for an *upper-bound* constraint k is accomplished by finding the lower and upper bounds on δ_k such that

$$
\begin{pmatrix} r_1 \\ r_2 \\ \vdots \\ r_k \\ \vdots \\ r_m \end{pmatrix} + \delta_k \begin{pmatrix} a'_{1j} \\ a'_{2j} \\ \vdots \\ a'_{kj} \\ \vdots \\ a'_{mj} \end{pmatrix} \geq \begin{pmatrix} 0 \\ 0 \\ \vdots \\ 0 \\ \vdots \\ 0 \end{pmatrix}
\tag{5.57}
$$

where r_i is the right-hand-side entry in row i of the optimal simplex tableau and a'_{ij} is the technical coefficient in row i for slack variable j, which is associated with constraint k.

The procedure for other types of constraints is very similar. For *equality* constraints, the procedure is identical except that there is no slack variable with which to work. In this case, the *artificial* variable for the equality constraint is used instead. In fact, this is the only time that artificial variables are needed once a feasible solution has been found.

Lower-bound constraints are handled in a slightly different manner. Consider the demand constraint for type 1 pipe from (5.40)

$$
X_1 + X_3 - S_3 = 12
$$

An increase in the surplus variable S_3 has the effect of *increasing* the production requirement. This is the opposite of the effect that the slack variable S_2 had on extrusion capacity. We would expect that the effect on the basis variables would be opposite as well. In general, right-hand-side ranging for a lower-bound constraint k is accomplished by finding the bounds on δ_k such that

$$
\begin{pmatrix} r_1 \\ r_2 \\ \vdots \\ r_k \\ \vdots \\ r_m \end{pmatrix} - \delta_k \begin{pmatrix} a'_{1j} \\ a'_{2j} \\ \vdots \\ a'_{kj} \\ \vdots \\ a'_{mj} \end{pmatrix} \geq \begin{pmatrix} 0 \\ 0 \\ \vdots \\ 0 \\ \vdots \\ 0 \end{pmatrix}
\tag{5.58}
$$

In our case

$$
\begin{pmatrix} \frac{24}{7} \\ \frac{80}{7} \\ 12 \\ \frac{32}{7} \end{pmatrix} - \delta_3 \begin{pmatrix} 5 \\ 0 \\ -1 \\ 0 \end{pmatrix} \geq \begin{pmatrix} 0 \\ 0 \\ 0 \\ 0 \end{pmatrix}
\tag{5.59}
$$

These relationships imply the following bounds on δ_3

$$\delta_3 \leq (\tfrac{24}{7})/5 = \tfrac{24}{35}$$

$$\delta_3 \leq (\tfrac{80}{7})/0 = +\infty$$

$$\delta_3 \geq -\tfrac{12}{1} = -12 \tag{5.60}$$

$$\delta_3 \leq (\tfrac{32}{7})/0 = +\infty$$

The effective bounds are

$$-12 \leq \delta_3 \leq \tfrac{24}{35} \tag{5.61}$$

This implies that the bounds on the new production requirement for type 1 pipe b'_3 are the following:

$$-12 \leq b'_3 - b_3 \leq \tfrac{24}{35}$$

$$-12 \leq b'_3 - 12 \leq 0.69$$

$$0 \leq b'_3 \leq 12.69 \tag{5.62}$$

The basis will not change so long as the market demands for type 1 pipe remain within these bounds. In addition, the shadow price of $50 remains valid in this range. For example, suppose that several contracts are canceled with the effect that market demands are reduced by 4000 feet of pipe. Because our variables are expressed in thousands of feet, we would expect total production costs to decrease by $50(4) = $200.

Technical Coefficients

The constraints in a linear programming model serve to define the boundaries of the feasible region. We have already discussed how changes in the right-hand-side quantity of a constraint can affect the optimal solution to the problem. These changes have the effect of creating new boundary equations parallel to the original one. The constraints can also be modified by changing the technical coefficients that multiply the decision variables. Altering these coefficients has the effect of changing the *slope* of the boundary equation represented by a constraint. New extreme points are defined, as in the case of changing the right-hand-side quantities; however, the general analysis is more complicated and beyond the scope of this text.

Nonetheless, we can say a few words about a special case. If a constraint is *nonbinding*, changes in the a_{ij} values can be made with no effect on the objective function so long as there is no change in the basis. For example, S_1 is in the optimal basis of the plastic-pipe example. Thus, the constraint on extrusion capacity in (5.40) at the Hometown plant is nonbinding, as shown below with the optimal values of the decision variables (i.e., $5(12) + 8(\tfrac{32}{7}) \leq 100$). At present, $a_{11} = 5$.

How much could a_{11} increase before all slack is consumed? In this case, the new coefficient could be as large as

$$\bar{a}_{11} = [100 - 8(\tfrac{32}{7})]/12 = 5.28 \tag{5.63}$$

Thus, processing of 1000 feet of type 1 pipe could increase by 0.28 hours before a new solution would be required.

Similarly, for type 2 pipe,

$$\bar{a}_{12} = [100 - 5(12)]/(\tfrac{32}{7}) = 8.75 \tag{5.64}$$

Processing time could increase by 0.75 hours per 1000 feet of type 2 pipe and the basis would not change, all other factors being status quo. The only effect would be to drive the slack time at Hometown to zero. Cases involving binding constraints involve more complicated logic and are beyond the scope of this text.

5.5 MULTIPLE OBJECTIVES

The presentation of linear programming has until now concentrated on problems in which there is one dominant objective. In the portfolio-mix problem we wanted to maximize return, whereas in the production-planning problem, the objective was to minimize costs. The discussion in Part I of the text indicated that there can be more than one objective for a given problem, and that the proper selection and consideration of these objectives is an important aspect of the decision-making process. As we shall see, linear programming can be useful for analyzing problems with multiple objectives.

Generating Noninferior Solutions

Numerous techniques are available for incorporating the consideration of multiple objectives in a decision problem. One set of techniques merely generates *noninferior* alternatives for the decision maker to consider. A feasible solution to a multiobjective programming problem is noninferior if there exists no other feasible solution that will yield an improvement in one objective without causing a degradation in at least one other objective.[5] Consider the following model incorporating two objectives:

$$\text{Max } Z_1 = X_1 + X_3$$
$$\text{Max } Z_2 = -50X_1 - 75X_2 - 60X_3 - 70X_4$$

subject to

$$
\begin{aligned}
X_2 + \qquad\quad X_4 &= 16 \\
5X_1 + 8X_2 \qquad\qquad &\le 100 \\
6X_3 + 7X_4 &\le 80 \\
X_1, X_2, X_3, X_4 \qquad\qquad &\ge 0
\end{aligned}
\tag{5.65}
$$

[5] An excellent presentation of the techniques incorporating multiple objectives can be found in Jared Cohen, *Multiobjective Programming and Planning*. New York: Academic Press, 1978.

Notice that (5.65) is the same model as (5.10), which was developed for the production-planning problem, except that the requirement on production of type 1 pipe has been elevated to the status of an objective. This objective might reflect the marketing department's desire to maximize customer service with type 1 pipe by ensuring that enough is produced to satisfy all demands. Notice that maximizing Z_2 is equivalent to minimizing total costs. These two objectives are conflicting, since costs can be minimized by eliminating type 1 pipe from the production plan. Therefore, some trade-offs between the objectives must be made.

One method of generating noninferior solutions to this problem is to multiply each objective function by a *weight*, W_k, and combine the resulting functions into a single objective function. Suppose some values for W_1 and W_2 are specified. Then the objective function for (5.65) may be written

$$\text{Max } Z = W_1(X_1 + X_3) + W_2(-50X_1 - 75X_2 - 60X_3 - 70X_4) \quad (5.66)$$

Suppose that the production of one unit of type 1 pipe can be related to the dollars of benefit the company can realize from the marketing standpoint; then (5.66) can be simplified to an objective function expressed in dollars

$$\text{Max } Z = W(X_1 + X_3) + (-50X_1 - 75X_2 - 60X_3 - 70X_4) \quad (5.67)$$

where W is the value that equates one unit of type 1 pipe to dollars of benefit. The values of the weight W in (5.67), or W_1 and W_2 in (5.66), can be varied in a systematic way to generate a series of alternatives for the decision maker to evaluate.

Another approach would be to incorporate the objectives as constraints in the model. Here one objective is arbitrarily chosen for optimization, and the others are made constraints. The model given by (5.10) is an example of this approach, in which the objective is to minimize costs, and the customer-service objective is made a constraint. The right-hand sides of the "objective constraints" are systematically varied to generate a series of noninferior solutions to evaluate.

Computers play an important role in this type of analysis. Computer programs can be developed to generate the noninferior solutions for any of the previously mentioned techniques. For example, with the "weighting" method, the computer could generate a series of weights, solve the corresponding linear programs, and print summarized results of the solutions for the decision maker. A linear programming subroutine would be only one module of a larger program designed to make the procedure as accessible and useful to the decision maker as possible. Nonetheless, the number of noninferior solutions to a realistic multiple-objective problem can be extremely large. Attempting to generate all of these solutions would not be practical in this case, even with a computer. Not only could the computation time be excessive, but the vast number of alternatives from which to choose might also be overwhelming. In most practical situations, we are reduced to generating only a subset of the noninferior solutions, and to running the risk of excluding one that would be desirable to the decision maker.

Incorporating Preferences

Techniques that incorporate personal preferences are intended to overcome the shortcoming of the generation techniques by limiting the number of alternatives for evaluation to those most likely to be desirable. One group of techniques attempts to estimate the decision maker's utility function and then seeks to optimize that function. It is usually difficult to derive an individual's utility function, especially for a decision problem involving a large number of decision variables. In addition, given our discussion in Chapter 2, it is likely that the utility function will be nonlinear, thereby complicating the solution process.

Another group of techniques involves the decision maker in the solution process. Computer programs have been developed to present noninferior solutions to the decision maker and to request information regarding the nature of the objective function trade-offs that would be desirable. With the information given, new noninferior solutions are generated and the process continues until the decision maker is unwilling to make any more trade-offs. The decision maker's utility function is never made explicit, but it is *implicitly* recognized by the responses made during the solution process.

A technique gaining in popularity is called *goal programming*. Here the decision maker must specify goals, or targets, for each objective. We then seek to minimize the deviation from the goals. The technique assumes that the decision maker has a linear utility function with respect to the objectives; that is, the marginal rate of substitution between the objectives is linear, regardless of the amount of deviation from the goals.

Consider the model given by (5.65). The objective for a goal program could be written

$$\text{Min } Z' = \sum_{k=1}^{2} |G_k - Z_k| \tag{5.68}$$

where G_k is the goal for objective k, and $\|$ represents the absolute value of the argument within. An assumption implicit in (5.68) is that the decision maker desires to meet the goals exactly. Unfortunately, (5.68) is nonlinear. An equivalent linear programming formulation would be

$$\text{Min } Z' = \sum_{k=1}^{2} (w^{k-}d_k^- + w_k^+ d_k^+)$$

subject to

$$
\begin{aligned}
X_2 \quad\quad + \quad X_4 \quad\quad\quad\quad\quad\quad &= 16 \\
5X_1 + 8X_2 \quad\quad\quad\quad\quad\quad\quad\quad &\le 100 \\
6X_3 + 7X_4 \quad\quad\quad\quad &\le 80 \\
X_1 \quad\quad + X_3 + d_1^- - d_1^+ \quad\quad &= 12 \\
50X_1 + 75X_2 + 60X_3 + 70X_4 + d_2^- - d_2^+ &= 1500 \\
X_1, X_2, X_3, X_4, d_1^-, d_1^+, d_2^-, d_2^+ \quad\quad &\ge 0
\end{aligned}
\tag{5.69}
$$

where d_k^- and d_k^+ are deviation variables, w_k^- and w_k^+ are weights, and the objectives are written as goal constraints in the model. In our example, the marketing department has set a goal of exactly 12,000 feet of type 1 pipe for customer demands, and manufacturing has set a goal of exactly \$1500 for total production cost.

The deviation variables for any goal constraint measure the amount of discrepancy between the value of the objective and the goal specified for it. For example, if the total production of type 1 pipe turns out to be 10,000 feet, $d_1^- = 2$ and $d_1^+ = 0$. Thus d_1^- picks up the underachievement of the goal, whereas d_1^+ picks up the overachievement. We are assured that we will never get a solution in which d_k^- and d_k^+ are *both* nonzero, since the objective is to minimize their sum. Even though there are an infinite number of combinations of d_1^- and d_1^+ — such as (2, 0), (3, 1), (5, 3), (105, 103), and others — the combination that minimizes the sum will always have one of d_1^- or d_1^+ at a zero level.

The weights used in a goal-programming model reflect the decision maker's utility for the various objectives. In particular, they measure the marginal rates of substitution between objectives and the degree of importance in attaining the goal of each objective relative to the others. For example, suppose we wish to standardize the weights so that we are minimizing the *percentage* deviation from the goals in each objective. This will avoid the problems associated with having goals with large magnitude differences. In our problem, the customer-service goal is only 12, whereas the total cost goal is 1500. An underachievement of 3 for customer service represents a deviation of 25%, whereas an overachievement of 3 for total costs represents a deviation of only 0.2%. Thus, let us assume for our problem that percentage deviations are of interest to the decision maker. The weights that would give "equal weighting" to each objective are given in (5.70).[6]

$$W_1^- = W_1^+ = \tfrac{1}{12} = 0.08333$$

$$W_2^- = W_2^+ = \tfrac{1}{1500} = 0.00067 \tag{5.70}$$

The solution to (5.69) with the weights given in (5.70) is found in Table 5.4. Notice that the customer service goal was met, but that the overachievement in the total-cost goal of \$242.86 represents a 16% deviation from the goal. It is interesting to note that this is the same solution we found for the model given by (5.10) in Table 5.1. Recall that we were minimizing total cost with a production requirement of at least 12,000 feet of type 1 pipe. Further elevating the importance of the customer-service objective relative to the total-cost objective for this set of goals would result in the same solution, since we have already achieved the customer-service goal.

---

[6] In this presentation we are assuming that it is desirable to meet the goals exactly. If, for example, the goal is to produce *at least* 12,000 feet of type 1 pipe, we could set $W_1^- = 0.08333$ and $W_1^+ = 0$. This is called "one-sided" goal programming.

Table 5.4　Goal Programming Analysis of the Production-Planning Problem

Objective	X_1	X_2	X_3	X_4	d_1^-	d_1^+	d_2^-	d_2^+	Customer Service	Total Costs
Equal weight to cost and service	12.00	4.57	0	11.43	0	0	0	242.86	12.00	$1742.86
Costs twice as important as service	7.14	4.57	0	11.43	4.86	0	0	0	7.14	$1500.00
Maximize service	12.69	4.57	0	11.43	37.31	0	0	1777.14	12.69	$1777.14
Minimize total costs	0	4.57	0	11.43	50	0	0	1142.86	0	$1142.86

Suppose the decision maker feels that achieving the total-cost goal is twice as important as achieving the customer-service goal. In this case the weights are given by

$$W_1^- = W_1^+ = \tfrac{1}{12} = 0.08333$$

$$W_2^- = W_2^+ = 2(\tfrac{1}{1500}) = 0.00134 \tag{5.71}$$

The results of this change are given in Table 5.4. The total cost goal was achieved, but the customer-service goal fell short by about 41%.

With respect to the last two solutions discussed, it appears that the decision maker must make some trade-offs. Both solutions are noninferior solutions; the only way to improve on one of the objectives is to lose ground with respect to the other. No solution "dominates" the other by being better with respect to all objectives. More solutions could be generated by changing the goals and repeating the analysis. For example, total cost goals of 1600 and 1700 could be tried to see what increases in the production of type 1 pipe could be generated. Using the model in this way resembles the generation techniques presented above.

A potential pitfall of goal programming is that it may generate an *inferior* solution. The analyst should be wary of any solution in which all deviation variables are zero. This means all goals are achieved. The danger is that raising the level of one goal may result in better performance with respect to that goal without impairing the performance of the other goals. In other words, the decision maker set goals that were too easy to achieve, given the resources available.

One way to reduce the possibility of this happening is to show the optimal value of each objective to the decision maker prior to setting the goals. This can be done by computing solutions to the model in which each objective is considered separately. In the goal-programming approach, the goal for a particular objective is set at some desired, but unachievable, level. The weights on the deviational variables for that goal are made very large and all other weights are set to zero.

For the total-cost objective in our example, the goal could be set to zero. In the case of customer service, since we wish to maximize that objective, a value of 50 could be used. These two solutions are shown in Table 5.4. Now the decision maker can see that realistic total cost goals fall in the range $1142.86 to $1777.14 and service goals in the range 0 to 12.69.

Goal programming is an important extension of linear programming analysis. It permits the consideration of multiple objectives and involves the decision maker in setting realistic goals. It also affords an opportunity to generate a series of noninferior solutions, or alternatives, from which to choose. In this respect it is a useful tool that helps decision makers in the decision-making process.

5.6 SUMMARY

Linear programming is a technique designed to select the optimal alternative(s) in a decision problem. Three key notions are implied in this statement. First, *selecting* the optimal alternative requires a series of well-defined steps designed to reach optimality in a finite number of iterations. We have shown how these calculations are performed for a technique called the simplex method. The use of linear programming for selecting the optimal alternative(s) requires a firm understanding of the economic implications of linear programming, as well as of the mechanical procedures of the simplex method. Section 5.2 served to underscore these economic underpinnings by introducing the concepts of duality. In addition, it was shown that there are potential computational savings by solving the dual if the primal model has more constraints than decision variables. Section 5.3 showed how the simplex procedure itself can pinpoint modeling deficiencies in which the model has no feasible solution or the solution is unbounded.

The simplex method can be performed manually for reasonably small problems. Most practical problems are large, however, and require a computer to solve them. Practical problems may require several hundred iterations before optimality is achieved. Even though it would be possible to solve problems of such size manually, it would take too much time and the accuracy of the result would, at best, be dubious. Nonetheless, computers employ procedures based on the simplex method because of its efficiency in finding optimal extreme points The output from these computer codes contains all of the information that linear programming can provide to the decision maker, including the postoptimality analyses presented in Section 5.4.

The second key notion regarding linear programming is implied by the word *optimal*. Linear programming selects optimal alternatives relative to a single objective function. In most decision problems, there is more than one objective to consider. If all objectives can be measured in common units, a single objective function can be constructed that will incorporate all objectives to be considered in the problem. For instance, if all objectives can be stated in terms of dollars, we can construct a single objective function that represents all objectives, as in the portfolio-mix problem in Section 5.1. Objectives frequently cannot all be stated in common terms, however. This is the case in a post office, where two objectives may be to maximize service and minimize costs. The costs are easy to measure, but service to the public is difficult to measure in dollar terms. Also, the two objectives are conflicting, in that it is unlikely that both can be achieved simultaneously. In these situations, the multiple-objective techniques presented in Section 5.5 can be used.

Finally, the *decision problem* typically crosses the boundaries of several functional areas in a business. This implies that more than one functional area must supply the data for the model and be a part of the final decision. A linear programming model may contain numerous constraints reflecting the capacity limitations or policies of various different functional areas in a business firm. The economic information resulting from a linear programming analysis is very useful for seeing the interactive nature of the decision process as it relates to these functional areas.

Consider the following model constructed to determine the optimal product mix in a firm. The objective is to maximize profits, and the decision variables X_j represent the number of units of product j to be produced per week.

$$\text{Max } Z = 10X_1 + 15X_2 + 25X_3 + 40X_4 \qquad \text{Total Profit}$$

subject to

$$
\begin{array}{llll}
2X_1 + & 3X_3 & \leq 500 \text{ lb} & \text{Raw material 1 capacity} \\
5X_2 + & 4X_4 \leq 700 \text{ lb} & & \text{Raw material 2 capacity} \\
3X_1 + 6X_2 + 8X_3 + 10X_4 \leq 2200 \text{ hr} & & & \text{Production capacity} \\
X_1 + X_2 & \geq 125 \text{ units} & & \text{Market requirements for product group 1} \\
X_3 + X_4 \geq 150 \text{ units} & & & \text{Market requirements for product group 2} \\
20X_1 + 30X_2 + 40X_3 + 60X_4 \leq \$11{,}500 & & & \text{Working capital capacity} \\
X_1, X_2, X_3, X_4 & \geq 0 & & (5.72)
\end{array}
$$

The model requires the inputs from at least the accounting, finance, marketing, and production areas. In addition to providing the alternative product mix that maximizes profits, the model enables managers to analyze important "what if" questions through postoptimality analysis. For hypothetical changes in the model parameters, the analysis demonstrates the impact on profits as well as the effect on other areas of the firm. Table 5.5 provides some example "what if" questions, and the areas (other than profits) in which there may be an impact as the result of parameter changes in (5.72).

It is obvious that linear programming for practical problems can provide decision-making information to a variety of functional disciplines.

Table 5.5 Example "What If" Questions That Could Be Analyzed With The Product-Mix Model

What If	Areas Potentially Affected
Raw material #1 is reduced to 400 lb because of material shortages	Production capacity, market requirements for Groups 1 and 2, working-capital requirements
Production capacity is increased to 2400 hr because of capital improvement	Raw-material requirements, working-capital requirements
Market requirements for group 1 are increased to 150 units because of a market-sales campaign	Raw-material capacities, production capacity, working-capital requirements
Wages are increased 8% because of a new labor contract	Raw-material capacities, production-capacity requirements, market requirements, working-capital requirements
New work methods decreased by 10% the time required to produce product group 1	Raw-material capacities, production capacity requirements, working-capital requirements

References Cohen, J.L. *Multiobjective Programming and Planning.* New York: Academic Press, 1978.

Dantzig, G.B. *Linear Programming and Extensions.* Princeton, N.J.: Princeton University Press, 1963.

Gass, S.I. *Linear Programming: Methods and Applications*, 4th ed. New York: McGraw-Hill, 1975.

Hadley, G. *Linear Programming.* Reading, Mass.: Addison-Wesley, 1962.

Hillier, F.S., and Lieberman, G.J. *Introduction to Operations Research*, 2nd ed. San Francisco: Holden Day, 1974.

Hughes, A.J., and Graiwog, D.E. *Linear Programming: An Emphasis on Decision Making.* Reading, Mass.: Addison-Wesley, 1973.

Lee, S. *Goal Programming for Decision Analysis.* Philadelphia: Auerbach Publishers, 1972.

Levin, R.I., and Lamone, R.P. *Linear Programming for Management Decisions.* Homewood, Ill.: Richard D. Irwin, 1969.

Spivey, W.A., and Thrall, R.M. *Linear Optimization.* New York: Holt, Rinehart and Winston, 1970.

Strum, J.E. *Introduction to Linear Programming.* San Francisco: Holden Day, 1972.

Wagner, H.M. *Principles of Operations Research*, 2nd ed. Englewood Cliffs, N.J.: Prentice-Hall, 1975.

1. Suppose that you have just formulated a linear programming model which your boss feels is an accurate representation of the problem he or she must solve. Your boss knows nothing of the simplex procedure you plan to use for solving it. In a few short paragraphs, provide an intuitive description of how the method works and describe the types of postoptimality analysis that could be done to provide more information for the boss's decision problem.

2. Define the following terms and indicate their significance to decision making with linear programming and the simplex method.
    (a) Pivot variable.
    (b) Pivot row.
    (c) Pivot element.
    (b) Degeneracy.
    (e) Cycling.

3. Provide an intuitive explanation, using the concept of "net contribution," of why the criterion for optimality for maximization problems is different from that for minimization problems.

4. The simplex method alters the basis at each iteration. What is a basis and why must there be as many variables in the basis as there are constraints in the model?

5. What is an artificial variable? Why are such models needed in some linear programming problems? What role do they play in situations in which the problem has no feasible solution?

6. Consider the following primal problem:

    $$\text{Min } Z = 5X_1 + 7X_2 \qquad \text{Costs}$$

    subject to

    $$
    \begin{aligned}
    2X_1 + 3X_2 &\geq 12 \qquad \text{Resource 1} \\
    8X_1 + 2X_2 &\geq 24 \qquad \text{Resource 2} \\
    6X_1 + 3X_2 &\geq 30 \qquad \text{Resource 3} \\
    X_1, X_2 &\geq 0
    \end{aligned}
    $$

    The dual problem would have as its first constraint

    $$2V_1 + 8V_2 + 6V_3 + L_1 = 5 \qquad \text{Product 1}$$

    where L_1 is the dual *slack* variable associated with product 1 in the primal problem. Provide an economic interpretation for L_1 as we did for the dual *surplus* variable in the portfolio-mix problem. Keep in mind that the primal problem here is a cost-minimization problem.

7. The duality theorems provide a useful economic interpretation of linear programming analysis. Provide an intuitive explanation of the duality theorems to emphasize the economic relationship between the primal and dual problems.

8. In the portfolio-mix problem we found that the shadow price for cash resources is $0.04. The return for each dollar invested in portfolio 1 is $0.06, however, and for portfolio 2 it is $0.08. It first appears that there is a contradiction. Explain why this result is reasonable for the portfolio-mix problem and why this can happen in any linear programming problem.

9. When we discussed sensitivity of the objective-function coefficients, we presented the analysis in the context of a maximization problem. How would the procedure for finding the bounds on δ_j have to change if the original problem were a minimization problem?

10. Explain how the simplex method can help point out the deficiencies in model formulation.

11. Why is it important to restrict attention to "noninferior" solutions (or alternatives) when analyzing a decision problem with multiple objectives? What is the difference between a noninferior solution and an inferior solution in this regard?

12. Consider the following alternatives and the corresponding values of the three objectives you consider important:

	Objectives		
Alternative	G_1	G_2	G_3
A_1	40	107	15
A_2	70	95	8
A_3	30	98	13
A_4	80	115	10

Assume that you wish to maximize each of the objectives. That is, the greater the objective function value for any objective, the better off you are. Are any *inferior* alternatives shown above? Explain.

13. Compare and contrast the technique of objective-function "weighting" as used in Equation (5.66) with that of goal programming for analyzing multiple-objective problems.

Problems 1. Consider the following linear programming problem:

$$\text{Max } Z = 8X_1 + 10X_2$$

subject to

$$X_1 + 4X_2 \leq 40$$

$$3X_1 + 2X_2 \leq 60$$

$$X_2 \leq 2X_1 + 4$$

$$X_1, X_2 \geq 0$$

(a) Solve the problem graphically.

(b) Solve the problem using the simplex method. After each iteration, note the specific extreme point in the current basis on the graph of the feasible region.

2. Solve the following linear programming model by the simplex method:

$$\text{Max } Z = 2X_1 + 10X_2 + 4X_3 + 6X_4$$

subject to

$$X_1 + 6X_2 + 3X_3 + 7X_4 \leq 10$$
$$X_1 + 3X_2 + 8X_3 + 4X_4 \leq 5$$
$$X_1, X_2, X_3, X_4 \geq 0$$

3. Consider the following linear programming model:

$$\text{Max } Z = 10X_1 + 2X_2$$

subject to

$$8X_1 + 4X_2 \leq 32$$
$$6X_1 + 8X_2 \leq 48$$
$$4X_1 + 6X_2 \geq 24$$
$$X_1, X_2 \geq 0$$

Solve this problem using the simplex method and verify your results graphically. Notice that you will have to use the big M method in this maximization problem.

4. Refer to the model in Problem 3. Using the notions of postoptimality analysis in Section 5.4 of this chapter, answer the following questions:

(a) How much can the objective-function coefficient of X_1 *decrease* before there is a change in the optimal solution?

(b) What is the shadow price for the first constraint ($8X_1 + 4X_2 \leq 32$)? Over what range of values for the right-hand side of this constraint will that shadow price be valid?

(c) How much can the technical coefficient for X_2 in the second constraint ($6X_1 + 8X_2 \leq 48$) be increased before that constraint becomes binding?

5. Consider the following linear programming problem:

$$\text{Min } Z = 100X_1 + 60X_2$$

subject to

$$X_1 + X_2 \geq 10$$
$$5X_1 + X_2 \geq 20$$
$$2X_1 + 5X_2 \geq 40$$
$$X_1, X_2 \geq 0$$

(a) Solve the problem graphically.

(b) Solve the problem using the simplex method. Check your results with the graphic solution.

6. Refer to the model in Problem 5. Suppose that the objective function were stated as

$$\text{Max } Z = -100X_1 - 60X_2$$

Solve the model with the new objective function using the simplex method. Are the two model formulations equivalent? Notice that the objective function is bounded over the feasible region, even though the new model has an objective function to be maximized and there are no upper-bound constraints on the decision variables.

7. Solve the following linear programming model using the simplex method:

$$\text{Min } Z = 8X_1 + 2X_2 + 4X_3 + 15X_4$$

subject to

$$2X_1 - X_2 + 4X_3 + 5X_4 \geq 18$$

$$5X_1 - X_2 + 2X_3 + 10X_4 \geq 22$$

$$X_1, X_2, X_3, X_4 \qquad \geq 0$$

8. The Slender Look Company makes skirts, dresses, and suits for women needing petite sizes of clothes. Recently, a new polyester knit fabric was introduced to the clothing industry, and Slender Look decided to manufacture a line of their products with this material. They have devoted 100 hours of their cutting capacity and 120 hours of their sewing capacity per week to the new line. In addition, the company will buy only 70 square yards of the new material per week until the market demands for the new product line can be assessed. Relevant production data are as follows:

Product	Process Time, Hours		Material, Yards
	Cutting	Sewing	
Skirt	$\frac{1}{2}$	1	1
Dress	1	4	2
Suit	6	10	6

Each skirt sold nets $5 profit, whereas each dress and suit sold nets $15 and $25 profit, respectively. Slender Look wishes to maximize its profits.

(a) Formulate the linear programming model.

(b) Use the simplex method to solve the problem.

(c) Assuming that the market potential exceeds the production output, which of the three resources would you recommend expanding first? Why? How much can you expand that resource before the product mix (basis) changes?

9. The procurement manager of a company that manufactures special gasoline additives must determine the proper amounts of each raw material to purchase for the production of one of its products. Three raw materials are available. Each gallon of the *finished* product must have at least a combustion point of 220°F. In addition, the gamma content (which causes hydrocarbon pollution) cannot exceed 6% of volume. The zeta content (which is good for cleaning the internal moving parts of engines) must be at least 12% by volume. Each raw material contains these elements in varying amounts, as shown below.

	Raw Material		
	A	B	C
Combustion point, °F	200	180	280
Gamma content, %	4	3	10
Zeta content, %	20	10	8

Raw material A costs $0.60 per gallon, whereas raw materials B and C cost $0.40 and $0.50 per gallon, respectively. The procurement manager wishes to minimize the cost of raw materials per gallon of product. Use linear programming to find the optimal proportions of each raw material to use in a gallon of finished product. *Hint*: Let your decision variables be expressed in terms of fractions of a gallon. The sum of the fractions must be equal to one.

10. The sectional-center post office in Hometown has recently been told to hire enough employees to come up to its authorized complement levels. There had been a hiring freeze for the past 3 years. The post office must hire 40 letter-sorting-machine (LSM) operators, 60 scheme clerks, and 20 mail handlers. Each of these 120 new people must go through a training program, and it is felt that only a fraction of the total can be trained in the next 4-week accounting period. Postal managers are faced with choosing the best mix of new positions to fill during the upcoming accounting period.

The training program for each employee is given below. Classroom hours reflect sessions in general orientation, craft orientation, and specialty training.

LSM operators	*Hours*
Classroom	20
Training consoles (sorting)	40

Scheme clerks	Hours
Classroom	20
Scheming station	30

Mail handlers	
Classroom	15
Training consoles (loading)	10

There is a classroom capacity of only 800 man-hours per accounting period. Likewise, a maximum of 1000 man-hours of console training and 1200 man-hours of scheme training are possible in an accounting period.

Postal management would like to hire a mix of new employees that would maximize productivity. In this respect, it is generally agreed that LSM operators are twice as productive as any other employee because of the capital equipment with which they work. Thus, LSM operators are more desirable than scheme clerks or mail handlers with respect to hourly output.

(a) Formulate the linear programming model for this problem.
(b) Solve the model for the desired hiring mix.
(c) What is the shadow price on console capacity? What is the range of console capacity over which this shadow price is valid? Explain the significance of this information to postal management.
(d) Suppose there is a suggestion to increase the training time of scheme clerks at the scheming station. How much more time can be added to the present scheme training time before the optimal solution must change?

11. The Hometown Bank has $5000 in excess funds to invest. The financial analysts have assembled three different portfolios for consideration. Portfolio A will return $0.20 for each dollar invested. Portfolio B, a more risky investment, will return $0.35 on the dollar, whereas portfolio C, a blue-chip investment, will return only $0.15 per dollar invested. The bank officers must decide how many dollars to invest in each portfolio to maximize return.

The bank has certain policies relative to investment in portfolios such as these. In particular, the investment in portfolios A and B must not exceed three times the investment in portfolio C, the blue-chip stocks. Also, the investment in the risky portfolio B must not exceed 25% of the total investment in portfolios A and C. Finally, each portfolio has been assessed a risk factor. Portfolio A has 2 risk units, portfolio B has 5 risk units, and portfolio C has only 1 risk unit per dollar invested. The total number of risk units accumulated in the investment in portfolios A, B, and C cannot exceed 8000.

(a) Formulate the linear programming model in augmented form. You can write the entire model without any fractional values for the technological coefficients, a_{ij}.
(b) Solve for the optimal investment mix. *Note:* This problem is degenerate. To break ties in the pivot row, choose the first row (lowest row number) as the pivot row.

12. Consider the primal problem in Review Question 6.
    (a) Set up the dual problem, including all dual slack variables.
    (b) Solve the dual problem.
    (c) Specify the solution to the primal problem from the optimal dual tableau. Verify your answer by solving the primal problem graphically. What is the optimal value of the primal objective function? How does it compare to the optimal value of the dual objective function?
    (d) Verify the theorem on complementary slackness for your solutions to the primal and the dual.

13. Consider the model in Section 5.6. The model has four decision variables and six contraints. In situations like this, there can be a computational advantage in formulating and solving the dual problem. In this case, the dual problem will have six variables and only four constraints.
    (a) Formulate the dual problem. Augment the model with dual surplus and artificial variables.
    (b) Solve the dual problem. What is the solution to the primal problem?
    (c) Currently, there is $11,500 of available working capital. What is the shadow price on that capacity? How much can we increase working capital and still reap the benefits indicated by the shadow price? *Note:* The $11,500 appears in the objective function of the dual problem. Thus, you want to do a sensitivity analysis of a coefficient in the objective function.
    (d) The production department has a proposal for increasing capacity to 2400 hours. What is the expected increase in profits?

14. Consider Problem 12 of Chapter 4. Solve the problem with the simplex method.

15. Consider Problem 13 of Chapter 4.
    (a) Solve the problem with the simplex method.
    (b) The marketing department is uncertain as to the effects of price changes (or profit margins) on the production of chairs and rockers. What is the range of profit margins on chairs that will yield the same production plan, assuming price does not affect total sales. What about the range of profit margins for rockers?
    (c) The production department is contemplating an increase in finishing capacity to 250 hours at a cost of $150. What is the expected benefit?

16. A chemical manufacturer produces two chemicals, X and Y. Each ton of X requires $200 of working capital, whereas each ton of Y requires $400. Two primary raw materials are used in the production process. Each ton of X requires 7 tons of raw material 1, and each ton of Y requires 5 tons. Each ton of X requires 10 tons of raw material 2, and each ton of Y also requires 10 tons of raw material 2. The company has only $2000 of working capital, 35 tons of raw material 1, and 60 tons of raw material 2 available during the planning period.

The plant manager has two conflicting objectives: maximize profits and maximize the utilization of the expensive process equipment used to produce X and Y. Each ton of X yields $100 in profit and each ton of Y yields $80. Each ton of X uses only 30 hours of process time, whereas each ton of Y uses 50 hours.

(a) Using graphic methods, specify the feasible region for this problem. Identify the four alternatives (excluding the origin).

(b) For each alternative, specify the values of each objective function. Identify the alternative that maximizes profit and the one that maximizes utilization. Are any of the four alternatives inferior? Explain.

(c) Suppose the manager has specified a goal of $530 for profits and 260 hours for utilization. Formulate a goal-programming model assuming that the manager wishes to minimize the percentage deviations from the stated goals and that both objectives have equal weighting in this regard.

(d) Suppose profits are twice as important as utilization. Use the model developed in part c to find the best alternative. You may use a computer if you have access to one. If you solve the problem manually you will not have to add artificial variables for the goal constraints. Use the slack variables for the three technical constraints and the d^- deviation variables for the goal constraints to get an initial feasible solution.

17. Consider Problem 10. Suppose postal management has two primary objectives: maximize productivity and minimize the monthly wage bill. Each LSM operator gets $1000 per month, whereas each clerk and mail handler gets only $800 and $600, respectively. Suppose also that management has a goal of 120 for productivity and $20,000 for monthly wages.

(a) Formulate a goal-programming model for this problem.

(b) Discuss how you would use the model to help postal management select the appropriate mix of new employees. Bring into your discussion how you would formulate the weights for the deviational variables.

6

THE TRANSPORTATION MODEL

6.1 THE PROPERTIES OF THE TRANSPORTATION MODEL

6.2 THE STEPPING-STONE AND MODI METHODS

Problem Identification, Data Gathering, and Specification
  of Objectives
The Linear Programming Model
The Stepping-Stone Method
The Modified-Distribution (MODI) Method
Review of the Stepping-Stone and MODI Methods
Special Modeling Considerations

6.3 SUMMARY

References
Review Questions
Problems

Linear programming models are useful in a wide variety of decision-making situations. In the last chapter, we saw that the simplex method is an efficient algorithm for solving linear programming models generally. Efficiency is directly related to the computational effort required to reach an optimal solution to the model. In this chapter, we discuss a certain class of linear programming models for which there exist solution methods more efficient than the simplex method.

6.1 THE PROPERTIES OF THE TRANSPORTATION MODEL

The solution methods we will discuss are really adaptations of the simplex method that take advantage of the special structure of transportation models. In general, the problem these models address is the allocation or assignment of capacity to specific demand requirements in such a way that all capacity and demands are met exactly. More specifically, there are m sources of capacity, $i = 1, 2, \ldots, m$, with source i capable of supplying s_i units of capacity. In addition, there are n demand requirements, $j = 1, 2, \ldots, n$, with the jth one demanding r_j units of demand. The cost of allocating one unit of capacity i to satisfy one unit of requirement j is c_{ij}. In mathematical terms, the model may be written as follows:

$$\text{Min } Z = \sum_{i=1}^{m} \sum_{j=1}^{n} c_{ij} X_{ij}$$

subject to

$$\sum_{j=1}^{n} X_{ij} = s_i, \qquad i = 1, 2, \ldots, m \text{ (capacity)} \tag{6.1}$$

$$\sum_{i=1}^{m} X_{ij} = r_j, \qquad j = 1, 2, \ldots, n \text{ (requirement)}$$

$$X_{ij} \geq 0 \qquad \text{for all } i, j$$

In (6.1), X_{ij} represents the quantity of capacity i used to satisfy requirement j. In order to ensure a feasible solution,

$$\sum_{i=1}^{m} s_i = \sum_{j=1}^{n} r_j \tag{6.2}$$

In addition, s_i and r_j can have any positive values, and m does not have to equal n. Each source i can be used to satisfy all, part, or none of any requirement j, and each requirement j can be satisfied by more than one source i. In Section 6.2 we discuss simple modifications to transportation models in cases where total capacity does not equal total requirements.

Table 6.1 Initial Simplex Tableau

		Source 1				Source 2				Artificial Variables						
C_j		C_{11}	C_{12}	$\cdots$	C_{1n}	C_{21}	C_{22}	$\cdots$	C_{2n}	M	M	$\cdots$	M	M	$\cdots$	M	
	Basis	X_{11}	X_{12}	$\cdots$	X_{1n}	X_{21}	X_{22}	$\cdots$	X_{2n}	A_1	A_2	$\cdots$	A_{m+1}	A_{m+2}	$\cdots$	A_{m+n}	R
M	A_1	1				1				1							s_1
M	A_2		1				1				1						s_2
$\cdots$	$\vdots$			$\cdots$				$\cdots$				$\cdots$					$\vdots$
M	A_{m+1}	1				1							1				r_1
M	A_{m+2}		1				1							1			r_2
$\cdots$	$\vdots$			$\ddots$				$\ddots$							$\ddots$		$\vdots$
M	A_{m+n}				1				1							1	r_n
	z_j	$2M$	$2M$	$\cdots$	$2M$	$2M$	$2M$	$\cdots$	$2M$	M	M	$\cdots$	M	M	$\cdots$	M	
	$c_j - z_j$	$C_{11}-2M$	$C_{12}-2M$	$\cdots$	$C_{1n}-2M$	$C_{21}-2M$	$C_{22}-2M$	$\cdots$	$C_{2n}-2M$	0	0	$\cdots$	0	0	$\cdots$	0	

The transportation model has been considerably used in the area of distribution. The typical problem involves the allocation of a particular commodity produced at a number of factories (sources) to a number of warehouses with certain demands (requirements) in such a way that total transportation costs are minimized (see Chapter 4, Figure 4.1). The resulting allocation of each factory's output to the warehouses is called a distribution pattern. The transportation model can also be used to determine optimal distribution patterns between warehouses and retail outlets. It has been used as well for problems such as production planning, allocation of contracts to bidders, and vehicle allocation (see Problems 1, 2, 4, and 9).

Although the model given by (6.1) can be solved with the simplex method presented in Chapter 5, it has special properties that are exploited by the more efficient, special-purpose solution techniques presented in this chapter. Consider Table 6.1, which contains the initial simplex tableau for (6.1) augmented with artificial variables. Notice that all the technological coefficients, a_{kl}, ($k = 1, 2, \ldots, m + n, l = 1, 2, \ldots, mn$), are either 0 or 1 in the initial tableau. This implies that transforming the pivot-column vector into a unit vector (to introduce a nonbasic variable into the basis on the first iteration) involves only a simple subtraction of the pivot row from the other row containing a 1 in the pivot column. For example, suppose we wanted to introduce X_{11} from Table 6.1 into the basis. Let row 1 be the pivot row. To transform the column vector for X_{11} into a unit vector, we need only subtract row 1 from row $m + 1$. No division or multiplication is required.

The resulting column vectors after the first iteration for X_{11}, X_{12}, X_{1n}, A_1, and R are shown in Table 6.2. Notice that the transformed technical coefficients a'_{kl} in each column vector of Table 6.2 are either $-1, 0$, or $+1$. This will hold true for any iteration. Thus, generating a new basis will only require simple additions or subtractions, and we will never need to multiply or divide to transform the

Table 6.2 Selected Column Vectors After the First Iteration

Row	X_{11}	X_{12}	X_{1n}	A_1	R
1	1	1	1	1	s_1
2	0	0	0	0	s_2
$\vdots$	$\vdots$	$\vdots$	$\vdots$	$\vdots$	$\vdots$
$m + 1$	0	-1	-1	-1	$r_1 - s_1$
$m + 2$	0	1	0	0	r_2
$m + 3$	0	0	0	0	r_3
$\vdots$	$\vdots$	$\vdots$	$\vdots$	$\vdots$	$\vdots$
$m + n$	0	0	1	0	r_n

pivot column to a unit vector. The stepping stone and modified distribution methods (Section 6.2) take advantage of this simplification.

Another property of (6.1) is that the decision variables X_{ij} will be integer valued provided the parameters s_i and r_j are integer valued.[1] Since the transformations required to generate a new basis require only additions and subtractions, the revised entries in the R column vector will always be the result of additions or subtractions of integer quantities (note the entry in row $m + 1$ of column R in Table 6.2). Thus, the entries in the R column vector will always be integer valued. The maximum value that the new basic variable X_{ij}, corresponding to column l in the tableau, can attain in any iteration is given by

$$X_{ij} = \Min_k \left(\frac{b_k}{a'_{kl}} \right) \qquad k = 1, 2, \ldots, m + n \qquad (6.3)$$

where $a'_{kl} > 0$ and b_k refers to the kth element in column vector R. Consequently, X_{ij} will always be integer valued, because b_k will always be integer valued and a'_{kl} for the pivot row will be $+1$. Notice that we have not required the values of X_{ij} to be integer; however, they will always have integer values because of the structure of (6.1), provided the parameters s_i and r_j are integers. This property also simplifies the solution process, and the techniques presented in this chapter will take advantage of this.

6.2   THE STEPPING-STONE AND MODI METHODS

We begin this section by defining a distribution problem and formulating it as a linear programming model. The stepping-stone method, and the more efficient modified distribution (MODI) method, which take advantage of the special structure of these models, will be presented next. Finally, we will discuss several special modeling considerations in this regard.

Problem Identification, Data Gathering, and Specification of Objectives

Plastique, Inc., has two plants that produce various sizes of plastic pipe for use in the construction of new houses and office buildings. Recently, management decided to build a new plant in Milwaukee. Even with this new capacity, demand for the products at each of the four distribution centers exceeds the capability to produce them.

---

[1] Without loss of generality, we will assume that all s_i and r_j are integer valued in this chapter. If values of the parameters s_i, r_j, or both in a transportation model are not integer, we can scale the parameters by multiplying *all* parameters by a suitable constant to make them integer. For example, suppose that s_1 has the most significant digits beyond the decimal point in 11.275. If we multiply all s_i and r_j by 1000, the newly scaled parameters will all be integer. Of course, we must remember to divide the values of X_{ij} by 1000 when we have found the optimal solution.

With the advent of the new plant, the distribution pattern between the three plants and the four distribution centers must be determined. Because of the pipe's bulky nature, management is most concerned about type 1 pipe and wants to determine a minimum-cost shipping pattern for that product. The shipping costs per 100 feet of type 1 pipe from each plant to each distribution center are shown in Table 6.3. In each case, the rate is based on the most economical mode of transportation, given certain minimum service requirements.

Table 6.3   Distribution Costs from Each Plant to Each Distribution Center

| | Distribution Center | | | |
Plant	Atlanta	Denver	St. Louis	Tulsa
Chicago	$10	$ 5	$ 7	$8
Dallas	6	4	8	5
Milwaukee	9	12	10	7

Because demand for all products exceeds the capacity to produce them, a linear programming model was used to determine the product mix that would maximize profits.[2] The planned output per month, as given by the linear programming model for type 1 pipe at each plant, is given in Table 6.4.

Table 6.4   Plant Capacities for the Plastique, Inc., Distribution Problem

Plant	Capacity of Type 1 Pipe, hundreds of feet per month
Chicago	$s_1 = 1500$
Dallas	$s_2 = 1250$
Milwaukee	$s_3 = 2250$
	Total capacity 5000

The total output of the three-plant system is 5000 feet per month (in hundreds) of type 1 pipe. The demand for type 1 pipe at each distribution center was estimated

[2] If the transportation costs are linearly related to the shipping quantities, a linear programming model could be used to solve the product-mix and distribution problems simultaneously. In this case, suppose that, prior to stating the cost in the contract, the transportation carriers require some commitment on total footage shipped each month from each plant (capacities). Each plant deals with only one carrier. This situation would cause nonlinearities in the objective function of the linear program because costs would be a function of a decision variable. This necessitates the two-stage approach in this example.

with a linear-regression model. The total capacity of 5000 feet was allocated to each distribution center in proportion to the forecasted demand at each center. In no case was the allocation in excess of the forecasted demand. The allocated requirements are shown in Table 6.5.

Table 6.5 Distribution-Center Requirements for the Plastique, Inc., Distribution Problem

Distribution Center	Requirements of Type 1 Pipe, hundreds of feet per month
Atlanta	$r_1 = 1100$
Denver	$r_2 = 800$
St. Louis	$r_3 = 1900$
Tulsa	$r_4 = 1200$
Total requirements	5000

The Linear Programming Model

The distribution problem facing Plastique can be formulated as a linear programming model. Let X_{ij} be the quantity of type 1 pipe (in hundreds of feet) shipped from plant i to distribution center j for $i = 1, 2, 3$ and $j = 1, 2, 3, 4$. The objective function can be written as

$$\begin{aligned}
\text{Min } Z = {} & 10X_{11} + 5X_{12} + 7X_{13} + 8X_{14} \\
& + 6X_{21} + 4X_{22} + 8X_{23} + 5X_{24} \\
& + 9X_{31} + 12X_{32} + 10X_{33} + 7X_{34}
\end{aligned} \tag{6.4}$$

The constraints on the capacities of each plant are

$$\begin{aligned}
X_{11} + X_{12} + X_{13} + X_{14} &= 1500 & \text{Chicago} \\
X_{21} + X_{22} + X_{23} + X_{24} &= 1250 & \text{Dallas} \\
X_{31} + X_{32} + X_{33} + X_{34} &= 2250 & \text{Milwaukee}
\end{aligned} \tag{6.5}$$

The constraints ensuring that each distribution center receives its allocated requirements are

$$\begin{aligned}
X_{11} + X_{21} + X_{31} &= 1100 & \text{Atlanta} \\
X_{12} + X_{22} + X_{32} &= 800 & \text{Denver} \\
X_{13} + X_{23} + X_{33} &= 1900 & \text{St. Louis} \\
X_{14} + X_{24} + X_{34} &= 1200 & \text{Tulsa}
\end{aligned} \tag{6.6}$$

In addition, X_{ij} for all i and j must be nonnegative.

Notice that $\sum_{i=1}^{m} s_i = \sum_{j=1}^{n} r_j$, and that the technological coefficients in the constraints (a_{ij}) are equal to 1. Recall from Section 6.1 that if all s_is and r_js are integers, the optimal solution to the model will also be integer valued. The solution can be found by using the simplex method presented in Chapter 5.

The Stepping-Stone Method

Although we already have a method for solving our example problem, the augmented model has twelve decision variables and seven artificial variables (one for each constraint). The regular simplex method involves more work than necessary for problems such as this. The stepping-stone method is based on the regular simplex method but takes advantage of the special structure of these problems to offer an approach that is much easier to apply. The method gets its name from the manner in which the pivot variable is selected in Step 3. As in the regular simplex method, there are several steps in the solution procedure.

Step 1. Set Up the Initial Tableau The initial tableau is a matrix of cells, showing the transportation costs per unit (100 feet of type 1 pipe) between each plant and distribution center, and showing the capacities and requirements at each plant and center, respectively. The costs are in the squares at the upper right-hand corner of each cell. The initial tableau should always ensure that $\sum_{i=1}^{m} s_i = \sum_{j=1}^{n} r_j$. In our problem, this condition is met without any modification to the tableau. Later, we discuss the case in which $\sum_{i=1}^{m} s_i \neq \sum_{j=1}^{n} r_j$.

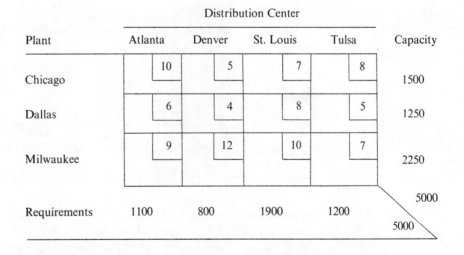

Distribution Center					
Plant	Atlanta	Denver	St. Louis	Tulsa	Capacity
Chicago	10	5	7	8	1500
Dallas	6	4	8	5	1250
Milwaukee	9	12	10	7	2250
					5000
Requirements	1100	800	1900	1200	5000

The matrix provides a convenient way of representing a solution to the problem. A numeric quantity allocated to the cell at the intersection of row i and column j represents a shipment in that amount from plant i to distribution center j. The summation of these quantities along any row (plant) must equal the stated capacity of that row. The summation of these quantities down any column (center) must equal the requirement of that column. This ensures that the constraints on plant capacities and center requirements are not violated. These constraints are called *rim conditions.* The next step provides us with an initial solution to the problem.

Step 2.   Determine an Initial Solution   As in the simplex method, the transportation method requires an initial solution that is subsequently modified in an iterative manner until the optimal solution is determined. We will discuss two approaches to determining an initial solution to a transportation problem: the *northwest-corner method* and *Vogel's approximation method* (VAM).

The northwest-corner method is the quickest method for determining an initial solution to a transportation problem. Starting with the cell in the upper left-hand corner of the initial tableau (northwest corner), we allocate as much as we can without exceeding the capacity of the first row or the requirements of the first column. In our example, this satisfies the requirements of Atlanta, and thus the first column is therefore eliminated from further consideration (shaded), as follows:

Distribution Center

Plant	Atlanta	Denver	St. Louis	Tulsa	Capacity
Chicago	10 1100	5	7	8	1500
Dallas	6	4	8	5	1250
Milwaukee	9	12	10	7	2250
					5000
Requirements	1100	800	1900	1200	5000

With each allocation, we eliminate either a row or a column. If the last allocation was made to cell (i, j), the next allocation would be to either cell $(i + 1, j)$ or cell $(i, j + 1)$, depending on whether a row or column, respectively, was eliminated. Thus, the next allocation should be from Chicago to Denver. Since we only have 400 units of capacity left in Chicago, and Denver requires 800 units, we allocate the remaining 400 units to Denver and eliminate Chicago from further consideration.

Distribution Center

Plant	Atlanta	Denver	St. Louis	Tulsa	Capacity
Chicago	10 1100	5 400	7	8	1500
Dallas	6	4	8	5	1250
Milwaukee	9	12	10	7	2250
Requirements	1100	800	1900	1200	5000 5000

Moving to the next row, the cell to be allocated is Dallas–Denver. The maximum we can allocate here is 400 units, which would just meet Denver's requirement. Because the capacity at Dallas is far in excess of 400 units, we allocate the 400 units and eliminate Denver from the matrix.

Distribution Center

Plant	Atlanta	Denver	St. Louis	Tulsa	Capacity
Chicago	10 1100	5 400	7	8	1500
Dallas	6	4 400	8	5	1250
Milwaukee	9	12	10	7	2250
Requirements	1100	800	1900	1200	5000 5000

There are 850 units of capacity left at Dallas, so the next allocation is the Dallas–St. Louis cell, in the amount of 850.

Distribution Center

Plant	Atlanta	Denver	St. Louis	Tulsa	Capacity
Chicago	10 1100	5 400	7	8	1500
Dallas	6	4 400	8 850	5	1250
Milwaukee	9	12	10	7	2250
					5000
Requirements	1100	800	1900	1200	5000

The remaining allocations are now clear. Milwaukee must ship 1050 units to St. Louis and 1200 units to Tulsa. The result of the northwest-corner method for arriving at an *initial* solution is as follows:

Distribution Center

Plant	Atlanta	Denver	St. Louis	Tulsa	Capacity
Chicago	10 1100	5 400	7	8	1500
Dallas	6	4 400	8 850	5	1250
Milwaukee	9	12	10 1050	7 1200	2250
					5000
Requirements	1100	800	1900	1200	5000

Once an initial solution has been obtained, several conditions must be checked. First, make sure that the sum of the allocations along each row equals the capacity of each row and that the sum of the allocations down each column equals the requirement of each column. The solution must satisfy these *rim conditions*. In our example, the rim conditions are satisfied. We could not achieve this if the sum of the capacities did not equal the sum of the requirements.

Second, successful application of the transportation method requires that there must be $m + n - 1$ allocated cells in any solution. In our case, $m + n - 1 = 3 + 4 - 1 = 6$. Note that 6 cells have allocations in our initial solution. If fewer than $m + n - 1$ cells are allocated, a degenerate condition exists. We will discuss degeneracy later.

Finally, the total cost of the initial solution is found by multiplying the allocation in each cell by the cost in the upper right-hand corner. In our example, this amounts to

$$1100\,(10) + 400\,(5) + 400\,(4) + 850\,(8) + 1050\,(10) + 1200\,(7) = \$40,300.$$

Although the northwest-corner method is an easy way to derive an initial solution, the solution is usually far from optimal. This can be expected because we did not use any cost information in arriving at the initial solution. This implies that we may yet face considerable work in determining the optimal solution. Some of this work can be saved by finding a better initial solution. Although *Vogel's approximation method* (VAM) involves more work than the northwest-corner method, because it recognizes the costs involved, it normally provides a solution that, if not optimal, is close to optimal.

We begin by computing a penalty for each row and column in the matrix. The penalty for a given row is merely the difference between the smallest cost element in the row and the *next largest* cost element in that row. Similarly, the penalty for a given column is the difference between the lowest cost element in the column and the next largest cost element in that column. The penalties for the rows and columns in our example problem are enclosed in circles.

The penalties are similar to opportunity costs because they indicate the per-unit increase in costs if we do not allocate all we can to the lowest cost cell in any row or column. In making our first allocation, it makes sense to choose that

Distribution Center

Plant	Atlanta	Denver	St. Louis	Tulsa	Capacity
Chicago	10	5	7	8	1500 ②
Dallas	6	4	8	5	1250 ①
Milwaukee	9	12	10	7	2250 ②
					5000
Requirements	1100 ③	800 ①	1900 ①	1200 ②	5000

row or column with the largest penalty. In our problem, this turns out to be column 1. We allocate as much as we can to the lowest cost cell in column 1: Dallas–Atlanta. Because Atlanta requires 1100 units and Dallas has a capacity of 1250 units, we allocate 1100 units to the Dallas–Atlanta route and eliminate Atlanta from further consideration.

Distribution Center

Plant	Atlanta	Denver	St. Louis	Tulsa	Capacity
Chicago	10	5	7	8	1500 ②
Dallas	6 1100	4	8	5	1250 ①
Milwaukee	9	12	10	7	2250 ③
					5000
Requirements	1100	800 ①	1900 ①	1200 ②	5000

Once an allocation has been made, the penalties must be recomputed. In our example, the only penalty that changes is the one for the Milwaukee row, as shown above. A penalty of 3 is the largest, and the next allocation is made to the

Distribution Center

Plant	Atlanta	Denver	St. Louis	Tulsa	Capacity
Chicago	10	5	7	8	1500 ②
Dallas	6 1100	4	8	5	1250 ④
Milwaukee	9	12	10	7 1200	2250 ②
					5000
Requirements	1100	800 ①	1900 ①	1200	5000

Milwaukee row in the Tulsa cell because it has the lowest cost. Milwaukee can satisfy all of Tulsa's requirements, and thus we allocate 1200 units from Milwaukee to Tulsa and eliminate Tulsa from further consideration.

The highest penalty is now in the Dallas row. We have already allocated 1100 units to Atlanta, so Dallas has only 150 units of capacity remaining. We allocate these 150 units to the Dallas–Denver route and eliminate Dallas from the matrix.

Distribution Center

Plant	Atlanta	Denver	St. Louis	Tulsa	Capacity
Chicago	10	5	7	8	1500 ②
Dallas	6 / 1100	4 / 150	8	5	1250
Milwaukee	9	12	10	7 / 1200	2250 ②
Requirements	1100	800 ⑦	1900 ③	1200	5000 / 5000

The new penalties indicate that we should now allocate 650 units to the Chicago–Denver route.

Distribution Center

Plant	Atlanta	Denver	St. Louis	Tulsa	Capacity
Chicago	10	5 / 650	7	8	1500
Dallas	6 / 1100	4 / 150	8	5	1250
Milwaukee	9	12	10	7 / 1200	2250
Requirements	1100	800	1900	1200	5000 / 5000

The remaining allocations are now obvious. In order to satisfy the requirements at St. Louis, Chicago, and Milwaukee must ship 850 units and 1050 units, respectively. The VAM initial solution is as follows:

	Distribution Center				
Plant	Atlanta	Denver	St. Louis	Tulsa	Capacity
Chicago	10	5	7	8	1500
		650	850		
Dallas	6	4	8	5	1250
	1100	150			
Milwaukee	9	12	10	7	2250
			1050	1200	
Requirements	1100	800	1900	1200	5000 / 5000

Notice that all rim conditions are satisfied and that 6 cells are allocated. In addition, the total cost of this solution is $35,300. This is a 14% reduction in total cost as compared to the northwest-corner solution. Although more calculations will be necessary to reach an *optimal* solution in this example, the VAM initial solution tends to minimize those calculations by getting us closer to optimality at the start. The major disadvantage of the method is the effort required to find the initial solution itself. In most cases, the extra effort is worth it.

Step 3.   Select the Pivot Variable The stepping-stone method is an iterative procedure that exchanges *one* variable that is in the basis (a positive quantity shipped from a plant to a distribution center), with *one* variable that is not in the

Table 6.6   Vogel's Approximation Method: Initial Solution to the Plastique, Inc., Distribution Problem

	Distribution Center			
Plant	Atlanta	Denver	St. Louis	Tulsa
Chicago	$X_{11} = 0$	$X_{12} = 650$	$X_{13} = 850$	$X_{14} = 0$
Dallas	$X_{21} = 1100$	$X_{22} = 150$	$X_{23} = 0$	$X_{24} = 0$
Milwaukee	$X_{31} = 0$	$X_{32} = 0$	$X_{33} = 1050$	$X_{34} = 1200$

basis (a cell with no allocation) in such a way that the objective criterion (minimal total transportation costs) is improved.[3] We will demonstrate the procedure using the VAM initial solution in Table 6.6.

Each variable with a value of zero is a candidate for inclusion in a new solution. The idea is to replace one of the variables now in the solution (drive it to zero) with one of the variables that is at a zero level. This leads us to the following questions, which must be answered in this and the following step:

1. Which nonbasic variable should be included in the solution?
2. Which basic variable should be made a nonbasic variable?

To answer the first question, recall that in the simplex method for minimization problems, the nonbasic variable that makes the largest per-unit cost reduction is selected to be a basic variable in the next iteration. In other words, the non-basic variable with the most negative net contribution is selected as the *pivot variable*. In terms of the notation we have introduced for the transportation model, the net contribution is equal to the difference between c_{ij}, the cost of shipping one unit from plant i to distribution center j, and z_{ij}, the opportunity cost (or per-unit savings) of a change of one unit in the shipments of certain plants affected by the inclusion of the new route from plant i to center j. The quantity $c_{ij} - z_{ij}$ must be calculated for each nonbasic variable at each iteration. The per-unit cost c_{ij} is given; however, the z_{ij} requires more analysis.

Consider the initial tableau for our problem containing the VAM initial solution.

Distribution Center

Plant	Atlanta	Denver	St. Louis	Tulsa	Capacity
Chicago	10	5	7	8	1500
		650	850	√	
Dallas	6	4	8	5	1250
	1100	150			
Milwaukee	9	12	10	7	2250
			1050	1200	
Requirements	1100	800	1900	1200	5000 / 5000

---

[3] In certain situations, the introduction of one nonbasic variable drives more than one basic variable to zero. This indicates a degenerate condition. The procedure for coping with this situation will be discussed later.

Suppose we want to see if there is any advantage in creating a route from Chicago to Tulsa. The affected "zero-cell" (nonbasic variable X_{14}) is denoted by a check ($\checkmark$). For purposes of calculating $c_{14} - z_{14}$, we hypothesize a shipment of 1 unit from Chicago to Tulsa. Tulsa requires only 1200 units, so we must *decrease* the shipment from Milwaukee to Tulsa by 1 unit. This leaves Milwaukee 1 unit short of its capacity of 2250. In order to utilize its capacity fully, we must increase its shipment to St. Louis by 1 unit. In so doing, St. Louis is now getting 1 more unit than it requires. In order to compensate, we must decrease the shipment from Chicago to St. Louis by 1 unit. No other shipments are affected. These adjustments are shown in the following matrix:

Distribution Center

Plant	Atlanta	Denver	St. Louis	Tulsa		Capacity
Chicago	10	5	7	$\checkmark$	8	1500
		650	849		1	
Dallas	6	4	8		5	1250
	1100	150				
Milwaukee	9	12	10		7	2250
			1051		1199	
						5000
Requirements	1100	800	1900	1200		5000
						5000

Note that the sum along each row equals the capacity of the row, and that the sum down each column equals the requirement of the column. Also note that, with the exception of the zero-cell being evaluated, the only cells affected are *allocated* cells. In computing z_{ij}, we want only to assess the impact on the *basic* variables.

Once we have determined the affected basic variables, we can calculate the net contribution of variable X_{14}. This calculation is shown in Table 6.7. Subtracting 1 unit from the Milwaukee–Tulsa and Chicago–St. Louis shipments represents a savings of $14. The Milwaukee–St. Louis shipment must be increased by 1 unit, which will cost $10. Therefore, the net savings resulting from opening a new route from Chicago to Tulsa is $4 per unit. In other words, $z_{14} = \$4$. Since it costs $8 to ship one unit from Chicago to Tulsa, the net contribution $c_{14} - z_{14} = \$8 - \$4 = \$4$, as shown in Table 6.7.

Obviously, opening a route between Chicago and Tulsa would not be profitable. It would cost an additional $4 per unit shipped on that route, relative to our

Table 6.7   Net Contribution for the Chicago–Tulsa Route

	Shipment Change	Cost Changes	
Add 1 unit	Chicago–Tulsa	+$8	cost increase
Subtract 1 unit	Milwaukee–Tulsa	−$7	cost savings
Add 1 unit	Milwaukee–St. Louis	+$10	cost increase
Subtract 1 unit	Chicago–St. Louis	−$7	cost savings
	Net contribution	+$4	$(c_{14} - z_{14})$

current solution. Other zero-cells must be evaluated, however. We will use the same method for evaluating these cells as we did for Chicago–Tulsa.

The stepping-stone method gets its name from this procedure. In general terms, we begin with the zero-cell to be evaluated by hypothetically allocating 1 unit, then adjusting currently allocated cells to balance the affected row capacities and column requirements alternately. In this respect, the matrix can be viewed as a pond with the allocated cells as *stepping stones*. Starting with the zero-cell, the idea is to move from allocated cell to allocated cell, each time moving in right angles to the last move, subtracting and adding 1 unit to the shipments in an alternating fashion, in such a way that we once again end up at the zero-cell. In so doing, a *loop* is created and all rim conditions are satisfied. Fortunately, there is only one loop for any given zero-cell. Once the loop is found, the net contribution can be calculated.

The loop for the Chicago–Tulsa zero-cell is shown in the following diagram, in which ★ indicates an allocated cell. Note that the loop moves in right-angle directions from each allocated cell in the loop.

	Distribution Center			
Plant	Atlanta	Denver	St. Louis	Tulsa
Chicago		★	★	✓
Dallas	★	★		
Milwaukee			★	★

The loops for the remaining zero-cells are shown in Table 6.8. Note that some loops are more complicated than others. The Dallas–Tulsa loop crosses itself, which is permissible as long as the intersection is at a right angle. The Milwaukee–

Table 6.8   Loops for the Remaining Zero-Cells

1.   Chicago–Atlanta

2.   Dallas–St. Louis

3.   Dallas–Tulsa

4.   Milwaukee–Atlanta

5.   Milwaukee–Denver

Table 6.9 Net Contributions: Remaining Routes

	Shipment Change	Cost Changes
	1. Chicago–Atlanta	
Add 1 unit	Chicago–Atlanta	+$10 cost increase
Subtract 1 unit	Dallas–Atlanta	−$6 cost savings
Add 1 unit	Dallas–Denver	+$4 cost increase
Subtract 1 unit	Chicago–Denver	−$5 cost savings
	Net contribution	+$3 $(C_{11} - Z_{11})$
	2. Dallas–St. Louis	
Add 1 unit	Dallas–St. Louis	+$8 cost increase
Subtract 1 unit	Dallas–Denver	−$4 cost savings
Add 1 unit	Chicago–Denver	+$5 cost increase
Subtract 1 unit	Chicago–St. Louis	−$7 cost savings
	Net contribution	+$2 $(C_{23} - Z_{23})$
	3. Dallas–Tulsa	
Add 1 unit	Dallas–Tulsa	+$5 cost increase
Subtract 1 unit	Milwaukee–Tulsa	−$7 cost savings
Add 1 unit	Milwaukee–St. Louis	+$10 cost savings
Subtract 1 unit	Chicago–St. Louis	−$7 cost savings
Add 1 unit	Chicago–Denver	+$5 cost increase
Subtract 1 unit	Dallas–Denver	−$4 cost savings
	Net contribution	+$1 $(C_{24} - Z_{24})$
	4. Milwaukee–Atlanta	
Add 1 unit	Milwaukee–Atlanta	+$9 cost increase
Subtract 1 unit	Dallas–Atlanta	−$6 cost savings
Add 1 unit	Dallas–Denver	+$4 cost increase
Subtract 1 unit	Chicago–Denver	−$5 cost savings
Add 1 unit	Chicago–St. Louis	+$7 cost increase
Subtract 1 unit	Milwaukee–St. Louis	−$10 cost savings
	Net contribution	−$1 $(C_{31} - Z_{31})$
	5. Milwaukee–Denver	
Add 1 unit	Milwaukee–Denver	+$12 cost increase
Subtract 1 unit	Chicago–Denver	−$5 cost savings
Add 1 unit	Chicago–St. Louis	+$7 cost increase
Subtract 1 unit	Milwaukee–St. Louis	−$10 cost savings
	Net contribution	+$4 $(C_{32} - Z_{32})$

Denver loop passes over the cell allocated for Dallas–Denver. If it had stopped there, the only next move would have been Dallas–Atlanta; however, no right-angle move to an allocated cell could have been made from that position. Finally, it should be mentioned that the loop can be traversed in two directions. The arrows in Table 6.8 indicate one possible direction; the reverse direction is also permissible.

Once the loop for a given zero-cell has been identified, the net contribution can be calculated. Table 6.9 contains the net contribution calculations for the remaining zero-cells. Note that the cost contributions alternate in sign as we traverse each loop, depending on whether we are adding or subtracting a unit from an existing shipment. After a little practice, finding the loops and computing the net contributions can be done mentally. The extra matrices and calculations are shown in Tables 6.8 and 6.9.

We can now answer the first question posed earlier. We should select as the pivot variable the variable with most negative net contribution. For our example, the pivot variable is X_{31}, representing the Milwaukee–Atlanta route. For each additional unit shipped along that new route, we can save \$1 relative to our current solution.

Step 4. Generate a New Solution To answer the second question posed earlier, we must determine which basic variable will leave the basis as we introduce the new route to the solution. This amounts to determining which present shipment will be reduced to zero as we increase the quantity shipped along the new route. Consider the following tableau, which contains the initial VAM solution and the loop for the Milwaukee–Atlanta route:

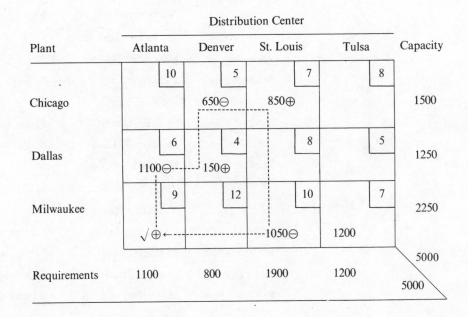

The plus or minus in the circle of each cell in the loop indicates that a unit must be added or subtracted from the corresponding shipment in that cell in order to satisfy the rim conditions. Note that each row and column affected has one plus cell and one minus cell. Each plus and minus corresponds to a plus and minus in the calculation of the net contribution for the Milwaukee–Atlanta route in Table 6.9.

We can save $1 for each unit shipped along the new route, so we would like to ship as many units as we can, keeping in mind that we do not want to cause any present shipments (basic variables) to go negative. Thus, in order to determine the maximum shipment along the new route, we must examine the shipments in the loop for which units must be subtracted. In particular, the *maximum* amount that can be shipped from Milwaukee to Atlanta is equal to the *minimum* shipment found in the cells with a minus. With reference to the last tableau, the shipment from Milwaukee to Atlanta = Min(1100, 650, 1050) = 650. Thus, the shipment that will be reduced to zero in the new solution is Chicago–Denver (variable X_{12}).

The new solution is found by traversing the loop, adding 650 units to each plus cell, and subtracting 650 units from each minus cell. The new solution is shown in the following tableau:

Plant	Distribution Center				Capacity
	Atlanta	Denver	St. Louis	Tulsa	
Chicago	10	5	7	8	1500
			1500		
Dallas	6	4	8	5	1250
	450	800			
Milwaukee	9	12	10	7	2250
	650		400	1200	
Requirements	1100	800	1900	1200	5000
					5000

Note that all rim conditions are satisfied, and that there are still 6 allocated cells. The cost of the new solution is $34,650. Recall that the initial solution cost $35,300. As expected, we have reduced costs by $650 because the net contribution for Milwaukee–Atlanta was −$1 and we allocated 650 units to that route.

Step 5 Check for Optimality The present solution is optimal if the net contribution for each zero-cell, $c_{ij} - z_{ij}$, is positive or zero. After each new solution, the loops and net contributions for each zero-cell must be reevaluated using the stepping-stone method. The new net contributions are in the lower left-hand corner of each zero-cell in the following matrix; the basic variables are circled:

Distribution Center

Plant	Atlanta	Denver	St. Louis	Tulsa	Capacity
Chicago	10 +4	5 +1	7 (1500)	8 +4	1500
Dallas	6 (450)	4 (800)	8 +1	5 +1	1250
Milwaukee	9 (650)	12 +5	10 (400)	7 (1200)	2250
					5000
Requirements	1100	800	1900	1200	5000

Because all net contributions are positive, the present solution is optimal. If one or more net contribution were negative, we would have to repeat steps 3, 4, and 5 until the criterion for optimality was met.

As for Plastique, Inc., the distribution pattern for the production system, including the new plant at Milwaukee, has been determined, as shown in Table 6.10.

Table 6.10 Optimal Distribution Pattern for Plastique, Inc.

Route		Quantity, hundreds
From	To	of feet of type 1 pipe
Chicago	St. Louis	1500
Dallas	Atlanta	450
Dallas	Denver	800
Milwaukee	Atlanta	650
Milwaukee	St. Louis	400
Milwaukee	Tulsa	1200
Total cost of distribution: $34,650		

It is interesting to note that two low-cost routes, Chicago–Denver and Dallas–Tulsa, are not used. This serves to emphasize that the solution to these problems is not always intuitively obvious.

The Modified-Distribution (MODI) Method

As we have just seen, the stepping-stone method is an improvement over the simplex method for models that can be solved manually. The stepping-stone method requires that we compute the loop for every nonbasic variable so that the pivot variable can be determined. More efficient methods for selecting the pivot variable are available. These methods are based on the *dual* of the transportation model and the property of complementary slackness (see Chapter 5, Section 5.2). A variety of computerized methods for efficiently solving large-scale transportation models employ the concepts of duality. We will first develop the dual for the transportation model, then demonstrate the modified-distribution (MODI) method, which is based on the dual.

The Dual Consider the model given by (6.1) with the side condition (6.2). All of the constraints of the model are equalities, so we must convert each constraint to an equivalent pair of upper-bound and lower-bound constraints before we can formulate the dual (see Section 5.2). After converting all of the upper-bound constraints to lower-bound constraints, we get (6.7), which is of the standard form of (5.28)

$$\text{Min } Z = \sum_{i=1}^{n} \sum_{j=1}^{m} c_{ij} X_{ij}$$

subject to

$$\sum_{j=1}^{n} X_{ij} \geq s_i \qquad i = 1, 2, \ldots, m$$

$$\sum_{j=1}^{n} (-1) X_{ij} \geq -s_i \qquad i = 1, 2, \ldots, m \qquad (6.7)$$

$$\sum_{i=1}^{m} X_{ij} \geq r_j \qquad j = 1, 2, \ldots, n$$

$$\sum_{i=1}^{m} (-1) X_{ij} \geq -r_j \qquad j = 1, 2, \ldots, n$$

$$X_{ij} \geq 0 \qquad \text{for all } i, j$$

In the dual formulation, there must be a dual variable for each row in the primal model. Let U_i^+ and U_i^- be the dual variables corresponding to the source i constraints, where the right-hand side in (6.7) is positive and negative, respectively. Similarly, define V_j^+ and V_j^- for the requirement constraints in (6.7). We have defined these two sets of dual variables to ease the development of the MODI method. The dual model is given by

$$\text{Max } Z' = \sum_{i=1}^{m} (U_i^+ - U_i^-)s_i + \sum_{j=1}^{n} (V_j^+ - V_j^-)r_j$$

subject to

$$(U_i^+ - U_i^-) + (V_j^+ - V_j^-) \leq c_{ij} \qquad \text{for all } i, j$$

$$U_i^+, U_i^-, V_j^+, V_j^- \geq 0 \qquad \text{for all } i, j$$

(6.8)

Note that in (6.8), U_i^+ and U_i^- always appear *together* in the objective function and in any constraint involving source i. In effect, they act as one variable, which can take on positive or negative values. Either one, or the other—but never both—will be in the optimal basis, because one is the negative of the other.[4] If, for example, $U_i^+ = 0$ and $U_i^- = 5$, the net result is -5 for the two variables. The same can be said for V_j^+ and V_j^-. Since we will not be using the simplex method presented in Chapter 5 for solving (6.7), we can simplify (6.7) by introducing a new set of variables that is unrestricted in sign.

$$U_i = U_i^+ - U_i^- \qquad i = 1, 2, \ldots, m$$

$$V_j = V_j^+ - V_j^- \qquad j = 1, 2, \ldots, n$$

(6.9)

The dual variables are shadow prices for the resources (capacities) and requirements. That is, U_i is the relative implicit contribution (value) of an additional unit of capacity at source i, and V_j is the relative implicit contribution of an additional unit shipped to requirement j.

The revised dual model can now be written as

$$\text{Max } Z' = \sum_{i=1}^{m} U_i s_i + \sum_{j=1}^{n} V_j r_j$$

subject to

$$U_i + V_j \leq c_{ij} \qquad \text{for all } i, j$$

$$U_i, V_j \qquad \qquad \text{Unrestricted in sign for all } i, j$$

(6.10)

---

[4] Since both variables always appear together in any constraint for source i, if we force the column vector for U_i^+ into a unit vector, the column vector for U_i^- will be similar to a unit vector but will have a -1 in the pivot row and thus cannot be part of the basis. The same holds true for forcing U_i^- into the basis.

As an example of (6.10), the dual model corresponding to (6.4), (6.5), and (6.6) for the Plastique, Inc., distribution problem is

$$\text{Max } Z' = 1500U_1 + 1250U_2 + 2250U_3$$
$$+ 1100V_1 + 800V_2 + 1900V_3 + 1200V_4$$

subject to

$$\begin{array}{llll}
U_1 & + V_1 & & \leq 10 \\
U_1 & + V_2 & & \leq 5 \\
U_1 & + V_3 & & \leq 7 \\
U_1 & + V_4 & & \leq 8 \\
U_2 & + V_1 & & \leq 6 \\
U_2 & + V_2 & & \leq 4 \\
U_2 & + V_3 & & \leq 8 \\
U_2 & + V_4 & & \leq 5 \\
U_3 + V_1 & & & \leq 9 \\
U_3 & + V_2 & & \leq 12 \\
U_3 & + V_3 & & \leq 10 \\
U_3 & + V_4 & & \leq 7
\end{array}$$

(6.11)

$$U_1, U_2, U_3, V_1, V_2, V_3, V_4 \text{ Unrestricted in sign for all } i, j$$

Application of the MODI Method The dual formulation can be very useful for solving transportation models. In general, the duality theorems of Section 5.2 state that (1) if a solution X_{ij} for all (i, j) is feasible with respect to (6.1), (2) if solutions U_i and V_j for all (i, j) are feasible with respect to (6.10), and (3) if

$$X_{ij}(c_{ij} - U_i - V_j) = 0 \qquad \text{for all } i, j \tag{6.12}$$

then X_{ij} constitutes an *optimal* solution to (6.1). The relationship in (6.12) is the property of *complementary slackness* for a transportation model. It states that if $X_{ij} > 0$ and is feasible in (6.1), then the combined value of a unit of capacity at source $i\,(U_i)$ and a unit shipped to requirement $j\,(V_j)$ must *equal* the cost to transport that unit from source i to requirement $j\,(c_{ij})$. Whenever $U_i + V_j < c_{ij}$, it would *not* be optimal to have $X_{ij} > 0$ because it would cost us more to ship the unit on a route from i to j than it is worth (in a relative sense) at source i and under requirement j. Finally, if we ever had $U_i + V_j > c_{ij}$ for some $X_{ij} = 0$, we would certainly want to create the route from i to j (make $X_{ij} > 0$), because the combined relative value of a unit at source i and requirement j exceeds the cost to ship it from i to j. Of course, if $U_i + V_j > c_{ij}$, we know we do not have an optimal solution for another reason—U_i and V_j are not feasible in (6.10).

Based on the previous discussion, it is now apparent that the opportunity cost of shipping one unit from source i to requirement j, z_{ij}, used in the stepping-stone method, is equal to $U_i + V_j$, the sum of the dual variables associated with source i and requirement j. Consequently, $(c_{ij} - U_i - V_j)$ is the per-unit net contribution to the objective function for opening a route from i to j. Let us define

$$\Delta_{ij} = c_{ij} - U_i - V_j \qquad \text{for all } i, j \qquad (6.13)$$

Table 6.11 summarizes our previous discussion.[5]

Table 6.11 Interpretation of Various Values for the Net Contribution

Condition	Corresponding Value of Primal Variable	Interpretation
(a) $\Delta_{ij} = 0$	$X_{ij} > 0$	X_{ij} is currently in the basis of the primal model
(b) $\Delta_{ij} > 0$	$X_{ij} = 0$	Given the present values of U_i and V_j, it is not desirable to put X_{ij} into the basis of the primal model at this time
(c) $\Delta_{ij} < 0$	$X_{ij} = 0$	Given the present value of U_i and V_i, X_{ij} is a candidate for inclusion in the basis of the primal model

Let us apply this logic to the VAM initial solution of the Plastique, Inc., distribution problem. Using Table 6.6, the dual model given by (6.11), (6.13), and condition a of Table 6.11, we have the following system of linear equations (one for each basic variable):

$$
\begin{aligned}
U_1 \quad &+ V_2 \qquad\qquad\qquad\quad = 5 \\
U_1 \quad &\qquad + V_3 \qquad\qquad\quad = 7 \\
U_2 + V_1 \quad &\qquad\qquad\qquad\qquad = 6 \\
U_2 \quad &+ V_2 \qquad\qquad\qquad = 4 \\
U_3 \quad &\qquad + V_3 \qquad\qquad = 10 \\
U_3 \quad &\qquad\qquad + V_4 \quad = 7
\end{aligned}
\qquad (6.14)
$$

We can solve (6.14) for trial values of U_i and V_j. Note that we have seven variables but only six equations. Six of the variables can be solved in terms of the seventh. Then, no matter which value we choose for the seventh variable, the other six variables will assume values *relative* to it (recall that U_i and V_j are unrestricted in sign). We will arbitrarily choose to assign U_1 a value of zero to simplify calculations. Given that $U_1 = 0$, V_2 and V_3 can be computed immediately.

---

[5] If the model is degenerate, we may get a situation in which $\Delta_{ij} = 0$ and $X_{ij} = 0$. We will discuss degeneracy later. To simplify the discussion here, we will assume that the model is not degenerate.

Given V_2, U_2 and then V_1 can be calculated. Finally, given V_3, U_3 and then V_4 can be determined. This results in the following trial values for U_i and V_j:

$$U_1 = 0 \qquad V_1 = 7$$
$$U_2 = -1 \qquad V_2 = 5$$
$$U_3 = 3 \qquad V_3 = 7$$
$$V_4 = 4$$

Table 6.12 contains the net contributions for all variables, using Table 6.3 and (6.13). Compare the results of the nonbasic variables with those in Tables 6.7 and 6.9. We have been able to calculate the net contributions of the nonbasic variables without the effort of determining the loops for each one. Since $\Delta_{31} < 0$ we know that it would pay to open the route from 3 to 1 (Milwaukee to Atlanta). We can now continue as we did in the stepping-stone method to generate a new solution to the model.

Table 6.12   Net Contributions Using the Dual Variables

Basic Variables	Nonbasic Variables
$\Delta_{12} = 5 - 0 - 5 = 0$	$\Delta_{11} = 10 - 0 - 7 = 3$
$\Delta_{13} = 7 - 0 - 7 = 0$	$\Delta_{14} = 8 - 0 - 4 = 4$
$\Delta_{21} = 6 + 1 - 7 = 0$	$\Delta_{23} = 8 + 1 - 7 = 2$
$\Delta_{22} = 4 + 1 - 5 = 0$	$\Delta_{24} = 5 + 1 - 4 = 2$
$\Delta_{33} = 10 - 3 - 7 = 0$	$\Delta_{31} = 9 - 3 - 7 = -1$
$\Delta_{34} = 7 - 3 - 4 = 0$	$\Delta_{32} = 12 - 3 - 5 = 4$

The MODI method can be streamlined even further, so as to avoid having to write out all the equations in (6.14). With respect to the steps in the stepping-stone method, we can modify the transportation tableau in Step 1 to include an extra column for U_i and an extra row for V_j.

Step 2 is the same as the stepping-stone method. In our example, we have used the VAM initial solution. In Step 3, however, we compute U_i, V_j, and Δ_{ij} rather than finding the loops for each nonbasic variable as in the stepping-stone method. The dual variables U_i and V_j can be easily computed in the tableau, given $U_1 = 0$. Simply scan the first row until you encounter an allocated cell in column j and compute the corresponding V_j using the relationship $V_j = c_{1j}$. Do this for each allocated cell in row 1. Thereafter, use the relationship $U_i + V_j = c_{ij}$ for each allocated cell in rows 2 and 3, until all U_i and V_j have been calculated. The net contributions Δ_{ij} for each zero cell can now be easily calculated using (6.13). These quantities are shown in the lower left-hand corners of the zero cells.

Distribution Center

Plant	Atlanta	Denver	St. Louis	Tulsa	Capacity	U_i
Chicago	10 +3	5 (650)	7 (850)	8 +4	1500	0
Dallas	6 (1100)	4 (150)	8 +2	5 +2	1250	−1
Milwaukee	9 −1	12 +4	10 (1050)	7 (1200)	2250	3
Requirements	1100	800	1900	1200	5000 / 5000	
V_j	7	5	7	4		

Step 4; generating a new solution, and Step 5, checking for optimality, are identical to the stepping-stone method. With respect to the Plastique, Inc., distribution problem, the Milwaukee–Atlanta route should be opened and the application of Step 4 results in the MODI tableau in Table 6.13. We see that this solution is optimal because $\Delta_{ij} \geq 0$ for all nonbasic variables.

The MODI method is identical to the stepping-stone method with the exception of Step 3—selecting the pivot variable. The MODI method employs the

Table 6.13 Optimal MODI Tableau for the Plastique, Inc., Distribution Problem

Distribution Center

Plant	Atlanta	Denver	St. Louis	Tulsa	Capacity	U_i
Chicago	10 +4	5 +1	7 (1500)	8 +4	1500	0
Dallas	6 (450)	4 (800)	8 +1	5 +1	1250	0
Milwaukee	9 (650)	12 +5	10 (400)	7 (1200)	2250	3
Requirements	1100	800	1900	1200	5000 / 5000	
V_j	6	4	7	4		

theorems of duality to minimize the effort required to select pivot variables. Note that we do not eliminate the need to find loops. Nonetheless, we need only find *one* loop at each iteration (for the pivot variable), as opposed to finding the loop for each nonbasic variable at each iteration as in the stepping-stone method. The consequence is that the MODI method offers enormous computational advantages for large-scale transportation models. Many computer codes using these concepts are available for large transportation problems.

Review of the Stepping-Stone and MODI Methods

We have seen that the stepping-stone method is an iterative procedure based on the simplex method. The steps in the solution process follow.

Step 1. Set Up the Initial Tableau Design a matrix that has a source for each row and a demand for each column. Put the cost of allocating one unit of capacity i to demand j in the upper right-hand corner of cell ij for $i = 1, 2, \ldots, m$, and $j = 1, 2, \ldots, n$. Put the capacity s_i of each source at the end of its row and the requirement r_j of each demand at the bottom of its column. Make sure that

$$\sum_{i=1}^{m} s_i = \sum_{j=1}^{n} r_j$$

Step 2. Determine an Initial Solution This can be accomplished with the northwest-corner method or Vogel's approximation method. The northwest-corner method is as follows:

1. Allocate as much as possible to the cell in the upper left-hand corner of the matrix. Do not violate the rim conditions. This will eliminate either a row or a column from further consideration.
2. If a row is eliminated, move down one row and allocate as much as possible to that cell. If a column is eliminated, move to the next column and allocate as much as possible to that cell. If both a row and column are eliminated, move diagonally downward to the next row and column and make an allocation to that cell. In any case, the maximum allocation is equal to the minimum of the remaining capacity of the row and the remaining requirement of the column.
3. Repeat number 2 until a complete initial solution is obtained. Check to be sure that all rim conditions are satisfied, and that $m + n - 1$ cells are allocated.

Vogel's approximation method is as follows:

1. For each row, compute the difference between the smallest-cost element and the next largest-cost element of the row. Repeat for each column. These can be considered penalties for not making an allocation to the lowest-cost cell.
2. Find the largest penalty. Allocate as much as possible to the lowest-cost cell in the corresponding row or column. This will eliminate a row or column from further consideration.

3. Repeat numbers 1 and 2 until a complete initial solution is obtained. Check to be sure that all rim conditions are satisfied, and that $m + n - 1$ cells are allocated.

Step 3. Select the Pivot Variable For each zero-cell, find the loop using the stepping-stone method. Compute the net contribution of each zero-cell by traversing the loop, adding the c_{ij}s for cells that must have units added, and subtracting the c_{ij}s for cells that must have units subtracted. Select the cell with the most negative net contribution for entry into the solution.

Step 4. Generate a New Solution The maximum quantity to be allocated to the chosen cell is the minimum of the allocations to the cells for which units must be subtracted in the loop for the pivot variable. Allocate the quantity to the chosen cell, adjusting the allocations of every cell in the loop to satisfy the rim conditions.

Step 5. Check for Optimality If the net contributions of all zero-cells are positive or zero, the present solution is optimal. If not, repeat Steps 3, 4, and 5 until the criterion for optimality is met.

The MODI method is similar to the stepping-stone method except for Step 3.

Step 1. Set up the Initial Tableau This is the same as in the stepping-stone method, except that an extra column for U_i and an extra row for V_j are added.

Step 2. Determine an Initial Solution This is the same as in the stepping-stone method.

Step 3. Select the Pivot Variable Set $U_1 = 0$. Compute the remaining dual variables $U_2, U_3, \ldots, V_1, V_2, \ldots$, such that $U_i + V_j = c_{ij}$ for all occupied cells in the matrix. Compute the net contribution $\Delta_{ij} = c_{ij} - U_i - V_j$ for all zero cells (nonbasic variables).

Step 4. Generate a New Solution This is the same as in the stepping-stone method.

Step 5. Check for Optimality This is the same as in the stepping-stone method.

Special Modeling Considerations

We will now discuss several special situations that require slight modifications to the transportation matrix. Modification to the *size* of the initial matrix is required for situations in which total supply does not equal total requirements. Modifications to the *costs* in the initial matrix are needed when some unacceptable allocations exist or when the objective is to maximize some criterion such as total profits or revenues. The *allocations* in the matrix at any iteration must be adjusted somewhat when degeneracy occurs during the solution process.

Total Supply Is Not Equal to Total Demand The stepping-stone and MODI methods rely on the fact that $\sum_{i=1}^{m} s_i = \sum_{j=1}^{n} r_j$. If this is not the case, an additional row or column must be added to the initial matrix, with an additional capacity or requirement such as that in the modified matrix the total supply equals the total requirements. Only *one* additional dummy row or column need ever be added. An additional row implies that $\sum_{i=1}^{m} s_i < \sum_{j=1}^{n} r_j$ in the original problem, and that not all requirements will be satisfied in the optimal solution. An additional column implies that $\sum_{i=1}^{m} s_i > \sum_{j=1}^{n} r_j$ in the original problem, and that the capacity of the sources will not be fully utilized in the optimal solution. There is usually no preference as to which requirement will not be met or which capacity will not be utilized, and therefore the costs in the cells of the new column or row are usually zero.

Suppose, for example, that the new plant to be built in Milwaukee for Plastique, Inc., is to have a capacity of 2500 units per month, as opposed to the 2250 units in the previous example. Now, $\sum_{i=1}^{3} s_i = 5250$, and $\sum_{j=1}^{4} r_j = 5000$. Since total supply exceeds total requirements by 250 units, an additional column, representing a dummy demand of 250 units per month, must be added to the initial matrix. The modified matrix is shown here, with the northwest-corner-method initial solution.

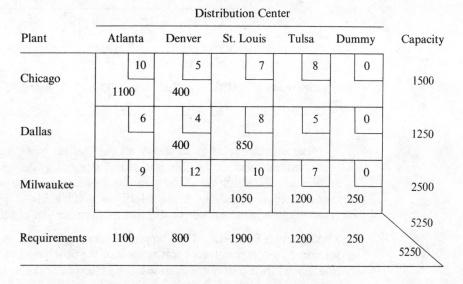

Plant	Atlanta	Denver	St. Louis	Tulsa	Dummy	Capacity
Chicago	10 / 1100	5 / 400	7	8	0	1500
Dallas	6	4 / 400	8 / 850	5	0	1250
Milwaukee	9	12	10 / 1050	7 / 1200	0 / 250	2500
Requirements	1100	800	1900	1200	250	5250 / 5250

Distribution Center

The solution procedures presented earlier can now be applied to the modified matrix. The optimal solution will specify how the unused capacity of 250 units should be distributed among the three plants. The solution of this modified problem is left as an exercise (see Problem 5).

Unacceptable Allocations   Quite often in the sort of allocation problems that can be analyzed with the transportation model, certain allocations are undesirable or impossible. In situations such as this, a large fictitious cost M can be assigned to the cells corresponding to the unacceptable allocations. This cost is much larger than any other cost in the matrix. Once the initial matrix has been modified in this way, standard procedures for solving transportation models can be used to find the optimal allocations.

The modification to the initial matrix can be seen in the following example. Suppose that the rail carriers serving Dallas and Milwaukee have informed Plastique, Inc., that they cannot serve the Dallas–Denver and the Milwaukee–Tulsa routes. Because these two routes cannot be used, the costs in the initial matrix must be modified as follows:

Distribution Center

Plant	Atlanta	Denver	St. Louis	Tulsa	Dummy	Capacity
Chicago	10	5	7	8	0	1500
		800	700			
Dallas	6	M	8	5	0	1250
	50			1200		
Milwaukee	9	12	10	M	0	2500
	1050		1200		250	
Requirements	1100	800	1900	1200	250	5250
						5250

The optimal solution is shown in the matrix. Note that the unacceptable routes are not part of the solution. Nonetheless, they may be in the solution at some intermediate phase of the solution process. If, for instance, the northwest-corner method is used, the initial solution would include both of the unacceptable routes. Subsequent iterations will drive these routes out of the solution.

Maximization Problems The stepping-stone and MODI methods are designed for minimization problems because most of the problems analyzed by transportation models have cost minimization as an objective. Maximization problems, however, can also be analyzed with these techniques. One way in which this can be done is to use the original objective-function coefficients (profits, revenues, or some other criterion to be maximized), and change the criterion for optimality to the following: the present solution is optimal if all $c_{ij} - z_{ij}$ are zero or negative. The pivot variable at each iteration is the one with the largest (most positive) net contribution Δ_{ij}.

Perhaps a less confusing and simpler approach is to compute the *opportunity costs* of each column. The opportunity cost for each cell in a given column is computed by subtracting the profit (or revenue, and so forth) element in each cell from the largest profit element in the column. The cell with the largest profit will have a zero opportunity cost. We seek to minimize total opportunity costs of the modified problem; for this, either of the procedures we used for the Plastique, Inc., example would work. See Problem 7 for a maximization problem that can be solved with a transportation model.

Degeneracy   Whenever a solution (intermediate or optimal) involves fewer than $m + n - 1$ allocated cells, it is *degenerate*. This can happen when determining an initial solution, or at any iteration in which the introduction of a new variable drives more than one basic variable to zero. The latter situation occurs when two or more "minus cells" in the loop have the same minimum quantity allocated. Allocating this minimum quantity to the new cell drives the present allocations of more then one cell in the loop to zero.

If fewer than $m + n - 1$ cells are allocated, it is impossible to find the loop for one or more zero-cells in the next iteration. Unless something is done, the solution procedure grinds to a halt.

There is a simple way to overcome degeneracy when solving a transportation model: whenever degeneracy occurs, allocate a minute quantity ε to as many cells as required so as to have $m + n - 1$ allocated cells once again. The quantity is so small that if a cell has an allocation of ε in the final solution, it is considered to be zero. These ε allocations must be made to zero-cells for which no loop can be found. Thereafter, any cell with an ε is considered to be in the basis and can be used to find loops for the zero-cells. The solution procedures presented earlier can then be applied.

Consider the following matrix, which contains an intermediate solution to a transportation model:

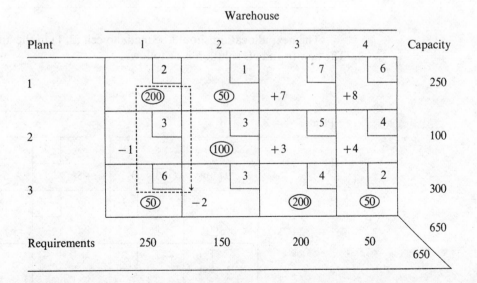

The obvious allocation should be made to cell (3, 2), as indicated by the net contributions shown in the lower left-hand corner of each zero-cell. But note that the two minus-cells in the loop contain the same minimal quantity, 50. By allocating

50 to cell (3, 2), both cells (3, 1) and (1, 2) become zero. This leaves us with only five allocated cells when six are required. Consequently, the only zero-cells for which we can find loops are (2, 3) and (2, 4). To overcome this problem, we can choose any cell for which we cannot find a loop and allocate ε to it. We might as well choose from these cells the one with the lowest cost. This turns out to be (1, 2), as shown in the following:

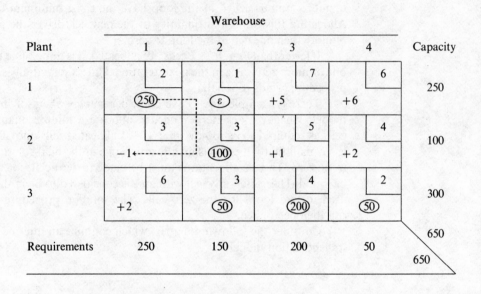

The next allocation should be made to cell (2, 1) in the amount of 100 units. The new (optimal) solution is as follows:

Note that cell (1, 2) has a quantity of $100 + \varepsilon$ in it; however, the ε is so small that plant 1 ships exactly 100 units to warehouse 2. Sometimes the ε appears in a minus cell in the loop corresponding to a zero-cell with the most negative net contribution. In such cases, the new cell gets an allocation of ε, and the total cost of the solution stays the same as before. In some problems, this may happen several times before the criterion for optimality is met.

6.3 SUMMARY

In this chapter we introduced the transportation model, which is one of a special class of linear programming models. Although the simplex method presented in Chapter 5 can be used to solve this model, the special-purpose solution techniques presented in this chapter are much more efficient than the simplex method. The added efficiency comes from taking advantage of the special properties of the transportation model. The first property—that the column vector of any nonbasic variable at any iteration will contain only transformed technological coefficients of $-1, 0,$ or 1—implies that the row operations needed to force the column vector of the pivot variable into a unit vector require only addition or subtraction. The second property—that the optimal solution will be integer-valued provided the source capacities and the requirements are integer-valued—makes manual computations easier. These two properties allow us to use the matrix or tableau format to reduce greatly the complexity of the problem. If we had to solve a problem that could be modeled in the form of (6.1), the simplex tableau would have $m + n$ rows, mn columns for the decision variables, and $m + n$ columns for the artificial variables, as shown in Table 6.1. The tableau for a transportation model would have only m rows and n columns. In addition, we would have to drive all $m + n$ artificial variables out of the basis using the simplex method before we would have our first feasible solution, whereas the northwest-corner method or Vogel's approximation method gives us a quick, initial, feasible solution to transportation models without the involvement of artificial variables. Subsequent iterations can be done in the tableau through simple additions or subtractions.

We have presented both the stepping-stone and MODI methods for solving transportation models for a particular reason. Although the MODI method is more efficient, the stepping-stone method allowed us to introduce the concepts of the loop for nonbasic variables and, in a straightforward manner, to present the concept of net contribution in transportation models. Using the theorems of duality, the MODI method eliminates the need for finding loops for each nonbasic variable at each iteration by computing net contributions directly from dual variables. Because of the significant computational savings involved, various computer routines are available that use the dual formulation of the transportation model.

With regard to the use of the computer, it should be pointed out that nobody solves problems of practical size by manual methods. In this chapter and the previous chapters on linear programming, we have concentrated on small-scale problems so that the principles associated with the various techniques could be easily presented and understood. Nonetheless, computer codes are available that quickly and efficiently perform the calculations to yield a solution to a model. Some codes actually prepare the data for the constraints and objective function with a routine called a "matrix generator" and then solve the problem. The necessary data for a particular problem can be stored on "disk files" or magnetic tape, and with a minimum of additional input from the decision maker, the computer codes can execute the matrix generator subroutine, the optimizing subroutine, and a report generator that provides the solution in a format useful to management. Linear programming models in general, and transportation models in particular would not be practical without the computer. The intelligent *use* of the solutions requires a firm understanding of the principles and assumptions associated with the techniques by which they are reached.

This chapter actually provides a bridge between the simplex method for solving general linear programming models in Chapter 5, and the methods for solving integer programming models in Chapter 7. The fact that in transportation models the optimal solution will be integer-valued provided the source capacities and requirements are integer-valued allows us to use these models to analyze problems in which only integer-valued decision variables make sense, provided the problems can be modeled in the general form given in (6.1). The discussion, examples, and problems in this chapter demonstrate the wide variety of problems that can be analyzed with these models. In the next chapter we will discuss methods for solving integer programming models that cannot be solved with the techniques presented in this chapter.

References   Dantzig, G.B., *Linear Programming and Extensions*, Princeton, N.J.: Princeton University Press, 1963.

Gass, S.I., *Linear Programming: Methods and Applications*, 4th ed. New York: McGraw-Hill, 1975.

Hadley, G., *Linear Programming*, Reading, Mass.: Addison-Wesley, 1962.

Hillier, F.S., and Lieberman, G.J., *Introduction to Operations Research*, 2nd ed. San Francisco: Holden Day, 1974.

Hughes, A.J., and Graiwog, D.E., *Linear Programming: An Emphasis on Decision Making*, Reading, Mass.: Addison-Wesley, 1973.

Levin, R.I., and Lamone, R.P., *Linear Programming for Management Decisions*, Homewood, Ill.: Richard D. Irwin, 1969.

Spivey, W.A., and Thrall, R.M., *Linear Optimization*, New York: Holt, Rinehart and Winston, 1970.

Strum, J.E., *Introduction to Linear Programming*, San Francisco: Holden Day, 1972.

Wagner, H.M., *Principles of Operations Research*, 2nd ed. Englewood Cliffs, N.J.: Prentice-Hall, 1975.

Review Questions

1. Explain why the optimal solution to a transportation model will be integer-valued provided the source capacities and requirements are integer-valued.

2. Transportation models can be solved with linear programming, the stepping-stone method, and the MODI method. Discuss the advantages of the stepping-stone method over the regular simplex method in lieu for selecting alternatives in a transportation problem.

3. The stepping-stone method is an adaptation of the simplex method of linear programming. With this in mind, state the assumptions one must make in utilizing a transportation model. Do you feel these assumptions are too restrictive or limiting for the transportation model to be useful in practice? Explain.

4. What are the advantages of using the MODI method in lieu of the stepping-stone method?

5. Why is it so important to have the total supply equal to the total requirements in a transportation model to be solved using the stepping-stone or MODI methods?

6. What trade-offs must one consider in choosing between the northwest-corner method and Vogel's approximation method for determining an initial solution to a transportation model?

7. What is the relationship between the dual variables U_i and V_j, and z_{ij}—the opportunity-cost of shipping 1 unit from source i to requirement j—used in the stepping-stone method? Given the definitions of U_i and V_j, provide an intuitive explanation of this relationship.

8. You have been chosen to resolve a distribution problem facing your company. You have suggested a transportation model to evaluate and select alternatives. Your boss would like to know a little about the method of solution. Explain, in simple terminology, the logic of the stepping-stone method for finding loops and net contributions. Use an example tableau if necessary.

9. Suppose that the total requirements of the distribution centers exceed the total capacity of the three plants in the Plastique, Inc., problem. Discuss how you would modify the initial tableau to account for this.

10. Suppose Plastique, Inc., wishes to decrease the capacity of the Dallas plant by 1 unit. What is the expected effect on total transportation costs? Give an explanation of your answer.

Problems

1. The production manager of a machine shop would like to determine the monthly production of each of four high-volume products on machines 1, 2, and 3. Each machine can produce at the same rate; however, the per-unit

cost of production for each product varies according to the machine used. These cost variances are due to the reject rate on each machine, the utility costs to run them, and the ability of the operator assigned to them. Setup costs are inconsequential because each machine can produce more than one product in a month without significant downtime for setups. The production costs per unit (in dollars), the monthly capacities of each machine, and the monthly product requirements are shown in Table P6.1.

(a) Formulate the transportation model for this problem.

(b) Using the northwest-corner method to find an initial feasible solution, use the stepping-stone method to find the optimal production plan.

(c) Use Vogel's approximation method to find an initial feasible solution. How much better is this solution compared to the northwest-corner solution? How many more iterations are required to find the optimal solution?

Table P6.1

Costs	Product			
Machine	A	B	C	D
1	$1.60	$1.65	$1.55	$1.70
2	$1.20	$1.55	$1.75	$1.40
3	$1.50	$2.00	$1.95	$1.60

Capacities

Machine	Units per Month
1	2200
2	1500
3	1550

Requirements

Product	Units per Month
A	1000
B	3000
C	750
D	500

2. Consider Problem 1. Using the northwest-corner method to find an initial feasible solution, use the MODI method to find the optimal production plan. Discuss the difference in efficiency between MODI and the stepping-stone method, based on your experiences in Problem 1.

3. The Cryevski Corporation has two plants, which service three regional warehouses. Management wishes to find a shipping pattern that minimizes the cost of transportation. The weekly capacities of each plant, the weekly requirements at each warehouse, and the per-unit shipping costs are given in Table P6.2.

   (a) Set up the linear programming model for this transportation problem, including all artificial variables.
   (b) Solve the model using the simplex method.
   (c) Solve the model using the MODI method of linear programming.
   (d) Discuss the advantages of the MODI method over the simplex method for this model.

Table P6.2

Plant	Capacity	Warehouse	Requirement
Columbus	3000	Chicago	1200
Richmond	2000	Cleveland	2100
		Buffalo	1700

Shipping Costs, $ per unit

Warehouse

Plant	Chicago	Cleveland	Buffalo
Columbus	$4	$3	$6
Richmond	$6	$4	$8

4. The production manager of a certain manufacturing firm must recommend a production plan for the next three quarters. Output capabilities and sales requirements have been reduced to man-hours as a unit of measurement. Regular time and overtime can be used for each quarter; however, the firm has certain policies regarding their use: (1) Regular-time capacity in quarter t can be used to satisfy sales requirements in quarters $t, t + 1, \ldots$; however, it cannot be used to satisfy previous requirements in quarters $t - 1, t - 2$, $\ldots$. (2) Overtime capacity in quarter t can be used to satisfy requirements in quarters $t, t - 1, t - 2, \ldots$. This cannot be used to satisfy future requirements, however. Thus, regular-time capacity can be used to satisfy current and future requirements, whereas overtime capacity can be used only to satisfy current requirements and back-orders.

The cost to produce 1 hour of requirements on regular time in quarter t (including materials and labor) is \$10. If that hour of production is held in inventory for sale in quarter $t + 1$, the total cost is \$14, to account for inventory carrying charges. It costs \$13 to use 1 hour of overtime capacity in quarter t, and \$15 to use it to satisfy a back-order from quarter $t - 1$. The cost matrix is shown in Table P6.3a, where M designates an unacceptable allocation. The sales requirements in quarters 1, 2, and 3 are 4000, 8000, and 7000 man-hours, respectively. The present plan for each quarter is given in Table P6.3b.

Table P6.3a

		Sales Requirements		
Type of Capacity		Quarter 1	Quarter 2	Quarter 3
Quarter 1	Regular time	\$10	\$14	\$18
	Overtime	\$13	M	M
Quarter 2	Regular time	M	\$10	\$14
	Overtime	\$15	\$13	M
Quarter 3	Regular time	M	M	\$10
	Overtime	\$17	\$15	\$13

Table P6.3b

		Capacity, hours
Quarter 1	Regular time	6,000
	Overtime	1,000
Quarter 2	Regular time	5,500
	Overtime	500
Quarter 3	Regular time	5,500
	Overtime	500
	Total	19,000

(a) Formulate the transportation model for this problem. Use the northwest-corner method to find an initial solution. You will have two allocations to a cell with an M. Solve the model using the MODI method.

5. Consider the Plastique, Inc., distribution problem of Section 6.2, in which capacity exceeds requirements.
   (a) Solve the problem starting with the given northwest-corner method initial solution, using either the stepping-stone method or the MODI method.
   (b) Determine the initial solution using VAM.
   (c) Compare the two initial solutions and discuss the advantages and disadvantages of VAM for this problem.

6. The city of Hometown has asked for bids on four construction projects. The deadline for awarding the contracts is rapidly approaching, and the city would like to award the contracts to the four companies that tendered bids. Two of the companies, *A* and *D*, have indicated that they would be willing to accept, at most, two of the contracts, whereas companies *B* and *C* will be able to accept only one contract each. The city, however, wishes to award the contracts in such a way that the total cost of the four contracts is minimized. Only one contractor can be awarded a given contract, but two contractors

Table P6.4

Contractor	Contract			
	1	2	3	4
A	10	50	30	70
B	20	40	25	60
C	12	55	35	65
D	11	42	28	67

can be awarded more than one contract, as previously noted. The bids (in thousands) are shown in Table P6.4.
   (a) Solve this problem using the MODI method. You will need to modify the initial tableau to include a dummy "contract" with a requirement of 2. This problem involves considerable degeneracy; therefore, make sure that $m + n - 1$ cells are allocated at each iteration. Put ε in low-cost cells for which no loop can be found.

7. The Able Company has four warehouses located across the country. Each warehouse stocks a certain commodity that is needed by five retailers. Depending on the transportation costs and prices the retailers are willing to pay, the profit per unit differs according to the warehouse from which it is shipped and the retailer who buys it. The profits per unit are given in Table P6.5a. The availability of the commodity (in units) and the requirements of each retailer are shown in Table P6.5b.

Table P6.5a

Warehouse		Retailer				
		1	2	3	4	5
A		4	5	2	6	6
B		3	4	3	7	5
C		5	7	6	8	7
D		2	6	4	5	4

Table P6.5b

Warehouse	Availability	Retailer	Requirement
A	200	1	150
B	200	2	200
C	100	3	250
D	300	4	100
Total	800	5	300
		Total	1000

(a) Determine the shipping pattern that maximizes profits.

(b) Suppose Able cannot ship from warehouse C to retailer 3 because of problems in finding suitable carriers. Would this change your recommendation in part a? If so, find the new shipping pattern. *Note.* You may use the solution to part a as an initial solution.

8. Consider Problem 1. Given the optimal production plan, answer the following questions. After each answer return to the original conditions in Problem 1.

(a) A methods-improvement task force has indicated that better methods employed by the operator of machine 1 on product D could result in a lower per-unit cost. How much would the per-unit cost have to decrease before it would be advisable to have machine 1 produce product D?

(b) How much would the per-unit cost of producing product B on machine 2 have to increase before the present solution would no longer be optimal?

9. The Acme Car Rental Company rents cars in various cities. Currently, cities 1, 2, 3, and 4 have a surplus of cars, and cities A, B, C, and D have a need for more cars. Management would like to reallocate the cars in such a

way that the total distance traveled is minimized. The mileage, car availabilities, and car requirements are given in Table P6.6.

Table P6.6

Mileage	To City			
From City	A	B	C	D
1	10	10	20	25
2	20	15	8	10
3	15	40	10	15
4	8	20	4	16

Car Availability	
City	Number of Cars Available
1	2
2	8
3	4
4	6

Car Requirements	
City	Number of Cars Required
A	5
B	7
C	3
D	4

(a) Formulate the transportation model for this problem. Note that
supply exceeds requirements. Solve the model for the optimal allocation of cars.

Problems 10 through 13 are called linear-assignment problems. They are
special cases of the transportation problem. In each case, the rim values b_i and r_j
are equal to unity. The decision variables X_{ij} take on values of either unity or zero.
The use of the stepping-stone or MODI methods involves a considerable amount
of degeneracy.

10. The postmaster of Hometown must award four contracts for truck routes.
Policy says that a trucking firm can be awarded at most one truck route, and
that each route must be awarded to only one trucking firm. Four trucking

firms have tendered bids for the four routes. The bids, expressed in tens of thousands of dollars, are given in Table P6.7. If the postmaster's objective is to minimize the total cost of the contracts, which routes should each trucking firm get? Use the MODI method to get your answer.

Table P6.7

Trucking Firm	Route			
	A	B	C	D
1	$ 5	$ 3	$8	$10
2	$12	$10	$9	$ 8
3	$15	$ 7	$6	$ 9
4	$ 9	$ 5	$7	$12

11. The production supervisor at the Kramer Manufacturing Corporation has three custom orders to get out of the shop as fast as possible. Although the three orders are behind their promised delivery dates, each job has only one operation remaining. The supervisor has three available machinists to do the required work; however, each machinist has a different productivity. The supervisor recognizes the need to assign each employee to a different order because the nature of the work precludes any advantage to assigning more than one person to an order at a time. In order to get the three orders to the customers as soon as possible, the supervisor must minimize the total time needed to finish the required work. The estimated time (in hours) required for each machinist to perform the remaining work on each order is shown in Table P6.8.

Table P6.8

Machinist	Order		
	1	2	3
Abbott	10	6	15
Baker	12	7	18
Collins	11	4	20

(a) Set up the assignment problem as a linear programming model, augmented with all artificial variables.

(b) Solve the same problem using the MODI method presented in this chapter.

12. A district court has four dockets of cases packaged according to the nature of the legalities associated with each case. Unfortunately, there are only three judges. The district court is able to estimate the number of days each judge would take to clear the cases on any docket. These estimates, based upon prior experiences, are provided in Table P6.9. If the objective is to minimize

Table P6.9

Judge	Docket			
	1	2	3	4
A	20	10	30	18
B	25	9	27	22
C	17	15	25	14

the total time of hearing all the cases on the dockets, use the MODI method to assign judges to dockets and to determine which docket will have to wait until a judge is available.

13. The Acme Oil Company has recently begun drilling operations at seven new sites in Texas, Oklahoma, and the Gulf of Mexico. In order to ensure that the drilling operations are kept on schedule, Acme wants to send a troubleshooter to each site. Currently, there are eight troubleshooters at sites where the drilling is almost completed. It is desired to get seven of the troubleshooters to the seven new sites in such a way that the total distance traveled by the troubleshooters is minimized. The distances (in miles) are shown in Table P6.10. Recommend an assignment of troubleshooters to drilling sites so as to minimize the total distance traveled.

Table P6.10

Troubleshooter	Site						
	1	2	3	4	5	6	7
A	500	300	1050	700	900	750	400
B	850	250	1100	800	1050	600	700
C	600	500	800	850	1000	675	500
D	550	300	1000	750	950	675	475
E	900	350	975	1000	1100	650	425
F	875	400	1150	725	875	800	600
G	650	325	1025	675	925	775	500
H	700	450	875	725	1000	625	450

7

INTEGER PROGRAMMING METHODS

7.1 EXAMPLES OF INTEGER PROGRAMMING MODELS

Capital Budgeting
Plant Location
Production Scheduling

7.2 CUTTING-PLANE METHOD

Steps in the Cutting-Plane Method
Summary of the Cutting-Plane Method
Practical Considerations of Cutting-Plane Methods

7.3 BRANCH-AND-BOUND

Steps in the Branch-and-Bound Method
Finding the Optimal Solution
Summary of the Branch-and-Bound Method
Practical Considerations of Branch-and-Bound Methods

7.4 SUMMARY

References
Review Questions
Problems

Many practical problems involve decision variables that must be integer-valued. Linear programming techniques such as the simplex method do not guarantee integer-valued solutions unless the model has a special structure, such as those presented in Chapter 6, for example. Integer programming models require all of the assumptions implicit in linear programming models except that certain specified variables must be nonnegative integers in the optimal solution. If all of the variables must be integer-valued, the model is a *pure*-integer programming model, whereas if only a subset of the variables must be integer, the model is called a *mixed*-integer programming model.

Numerous techniques have been developed for solving integer programming models. You might wonder why a regular linear programming model could not be used, with the resulting values of the decision variables "rounded off" to the nearest integer value. Although this sounds reasonable, we must consider the implications of this approach. Suppose we had a linear programming model with n variables that must be integer-valued, and of which $k \leq n$ have fractional values in the optimal linear programming solution. Simply rounding each of the k decision variables to the nearest integer value might cause infeasibility with respect to a number of constraints in the model. To ensure a feasible integer solution with this intuitive approach, we should evaluate a multitude of solutions, keeping each of the $n - k$ integer-valued decision variables at their present values, and systematically adjusting each of the k variables to its "next lower integer value" and then to its "next higher integer value." Thus, we must evaluate 2^k different integer solutions for feasibility, selecting the feasible integer solution that is best with respect to the objective function. This can be a very tedious task for a model of reasonable dimensions. For example, if $k = 16$, there would be 65,536 solutions to check for feasibility.

Even if we had the patience to perform all of the feasibility checks, we would not be guaranteed an *optimal* integer solution because we have not considered adjustment of the $n - k$ variables that had integer values in the original linear programming solution. By way of example, consider the media-mix model of Chapter 4, which is reproduced in (7.1). Suppose

$$\text{Min } Z = 2000X_1 + 3500X_2$$

subject to

$$50{,}000X_1 + 30{,}000X_2 \geq 900{,}000$$
$$10X_1 + \quad 15X_2 \geq \quad 300 \qquad (7.1)$$
$$X_1 \qquad\qquad \leq \quad 22$$
$$X_2 \leq \quad 25$$
$$X_1, X_2 \qquad\quad \geq \quad 0$$

and that we desire an integer solution to the model. The linear programming solution yields $(X_1, X_2) = (22, 5.33)$, and $Z = \$62,666.67$. According to our previous discussion, $n = 2$, $k = 1$, and we would examine only two integer solutions for feasibility: $(22, 5)$ and $(22, 6)$. The solution $(22, 5)$ is infeasible with respect to the second constraint of (7.1). Thus, we are left with $(22, 6)$, which is feasible and yields $Z = \$65,000$. The optimal integer solution is $(21, 6)$, however, with $Z = \$63,000$. Even though the model is small and the optimal solution can easily be found by trial and error, the example demonstrates that optimal integer solutions cannot always be found simply by rounding off the fractional-valued decision variables to the nearest integer value. In this chapter, we will present two approaches for solving integer programming models: the *cutting-plane method* and the *branch-and-bound method*.

7.1   EXAMPLES OF INTEGER PROGRAMMING MODELS

Integer programming applications can be found in all of the major functional areas of a business. The following examples will demonstrate the variety of these applications, as well as the nature of certain constraint types that are typically required.

Capital Budgeting

Capital budgeting involves the selection of a set of projects or investments such that expected return is maximized and the capital available for investment is not exceeded. Since it normally does not make sense to invest in fractional projects, the decision variable for project i, X_i, must be either one or zero in the optimal solution. If X_i equals one, project i is accepted, whereas if X_i equals zero, the project is rejected.

Consider the following pure integer programming model:

$$\text{Max } Z = \sum_{i=1}^{m} c_i X_i$$

subject to

$$\sum_{i=1}^{m} a_i X_i \le B \qquad\qquad (7.2)$$

$$X_i = 0, 1, \qquad i = 1, 2, \ldots, m$$

where c_i is the discounted return over the life of project i, a_i is the capital outlay for project i, and B is the capital budget.

The optimal solution to the foregoing model might be found by inspection if m is not very large; however, other constraints on the projects may make solution by inspection or trial-and-error methods frustrating. For example, suppose that it is undesirable to invest in *both* projects 3 and 4. These projects could be alternative approaches to resolving a certain bottleneck in production. It would not make sense to invest in both projects. The following constraint could be added to the model:

$$X_3 + X_4 \leq 1 \tag{7.3}$$

If X_3 is one in the optimal solution, X_4 must be zero, and vice versa. This constraint is an example of a constraint for *mutually exclusive* projects.

Some projects may be contingent on the acceptance of other projects. For example, project 7 may be the expansion of a loading dock, and project 10 may be the purchase of five new tractor-trailer rigs. The new trucks could not be used unless the loading dock is expanded. A new constraint, called a *contingency* constraint must be added to the model.

$$X_{10} \leq X_7$$

or

$$X_{10} - X_7 \leq 0 \tag{7.4}$$

Thus, if X_7 equals one, X_{10} can be zero or one. If X_7 equals zero, X_{10} must also be zero.

The capital-budgeting model that we have presented, including the mutually exclusive constraints and the contingency constraints, is a special case of the so-called *knapsack model*. The model gets its name from the problem faced by a traveler who must pack a knapsack with items for a trip. Each of the m available items has a value c_i and has a certain weight, a_i pounds. The maximum allowable payload is B pounds. Of course, there could be budgetary constraints and *mutually exclusive* and *contingency* constraints. The objective is to determine the payload that maximizes the total value. This model has application for cargo-loading problems as well as for capital budgeting.

Plant Location

In Chapter 6 we discussed a transportation model that could be used to determine optimal shipping patterns from m plants to n distribution centers. The transportation model assumes that the m plants have already been located, and that the total capacity of the system is known a priori. A plant-location model is a generalization of the transportation model in which the objective is to determine the locations of the m plants as well as the shipping pattern in such a way that total costs are minimized. Suppose there is a significant fixed charge F_i for opening a plant at site i. These costs could consist of construction and land costs, which may vary across the country. In addition, a plant at site i will have a capacity of s_i units per period. Each distribution center j has a requirement of r_j units per period. Finally, it costs c_{ij} to manufacture and ship one unit of output from site i to distribution center j.

We can formulate this problem as a pure-integer programming model. Let

$$Y_i = \begin{cases} 1 \text{ if site } i \text{ is selected} \\ 0 \text{ otherwise} \end{cases}$$

X_{ij} = quantity shipped from site i to distribution center j

The complete model can now be written as

$$\text{Min } Z = \sum_{i=1}^{m} F_i y_i + \sum_{i=1}^{m} \sum_{j=1}^{n} c_{ij} X_{ij}$$

subject to

$$\sum_{j=1}^{n} X_{ij} \leq s_i y_i \qquad i = 1, 2, \ldots, m \qquad \text{(supply)}$$

$$\sum_{i=1}^{m} X_{ij} = r_j \qquad j = 1, 2, \ldots, n \qquad \text{(demand)}$$

$$Y_i = 0, 1 \qquad \text{for all } i$$

$$X_{ij} = \text{nonnegative integer} \qquad \text{for all } i, j$$

(7.5)

Note that this model is very similar to the transportation model presented in Chapter 6. The only difference is the addition of the binary variables Y_i in the objective function and the supply constraints. The supply constraints ensure that the capacity of site i is used only if a plant is located there. If it is not necessary to require integer-valued X_{ij}s, the model would be a *mixed-integer* programming model.

Production Scheduling

Integer programming problems are frequently encountered in the area of production and operations management. Managers are often faced with problems involving discrete quantities such as batch sizes, machines, machine setups, and, of course, production personnel. As an example, we will consider a production-scheduling problem in which there are m jobs, $i = 1, 2, \ldots, m$ currently available for processing. Each job has n_i operations to be completed. The factory has K machine centers, $k = 1, 2, \ldots, K$, through which the m jobs must be sequenced. No job requires the same machine center more than once. The objective is to determine the starting times of each job at each machine on which it must be processed in such a way that the total time required for processing the m jobs is minimized. We will see that the model for this problem is a mixed-integer programming model.

There are two basic types of constraints in this model: *precedence* constraints and *machine interference* constraints. Starting with the precedence constraints, let X_{ijk} be the starting time of job i, operation j, on machine k. Also, let p_{ijk} be the total processing and setup time for job i, operation j, on machine k. Then, given the routing for job i, certain operations must precede certain other operations in the normal production sequence. Thus, if operation 5 of job 2 on machine 7 must *precede* operation 6 on machine 3, we have the following constraint:

$$X_{257} + p_{257} \leq X_{263} \tag{7.6}$$

This constraint ensures that the starting time of the sixth operation on job 2 is at least as large as the starting time of the fifth operation plus the processing and setup time for the fifth operation. All such precedence relationships must be specified for each job.

The machine-interference constraints ensure that two or more jobs are not scheduled on the same machine at the same time. These constraints provide an example of *either-or* constraints, which are commonly encountered in integer programming models. In order that operation 3 of job 4 and operation 8 of job 6 are not scheduled simultaneously on machine 2, either

$$X_{432} \geq X_{682} + p_{682} \qquad \text{(job 6 precedes job 4)}$$

or $\hspace{9cm}$ (7.7)

$$X_{682} \geq X_{432} + p_{432} \qquad \text{(job 4 precedes job 6)}$$

Unfortunately, the constraints in (7.7) are inconsistent. Both cannot be satisfied simultaneously. Suppose that $p_{682} = 10$ and $p_{432} = 5$, and that X_{682} is chosen to be 30. The first constraint implies that $X_{432} \geq 40$ and that job 6 precedes job 4; however, the second constraint implies that $X_{682} \geq 45$, which is a contradiction. This contradiction is present no matter what positive values are chosen for X_{432} or X_{682}.

In order to overcome this difficulty, we introduce a binary variable, Y_{ilk}, such that

$$Y_{ilk} = \begin{cases} 1 \text{ if job } i \text{ precedes job } l \text{ on machine } k \\ 0 \text{ otherwise} \end{cases}$$

Now, let M be a very large positive number. Then we can write the either-or constraints as

$$MY_{462} + X_{432} \geq X_{682} + p_{682}$$
$$M(1 - Y_{462}) + X_{682} \geq X_{432} + p_{432} \tag{7.8}$$

If $Y_{462} = 1$, the first constraint is made redundant and the second constraint is binding. Similarly, if $Y_{462} = 0$, the first constraint is binding and the second constraint is redundant.

Using our previous example, job 6 precedes job 4, which implies that $Y_{462} = 0$ and

$$0 + X_{432} \geq 40$$

$$M + X_{682} \geq X_{432} + 5$$

Now X_{432} can take on any feasible value without causing a contradiction in the constraints. $M + X_{682}$ is certainly larger than $X_{432} + 5$. These machine-interference constraints must be specified for each machine and for all jobs for which there may be a potential conflict.

As stated earlier, the objective is to minimize the total time required for processing all m jobs. Because of this particular objective, another set of constraints must be specified. We wish to ensure that the completion time of each job is as small as possible. Suppose that operation 7 on machine 4 is the *last* operation for job 3. Then, if T is the total time to minimize, we have

$$X_{374} + p_{374} \leq T \tag{7.9}$$

where T is a variable. A similar constraint must be specified for each job.

The model, then, consists of the objective function

$$\text{Min } Z = T \tag{7.10}$$

plus all the precedence, machine interference, and completion-time constraints in the form of (7.6), (7.8), and (7.9), respectively. Of course, all variables X_{ijk} must be nonnegative, and all Y_{ilk} must be zero or one. This model is an example of a *mixed-integer* programming model because X_{ijk} can take on continuous values (fractions of hours are permitted, for example); however Y_{ilk} must be integer-valued.

The models presented in this section are examples of the variety of applications of integer programming models. The rest of the chapter is devoted to the presentation of solution methodologies for models such as these.

7.2   CUTTING-PLANE METHOD

The cutting-plane method is an iterative approach for solving *pure*-integer programming models; it makes use of the simplex method of linear programming Recall from Chapter 5 that the constraints of a linear programming model define a *feasible region* for the selection of alternatives. Unfortunately, the feasible region contains alternatives for which fractional values for the decision variables are permissible. At each iteration, the cutting-plane approach generates a new constraint that eliminates (makes infeasible) certain noninteger alternatives in such a way that all pure-integer alternatives remain feasible. The process continues until the simplex method finds the optimal integer solution.

We will now demonstrate the steps in the cutting plans method by applying it to the following product-mix model:

$$\text{Max } Z = 6X_1 + 5X_2 \qquad \text{Profits}$$

subject to

$$9X_1 + 3X_2 \leq 18 \qquad \text{Resource 1} \tag{7.11}$$

$$\tfrac{4}{5}X_1 + \tfrac{4}{5}X_2 \leq 2\tfrac{2}{5} \qquad \text{Resource 2}$$

$$X_1, X_2 \geq 0 \text{ and integer}$$

Steps in the Cutting-Plane Method

Step 1. Integerize the Original Constraints   The cutting-plane method requires that all constraints have integer coefficients and right-hand sides. Any model can easily be transformed to satisfy this requirement by multiplying both sides of each constraint by a suitable constant. For example, the first constraint in our model is already in integer form; however, the second constraint can be multiplied by 5 to satisfy the requirement—that is,

$$5(\tfrac{4}{5})X_1 + 5(\tfrac{4}{5})X_2 \le 5(\tfrac{12}{5})$$

or

$$4X_1 + 4X_2 \le 12 \tag{7.12}$$

Note that we could have multiplied the constraint by $\tfrac{5}{4}$ and also arrived at an integer form. It makes no difference which constant is used because the relationship between X_1 and X_2 is not affected.

The complete model, in augmented form, can now be written

$$\text{Max } Z = 6X_1 + 5X_2 + 0S_1 + 0S_2$$

subject to

$$
\begin{aligned}
9X_1 + 3X_2 + S_1 \quad\;\;\; &= 18 \qquad \text{Resource 1} \tag{7.13}\\
4X_1 + 4X_2 \quad\;\; + S_2 &= 12 \qquad \text{Resource 2}\\
X_1, X_2, S_1, S_2 \quad\;\; &\ge 0 \qquad \text{and integer}
\end{aligned}
$$

Step 2. Solve the Linear Programming Model   If it were not for the integer requirements, the augmented model in the previous step would be an ordinary linear programming model. In this step we solve the model as if it were an ordinary linear programming model. If the resulting solution is integer-valued, the optimal solution has been found. If not, we must proceed to Step 3.

The initial simplex tableau for our example problem follows. Applying the standard simplex procedure for maximization problems we find that the pivot variable is X_1, the pivot row is row 1, and the pivot element is 9.

c_j	Basis	6 X_1	5 X_2	0 S_1	0 S_2	R	Ratio
→0	S_1	⑨	3	1	0	18	2
0	S_2	4	4	0	1	12	3
	z_j	0	0	0	0	0	
	$c_j - z_j$	6	5	0	0		

After the necessary row operations, we arrive at the following tableau:

c_j	Basis	6 X_1	5 X_2	0 S_1	0 S_2	R	Ratio
6	X_1	1	$\frac{1}{3}$	$\frac{1}{9}$	0	2	6
→ 0	S_2	0	$\boxed{\frac{8}{3}}$	$-\frac{4}{9}$	1	4	$\frac{12}{8} = \frac{3}{2}$
	z_j	6	2	$\frac{2}{3}$	0	12	
	$c_j - z_j$	0	3 ↑	$-\frac{2}{3}$	0		

Note that the present solution is integer-valued. The criterion for optimality has not been met, however. We must continue by introducing X_2 to the basis, thereby replacing S_2. The final tableau follows.

c_j	Basis	X_1	X_2	S_1	S_2	R	Ratio
6	X_1	1	0	$\frac{1}{6}$	$-\frac{1}{8}$	$\frac{3}{2}$	
5	X_2	0	1	$-\frac{1}{6}$	$\frac{3}{8}$	$\frac{3}{2}$	
	z_j	6	5	$\frac{1}{6}$	$\frac{9}{8}$	$\frac{33}{2}$	
	$c_j - z_j$	0	0	$-\frac{1}{6}$	$-\frac{9}{8}$		

The optimal solution to the linear programming model (no integer restrictions) is

$$X_1 = \tfrac{3}{2}$$
$$X_2 = \tfrac{3}{2}$$
$$S_1 = 0$$
$$S_2 = 0$$
$$Z = \tfrac{33}{2}$$

It is obvious that we do not have the optimal integer solution. This is verified by Figure 7.1. The dark circles represent the feasible integer solutions to the model. The feasible region defined by the constraints allows fractional solutions, however, and one of these solutions has been chosen by the simplex method as the optimal solution to the linear programming model. The object of the next step is to re-define the feasible region so as to make the previous noninteger solution infeasible while retaining all feasible integer solutions.

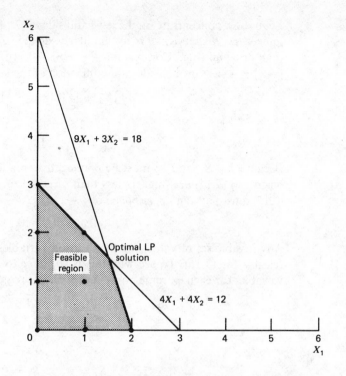

Figure 7.1 Feasible integer solutions for the integer product-mix problem.

Step 3. Construct the Cutting-Plane Constraint We failed to get an integer solution in the previous step, and we must therefore modify the model in such a way that the previous solution is infeasible. We can do this by adding a new constraint, or cutting plane, to the model. We begin by determining the variable in the previous solution with the largest fractional value. In our example,

$$X_1 = \tfrac{3}{2} = 1\tfrac{1}{2}$$

$$X_2 = \tfrac{3}{2} = 1\tfrac{1}{2}$$

$$S_1 = 0$$

$$S_2 = 0$$

Because we have a tie between X_1 and X_2, we arbitrarily choose X_1. Note that the slack variables are also considered in this step, because in a pure-integer programming model all slack and surplus variables must also be integer-valued in the optimal solution.

Having chosen X_1, consider the equation in the optimal linear programming tableau corresponding to X_1

$$X_1 + \tfrac{1}{6}S_1 - \tfrac{1}{8}S_2 = \tfrac{3}{2} \tag{7.14}$$

Let us now concentrate on the left-hand side of (7.14). Define $[a'_{ij}]$ to be the largest integer *less than or equal to* a'_{ij}. Similarly, define $[b'_i]$ to be the largest integer less than or equal to b'_i. For example, $[\frac{2}{3}] = 0$, $[\frac{5}{3}] = 1$, $[8.4] = 8$, $[-\frac{12}{5}] = -3$, and $[-\frac{1}{7}] = -1$. Now consider a modification of the left side of (7.14)—that is,

$$[1]X_1 + [\tfrac{1}{6}]S_1 + [-\tfrac{1}{8}]S_2$$

or

$$X_1 + 0S_1 - 1S_2 \tag{7.15}$$

Because X_1, S_1, and S_2 must be nonnegative in a feasible solution, and the coefficients in (7.15) are integers less than or equal to those of the left side of (7.14), (7.15) must have an *upper bound* of $\frac{3}{2}$

$$X_1 + 0S_1 - 1S_2 \leq \tfrac{3}{2} \tag{7.16}$$

Any feasible set of values for the decision variables with respect to (7.14) is also feasible for (7.16). To see why this is so, refer to Figure 7.1. The values of the variables for each extreme point in the feasible region are as follows:

(1)	(2)	(3)	(4)
$X_1 = 0$	$X_1 = 0$	$X_1 = \frac{3}{2}$	$X_1 = 2$
$X_2 = 0$	$X_2 = 3$	$X_2 = \frac{3}{2}$	$X_2 = 0$
$S_1 = 18$	$S_1 = 9$	$S_1 = 0$	$S_1 = 0$
$S_2 = 12$	$S_2 = 0$	$S_2 = 0$	$S_2 = 4$

Both relationships for X_1—(7.14) and (7.16)—are satisfied for these four solutions to the model, as shown in Table 7.1.

Table 7.1 Calculations Showing that Both Relationships for X_1 are Satisfied for the Four Extreme-Point Solutions

Extreme Point	Relationships for X_1	
	$X_1 + \frac{1}{6}S_1 - \frac{1}{8}S_2 = \frac{3}{2}$	$X_1 + 0S_1 - 1S_2 \leq \frac{3}{2}$
1	$0 + \frac{1}{6}(18) - \frac{1}{8}(12) = \frac{3}{2}$	$0 + 0(18) - 1(12) \leq \frac{3}{2}$
	$\frac{3}{2} = \frac{3}{2}$	$-12 < \frac{3}{2}$
2	$0 + \frac{1}{6}(9) - \frac{1}{8}(0) = \frac{3}{2}$	$0 + 0(9) - 1(0) \leq \frac{3}{2}$
	$\frac{3}{2} = \frac{3}{2}$	$0 < \frac{3}{2}$
3	$\frac{3}{2} + \frac{1}{6}(0) - \frac{1}{8}(0) = \frac{3}{2}$	$\frac{3}{2} + 0(0) - 1(0) \leq \frac{3}{2}$
	$\frac{3}{2} = \frac{3}{2}$	$\frac{3}{2} = \frac{3}{2}$
4	$2 + \frac{1}{6}(0) - \frac{1}{8}(4) = \frac{3}{2}$	$2 + 0(0) - 1(4) \leq \frac{3}{2}$
	$\frac{3}{2} = \frac{3}{2}$	$-2 < \frac{3}{2}$

Unfortunately, (7.16) still allows noninteger values for X_1 (see extreme point 3 in Table 7.1). In an optimal solution to the integer programming model, however, the left-hand side of (7.16) will be integer-valued, because X_1, S_1, and S_2 will be integer-valued, and their coefficients are integral. Consequently, if we make the right-hand side of (7.16) an integer in the same way we did the coefficients of the left-hand side, any feasible integer solution will satisfy the new relationship but the current linear programming solution will be infeasible. The new relationship is given by

$$X_1 + 0S_1 - 1S_2 \leq [\tfrac{3}{2}]$$

or

$$X_1 + 0S_1 - S_2 \leq 1 \tag{7.17}$$

Note that the solution to the linear programming model (extreme point 3) is no longer feasible with respect to (7.17). With the addition of this constraint, we have *cut* the current optimal linear programming solution from the feasible region.

Although we could use this new relationship for X_1 as the *cutting plane*, it is more convenient to represent it as a function of the nonbasic variables only. We can accomplish this by subtracting the original equation for X_1 from the new relationship, augmented with a new slack variable S_3

$$X_1 + 0S_1 - 1S_2 + S_3 = 1 \qquad \text{New equation}$$
$$\underline{-(X_1 + \tfrac{1}{6}S_1 - \tfrac{1}{8}S_2 \qquad = \tfrac{3}{2})} \qquad \text{Original equation}$$
$$0X_1 - \tfrac{1}{6}S_1 - \tfrac{7}{8}S_2 + S_3 = -\tfrac{1}{2} \qquad \text{Cutting plane}$$

Since the Simplex method requires that all right-hand sides are positive, we multiply the cutting plane by -1 to yield

$$(\tfrac{1}{6})S_1 + (\tfrac{7}{8})S_2 - S_3 = \tfrac{1}{2} \tag{7.18}$$

Note that we added a new variable, S_3, to the model.

Let us now see what the cutting plane does to the feasible region when it is added to the model. In order to graph the cutting plane in this example we must make some substitutions. Note that (7.18) can be written as

$$(\tfrac{1}{6})S_1 + (\tfrac{7}{8})S_2 \geq \tfrac{1}{2}$$

because S_3 behaves like a surplus variable. Also, from the original augmented model given by (7.13), we have

$$S_1 = 18 - 9X_1 - 3X_2$$
$$S_2 = 12 - 4X_1 - 4X_2$$

Substituting for S_1 and S_2 in (7.18) results in

$$\tfrac{1}{6}(18 - 9X_1 - 3X_2) + \tfrac{7}{8}(12 - 4X_1 - 4X_2) \geq \tfrac{1}{2}$$
$$3 - \tfrac{3}{2}X_1 - \tfrac{1}{2}X_2 + \tfrac{21}{2} - \tfrac{7}{2}X_1 - \tfrac{7}{2}X_2 \geq \tfrac{1}{2}$$
$$- 5X_1 - 4X_2 \geq -13$$
$$5X_1 + 4X_2 \leq 13 \tag{7.19}$$

This new constraint (7.19) can now be graphed to demonstrate the effect of the cutting plane, as shown in Figure 7.2. The previous linear programming solution is now infeasible. Nonetheless, every integer alternative is still feasible. Thus, the new constraint cuts off the current linear programming solution but does not affect the feasibility of the integer solutions.

Step 4. Solve the Modified Model   The modified model can now be written as

$$\text{Max } Z = 6X_1 + 5X_2 + 0S_1 + 0S_2 + 0S_3$$

subject to

$$
\begin{aligned}
9X_1 + 3X_2 + \; S_1 \qquad\qquad\;\; &= 18 \qquad \text{Resource 1} \\
4X_1 + 4X_2 \qquad + \; S_2 \qquad\;\; &= 12 \qquad \text{Resource 2} \\
\tfrac{1}{6}S_1 + \tfrac{7}{8}S_2 - S_3 &= \tfrac{1}{2} \qquad \text{Cutting plane} \\
X_1, X_2, S_1, S_2, S_3 \qquad\qquad\;\; &\geq 0 \text{ and integer}
\end{aligned}
$$

(7.20)

Fortunately, we do not have to start from scratch to solve the modified model. We begin by adding the new cutting plane to the previous optimal simplex tableau. Keep in mind that this new tableau does not portray a feasible solution

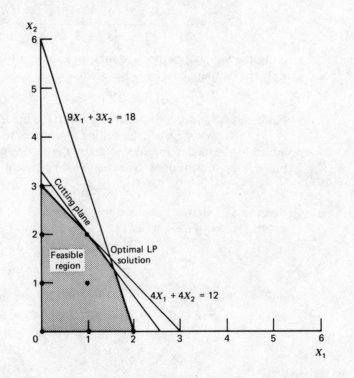

Figure 7.2   Effect of adding the cutting plane to the integer product-mix model.

to the modified model, because $X_1 = \frac{3}{2}$, $X_2 = \frac{3}{2}$ is no longer feasible. In addition, because there are now *three* constraints, there must be *three* variables in the basis. At present, there are only two variables in the basis. Finally, the $c_j - z_j$ values are the same ones found in the previous simplex tableau.

c_j	Basis	6 X_1	5 X_2	0 S_1	0 S_2	0 S_3	R
6	X_1	1	0	$\frac{1}{6}$	$-\frac{1}{8}$	0	$\frac{3}{2}$
5	X_2	0	1	$-\frac{1}{6}$	$\frac{3}{8}$	0	$\frac{3}{2}$
—	—	0	0	$\frac{1}{6}$	$\frac{7}{8}$	-1	$\frac{1}{2}$
	z_j	6	5	$\frac{1}{6}$	$\frac{9}{8}$	—	$\frac{33}{2}$
	$c_j - z_j$	0	0	$-\frac{1}{6}$	$-\frac{9}{8}$	—	

We can use the simplex method to get a feasible solution to the modified model. We must select a pivot row and a pivot variable. Row 3 is not represented by a basic variable, so it makes sense to select it as the pivot row. In general, the following rule applies: select the new cutting plane constraint as the pivot row.

For the pivot variable, we would like to select the nonbasic variable that, when entered into the basis, will result in a value of the objective function as close as possible to the optimal value in the linear programming solution. In the present linear programming solution, $Z = \frac{33}{2}$. But the cutting plane renders the optimal solution to the linear program infeasible. Thus, we would expect that the optimal integer solution will yield $Z < \frac{33}{2}$. How much will each nonbasic variable detract from the value of the objective function? The answer lies in the $c_j - z_j$ row. Note that the net contribution per unit of S_1 is only $-\frac{1}{6}$. Each unit of S_1 introduced into the basis only reduces the value of the objective function by $\frac{1}{6}$ dollars. Choosing S_2 would reduce Z by $\frac{9}{8}$ dollars per unit. We could not choose S_3 for the pivot variable because of the -1 coefficient in the pivot row. In general, the following rule applies for determining the pivot variable: select the nonbasic variable with the largest $c_j - z_j$ value as the pivot variable provided the pivot element is positive. In minimization problems, choose the nonbasic variable with the smallest $c_j - z_j$ value. In all cases, the $c_j - z_j$ values come from the previously optimal simplex tableau and the pivot element must be positive.

Now that we have selected a pivot variable and a pivot row, we can perform the usual row operations to arrive at a new basis. The new tableau is shown below. Note that because the cutting-plane constraint (7.18) did not include any basic variables, the insertion of S_1 into the basis did not make any basic variables nonbasic. Thus, the form of the cutting plane—in terms of nonbasic variables only, as opposed to the equivalent form (7.17)—simplifies the calculations required for getting a new basis.

c_j	Basis	6 X_1	5 X_2	0 S_1	0 S_2	0 S_3	R
6	X_1	1	0	0	-1	1	1
5	X_2	0	1	0	$\frac{10}{8}$	-1	2
0	S_1	0	0	1	$\frac{42}{8}$	-6	3
	z_j	6	5	0	$\frac{2}{8}$	1	16
	$c_j - z_j$	0	0	0	$-\frac{2}{8}$	-1	

In our example, the simplex criterion for optimality has been met after one iteration. If it had not been met, we would have had to continue with the simplex procedure until all $c_j - z_j \leq 0$. In addition, all variables have integer values, and we have thus found the optimal solution to the pure-integer model, as shown here.

$$X_1 = 1 \quad S_2 = 0$$
$$X_2 = 2 \quad S_3 = 0$$
$$S_1 = 3 \quad Z = 16$$

If one or more of the variables had a fractional value, we would have had to repeat Steps 3 and 4 until a pure-integer solution was found.

Summary of the Cutting-Plane Method

The cutting-plane method of integer programming is an iterative approach that makes use of additional constraints and standard linear programming techniques to arrive ultimately at a pure-integer solution. The following steps apply to any pure-integer model:

Step 1. *Integerize the original constraints.* Multiply each constraint by an appropriate constant such that all a_{ij}s and b_is are integers. Augment the model to include slack, surplus, and artificial variables as needed.

Step 2. *Solve the linear programming model.* Solve the model defined in Step 1 as if it were a regular linear programming model. If the optimal values of all variables are integer, stop. If not, proceed to Step 3.

Step 3. *Construct the cutting-plane constraint.* Select the basic variable with the largest fractional part in the last optimal simplex tableau. Suppose it is X_k in row i. Let $[a'_{ij}] + f_{ij} = a'_{ij}$, and $[b_i'] + f = b_i'$ where $0 \leq f_{ij} \leq 1$ and $0 < f < 1$. Construct a new constraint

$$\sum_{j \text{ nonbasic}} f_{ij} X_j - S_l = f$$

where the summation is over all the nonbasic variables and S_l is a new surplus variable. This formulation is identical to the more intuitive approach presented earlier.

Step 4. *Solve the modified model.* Insert new cutting-plane constraint into the model and solve for the new values of the decision variables. This can be accomplished by adding the new constraint to the last optimal simplex tableau. Select the new constraint as the pivot row and the nonbasic variable with the largest $c_j - z_j$ value as the pivot variable for a maximization problem, provided the pivot element is positive. If in the resulting solution all variables have integer values, stop. If not, go back to Step 3.

Practical Considerations of Cutting-Plane Methods

Although the cutting-plane method presented in this chapter is a theoretically sound approach for solving pure-integer programming models, there are some potential pitfalls with its use in practice. In the first place, the algorithm is guaranteed to converge to an integer solution in a finite number of iterations. The word *finite* is misleading, however. The number *2 billion* is a finite number. The algorithm has a tendency to require numerous iterations and is thus expensive to use in practice. In many instances, each cutting plane causes only a very small change in the feasible region and, consequently, in the objective function. Its success at finding a solution in a reasonable number of iterations seems to depend on the structure of the model; this is a disconcerting situation.

Second, the algorithm adds a new constraint to the model after each optimization. Because quite a few iterations may be required for reaching a feasible integer solution, many constraints could be appended to the model. We know that the computational effort required for the solution of a linear programming model is related to the number of constraints in the model. Thus, at each iteration, the model becomes more unwieldy and requires more computer time to get to the next iteration.

Another consideration is that we do not have a feasible integer solution until the very end of the solution. If the solution process must be prematurely terminated because of excessive computational costs, no feasible integer solution will be available because the last simplex tableau will contain (at best) only a partial integer solution. Of course, the solution at any iteration satisfies all the constraints in the original model except the integer restrictions. Nonetheless, it would be comforting to have a procedure that proceeded from integer extreme point to integer extreme point in a manner analogous to the simplex method for continuous linear programming models. The cutting-plane method does not fill that bill.

Finally, computer codes are required to solve problems of practical size or, for that matter, reasonable textbook problems. The example model in this section of the chapter should not be considered a problem of realistic dimensions. Nonetheless, we could easily present the concept of creating the new cutting constraint by working manually with the fractional parts of the a'_{ij}s and b'_i. Unfortunately, the computer must convert these fractional parts to decimals, introducing the potential for round-off errors. Since many iterations may be required, the cutting-plane method is particularly susceptible to round-off errors. In extreme cases, the ultimate "solution" is not feasible with respect to the original model. The double-precision arithmetic option available for most computers is only a partial remedy for this problem because, for models requiring a large number of iterations, the same round-off problem can still occur and more computer core is required.

There are several variants of the cutting-plane method. The procedure we presented in this section is an example of these variants. We will now turn to a completely different approach to solving integer programming models.

7.3 BRANCH-AND-BOUND

The two variable problems we used for demonstrating the cutting plane method could have been solved by complete enumeration. That is, we could have tried every feasible integer alternative and evaluated it in the objective function, choosing the one that yielded the largest value. Of course, for larger problems, the number of alternatives to evaluate would be prohibitive. Thus, it would be intuitively appealing to find a method that separates the total number of feasible solutions into subsets, and then *implicitly* enumerates all feasible solutions within each subset. The *branch-and-bound* method partitions (branches) a feasible subset of solutions to an integer programming model and then determines minimum and maximum values (bounds) on the objective function value by implicitly evaluating all solutions in that subset. A subset of feasible solutions is pruned (fathomed) from further consideration when it can be shown that the best integer solution in that subset has already been found or, when it is, it will be no better than an integer solution in another subset. All of this terminology suggests the image of a tree in which branches are added and then later pruned until the optimal solution is found. The terminology will more clearly be defined as we proceed through our example.

Steps in the Branch-and-Bound Method

Step 1. Initialization Perhaps the best way to introduce this approach is to apply it to a simple problem, following an intuitive argument. Later we will summarize the approach in more general terms. Consider the following pure-integer programming model:

$$\text{Max } 50X_1 + 30X_2 \qquad \text{Profits}$$

subject to

$$6X_1 + 13X_2 \leq 70 \qquad \text{Resource 1} \qquad (7.21)$$

$$5X_1 + 2X_2 \leq 33 \qquad \text{Resource 2}$$

$$X_1, X_2 \qquad \geq 0 \text{ and integer}$$

The model has been kept small so that solutions can be obtained graphically. It should be kept in mind throughout this presentation that the simplex method can be used for more elaborate models.

Figure 7.3 shows the feasible region and the optimal linear programming solution for the example model, ignoring the integer restrictions. The dark circles represent the feasible integer alternatives. The current solution

$$X_1' = 5.45$$

$$X_2 = 2.87$$

$$Z = 358.74$$

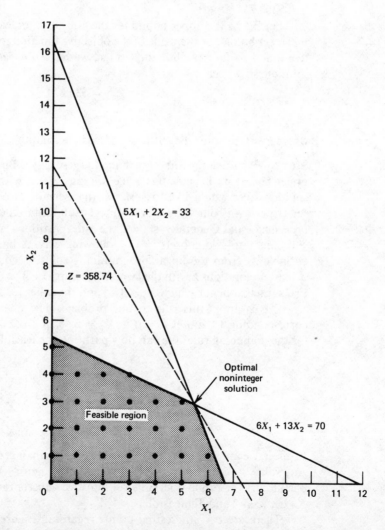

Figure 7.3 Feasible region and optimal noninteger solution for branch-and-bound example.

does not satisfy the integer restrictions on the decision variables, so we will use the method of branch-and-bound to find the optimal integer solution.

Although the noninteger solution is not a feasible solution for the pure-integer model, it does provide us with some valuable information. We now know that the optimal *integer* solution will not yield a value for the objective function greater than \$358.74. This can be verified by noticing where the feasible integer alternatives are located in the feasible region relative to the iso-profit line in Figure 7.3. In effect, we have found an *upper bound* on the objective function value. Also, because we do not yet have a feasible integer solution, the *lower bound* on the objective function can be set at minus infinity ($-\infty$). Thus, we know that the objective function value for the optimal integer alternative will lie between $-\infty$ and \$358.74.

Let Z_u^k be the upper bound for the kth subset of feasible solutions and Z_L be the lower bound, or the value of the objective function for the best integer alternative found so far. At this initial stage, we have not yet found a feasible integer solution, so we set

$$Z_u^0 = \$358.74$$

$$Z_L = -\infty$$

where $k = 0$ denotes the entire set of feasible solutions.

Step 2.   Partition the Subset with the Largest Upper Bound   Since Z_u^0 is the only upper bound we have at this stage, we must work with the entire set of feasible solutions. We would like to *partition* that set into two subsets in an attempt to "narrow down" our search for an integer solution to the model. We do this with a *branching rule*. Generally stated, the rule partitions a given subset of feasible solutions into two subsets in the following way. Arbitrarily select a noninteger variable X_j from the linear programming solution corresponding to the subset of feasible solutions k with the largest Z_u^k. Suppose $X_j = b'$. Partition subset k into two subsets: one for which $X_j \leq [b']$ and the other for which $X_j \geq [b'] + 1$.

Let us apply this rule to our problem. The linear programming solution corresponding to subset $k = 0$ is $X_1 = 5.45$, $X_2 = 2.87$. Arbitrarily choose X_2 for the branching rule. We can now partition the feasible region into two subsets.

Subset 1	Subset 2
$6X_1 + 13X_2 \leq 70$	$6X_1 + 13X_2 \leq 70$
$5X_1 + 2X_2 \leq 33$	$5X_1 + 2X_2 \leq 33$
$X_2 \leq 2$	$X_2 \geq 3$

In effect, we are saying that X_2 cannot be larger than 2, or it cannot be less than 3. Any value of X_2 between 2 and 3 is infeasible. Figure 7.4 shows how we have now partitioned the original feasible set into two subsets rendering all solutions with X_2 between 2 and 3 infeasible.

There are two interesting points regarding Figure 7.4. First, the branching rule has not eliminated any feasible integer solutions from further consideration.

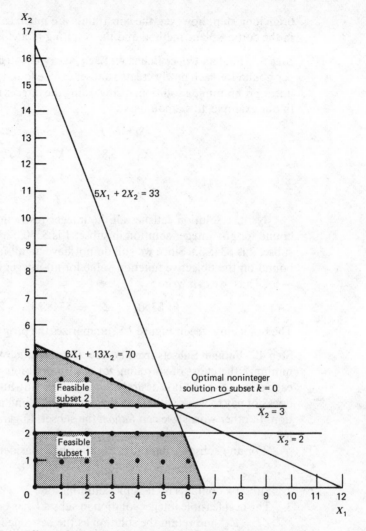

Figure 7.4 Effects of the branching rule on the original feasible region.

We have only eliminated *fractional* values of X_2 between 2 and 3. Second, the new constraints that are added behave like *cutting planes* except that they will always be perpendicular to one of the axes. Recall that with the cutting-plane method, the new constraints that must be added at each iteration can intersect the axes at various different angles. In addition, the new constraints in the branch-and-bound method are mutually exclusive. That is, each new constraint formed in the partitioning step involves only the variable chosen in the branching rule. In contrast, the cutting-plane method generates constraints involving more than one variable and these constraints must be continually added to the model to be solved. Thus, the branch-and-bound method introduces new constraints at each branching step; however, the constraints are much easier to construct than those in the cutting-plane method and the resulting model is easier to solve in general.

Step 3.   Find an Upper Bound on Each Newly Created Subset   A reasonable upper bound for each newly created subset can be found by determining the optimal linear programming solution, disregarding the integer restrictions on the variables. In our example, this amounts to:

Subset 1	*Subset 2*
$X_1 = 5.8$	$X_1 = 5.167$
$X_2 = 2$	$X_2 = 3$
$Z = \$350$	$Z = \$348.33$

Neither solution satisfies all the integer restrictions. Nonetheless, the upper bound for any integer solution in subset 1 is $350. Similarly, the upper bound for subset 2 is $348.33. Since we still do not have an all-integer alternative, the lower bound on the objective function value for all-integer alternatives must remain at $-\infty$. Thus, we can write

$$Z_u^{\,1} = \$350, \qquad Z_u^{\,2} = \$348.33, \qquad Z_L = -\infty$$

The branching tree in Figure 7.5 summarizes the progress we have made.

Step 4.   Fathom Subsets from Further Consideration Where Possible   In order to minimize the effort of searching for the optimal integer solution, we must check each subset to see if it is desirable to explore it any further. If we determine that it does not pay to work with it any longer, we can eliminate it from further consideration. In other words, we can *fathom* the subset. In general, we apply the following tests:

For any subset k, fathom it from further consideration if

1. $Z_u^{\,k} \le Z_L$, or
2.   Subset k contains no feasible solutions, or
3.   The best feasible integer solution in subset k has been found. If $Z_L < Z_u^{\,k}$, reset $Z_L = Z_u^{\,k}$ and retain the solution as the best one found so far.

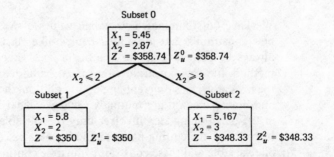

Figure 7.5   Branching tree for the first partition.

If $Z_u^k \leq Z_L$, the implication is that an integer solution has already been found that yields an objective function value at least as large as the upper bound for subset k. It does not pay to explore subset k any further. Similarly, with respect to the second test, if no feasible integer solutions are contained in subset k it can be fathomed. Finally, if the best integer solution in the subset has been found, we must retain it for comparison with other subsets. By definition, there is no need to look for more integer solutions in subset k, and we can fathom it from further consideration.

Unfortunately, at this stage in our example, we cannot fathom subset 1 or subset 2. Both Z_u^1 and Z_u^2 exceed Z_L, a feasible solution (albeit noninteger) has been found in each subset, and no integer solutions have been found. Thus, we must explore both of these subsets further.

Step 5.   Stop the Procedure When All Subsets Have Been Fathomed   Although it is premature to present this step in the chronology of our example problem, we state it here for completeness. Since we have two unfathomed subsets to evaluate, we must go back to Step 2 and continue the procedure. Obviously, if all subsets have been fathomed, the optimal integer solution has been identified.

Finding the Optimal Solution

The optimal solution has not yet been identified, so we must repeat Steps 2 through 5 until it is found. Returning to Step 2, we select subset 1 for further branching because $Z_u^1 = \$350 > Z_u^2 = \$348.33$. Since $X_1 = 5.8$ is the only noninteger variable in the linear programming solution for subset 1, we select it to partition the subset into two more subsets.

	Subset 3	*Subset 4*
	$6X_1 + 13X_2 \leq 70$	$6X_1 + 13X_2 \leq 70$
	$5X_1 + 2X_2 \leq 33$	$5X_1 + 2X_2 \leq 33$
	$X_2 \leq 2$	$X_2 \leq 2$
	$X_1 \leq 5$	$X_1 \geq 6$

Figure 7.6 shows the feasible regions for each of the new subsets.

Proceeding to Step 3, we solve the linear programming model for each subset as if there were no integer restrictions. The two solutions are shown below.

Subset 3	*Subset 4*
$X_1 = 5$	$X_1 = 6$
$X_2 = 2$	$X_2 = 1.5$
$Z = \$310$	$Z = \$345$

The upper bounds for each subset can now be specified as $Z_u^3 = \$310$ and $Z_u^4 = \$345$. The effect of this second level of branching can be seen in Figure 7.7.

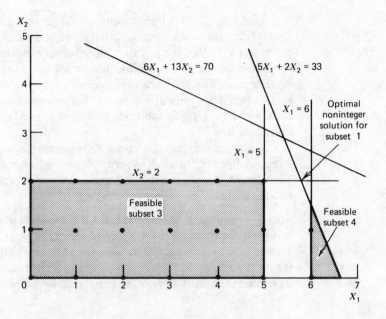

Figure 7.6 Effects of the branching rule on subset 1.

We must now check to see if any of the subsets can be fathomed. Subset 3 can be fathomed because the best integer solution in the subset has been found and $Z_u^3 > Z_L = -\infty$. Thus, we set $Z_L = Z_u^3 = \$310$ and retain $X_1 = 5$ and $X_2 = 2$ as the best integer solution found so far. Even though we have found an integer solution at this stage, we cannot stop the procedure because two subsets (2 and 4) have upper bounds greater than $Z_L = \$310$. There could be a better solution in

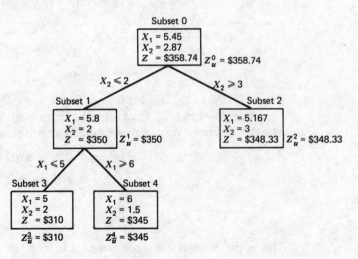

Figure 7.7 Branching tree after the second partition.

one of those subsets. In particular, neither subset 2 nor subset 4 can be fathomed, so we must go back to Step 2 and partition another subset.

Since $Z_u^2 = \$348.33 > Z_u^4 = \$345$, we select subset 2 for further partitioning. From the optimal linear programming solution shown in Figure 7.7, X_1 is chosen as the basis for the partition. The newly created subsets become

Subset 5	Subset 6
$6X_1 + 13X_2 \leq 70$	$6X_1 + 13X_2 \leq 70$
$5X_1 + 2X_2 \leq 33$	$5X_1 + 2X_2 \leq 33$
$X_2 \geq 3$	$X_2 \geq 3$
$X_1 \leq 5$	$X_1 \geq 6$

Figure 7.8 shows the feasible regions for each of the new subsets. Note that the optimal noninteger solution for subset 2 has been rendered infeasible without disturbing any feasible integer solutions. In addition, it is obvious that subset 6 contains no feasible solutions.

The results of the bounding and fathoming steps for subsets 5 and 6 are summarized in Figure 7.9. Note that subset 3 has been fathomed and its solution has provided the lower bound for the solution process so far. Subset 6 can be

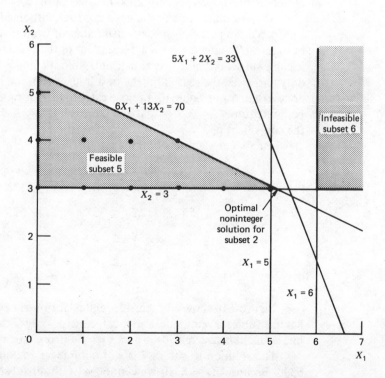

Figure 7.8 Effects of the branching rule on subset 2.

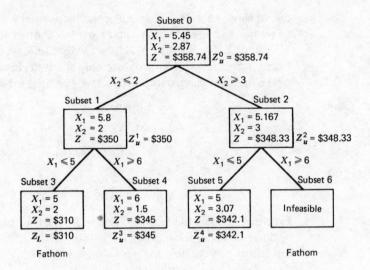

Figure 7.9   Branching tree after the third partition.

fathomed because it contains no feasible solutions (the second fathoming test). No other subsets can be fathomed because both $Z_u{}^5$ and $Z_u{}^4$ exceed Z_L.

At this point, two subsets have not been fathomed. The largest upper bound is $Z_u{}^4$. We can partition subset 4 using the constraints $X_2 \leq 1$ and $X_2 \geq 2$. Notice in Figure 7.9 that subset 4 is a descendant of the branch $X_2 \leq 2$ from the original feasible subset 0. These new constraints do not conflict with that branch. We have only narrowed the search for the best integer solution in subset 4 to values of X_1 no less than 6 and values of X_2 no greater than 1, or *equal* to 2. The reason subset 8 below requires $X_2 = 2$ is that the constraints $X_2 \leq 2$ and $X_2 \geq 2$ together are the equivalent of $X_2 = 2$.

The two new subsets become

Subset 7   Subset 8

$$6X_1 + 13X_2 \leq 70 \qquad 6X_1 + 13X_2 \leq 70$$

$$5X_1 + 2X_2 \leq 33 \qquad 5X_1 + 2X_2 \leq 33$$

$$X_2 \leq 2 \qquad\qquad X_2 \leq 2$$

$$X_1 \qquad \geq 6 \qquad X_1 \qquad \geq 6$$

$$X_2 \leq 1 \qquad\qquad X_2 \geq 2$$

Figure 7.10 shows the feasible regions for these new subsets. Note that subset 8 is infeasible for our model and that it consists only of the points along the straight-line segment between $X_1 = 6$ and $X_1 = \frac{22}{3}$ (from the first constraint with $X_2 = 2$).

The solution to subset 7 is still noninteger, yielding an upper bound $Z_u{}^7 = \$340$. Because $Z_L = \$310$ we cannot yet fathom subset 7. Subset 8 is infeasible, however, and as such can be fathomed (the second test). The next branch must be

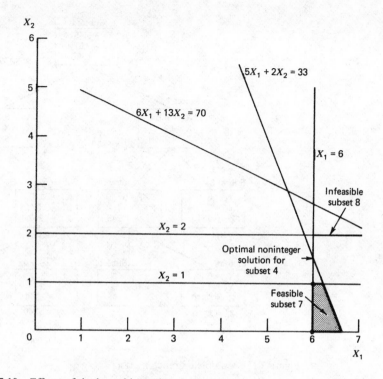

Figure 7.10 Effects of the branching rule on subset 3.

made from subset 5 because $Z_u^5 > Z_u^7$. As it turns out, this is the last subset that must be partitioned. Figure 7.11 shows the complete branching tree for our example problem.

The optimal solution of subset 9 is integer-valued and, because $Z_u^9 = \$340$ is greater than the current value of the lower bound $Z_L = \$310$, we set $Z_L = \$340$ and fathom subset 9. Consequently, subset 7 can also be fathomed because $Z_u^7 = Z_L$. We no longer need to consider subset 7. Similarly, even though the optimal alternative in subset 10 is integer-valued, $Z_u^{10} = \$270$ is less than the current lower bound $Z_L = \$340$. Thus, subset 10 can be fathomed. Because all subsets have been fathomed, we can now declare that $X_1 = 5, X_2 = 3$ is the optimal integer solution to our model because it corresponds to the current value of the lower bound.

Summary of the Branch-and-Bound Method

The branch-and-bound method for solving integer programming maximization models can be summarized as follows:

Step 1. *Initialization.* Solve the model without integer restrictions using standard linear programming methods. If the optimal solution is integer, stop. If not, set Z_u^0 equal to the value of the objective function. Set $Z_L = -\infty$.

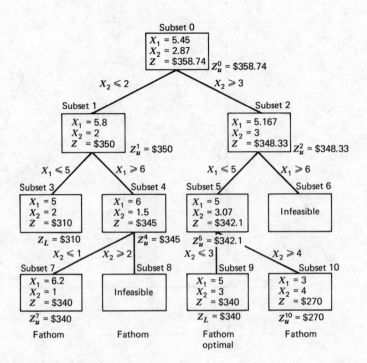

Figure 7.11 Complete branching tree.

Step 2. *Partition the Subset with the Largest Upper Bound.* Arbitrarily select a noninteger variable X_j from the linear programming solution corresponding to the subset of feasible solutions k with the largest Z_u^k. Suppose $X_j = b'$. Partition subset k into two subsets: one for which $X_j \leq [b']$ and the other for which $X_j \geq [b'] + 1$, where $[b']$ refers to the largest integer portion of b'.

Step 3. *Find an Upper Bound on Each Newly Created Subset.* The upper bound for each subset is found by solving the linear programming model without integer restrictions subject to the feasible region defined by each subset. Set $Z_u^k = Z$ for each subset k.

Step 4. *Fathom Subsets Where Possible.* For any subset k, fathom it from further consideration if:

1. $Z_u^k \leq Z_L$, or
2. Subset k contains no feasible solutions, or
3. The best feasible integer solution in subset k has been found. If $Z_L < Z_u^k$, reset $Z_L = Z_u^k$ and retain the solution as the best one found so far.

Step 5. *Stop the Procedure When All Subsets Have Been Fathomed.* When all subsets have been fathomed, the optimal integer solution is the one that corresponds to the current value of Z_L. If all subsets have not been fathomed, return to Step 2 and continue the procedure.

Practical Considerations of Branch-and-Bound Methods

Branch-and-bound methods for solving integer programming models use implicit enumeration of feasible integer alternatives to reduce the computational effort required to find the optimal integer alternative. This procedure works well for moderate-sized models – with about 50 integer variables and 30 constraints, for example. Unfortunately, many practical models exceed these modest dimensions. Consequently, the number of iterations may get prohibitively large because we may have to follow many branches to their tips before we can fathom them. Some of the computational burden can be relieved if we use a tolerance factor $\varepsilon > 0$ such that we would be willing to terminate the procedure if the largest upper bound at any iteration $Z_u{}^k$ were within ε of the current value of the lower bound Z_L. Of course, we could not state that we have the optimal solution in that event.

On a more positive note, integer alternatives are determined periodically throughout the solution process. If the procedure must be terminated prematurely because of the cost of computation, the solution corresponding to the current value of the lower bound may be of some use to the decision maker. Recall that when the cutting-plane method is used, no integer solution is available until the final iteration.

Another point to consider is that the branch-and-bound method can be used to solve *mixed-integer* programming models. Recall that a mixed-integer-programming model has integer restrictions on only a portion of the decision variables. The procedure is the same as the one we have presented, except that the branching step only considers those variables with integer restrictions. It does not matter what values the continuous variables have so long as they are feasible. The cutting-plane method can also be used for mixed-integer models but, in general, it is not as efficient.

Finally, the branch-and-bound method can be used to solve models with objective functions to be minimized. All we must do is reverse the roles of $Z_u{}^k$ and Z_L. We now define $Z_L{}^k$ to be the lower bound for subset k and Z_u to be the upper bound determined by the objective function value of the best integer solution found so far. In the initialization step, set $Z_L{}^0$ at the value of the objective function and $Z_u = +\infty$. For Step 2, select the subset k for which $Z_L{}^k$ is the smallest and partition it as before. The bounds for each newly created subset are found by using standard linear programming methods and setting the *lower bounds* equal to the corresponding values of the objective function in each case. Only tests one and three of the fathoming step are affected as follows:

1. Fathom subset k if $Z_u \leq Z_L{}^k$.
2. Fathom subset k if the best integer solution in subset k has been found. If $Z_L{}^k < Z_u$, reset $Z_u = Z_L{}^k$ and retain the solution as the best one found so far.

The only change to the last step is to declare the solution corresponding to the current value of Z_u the optimal solution if all subsets have been fathomed.

7.4 SUMMARY

In this chapter, we have presented two approaches to solving integer programming models. Simple two-variable models were used so that the mechanical aspects of the cutting-plane and branch-and-bound methods could be easily followed. Unfortunately, most practical models like those presented in the first part of this chapter involve many more variables and constraints. As such, computer codes are required to solve these models. Because of the integer restrictions on the variables, these codes are much less efficient than the simplex method. Usually, significant computer time is needed to solve these models. Consequently, applications to date have involved models with only a limited number of integer variables. Most codes are based on the branch-and-bound method because the cutting-plane method, which has met with only limited success so far, is too dependent on the model structure. Nonetheless, research is continuing in an effort to find more efficient methods based on these two approaches.

We should not lose sight of the possibility of finding near-optimal solutions that may be satisfactory to the decision maker. One approach would be to find a solution by inspection. In the simple examples of this chapter, an optimal solution could easily have been determined by trying a few of the pure integer alternatives lying close to the extreme points of the feasible regions. In larger, more complex cases, solution by inspection can only result, at best, in a satisfactory but not optimal solution.

Another approach is to solve the model without integer restrictions using the simplex method and then round off the variables to the nearest integer value such that the constraints are not violated. For large models, this procedure may not be as simple as it sounds because of all the possible combinations of values for the decision variables. In addition, it cannot be assured that the optimal solution will be found.

Finally, a significant amount of research is being devoted to the development of *heuristic* procedures for solving integer programming models. These procedures cannot guarantee an optimal solution, but they promise to be superior to the use of inspection—or simplex and then rounding-off—and should take less computational effort than the cutting-plane and branch-and-bound methods.

References Balinski, M.L., "Integer Programming: Methods, Uses, Computation," *Management Science*, Vol. 12 (1965), pp. 253–313.

Efroymson, M.A., and Ray, T.L., "A Branch-Bound Algorithm for Plant Location," *Operations Research*, Vol. 14 (1966), pp. 361–368.

Faaland, B., "An Integer Programming Algorithm for Portfolio Selection," *Management Science*, Vol. 20 (1974), pp. 1376–1384.

Geoffrion, A.M., and Marsten, R.E., "Integer Programming: A Framework and State-of-the-Art Survey," *Management Science*, Vol. 18 (1972), pp. 465–491.

Gomory, R.E., "An Algorithm for Integer Solutions to Linear Programs," in *Recent Advances in Mathematical Programming*, L. Graves and P. Wolfe (eds.), New York: McGraw-Hill, 1963, pp. 269–302.

Hadley, G., *Nonlinear and Dynamic Programming*, Reading, Mass.: Addison-Wesley, 1964.

Hillier, F.S., and Lieberman, G.J., *Introduction to Operations Research*, 2d ed., San Francisco: Holden Day, 1974.

Khumawala, B.M., "An Efficient Branch-and-Bound Algorithm for the Warehouse Location Problem," *Management Science*, Vol. 18 (1972), pp. B-718–B-731.

Kolesar, P.J., "A Branch-and-Bound Algorithm for the Knapsack Problem," *Management Science*, Vol. 13 (1967), pp. 723–735.

Lawler, E.L., and Wood, D.E., "Branch-and-Bound Methods: A Survey," *Operations Research*, Vol. 14 (1966), pp. 699–719.

Taha, H.A., *Integer Programming: Theory, Applications and Computations*, New York: Academic Press, 1975.

Trauth, C.A., and Woolsey, R.E., "Integer Linear Programming: A Study in Computational Efficiency," *Management Science*, Vol. 15 (1969), pp. 481–492.

Wagner, H.M., "An Integer Linear Programming Model for Machine Scheduling," *Naval Research Logistics Quarterly*, Vol. 6 (1959), pp. 131–140.

Wagner, H.M., *Principles of Operations Research*, 2d. ed., Englewood Cliffs, N.J.: Prentice-Hall, 1975.

Weingartner, H.M., "Capital Budgeting of Interrelated Projects: Survey and Synthesis," *Management Science*, Vol. 12 (1966), pp. 485–516.

Review Questions

1. Suppose your company is in the process of selecting new locations for two new plants. Explain to management why an integer programming model would be appropriate for selecting the optimal alternatives.

2. Many practical decision problems involve decision variables that, by their very nature, should be integer-valued in the final solution. Compare and contrast linear programming and integer-programming methods for solving problems such as these. Discuss the advantages and disadvantages of each approach.

3. Describe, in general terms, a decision problem that could be analyzed with an integer programming model. Specify the variables that must be integer-valued. Do not use any of the examples presented in this chapter.

4. Suppose you are in a position to recommend a solution procedure for a certain pure-integer programming model. Management is not familiar with integer programming technology. Explain, in lay terms, how the cutting-plane method works and how the new cutting constraint is developed.

5. Explain why it is more convenient to express the cutting plane in terms of nonbasic variables only.

6. Management has never heard of the method of branch and bound. In general terms, explain the basic idea behind the branch-and-bound technique.

7. Explain why, in a maximization problem, finding the continuous linear-programming solution for a given subset provides a good upper bound on the feasible integer alternatives in that subset.

8. Graph the effects of using the branching rule on subset 5 of Figure 7.11. Verify that the optimal integer solution is $X_1 = 5$ and $X_2 = 3$.

9. Compare and contrast the cutting-plane method and the branch-and-bound method. Discuss the advantages and disadvantages of each.

10. Consider the statement: "Integer programming methods are of academic interest only. Managers should stick to linear programming codes." Do you agree or disagree? Discuss your reasons.

Problems

1. A small manufacturing concern is facing more demand for its two products than it can supply. Consequently, the manager would like to produce as much as possible so that profits are maximized. Each product must be processed in two critical departments. Product 1 requires two employees in department A and five employees in department B per day. Product 2 requires two employees in department A and three employees in department B per day. Department A has eight employees, and department B has fifteen employees who report to work on a daily basis. Each unit of product 1 generates $4 in profit, whereas each unit of product 2 generates $3 in profit.
   (a) Formulate the pure-integer programming model for this problem.
   (b) Solve for the optimal alternative using the cutting-plane method.

2. Consider the following pure-integer programming model:

$$\text{Max } Z = 4X + 5Y$$

subject to

$$5X + 3Y \leq 32$$
$$2X + 3Y \leq 18$$
$$X, Y \geq 0 \text{ and integer}$$

   (a) Using the cutting-plane method, determine the first cutting plane to this model. Graph the original feasible region and the effect of the cutting plane on it.
   (b) Specify the second cutting plane to this model.

3. Consider the following pure-integer programming model:

$$\text{Max } 30X_1 + 50X_2$$

subject to

$$\tfrac{2}{5}X_1 + \tfrac{1}{5}X_2 \leq 2$$
$$4X_1 + 10X_2 \leq 40$$
$$X_1, X_2 \geq 0 \text{ and integer}$$

(a) Graph the feasible region for this model showing all feasible integer alternatives. Identify the optimal noninteger solution.

(b) Determine the first cutting plane to this model using the cutting-plane method. Graph the cutting plane and show that no feasible integer alternatives are made infeasible.

(c) Determine the second cutting plane.

4. The ACME motion picture company is planning to film a torrid love scene and chase in Milano, Italy. Transportation for the leading actors and actresses has already been arranged. Transportation for the seconds and stunt drivers and their baggage must still be determined. Two types of aircraft can be rented. Type 1 can carry 1 ton of luggage and 12 passengers for a rental fee of $8000 per plane. Type 2 can carry 1 ton of luggage and 5 passengers for a rental fee of $5000 per plane. Enough transportation capacity must be available to carry at least 8 tons of luggage and at least 60 people. The idea is to determine the number of airplanes of each type so that enough capacity is available and costs are minimized.

(a) Formulate the pure-integer programming model for this problem.

(b) Determine the optimal alternative using the cutting-plane method.

5. Consider the following pure-integer programming model:

$$\text{Max } Z = 40X + 30Y$$

subject to

$$4X + 5Y \leq 20$$

$$6X + 3Y \leq 18$$

$$X, Y \geq 0 \text{ and integer}$$

(a) Graph the feasible region for this model and specify all pure-integer alternatives.

(b) Determine the optimal alternative using branch-and-bound. You may solve the subsets using graphic methods. Show the effects of each partition graphically.

6. The sales manager of a cosmetics firm must select an advertising campaign for a new lipstick. The art department has developed an advertisement that can be placed into two popular magazines. The market research department has estimated that each ad placed in magazine 1 will provide exposure to 30,000 readers, whereas each ad placed in magazine 2 will provide exposure to only 20,000 readers. An ad costs $500 in magazine 1 and only $400 in magazine 2. The total budget for ads this month is $2000. Magazine 1 will allow at most three ads per issue, while magazine 2 will allow a maximum of four ads per issue. Finally, the teenage market for the new lipstick is considered an important determinant for the success of the new product. Consequently, each ad in magazine 1 reaches 3000 teenage female readers, whereas each ad in magazine 2 reaches 5000 teenage female readers. It is felt that the advertising campaign should reach *at least* 15,000 teenage female readers,

    (a) Formulate a pure-integer programming model designed to determine the number of ads to place in each magazine such that total readership exposure is maximized.

    (b) Graph the feasible region for this model, indicating all feasible integer alternatives.

    (c) Solve the model using the method of branch-and-bound. You may use graphic methods to determine the upper bounds for each subset.

7. Consider the following pure-integer model:

$$\text{Min } Z = 5X + 2Y$$

subject to

$$6X + 2Y \geq 12$$

$$5X + 4Y \geq 20$$

$$Y \geq X$$

$$X, Y \geq 0 \text{ and integer}$$

    (a) Graph the feasible region for this model.

    (b) Determine the optimal alternative using branch-and-bound.

8. Consider Problem 3.

    (a) Solve the model using branch-and-bound. You may use graphic methods to determine the upper bounds for each subset.

    (b) Compare your experiences using the cutting-plane method and the branch-and-bound method for the same problem.

9. Suppose that the following product mix has been developed for a small firm:

$$\text{Max } Z = 40X_1 + 30X_2 \qquad \text{Profits}$$

subject to

$$8X_1 + 4X_2 \leq 32 \qquad \text{Resource 1}$$

$$6X_1 + 5X_2 \leq 30 \qquad \text{Resource 2}$$

$$X_2 \leq 4 \qquad \text{Demand limit}$$

$$X_1, X_2 \geq 0$$

$$X_1 \text{ integer}$$

This is an example of a mixed-integer programming model.

    (a) Graph the feasible region for this model.

    (b) Determine the optimal solution using the branch-and-bound method. Keep in mind you will only have to partition the subsets on the basis of X_1. Continuous values of X_2 are permissible.

10. Your company is considering the construction of one or more new plants. Three sites have been determined and a plant design for each site has been developed. At present, four distribution centers located around the country

must be serviced by the added plant capacity. The intent is to select the location(s) such that construction, land, and distribution costs are minimized subject to the restrictions that plant capacity is not exceeded and all demand at the distribution centers is satisfied. Plant construction and land costs are $3MM, $4.5MM, and $3.75MM for sites A, B, and C respectively. In addition, the costs in Table P7.1a represent the per-unit distribution cost from each

Table P7.1a Distribution Center

Site	1	2	3	4
A	$1.00	$1.50	$0.75	$1.25
B	$1.30	$1.60	$1.00	$1.10
C	$1.00	$0.95	$1.10	$1.00

Table P7.1b

Distribution Center	Annual Demand (MM)	Site	Annual Capacity (MM)
1	2	A	7
2	4	B	8
3	3	C	5
4	3		Total 20
Total 12			

site to each distribution center using the appropriate mode of transportation. Finally, the demands at each distribution center and the capacities at each site are given in Table P7.1b.

    (a) Formulate the pure-integer programming model for this plant location model. Identify each variable in the model and completely specify the objective function and all constraints.

11. The management of the Kramer Company is faced with a capital investment decision. The present plant is old and outdated. Managers must decide whether or not to build a new plant. If they decide to build a new plant, they must choose one of five locations for the plant. If they decide against the new plant. they could decide to expand the present plant to increase its output or just modernize the existing plant. Some modernization will take place if expansion is chosen, so management has decided that to do both expansion and modernization would not be desirable.

(a) Let X_i be the decision variable for alternative i (there are seven alternatives). Also, let c_i be the present value of the returns over the life of alternative i. If there is a total of B dollars available for investment, formulate the integer programming model for this problem.

12. A manager of the Hometown Bank must determine a daily work-force schedule for encoding clerks such that all the checks arriving in a given 2-hour period are processed and the total work force is minimized. An encoding clerk processes checks using a machine that prints the dollar total of the check in magnetic ink for further sorting and classification. Each full-time clerk must be assigned to one of three tours of duty: 8 A.M.–4 P.M., 12 N–8 P.M. and 2 P.M.–10 P.M. Each part-time clerk must be assigned to one of two tours: 10 A.M.–2 P.M. or 11 A.M.–3 P.M. Each part-time clerk processes p checks in 2 hours and each full-time clerk processes p' checks in 2 hours where $p' > p$. In order to maintain a flexible work force, at least 30% of the workers must be part-time. Bank messengers pick up unprocessed checks at the branch offices and deposit them at the Hometown Bank every 2 hours. This bihourly volume, based on historical records, is given by D_t where $t = 1, 2, \ldots, 7$ represents the seven bihourly intervals in a working day. The check-processing capacity of the department in interval t must be at least as great as the number of checks arriving in interval t, D_t.

Finally, all encoding machines must be cleaned and maintained on a periodic basis. There are a total of N encoding machines, one for each clerk. Consequently, between the hours of 8 A.M. and 12 noon, only $n < N$ machines are available for processing because of the maintenance program.

(a) Let X_{ij} denote the quantity of encoder clerks of type i (full-time or part-time) assigned to work during shift j (8 A.M.–4 P.M., 12 N–8 P.M., 2 P.M.–10 P.M., 10 A.M.–2 P.M., 11 A.M.–3 P.M.). There are only five decision variables in this problem. Formulate an integer programming model with the objective of minimizing the total number of employees in the work force.

13. A certain organization must decide which of 10 projects, $i = 1, 2, \ldots, 10$, it should undertake over the next five years, $j = 1, 2, \ldots, 5$. Each project i will consume a_{ij} dollars in year j. The organization has B_j dollars to invest each year, $j = 1, 2, \ldots, 5$. These budgets cannot be exceeded in any year. Also, it has been estimated that each project i will provide c_i dollars in return, discounted over the projected life of the project.

Several relationships between the projects must be considered. Projects 1, 2, 3, and 4 are all alternatives to remedy the same problem; thus, only one, if any, should be undertaken in this group. If project 4 is selected, then projects 7 *and* 9 must also be selected. If project 4 is not selected, projects 7 and 9 cannot be undertaken. If project 2 is selected, then project 8 may be selected if desirable; however, project 8 cannot be selected unless project 2 is selected first. All other projects can be treated independently of the rest.

(a) The objective is to maximize the total discounted returns of the projects selected. Define suitable decision variables. Formulate the integer programming model for this problem.

14. The production manager of a small job shop must determine a schedule for three jobs (A, B, and C) available for processing. There are three machines in the shop (1, 2, and 3) and, at present, all are idle and available for processing. The total processing time, including setup time for job i, operation j, on machine k is given by p_{ijk}. The routing for each job is given in the body of Table P7.2.

Table P7.2

Job	Operation (1)	(2)	(3)
A	1	3	2
B	2	3	1
C	1	2	3

(a) Let X_{ijk} be the starting time of job i, operation j, on machine k. Formulate a mixed-integer programming model to minimize the total time to process all three jobs, recognizing the precedence and machine-interference constraints.

15. The Acme Trucking Company has a fleet of three trucks. Each truck j has a capacity of b_j cubic feet and a weight limit of d_j pounds. A certain customer has placed an order for five items stored in the warehouse at Acme. Each product i consumes a_i cubic feet and weighs g_i pounds. Each product i delivered to the customer yields c_i dollars of profit for Acme.

(a) Formulate the integer programming model that will maximize profits subject to the limitations on the space and weight capacities.

8

METHODS OF NETWORK ANALYSIS

8.1 NETWORK MODELS

Network Terminology
Applications of Network Models

8.2 SIMPLE NETWORK-OPTIMIZATION METHODS

Shortest-Route Problem
Maximal-Flow Problem

8.3 PROJECT PLANNING AND CONTROL METHODS

The Critical-Path Method
The Program Evaluation and Review Technique
Review of Project Network Methods

8.4 SUMMARY

References
Review Questions
Problems

We saw in the previous chapters that a number of quantitative methods are useful for selecting optimal alternatives and that the structure of the model is an important determinant of the particular technique to use. In this respect, an important class of models can be applied in planning transportation systems, communications systems, and large-scale projects. The common feature of these models is that each one is a representation of a *network*. Although techniques such as linear programming, integer programming, and dynamic programming can be used to solve network models, we will see that some techniques are much more efficient than these—they take advantage of the special structure of networks.

8.1 NETWORK MODELS

Network models can be used to analyze a wide variety of decision problems. The special-purpose techniques presented in this chapter will not be utilized by the decision maker unless the problem is recognized as a network problem in Step 1 of the decision-making process. To facilitate the task of problem recognition, we will introduce the special jargon of network theory in this section, followed by some examples of the applications of network models.

Network Terminology

A *network* is defined as a set of *nodes* connected by *branches* with a *flow* of some type in the branches. Consider Figure 8.1, which is an example of a network of roads connecting seven cities. In our example, the nodes are the cities, the branches are the roads, and the flow is measured in the number of vehicles.

The *flow capacity* of a branch is the maximum allowable flow in a branch in a specified direction. If the flow capacity is zero in a specified direction, the branch is said to be *oriented*. For example, branch *AD*, in Figure 8.1 may have a maximal

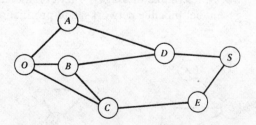

Figure 8.1 Network of roads.

flow of 1000 vehicles per hour in the direction $A \to D$ or 1000 vehicles per hour in the direction $D \to A$. Thus, vehicles can flow in either direction of that branch. Alternatively, branch CE may represent a one-way road with a capacity of 500 vehicles per hour in the direction $C \to E$ and zero vehicles per hour from $E \to C$. In this case, branch CE is an *oriented* branch.

A *source node* is defined as a node with all its flows oriented away from it. Node O in Figure 8.1 could be a source node if branches OA, OB, and OC are oriented away from it. Similarly, a *sink node* is a node whose branches are oriented toward it. Node S in Figure 8.1 could be a sink node if OS and ES are oriented toward it. Intuitively, source nodes generate the flows while sink nodes absorb the flows.

A network is called a *connected network* if *any* pair of nodes can be linked by traversing a series of branches in the network. Figure 8.1 is an example of a connected network. The network in Figure 8.2, however, is not a connected network. There is no way to link node B, for example, to node D.

Although this terminology may seem a little foreign at this time, we will see that if a problem can be structured as a network, considerable computational effort can be avoided when selecting the optimal alternative.

Applications of Network Models

Shortest Route   Network models have been applied in a wide variety of decision-making problems. One such problem is the so-called *shortest route* problem. For example, given a network of cities and major arterial intersections with the connecting roads or air lanes, find the route from source to sink that minimizes the total distance traveled. Alternatively, the objective could be to minimize time or costs. The transportation industry frequently uses network models to find the shortest route for trucks or airplanes between two designated cities, for example.

Maximal Flow   Shortest-route network models typically assume unlimited flows along the branches. The *maximal-flow* problem, however, is concerned with the flow capacity of a network. Given a network with the flow capacities of each of the branches, the objective is to determine the maximum attainable flow from source to sink. Network models can be used to solve maximal-flow problems in a wide variety of settings. The flows could be vehicles or aircraft in transportation networks, telephone messages or letters in communications networks, oil or natural gas in fuel-pipeline networks, and production orders in manufacturing networks.

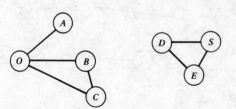

Figure 8.2   Nonconnected network.

Large Projects A network model need not always represent a physical network. It may just be a diagrammatic representation of a more abstract entity. For example, the network could represent a large complex project where the branches are activities that must be performed and each node is an event signifying the completion of one or more activities that flow into it and/or the start of other activities that flow out of it. In this respect, the network specifies the interrelationships among all the activities in a large project. Special network techniques such as the *program evaluation and review technique* (PERT) and the *critical-path method* (CPM) aid in determining (1) the minimum (expected) completion time of the project, (2) the minimum cost of completing the project, and (3) those activities that can be delayed without delaying the completion time of the entire project. Network methods have been used to analyze large projects such as the construction of skyscrapers, bridges, jumbo airliners, ships, and ballistic missile systems.

The remainder of this chapter focuses on the use of network methods to select optimal alternatives for each of these three problem areas.

8.2   SIMPLE NETWORK-OPTIMIZATION METHODS

In this section, we present simple methods for analyzing the shortest-route and maximal-flow problems. In each case, an example problem will be presented followed by an intuitive discussion of the solution process.

Shortest-Route Problem

The Kramer Merchandising Corporation ships various consumer products to a number of retail outlets throughout the United States. Recently, a new outlet store has been constructed on the West Coast. The traffic department at Kramer must determine the least-cost shipping route from the company's East Coast location to the new outlet store on the West Coast.

The merchandise is shipped in crates amenable to both air and truck transport. Five cities between the origin and destination cities are considered major transportation hubs. Staff members in the traffic department have determined the shipping rates per crate between each of the transportation hubs. The rate between each city reflects the most economical mode of transport (air carrier or truck carrier) with consideration for service and reliability. The problem is to find the route that minimizes the total cost per crate.

The Network Model The problem can be analyzed with a network model. Figure 8.3 shows the network with the cost of transportation per crate along each branch. City O is the origin (source) of the shipments and city S is the destination (sink) for the shipments. Thus, only branches OA, OB, OD, CS, DS, and ES are oriented because there can be no flow into the source or out of the sink nodes. All other branches have no orientation. Note that Figure 8.3 depicts a connected network.

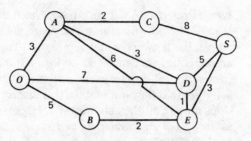

Figure 8.3 Network for the Kramer Shipping problem.

Let us now develop the model for the network in Figure 8.3. Let X_{ij} be the flow of crates from node i to node j. We are only interested in finding the shortest (minimum-cost) route, and therefore we will constrain X_{ij} to be either 0 or 1. Thus, we will find the best route for one crate with our model.

The constraints of the model involve the flow at each node in the network. Because no flow enters the origin and our decision variables are constrained to be 0 or 1, we constrain the flow out of the origin to be one crate.

$$X_{OA} + X_{OB} + X_{OD} = 1 \qquad \text{Node } O$$

The constraint says that the flow from the origin to city A, or to city B, or to city C must equal one crate. The equality constraint guarantees that one of the three branches will be a part of the shortest route.

For all nodes other than the origin and the sink, we must now ensure that any flow into a node must leave that node. Thus, the following constraints must be included:

Flow Out		Flow In	
$X_{AC} + X_{AD} + X_{AE}$	$= X_{OA} + X_{CA} + X_{DA} + X_{EA}$		Node A
X_{BE}	$= X_{OB} + X_{EB}$		Node B
$X_{CA} + X_{CS}$	$= X_{AC}$		Node C
$X_{DA} + X_{DE} + X_{DS}$	$= X_{OD} + X_{AD} + X_{ED}$		Node D
$X_{EA} + X_{EB} + X_{ED} + X_{ES}$	$= X_{AE} + X_{BE} + X_{DE}$		Node E
1	$= X_{CS} + X_{DS} + X_{ES}$		Node S

Note that the constraints do not include variables of the form X_{io} or X_{Sj} because this would be contrary to the definitions of source and sink nodes. In addition, the constraint for node S is actually redundant and can be eliminated. This can be seen by adding the constraints for nodes A through E. The result, after canceling variables that appear on both sides of the equality sign, is

$$X_{CS} + X_{DS} + X_{ES} = X_{OA} + X_{OB} + X_{OD}$$

Since $X_{OA} + X_{OB} + X_{OD} = 1$, we conclude that the constraint for node S is implied by the constraints for nodes A through E and the flow constraint for the origin, node O.

Finally, the objective function can be written

$$
\begin{aligned}
\text{Min } Z = \quad & 3X_{OA} + 5X_{OB} + 7X_{OD} \\
& + 2X_{AC} + 3X_{AD} + 6X_{AE} \\
& + 2X_{BE} + 2X_{CA} + 8X_{CS} \\
& + 3X_{DA} + 1X_{DE} + 5X_{DS} \\
& + 6X_{EA} + 2X_{EB} + 1X_{ED} + 3X_{ES}
\end{aligned}
$$

The model, exclusive of nonnegativity constraints and artificial variables, can be summarized in the tableau in Table 8.1.

The tableau reveals an interesting aspect of our model. Note that each column vector consists of, *at most*, two nonzero entries, either $a + 1$ or -1. If there are two entries, there is always $a + 1$ *and* $a - 1$. Whenever a model satisfies these conditions, it satisfies the conditions for a network. This follows from the flow constraints.

Any variable X_{ij} representing a flow from i to j appears in the constraint for node i as a *flow out* of node i and in the constraint for node j as a *flow into* node j. Thus, X_{ij} appears on opposite sides of the equality sign in the two constraints. Consequently, since $a_{ij} = 1$ in the model, the column vector for X_{ij} will have an entry of $+1$ in the row for node i and -1 in the row for node j in Table 8.1. Those variables representing a flow into the sink node will have only one entry in their column vector because there is no flow out of the sink node to other nodes in the network.

The model we have specified is actually a linear programming model and could be solved using the simplex method. It turns out that if a *unique* optimal solution exists to a network model, it must be *interger-valued*. For example,

Table 8.1 Simplex Tableau for the Network Model

Cost	3	5	7	2	3	6	2	2	8	3	1	5	6	2	1	3	
Node	X_{OA}	X_{OB}	X_{OD}	X_{AC}	X_{AD}	X_{AE}	X_{BE}	X_{CA}	X_{CS}	X_{DA}	X_{DE}	X_{DS}	X_{EA}	X_{EB}	X_{ED}	X_{ES}	R
O	1	1	1	0	0	0	0	0	0	0	0	0	0	0	0	0	$= 1$
A	-1	0	0	1	1	1	0	-1	0	-1	0	0	-1	0	0	0	$= 0$
B	0	-1	0	0	0	0	1	0	0	0	0	0	0	-1	0	0	$= 0$
C	0	0	0	-1	0	0	0	1	1	0	0	0	0	0	0	0	$= 0$
D	0	0	-1	0	-1	0	0	0	0	1	1	1	0	0	-1	0	$= 0$
E	0	0	0	0	0	-1	-1	0	0	0	-1	0	1	1	1	1	$= 0$

suppose that the route O-B-E-S is a unique optimal solution to our model. Then, $X_{OB} = X_{BE} = X_{ES} = 1$ and all other $X_{ij} = 0$. This must be the case for the same reason we presented for the transportation model, and that argument will not be repeated here (see Section 6.1).

Solution Method   Although the simplex method could be used to solve our model, more efficient methods take advantage of its special structure. The procedure we present next is perhaps the most simple and intuitive. The method begins by finding the nearest (least-cost) node to the source node. The flow along the branch connecting it to the source is assumed to be in the direction of the source node *to* the new node just assigned. All other branches to the new node are eliminated from further consideration (all flows along these branches are made zero). Identify the source node and the new node as *assigned nodes*.

Next, find the unassigned nodes nearest to each of the assigned nodes. From these new unassigned nodes, select the node nearest to the *source node*. Activate the flow along the branch from the nearest assigned node to the new node and eliminate from further consideration any other branches to the new node. Identify the new node as an *assigned* node. Continue in this manner until all branches have been activated or eliminated. The result is the optimal solution to the model.

The solution procedure makes use of a tableau that contains the cost (distance) for each branch. The tableau, which is based on the network diagram in Figure 8.3, is updated each time a new node is assigned.

From Node	To Node					
	A	B	C	D	E	S
* O	3	5	—	7	—	—
A	—	—	2	3	6	—
B	—	—	—	—	2	—
C	2	—	—	—	—	8
D	3	—	—	—	1	5
E	6	2	—	1	—	3

A dash $(-)$ in the tableau indicates that there is no branch between the two nodes in question. In addition, the source node (node O) is in the first row but does not appear in a column because nothing flows *into* a source node. Similarly, the sink node (node S) is in the last column but does not appear in a row because nothing flows *out of* a sink node. The nonzero entries are the costs associated with each branch in the network, c_{ij}.

We begin by making the source node an assigned node. This is indicated by the * in row O of the tableau. Next, find the unassigned node that is the closest (least-cost) to the source node by scanning the nonzero entries in row O. Node A is obviously the best choice, so we make node A an assigned node, circle the cost element 3 in row O, and eliminate any branches that flow into node A. In the new tableau we have replaced the costs for branches CA, DA, and EA with dashes because we will no longer consider them.

		To Node				
From Node	A	B	C	D	E	S
* O	③	5	—	7	—	—
* A	—	—	2	3	6	—
B	—	—	—	—	2	—
C	—	—	—	—	—	8
D	—	—	—	—	1	5
E	—	2	—	1	—	3
d_j	$3					

We have also added a new row, d_j, which indicates the least cumulative cost of going from the source node to node j in the network. At this stage, $d_A = \$3$ indicates that branch OA is the least-cost way to get to node A. This is why we can eliminate branches CA, DA, and EA; if the optimal route includes node A, no other route includes branches flowing *into* node A that will be less costly. This can be verified by examining Figure 8.4, where the network diagram for the Kramer problem has been reproduced for convenience. The *next* best route from the origin to node A is ODA at a cost of \$10.

We now have two assigned nodes, O and A. The node closest to node O is node B at a cost of \$5. The node closest to node A is node C. The cost of going from node O to node C is equal to the cost of going from node O to node A plus the cost of going from node A to node C. This is easily computed from the tableau as

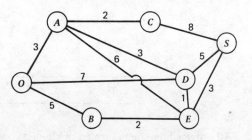

Figure 8.4 Kramer Shipping network.

$d_A + c_{AC} = \$3 + \$2 = \$5$. Since we have a tie (both new nodes are equally "distant" from the origin), we can assign both nodes B and C and set $d_B = d_C = \$5$. In addition, we can eliminate all branches flowing into nodes B and C that have not been circled. The new tableau is as follows:

From Node	To Node					
	A	B	C	D	E	S
* O	③	⑤	—	7	—	—
* A	—	—	②	3	6	—
* B	—	—	—	—	2	—
* C	—	—	—	—	—	8
D	—	—	—	—	1	5
E	—	—	—	1	—	3
d_j	\$3	\$5	\$5			

The assigned nodes are O, A, B, C. The node closest to node O is node D at a cost of \$7. Node D is also closest to node A at a total cumulative cost of $d_A + c_{AD} = \$3 + \$3 = \$6$. Node E is closest to node B with a total cumulative cost of $d_B + c_{BE} = \$5 + \$2 = \$7$. The total cumulative cost to node S via node C is \$13. Therefore, we assign node D because it has the lowest total cumulative cost, set $d_D = \$6$, eliminate all branches into node D, and circle c_{AD}. The new tableau is as follows:

From Node	To Node					
	A	B	C	D	E	S
O	③	⑤	—	—	—	—
* A	—	—	②	③	6	—
* B	—	—	—	—	2	—
* C	—	—	—	—	—	8
* D	—	—	—	—	1	5
E	—	—	—	—	—	3
d_j	\$3	\$5	\$5	\$6		

All entries have been circled in row O, so we can eliminate node O from the set of assigned nodes. We must now find the unassigned nodes closest to each of the assigned nodes A, B, C, and D. There is a tie for the lowest cumulative cost ($7) to node E between nodes B and D. Thus, we assign node E, set $d_E = \$7$, circle both c_{BE} and c_{DE}, and eliminate all other branches into node E. The result is given below. Note that nodes A and B can be eliminated from the set of assigned nodes.

			To Node			
From Node	A	B	C	D	E	S
O	③	⑤	—	—	—	—
A	—	—	②	③	—	—
B	—	—	—	—	②	—
* C	—	—	—	—	—	8
* D	—	—	—	—	①	5
* E	—	—	—	—	—	3
d_j	$3	$5	$5	$6	$7	

Node S is the only unassigned node. Since $d_C + c_{CS} > d_D + c_{DS} > d_E + c_{ES} = \$10$, we circle c_{ES} and eliminate all other branches into node S. The final tableau is as follows:

			To Node			
From Node	A	B	C	D	E	S
O	③	⑤	—	—	—	—
A	—	—	②	③	—	—
B	—	—	—	—	②	—
C	—	—	—	—	—	—
D	—	—	—	—	①	—
E	—	—	—	—	—	③
d_j	$3	$5	$5	$6	$7	$10

The optimal solution can be assembled from the information in the last tableau. We start at the sink node and work toward the source node. We find all the circled entries in column S. In this case there is only the one in row E. This means that the optimal solution contains branch ES. We must now find the best way to get to node E. Searching column E we find two circled elements, one in row B and the other in row D. This implies that we will have more than one optimal solution to our model. Let us first choose node D. Thus, the route so far is DES.

The best way to get to node D is from node A because c_{AD} is the only circled element in column D. Similarly, the best way to get to node A is to go straight from the origin. Therefore, one of the optimal routes in $OADES$.

Following the same procedure, the other optimal route is $OBES$. Since $d_s =$ $10, the cost of the optimal routes is $10 per crate.

Summary of the Shortest-Route Method   Having seen a straightforward application of the shortest-route method, let us review the procedure in a more general manner. Define set A to be the set of assigned nodes. In addition, define O to be the source node and S the sink node. We can now begin the procedure.

Step 1.   Prepare a matrix from the connected network representation of the problem. If there are n nodes in the network, there will be $n - 1$ rows, one for each node excluding node S, and $n - 1$ columns, one for each node excluding node O. Cell i, j of the matrix contains the cost (distance) of going from node i to node j. Put a dash in the matrix wherever there can be no flow from i to j.

Step 2.   Initialize set A to contain the source node, $A : O$.

Step 3.   Scan row O of the matrix for the lowest-cost element. Suppose it is element c_{Oj}. Circle element c_{Oj}, eliminate from the matrix all other cost elements corresponding to flows to node j, and set $d_j = c_{Oj}$. Add node j to the set of assigned nodes, $A : O, j$.

Step 4.   If set A contains node S, stop. The shortest route can be found by tracing back through the matrix starting from node S. The optimal cost is given by d_S. Otherwise, go to Step 5.

Step 5.   Scan each row in the matrix corresponding to the nodes in set A for the minimum-cost element. Each minimum-cost element corresponds to a branch from an assigned node to an unassigned node. Find the unassigned node that represents the least-cost link *to the source node* O. Suppose this is node k and the closest assigned node is j. Circle cost element c_{jk}, eliminate all other cost elements in the column corresponding to node k that are not circled, and set $d_k = d_j + c_{jk}$. Add node k to set $A : O, \ldots, j, k, \ldots$. In the event of ties between nodes k and k', add both nodes to set A, eliminate all cost elements in column k' that are not circled, and set $d_{k'} = d_m + c_{m,k'}$, where m is the closest assigned node to k'. Repeat Steps 4 and 5 until the optimal route has been identified.

MAXIMAL-FLOW PROBLEM

The method for solving the shortest-route problem did not specifically recognize capacity limitations on the flow through the branches in the network. The maximal-flow problem, however, is concerned with finding the maximal flow from source to sink in a connected network. Each branch has an upper limit on flow in a given direction called its *flow capacity*. Let c_{ij}^k designate the *remaining* flow capacity along branch i, j in the direction $i \rightarrow j$ at the kth iteration. At the start of the procedure, $k = 0$ and c_{ij}^0 designates the total flow capacity of the branch in the $i \rightarrow j$ direction. These initial conditions are represented in the following network diagram:

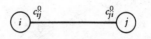

If $c_{ij}^0 = 0$ we say that the branch is *oriented* in the direction $j \rightarrow i$.

At each iteration k, the procedure selects any series of branches forming a path from source to sink. The maximal flow along the path is the *minimum* of the remaining capacities of the branches in the path. Suppose that this minimum value is f. Then, for each branch ij in the path where the flow proceeds in the direction $i \rightarrow j$, the remaining capacities are updated as follows:

$$c_{ij}^k = c_{ij}^{k-1} - f$$
$$c_{ji}^k = c_{ji}^{k-1} + f \qquad (8.1)$$

All other branches not a part of the path are not affected, and their remaining capacities at the kth iteration are the same as they were at iteration $k - 1$. Obviously, if $c_{ij}^k = 0$ there can be no more flow in the direction $i \rightarrow j$ along that branch.

Note that the remaining capacity is *increased* in the opposite direction, $j \rightarrow i$. This enables us to keep track of the magnitude of the flow in the branch and subsequently to fine tune the solution to determine the maximal flow in the network. We will see how to fine tune the solution later. To determine the flow in a branch at the kth iteration, we can compute $\alpha_{ji}^k = c_{ji}^0 - c_{ji}^k$. If $\alpha_{ji}^k > 0$, the flow is equal to α_{ji}^k in the direction $j \rightarrow i$. If $\alpha_{ji}^k < 0$, the flow is $|\alpha_{ji}^k|$ in the direction $i \rightarrow j$. Of course, if $\alpha_{ji}^k = 0$, there is no flow in the branch at the kth iteration.

As an example of a maximal-flow problem, consider the Krood Oil Company, which owns and operates a network of fuel pipelines and pumping stations. The pipelines are the branches and the pumping stations are the nodes. Krood managers are considering the addition of a new pumping station (node D in Figure 8.5); consequently, they are interested in finding how many barrels of oil per day they would be able to transport from a particular wellhead (node O) to the port (node S) where the oil tankers are kept.

The flow capacities (in thousands of barrels per day) are shown above each branch. The capacities for branches AD, BD, and DS are hypothetical at this point because these branches would be a part of the new addition to the network. Krood wants to determine the required capacities of these pipelines through network analysis. Note that all branches in the network are oriented.

Solution Method We begin by arbitrarily selecting a path from the source to the sink. Suppose we select $CADS$. Figure 8.5 indicates that the maximum flow along this path is 2 because branch AD has a capacity limit of 2. We now update the

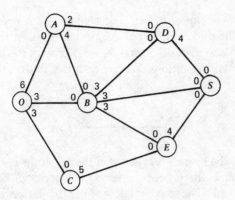

Figure 8.5 Network for the Krood Oil Company.

remaining capacities of each branch along the path to reflect a flow of 2. All other branch capacities remain the same at this iteration. The new network is shown below. The value in the box by the sink node is the total cumulative flow through the network.

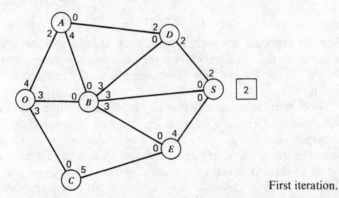

First iteration.

We now select another path through the network. Obviously, we cannot include branch AD in the direction $A \rightarrow D$ in the new path because it has no more capacity available. Let us choose $OABDS$ for the second iteration. The limiting branch is DS with a remaining capacity of 2. The resulting network is as follows:

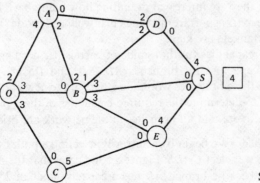

Second iteration.

Next, we assign a flow of 2 to path *OABS*. In this case, both branches *OA* and *AB* limit the flow along this path. This results in the following network:

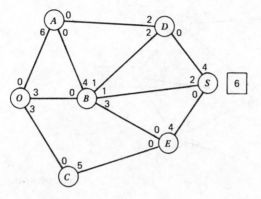

Third iteration.

Following this procedure, the next two iterations are:

Iteration 4.   Assign a flow of 3 to *OBES*.
Iteration 5.   Assign a flow of 1 to *OCES*.

The resulting network is as follows:

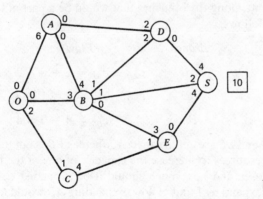

Resulting network.

At this point, it seems that the maximal flow has been found, but this is not the case. Even though each path has at least one branch ij, with zero remaining capacity c_{ij}^5 in the feasible direction of flow, we can treat c_{ji}^5 as if it were a hypothetical remaining capacity in the opposite direction. In other words, we tentatively assume that we can assign a flow in the opposite direction along the branches with zero remaining capacity to see if we can find another path from the source to the sink. In our problem, *OCEBS* is such a path. We treat the remaining capacity along branch BE as 3 in the direction $E \to B$. The maximum flow we can assign to this path is 1 because of branch BS. The final network is as follows:

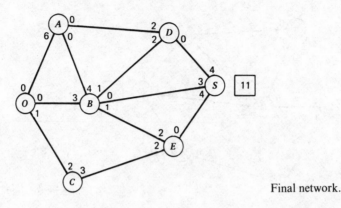

Final network.

Note that branch BE now has a remaining capacity of 1 in the feasible direction $B \to E$. In effect, we have canceled one unit of flow in branch BE in the direction $B \to E$, thereby reallocating the flows in three paths. We have subtracted one unit of flow along the path $OBES$ and added one unit of flow to each of the paths OBS; and $OCES$. The result is a net increase of one unit of flow for the entire network. Because no other paths lend themselves to this "fine tuning," the Krood Oil Company can expect to transport 11,000 barrels of oil a day to the seaport.

The flow in each branch can be determined from the final network. In particular, the flows along the branches that would be a part of the new addition are computed as follows:

Branch	Flow
AD	$c_{AD}^0 - c_{AD}^6 = 2 - 0 = 2$
BD	$c_{BD}^0 - c_{BD}^6 = 3 - 1 = 2$
DS	$c_{DS}^0 - c_{DS}^6 = 4 - 0 = 4$

Both AD and DS are at full capacity, whereas BD is not fully utilized. If Krood had enough resources to increase the capacity of one of the branches, which one should be chosen and how much should it be expanded? Certainly they would choose DS to expand by 1 unit of flow. Expanding AD would not yield any increase in total network flow unless DS were expanded also. The expansion of DS by 1 unit of flow will allow the full utilization of branches OC and BD because we could find another path, $OCEBDS$, with a capacity of 1 unit of flow. Because the flow is in the reverse direction for branch BE, we would be canceling another unit of flow along path $OBES$ and increasing the flow along paths $OBDS$ and $OCES$. The net result would be a total flow of 12,000 barrels per day through the network.

Let us now return to the original network for the Krood Oil Company in Figure 8.5. Suppose we were only interested in finding the maximal flow through

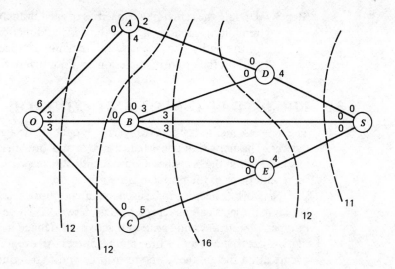

Figure 8.6 Initial Krood Oil network with example cuts and cut values.

the network and we were not concerned with determining the utilization of specific branches. In this instance, we could make use of the *max-flow min-cut theorem*. A *cut* is any subset of oriented branches that contains *at least* one branch of every path from source to origin. The *cut value*, which is the sum of the capacities of the branches in the subset in the direction specified, provides an *upper bound* on the flow through a network with only one source and sink. The max-flow min-cut theorem states that the maximum flow through a network is equal to the minimum cut value for any of the cuts in the network.

Figure 8.6 shows the original Krood Oil Company network with some example cuts and cut values. Note that the minimum cut value equals the maximal flow of 11,000 barrels through the network. The max-flow min-cut theorem can also be useful during the solution procedure we demonstrated earlier. Whenever the minimum cut value of the *remaining capacities* is zero, we need no longer search for a path with positive flow from source to sink. The optimal flow pattern has already been found.

Review of the Maximal-Flow Method The procedure for finding the flow pattern that results in the maximal flow through a connected network with only one source and sink can be summarized in the following steps:

Step 1. Arbitrarily select a path from source to sink with strictly positive flow capacity. That is, for each branch $c_{ij}^k > 0$ or $c_{ji}^k > 0$ depending on the desired flow through the branch. If no such path exists, the existing flow pattern must be optimal.

Step 2. Search the path for the branch with the smallest remaining capacity. Let f be the value of that smallest remaining capacity. Assign a flow of f to the path.

Step 3. Update the remaining capacities of each branch in the path. Decrease the remaining capacity by f in the desired direction of flow for each branch in the path. Also, increase the remaining capacity of each branch in the path in the opposite direction by f. Return to Step 1.

8.3 PROJECT PLANNING AND CONTROL METHODS

The network methods we have presented so far are designed to select *optimal* alternatives. The networks consisted of nodes and branches where there was a flow of some kind in the branches. Consequently, the networks were readily identifiable representations of the problem situation.

Network concepts can be used to manage more abstract situations. In particular, large projects can be represented as networks. These projects consist of a large number of *activities* and *events*. An activity is defined as any recognizable portion of a project that consumes time and resources. An event is an accomplishment that occurs at an instantaneous point in time and that requires no time or resources. In terms of network terminology, the activities are the branches and the events are the nodes. The network, then, is a diagram of the entire project showing the interrelationships of all the activities and events.

Network concepts applied to large projects are useful in keeping managers informed as to the progress of the project and aid in coordinating the various activities of the overall job. Managers are made aware of those activities that are critical to completing the project on time. In general, large-project networks provide a useful information source so that management can make efficient decisions regarding the project.

In this section, we present two methods for large-project planning and control. The first, the critical-path method (CPM), is most often used when the organization has completed a number of similar projects in the past and management is able to estimate with certainty how long the activity will take. The second approach, the program evaluation and review technique (PERT), is used when management is uncertain as to how long the activity will take, and probability distributions of the time duration must be assigned to each activity. Although the two methods are very similar, there is enough of a difference to warrant separate treatment.

The Critical-Path Method

Goliath Manufacturing Company manufactures heavy earth-moving equipment. Although the company has a large number of products in its product line, one product in particular—a giant land-mover used in strip-mining—is only ordered on a special basis because of the infrequent demand and the high cost of production. CPM is used to help management coordinate the complex project represented by the construction of the land-mover. The activities, their predecessors, and the time durations are given in Table 8.2.

The network is shown in Figure 8.7. The activity durations, expressed in weeks, are shown above each activity branch in the network. The arrowheads reflect the

Table 8.2 Activities in the Construction of the Goliath Land-mover

Activity	Description	Predecessors	Duration, weeks
A	Finalize customer options and specifications	—	4
B	Procure raw materials	—	20
C	Develop test specifications	A	5
D	Manufacture chassis components	A, B	35
E	Manufacture power-train components	A, B	44
F	Assemble chassis	D	5
G	Assemble power train to chassis	E, F	6
H	Tests and quality checks	C, G	2

sequence of the activities. For example, we cannot achieve event 5 until we have achieved events 3 and 4 and performed activities E and F. No activity leaving a node can be started until all activities leading into the node have been completed.

Notice that there is an extra activity, activity X, in Figure 8.7. Activity X is a *dummy activity*. A dummy activity consumes no time or resources and is used only to impose a precedence relationship between two or more real activities in a project. When constructing a project network, *only one branch* can be used to connect two nodes directly. Quite often the situation arises where two concurrent activities have a common event as a starting point and both must be completed before a certain other event can be achieved. This is the case with activities A and

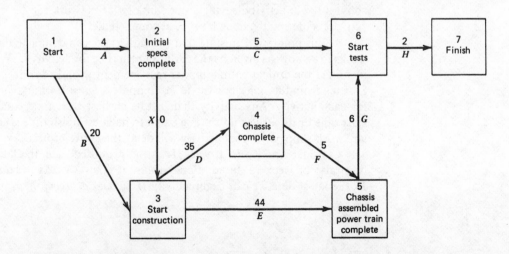

Figure 8.7 Network representation of the Goliath Land-mover project.

B. Finalizing the customer options and specifications can be done concurrently with the procurement of the raw materials; however, both of these activities must be completed before event 3, the start of construction, can be realized. To avoid two activities directly connecting nodes 1 and 3, we create node 2 and insert a dummy activity between nodes 2 and 3. This has the effect of requiring that event 3 cannot be realized until both activities *A* and *B* are completed.

Identifying the Critical Path   Suppose that a customer order has just been accepted for a Goliath land-mover. How long will it take to construct the land-mover? Merely summing all of the activity times will not do because many of the activities can be performed concurrently. A certain sequence of activities determines the total length of the project. This sequence of activities from the starting node to the finishing node is called the *critical path.*

We must analyze the network to find the critical path. Starting with the source node (node 1), compute an *earliest start* and *earliest finish* time for each activity. Consider activity *A.* The earliest this activity can begin is at time zero. The earliest the activity can be completed is 4 weeks from now. This information is recorded above the arrow representing activity *A* as shown in Figure 8.8.

In general, the earliest start time for activity *j* leaving node *k* is equal to the *largest* of the earliest finish times of those activities entering node *k.* The *earliest finish* time for activity *j* is computed as $EF_j = ES_j + t_j,$

where

EF_j = earliest finish time for activity *j*
ES_j = earliest start time for activity *j*
  t_j = time duration of activity *j*

These computations are shown for the entire network in Figure 8.9. Note that the early start time for activities *D* and *E* is 20 weeks because of the early finish time for activity *B.* No activity leaving a node in a *CPM* network can be started until all activities entering the node have been completed.

At this point, we can state that the earliest we can complete the project is 72 weeks from now, as given by the earliest finish time for activity *H.* We have not yet identified the critical path. Suppose management promises delivery in 72 weeks. Starting from the sink node (node 7), compute a *latest start* and *latest finish* time for each activity. Any activity that has its earliest start time equal to its latest start time or its earliest finish time equal to its latest finish time is critical because any work slippage on that activity will delay the entire project.

Consider activity *H.* If week 72 is the promised date, the latest finish date must also be week 72. In addition, because it takes 2 weeks to complete activity *H,* the latest date we can begin activity *H without delaying the rest of the project*

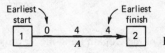

Figure 8.8   Earliest start and finish times for activity **A.**

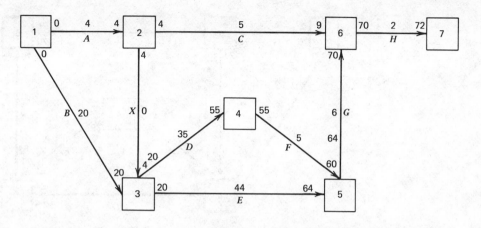

Figure 8.9 Early start and early finish times for the Goliath Land-mover project.

is week 70. Record this information *below* the arrow, as shown in Figure 8.10 for activity H.

In general, the latest finish time for activity j entering node k is equal to the *smallest* of the latest start times of the activities leaving node k. The latest start time for activity j is computed by

$$LS_j = LF_j - t_j$$

where

LS_j = latest start time of activity j
LF_j = latest finish time of activity j

These computations for the entire network are shown in Figure 8.11. Note that the latest finish time for activity B is 20 weeks because of the latest start time for activity E.

We can now compute the *slack* associated with each activity. Slack is the amount of time an activity can be delayed without delaying the entire project. The slack for activity j is given by

$$S_j = LF_j - EF_j = LS_j - ES_j$$

Table 8.3 gives the slack for each activity in the network. This information enables management to allocate resources more efficiently among projects and among

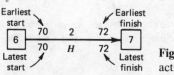

Figure 8.10 Earliest and latest start and finish times for activity H.

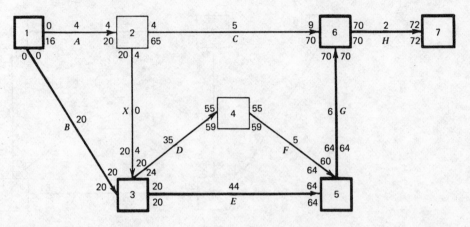

Figure 8.11   Earliest and latest start and finish times and critical path for the Goliath Land-mover project.

activities within the same project. For example, the start of activity *A* can be delayed 16 weeks without lengthening the project. The resources normally used on this activity can be assigned to another project until week 16. In addition, when we are 55 weeks into the project, some resources used on activity *F* can be assigned to activity *E* to help get caught up if we fall behind schedule there, as long as they are reassigned to activity *F* by the 59th week of the project.

Once the slack for each activity has been computed, the critical path can be easily identified. *Each activity on the critical path has zero slack.*[1] In our example, the critical path is *BEGH* as evidenced in Table 8.3 and Figure 8.11. The critical path has special significance because if we fall behind schedule on any of these activities the entire project will be delayed. Management should focus attention on these activities to make sure they are completed on schedule. The other activities should not be ignored however, because if the slack on an activity is consumed, that activity becomes critical to the completion of the project on time. Normally, the progress on the project is frequently reviewed to see if the critical path has changed.

Although the critical path can be identified by computing the slack for each activity, the critical path in small networks (such as our example) can be determined by finding the *longest* path (with respect to time) from the source to sink node. Because the slack information is so important to management, CPM computer codes automatically provide the slack information on each activity. The critical path is a by-product of this information. This is much easier than searching for the longest time path in a large network. Nonetheless, the critical path is the longest

---

[1] If the promised date was chosen to be greater than the earliest finish time of the last activity, the slack for each activity on the critical path will be equal and greater than zero. The slacks for all other activities will be greater.

Table 8.3 Slack Time for Each Activity in the Goliath Land-mover Project

Activity	Latest Finish	Earliest Finish	Latest Start	Earliest Start	Slack, weeks
A	20	4	16	0	16
B	20	20	0	0	0
C	70	9	65	4	61
D	59	55	24	20	4
E	64	64	20	20	0
F	64	60	59	55	4
G	70	70	64	64	0
H	72	72	70	70	0
X	20	4	20	4	16

time path in the network, and its length determines the minimum project duration, as shown in Table 8.4 for our example.

Cost-Time Trade-offs During the normal course of a large project, many circumstances typically cause one or more activities to fall behind schedule. It may then be desirable to expedite, or *crash*, some of the activities to get back on schedule. It costs more to crash an activity than to allow it to proceed at its normal pace, however, and important cost-time trade-offs must be considered by the project management.

Four cost-time parameters are associated with each activity: *normal time*, *normal cost*, *crash time*, and *crash cost*. The crash time for an activity is the *minimum* duration that can be achieved through the use of time-reduction options such as

Table 8.4 Total Time Durations of the Paths in the Goliath Land-mover Example

Path	Total Time, weeks
ACH	11
AXDFGH	52
AXEGH	56
BDFGH	68
BEGH (critical)	72

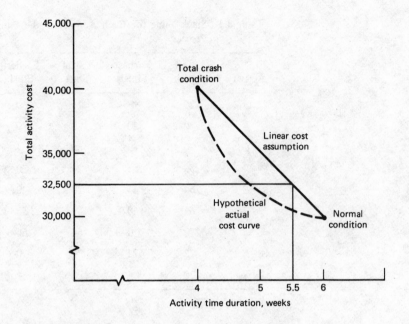

Figure 8.12 Cost-time relationships in a CPM cost-time analysis.

enlarged work crews, overtime, and subcontracting. The crash cost is the cost to achieve the minimum activity time.

In a CPM cost-time analysis, we assume that there is a *linear* increase in costs as the activity time is reduced from its normal time. For example, suppose that the normal time is 6 weeks at a cost of $30,000 for activity *G* in the Goliath land-mover example. If the crash time is 4 weeks at a total crash cost of $40,000, the net reduction in time is 2 weeks at a net increase in costs of $10,000. We assume that it costs $10,000/2 = $5000 per week to crash activity *G*. This assumption of linear marginal cost increases is shown in Figure 8.12 along with a hypothetical "actual" marginal cost curve for activity *G*. Thus, if activity *G* is crashed by only $\frac{1}{2}$ week, the estimated total cost is $32,500. Even though the actual costs would be much less in this example, the linear assumption is usually adequate in most cases.

Table 8.5 contains the cost and time data for the Goliath land-mover example. The cost to crash per week is given by

$$\text{Cost to crash per week} = \frac{\text{Crash cost} - \text{Normal cost}}{\text{Normal time} - \text{Crash time}}$$

In addition, project indirect costs amount to $3500 per week.

As an example of a CPM cost-time trade-off analysis, suppose that Goliath has accepted an order for a land-mover with a promised date of 64 weeks from now. In addition, a penalty clause awards the customer $10,000 per week that the project is late. Considering that the critical path is 72 weeks (Figure 8.11), it

Table 8.5 Cost and Time Data for the Goliath Land-mover Example

Activity	Normal Time, weeks	Normal Cost	Crash Time, weeks	Crash Cost	Maximum Time Reduction, weeks	Cost to Crash per Week
A	4	$ 2,000	3	$ 3,000	1	$1,000
B	20	$100,000	15	$116,000	5	$3,200
C	5	$ 4,000	3	$ 6,000	2	$1,000
D	35	$105,000	30	$120,000	5	$3,000
E	44	$ 88,000	37	$107,600	7	$2,800
F	5	$ 10,000	4	$ 13,000	1	$3,000
G	6	$ 30,000	4	$ 40,000	2	$5,000
H	2	$ 2,000	1	$ 3,500	1	$1,500
	Total	$341,000	Total	$409,100		

would seem that Goliath should not have accepted the order. As Table 8.5 indicates, however, any activity in the project could be expedited for a certain increase in direct costs. For every week the project duration is decreased up to week 64, Goliath avoids one week's worth of penalty and indirect costs, or $13,500. If the project duration is reduced beyond week 64, the savings are only the weekly indirect costs of $3500. The objective, then, is to determine the project duration that minimizes total project costs.

Although the first impulse may be to crash *all* activities to their limit, this would be unnecessarily costly. Because the critical path determines the project duration, it makes more sense to concentrate on crashing the activities along the critical path. In applying the logic, we make use of the following guidelines:

1. Choose the activity on the critical path(s) that is the cheapest to crash per week.
2. Reduce the time on this activity until either it cannot be reduced any further or another path becomes critical. If more than one path is critical it may be necessary to reduce more than one activity simultaneously.
3. Reduce the activity (activities) so long as the increase in project direct costs is less than the savings generated by the reduction in project duration.

Figure 8.13 shows the network changes required to arrive at the minimum-cost project duration of 62 weeks. The critical paths are shown by the heavy dark arrows. Table 8.6 summarizes the crash strategies and provides the total cost information. Column 5 gives the total project direct costs before crashing the corresponding activity for a particular trial. Column 9 is merely the sum of columns 5 through 8.

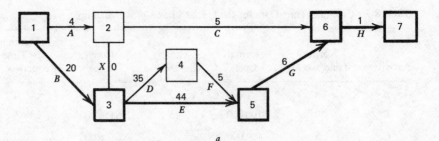

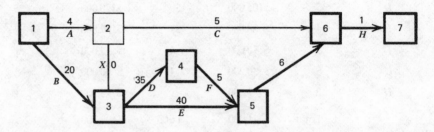

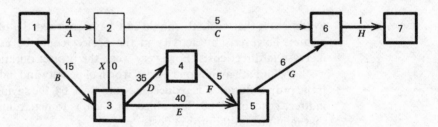

Figure 8.13 Network changes in cost-time analysis. Project durations: (*a*) 71 weeks; (*b*) 67 weeks; (*c*) 62 weeks.

Table 8.6 Cost-Time Analysis for the Goliath Land-mover Example

	1	2	3	4	5	6	7	8	9
Trial	Crash Activity	Resulting Critical Path	Time Reduction. weeks	Project Duration, weeks	Project Direct Costs	Added Crash Costs	Indirect Costs	Penalty Costs	Total Project Costs
0	—	*BEGH*	—	72	$341,000	—	$252,000	$80,000	$673,000
1	*H*	*BEGH*	1	71	$341,000	$ 1,500	$248,500	$70,000	$661,000
2	*E*	*BDFGH* *BEGH*	4	67	$342,500	$11,200	$234,500	$30,000	$618,200
3	*B*	*BDFGH* *BEGH*	5	62	$353,700	$16,000	$217,000	$0	$586,700

Activity *H* was chosen first because it is the cheapest to crash per week of the activities on the critical path *BEGH* (see Table 8.5). The critical path remains unchanged after the reduction in *H*. *E* is the next most inexpensive to crash, and it was chosen next in trial 2. It can only be reduced 4 weeks, however, because path *BDFGH* also becomes critical (see Figure 8.13*b*). In trial 3 we crash activity *B* by 5 weeks. The total project duration is now 62 weeks at a total cost of $586,700. At this point we can only save the $3500 per week of indirect costs by shortening the project 1 week. If we try to shorten activity *E* any further we must also shorten activity *D* or *F* simultaneously. The weekly cost would be $5800. Also, we could crash activity *G* for only $5000 per week. Both of these alternatives are not very interesting because the weekly cost would exceed the weekly benefits from reducing indirect costs.

The analysis indicates that Goliath should schedule the project completion date 2 weeks before the promised date in the contract. Figure 8.13*c* shows the new activity times for the project. Given these times, early start, early finish, latest start, latest finish, and slack times can be computed for each activity. It should be reemphasized, however, that the project now has *two* critical paths; thus, management must avoid any delays along activities *B*, *D*, *E*, *F*, *G*, and *H*.

The Program Evaluation and Review Technique

Frequently, managers are not certain as to the duration of a project because the project is a new experience for the company or it is performed so infrequently that work methods or production processes have changed significantly since the last time the project was attempted. In this situation, the activity times can be treated as random variables subject to some probability distribution. The program evaluation and review technique (PERT) recognizes this uncertainty when arriving at expected activity times. Once the activity times have been determined, activity slacks can be computed and the critical path identified as in the CPM approach. Because the activity-time estimation is the major difference between CPM and PERT, we concentrate on that issue in the following discussion.

Activity-Time Estimation   The original version of PERT required that project management develop three time estimates for *each activity* where there is uncertainty as to the duration. These estimates are then used to describe the probability distribution for the activity time. The three time estimates are

a—The *most optimistic* time. This would be the activity time if everything progressed at an ideal pace. The probability of achieving the activity in less time than this should be no more than 0.01.

m—The *most likely* time. This would be the activity time under normal conditions.

b—The *most pessimistic* time. This would be the activity time if significant delays or other work stoppages occurred. The probability of requiring more time than this is only 0.01.

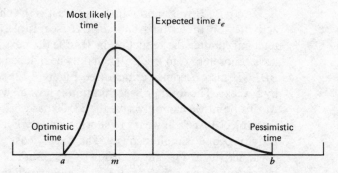

Figure 8.14   Probability distribution for an activity showing the three time estimates and the expected time.

The three time estimates for an uncertain activity can be used to define a probability distribution as shown in Figure 8.14. PERT assumes that the distribution is a *Beta distribution*. Although this choice is somewhat arbitrary, the Beta distribution is nonsymmetric and allows the most likely time (or mode of the distribution) to move freely between the most optimistic and most pessimistic time estimates. If a symmetric probability density function were used instead, the mode and the mean would be coincidental, requiring the most likely time estimate always to be halfway between the most optimistic and most pessimistic time estimates. The Beta distribution allows flexibility in choosing the time estimates.

The three time estimates for a given activity are used to compute two parameters of the probability distribution of activity times. One parameter is the *expected activity time*. The expected time t_e for a given activity with a Beta distribution is approximately

$$t_e = \frac{a + 4m + b}{6} \tag{8.2}$$

The expected activity times are used to determine the activity slacks and critical path in a PERT network analysis.

Another parameter important in a PERT analysis is the *variance* of each activity. The variance represents the degree of uncertainty associated with the activity duration. To estimate this parameter, PERT assumes that the standard deviation of the activity's Beta distribution is one-sixth the range of possible activity times, or

$$\sigma = (b - a)/6 \tag{8.3}$$

This assumption seems reasonable because the outer extremeties of many probability distributions lie about 3 standard deviations from the mean. This implies that there are about 6 standard deviations between the tails of the distribution. Consequently, the variance is

$$\sigma^2 = (b - a)^2/36 \tag{8.4}$$

Table 8.7 PERT Activity Time Data for the Goliath Land-mover Example

Activity	Most Optimistic (a)	Most Likely (m)	Most Pessimistic (b)	t_e	σ^2
A	1	3	11	4	2.78
B	14	20	26	20	4.00
C	2	4	12	5	2.78
D	22	36	44	35	13.44
E	40	44	48	44	1.78
F	1	4	13	5	4.00
G	4	5	12	6	1.78
H	2	2	2	2	0

As we will see, the variance will be useful in making probability statements about the project duration.

PERT Probability Concepts Consider the Goliath land-mover example we analyzed with CPM. Suppose that this is the first time that the project has ever been attempted. As such, management is uncertain about the activity times in the project. Table 8.7 contains the three time estimates, expected time, and variance for each activity. The time estimates were chosen so that the expected activity times equal the normal activity times used in the CPM analysis. Consequently, Figure 8.11 represents the project network where the t_e for each activity is written above each arrow. Note in Table 8.7 that there is no uncertainty in the time estimate for activity H in this example: thus, the variance is zero.

By just looking at Figure 8.11 it would seem that everything is the same as it was before in the CPM analysis. The difference, however, is that the activity times we use in a PERT analysis are the *means* of activity time *probability distributions*. This implies that the actual *project* duration is a random variable subject to some probability distribution, whereas before we assumed that the project duration was a certainty. In a PERT analysis, we assume that

1. The activity times are *statistically independent*.
2. The expected value and variance of the project-completion time are equal to the sum of the expected times and variance of the activities on the *critical path*.
3. The probability distribution of the project-completion time is a *normal distribution*. This arises from the *central-limit theorem*, which states that the distribution of a sum of independent random variables approaches the normal distribution as the number of variables gets large.

We now have a convenient way to make probability statements about the completion time of the project. Let T_c be the sum of the expected activity times along the *critical path* and $\sigma_c{}^2$ be the sum of the activity variances along the critical path. Then, to find the probability of completing the project in T weeks or less, we compute

$$z = \frac{T - T_c}{\sigma_c} \tag{8.5}$$

and look up z in the table for the area under the normal curve.

For example, using Table 8.7 and Figure 8.11, the critical path is *BEGH* and

$$T_c = 20 + 44 + 6 + 2 = 72 \text{ weeks}$$

$$\sigma_c{}^2 = 4 + 1.78 + 1.78 + 0 = 7.56 \text{ weeks}^2$$

or

$$\sigma_c = \sqrt{7.56} = 2.75 \text{ weeks}$$

Suppose management is interested in giving the land-mover customer a delivery-promise date. In particular, management would like to assess the chances of completing the project within a 76-week deadline. Using (8.5), we compute the normal deviate

$$z = \frac{76 - 72}{2.75} = 1.45$$

Looking up this value of z in the normal table indicates that there is a 93% chance that the project will be completed within 76 weeks. In this way, managers can use

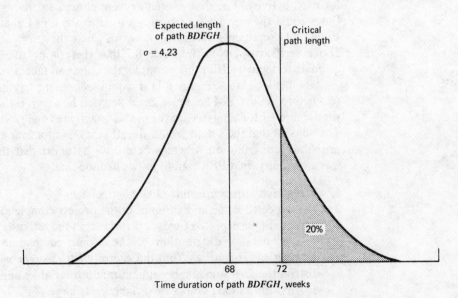

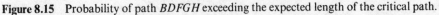

Figure 8.15 Probability of path *BDFGH* exceeding the expected length of the critical path.

these probability concepts to set contract promise dates or merely assess the chances of achieving a given scheduled completion date.

All of the above analysis assumes that *BEGH* will remain the critical path throughout the project. Consider the path *BDFGH*, which has a total expected length of 68 weeks. Using Table 8.7, the sum of the variances along this path is 23.22 weeks^2 as compared to 7.56 weeks^2 for the critical path. This implies that managers are collectively more uncertain about the activity times in path *BDFGH* than they are for the critical path. The managerial consequence is that there is a good chance that *BDFGH* will exceed the expected length of the critical path. The probability of this occurring is 20%, as shown in Figure 8.15. Thus, managerial attention should focus on "near-critical" paths with high variances as well as on the critical path, frequently checking the progress to avoid unnecessary delays in the total project.

Review of Project Network Methods

The procedure for analyzing CPM or PERT networks can be summarized as follows:

Step 1. Determine the activities and the precedence relationships for the project.
Step 2. Draw the network consisting of the activities determined in Step 1.
Step 3. Estimate the expected times for each activity. In a PERT analysis, also estimate the variances.
Step 4. Compute the earliest start and finish times and the latest start and finish times for each activity. Compute the slack for each activity and define the critical path.
Step 5. In a PERT analysis, compute the probability of achieving a given project-completion date.

In a CPM cost-time analysis to determine the minimum-cost project duration, successively crash the least expensive activities along the critical path in such a way that the added crash costs are less than the savings in indirect and penalty costs. Variations of PERT can allow single activity-time estimates and activity-cost information for a cost-time analysis analogous to the CPM procedure.

8.4 SUMMARY

Network methods have a good potential as managerial decision-making aids. If it is realized in the problem-recognition stage of the decision-making process that a problem can be modeled as a network, efficient solution procedures that take advantage of the special model structure can be utilized. We have demonstrated some of the simple optimum-seeking methods in this chapter, but this does not completely exhaust the list of available techniques. New and better methods useful to decision makers continue to be a focus of research in this area.

Network theory can also be applied to the management of large-scale projects. We have seen that CPM and PERT help identify potential trouble spots in a project through the identification of the critical path. These techniques improve project coordination and enable the efficient use of resources. Although network methods can be used to determine the minimum-cost project duration, perhaps the largest benefit comes from the information feedback on project progress and added control of the project as a whole. By far, this is the largest application of network methods in the business world.

Of course, the computer plays an important role here. CPM and PERT software packages provide reports on activity slack and other information useful for activity scheduling such as early start and finish times, late start and finish times, and resource needs per time period. Some routines actually schedule the activities when there are capacity constraints to consider. The discussion in this chapter assumed there were no resource constraints. One of the greatest advantages of computer use is the capability to *update* the network to reflect changes in activity progress. This is no easy task for realistic projects because of the large number of interrelated activities. Nonetheless, the successful implementation of network methods in general does not depend only on the availability of computer routines, but also on management's basic understanding of the techniques the computer uses.

The last five chapters have dealt with techniques that implicitly enumerate the alternatives and select the alternative(s) that optimize some linear objective function. The next chapter will present various techniques useful for analyzing problems where the objective function is nonlinear.

References Battersby, A., *Network Analysis for Planning and Scheduling*, 3d ed., New York: John Wiley & Sons, 1970.

Elmagrahby, S.E., "The Theory of Networks and Management Science, Parts I and II," *Management Science*, Vol. 17 (1970), pp. 1–34 and B-54–B-71.

Ford, L.R., Jr., and Fulkerson, D.R., *Flow in Networks*, Princeton, N.J.: Princeton University Press, 1962.

Frank, H., and Frisch., I.T., *Communications, Transmission and Transportation Networks*, Reading, Mass.: Addison-Wesley, 1971.

Hillier, F.S., and Lieberman, G.J., *Introduction to Operations Research*, 2d ed., San Francisco: Holden Day, 1974.

Hoare, H.R., *Project Management Using Network Analysis*, Maidenhead, England: McGraw-Hill, 1973.

Kelley, J.E., Jr., "Critical-Path Planning and Scheduling: Mathematical Basis," *Operations Research*, Vol. 9 (1961), pp. 296–320.

Levin, R., and Kirkpatrick, C.A., *Planning and Control with PERT/CPM*, New York: McGraw-Hill, 1966.

Wagner, H.M., *Principles of Operations Research*, 2d ed., Englewood Cliffs, N.J.: Prentice-Hall, 1975.

Whitehouse, G.E., *Systems Analysis and Design Using Network Techniques*, Englewood Cliffs, N.J.: Prentice-Hall, 1973.

Yen, J.Y., "An Algorithm for Finding Shortest Routes from all Source Nodes to a Given Destination in General Networks," *Quart. of Applied Math.*, Vol. 27 (1969), pp. 526–530.

Review Questions

1. Why is it advantageous to recognize a decision problem as having the structure of a network?

2. What are the advantages of using the shortest-route method in lieu of linear programming?

3. In the maximum-flow method, the remaining capacity of a branch is updated after a flow has been assigned to the branch. If the assigned flow on branch ij is in the direction $i \rightarrow j$, c_{ij} is decremented while c_{ji} is incremented. Explain why these two adjustments must be made in this procedure.

4. Intuitively explain why the max-flow min-cut theorem provides the value of the maximum flow through a network with one source and sink.

5. Why is the critical path of such importance in large project scheduling and control? Can the critical path change during the project? Why?

6. Your construction company has a new contract to build an office building. The company frequently builds this particular design. Which network planning method, PERT or CPM, most closely fits this situation? Why? What types of analysis can you do?

7. Why is the normal distribution not particularly well suited for describing the uncertainty in time estimates for particular activities in a PERT network?

8. Suppose that you are trying to convince management that project planning techniques (PERT or CPM) would be useful to them. Some of the managers have voiced the following concerns:
   (a) There is a tendency for the technicians to handle the operation of the technique; thus, management will not use it very much.
   (b) It puts pressure on managers because everyone knows where the critical path is. Managers of activities along the critical path are in the "spotlight," and if their activity is delayed, the cost of the delay is on their shoulders alone.
   (c) The introduction of network-planning techniques may require new communication channels and systems procedures.

   Comment on each of these concerns.

Problems

1. Consider the network shown in Figure P8.1.
   (a) Find the shortest route from source to sink using the shortest-route method.
   (b) Verify your solution by enumerating all paths completely.

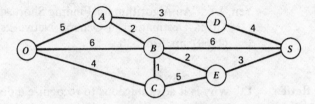

Figure P8.1   Hypothetical network.

2.   The Acme Automotive Parts Company has recently opened a new warehouse in Sunset City. The traffic manager feels that the present route taken by the trucks supplying the new warehouse can be improved. Trucks take the route *OAFS* where *O* is the plant at Orion Junction and *S* is the warehouse. Although the roads are reasonably straight and well maintained, the manager objects to the distance traveled. A recent study indicates that the cost of this transportation system is greatly affected by the distances the trucks travel. These costs primarily consist of maintenance, replacement, and driver wages. Because the truck fleet makes many trips to Sunset City annually, significant cost reductions can be expected for each mile the route is reduced. The diagram in Figure P8.2 is an abstraction of the road network between Orion and Sunset. Although the branches are all straight lines, the actual roads may have numerous curves or hills. It can be safely assumed that the rate of speed along any road is the same. The diagram shows the distance, in miles, of each road segment.

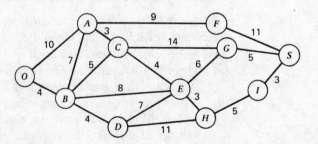

Figure P8.2   Road network between Orion and Sunset.

   (a)   Use the shortest-route method to find the best route from origin to sink.

   (b)   What other considerations should the manager make before authorizing a new route?

3.   A certain manufacturing company is considering the installation of an automated conveyor system to move various heavy products finished in department *O* through the rest of the plant to department *S*, the shipping

area. Because of the physical setup of the plant, the conveyor must be constructed in links. The cost of the construction of a link depends on the path the link takes. Three alternative "routes" for the conveyor have been proposed: *OADS*, *OBDS*, and *OCS*. Management would like to find the least-cost conveyor system as a prelude to arriving at a final decision to automate handling these products. The problem is seen to be a matter of finding the shortest route in the network diagram in Figure P8.3. The costs (in tens of thousands of dollars) are shown by each link.

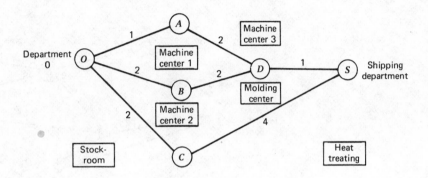

Figure P8.3 Alternative conveyer routes.

(a) Formulate the linear programming model for finding the minimum-cost path.

(b) Solve the model for the optimum path.

(c) Although this problem can be solved by inspection, discuss the advantages of using the shortest-route method instead of linear programming models for this problem.

4. Consider a network with the flow capacities shown in Figure P8.4.

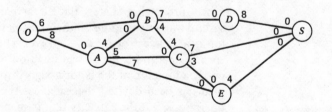

Figure P8.4 Hypothetical network with flow capacities.

(a) What is the maximal flow in this network? Use the min-cut max-flow theorem.

(b) What is the specific flow along each branch in the network?

5. Every time the Sunset OX football team plays a game, over 60,000 fans jam the stadium. The officer in charge of traffic control after the game is always fighting traffic jams caused by fans eager to leave the stadium area. A proposal was made to make certain streets one-way to increase traffic flow. The largest amount of traffic proceeds from the north end of the stadium to the northbound interstate system, so the officer has decided to try the proposal for those streets leading from the stadium to the northbound interstate. The network diagram in Figure P8.5 depicts the road system and the estimated flow in thousands of automobiles per hour for each street.

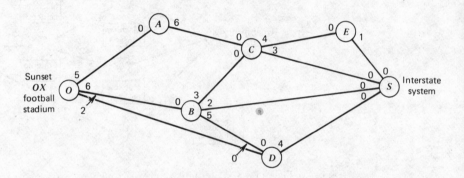

Figure P8.5 Road system between Sunset OX football stadium and interstate system.

(a) In order for the new traffic proposal to work, the flow must be at least 12,000 automobiles per hour. Will the proposal be successful?

(b) Which streets are bottlenecks in the new proposal? If you could increase the flow in one of the bottleneck streets at a certain cost per 1000 increase in flow, which one would you choose and how much would you want to increase the flow? Why?

6. The management of a parcel delivery service is in the final stages of designing a new processing center. Parcels arrive at the incoming dock, are sorted several times depending on their destination, and then are loaded into trucks for local delivery or interstate travel. The processing capacity of the various sorting operations is partly a function of material-handling equipment and partly a function of the labor assigned to the various operations. A tentative plan has been devised that specifies the processing capacity of the sorting operations, but the capacity requirements of the shipping dock have not yet been determined. Of course, these requirements are a function of the flow of parcels through the processing network. The network diagram in Figure P8.6 depicts the processing system where the branches represent the operations and the nodes represent separation points for the parcels. The capacities are expressed in hundreds of parcels per hour.

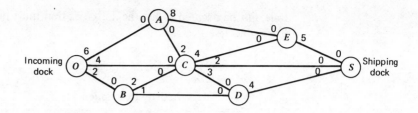

Figure P8.6 Processing system.

   (a)   What is the maximal flow in parcels per hour that the shipping dock must handle?

   (b)   Do any operations appear to have too much capacity? Is this necessarily bad in this case?

   (c)   If you wanted to fine tune the system to achieve the total input flow of 1200 packages per hour, which operations would you want to expand and by how much?

7. Consider the CPM network diagram of a large project shown in Figure P8.7. The time estimates are in weeks.

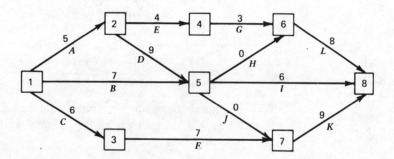

Figure P8.7 Network describing a large project system.

   (a)   Compute the earliest and latest start times and the earliest and latest finish times for each activity.

   (b)   Compute the slack for each activity.

   (c)   What is the critical path? Are other paths worthy of close attention? Why?

8. Ignatius R. Withet has recently been informed that Hopeful Electronics has just been awarded a new contract for electronic parts. Withet was put in charge of planning for hiring of some new personnel. His duties were to make sure that the firm had a new secretary and a new managerial assistant to work on the new project within 7 weeks. Withet was not sure if this could be done, but he decided to list the activities that must take place to achieve the firm's objective.

	Activity Description	Estimated Duration, weeks
A	College interviewing for new managerial assistant	3
B	Renovate old storage area into offices for assistant and secretary	5
C	Place ad for secretary and interview applicants	4
D	Interview managerial assistant applicants	2
E	Purchase new office equipment and supplies for new office	2
F	Check references for secretarial applicants and make final selection	1
G	Check references for managerial assistant applicants and make final selection	1
H	Orientation meetings and paperwork to get new employees on payroll	1

Withet realized that some activities could be taking place simultaneously. In fact, he made the following table to show which activities must immediately precede others:

Activity	Activities that Must Immediately Precede the One Listed
A	None
B	None
C	None
D	A
E	B
F	C
G	D
H	E, F, G

At that point, Withet was not sure if he could get all of this done in 7 weeks when the project must begin. He knew that the company would incur added costs of $200 per week for each week the project started late. I.M. Twinkle, who seemed to have flashes of brilliance every now and then, pointed out two potential time-savers:

1. Employ Aztec, Inc., a renowned employment agency, to locate some good secretarial prospects. It would save 2 weeks in activity C and cost the firm an additional $50.
2. By adding a few more workers for a while, activity B—the renovation of the old storage area into an office—could be shortened by 1 week at an additional cost of $150 to the firm.

Help Withet by answering the following questions:
   (a) Will the project be completed on time without the timesaving ideas? If not, how much will it be late?
   (b) If it will be late, what additional expenditures should be made to get the project completed on time least expensively?

9. The CPM network diagram in Figure P8.8 was prepared for the production and assembly of a certain special customer order.

Activity	Normal Time, days	Normal Cost	Crash Time, days	Crash Cost
A	4	$1000	3	$1300
B	7	1400	4	2000
C	5	2000	4	2700
D	6	1200	5	1400
E	3	900	2	1100
F	11	2500	6	4000
G	4	800	3	1450
H	3	300	1	500

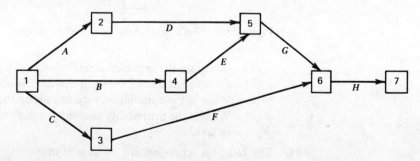

Figure P8.8 Production and assembly network.

The firm will experience a penalty of $100 per day starting on the thirteenth day from now. The project's indirect costs are estimated to be $300 per day. When would you recommend that the company plan to complete the project and what would the resultant critical path be?

10. The PERT network diagram and the associated data in Figure P8.9 have been prepared for the design of a new product.

| | Time Estimates, weeks | | |
Activity	a	m	b
A	3	5	7
B	2	4	6
C	6	7	8
D	2	3	8
E	4	8	12
F	4	5	6
G	4	10	12
H	7	7	7
I	1	4	5
J	1	2	3

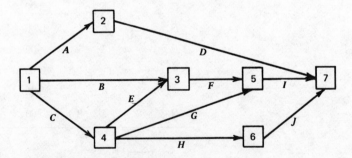

Figure P8.9   PERT network for new product designs.

(a) Compute the expected time for each activity.
(b) Compute the slack for each activity. Specify the critical path.
(c) What is the cumulative variance along the critical path?
(d) What is the probability that the project will be completed in 20 weeks or less?

11. The business school faculty of a large university is interested in conducting a conference on the use of quantitative methods for decision making. In

order to coordinate the project, it was decided to use a PERT network. The major activities and time estimates for each were carefully compiled, as follows:

	Activity Description	a	m	b	Activities that Must Precede
A	Design conference meetings and theme	1	2	3	None
B	Design front cover of conference proceedings	0.5	1	4	A
C	Design brochure and request for papers	0.5	2	4	A
D	Compile list of distinguished speakers	3	4	7	A
E	Finalize brochure and print it	2	3	4	C, D
F	Make travel arrangements for distinguished speakers	1	2	3	D
G	Send brochures	1	3	5	E
H	Receive papers for conference	10	12	16	G
I	Edit papers and assemble proceedings	3	4	6	H
J	Print proceedings	1.5	2	3	B, I

- (a) What is the critical path?
- (b) The faculty hopes to meet a deadline of 30 weeks because hotel and conference facilities have to be reserved now. What are the chances of meeting the deadline?

12. Consider the PERT network in Figure P8.10 where the expected times for each activity are shown. The company loses $1000 for every week the project

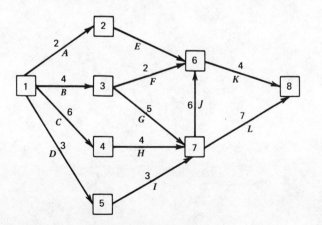

Figure P8.10 PERT network for project analysis.

lasts beyond 17 weeks. For each of the following proposals taken *independently*, discuss why or why not they are a good idea.

(a) Activity H can be reduced to 1 week by using overtime and extra labor at a total cost of $2000.

(b) Activity J can be reduced to 3 weeks by taking resources from activity L, thereby increasing its expected time to 10 weeks at no additional cost.

(c) Activity G can be reduced to 2 weeks at a total cost of $1000.

(d) Activity K can be reduced to 1 week by taking resources from activity L, thereby increasing its expected time to 9 weeks at no additional cost.

9

CLASSICAL OPTIMIZATION

9.1 OPTIMIZING FUNCTIONS OF ONE DECISION VARIABLE

Some Examples of Optimization Using Single-Variable Calculus

First and Second Derivatives and Optimization
Convex and Concave Functions
An Additional Comment

9.2 UNCONSTRAINED OPTIMA FOR FUNCTIONS OF MANY VARIABLES

Partial Derivatives, Total Differentials, and Maximization
Maximizing Functions of Many Variables

9.3 CONSTRAINED OPTIMIZATION: EQUALITY CONSTRAINTS

The Lot-Size Model With Equality Constraints
The Stock-and-Bond Investment Problem with Equality Constraints

9.4 CONSTRAINED OPTIMIZATION: INEQUALITY CONSTRAINTS

9.5 REVIEW AND SUMMARY

References
Review Questions
Problems

This chapter reviews the standard techniques of single-variable differential calculus as they apply to optimizing a decision criterion and extends these techniques to problems involving more than one decision variable.

9.1 OPTIMIZING FUNCTIONS OF ONE DECISION VARIABLE

Some Examples of Optimization Using Single-Variable Calculus

In this section we present three business decision situations where models involving single-variable calculus can be used to optimize a decision. These examples will then serve as the focal point for both extension and generalization in the remainder of this chapter.

The Lot-Size Model   One of the most venerable applications of calculus to the optimization of a business decision arises in the context of inventory planning. The lot-size model, which we will discuss here, has many applications in a wide variety of businesses. These include situations where it is strictly and unambiguously applicable and other situations where it serves as a convenient approximation to a more "realistic" but more complicated model. The lot-size model is not only useful in practice, it also represents a straightforward illustration of how a model can be formulated and analyzed.

A large furniture-manufacturing firm uses a substantial amount of paints, varnishes, and thinners in its daily production operations. During one of its periodic cost-reduction programs, the company management noticed a large investment in inventories of these supplies and raised the question of whether the investment in inventory was worthwhile. A study team was formed to answer the question.

The study team focused attention first on inventory item P724, the most commonly used polyurethane varnish, and developed a model for inventory policy with respect to this item. It was soon determined that the issue was the proper amount (5-gallon cans of P724) to order when restocking. To analyze the problem the team developed the total cost per year associated with item P724.

The total cost (K_T) was the sum of the cost to place orders (K_O), the cost to carry inventory (K_I), and the cost of the material (K_M). Symbolically, the yearly cost is $K_T = K_O + K_I + K_M$. Demand for item P724 was assumed to occur at uniform rate of d 5-gallon cans per year. (This assumption implies that the weekly rate is $(\frac{1}{52})d$.) In addition, it was assumed that annual demand for P724 was known with certainty. Although in reality this was not the case, the annual forecasts in the past were very accurate and the assumption of certainty was made to simplify the analysis.

The cost to order is simply the cost to place a single order, C_O, times the number of orders placed in a year. If each order placed is for X items, the average number of orders placed during a year is d/X and

$$K_O = C_O \frac{d}{X}$$

The cost to carry inventory is simply the cost to carry one unit in inventory times the average number of units carried during the year. The maximum level of inventory achieved during the year depends on the order quantity X. Let us define a *cycle* to be the time between the receipt of an order quantity and the arrival of the next order quantity. If inventory is replenished immediately when it runs out, then the maximum inventory in any cycle is X. This result follows from our assumption of certainty of demand, which implies we need no safety stocks, and an additional assumption that the entire quantity of X units will be delivered on time.

Because demand occurs at a constant rate of d per year, and we are going to order X units each time we place an order, each order will last X/d years. Figure 9.1 shows the maximum inventory occurring at $t = 0, X/d, 2X/d, \ldots$. Note that the inventory level during each cycle takes on the shape of a triangle. This follows from our assumption of a uniform annual rate of demand. For example, inventory is built up to X at time $t = 0$ and is depleted to zero at time $t = X/d$. What is the

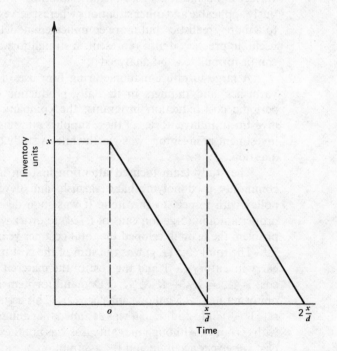

Figure 9.1 Inventory as a function of time.

average inventory level during this cycle? Intuitively, it would be $X/2$ since we start with X units and end with 0 units, the average of which is $X/2$. More rigorously, the average inventory is equal to the area of the triangle divided by the length of the inventory cycle. Thus, we have for the nth inventory cycle

$$\frac{\frac{1}{2}(X)\left(\frac{nX}{d} - \frac{(n-1)X}{d}\right)}{\left(\frac{nX}{d} - \frac{(n-1)X}{d}\right)} = \frac{X}{2}$$

The area of the triangle is in terms of units of P724 times years in a cycle. When we divide by the length of a cycle in years, we are left with average units in inventory during a cycle. Consequently, if there are $X/2$ units in inventory on the average in each cycle, it follows that the average inventory for the year is $X/2$.

The cost to carry inventory is commonly held to be proportional to the *value* of the inventory. If the value of a unit of inventory is C_P and the cost to carry inventory expressed as a percentage of that cost k, the annual cost to carry inventory is given by

$$K_I = kC_P \frac{X}{2}$$

The annual cost of the material is just the value per unit C_P times the number of units used during the year or

$$K_M = C_P d$$

Now, because C_O, C_P, k, and d have known values, we can write the total cost of inventory as

$$K_T = C_O \frac{d}{X} + kC_P \frac{X}{2} + C_P d \tag{9.1}$$

which is a function of the single variable X.

Note that in (9.1) the third term, the cost of the material, is constant and therefore does not depend on X. The costs associated with inventory *but not material* are

$$K_T^* = K_T - K_M = C_O \frac{d}{X} + kC_P \frac{X}{2} \tag{9.2}$$

These costs are plotted on Figure 9.2 for the case where $C_O = \$4$, $C_P = \$20$, $k = 0.10$, and $d = 50$ units.

To find the value of X that minimizes K_T^* we take the first derivative of K_T^* and set it equal to zero and solve for X. To this end

$$\frac{dK_T^*}{dX} = -\frac{C_O d}{X^2} + \frac{kC_P}{2} = 0 \tag{9.3}$$

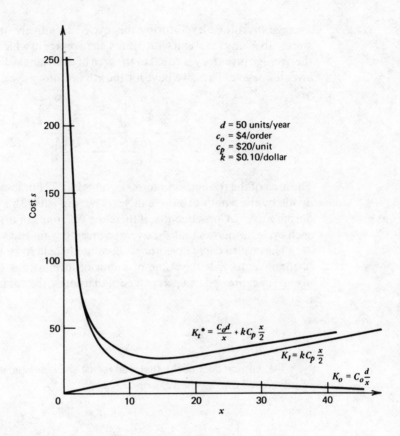

Figure 9.2 Inventory costs as a function of X.

and

$$X = \sqrt{\frac{2C_O d}{k C_P}} \tag{9.4}$$

is the optimal ordering amount. The relationship in (9.4) is commonly referred to as the economic lot-size model. Let us designate this value as X_O for further reference.

From the graph in Figure 9.2 we know that $X = X_O$ will produce the minimum cost (as opposed to the maximum), but the second derivative test can be performed to check this. From (9.3) we have

$$\frac{d^2 K_T{}^*}{dX^2} = + \frac{2C_O d}{X^3}$$

Clearly, for $X = X_O$, $d^2 K_T{}^*/dX^2 > 0$, indicating that $X = X_O$ is indeed a minimum, because X_O will always be positive for positive values of C_O, d, k, and C_P.

The optimal value of total inventory cost is

$$K_T{}^* = C_O \frac{d}{X_O} + kC_P \frac{X_O}{2}$$

$$= \frac{C_O d}{\sqrt{\dfrac{2C_O d}{kC_P}}} + \frac{kC_P}{2} \sqrt{\frac{2C_O d}{kC_P}}$$

$$= \tfrac{1}{2}\sqrt{2C_O dkC_P} + \tfrac{1}{2}\sqrt{2C_O dkC_P} \qquad (9.5)$$

Note in (9.5) that at optimality the annual inventory-carrying cost is equal to the annual ordering cost. The total cost is $K_T{}^* = \sqrt{2C_O dkC_P}$.

In addition to illustrating the use of single-variable calculus in a decision problem, the lot-size model has several important features that make it far more useful in practice than it would appear on the surface. Examination of the graph of $K_T{}^*$ in Figure 9.2 shows that the cost function is very shallow in the neighborhood of the optimal solution. Therefore, if in practice a mistake is made in estimating the costs or annual demand and the quantity actually ordered is not the true optimal order quantity, the cost will not increase dramatically. To see why this is the case, let $X = \theta X_O$ be an arbitrary order quantity. (For example, if $\theta = 1.05$ then the arbitrary quantity is 5% greater than the optimal order quantity.) Then the cost is

$$C_O \frac{d}{\theta X_O} + kC_P \frac{\theta X_O}{2} = \frac{1}{\theta}\frac{1}{2}\sqrt{2C_O dkC_p} + \theta \frac{1}{2}\sqrt{2C_O dkC_p}$$

$$= \frac{1}{2}\left(\frac{1}{\theta} + \theta\right)\sqrt{2C_O dkC_p}$$

Thus $\frac{100}{2}[(1/\theta + \theta) - 1]$ represents the percent that costs are increased if the wrong order quantity is used. Table 9.1 shows the percentage increase in costs for various values of θ. Note when $\theta = 0.85$, or the lot size used is 15% less than the optimal lot size, the inventory cost is increased by only 1.32%. Indeed, the cost function is very "flat" in the neighborhood of X_O.

The analysis in Table 9.1 demonstrates the economic lot-size model's insensitivity to "errors." Any inventory situation will have a balancing of costs: the cost to place orders and the cost to carry inventory. Even if there is nonuniform demand, uncertainties in demand, nonproportional costs, stockout costs, etc., the lot-size model will give approximate solutions that give the analyst some hints as to the kinds of savings that are possible from efficient inventory management.

Investing in Bonds and Stocks The theory of finance suggests that investors seek to maximize the expected utility of wealth by investing in bonds and a well-diversified portfolio of common stocks. The returns from bonds are looked at as risk-free and those from a stock portfolio as risky. Suppose that an investor has M dollars to invest and wants to determine the amount X to invest in stocks. The

Table 9.1 Percentage Increase in Total Inventory Costs as Function of θ

θ	Increase in Costs, %
0.85	1.32
0.90	0.56
0.95	0.13
1.00	0.00
1.05	0.12
1.10	0.45
1.15	0.98

rate of return on bonds is a *certain* amount r_b per dollar of investment. The return per dollar invested in stocks is $\tilde{R}_S$, a random variable, with $E(\tilde{R}_S) = r_S$ and $\text{Var}(\tilde{R}_S) = \sigma_S{}^2$.

The total return to the investor will be

$$\tilde{R}_T = (M - X)r_b + X\tilde{R}_S$$

and therefore

$$E(\tilde{R}_T) = (M - X)r_b + Xr_S \tag{9.6}$$

and

$$\text{Var}(\tilde{R}_T) = X^2\sigma_S{}^2 \tag{9.7}$$

A given investor in formulating this decision problem uses the idea of a certainty equivalent developed in Chapter 2. Thus, we seek to find

$$\underset{X}{\text{Max}}[M + E(\tilde{R}_T) - K\,\text{Var}(\tilde{R}_T)] \tag{9.8}$$

where the term in the brackets is the certainty equivalent of end-of-period wealth. The parameter K (discussed in Chapter 2) characterizes the trade-off of risk and return. Substituting (9.6) and (9.7) in (9.8), the objective becomes

$$\underset{X}{\text{Max}}[M + (M - X)r_b + Xr_S - KX^2\sigma_S{}^2]$$

Now, applying the usual methods of calculus we get, as a condition for maximization

$$-r_b + r_S - 2KX\sigma_S{}^2 = 0$$

or

$$X = \frac{r_S - r_b}{2K\sigma_S{}^2} \tag{9.9}$$

The second derivative test yields

$$-2K\sigma_S^2 < 0$$

which denotes a maximum and will hold as long as $K > 0$.

Suppose that $M = \$100,000$, $r_S = 0.12$, $r_b = 0.08$, $\sigma_S^2 = 0.0064$, and $K = 0.0001$.

Then

$$X = \frac{0.12 - 0.08}{2(0.0001)(0.0064)} = \$31,250$$

Then we would have $M - X = \$68,750$ and the maximum value of the certainty equivalent would be

$$\$100,000 + 68,750(0.08) + 31,250(0.12) - (0.0001)(31,250)^2(0.0064)$$

$$= 100,000 + 5500.00 + 3750.00 - 625.00$$

$$= \$108,625.00$$

The expected return (including the return of the original investment of $100,000), which differs from the certainty equivalent, is $105,500.00 + \$3750.00 = \$109,250.00$.

Figure 9.3 shows the graph of the certainty equivalent. Note from (9.9) that as the variance of the common-stock investment increases, the amount invested in stocks decreases. Furthermore, as the value of K increases, the investment in common stocks decreases.

Because r_S would be greater than r_b in most practical situations, and because K and σ_S^2 are positive, it follows that $X \geq 0$. That is, there will never be negative investment in stocks. With K and σ_S^2 sufficiently small, however, X could exceed M. That is, if K were small this would mean that the investor had a great tolerance for risk and would therefore seek investments that more nearly maximized the *expected return* from investments. Common stock yields a greater expected return, and there would be a tendency to invest large amounts in common stock. By choosing $X > M$ we have a situation where the investor borrows money at r_b (a negative investment) and invests these funds, along with other funds M, in common stocks.

Although the model developed in this section is simple, it does illustrate the way in which the tolerance for risk, the expected returns, and the variance of returns affects the choice of an investment portfolio.

Optimal Sales Force In Chapter 1 we discussed the decision problem of Prefinishing Corporation. Alternative A_5—the complex alternative—involved hiring an additional salesperson and incorporating a number of additional changes leading to a substantial increase in the profits. After implementing the complex alternative, Mr. Yef decided that he was too narrow in his look at alternatives. He raised the question of whether he should add more than one salesperson.

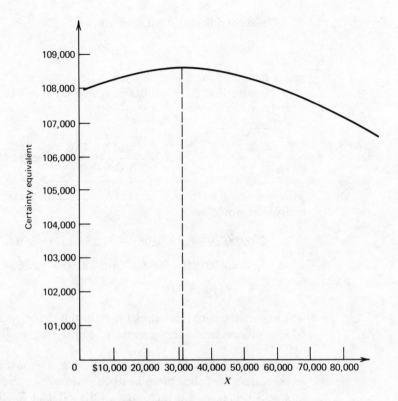

Figure 9.3 Certainty equivalent function for the investment problem.

After a careful study of the productivity of salespeople, Mr. Yef determined that the dollar value of sales S was related to the number of salespeople X by the following function:

$$S = \begin{cases} \$209,000 - \dfrac{\$198,000}{X} & X \geq 1 \\[2mm] 0 & X < 1 \end{cases}$$

The profit per month *before interest charges and taxes*, and assuming $X \geq 1$, is

$$\pi^* = \tfrac{1}{2}S - 23,760 - 2,000X$$

$$= 104,500 - \frac{99,000}{x} - 23,760 - 2,000X$$

It is shown in Figure 9.4.

The profit is maximized when

$$\frac{d\pi^*}{dX} = \frac{99,000}{X^2} - 2,000 = 0$$

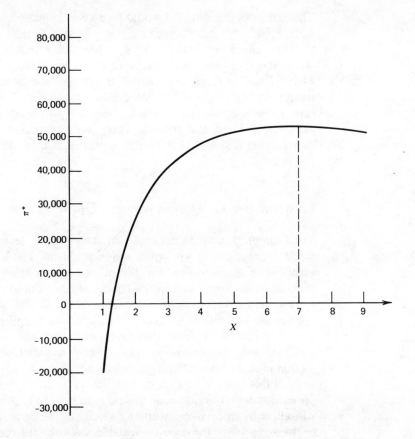

Figure 9.4 Profit per month before interest and taxes as a function of salespeople.

or when

$$X = \sqrt{\frac{99,000}{2,000}}$$

$$\doteq 7$$

Since

$$\frac{d^2\pi^*}{dX^2} = -\frac{198,000}{X^3} < 0,$$

it follows that $X \doteq 7$ yields a maximum profit.

The profit before interest charges and taxes would be

$$\pi^* = 104,500 - \frac{99,000}{7} - 23,760 - 2,000(7)$$

$$= \$52,597$$

This indicates that Mr. Yef would be able to increase his profits substantially by adding five more salespeople to his present sales force.

The calculation was revealing to Mr. Yef. Although such an increase in the size of the sales force would be profitable, it represented a very serious move that Mr. Yef had to examine carefully. It required increasing sales to \$180,714 per month or an increase of 64% over his existing sales. This meant that productive capacity would have to be added, financing arranged, and workers, as well as salespeople, hired and trained. This would take time and planning. Mr. Yef therefore set it as a goal to be accomplished in an orderly fashion over the next five years.

First and Second Derivatives and Optimization

The example situations presented in the previous section illustrate the use of single-variable calculus in optimization problems. The lot-size example was concerned with minimization and the other two examples with maximization. All three examples used the second-derivative test to determine if an optimum had been found by setting the first derivative equal to zero. All three examples made implicit use of the fact that there was a single local optimum and that there were no constraints on the values that the decision variable could take.

In this section, we wish to discuss the optimization procedures of the previous section in more abstract and general terms. This will allow us, in subsequent sections of this chapter, to develop parallels between the concepts of single-variable optimization and similar concepts that are used in multivariable optimization. It will allow us to develop intuition, which will be helpful in finding solutions to problems in which the decision variables are subject to constraints.

Consider a continuous function $f(X)$ of a single decision variable X defined over the domain $a \leq X \leq b$. It is convenient to think of this function as representing a decision problem under certainty—a single state of nature—with an infinite set of decision alternatives. The decision criterion may be either the maximization of $f(X)$ or the minimization of $f(X)$. The following discussion will be in terms of maximization. Minimization problems can be solved merely by maximizing $g(X) = -f(X)$.

The function $f(X)$ takes on its *global* maximum (there may be more than one) at X_O ($a \leq X_O \leq b$) if $f(X) \leq f(X_O)$ for all X in the interval. A *local* maximum X_l occurs if $f(X) \leq f(X_l)$ for every point X that is *close* to X_l. When searching for the value of X that maximizes $f(X)$ in a decision problem, we must make sure that the selected X corresponds to the global and not the local maximum. Although this may seem an obvious admonition, it takes on importance because of the way in which the search for X_O takes place.

The statement that $f(X) \leq f(X_O)$ for all $a \leq X \leq b$ does little to help find the value of X_O. There are an infinite number of points in the interval (a, b), and some techniques more sophisticated than total enumeration are therefore necessary. These techniques are found in the traditional methods of calculus. The first and second derivatives are important tools in an efficient search for X_o. The potential candidates for X_O are the points that produce local maxima and the end points of the interval (a, b). The points that produce local maxima can be found using the first derivative and the second derivative. The function can be evaluated at these points and at the end points and the value of X_O then determined.

A *necessary* condition for a local maximum in (a, b) is that

$$f'(X) = 0 \qquad\qquad (9.10)$$

The solution of (9.10) will produce all internal candidates for X_O—excluding end points. Some of these points may be local *minima* or *inflection* points so it is necessary to check these candidates further.

Consider Figure 9.5 where five candidates for the position of X_O have been determined, The points X_1, X_2, and X_3 are determined from (9.10), whereas a and b are the end points that must be evaluated. Note that for ε arbitrarily small, as one moves from $X_1 - \varepsilon$ to X_1 the derivative decreases from a positive value to zero and as one moves from X_1 to $X_1 + \varepsilon$ the derivative decreases from zero to a negative value. Therefore, at the point X_1, the derivative is decreasing and the second derivative, $f''(X_1)$ is negative. That is, $f''(X_1) < 0$ indicates a local maximum. On the other hand, at X_2 we would find that the derivative is increasing and therefore $f''(X_2) > 0$. That is, $f''(X_2) > 0$ indicates a local minimum. The point X_3 is an inflection point and will have $f''(X_3) = 0$. (In general, $f''(X) = 0$ does not imply an inflection point; instead, it supplies no information on whether X is a maximum, a minimum, or an inflection point.)

Using the results of the previous paragraph, we can suggest a procedure for finding X_O.

Step 1.   Find all X_i for which $f'(X_i) = 0$. This is the set of X_is that satisfy the so-called first-order conditions. Let this set be denoted by F.

Step 2.   For each $X_i \varepsilon F$, calculate $f''(X_i)$. Eliminate all candidates for which $f''(X_i) > 0$. The remaining candidates satisfy both the first- and second-order conditions. Let this set be denoted by FS.

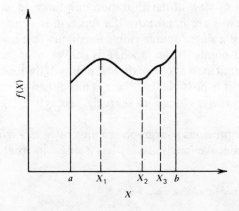

Figure 9.5   Hypothetical objective function and candidates for optimization.

Step 3. Evaluate $f(X)$ for all $X \varepsilon FSU(a, b)$.[1] Select X_O such that $f(X) \leq f(X_O)$ for all $X \varepsilon FSU(a, b)$.

In the examples shown in the previous section, we found that $f'(X) = 0$ yielded only one value of X, and therefore the procedure was vastly simplified. Furthermore, in all examples, the second derivative test yielded $f''(X) < 0$ so no ambiguity was introduced. Also, all three samples implicitly assumed that the domain was $0 \leq X \leq \infty$. Only one end point was relevant in each example. The selection of $X_O = 0$ in the inventory problem was ruled out without further thought because the ordering costs approached infinity as X approached zero. In the portfolio case it is not readily apparent that $X = 0$ produces a lower certainty equivalent, but when $X = 0$ we have the certainty equivalent equal to Mr_b and when $X = r_S - r_b/2K\sigma_S^2$, we have the certainty equivalent equal to $Mr_b + (r_S - r_b)^2/4K\sigma_S^2$, therefore, the point $X = 0$ is ruled out as the optimal decision. Finally, in the prefinishing example, when $X < 1$ sales are zero and negative profit is made. This characteristic was implicitly considered in deriving the optimal solution to the example.

Convex and Concave Functions

Two important concepts in our subsequent discussions are *convexity* and *concavity* of functions. A function is *convex* over the interval (a, b) if the tangent to the function at $a \leq X \leq b$ lies below the function. Conversely, a function is *concave* over the interval (a, b) if the tangent lies on or above the function. Alternate definitions of convexity and concavity are that $f''(X) \geq 0$ for $a \leq X \leq b$ and $f''(X) \leq 0$, respectively. The concepts of convexity and concavity are refined further by defining *strict* convexity as $f''(X) > 0$ and strict concavity as $f''(X) < 0$ for $a \leq X \leq b$.

Using these ideas we can see that for $0 \leq X < \infty$, the inventory cost function, as shown in Figure 9.2, is convex. Furthermore, it is strictly convex. The certainty equivalent function for the portfolio problem, as shown in Figure 9.3, is strictly concave on the interval $0 \leq X < \infty$. The profit function for prefinishing is concave on the interval $0 \leq X < 1$ and strictly concave for $1 \leq X < \infty$.

From the point of view of maximization of a function, concavity and strict concavity over intervals are important. If a function is strictly concave over the interval (a, b), there is a single unique global maximum that may be either internal or at one of the end points. If the function is convex over the interval, a global maximum must occur at least at one of the end points. If the function is concave but not strictly concave, it is possible that there is more than one maximum. Convex functions and strictly convex functions share the property that the maximum must occur at end points.

The ideas of the previous paragraph are illustrated in Figure 9.6. Figure 9.6a shows two strictly concave functions; A_1 has a single internal maximum and A_2

---

[1] $FSU(a, b)$ is the set formed by adding a and b to FS.

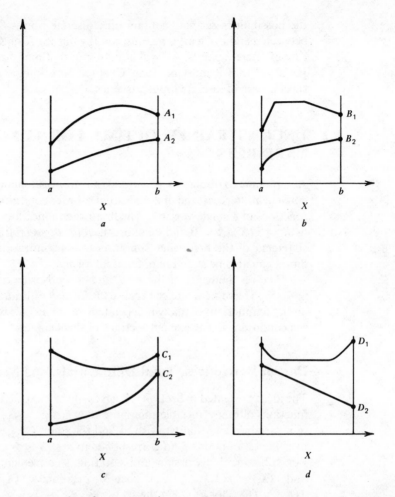

Figure 9.6 Examples of concave and convex functions. (*a*) Strictly concave functions. (*b*) (Not strictly) concave functions. (*c*) Strictly convex functions. (*d*) (Not strictly) convex functions.

has the maximum at the end point of the interval. Figure 9.6*b* shows two concave functions. Function B_1 has multiple maxima while B_2 has a single end-point maxima. Figures 9.6*c* and 9.6*d* illustrate the property that convex functions have maxima at the end points regardless of whether the convexity is strict or not.

An Additional Comment

Our discussion of maximizing of functions of a single-decision variable has been concerned with choosing X_O from a continuous set of possibilities denoted by the interval (*a*, *b*). We will discuss some important properties of possibilities sets in detail in the next section. At this point, we wish only to state that in some instances, the possibilities set may contain only discrete points—for example, the integers between a and b. Clearly, we must modify our thinking somewhat to deal with the case of discrete points. We will not attempt that modification here but will merely point out that it must be done. Chapter 7 on integer programming discusses a specific case of discrete input variables.

9.2   UNCONSTRAINED OPTIMA FOR FUNCTIONS OF MANY VARIABLES

As a prelude to discussion of the maximization of functions of many variables, it is convenient to recast the first- and second-order conditions for the maximization of functions of a single variable. The first-order condition $f'(X) = 0$ can be restated as $df = f'(X)dX = 0$, and therefore the *total differential df* $= 0$ must be an alternate statement of the first-order condition for maximization. The second-order condition can also be stated in differential form as $d^2f = f''(X)(dX)^2 < 0$.

The restatements of the first- and second-order conditions of the previous paragraph have significance because the form $df = 0$, and $d^2f < 0$ has equal applicability to functions of many independent variables. We will use these statements of the conditions in subsequent sections of this chapter.

Partial Derivatives, Total Differentials, and Maximization

The ideas presented in Section 9.1 can easily be extended to the case of maximizing functions of many variables. Suppose that $f(X_1, \ldots, X_n)$ is a continuous function of n variables and that we wish to find the point $(X_{o1}, \ldots, X_{on})$ that maximizes f over the set of points S. (S corresponds to $a \leq X \leq b$ in the single-variable case.) For subsequent discussion and notational convenience, let $\mathbf{X}_i = (X_{i1}, \ldots, X_{in})$ and $f(\mathbf{X}_i) = f(X_{i1}, \ldots, X_{in})$. Then $\mathbf{X}_o$ maximizes $f(\mathbf{X}_i)$ if $\mathbf{X}_o$ is in the set S and $f(\mathbf{X}_i) \leq f(\mathbf{X}_o)$ for all X_i in the set S.

Again, as in the case of a single variable, we must carefully distinguish between global and local maxima. With multiple variables the procedure is somewhat more complicated than with a single variable, but the basic idea is the same. A search is made for all local maxima within the set S. Then these, along with all of the points on the *boundary* of S, are evaluated and the global maximum is determined.

First let us consider the search for internal maxima. To begin, let us assume that $S = R^n$ (that is, the X_{ij} can take on any real value). Then the first-order conditions for $\mathbf{X}_i$ to maximize $f(\mathbf{X}_i)$ are

$$f_1(\mathbf{X}_i) = 0, \ f_2(\mathbf{X}_i) = 0, \ldots, f_n(\mathbf{X}_i) = 0 \qquad (9.11)$$

where $f_k(\mathbf{X}_i)$ is the first partial derivative of f with respect to the kth variable. These conditions, necessitating the solution of n simultaneous equations, correspond to the first-order condition that $f'(X_i) = 0$ for the function of a single variable.

The total differential at the point $\mathbf{X}_i$ is

$$df = f_1(\mathbf{X}_i)dX_{i1} + f_2(\mathbf{X}_i)dX_{i2} + \cdots + f_n(\mathbf{X}_i)dX_{in} \tag{9.12}$$

It therefore follows that $df = 0$ if (9.11) holds.

It is instructive to look at (9.12) intuitively. If we consider the dX_{ij} in (9.12) to be arbitrarily small but nonzero, then for $df = 0$ we must have $f_k(\mathbf{X}_i) = 0$ for all k. Note that we need not have all dX_{ij} the same size or sign. Some dX_{ij} could be bigger than others, some could be positive, and some could be negative. To see what this means, consider a two-dimensional problem. Figure 9.7 shows the X_1X_2 plane and the point $\mathbf{X}_i = (X_{i1}, X_{i2})$ that we have determined to be a local maximum. A close neighborhood around the point is sketched. Included in the neighborhood are five other points labeled A, B, C, D, and E. For point A, we have $dX_{i1} < 0$ and $dX_{i2} < 0$; for point B, $dX_{i1} > 0$, $dX_{i2} < 0$; for point C, $dX_{i1} > 0$, $dX_{i2} = 0$; for D, $dX_{i1} = 0$, $dX_{i2} > 0$; and for E, $dX_{i1} < 0$, $dX_{i2} > 0$. The sizes and signs of these small changes indicate the *direction* that they lie from point $\mathbf{X}_i$. If we move from the point specified by a letter toward $\mathbf{X}_i$ in a straight line we will keep the signs of the dX_{ij} terms as well as their ratios constant. Thus, the only way we can be assured that df will approach zero as we move toward $\mathbf{X}_i$ from any direction is if $f_1(\mathbf{X}_i) = f_2(\mathbf{X}_i) = 0$.

The reasoning of the previous paragraph can now be used to look at second-order conditions for a maximum. Suppose we start at *any* point in the region shown in Figure 9.7 and move on the straight line toward $\mathbf{X}_i$. If the point $\mathbf{X}_i$ denoted a maximum we would find that as we moved toward $\mathbf{X}_i$, f would increase by smaller and smaller amounts until we reached $\mathbf{X}_i$; if we then continued *in the same direction* the function would decrease by larger and larger amounts. This behavior indicates that if a plane were constructed so that it was perpendicular to

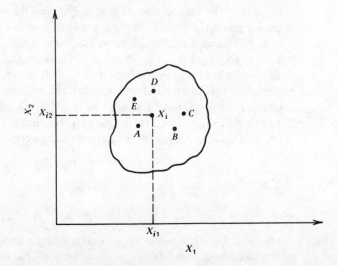

Figure 9.7 Hypothetical region near the maximum.

the X_1X_2 plane and passed through *any* point in the close region and the point $\mathbf{X}_i$, the intersection of that plane and f would produce a function whose second derivative was negative at the point $\mathbf{X}_i$. These ideas carry over into the second-order condition for a maximum of a function of n variables. It is

$$d^2f = f_{11}(\mathbf{X}_i)(dX_{i1})^2 + f_{22}(\mathbf{X}_i)(dX_{i2})^2 + \cdots + f_{nn}(\mathbf{X}_i)(dX_{in})^2$$
$$+ 2f_{12}(\mathbf{X}_i)(dX_{i1}dX_{i2}) + 2f_{13}(\mathbf{X}_i)dX_{i1}\,dX_{i3}) + \cdots$$
$$+ 2f_{n-1\,n}(\mathbf{X}_i)dX_{in-1}dX_{in} < 0 \tag{9.13}$$

where $f_{kl}(\mathbf{X}_i)$ is the second partial derivative with respect to the lth variable (the first partial being taken with respect to the kth variable).

The condition expressed in (9.13) has little direct appeal. It looks too complicated to be particularly useful. But some analysis of the special case of two variables is worthwhile. For this case we have

$$d^2f = f_{11}(\mathbf{X}_i)(dX_{i1})^2 + f_{22}(\mathbf{X}_i)(dX_{i2})^2 + 2f_{12}(\mathbf{X}_i)(dX_{i1}dX_{i2}) < 0 \tag{9.14}$$

which by algebraic manipulation can be written as

$$d^2f = f_{11}(\mathbf{X}_i)\left[dX_{i1} + \frac{f_{12}(\mathbf{X}_i)}{f_{11}(\mathbf{X}_i)}dX_{i2}\right]^2 + \left[\frac{f_{11}(\mathbf{X}_i)f_{22}(\mathbf{X}_i) - [f_{12}(\mathbf{X}_i)]^2}{f_{11}(X_i)}\right]$$
$$\times (dX_{i2})^2 < 0 \tag{9.15}$$

Note that the sign of d^2f is determined by $f_{11}(\mathbf{X}_i)$ and $f_{11}(\mathbf{X}_i)f_{22}(\mathbf{X}_i) - [f_{12}(\mathbf{X}_i)]^2$. To understand (9.15) further consider a plane perpendicular to the X_2 axis and passing through the point $\mathbf{X}_i$ (use Figure 9.7 as a reference). If $\mathbf{X}_i$ is a maximum of $f(\mathbf{X})$ the intersection of this plane and the surface $f(\mathbf{X})$ will form a function with its maximum at $\mathbf{X}_i$. Thus, the second derivative of the function formed by the intersection will be $f_{11}(\mathbf{X}_i)$ and we will have $f_{11}(\mathbf{X}_i) < 0$. If we now pass a plane through $\mathbf{X}_i$ and perpendicular to the X_1 axis we will conclude that if $\mathbf{X}_i$ produced a maximum we would have $f_{22}(\mathbf{X}_i) < 0$. Note that if $f_{11}(\mathbf{X}_i) < 0$ and $f_{11}(\mathbf{X}_i)f_{22}(\mathbf{X}_i) - [f_{12}(\mathbf{X}_i)]^2 > 0$ we are *assured*, from (9.15), that $d^2f < 0$. Let us look at the case where $f_{11}(\mathbf{X}_i) < 0$ but $f_{11}(\mathbf{X}_i)f_{22}(\mathbf{X}_i) - [f_{12}(\mathbf{X}_i)]^2 < 0$. Certainly the latter condition would hold for two cases: (1) $f_{22}(\mathbf{X}_i) > 0$ and (2) where $f_{22}(\mathbf{X}_i) < 0$ but $[f_{12}(\mathbf{X}_i)]^2 > f_{11}(\mathbf{X}_i)f_{22}(\mathbf{X}_i)$. For case 1 we definitely do not have a maximum. For case 2 it *may* be true that d^2f will be less than zero for *some* (dX_{i1}, dX_{i2}) *but not for all*. Therefore, we can conclude that

$$f_{11}(\mathbf{X}_i) < 0$$

and

$$f_{11}(\mathbf{X}_i)f_{22}(\mathbf{X}_i) - f_{12}(\mathbf{X}_i)^2 > 0 \tag{9.16}$$

are second-order conditions for determining a maximum in the case of two input variables. Equation 9.16 is equivalent to (9.14) but has the advantage that it is easily applied.

Before going on to discuss functions of more than two variables, some examples will help to illustrate the points just made.

The lot-size model we introduced in Section 9.1 can be extended to two variables. The extension will produce a very simple application of the ideas of this section. The portfolio example from Section 9.1 can also be extended. The extension will produce a more complicated application.

The Lot-Size Model Extended Suppose we extend the lot-size model by considering a two-item inventory with the cost

$$g(X_1, X_2) = \sum_{j=1}^{2} K_{Tj}^* = C_o \frac{d_i}{X_1} + kC_{p1} \frac{X_1}{2} + C_o \frac{d_2}{X_2} + kC_{p2} \frac{X_2}{2}$$

which we wish to minimize by choosing X_1 and X_2. To convert this problem to a maximization problem we form

$$f(X_1, X_2) = -g(X_1, X_2) = -\frac{C_o d_1}{X_1} - kC_{p1} \frac{X_1}{2} - \frac{C_o d_2}{X_2} - kC_{p2} \frac{X_2}{2} \quad (9.17)$$

Then the first-order conditions are

$$f_1(X_1, X_2) = \frac{C_o d_1}{X_1^2} - \frac{kC_{p1}}{2} = 0, f_2(X_1, X_2) = \frac{C_o d_2}{X_2^2} - \frac{kC_{p2}}{2} = 0 \quad (9.18)$$

which can be solved yielding

$$X_1 = \sqrt{\frac{2C_o d_1}{kC_{p1}}}$$

and $\qquad\qquad\qquad\qquad\qquad\qquad\qquad\qquad\qquad\qquad\qquad\qquad (9.19)$

$$X_2 = \sqrt{\frac{2C_o d_2}{kC_{p2}}}$$

To check the second-order conditions form

$$f_{11}(X_1, X_2) = -\frac{2C_o d_1}{X_1^3}, f_{22}(X_1, X_2) = -\frac{2C_o d_2}{X_2^3}, f_{12}(X_1, X_2) = 0$$

Then

$$f_{11}\left(\sqrt{\frac{2C_o d_1}{kC_{p1}}}, \sqrt{\frac{2C_o d_2}{kC_{p2}}}\right) < 0$$

$$f_{22}\left(\sqrt{\frac{2C_o d_1}{kC_{p1}}}, \sqrt{\frac{2C_o d_2}{kC_{p2}}}\right) < 0$$

and

$$f_{11}\left(\sqrt{\frac{2C_o d_1}{kC_{p1}}}, \sqrt{\frac{2C_o d_2}{kC_{p2}}}\right) f_{22}\left(\sqrt{\frac{2C_o d_1}{kC_{p1}}}, \sqrt{\frac{2C_o d_2}{kC_{p2}}}\right) - f_{12}\left(\sqrt{\frac{2C_o d_1}{kC_{p1}}}, \sqrt{\frac{2C_o d_2}{kC_{p2}}}\right)^2 > 0$$

The solution is a maximum.

The first-order conditions shown in (9.18) have an important feature. The decision variables each occur only in one equation. Therefore, the solution to the set of equations (9.18) is simple.

The practical upshot of the model formulation is that each inventory item can be treated in isolation of the others. We do not need to worry about interactions.

Investing in Bonds and Stocks Next extend the bond and stock example to include two stocks as candidates for selection as opposed to a well-diversified portfolio of stocks. Let r_b be the return on bonds, r_{S1} and r_{S2} be the expected returns on stocks 1 and 2, σ_{S1}^2 and σ_{S2}^2 be the variances of returns on stocks 1 and 2. We will add a covariance between returns on stocks 1 and 2 and call it $\rho\sigma_{S1}\sigma_{S2}$ where $-1 \leq \rho \leq 1$ is the correlation between returns on stock 1 and stock 2.

If X_1 is the amount invested in stock 1 and X_2 the amount invested in stock 2, then

$$\tilde{R}_T = (M - X_1 - X_2)r_b + X_1\tilde{R}_{S1} + X_2\tilde{R}_{S2}$$

and therefore

$$E(\tilde{R}_T) = (M - X_1 - X_2)r_b + X_1 r_{S1} + X_2 r_{S2}$$

and

$$\text{Var}(\tilde{R}_T) = X_1^2\sigma_{S1}^2 + 2\rho\sigma_{S1}\sigma_{S2}X_1X_2 + X_2^2\sigma_{S2}^2$$

where M is again the total funds available.

The certainty equivalent is

$$f(X_1, X_2) = M + (M - X_1 - X_2)r_b + X_1 r_{S1} + X_2 r_{S2}$$
$$- K(X_1^2\sigma_{S1}^2 + 2\rho\sigma_{S1}\sigma_{S2}X_1X_2 + X_2^2\sigma_{S2}^2)$$

The first-order conditions are

$$f_1(X_1, X_2) = -r_b + r_{S1} - 2KX_1\sigma_{S1}^2 - 2K\rho\sigma_{S1}\sigma_{S2}X_2 = 0 \qquad (9.20)$$

and

$$f_2(X_1, X_2) = -r_b + r_{S2} - 2KX_2\sigma_{S2}^2 - 2K\rho\sigma_{S1}\sigma_{S2}X_1 = 0 \qquad (9.21)$$

Equations 9.20 and 9.21 must now be solved simultaneously. The solution is

$$X_1 = \frac{(r_{S1} - r_b)\sigma_{S2}^2 - (r_{S2} - r_b)\rho\sigma_{S1}\sigma_{S2}}{2K\sigma_{S1}^2\sigma_{S2}^2(1 - \rho^2)}$$

$$X_2 = \frac{(r_{S2} - r_b)\sigma_{S1}^2 - (r_{S1} - r_b)\rho\sigma_{S1}\sigma_{S2}}{2K\sigma_{S2}^2\sigma_{S2}^2(1 - \rho^2)} \qquad (9.22)$$

Because the formulas for the first-order conditions are quite complicated, we will study an example to get the flavor of the analysis. To this end, let $r_{s1} = 0.12$,

$\sigma_{s1}^2 = 0.0064$, $r_{S2} = 0.14$, $\sigma_{S2}^2 = 0.0100$, $\rho = 0.5$, and $K = 0.0001$. Again, as in the previous example, assume $M = \$100,000$. Then using (9.22) we have

$$X_1 = \frac{(0.04)(0.0100) - (0.06)(0.5)(0.08)(0.10)}{2(0.0001)(0.0064)(0.0100)(1 - 0.25)} = \frac{16 \times 10^{-5}}{9.6 \times 10^{-9}} = \$16,666.67$$

$$X_2 = \frac{(0.06)(0.0064) - (0.04)(0.5)(0.08)(0.10)}{2(0.0001)(0.0064)(0.0100)(1 - 0.25)} = \frac{22.4 \times 10^{-5}}{9.6 \times 10^{-9}} = \$23,333.33$$

This means that the amount invested in bonds is $M - X_1 - X_2 = \$100,000 - \$16,666.67 - \$23,333.33 = \$60,000.00$.

Now, let us check the second-order condition. From (9.20) and (9.21) we have

$$f_{11}(X_1, X_2) = -2K\sigma_{S1}^2, f_{22}(X_1, X_2) = -2K\sigma_{S2}^2, f_{12}(X_1, X_2) = -2K\rho_{S1}\sigma_{S2}$$

$$(9.23)$$

Then using the second-order conditions (9.16) we have

$$f_{11}(16,666.67, 23,333.33) = -2(0.0001)(0.0064) < 0$$

$$f_{22}(16,666.67, 23,333.33) = -2(0.0001)(0.01) < 0$$

and

$$f_{12}(16,666.67, 23,333.33) = -2(0.0001)(0.5)(0.08)(0.10) < 0$$

Therefore,

$$f_{11}(16,666.67, 23,333.33)f_{22}(16,666.67, 23,333.33) - [f_{12}(16,666.67, 23,333.33)]^2$$

$$= 2.56 \times 10^{-12} - .64 \times 10^{-2}$$

$$= 1.92 \times 10^{-12}$$

which is greater than zero, and the second-order conditions indicate that the solution is a maximum.

The second-order conditions from this example provide some added insight into the model. From (9.23) it is clear that $f_{11}(X_1, X_2) < 0$ for all (X_1, X_2). Also,

$$f_{11}(X_1, X_2)f_{22}(X_1, X_2) - [f_{12}(X_1, X_2)]^2$$

$$= 4K^2\sigma_{S1}^2\sigma_{S2}^2 - 4K^2\rho^2\sigma_{S1}^2\sigma_{S2}^2$$

$$= 4K^2\sigma_{S1}^2\sigma_{S2}^2(1 - \rho^2) > 0 \qquad \text{provided } |\rho| \neq 1$$

Therefore, this condition will hold for any value of (X_1, X_2). This means that one need not worry about the model producing a minimum of the certainty equivalent if the parameter values r_b, r_{S1}, r_{S2}, σ_{S1}^2, σ_{S2}^2, ρ, and K should change.

It is interesting to study the effects of parameter changes on the values of X_1 and X_2 that are produced by the model. Let us look at a few. First, suppose all parameters are the same as in the example above except $\rho = -0.5$. The solutions (9.22) become

$$X_1 = \frac{(0.04)(0.0100) + (0.06)(0.5)(0.08)(0.10)}{2(0.0001)(0.0064)(0.0100)(1 - 0.25)} = \frac{64 \times 10^{-5}}{9.6 \times 10^{-9}} = \$66,666.67$$

$$X_2 = \frac{(0.06)(0.0064) + (0.04)(0.5)(0.08)(0.10)}{2(0.0001)(0.0064)(0.0100)(1 - 0.25)} = \frac{54.4 \times 10^{-5}}{9.6 \times 10^{-9}} = \$56,666.67$$

Note that in this case greater amounts of the stocks were purchased. In fact, since $X_1 + X_2 > \$100,000$, the solution implies that the investor should borrow to invest in the stocks. This is a manifestation of the fact that a negative correlation between returns tends to reduce the risk that accompanies the combined return from the two stock investments.

A second example will show another aspect of the model. Suppose $\rho = 0.95$. Then

$$X_1 = \frac{(0.04)(0.0100) - (0.06)(0.95)(0.08)(0.10)}{2(0.0001)(0.0064)(0.0100)(1 - 0.7225)} = \frac{-5.6 \times 10^{-5}}{3.6 \times 10^{-9}} = -\$15,555.56$$

$$X_2 = \frac{(0.06)(0.0064) - (0.04)(0.95)(0.08)(0.10)}{2(0.0001)(0.0064)(0.0100)(1 - 0.7225)} = \frac{8.0 \times 10^{-5}}{3.6 \times 10^{-9}} = \$22,222.22$$

and the investment in bonds is $\$100,000 + 15,555.56 - 22,222.22 = \$93,333.34$.

At first glance, this result seems unreasonable. The investment in stock 1 is negative! There is, however, an interpretation that makes sense. A negative value of bonds indicates that the investor should borrow money to invest in stocks. A negative value of X_1 indicates that stock 1 should be sold in the amount of $\$15,555.56$ and the proceeds used along with the initial $\$100,000$ to invest in stock 2 and bonds. (In the parlance of finance, selling the stock is referred to as "selling short." The stock is sold even though it is not owned. The funds obtained are used to invest in other securities and the earnings and proceeds are then used at a later date to buy the stock and deliver it to the new owner.)

Maximizing Functions of Many Variables

The first-order conditions (9.11) and the second-order conditions (9.13) hold with generality for functions of more than two input variables. As n gets large, however, the equations of the first-order conditions becomes more difficult to solve. Furthermore, although second-order conditions for functions of n variables can be developed (and are extensions of (9.16)), they require mathematics beyond the scope of this book; we would face severe pedagogical problems if we proceeded. Therefore, we will leave our present discussion of unrestrained maximization with the caveat that the general ideas relevant to n-variable maximization are the same as those we have heretofore discussed.

In the next two sections (9.3 and 9.4) we will discuss maximization of functions with equality and inequality constraints. Again, the mathematics of the second-order conditions provides mathematical difficulty beyond the scope of this text. We will not try to discuss this matter but leave it to more advanced works. (See the references at the end of this chapter).

9.3 CONSTRAINED OPTIMIZATION: EQUALITY CONSTRAINTS

Up to this point, we have only discussed finding local maxima where the set of possibilities for X_i is unlimited. We next consider the case where equality constraints limit the set of alternatives.

To illustrate the constrained-optimization problem, we will make another extension to the lot-size model. We will also extend the portfolio example.

The Lot-Size Model with Equality Constraints

With no restrictions on the decision variables X_1 and X_2, the optimum is found from (9.19) to be

$$X_1 = \sqrt{\frac{2C_o d_1}{k C_{p1}}}, \; X_2 = \sqrt{\frac{2C_o d_2}{k C_{p2}}} \qquad (9.24)$$

Suppose that there is a restriction on the average dollar value of inventory held for the two products; that is, average inventory must be equal to I. Then we seek a set of values (X_1, X_2) that minimizes costs subject to the restriction that

$$I = C_{p1} \frac{X_1}{2} + C_{p2} \frac{X_2}{2} \qquad (9.25)$$

One approach to solving this problem would be to solve (9.25) for X_2 in terms of X_1 and then substitute into the original cost function, (9.17),

$$h(X_1) = f\left(X_1, \frac{2I - C_{p1} X_1}{C_{p2}}\right)$$

$$= -\frac{C_o d_1}{X_1} - k C_{p1} \frac{X_1}{2} - \frac{C_o d_2 C_{p2}}{2I - C_{p1} X_1} - \frac{k}{2}(2I - C_{p1} X_1) \qquad (9.26)$$

which is a function of X_1 only.

Then differentiating (9.26), we have

$$h'(X_1) = \frac{C_o d_1}{X_1{}^2} - \frac{k C_{p1}}{2} - \frac{C_o d_2 C_{p2} C_{p1}}{(2I - C_{p1} X_1)^2} + \frac{k C_{p1}}{2} = 0 \qquad (9.27)$$

which must be solved for X_1. After obtaining the solution for X_1, (9.25) can be used to find X_2.

Note that (9.27) does not lend itself to an easy solution. Although (9.27) could be solved, it would be desirable to find a better way to solve this problem. This need to search for a better way becomes even more apparent when we add a third variable X_3 and find our straightforward approach virtually unworkable.

LaGrange Multipliers and a Single Equality Constraint   The method of *LaGrange multipliers* offers a better approach to this problem and makes it easy to find a solution. It is a very general method and has a wide variety of applications. It is important to note, however, that it does not always lead to improved computational efficiency but almost always leads to important interpretations. We will illustrate the method, then explain why it works, show how it can be interpreted, and give some indication of its limitations.

Create a new variable λ and define a new function

$$L(X_1, X_2, \lambda) = f(X_1, X_2) - \lambda\left(\frac{C_{p1}X_1}{2} + \frac{C_{p2}X_2}{2} - I\right) \tag{9.28}$$

Now proceed to maximize $L(X_1, X_2, \lambda)$ by the usual procedures. That is

$$L_1(X_1, X_2, \lambda) = \frac{C_o d_1}{X_1^2} - \frac{kC_{p1}}{2} - \frac{\lambda C_{p1}}{2} = 0 \tag{9.29a}$$

$$L_2(X_1, \ X_2, \ \lambda) = \frac{C_o d_2}{X_2^2} - \frac{kC_{p2}}{2} - \frac{\lambda C_{p2}}{2} = 0 \tag{9.29b}$$

$$L_3(X_1, X_2, \lambda) = -\left(\frac{C_{p1}X_1}{2} + \frac{C_{p2}X_2}{2} - I\right) = 0 \tag{9.29c}$$

define the first-order conditions. Equations 9.29a and 9.29b can be solved in terms of λ yielding

$$X_1 = \sqrt{\frac{2C_o d_1}{(k + \lambda)C_{p1}}}, X_2 = \sqrt{\frac{2C_o d_2}{(k + \lambda)C_{p2}}} \tag{9.30}$$

Now substitute (9.30) into (9.29c) getting

$$-\left(\frac{C_{p1}}{2}\sqrt{\frac{2C_o d_1}{(k + \lambda)C_{p1}}} + \frac{C_{p2}}{2}\sqrt{\frac{2C_o d_2}{(k + \lambda)C_{p2}}} - I\right) = 0$$

which can be solved for λ, yielding

$$\lambda = -k + \frac{1}{I^2}\left(\sqrt{\frac{C_o d_1 C_{p1}}{2}} + \sqrt{\frac{C_o d_2 C_{p2}}{2}}\right)^2 \tag{9.31}$$

Then, using (9.31), equation (9.30) can be written as

$$X_1 = \omega\sqrt{\frac{2C_o d_1}{kC_{p1}}}, X_2 = \omega\sqrt{\frac{2C_o d_2}{kC_{p2}}} \tag{9.32a}$$

where

$$\omega = I/\tfrac{1}{2}\left(C_{p1}\sqrt{\frac{2C_o d_1}{kC_{p1}}} + C_{p2}\sqrt{\frac{2C_o d_2}{kC_{p2}}}\right) \tag{9.32b}$$

Note that ω can be easily determined from (9.32b), and knowing ω X_1 and X_2 can be easily determined from (9.32a). An example will illustrate the calculations.

Consider a two-product inventory with $C_o = \$10$, $k = 0.20$, $d_1 = 500$, $d_2 = 1000$, $C_{p1} = \$2$, $C_{p2} = \$1$, and $I = \$200$. If the constraint on inventory were ignored we would have $X_1 = 158.1139$ and $X_2 = 316.2278$ using (9.24). Note that these values for X_1 and X_2 would result in an average inventory investment in excess of $200.

From (9.32b), $\omega = 200/\frac{1}{2}(2\sqrt{2(10)(500)/0.20(2)} + 1\sqrt{2(10)(1000)/0.20(1)}) = 0.63246$ and from (9.32a) $X_1 = 0.63246\sqrt{2(10)(500)/0.20(2)} \doteq 100.000$, $X_2 = 0.63246\sqrt{2(10)(1000)/0.20(1)} \doteq 200.000$. The average investment now equals $\$200[\$2(100)/2 + \$1(200)/2 = \$200]$.

Why does the LaGrange multiplier technique work? To find the answer to this question, let us look at the problem somewhat abstractly. Suppose we wish to maximize $f(X_1, X_2)$ subject to the equality constraint $h(X_1, X_2) = 0$. The standard first-order condition

$$df = f_1 dX_1 + f_2 dX_2 = 0 \tag{9.33}$$

must hold for a maximum. But it must be remembered that dX_1 and dX_2 are not independent because of the side condition $h(X_1, X_2) = 0$. They are related by

$$dh = h_1 dX_1 + h_2 dX_2 = 0 \tag{9.34}$$

Therefore, (9.33) and (9.34) produce the condition that

$$\frac{f_1}{f_2} = \frac{h_1}{h_2} \tag{9.35}$$

as a single equation that must hold for optimality. Combining (9.35) with the original restriction $h(X_1, X_2) = 0$ produces two equations in two unknowns that are necessary for optimality.

Now consider the LaGrange multiplier approach, which indicates that $L(X_1, X_2, \lambda) = f(X_1, X_2) - \lambda h(X_1, X_2)$ should be formed and maximized. The first-order conditions are

$$L_1(X_1, X_2, \lambda) = f_1(X_1, X_2) - \lambda h_1(X_1, X_2) = 0 \tag{9.36a}$$

$$L_2(X_1, X_2, \lambda) = f_2(X_1, X_2) - \lambda h_2(X_1, X_2) = 0 \tag{9.36b}$$

$$L_3(X_1, X_2, \lambda) = -h(X_1, X_2) = 0 \tag{9.36c}$$

Combining (9.36a) and (9.36b) produces

$$\frac{f_1}{f_2} = \frac{h_1}{h_2}$$

which is identical to (9.35). Furthermore, the condition (9.36c) is merely the original constraint. So the LaGrange multiplier technique produces exactly the same answer that the "classic" technique would produce.

The interpretation of the LaGrange multiplier technique offers significant appeal for use in business and economic problems. The multiplier itself has economic meaning. Reconsider the inventory problem and equation (9.28).

Because the solution of the problem is constrained to the case where $C_{p1}X_1/2 + C_{p2}X_2/2 - I = 0$, it follows that the second term in the right-hand side of (9.28) is zero, and therefore $L(X_1, X_2, \lambda)$ is, when evaluated at feasible points, the negative of the cost function. Therefore,

$$\frac{dL(X_1, X_2, \lambda)}{dI} = \lambda \tag{9.37}$$

is the rate of change of the optimal value of the objective function with respect to the inventory limitation (I). Stated in first differences, (9.37) can be approximated by

$$\Delta L(X_1, X_2, \lambda) = \lambda \Delta I \tag{9.38}$$

indicating the change in (the negative of) the optimal cost is equal to the LaGrange multiplier times the change in the constraint. With respect to the example, we have, from equation (9.31),

$$\lambda = -0.20 + \frac{1}{(200)^2} \left(\sqrt{\frac{10(500)(2)}{2}} + \sqrt{\frac{10(1000)(1)}{2}} \right)^2$$

$$\doteq -0.20 + 0.50$$

$$= 0.30$$

Thus, we know that if the constraint is increased by \$1 from \$200 to \$201, the optimal cost will *fall* by approximately $0.30(\$1) = \$0.30$.

There is another aspect of this problem where the use of the LaGrange multipliers leads to an important interpretation. The constrained optimal solution to the inventory problem appeared in equation (9.30) and is similar to the unconstrained optimal order quantity (9.24) with the exception that the inventory-carrying cost parameter k is replaced by $k + \lambda$. That is, (9.30) computes optimal inventories *as if* the cost to carry inventory were $k + \lambda = 0.20 + 0.30 = 0.50$. Thus, $k + \lambda$ is the implicit cost to carry inventory as witnessed by the amount ordered under the constrained case.

All is not a bed of roses with the LaGrange multiplier technique. In some instances, the computations to get the problem solution are not reduced significantly. Consider the two-item inventory problem just discussed, but assume that there is a limitation on storage of maximum inventory rather than on the dollar value of inventory investment. Furthermore, assume that the unconstrained optimal inventory will exceed the storage-space limitation. In this case, even though the amount of storage represents an upper limit for X_1 and X_2, we will want to use all the available storage. We then have a problem with an equality constraint on storage. If S_1 and S_2 are the space requirements to store one unit of items 1 and 2, the constraint will be

$$S_1 X_1 + S_2 X_2 = S$$

where S is the total space availability. The problem then becomes one of maximizing

$$L(X_1, X_2, \lambda) = -\frac{C_o d_1}{X_1} - kC_{p1}\frac{X_1}{2} - \frac{C_o d_2}{X_2} - kC_{p2}\frac{X_2}{2} - \lambda(S_1 X_1 + S_2 X_2 - S)$$

The first-order conditions are

$$L_1(X_1, X_2, \lambda) = \frac{C_o d_1}{X_1^2} - \frac{kC_{p1}}{2} - \lambda S_1 = 0$$

$$L_2(X_1, X_2, \lambda) = \frac{C_o d_2}{X_2^2} - \frac{kC_{p2}}{2} - \lambda S_2 = 0$$

$$L_3(X_1, X_2, \lambda) = -(S_1 X_1 + S_2 X_2 - S) = 0$$

The solutions to the first two equations are

$$X_1 = \sqrt{\frac{2C_o d_1}{kC_{p1} + \lambda S_1}}, X_2 = \sqrt{\frac{2C_o d_2}{kC_{p2} + \lambda S_2}}$$

Substituting these values into the third of the first-order conditions yields

$$S_1 \sqrt{\frac{2C_o d_1}{kC_{p1} + \lambda S_1}} + S_2 \sqrt{\frac{2C_o d_2}{kC_{p2} + \lambda S_2}} = S$$

which cannot be solved *in closed form* for λ. To be sure, the equation can be solved by trial-and-error procedures, but the point we wish to establish is that the computation is not easy.

LaGrange Multipliers and More Than One Constraint   The example that we used in the last section to illustrate the LaGrange multiplier technique did not illustrate the generality of the method. It involved only two decision variables and a single equality constraint, whereas the method can be shown to apply to cases where there are n variables and not more than $n - 1$ equality constraints. The example discussed an objective function that was separable in the variables, whereas in the general case the objective function need not be separable into parts with each part being a function of only one variable. In this section, we will briefly discuss the greater generality that the technique can handle.

Consider an inventory system with n items. The total cost of the system is

$$f(\mathbf{X}) = \sum_{j=1}^{n} \left(\frac{C_o d_j}{X_j} + kC_{pj}\frac{X_j}{2} \right) \tag{9.39}$$

where the subscript j denotes the jth item. Suppose two constraints are put on the system: (1) an average dollar inventory constraint and (2) a storage-space maximum constraint.

The inventory dollar constraint can be expressed as

$$\sum_{j=1}^{n} C_{pj}\frac{X_j}{2} - I = 0 \tag{9.40}$$

and the space constraint as

$$\sum_{j=1}^{n} S_j X_j - S = 0 \tag{9.41}$$

In this case, two LaGrange multipliers λ and μ can be defined and the function

$$L(\mathbf{X}, \lambda, \mu) = -\sum_{j=1}^{n} \left(\frac{C_o d_j}{X_j} + kC_{pj} \frac{X_j}{2} \right) - \lambda \left(\sum_{j=1}^{n} C_{pj} \frac{X_j}{2} - I \right) - \mu \left(\sum_{j=1}^{n} S_j X_j - S \right) \tag{9.42}$$

formed. The first-order conditions can now be developed as

$$L_k(\mathbf{X}, \lambda, \mu) = \frac{C_o d_k}{X_k^2} - \frac{kC_{pk}}{2} - \frac{\lambda C_{pk}}{2} - \mu S_k = 0 \qquad k = 1, \ldots, n \tag{9.43a}$$

$$L_{n+1}(\mathbf{X}, \lambda, \mu) = -\left(\sum_{j=1}^{n} C_{pj} \frac{X_j}{2} - I \right) = 0 \tag{9.43b}$$

$$L_{n+2}(\mathbf{X}, \lambda, \mu) = -\left(\sum_{j=1}^{n} S_j X_j - S \right) = 0 \tag{9.43c}$$

The solution to (9.43a) to (9.43c) will not be easy. It can be accomplished in the following way. First solve (9.43a) for X_k. The solution for each X_k will be in terms of λ, μ and known parameters (i.e., C_o, d_k, k, C_{pk}, S_k). Then substitute these solutions into (9.43b) and (9.43c), which will then become functions of λ and μ only. These last two equations can be solved for λ and μ and, upon having obtained the solution values, X_k can be determined from equation (9.43a).

Although the general principles of solving (9.43a) to (9.43c) are straightforward, the practical facts are different. An example will illustrate the problem.

Table 9.2 describes the data for an inventory system. The LaGrangean is

$$L(X_1, X_2, X_3, \lambda, \mu) = -\frac{5,000}{X_1} - 0.2X_1 - \frac{10,000}{X_2} - 0.1X_2 - \frac{10,000}{X_3} - 0.01X_3$$
$$- \lambda(X_1 + 0.5X_2 + 0.5X_3 - 200)$$
$$- \mu(0.5X_1 + X_2 + 2X_3 - 200)$$

Table 9.2 Data for Inventory Example

j	d_j	C_{pj}	S_j	$C_o = \$10, k = 0.20$
1	500	\$2	0.5 ft^2	$I = \$200$
2	1,000	\$1	1.0	$S = 200 \text{ ft}^2$
3	1,000	\$1	2.0	

and the first-order conditions are

$$L_1(X_1, X_2, X_3, \lambda, \mu) = \frac{5{,}000}{X_1^2} - 0.2 - \lambda - 0.5\mu = 0$$

$$L_2(X_1, X_2, X_3, \lambda, \mu) = \frac{10{,}000}{X_2^2} - 0.1 - 0.5\lambda - \mu = 0$$

$$L_3(X_1, X_2, X_3, \lambda, \mu) = \frac{10{,}000}{X_2^2} - 0.1 - 0.5\lambda - 2\mu = 0$$

$$L_4(X_1, X_2, X_3, \lambda, \mu) = -(X_1 + 0.5X_2 + 0.5X_3 - 200) = 0$$

$$L_5(X_1, X_2, X_3, \lambda, \mu) = -(0.5X_1 + X_2 + 2X_3 - 200) = 0$$

From the first three first-order conditions we have

$$X_1 = \sqrt{\frac{5{,}000}{0.2 + \lambda + 0.5\mu}},\ X_2 = \sqrt{\frac{10{,}000}{0.1 + 0.5\lambda + \mu}},\ X_3 = \sqrt{\frac{10{,}000}{0.1 + 0.5\lambda + 2\mu}}$$

Substituting these into the fourth and fifth first-order conditions yields

$$\sqrt{\frac{5{,}000}{0.2 + \lambda + 0.5\mu}} + 0.5\sqrt{\frac{10{,}000}{0.1 + 0.5\lambda + \mu}} + 0.5\sqrt{\frac{10{,}000}{0.1 + 0.5\lambda + 2\mu}} - 200 = 0$$

and

$$0.5\sqrt{\frac{5{,}000}{0.2 + \lambda + 0.5\mu}} + \sqrt{\frac{10{,}000}{0.1 + 0.5\lambda + \mu}} + 2\sqrt{\frac{10{,}000}{0.1 + 0.5\lambda + 2\mu}} - 200 = 0$$

which must be solved simultaneously.

The two equations in λ and μ are formidable indeed, and solution is not easy. We will not attempt solution because solving simultaneous nonlinear equations is beyond the scope of this text. The example should illustrate both the technique of using multiple constraints within the LaGrange multiplier context and the fact that as more variables and constraints are added to the problem, the solution becomes progressively more difficult. Easy solutions are obtained only in special cases.

The Stock-and-Bond Investment Problem with Equality Constraints

The concepts of LaGrange multipliers can be applied to the portfolio selection problem of this chapter. Suppose that we formulate the LaGrangean as

$$L(X_1, X_2, X_3, \lambda) = M + X_3 r_b + X_1 r_{S1} + X_2 r_{S2}$$

$$- K(X_1^2 \sigma_{S1}^2 + 2\rho \sigma_{S1} \sigma_{S2} X_1 X_2 + X_2^2 \sigma_{S2}^2).$$

$$- \lambda(X_1 + X_2 + X_3 - M)$$

where X_3 is the investment in bonds (formerly treated implicitly as $M - X_1 - X_2$). Then the first-order conditions are

$$L_1(X_1, X_2, X_3, \lambda) = r_{S1} - 2K\sigma_{S1}^2 X_1 - 2K\rho\sigma_{S1}\sigma_{S2}X_2 - \lambda = 0$$

$$L_2(X_1, X_2, X_3, \lambda) = r_{S2} - 2K\rho\sigma_{S1}\sigma_{S2}X_1 - 2K\sigma_{S2}^2 X_2 - \lambda = 0$$

$$L_3(X_1, X_2, X_3, \lambda) = r_b - \lambda \qquad\qquad\qquad = 0$$

$$L_4(X_1, X_2, X_3, \lambda) = -(X_1 + X_2 + X_3 - M) \qquad\quad = 0$$

Note that the third first-order condition yields $\lambda = r_b$ and then, substituting into the first and second equations and solving, we produce the result previously shown in (9.22).

Although the solution is the same as was produced in the first formulation, the LaGrange multiplier approach does offer some added insight. We know that

$$\frac{dL(X_1, X_2, X_3, \lambda)}{dM} = 1 + \lambda = 1 + r_b$$

Thus, the rate of change of the optimal certainty equivalent with respect to the amount of funds available is $1 + r_b$. If \$1 in added funds were available the certainty equivalent would increase by \$$1 + r_b$. It is worthwhile to attempt a verbal rationalization of this result. Note that $\lambda = r_b$ *regardless of the values of the parameters in the problem.* Even though the parameter values can have an influence on the values of X_1, X_2, and $X_3 (= M - X_1 - X_2)$, as we saw in the previous discussion of this problem, the rate of change of the objective function stays constant at $1 + r_b$ as M is increased. This reflects the fact that as M is increased, the optimal solution will call for the added funds to be placed in bond investment if $X_3 > 0$ and to reduce borrowing if $X_3 < 0$. In either case, the objective function will increase by $1 + r_b$.

The opportunity for bond investment plays a key role in the example. It offers a riskless investment—that is, the variance of return is zero. Let us see what would happen if the bond investment were not allowed as a possibility and the amount M must be divided between investment in the two stocks. Then the LaGrangean would be

$$L(X_1, X_2, \lambda) = M + X_1 r_{S1} + X_2 r_{S2} - K(X_1^2\sigma_{S1}^2 + 2\rho\sigma_{S1}\sigma_{S2}X_1 X_2 + X_2^2\sigma_{S2}^2)$$
$$- \lambda(X_1 + X_2 - M)$$

and the first-order conditions are

$$L_1(X_1, X_2, \lambda) = r_{S1} - 2K\sigma_{S1}^2 X_1 - 2K\rho\sigma_{S1}\sigma_{S2}X_2 - \lambda = 0$$

$$L_2(X_1 X_2, \lambda) = r_{S2} - 2K\rho\sigma_{S1}\sigma_{S2}X_1 - 2K\sigma_{S2}^2 X_2 - \lambda = 0$$

$$L_3(X_1, X_2, \lambda) = -(X_1 + X_2 - M) = 0$$

The solution to this set of equations is

$$X_1 = \frac{r_{S1} - r_{S2} + 2KM(\sigma_{S2}^2 - \rho\sigma_{S1}\sigma_{S2})}{2K(\sigma_{S1}^2 - 2\rho\sigma_{S1}\sigma_{S2} + \sigma_{S2}^2)}$$

$$X_2 = \frac{2KM(\sigma_{S1}^2 - \rho\sigma_{S1}\sigma_{S2}) - (r_{S1} - r_{S2})}{2K(\sigma_{S1}^2 - 2\rho\sigma_{S1}\sigma_{S2} + \sigma_{S2}^2)}$$

$$\lambda = r_{S1} + \frac{(r_{S2} - r_{S1})(\sigma_{S1}^2 - \rho\sigma_{S1}\sigma_{S2}) - 2KM\sigma_{S1}^2\sigma_{S2}^2(1 - \rho^2)}{(\sigma_{S1}^2 - 2\rho\sigma_{S1}\sigma_{S2} + \sigma_{S2}^2)}$$

Using the same numerical values of the parameters used in previous examples (i.e., $r_{S1} = 0.12$, $r_{S2} = 0.14$, $\sigma_{S1}^2 = 0.0064$, $\sigma_{S2}^2 = 0.0100$, $K = 0.0001$, $\rho = 0.5$) the solution becomes

$$X_1 = \$ -11904.762 + 0.71428M$$

$$X_2 = \$11904.762 + 0.28572M$$

$$\lambda = 0.125714 - 0.0000011429M$$

Note that as M is increased, the rate of change of the certainty equivalent $1 + \lambda$ decreases at a decreasing rate. This reflects the fact that risk is being added at a faster rate than return. In the case where bond investment was possible, added funds were invested in bonds that did not add to risk. Therefore, the certainty equivalent increased. In the present example, when funds are added they *must* be invested in risky securities and therefore add to risk and reduce the certainty equivalent.

9.4 CONSTRAINED OPTIMIZATION: INEQUALITY CONSTRAINTS

The lot-size model we have discussed in this chapter serves as a convenient example where an inequality constraint may be operating. Suppose in formulating a "dollar value" constraint on inventory investment we replaced (9.25) by

$$C_{p1}\frac{X_1}{2} + C_{p2}\frac{X_2}{2} \le I$$

This is a reasonable constraint from a management point of view. If the unconstrained optimum values for X_1 and X_2 were such that the constraint was satisfied, the optimum values would be used as the lot sizes. On the other hand, if the unconstrained optimal values of X_1 and X_2 did not satisfy the constraint, they would have to be modified in order to do so.

This suggests that there are two ways we might proceed to solve this problem. First, the constraint may be ignored and the problem solved. If the solution then satisfies the constraint, we are done. If it does not satisfy the constraint, the solution to the problem must lie on the constraint, and we can solve the problem with the equality constraint and the LaGrange multiplier approach.

The second approach would be to solve the problem with the equality constraint. If the value of the LaGrange multiplier is positive, the optimal solution has been found. If it is negative, then as I is decreased, the value of the objective function increases; a decrease in I is equivalent to placing the solution within the original constraint, so the unconstrained solution must be optimal.

To illustrate the situation, let $I = \$500$, $C_o = \$10$, $k = 0.20$, $d_1 = 500$, $d_2 = 1000$, $C_{p1} = \$2$, $C_{p2} = \$1$. Now use the first approach—solve for the unconstrained values of X_1 and X_2. We previously calculated these to be $X_1 = 158.1139$, $X_2 = 316.2278$. Therefore,

$$C_{p1}\frac{X_1}{2} + C_{p2}\frac{X_2}{2} = 2\frac{158.1139}{2} + 1\frac{316.2278}{2} = \$474.3417 < I = \$500$$

and the unconstrained solution is optimal.

Using the second approach we can calculate the optimal solution with the equality constraint

$$\frac{C_{p1}X_1}{2} + \frac{C_{p2}X_2}{2} = X_1 + \tfrac{1}{2}X_2 = I = 500$$

Equations 9.31 and 9.32 can then be used to find the values of λ and X_1 and X_2. From (9.31) we have

$$\lambda = -0.20 + \frac{1}{(500)^2}\left(\sqrt{\frac{10(500)(2)}{2}} + \sqrt{\frac{19(1000)(1)}{2}}\right)^2 = -0.12$$

The change in the negative of total cost with a unit change in I is negative, and this indicates that if required inventory is reduced below $I = \$500$, the negative of total cost will increase—or total costs will decrease. Therefore, lower costs can be obtained if dollar value of inventory is less than $\$500$ or if the constraint is ignored. Therefore, the unconstrained solution is optimal.

More general techniques for solving nonlinear problems subject to inequality constraints are beyond the scope of this text. The interested reader is referred to the references at the end of this chapter.

9.5 REVIEW AND SUMMARY

This chapter has introduced a number of important concepts. A short review of them will be worthwhile.

The first concepts were *global* and *local* maximums. When a function has more than one local maximum, we have no "sure-fire" simple way of finding the global maximum from the set of local maxima and any potential boundary points that may be candidates. The function itself must be evaluated at each candidate for the global maximum.

Minimization problems can be converted to maximization problems by multiplying the function by -1 and then proceeding with the techniques of maximization.

The *first-order conditions* for a maximum are that $df = 0$ where df is the total differential of the function f. When there is a single variable, the first-order condition is equivalent to $df/dX = 0$. When there are n variables, the first-order condition $df = 0$ is equivalent to $f_1(\mathbf{X}) = f_2(\mathbf{X}) = \cdots = f_n(\mathbf{X}) = 0$; in other words, the first partial derivatives must be zero.

The *second-order conditions* distinguish between maxima, minima, and other points. The general condition for a maximum is $d^2 f < 0$. The latter expression, the second total differential being negative, is equivalent to $d^2 f /dX^2 < 0$ for a function of a single input variable. For functions of many input variables, the statement of equivalent conditions is complicated. We specified these equivalent conditions for functions of two input variables but noted that specification of the second-order conditions for functions of more than two input variables was beyond the scope of this text.

The ideas of *concavity* and *convexity* are important to maximization problems. A function is concave in the close neighborhood of a local maximum; it is convex in the neighborhood of a local minimum. Clearly, concavity and convexity can be expressed in terms of second differentials.

If it is can be shown that a function is *strictly* (the inequality holds) *concave* over the set of feasible values of the variables, then there is a single maximum, and the first-order conditions are necessary and sufficient to determine the maximum point. Thus, we are at times concerned with determining whether a function is strictly concave since it will tend to ease any computational problems associated with finding the maximum point.

The set of points S over which many-variable maximization takes place can be the result of a set of equalities or inequalities. The equality constraints can be dealt with by means of *LaGrange multipliers*. The first-order conditions for a maximum using the technique of LaGrange multipliers, as compared to "classic" techniques, may end up with little to be gained by way of computational efficiency, but in many cases the LaGrange technique offers valuable economic insight into the problem. The value of the LaGrange multiplier itself gives some indication about the unconstrained maximum. Maximization of functions with inequality constraints can be handled with a modification of the LaGrange multiplier technique.

References   Fiacco, A.V., and McCormick, G.P., *Nonlinear Programming: Sequential Unconstrained Minimization Techniques*, New York: John Wiley & Sons, 1968.

Hadley, G., *Nonlinear and Dynamic Programming*, Reading, Mass.: Addison-Wesley, 1964.

Himmelblau, D., *Applied Nonlinear Programming*, New York: McGraw-Hill, 1972.

Miller, R.E., *Modern Mathematical Methods for Economics and Business*, New York: Holt, Rinehart & Winston. 1972.

Simmons, D.M., *Nonlinear Programming for Operations Research*, Englewood Cliffs, N.J.: Prentice-Hall, 1975.

Teichroew, D., *An Introduction to Management Science: Deterministic Models*, New York: John Wiley & Sons, 1964.

Tucker, A.W., "Linear and Nonlinear Programming," *Operations Research*, Vol. 5 (1957), 244–257.

Wagner, H.M., *Principles of Operations Research*, 2nd ed., Englewood Cliffs, N.J.: Prentice-Hall, 1975.

Review Questions

1. Using the ideas of a certainty equivalent of ending wealth that were discussed in Chapter 2, justify Equation 8.

2. Distinguish between a global and local maximum. Explain why maximizing the negative of a function is equivalent to minimizing the function.

3. For a function of a single variable, explain the second derivative test for a local maximum and a local minimum.

4. Is the profit function for Prefinishing Corp. concave for $0 \le S < \infty$?

5. Explain the meaning of $df = 0$ and $d^2f < 0$ for two input variables in terms of directions of change. Use graphs to illustrate your points.

6. Explain the role of the second partial derivatives and cross partial derivatives in finding the maximum of a function of two input variables.

7. Suppose we have a function of two input variables subject to two equality constraints. How many points are in the set S? What can you say about maximizing a function of two input variables subject to three or more equality constraints?

8. For the investment problem with two stocks how do you know that the first-order conditions yield a maximum for *any* values of the parameter?

9. Describe a procedure for using LaGrange multipliers for solving an inequality constrained maximization problem.

10. What can you say about the size of S when it is defined by two inequality constraints in a problem that maximizes a function of two input variables? (Compare your answer with question 7.)

11. If you can determine that a function is concave over the constraint set, how does such knowledge help you to find the solution?

Problems

1. (a) Using Equation 9.2 plot the cost function for $C_o = \$50$, $d = 1000$, $k = 0.10$, $C_p = \$0.05$.   (b) Find the optimal solution.   (c) Plot the negative of the cost function from part a.

2. (a) For the data given in Problem 1, plot a graph with C_p on the horizontal axis and X_o on the vertical axis.   (b) Plot a graph with C_p on the horizontal axis and the optimal number of orders per year on the vertical axis.   (c) Plot a graph with C_p on the horizontal axis and the optimal average dollar value of inventory on the vertical axis.

3. From the data given in Problem 1, develop a formula that: (a) Relates X_o to the ratio of ordering to carrying costs. (b) Relates X_o to the demand given the ratio of ordering to carrying costs given in the problem.

4. (a) For the data given in Problem 1, calculate the ratio of the total orders per year to the average dollar value of inventory for the optimal solution. (b) Suppose the cost data were the same as in Problem 1 but another item in inventory had $d = 500$ and $C_p = \$1.00$. Calculate the ratio between the optimal total orders per year and the optimal average dollar value of inventory for this item. Compare your result with part a. (c) Can you prove that the result you obtained will occur regardless of the values of d and C_p for various items in inventory? (d) If you were called in to determine whether an inventory of many similar items was efficiently run, could you use the results of part c to make a quick check before you knew the values of C_o and k?

5. Suppose that the cost to carry a dollar of inventory k was an increasing function of average inventory. In particular, suppose $k = 0.001C_p X$. (a) Develop a formula for the optimal lot size. (b) Using the data of Problem 1, calculate the optimal lot size and optimal inventory cost.

6. (a) Given $r_S = 0.12$, $r_b = 0.08$, $K = 0.001$, use Equation 9.9 to plot the proportion of stock investment as a function of σ_S^2. Can you give an intuitive explanation of your result? (b) Plot the proportion of stock investment as a function of σ_S^2 if $K = 0.005$. Give an intuitive explanation of the difference between the results of parts a and b.

7. Extend the optimal sales force example for Prefinishing Corp. to the case where profit after interest and income taxes is the objective function. (Use the analysis of Chapter 1, the complex alternative, to develop the profit as a function of S then find the optimal value of S.)

8. Consider the function $f(X_1\, X_2) = -X_1{}^2 - 2X_2{}^2 - 3X_1 X_2$. Find $f_1(X_1, X_2)$, $f_2(X_1, X_2)$, $f_{11}(X_1, X_2)$, $f_{22}(X_1, X_2)$, $f_{12}(X_1, X_2)$, $f_{21}(X_1, X_2)$. Solve $f_1(X_1, X_2) = 0$ and $f_2(X_1, X_2) = 0$. Is this point a maximum?

9. Using Equation 9.14 as a starting point, derive Equation 9.15.

10. Is the point $(X_1, X_2) = (0, 0)$ a maximum point, a minimum point, or neither for the function $f(X_1, X_2) = -X_1{}^2 + X_2{}^2 + 10$?

11. Consider a two-item inventory problem with $C_o = \$10$, $k = 0.20$, $d_1 = 500$, $d_2 = 1000$, $C_{p1} = \$2$, $C_{p2} = \$1$, and constraint on total dollar value of average inventory of $I = \$200$. (These data are identical to the example given in Section 9.3). (a) Determine the reduction in cost that would be available if I were increased to $\$210$ by recalculating Equation 9.32. (b) Calculate

$$\int_{I=200}^{210} \left[-k + \frac{1}{I^2} \left(\sqrt{\frac{C_1 d_1 C_{p1}}{2}} + \sqrt{\frac{C_o d_2 C_{p2}}{2}} \right)^2 \right] dI$$

(See Equation 9.31.)

(c) Explain why the solutions to parts a and b are equal.

12. It is common for "practical" people to determine lot sizes for dollar-constrained inventory problems by the following method:
    (a) First calculate the unconstrained lot sizes for all items.
    (b) Determine the dollar value of average inventory (aggregated for all items) that would result from these lot sizes.
    (c) Calculate the ratio of the allowed dollar value of inventory (I in the symbol of this chapter) to the dollar value of optimal (aggregate) average inventory.
    (d) Multiply each unconstrained lot size by the ratio determined in step c. Show that this "practical" procedure is theoretically correct.

13. Consider the stock-and-bond investment model that allowed investment in two stocks. If $r_b = 0.08$, $r_{S1} = 0.12$, $r_{S2} = 0.14$, $\sigma_{S1}^2 = 0.0064$, $\sigma_{S2}^2 = 0.0100$, $K = 0.0001$, and M is increased from \$100,000 to \$110,000, by how much will the certainty equivalent increase? By how much will the expected return increase? By how much will the variance of return increase?

14. Consider the example of stock investment that did not allow bond investment. If $r_{S1} = 0.12$, $r_{S2} = 0.14$, $\sigma_{S1}^2 = 0.0064$, $\sigma_{S2}^2 = 0.0100$, $K = 0.0001$, and M increases from \$100,000 to \$110,000:   (a) By how much will the certainty equivalent increase?   (b) Calculate the ratio of the certainty equivalent to the value of M for $M = \$100,000$ and $M = \$110,000$:   (c) Calculate the ratio of M plus the expected return to M for $M = \$100,000$ and $M = \$110,000$.   (d) Calculate the ratio of the expected return to the variance of the return for $M = \$100,000$ and $M = \$110,000$.   (e) Explain the significance of each of the calculations in parts a to d.

15. Consider a firm that produces two products, A and B. The demand for product A is given by $d_A = a + bp_A + Cp_B$ where $b < 0$, $c > 0$, p_A is the price of product A, and p_B is the price of product B. The demand for product B is given by $d_B = e + fp_A + gp_B$ where $g < 0$ and $f > 0$. If the total costs of production are $C = m_A d_A + m_B d_B$ and the amount available for production is fixed at $C = C_0$, determine the optimal production amount of each product.

16. Consider the problem of the Prefinishing Corporation in Section 9.1. Mr. Yef has determined that for every dollar spent on advertising the total productivity of the salespeople will be increased by a factor of $1 + 2.20(A/A + 200)$ (that is, revenues will be $S(1 + 0.20(A/A + 200))$.   (a) Develop a profit (before interest and income taxes) function that includes both the number of salespeople and the advertising expenditure A as decision variables.
    (b) Determine the first-order conditions for a maximum.
    (c) Solve the system of equations. (*Hint*: The solution will require a graphical approach.)

Part III
STOCHASTIC MODELS

Part III introduces techniques that are useful for modeling situations where random variables play an important role in the determination of profits and costs. The techniques are of two distinct types: those that just predict outcomes and those that both predict outcomes and select alternatives.

Chapters 10 and 11 are concerned with predicting outcomes and are not concerned with optimizing techniques. Chapter 10 covers queuing theory. It shows the development of the formulas that are useful in predicting outcomes as well as the probability distributions of outcomes for simple problems involving waiting lines. Chapter 11 illustrates how outcomes can be predicted by simulation techniques for problems that cannot be easily analyzed by mathematical methods.

Chapters 12–14 introduce methods for optimizing stochastic decision problems. Chapter 12 introduces the computing philosophy and methodology known as dynamic programming. The approach is useful in a wide variety of business applications. The computing procedures used in dynamic programming make use of the concepts of *stages*, *states* of the system, and *policies*. These concepts have direct and transparent relationships to the business concepts you think of when you hear these words. The concepts of dynamic programming are then used in the analysis of problems under risk in Chapter 13. The concept of the value of information is introduced through an example involving forecasts and applied to a variety of situations. Chapter 14 shows how some multistage problems under risk can be translated into equivalent linear programming problems.

Chapter 15, the epilogue, takes a broad view of the entire text, but is essentially a description of our point of view in selecting alternatives and the place of quantitative methods in that endeavor. It is designed to reinforce, once again, a respect for the proper use of management science.

10

QUEUING THEORY

10.1 STRUCTURE OF QUEUING PROBLEMS

Input Source
Queue
Service Facilities
Decision Variables
Outcomes

10.2 THE EXPONENTIAL DISTRIBUTION AND THE BIRTH AND DEATH PROCESS

Characteristics of the Exponential Distribution
The Birth and Death Process

10.3 QUEUING MODELS BASED ON THE SIMPLE BIRTH AND DEATH PROCESS

Case 1: Single Server
Case 2: Multiple Servers

10.4 MODIFICATIONS TO THE ASSUMPTIONS OF THE SINGLE-SERVER MODEL

Unspecified Service-Time Distribution
Finite Input Source

10.5 THE ROLE OF QUEUING MODELS IN THE DECISION-MAKING PROCESS

The Design of a Banking System Using Queuing Theory
Objectives, Performance Measures, and Constraints
Model Construction
Prediction of Outcomes
Analysis of Outcomes
Analysis of a Work-Methods Proposal

10.6 SUMMARY

References
Review Questions
Problems
Appendixes

The decision-making process presented in Chapter 1 involves six steps. The chapters of Part II of the text presented techniques that simultaneously performed the last three steps: enumeration of alternatives, prediction of outcomes, and alternative selection. Although those models and techniques may be complex, the underlying assumption was that risk could be considered a minor factor in the decision analysis. In other words, a single state of nature was assumed to exist. Many decision problems exist where risk must play a major role, however, and in these cases it may not be possible to perform the last three steps of the decision process simultaneously because of the complexity involved. It may be necessary to perform each step separately, first enumerating the alternatives and then building a model to predict the outcomes. Depending on the problem, a second model may be needed to select the best alternative(s).

In this chapter we will study queuing problems that are quite prevalent in the business world. Estimating outcomes is difficult for these problems because often they are complex, nonlinear functions of the decision alternatives and states of nature. Queuing theory strives to derive explicit functional forms for the outcomes of interest. As we will see in subsequent sections, queuing problems can become quite complex and we are limited in our ability to derive these functional forms analytically. Nonetheless, for those cases where the outcomes can be derived, the problem of predicting outcomes reduces to estimating the *parameters* of the functions. In those situations where the functional forms are too complex to derive, simulation (Chapter 11) can be used to estimate the outcomes.

10.1 STRUCTURE OF QUEUING PROBLEMS

Queuing problems are perhaps the most plentiful and frequently encountered problems in existence. Figure 10.1 shows the elements common to every queuing problem. An *input source* generates potential customers for the *service system.* Those choosing to enter the service system enter a *queue* or waiting line. Customers are selected from the queue on the basis of a *priority discipline* and are then served by the *service facility*: a particular arrangement of people, machines, or both acting as *servers*. After the service has been performed, the customers leave the service system as served customers.

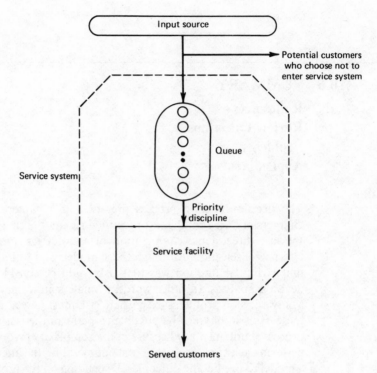

Figure 10.1   Elements of queuing problems.

Even though we have not yet discussed the elements of queuing problems in detail, it should be apparent that queuing problems are easy to find. Table 10.1 contains some problem descriptions that suggest a wide range of queuing problems. Note that the examples come from the traditional disciplines of marketing, finance, and production in the manufacturing as well as service industries. In many of the examples, the service system uses the traditional priority discipline *first come, first served*; in other cases, more complex priority schemes are used. Nonetheless, all of the examples cited in Table 10.1 have the same basic elements as shown in Figure 10.1. Let us now proceed to a more detailed discussion of each of the elements of the queuing problem.

Input Source

Intuitively, the input source is some mechanism that generates customers for the service system. Several characteristics of input sources, when identified, guide the model-building process: (1) *size*, (2) *arrival distribution*, and (3) *customer disposition*.

Size   An input source can be either *finite* or *infinite*. If the total number of customers in the service system at any point in time can be an appreciable proportion of the total potential customers that can be generated by the input source, the input

Table 10.1 Queuing Problem Examples

Problem Description	Customers	Priority Discipline[a]	Server(s)
1. Theater ticket sales	Theatergoers	FCFS	Ticket seller
2. Semitrailer loading/unloading	Semitrailer trucks	Varied	Conveyors and/or dock employees
3. Grocery store	Grocery shoppers	FCFS	Checkout clerks and bag packers
4. Catalog sales	Customer orders to be filled	FCFS	Order clerks
5. Banking	Bank patrons	FCFS	Bank tellers
6. Bank check processing	Checking account transactions	Varied	Bank clerks and/or computer
7. Machine maintenance	Machines needing repair or maintenance	Varied	Maintenance crew
8. Machine shop system	Customer production orders	Varied	Machines and employees
9. Typing pool	Reports to be typed	Varied	Secretaries with typewriters
10. Parking lot	Cars	FCFS	Parking lot spaces
11. Medical clinic	Medical patients	Varied	Doctor
12. Telephone exchange	Telephone calls	FCFS	Switchboard operator and/or electronic switching apparatus
13. Judicial system	Court cases	Varied	Judge

[a] FCFS means first come, first served.

source is said to be finite. For instance, consider a machine maintenance problem where the input source (consisting of machines that could fail) generates customers (failed machines) for the service system (maintenance crew). If the organization has 10 machines and 2 have failed, the input source consists of only 8 machines that could fail—a 20% reduction in size. This could have an appreciable effect on the rate at which the input source generates new customers.

Alternatively, an infinite input source is one in which the number of customers in the service system does not affect the rate at which the input source generates new customers. A grocery store checkout counter is a case in point because the population of potential grocery shoppers is not appreciably affected by the number of customers already in the store. It should be apparent from these two examples that the terms *finite* and *infinite* are approximations of reality, but, as we will see later, the complexity of a queuing model depends to a degree on the perceived size of the input source.

Arrival Distribution The arrival distribution is a probability distribution that describes either the number of customers that enter the service system per unit of time or the duration of time between customer arrivals (*interarrival times*). Of course, the more complex these distributions are, the more difficult it is to predict the outcomes analytically. We will concentrate on those distributions for which relatively simple functions for the outcomes have been derived.

Many times model builders use a Poisson distribution to describe a customer arrival process. Let $A(t)$ be the number of customer arrivals during an interval of time $(0, t)$. If λ designates the mean arrival rate (customer arrivals per unit of time) for a Poisson arrival process, the probability that there will be exactly n arrivals during the time interval $(0, t)$ is

$$P[A(t) = n] = \frac{(\lambda t)^n}{n!} e^{-\lambda t} \qquad \text{for } n = 0, 1, \ldots$$

Because the parameter of this Poisson distribution is λt (a function of time), $A(t)$ is said to be generated by a *Poisson process*. Suppose that $\lambda = 2$ customers per hour and we wish to specify the probability distribution of arrivals during a 1-hour

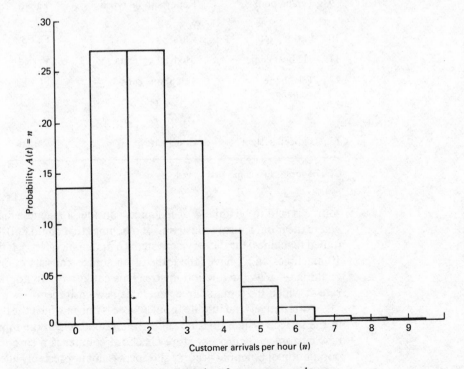

Figure 10.2   *Poisson distribution with* $\lambda = 2$ *customers per hour.*

period of time ($t = 1$). The distribution would look like the one in Figure 10.2 for the Poisson process with parameter $\lambda t = 2$. If we wanted to determine the distribution of arrivals for an 8-hour working day, the parameter value to use would be $\lambda t = 16$. The mean of the distribution is λt and its standard deviation is the square root of λt.

Sometimes it is more convenient to specify the arrival distribution in terms of customer *interarrival times*. Suppose that the input source generates customers according to a Poisson process with parameter λt. The probability that no customer will arrive during the interval $(0, t)$ is

$$P[A(t) = 0] = e^{-\lambda t}$$

This is equivalent to defining the probability that the first customer will arrive *more* than t time periods from now. Thus, the probability that the first customer will arrive in the interval $(0, t)$ is

$$F(t) = 1 - e^{-\lambda t} \tag{10.1}$$

where $F(t)$ is the distribution function of the arrival time t of the first customer. The density function is found by differentiating $F(t)$ to give

$$\frac{d}{dt} F(t) = f(t) = \lambda e^{-\lambda t} \qquad 0 \leq t < \infty \tag{10.2}$$

Specifically, $f(t)$ is called the *negative exponential* distribution with parameter λ and it is the distribution of the time interval between any two successive events (customer arrivals, for instance). Figure 10.3 shows how the negative exponential

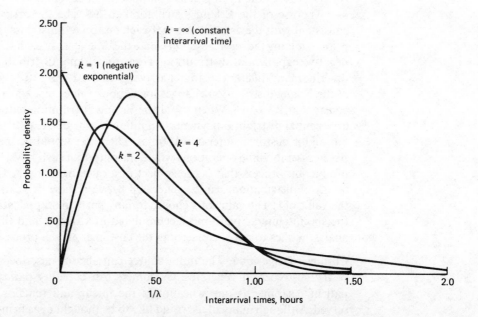

Figure 10.3 Erlang distribution for various values of k and constant mean of $1/\lambda$.

distribution places greater emphasis on relatively short interarrival times yet allows for the possibility of lengthy interarrival times. The mean *and* the standard deviation of the negative exponential distribution are equal to $1/\lambda$ (time periods per customer arrival). Thus, in the case of the Poisson-generated input, specification of the arrival distribution in terms of a Poisson process is equivalent to specifying the arrival distribution as a negative exponential distribution of interarrival times. Since these distributions are so basic to queuing theory, more will be said about the underlying assumptions of the Poisson process in Section 10.2.

Another distribution (actually a family of distributions) for which several queuing models have been developed is the *Erlang* distribution. Suppose that T_1, $T_2, \ldots, T_k$ are k independent random variables, each subject to an identical negative exponential distribution whose mean is $1/k\lambda$. Then their sum

$$S_k = T_1 + T_2 + \cdots + T_k$$

has an Erlang distribution with a mean of $1/\lambda$ and standard deviation of $1/\sqrt{k\lambda}$. The density function is

$$f(t) = \frac{(k\lambda)}{(k-1)!}\, t^{k-1} e^{-k\lambda t} \qquad \text{for } t \geq 0 \tag{10.3}$$

Thus the probability that S_k will not exceed a certain time duration T' is given by

$$P(S_k \leq T') = \int_0^{T'} \frac{(k\lambda)^k}{(k-1)!}\, t^{k-1} e^{-k\lambda t} dt \qquad T' \geq 0 \tag{10.4}$$

A derivation of the Erlang density function can be found in Appendix A10.1.

The use of the Erlang distribution to describe the arrival of customers is consistent with the assumption that each customer must pass through k "stages" prior to joining the service system where the time spent in each stage has an identical negative exponential distribution. Thus, the Erlang distribution can be used to describe many different customer arrival patterns. Figure 10.3 shows how the shape of the Erlang distribution changes for various values of k while keeping the mean constant at $1/\lambda = 0.5$. When $k = 1$ the Erlang distribution reduces to the negative exponential distribution, whereas an infinite value of k results in a *constant* distribution for customer interarrival times. The latter would be the case in machine-paced assembly-line operations where the output of such a system is the input to a production process that is the subject of a queuing analysis. Of course, a whole family of distributions can be generated between these two extremes by adjusting the value of k. The value of k chosen for any particular application will depend on the specific interarrival times accumulated in a sample and the assumptions the analyst wishes to make concerning the customer arrival process.

Customer Disposition The input source can also be described by the *disposition* of the customers it generates. Customers can be either patient or impatient. A patient customer is one who enters the queue and remains there until being served. Although many of us would like to be thought of as being patient, the most patient customers are those that are inanimate. For example, semitrailer truck vans waiting to be unloaded at a warehouse will wait in queue until served simply because there is no other place for them to go. Likewise, broken-down machines in a production system patiently wait in queue to be served by the maintenance crew.

Alternatively, an impatient customer is one who either enters the queue but leaves the system before being served (*reneging*), or estimates the waiting time and decides not to enter the system at all (*balking*). For example, a customer who enters the queue in front of a hot-dog stand between innings at a ballgame may leave the queue after 10 minutes without being served because the next inning has already begun. As opposed to this *reneging* customer, a *balking* customer may approach the hot-dog queue and decide that the wait would be too long and either return to the seat or try to find another stand with a smaller queue. The models in this chapter make the simplifying assumption that all customers are patient. The more difficult analysis of impatient customers is left to those texts devoted to a more detailed study of queuing.

Queue

The queue, or waiting line, can best be described by the constraints on its size. In this respect, the queue size can be *limited* or *unlimited*. A *limited* queue is constrained to be no larger than some finite number of customers. Consider an auto ferry where the number of cars waiting to be ferried across the lake is allowed to increase until the capacity of the ferry is reached. Extra cars may go to another ferry for service or come back several hours later. An extreme case of a limited queue is a parking lot or a drive-in movie theater where the maximum allowable queue size is zero.

Other queues are *unlimited* in size for all practical purposes. Such would be the case where space or other resource limitations do not impose a limitation on the queue length. A bank check-processing system or a catalog sales department for all practical purposes could entertain unlimited queue sizes (although this would probably not be good for business) because the customers (checks or sales orders) take up very little space.

Service Facilities

The service facilities are the devices that serve the customers and consist of one or more *servers*. The servers can be human (a telephone operator), machines (an automatic car wash), or a combination of both (a car ferry and crew). The facilities can be characterized by their *arrangement*, the *service time distribution*, and the *priority system*.

Arrangement   Service facilities can be arranged in a variety of ways. Figure 10.4 provides insight into the many possible arrangements one might find in a practical setting. The simplest of all arrangements is the single-channel, single-phase case: one server satisfies all customers. Examples of this situation would include theater ticket sales and a doctor serving patients.

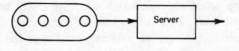

a

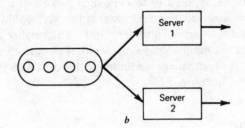

b

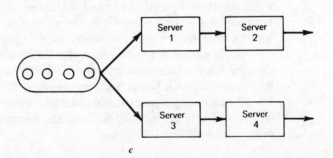

c

Figure 10.4 Examples of arrangements for service facilities. (*a*) Single channel, single phase. (*b*) Two channel, single phase. (*c*) Two channel, two phase.

A slightly more complex situation is the two-channel, single-phase arrangement where two servers perform the same service. Window tellers servicing banking customers and the loading of semitrailer vans at two bays in a loading dock are examples of this arrangement. Of course, this case can be easily extended to more than two channels or servers.

The two-channel, two-phase arrangement is symbolic of the kind of complexity that can be found in queuing problems. The customer enters any one of two service channels and is served by two different servers in series. Each channel provides the same service. Class registration at a university and many production systems take on this character. As in the other examples, this case can be extended to s channels and p phases. In addition, the customer could switch channels in some systems depending on server availabilities. All of this adds complexity to the modeling process and emphasizes the importance of proper problem recognition when analyzing queuing systems.

Service Time Distribution   The service time distribution describes the probabilistic nature of the rate of output of the service system. Although the rate of output could be expressed in terms of the number of customers served per unit of time, it is usually preferable to specify service capability in terms of the service time per customer. Two of the most often used distributions to describe service times are the negative exponential distribution

$$g(t) = \mu e^{-\mu t} \qquad \text{for } t \geq 0 \tag{10.5}$$

and the Erlang distribution

$$g(t) = \frac{(k\mu)^k}{(k-1)!} t^{k-1} e^{-k\mu t} \qquad \text{for } t \geq 0 \tag{10.6}$$

where μ is the expected number of customers completing service per unit of time. Figure 10.3 shows the shape of these functions.

The flexibility of the Erlang distribution to describe many different empirical situations emphasizes its importance. If $k = 1$ we have the negative exponential distribution that describes many practical situations. For intermediate values of k, $1 < k < \infty$, the Erlang distribution is useful for defining the service time of a customer who receives k identical repetitions of a particular service. This is the case of a production lot of k items (the customer) that is processed at a particular work center (the server) where the time duration of the activity to be performed for each item has a negative exponential distribution. Finally, if $k = \infty$ the Erlang distribution degenerates to the constant service time distribution that may, for example, be useful in transportation planning of subway systems where it can be assumed that the travel time between two given points is a constant. From this discussion it is apparent that the Erlang distribution adds a good degree of flexibility to queuing models.

Priority System   The priority system determines the next customer to be served when a server becomes available. The priority system makes use of *priority rules* to assign a priority to each customer at arrival. The most frequently encountered priority rule is first come, first served (FCFS). The customer at the head of the waiting line has the highest priority and so on down to the customer who last arrived. Not all priority rules are that equitable. In some production systems the jobs to be processed on a particular machine are assigned priorities on the basis of expected processing times (such as shortest processing times first) or due dates. The check-processing department in a bank may choose to process the checks of highest denominations first. Semitrailers may be unloaded on the basis of their contents and not when they arrived at the unloading dock. In some situations where the customers do not wait in a well-organized queue the priorities are actually assigned randomly.

The priority system can be more complicated than merely using a single priority rule to assign customer priorities. Computer programs awaiting processing may be given a priority by first assigning each program to a class depending on the expected run time (shortest run-time classes have highest priority) and then using FCFS within each class. In some manufacturing settings the priority system assigns each job to one of two classes: customer orders or orders for stock. Customer orders have the highest priority and jobs within each class are processed according to their earliest due date.

The priority system may also invoke a *preemptive* discipline. Preemption takes place when a customer of higher priority interrupts the service of another customer. Such may be the case in an emergency room at a hospital. As one can readily imagine, modeling queuing systems with complex priority systems is difficult. For all practical purposes, when the priority rule is not FCFS, simulation is the best approach for analysis.

Decision Variables

The previous discussion focused on the characteristics of queuing problems that enable the analyst to describe a problem prior to the model-building stage in the decision process. Once the model has been constructed, the analyst will use it to evaluate a number of decision alternatives for the specific problem at hand. These alternatives usually consist of a range of values for one or more of the following decision variables.

1. *Arrival rates.* The rates of customer arrivals can be affected by advertising, price changes, or adjusting the proportion of a given, finite population assigned to a certain service facility.
2. *Number of facilities.* How many tool cribs, secretarial pools, or restaurants along an interstate highway should we have?
3. *Facility arrangement.* At each facility, how many channels and phases should we have?
4. *Number of servers.* How many telephone lineworkers should be assigned to a repair crew? Many times this decision variable is closely linked to the facility arrangement decision.
5. *Server efficiency.* Server efficiency can be affected by the number of servers, the ratio of human to capital resources, and work methods and incentive programs.
6. *Priority system.* What priority rules should be used? Should we have more than one priority rule? Should preemption be allowed?

The choice of the best alternative for a given problem can be a complex task because of the interrelatedness of the decision variables. In addition, important cost versus service trade-offs must be evaluated. A queuing model must therefore provide information on expected costs and service to be useful.

Outcomes

Queuing models determine the *operating characteristics* of a system defined by the analyst. The distributions of these operating characteristics contribute to the evaluation of each alternative. Some of the more commonly considered characteristics are listed below.

1. *Queue length.* Large queues may indicate poor server performance or a need for more space. Small queues may imply too much server capacity.

2. *Number of customers in system.* This is the number of customers in the queue plus those being served. Large values imply congestion and possible customer dissatisfaction and a potential need for more service capacity.

3. *Waiting time in queue.* Long waiting times are directly related to customer dissatisfaction and potential loss of future revenues. Very small waiting times may indicate too much service capacity.

4. *Total time in system.* This is the total elapsed time from entry in the queue to completion of service. Large values of this statistic may indicate a change in priority rules is needed or capacity needs adjustment.

5. *Server idle time.* Idle time is directly related to cost; however, reducing idle time may have adverse effects on the other characteristics mentioned.

Both the means and variances of the above operating characteristics are usually of interest. Consider alternative A_1, which would result in a mean waiting time in queue slightly less than that resulting from alternative A_2. If the variance of the waiting time in queue for A_1 is much greater than that of A_2, the second alternative may be considered best simply because there is less risk of having a customer wait a long time in queue. Of course, as the queuing system gets more complicated, deriving the analytical forms of these distributions becomes extremely difficult if not impossible.

The outcomes in a decision analysis of a queuing system can be expressed in terms of the operating characteristics mentioned above. If costs and/or revenues can be associated with particular values of the operating characteristics and alternatives, the outcome of any alternative can be expressed in dollars. All too often it is difficult to put a dollar figure on a characteristic (how much does it cost to have an average of 5 minutes of waiting time in queue per customer?) so that the operating characteristics themselves plus the cost (if any) of the alternative become the outcome. In this case, the decision maker must often resort to a subjective assessment of the alternatives given the outcomes to make a final alternative selection.

10.2   THE EXPONENTIAL DISTRIBUTION AND THE BIRTH AND DEATH PROCESS

The exponential distribution is perhaps the single most important distribution in queuing theory.[1] It provides the foundations for the *birth and death process*, which

---

[1] In the remainder of this chapter we will refer to the *negative exponential* distribution as the *exponential* distribution.

in turn is the basis for many queuing models. This section will first discuss two important characteristics of the exponential distribution and then develop the principles of the simple birth and death process.

Characteristics of the Exponential Distribution

One interesting characteristic of the exponential distribution is its *lack of memory*. The interarrival time of the next customer does not depend on the arrival time of the last customer. We can state this condition more precisely in probabilistic terms for some interarrival time X. The conditional probability that X will exceed some time $T + \Delta T$, given X is greater than ΔT (the elapsed time since the last arrival), is

$$P(X > T + \Delta T \mid X > \Delta T) = \frac{P(X > T + \Delta T, X > \Delta T)}{P(X > \Delta T)} \quad \text{for } T, \Delta T > 0 \quad (10.7)$$

The numerator of the right-hand side is equivalent to $P(X > T + \Delta T)$, so that

$$P(X > T + \Delta T \mid X > \Delta T) = \frac{P(X > T + \Delta T)}{P(X > \Delta T)} \tag{10.8}$$

Recall from (10.1) that $P(X \leq T) = 1 - e^{-\lambda T}$ and hence $P(X > T) = e^{-\lambda T}$. Then

$$P(X > T + \Delta T \mid X > \Delta T) = \frac{e^{-\lambda(T + \Delta T)}}{e^{-\lambda \Delta T}} = e^{-\lambda T} = P(X > T) \tag{10.9}$$

Note that this probability is not a function of ΔT, the time that has already passed since the beginning of the current interval. Thus, the probability distribution of the remaining time until the next arrival is independent of the elapsed time since the last arrival. The corresponding result can be stated for an exponential service time distribution.

The second characteristic of interest allows us to approximate the probability that the next customer will arrive in the next small interval of time ΔT. Suppose T is now the time since the last arrival. Following from the lack of memory characteristic given in (10.9),

$$P(X \leq T + \Delta T \mid X > T) = P(X \leq \Delta T)$$

$$= 1 - e^{-\lambda \Delta T} \quad \text{for } T, \Delta T > 0 \tag{10.10}$$

The series expansion for $e^{-\lambda \Delta T}$ is given by

$$e^{-\lambda \Delta T} = 1 - \lambda \Delta T + \sum_{j=2}^{\infty} \frac{(-\lambda \Delta T)^j}{j!}$$

Let

$$0(\Delta T) = \sum_{j=2}^{\infty} \frac{(-\lambda \Delta T)^j}{j!}$$

Thus,

$$P(X \leq T + \Delta T \mid X > T) = 1 - [1 - \lambda \Delta T + 0(\Delta T)]$$
$$= \lambda \Delta T - 0(\Delta T)$$

The function $0(\Delta T)$ becomes negligible as ΔT gets small because ΔT is raised to the power j in the summation and $j!$ gets very large. The probability, then, can be approximated by[2]

$$P(X \leq T + \Delta T \mid X > T) \simeq \lambda \Delta T \qquad \text{for small } \Delta T \qquad (10.11)$$

This result shows that the probability of an arrival during the next (very small) interval ΔT is roughly *proportional* to ΔT. It should be noted that this probability is not affected by T, the elapsed time since the last arrival.

The Birth and Death Process

These two unique characteristics of the exponential distribution will be useful for determining the state *probabilities* of the simple birth and death process. Stated in terms of queuing systems, a *birth* is a new customer arrival and a *death* is a satisfied customer leaving the system. The purpose of this section is to determine the probability distribution of the number of customers n in the system at a particular instant of time. In other words, we wish to determine the probability that the system will be in state n at some instant of time. These probabilities will be useful in determining the distributions of the important operating characteristics for the queuing models to be developed later.

We shall make the following assumptions about the system:

1. The probability distribution of the remaining time until the next birth (arrival) is exponential with parameter λ.
2. Given $n \geq 1$, the probability distribution of the remaining time until the next death (serviced customer) is exponential with parameter μ.
3. Only one birth or death can occur during any given *small* interval of time Δt.

Given these assumptions, we know from the characteristics of the exponential distribution that the probability of a birth in Δt is approximately $\lambda \Delta t$ and the probability of a death in Δt is $\mu \Delta t$ for small Δt. Suppose the system is in state n at time $t + \Delta t$. This can happen in one of three ways:

1. The system is in state $n - 1$ at time t and there is a birth in time Δt.
2. The system is in state $n + 1$ at time t and there is a death in time Δt.
3. The system is in state n at time t and there is no birth or death in time Δt.

If $P_n(t)$ is the probability that the system will be in state n at time t, the probability that the system will be in state n at time $t + \Delta t$ can be written as the sum of the

---

[2] More precisely,

$$\lim_{\Delta T \to 0} \frac{P(X \leq T + \Delta T \mid X > T)}{\Delta T} = \lambda$$

joint probabilities of the three mutually exclusive and collectively exhaustive events above. The probability is

$$P_n(t + \Delta t) = P_{n-1}(t)(\lambda \Delta t)(1 - \mu \Delta t) + P_{n+1}(t)(\mu \Delta t)(1 - \lambda \Delta t)$$
$$+ P_n(t)(1 - \lambda \Delta t)(1 - \mu \Delta t) \qquad \text{for small } \Delta t. \qquad (10.12)$$

Expanding (10.12), and, since Δt is very small, recognizing that terms with $(\Delta t)^2$ are negligible (and also that they imply two events can occur in Δt), yields

$$P_n(t + \Delta t) = \lambda P_{n-1}(t)\Delta t + \mu P_{n+1}(t)\Delta t + P_n(t) - P_n(t)(\lambda + \mu)\Delta t \quad (10.13)$$

Subtracting $P_n(t)$ from both sides of (10.13) and dividing by Δt gives

$$\frac{P_n(t + \Delta t) - P_n(t)}{\Delta t} = \lambda P_{n-1}(t) + \mu P_{n+1}(t) - P_n(t)(\lambda + \mu) \qquad (10.14)$$

Taking the limit as $\Delta t \to 0$ results in the differential equation

$$\frac{dP_n(t)}{dt} = \lambda P_{n-1}(t) + \mu P_{n+1}(t) - P_n(t)(\lambda + \mu) \qquad (10.15)$$

It should be noted that a special case exists when $n = 0$. The only way the system can be in state 0 at time $t + \Delta t$ is (1) if it is in state 0 at time t and there is no birth in time Δt or (2) if it is in state 1 at time t and a death occurs in time Δt. Following the same procedure as before yields the differential equation

$$\frac{dP_0(t)}{dt} = \mu P_1(t) - \lambda P_0(t) \qquad (10.16)$$

Unfortunately, these differential equations must be solved to get the probabilities we seek. The whole process can be greatly simplified if we solve for the probabilities that will be in effect when the system is in *steady state*. In its early existence, the state of a queuing system, as represented by the number of customers in the system, is very dependent on the initial state and the time that has elapsed. After a sufficient operating time, the state of the system is essentially independent of the initial state and the elapsed time, provided that $\lambda > \mu$. At this point the system is said to have reached a steady state. The term *steady state* simply implies that for any state of the system ($n = 0, 1, 2, \ldots$) the expected rate of entering that state is equal to the expected rate of leaving that state.[3] Thus, the probability of being in state n is not changing with respect to time. Setting (10.15) and (10.16) equal to 0 and dropping t from all expressions we obtain

$$\mu P_1 - \lambda P_0 = 0 \qquad n = 0 \qquad (10.17)$$

$$\lambda P_{n-1} + \mu P_{n+1} - P_n(\lambda + \mu) = 0 \qquad n = 1, 2, \ldots \qquad (10.18)$$

---

[3] If this condition is not present the system is said to be in a *transient* condition. The solution of the state probabilities for this case is beyond the scope of this text.

The equations can be solved recursively in terms of P_0.

$$P_1 = \left(\frac{\lambda}{\mu}\right)P_0 \hspace{4cm} \text{State} = 0$$

$$P_2 = P_1\frac{(\lambda + \mu)}{\mu} - \left(\frac{\lambda}{\mu}\right)P_0 = \frac{\lambda(\lambda + \mu)}{\mu^2}P_0 - \left(\frac{\lambda}{\mu}\right)P_0 \hspace{1cm} = \left(\frac{\lambda}{\mu}\right)^2 P_0$$

$$\text{State} = 1$$

$$P_3 = P_2\frac{(\lambda + \mu)}{\mu} - \left(\frac{\lambda}{\mu}\right)P_1 = \left(\frac{\lambda}{\mu}\right)^2\frac{(\lambda + \mu)}{\mu}P_0 - \frac{\lambda}{\mu}\left(\frac{\lambda}{\mu}\right)P_0 \hspace{0.5cm} = \left(\frac{\lambda}{\mu}\right)^3 P_0$$

$$\text{State} = 2$$

$$\vdots$$

$$P_{r+1} = P_r\frac{(\lambda + \mu)}{\mu} - \frac{\lambda}{\mu}P_{r-1} = \left(\frac{\lambda}{\mu}\right)^r\frac{(\lambda + \mu)}{\mu}P_0 - \frac{\lambda}{\mu}\left(\frac{\lambda}{\mu}\right)^{r-1}P_0 = \left(\frac{\lambda}{\mu}\right)^r P_0$$

$$\text{State} = r$$

$$\vdots$$

Thus, for any general state n,

$$P_n = \left(\frac{\lambda}{\mu}\right)^n P_0 \tag{10.19}$$

and, since

$$\sum_{n=0}^{\infty} P_n = 1$$

we have

$$\left[\sum_{n=0}^{\infty}\left(\frac{\lambda}{\mu}\right)^n\right]P_0 = 1$$

Finally,

$$P_0 = \frac{1}{\displaystyle\sum_{n=0}^{\infty}\left(\frac{\lambda}{\mu}\right)^n} \tag{10.20}$$

Thus, given $\lambda < \mu$, which is necessary for a steady-state condition, all the steady-state probabilities can be computed from the above relationships. If we let $\rho = \lambda/\mu$ (and $\rho < 1$) we have

$$\sum_{n=0}^{\infty}\rho^n = \frac{1}{(1 - \rho)} \tag{10.21}$$

The state probabilities become

$$P_0 = \frac{1}{\left(\dfrac{1}{1 - \rho}\right)} = (1 - \rho) \hspace{1cm} n = 0 \tag{10.22}$$

$$P_n = \rho^n(1 - \rho) \hspace{2cm} n = 1, 2, \ldots \tag{10.23}$$

In the parlance of queuing theory, ρ is called the *traffic density* and must always be less than 1 if the steady-state condition is ever to be attained. If $\rho > 1$, the mean arrival rate λ is greater than the mean service rate μ and extremely large queues will result. In the queuing models developed in the next section we will always assume $\rho < 1$ so that the steady-state probabilities just derived may be used.

10.3 QUEUING MODELS BASED ON THE SIMPLE BIRTH AND DEATH PROCESS

In this section we discuss several queuing models that can be developed from the simple birth and death process principles. The complexity of the model depends on the number of servers, the arrival and service distributions, limits placed on the size of the queue or input source, and the number of service phases. Regardless of the nature of the service system, certain basic relationships between the operating characteristics will help to predict the outcomes in a decision problem.

Consider the following useful statistics from a queuing model:

L = expected number in the queuing system
L_q = expected queue length
W = expected waiting time in the system (including service)
W_q = expected waiting time in queue

It was first shown by Little[4] that

$$L = \lambda W \tag{10.24}$$

This relationship will hold for an unrestricted queue size and infinite input source and any number of servers. Intuitively, it says that the expected number of customers in the system at any time is equal to the mean arrival rate times the expected waiting time in the system. For example, if $\lambda = 5$ customers per minute and $W = 3$ minutes per customer, the expected number in the system is 15.

Similarly

$$L_q = \lambda W_q \tag{10.25}$$

In addition, the expected waiting time in the system is equal to the expected waiting time in queue plus the mean service time—that is,

$$W = W_q + \frac{1}{\mu} \tag{10.26}$$

These relationships simplify the model-building process because once we develop the expression for one of the four parameters L, L_q, W, W_q, the others can

---

[4] John D.C. Little, "A Proof for the Queuing Formula L = λW," *Operations Research, 9*, 3 (1961), pp. 383–387.

be immediately computed. We can now develop the models under the following conditions:

1. Interarrival and service times are exponentially distributed.
2. The input source is infinite.
3. There are no queue limitations.
4. There is single phase service.
5. There are s channels (or servers).
6. The service priority rule is first come, first served.

Case 1:   Single Server ($s = 1$)

In this case the state probabilities for the simple birth and death process can be applied directly. From (10.23) we have

$$P_n = (1 - \rho)\rho^n \qquad n = 0, 1, 2, \ldots$$

Therefore, the expected number in the queuing system is

$$L = \sum_{n=0}^{\infty} n(1 - \rho)\rho^n$$

or

$$L = (1 - \rho) \sum_{n=0}^{\infty} n\rho^n \tag{10.27}$$

Since $\displaystyle\sum_{n=0}^{\infty} n\rho^n = \frac{\rho}{(1 - \rho)^2}$ for $\rho < 1$, (10.27) can be written as

$$L = \frac{(1 - \rho)}{(1 - \rho)^2} \rho = \frac{\rho}{1 - \rho} = \frac{\lambda}{\mu - \lambda} \tag{10.28}$$

Using the relationship between L and W in (10.24),

$$W = \frac{L}{\lambda} = \frac{1}{\mu - \lambda}$$

Consequently, from (10.26),

$$W_q = W - \frac{1}{\mu} = \frac{1}{\mu - \lambda} - \frac{1}{\mu}$$

$$= \frac{\mu - (\mu - \lambda)}{\mu(\mu - \lambda)}$$

$$= \frac{\lambda}{\mu(\mu - \lambda)} \tag{10.29}$$

$$= \rho W \tag{10.30}$$

Finally, the average queue length is found by using (10.25), (10.28), and (10.29):

$$L_q = \frac{\lambda^2}{\mu(\mu - \lambda)}$$

or

$$L_q = \rho L \qquad\qquad (10.31)$$

Another system characteristic of interest to management is system idleness I. The proportion of time the system is *busy* is

$$B = \sum_{n=1}^{\infty} P_n$$

$$= 1 - P_0$$

$$= 1 - (1 - \rho) = \rho \qquad\qquad (10.32)$$

Thus, the proportion of time that the system is *idle* is simply the probability that there are no customers in the system.

$$I = 1 - B$$

$$= 1 - \rho$$

$$= P_0 \qquad\qquad (10.33)$$

Although we could discuss the probability distributions for all of the operating characteristics, in most cases it is the waiting time distributions that are of particular interest. It can be shown that the distribution of waiting time in the system ω is given by

$$P(\omega > t) = e^{-(\mu - \lambda)t} \qquad \text{for } t > 0 \qquad\qquad (10.34)$$

It is interesting to note that for this case with exponential interarrival and service times, the distribution of ω is also exponential. Given the distribution for ω, it can be shown that the distribution function for the waiting time in queue, ω_q, is

$$P(\omega_q > t) = \rho P(\omega > t)$$

$$= \rho e^{-(\mu - \lambda)t} \qquad \text{for } t > 0 \qquad\qquad (10.35)$$

Of course, the probability that there is no wait in the queue is

$$P(\omega_q = 0) = P_0 = 1 - \rho \qquad\qquad (10.36)$$

since, if there are no customers in the system, service can commence immediately.

Case 2: Multiple Servers ($s > 1$)

In the single-server case the mean rate of output for the system is μ when the server is busy. When there are s servers the output of the system will be $n\mu$ for $n < s$ customers in the system, and $s\mu$ for $n > s$ customers in the system. If the *traffic density* $\rho = \lambda/s\mu < 1$ the system will eventually achieve a steady-state condition and the general results for the birth and death process can be applied. The state probabilities are somewhat more complicated and become for this case (see Appendix A10.2 for details):

$$P_0 = \left[\sum_{n=0}^{s-1} \frac{(\lambda/\mu)^n}{n!} + \frac{(\lambda/\mu)^s}{s!} \left(\frac{1}{1-\rho} \right) \right]^{-1}$$

$$P_n = \begin{cases} \dfrac{(\lambda/\mu)^n}{n!} P_0 & 0 < n < s \\[4mm] \dfrac{(\lambda/\mu)^n}{s! s^{n-s}} P_0 & n \geq s \end{cases} \qquad (10.37)$$

To find the expected values L, L_q, W, and W_q all we need to do is find the expression for any one and use (10.24), (10.25), and (10.26) to get the others. The easiest one to compute is the expected number in queue. Recalling that $\rho = \lambda/\mu s$,

$$L_q = \sum_{n=s}^{\infty} (n-s) \frac{(\lambda/\mu)^n}{s! s^{n-s}} P_0$$

$$= P_0 \left(\frac{\lambda}{\mu} \right)^s \left(\frac{1}{s!} \right) \sum_{n=s}^{\infty} (n-s) \rho^{n-s} \qquad (10.38)$$

To help evaluate the summation, let $j = n - s$. Then

$$L_q = P_0 \left(\frac{\lambda}{\mu} \right)^s \left(\frac{1}{s!} \right) \sum_{j=0}^{\infty} j \rho^j \qquad (10.39)$$

Because the first term of the summation is zero, we can rewrite the expression as

$$L_q = P_0 \left(\frac{\lambda}{\mu} \right)^s \left(\frac{1}{s!} \right) \rho \sum_{j=1}^{\infty} j \rho^{j-1} \qquad (10.40)$$

The summation $\sum_{j=1}^{\infty} j \rho^{j-1} = (1-\rho)^{-2}$

$$L_q = \frac{P_0 \left(\dfrac{\lambda}{\mu} \right)^s \rho}{s!(1-\rho)^2} \qquad (10.41)$$

Using (10.25), the expected waiting time in queue is

$$W_q = \frac{L_q}{\lambda} = \frac{P_0 \left(\dfrac{\lambda}{\mu} \right)^s}{s!(1-\rho)^2 s\mu} \qquad (10.42)$$

Similarly, W and L can be calculated using (10.24) and (10.26). In addition, the proportion of time that a multiple-server, single-phase queuing system is completely busy is merely the probability there will be s or more customers in the system.

$$B = \sum_{n=s}^{\infty} P_n = 1 - \sum_{n=0}^{s-1} P_n \qquad (10.43)$$

Consequently, the proportion of the time that the system will be partially idle is

$$I = 1 - B$$

$$= 1 - \left(1 - \sum_{n=0}^{s-1} P_n\right) \qquad (10.44)$$

$$= \sum_{n=0}^{s-1} P_n$$

The waiting-time distribution functions for the multiple-server case are more complicated than those for the single-server case.[5] The distribution functions are[6]

$$P(\omega > t) = \left[1 + \frac{P_0\left(\dfrac{\lambda}{\mu}\right)^s}{s!(1-\rho)} \frac{1 - e^{-\mu t(s-1-\lambda/\mu)}}{(s-1-\lambda/\mu)} \right] e^{-\mu t} \qquad (10.45)$$

$$P(\omega_q > t) = B e^{-(s\mu - \lambda)t}$$

It is quite apparent that these distributions become complex as one diverges from the simple single-server case.

10.4 MODIFICATIONS TO THE ASSUMPTIONS OF THE SINGLE-SERVER MODEL

Several modifications to the assumptions of the single-server model serve to broaden its applicability. The basic assumptions are that interarrival and service times are exponentially distributed, the input source is infinite in size, the maximum queue length is unlimited, and the service priority rule is first come, first served (FCFS). In this section we will see how the model changes when the service-time distribution is unspecified and the input source is finite. We will retain the FCFS priority rule.

Unspecified Service-Time Distribution

Suppose that customers arrive according to a Poisson process with mean λ as before; however, the only information available on the service-time distribution is its mean $(1/\mu)$ and variance (σ^2). This generalization of the service-time assump-

---

[5] A mathematical derivation of these results can be found in P.M. Morse, *Queues, Inventories and Maintenance*, New York: John Wiley & Sons, 1962, pp. 106–107.

[6] When $s - 1 - \lambda/\mu = 0$, $(1 - e^{-\mu t(s-1-\lambda/\mu)}/s - 1 - \lambda/\mu)$ should be replaced by μt.

tions where $\rho = \lambda/\mu < 1$ yields the following expressions for the system characteristics:[7]

$$L_q = \frac{\lambda^2\sigma^2 + \rho^2}{2(1 - \rho)} = \frac{\lambda^2(\mu^2\sigma^2 + 1)}{2\mu(\mu - \lambda)}$$

$$W_q = \frac{L_q}{\lambda}$$

$$W = W_q + \frac{1}{\mu} \tag{10.46}$$

$$L = \lambda W = L_q + \rho$$

$$B = 1 - P_0 = 1 - (1 - \rho) = \rho$$

These results are important because they allow us to derive the expected values of the system characteristics for any service-time probability distribution given only its mean and variance. For example, if the service distribution is exponential with $\sigma^2 = (1/\mu)^2$, we obtain the same results as we had in (10.27) through (10.33). If the service times have a k-phase Erlang distribution with $\sigma^2 = (1/k\mu^2)$, the expression for the expected number in queue becomes

$$L_q = \frac{\lambda^2/k\mu^2 + \rho^2}{2(1 - \rho)} = \frac{1 + k}{2k}\left[\frac{\lambda^2}{\mu(\mu - \lambda)}\right] \tag{10.47}$$

Recalling that the Erlang distribution becomes the exponential distribution for $k = 1$ and that the bracketed term above is the expression for L_q with an exponential service-time distribution, it is interesting to note that L_q for the Erlang distribution will always be less than L_q for an exponential service distribution. This follows from the smaller variance associated with the Erlang distribution. Of course, if L_q is smaller, so will be L, W_q, and W.

A special case of the Erlang distribution is the constant service-time distribution where $k \to \infty$ and consequently $\sigma^2 = 0$. The expressions for this case become

$$L_q = \frac{\rho^2}{2(1 - \rho)} = \frac{\lambda^2}{2\mu(\mu - \lambda)}$$

$$W_q = \frac{L_q}{\lambda} = \frac{\lambda}{2\mu(\mu - \lambda)}$$

$$W = W_q + \frac{1}{\mu} = \frac{\lambda}{2\mu(\mu - \lambda)} + \frac{1}{\mu} = \frac{(2\mu - \lambda)}{2\mu(\mu - \lambda)}$$

$$L = \lambda W = \frac{\rho(2\mu - \lambda)}{2(\mu - \lambda)} \tag{10.48}$$

[7] Derivations of L_q and W_q can be found in R.B. Cooper, *Introduction to Queuing Theory*, New York: Macmillan, 1972, pp. 162–167.

Note that a system with a constant service time of $1/\mu$ will provide an expected waiting time in queue one-half of that of a system with exponential service times *averaging* $1/\mu$. The more consistent the service time, the smaller the customer waiting time.

Finite Input Source

Now consider a situation where all of the assumptions of the basic single-server model are valid except that the input source is *finite*. Suppose that there are N individuals (animate or inanimate) comprising the input source for a queuing problem. At any point in time these individuals are either customers of the service system or not. If the distribution of time that any *individual* spends outside the service system is exponential with mean $1/\lambda_o$ and there are now $n < N$ customers in the service system, the interarrival time distribution for the input source of $(N - n)$ individuals is exponential with mean $1/(N - n)\lambda_o$. If $n = N$ the mean interarrival time is infinite, and thus the probability of another customer entering the system is zero. Previously we used the parameter $1/\lambda$ to denote the mean interarrival time for an *infinite* input source. The mean interarrival rate for a finite input source will approach that of an infinite input source with mean $1/\lambda$ as N gets larger. Typically, if N exceeds 30, the single-server model with infinite input source is adequate, and one need not be concerned with estimating *individual* interarrival times.

Under steady-state conditions, the expected values of the system operating characteristics become

$$L_q = N - \frac{\lambda_o + \mu}{\lambda_o}(1 - P_0)$$

$$L = N - \frac{\mu}{\lambda_o}(1 - P_0)$$

$$W_q = L_q[(N - L)\lambda_o]^{-1} \tag{10.49}$$

$$W = L[(N - L)\lambda_o]^{-1}$$

$$B = 1 - P_0 = 1 - \left[\sum_{n=0}^{N} \frac{N!}{(N - n)!}\left(\frac{\lambda_o}{\mu}\right)^n\right]^{-1}$$

The term $[(N - L)\lambda_o]^{-1}$ is the mean interarrival rate of the input source in steady state.

This model is most often applied to machine maintenance problems where N machines must be serviced by a single repairperson (or crew). The time interval between breakdowns for a given machine is exponentially distributed with mean $1/\lambda_o$. Of course, this model assumes that the rate of failure for a machine is independent of how many times it has failed in the past or the specific age of the machine. That is the essence of the assumptions of the exponential distribution. More elaborate models can be constructed, but they are beyond the scope of this text.

10.5 THE ROLE OF QUEUING MODELS IN THE DECISION-MAKING PROCESS

Queuing models predict the outcomes for a given set of alternatives in a decision problem that can be formulated as a queuing problem. As such these models are purely descriptive, static (in the steady state), and stochastic. This section will demonstrate how these models can be effectively used within the context of the decision-making process. The first example deals with the design of a branch bank office, and the second example demonstrates the use of a finite-input source model in a machine-maintenance problem.

The Design of a Banking System Using Queuing Theory

The management of Hometown Bank has decided to build a branch office at the corner of Washington and Hamilton streets. One of the issues to be resolved is the design of the drive-in customer service system. In this system the customer drives up to a service window and transacts such business as depositing money into a savings or checking account, withdrawing money from the same, paying utility bills, or cashing checks. It is agreed that the design of the system is very important for generating new customers for the branch as well as retaining the customers once they open an account there.

Objectives, Performance Measures, and Constraints

There are two major conflicting objectives in this problem: cost and service. For instance, if the service system has many service windows the waiting time per customer will be very low. Alternatively, only one service window would cost much less to operate but the customers may have to spend an unacceptable amount of time waiting for service. Because the social costs of customer waiting are difficult to assess, it is decided that the objective should be to minimize the expected cost of operating the system subject to two constraints on customer service: (1) the average number of customers in the system should be less than six, and (2) the average customer should not have to wait more than 5 minutes for service. These constraints can be expressed mathematically as

$$L < 6 \text{ customers}$$

$$W_q \leq 5 \text{ minutes}$$

Model Construction

The model-construction phase of the decision-making process *for this problem* requires a predetermined list of alternatives and the appropriate data (or at least part of the data) a priori. Given this information let us follow the logic of selecting the appropriate models for this case.

It is recognized that the problem can be formulated as a queuing problem. Three alternatives have been proposed by management:

1. Single-manual-channel, single phase.
2. Two-manual-channels, single phase.
3. Single-computer-assisted-channel, single phase.[8]

The manual channels would require a clerk to check the accounts and records manually in transacting business, whereas the computer-assisted alternative would enable a clerk to retrieve the appropriate information electronically.

Given the nature of these alternatives it is decided that the model(s) should be *descriptive* because of the complexity involved. Also, the model(s) should be formulated in the steady state because the modeling would be simplified and the results would give management a reasonable idea of how the alternative designs would work. Thus, a *static* model is acceptable. Finally, because of variations in customer arrivals and service times, the model(s) should be *stochastic*. Reference to Table 3.1 of Chapter 3 indicates that a number of quantitative methods can be used to analyze descriptive-static-stochastic models. For a queuing problem, however, only *queuing theory* and *Monte Carlo simulation* (as we will see in the next chapter) make sense. Final choice between these methods depends on the nature of the arrival and service distributions.

Figures 10.5 and 10.6 show the results of a sample of customer arrivals and service times, respectively. The sample sizes in each case are 1000 and were taken

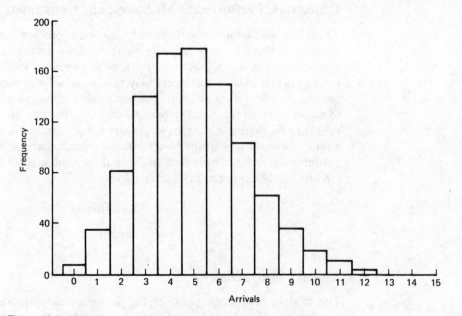

Figure 10.5 Distribution of arrivals during a 15-minute interval.

[8] Refer back to Figure 10.4 for a diagram of these alternative facility arrangements.

at another branch office thought to have about the same customer arrival pattern as the new one will have. The service times are for a single manual server. An estimate for the mean number of customers arriving during a 15-minute interval is calculated by dividing the total number of customers observed by the sample size, or

$$\hat{\lambda} = \frac{4997}{1000} \simeq 5 \text{ customers per 15-minute interval.}$$

A chi-square statistical test for goodness of fit verifies that the observed frequency distribution could have been generated by a Poisson distribution with a mean of 5 customers per 15 minute interval (or $\lambda = 0.33$ customers per minute). Thus, the customer interarrival time distribution can be assumed to be exponential with mean $1/\lambda = 3$ minutes per customer, or

$$f(t) = 0.33e^{-0.33t} \qquad t > 0 \tag{10.50}$$

Similarly, the service distribution in Figure 10.6 can be assumed to be an exponential distribution with mean of 2.4 minutes per customer (or $\mu = 0.42$ customers per minute). Thus,

$$g(t) = 0.42e^{-0.42t} \qquad t > 0 \tag{10.51}$$

Since both the interarrival and service time distributions are verified exponential distributions, queuing theory can be used to analyze the problem, and the models developed in this chapter are applicable.

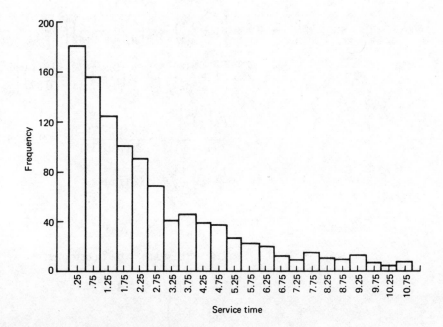

Figure 10.6 Distribution of service times.

Prediction of Outcomes

Having already enumerated the alternatives, we can proceed directly to the prediction of outcomes using the results of queuing theory developed earlier. The outcomes for each alternative are presented below and summarized in Table 10.2.

Single Manual Channel   Applying the single-channel results of (10.24) and (10.28) through (10.33), we find

$$\rho = \frac{\lambda}{\mu} = \frac{0.33}{0.42} = 0.78$$

$$L = \frac{\lambda}{\mu - \lambda} = \frac{0.33}{0.42 - 0.33} = 3.67 \text{ customers}$$

$$L_q = \rho L = 0.78(3.67) = 2.86 \text{ customers}$$

$$W = \frac{1}{\mu - \lambda} = \frac{1}{0.42 - 0.33} = 11.11 \text{ minutes}$$

$$W_q = \rho W = 0.78(11.11) = 8.67 \text{ minutes}$$

$$B = 1 - P_0 = \rho = 78\%$$

$$I = 1 - B = 22\% \text{ idleness}$$

Two Manual Channels   Applying the results of (10.24), (10.26), (10.37), and (10.41) through (10.44) we find

$$\rho = \frac{\lambda}{2\mu} = \frac{0.33}{0.84} = 0.39$$

$$P_0 = \left[1 + \left(\frac{\lambda}{\mu}\right) + \frac{1}{2} \left(\frac{\lambda}{\mu}\right)^2 \left(\frac{1}{1-\rho}\right) \right]^{-1}$$

$$= \left[1 + \left(\frac{0.33}{0.42}\right) + \frac{1}{2} \left(\frac{0.33}{0.42}\right)^2 \left(\frac{1}{1-0.39}\right) \right]^{-1} = 0.44$$

$$L_q = \frac{P_0 \left(\frac{\lambda}{\mu}\right)^2 \rho}{2!(1-\rho)^2} = \frac{0.44(0.78)^2(0.39)}{2(1-0.39)^2} = 0.14 \text{ customers}$$

$$W_q = \frac{L_q}{\lambda} = \frac{0.14}{0.33} = 0.42 \text{ minutes}$$

$$W = W_q + \frac{1}{\mu} = 0.42 + \frac{1}{0.42} = 2.8 \text{ minutes}$$

$$L = \lambda W = 0.33(2.8) = 0.92 \text{ customers}$$

$$I = P_0 + P_1$$

$$= P_0 \left(1 + \frac{\lambda}{\mu}\right)$$

$$= 0.44(1 + 0.78) = 78\% \text{ idleness}$$

Single Computer-Assisted Channel The computer-assist device is a teleprinter terminal connected to the central computer at the main office. Because of the input procedures (which are almost identical for any transaction) the service time per customer can be safely assumed to be a *constant* 2 minutes ($\mu = 0.50$ customers per minute). Using (10.33) and (10.48) we find

$$\rho = \frac{\lambda}{\mu} = \frac{0.33}{0.50} = 0.66$$

$$L_q = \frac{\rho^2}{2(1 - \rho)} = \frac{(0.66)^2}{2(1 - 0.66)} = 0.64 \text{ customers}$$

$$W_q = \frac{L_q}{\lambda} = \frac{0.64}{0.33} = 1.94 \text{ minutes}$$

$$W = W_q + \frac{1}{\mu} = 1.94 + \frac{1}{0.5} = 3.94 \text{ minutes}$$

$$L = \lambda W = 0.33(3.94) = 1.30 \text{ customers}$$

$$I = 1 - B = 1 - \rho = 34\% \text{ idleness}$$

Analysis of Outcomes

The results of the three models can be easily compared in Table 10.2. The costs were derived by assuming that the single-channel designs would each require a clerk at an annual salary of $7000. The two-channel design would then require two clerks for a total annual salary of $14,000. It would cost $10,000 for a single window that, when amortized over a 20-year period at a cost of capital of 10%, would result in an annual charge of $1175. The computer installation, in addition to the annual charge for the single-window facility, would require an annual lease charge of $5000 for the equipment. The service system is expected to operate 1040 hours per year.

Table 10.2 Comparison of Outcomes for Hometown Bank Example

Design	L	L_q	W	W_q	I	Personnel Cost/Year	Capital Cost/Year	Total Annual Cost	Cost/Hour
Single manual channel	3.67	2.86	11.11	8.67	22%	$7,000	$1,175	$8,175	$7·86
Two manual channels	0.92	0.14	2.80	0.42	78%	$14,000	$2,350	$16,350	$15·72
Single computer-assisted channel	1.30	0.64	3.94	1.94	34%	$7,000	$6,175	$13,175	$12·67

If annual operating costs were the only criterion, the single manual channel would be the best choice. But the average waiting time in queue for this alternative exceeds the service constraint imposed by management (W_q must not exceed 5 minutes). It is also interesting to compare the waiting-time distributions of the single manual channel with the two-manual-channel design because the latter apparently provides the best service. From (10.34) and (10.35), the waiting-time distributions for the single-manual-channel alternative are

$$P(\omega > t) = e^{-(\mu - \lambda)t} = e^{-0.09t} \qquad t \geq 0$$

$$P(\omega_q > t) = \rho P(\omega > t) = 0.78e^{-0.09t} \qquad t \geq 0$$

The distributions for the two-manual-channel alternative are computed from (10.43) and (10.45).

$$P(\omega > t) = \left[1 + \frac{P_0 \left(\dfrac{\lambda}{\mu}\right)^s}{s!(1 - \rho)} \frac{1 - e^{-t(s - 1 - \lambda/\mu)}}{(s - 1 - \lambda/\mu)} \right] e^{-\mu t}$$

$$= \left[1 + \frac{0.44 \left(\dfrac{0.33}{0.42}\right)^2}{2!(1 - 0.39)} \frac{1 - e^{-0.42t(1 - 0.78)}}{1 - 0.78} \right] e^{-0.42t}$$

$$= [2.01 - 1.01e^{-0.09t}]e^{-0.42t} \qquad t > 0$$

$$P(W_q > t) = Be^{-(s\mu - \lambda)t}$$

$$= (0.44 + 0.34)e^{-(0.84 - 0.33)t}$$

$$= 0.78e^{-0.51t} \qquad t > 0$$

Figure 10.7 shows these four distributions for various values of t. It is readily apparent that the two-manual-channel design is far superior with respect to service because its curves rapidly drop off as t increases. Moreover, there is about a 20% chance that a customer will have to wait in queue more than 16 minutes for the single-channel alternative, whereas no customer should ever have to wait more than 8 minutes for the two-channel design. Management now has much more information concerning these alternatives, because, even though W_q exceeds the stated limits by only 3.67 minutes, the waiting-time distributions for the single-server design indicate that some customers will have an unbearably long wait before service. We can assume that the curves for the computer-assisted design (constant service time) would be somewhere between the single-channel and two-channel alternatives in Figure 10.7.

Given the stated objectives, we conclude that management should build a single-channel system with a computer-assisted service station. Note, however, that this system would not provide the same level of service that the two-channel system does.

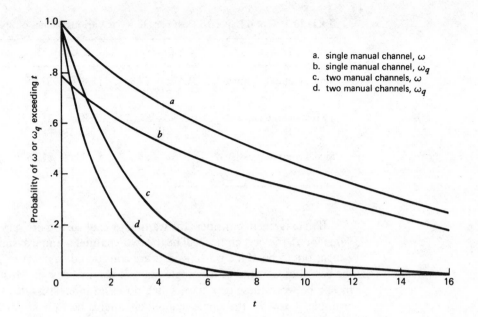

Figure 10.7 Waiting-time distributions for single-manual-channel and two-manual-channel designs. (*a*) Single manual channel ω. (*b*) Single manual channel ω_q. (*c*) Two manual channels ω_q. (*d*) Two manual channels ω_q.

Even though both the two-channel and the computer-assisted-channel designs satisfy the service constraints, the superior service performance of the two-channel system is not reflected in the analysis. Let us examine a more complicated problem where the service performance of the alternatives is given more weight in the analysis. Suppose that management is not certain about the number of customers that will use the new branch office. In particular, the mean arrival rate may be $\lambda = 0.25$ (relatively low customer usage), $\lambda = 0.33$, or $\lambda = 0.40$ (high customer usage). In addition, assume that a cost of α dollars per hour can be imputed to customer waiting time, so that the objective is to minimize total waiting plus operating costs. No constraints are placed on the operating characteristics. If the waiting costs C_ω are assumed to be linear with respect to the waiting time per customer, the expected cost of waiting per hour is

$$E(C_\omega) = \alpha\lambda E(\omega)$$

$$= \alpha\lambda W$$

$$= \alpha L \tag{10.52}$$

The outcomes for each alternative for each λ (state of nature) can now be evaluated given the models already presented. These results are given in Table 10.3. The computed values assume that $\alpha = \$4$ per hour.

Table 10.3 Total Expected Cost per Hour for Various Values of λ

Design	$\lambda = 0.25$	$\lambda = 0.33$	$\lambda = 0.40$
Single manual channel	$1.47\alpha + \$7.85$ $\$13.73$	$3.67\alpha + \$7.85$ $\$22.53$	$20\alpha + \$7.85$ $\$87.85$
Two manual channels	$0.65\alpha + \$15.72$ $\$18.32$	$0.92\alpha + \$15.72$ $\$19.40$	$1.23\alpha + \$15.72$ $\$20.64$
Single computer assisted channel	$0.75\alpha + \$12.67$ $\$15.67$	$1.30\alpha + \$12.67$ $\$17.87$	$2.4\alpha + \$12.67$ $\$22.27$

If management considers the waiting time of customers very costly (very large value for α), the best choice will be the two-channel manual system no matter what λ turns out to be. If the waiting costs are considered trivial (very small value for α) the best choice would be the single-manual-channel design. Most situations would have α between these extremes, which poses an interesting decision problem. For example, if $\alpha = \$4$, the single manual channel is best for $\lambda = 0.25$, the computer-assisted single-channel design is best for $\lambda = 0.33$, and the two-channel-manual system is best for $\lambda = 0.40$. Table 10.3 is seen to be a payoff matrix like that introduced in Figure 1.4 of Chapter 1.

Suppose that the estimated probability is 0.20 that λ will be 0.25, 0.50 for $\lambda = 0.33$, and 0.30 for $\lambda = 0.40$. Using expected costs as our measure of effectiveness, we can evaluate each of the alternatives as shown in Table 10.4.

In this example, the single computer-assisted channel alternative yields the minimum expected costs per hour; however, the two-manual-channel alternative is a close second. Nonetheless, the example demonstrates how the *outcomes* can be generated by queuing models and how they can be analyzed to arrive at a solution to the problem.[9]

Table 10.4 Expected Cost Analysis for the Hometown Bank Example

Alternative	Expected Cost
Single manual channel	$0.2(\$13.73) + 0.5(\$22.53) + 0.3(\$87.85) = \$40.37$
Two manual channels	$0.2(\$18.32) + 0.5(\$19.40) + 0.3(\$20.64) = \$19.56$
Single computer-assisted channel	$0.2(\$15.67) + 0.5(\$17.87) + 0.3(\$22.27) = \$18.75$

[9] See the problem section at the end of this chapter for more exercises involving the operating characteristics and service distributions for the Hometown Bank example.

Analysis of a Work-Methods Proposal

The industrial engineering department at Ace Manufacturing is preparing a proposal for a work-methods study aimed at increasing the productivity of the maintenance personnel. The expected benefits from the study must be documented in the proposal.

The industrial engineers decided that a particular machine shop that has been experiencing long delays in service should be used as a case example. One mechanic is assigned to the maintenance of 10 identical machines. When the mechanic is not needed for maintenance, she or he can be productively put to work elsewhere. Each machine has an exponential breakdown distribution with a mean time between breakdowns of 200 hours ($\lambda_o = 0.005$ machines per hour). Because of the high variability in the breakdown distribution, no preventive maintenance is performed. The service-time distribution is also exponential with a mean of $\mu_1 = 0.1$ machine per hour (or 10 hours per machine). It is anticipated that the study will result in a 20% increase in productivity. Thus, the mean service time per machine after the study would be 8 hours or $\mu_2 = 0.125$ machines per hour.

The finite-source model would be appropriate in this case. The results for $\mu_1 = 0.1$ are given below using (10.49) and can be compared to those of $\mu_2 = 0.125$ in Table 10.5.

$$P_0 = \left[\sum_{n=0}^{N} \frac{N!}{(N-n)!} \left(\frac{\lambda_o}{\mu_1} \right)^n \right]^{-1}$$

$$= \left[\sum_{n=0}^{10} \frac{10!}{(10-n)!} \left(\frac{0.005}{0.1} \right)^n \right]^{-1}$$

$$= 0.538$$

$$L_q = N - \frac{\lambda_o + \mu_1}{\lambda_o} (1 - P_0) = 10 - \frac{0.005 + 0.1}{0.005} (1 - 0.538)$$

$$= 0.30 \text{ machines}$$

$$L = N - \frac{\mu_1}{\lambda_o} (1 - P_0) = 10 - \frac{0.1}{0.005} (1 - 0.538)$$

$$= 0.76 \text{ machines}$$

$$W_q = L_q[(N-L)\lambda_o]^{-1} = \frac{0.30}{(10 - 0.76)(0.005)} = 6.94 \text{ hours}$$

$$W = L[(N-L)\lambda_o]^{-1} = \frac{0.76}{(10 - 0.76)(0.005)} = 16.45 \text{ hours}$$

$$I = 1 - B = P_0 = 54\%$$

A comparison of the steady-state operating characteristics for the two service rates reveals that a 20% improvement in productivity would result in a 29% reduction in waiting time in the system (4.81/16.45). Idle machines are costly

Table 10.5 Comparison of Operating Characteristics Before and After
the Proposed Study

Condition	L	L_q	W	W_q	I
Present ($\mu = 0.1$)	0.76	0.30	16.45	6.94	54%
New methods ($\mu = 0.125$)	0.55	0.20	11.64	4.23	62%

because they cannot generate revenues, and once they are repaired, the extra expediting efforts in trying to maintain production schedules, after the delay for repair, is expensive. In addition, the idle machinists must still be paid their normal rates. It should also be noted that the improved methods would increase the idleness of the mechanic—an advantageous situation because the mechanic can productively be put to work elsewhere. Thus, the queuing model provides the outcomes that are beneficial in estimating the benefits to be derived by the proposed study. Of course, these benefits must be weighed against the costs of developing and implementing the new methods.

10.6 SUMMARY

This chapter has discussed the role of queuing theory in the decision process. Problem recognition is the first step. All queuing problems have the same basic elements. The *input source*, which generates customers for the service system, can be described by its size, arrival-time distribution, and disposition of customers. The *queue*, or the line in which the customer must wait until selected for services, can have limitations as to its size. The *service facilities*, consisting of the servers, can be described by their arrangement, service-time distributions, and priority system. Proper identification of these elements is important for the model-building step that follows.

The second step is the specification of objectives, performance measures, and constraints. In queuing problems the objectives are usually a function of outcomes such as queue length, number of customers in the system, waiting time in queue, total time in system, and server idle time. Constraints may be imposed on the size of the queue, the average waiting time in queue, or the total number of customers in the system, for example,

Given these first two steps, model construction can begin. The model must relate each alternative (particular choice of values for the decision variables) to the outcomes. Typical decision variables include arrival rates, number of facilities, facility arrangement, number of servers, server efficiency, and priority rule. This chapter focused on the use of queuing theory to derive analytical functions for the outcomes of interest. We used the concepts of the simple birth and death process to derive the steady-state probabilities for the number of customers in the system. These probabilities enabled us to derive the expected values for the outcomes for the single-server and multiple-server, single-channel cases. We also derived the functional forms for the outcomes for an unspecified service-time distribution, and finite input source—all for the single-server case. More complicated models have been developed; these can be found in the references at the end of this chapter.

The next step, enumeration of alternatives, is often done simultaneously with the model-building step. This was the case in the Hometown Bank example where the three alternatives—single manual channel, two manual channels, and single computer-assisted channel—each required a different model. This need not always be the case. One model may suffice if the alternatives only deal with arrival rates, or server rates, for example.

Given the model(s) and the alternatives to evaluate, the outcomes can be computed. If the assumptions of the model(s) are valid, the outcomes can be easily computed using the analytical results from queuing theory. The outcomes can then be used in the final step, alternative selection. Although this chapter did not focus on alternative selection, the Hometown Bank problem provided an example of how this could be done using expected costs as the measure of effectiveness.

Queuing theory is a powerful tool for predicting outcomes in queuing problems. Analytical functions for the outcomes become very difficult, if not impossible, to derive as one digresses from the simple models presented in this chapter. Complex facility arrangements and priority rules other than first come, first served make the mathematics intractable in most cases. Queuing problems involving these complexities are best analyzed using simulation, which is the topic of the next chapter.

References

Bhat, U.N., "Sixty Years of Queuing Theory," *Management Science*, Vol. 15 (1968), pp. B280–B294.

Cooper, R.B., *Introduction to Queuing Theory*, New York: MacMillan, 1972.

Cox, D.R., and Smith, W.L., *Queues*, New York: John Wiley & Sons, 1961.

Hillier, F.S., and Lieberman, G.S., *Introduction to Operations Research*, 2d ed., San Francisco: Holden-Day, 1975.

Lee, A.M., *Applied Queuing Theory*, New York: St. Martin's Press, 1966.

Morse, P.M., *Queues, Inventories and Maintenance: The Analysis of Operations Systems with Variable Demand and Supply*, New York: John Wiley & Sons, 1958.

Prabhu, N.V., *Queues and Inventories: A Study of Their Basic Stochastic Processes*, New York: John Wiley & Sons, 1965.

Saaty, T.L., *Elements of Queuing Theory with Applications*, New York: McGraw-Hill, 1961.

Review Questions

1. Queuing theory strives to develop analytic expressions for the outcomes of interest in a queuing problem. Why is it advantageous to have analytic expressions for the outcomes? What are the limitations of attempting to derive analytic expressions for queuing problems in general?

2. For each of the following queuing situations, describe the nature of the input source and the usual service facilities arrangement:
   (a) Depositing or withdrawing money at a bank.
   (b) Typing pool.
   (c) Emergency clinic in a hospital.
   (d) Fast-food shop.

3. Priority systems involve priority rules. Discuss some priority rules that an emergency clinic at a hospital may use to process the patients. What trade-offs must be considered by hospital management?

4. Consider the design of a tollbooth system on an interstate highway. What are the decision variables? What operating characteristics would be of interest?

5. What is meant by the term *steady state*? Why is this condition important to queuing theory results? Discuss the problems of achieving steady state in a practical setting.

6. Of what importance is the *traffic density* to queuing systems?

7. The owner of a car-wash facility replaced a completely manual system with a machine-paced (automatic conveyor) system. The old system *averaged* 9 minutes per car (Poisson distribution), whereas the new system maintains a *constant* 9 minutes per car. The owner claims that the waiting time in queue was cut in half. Explain this result in light of what you know about single-server systems where customers arrive according to a Poisson process.

8. Prior to the development of queuing models, it must be determined if the arrival and service distributions can be approximated by some known theoretical distributions. Discuss, in detail, how you would do this.

9. Suppose someone said to you, "Queuing theory is too esoteric for practical use. The people who must make use of the results do not understand how they were derived. The assumptions that must be made are too limiting to result in anything useful." Discuss this statement in light of the material in this chapter and your understanding of the complexity of queuing problems.

10. Table 10.3 demonstrates how total expected costs per hour vary as the mean interarrival rate varies for the Hometown Bank example. The final choice of system design, however, depends on the value chosen for the parameter α. *Discuss* the considerations that would be made in choosing a value for α. Is it possible to empirically determine α? Alternatively, is α a subjective estimate of costs per minute of waiting time? Would a manager analyzing this problem be more interested in a specific value for α or a range of values for α? How would the range of values be used to select the best system design?

Problems   1. The automobile registration desk in the Motor Vehicle Department can service a customer every 5 minutes on the average. An average of 10 customers arrive every hour. The service times are exponentially distributed and the arrivals follow a Poisson distribution. Calculate the following operating characteristics:

  (a)   Average waiting time in the queue.
  (b)   Average waiting time in the system.
  (c)   Average length of the queue.
  (d)   Average number in the system.
  (e)   Probability that the waiting time in the queue will exceed 2 minutes.
  (f)   Probability that the waiting time in the system will exceed 10 minutes.
  (g)   The proportion of time that the system will be idle.

2. The owner of a car-cleaning company is contemplating a modification to the washing operation. It is estimated that the washing operation (after modification) would yield exponential service times with a mean of 1 minute and 40 seconds per car. A sample of customer arrivals during 10-minute intervals resulted in the following distribution:

Customer Arrivals	Number of Occurrences
0	22
1	72
2	157
3	185
4	196
5	156
6	94
7	60
8	27
9	23
10	3
11	2
12	3
	1000

  (a)   Compute the mean *interarrival* time in minutes per car.
  (b)   Verify that the arrival distribution is Poisson.
  (c)   Compute the traffic density ρ.
  (d)   Compute the operating characteristics assuming that the system can be modeled as a single-server system.

3. Suppose that the manager of the car wash in Problem 2 is considering an advertising campaign that involves a price reduction for a car wash. The new arrival distribution is expected to be a Poisson process with a mean of 0.5 customers per minute. Assuming that the new modification to the washing operation is installed, compute the expected operating characteristics. Compare them to the operating characteristics without the advertising campaign (Problem 2). Discuss the considerations the manager would make in deciding if the advertising campaign should be conducted.

4. There are four bays for loading trucks at a warehouse. Trucks arrive at the warehouse and can be serviced at any one of the four bays. A dock worker is

assigned to each bay and is responsible for loading the truck. It takes a dock worker an average of 1 hour to load a truck completely. The loading times follow an exponential distribution. The trucks arrive according to a Poisson distribution with a mean of three trucks per hour. Calculate the following operating characteristics:

    (a)   Average waiting time in the queue.

    (b)   Average waiting time in the system.

    (c)   Average length of the queue.

    (d)   Average number in the system.

    (e)   The probability that there will be no trucks in the system.

    (f)   Probability that the waiting time in the queue will exceed 3 hours.

    (g)   Probability that the waiting time in the system will exceed 4 hours.

5. In Problem 4, suppose that it is proposed that an additional loading bay is added to the system. Amortized capital costs and employee wages amount to $40 per hour. The cost of idle trucks (trucks waiting in queue and being loaded) is $50 per hour reflecting driver wages and equipment charges. Which of the two systems would result in a lower cost per hour?

6. The managers of the Hometown Bank are not certain as to the customer demand for their new branch office. In particular, the mean arrival rate may be as low as 0.25 customers per minute or as large as 0.40 customers per minute. It is generally agreed that the arrivals will be Poisson. Using the same service time data as given in Section 10.5 and for $\lambda = 0.25$ and 0.40,

    (a)   Compute the operating characteristics for single manual channel, two manual channels, and single computer-assisted channel.

    (b)   Compare and contrast these results with those given in Section 10.5.

    (c)   With reference to Table 10.3, what values of α would result in a choice of the single manual channel, the two manual channels, or the computer-assisted channel?

7. Suppose that a sampling of actual service times for the single manual channel in the Hometown Bank example of Section 10.5 indicates that the mean service time per customer $(1/\mu)$ is 2.4 minutes per customer with a variance of 4 minutes. The distribution is not a negative exponential and thus must remain unspecified. Suppose that the arrival rate is $\lambda = 0.33$ customers per minute from a Poisson distribution. Compute the following:

    (a)   The average queue length.

    (b)   The average wait in the queue.

    (c)   The average wait in the system.

    (d)   The average number in the system.

    (e)   The proportion of time that the server is busy.

    (f)   Compare these results to those in Section 10.5. Explain the discrepancies.

8. A certain automobile service and repair shop has a stock clerk who supplies the mechanics requiring parts for the autos they are servicing. The shop employs 10 mechanics. On the average, each mechanic requires something from the stockroom every hour. The stock clerk services requests in 6 minutes on the average. The management is considering installing a new stockpicking procedure that would reduce the average service time to 3 minutes per request. If the idle mechanics cost $10 per hour, and if the new procedure costs $8 per hour, should the new system be installed? Assume the arrival rate is Poisson and the service rates are exponential.

9. In Problem 8, suppose that the shop employs 50 mechanics. Would the proposed system be economic in this case? Assume $\lambda = 9.1$ mechanics per hour.

10. The industrial engineers of a job shop are studying work methods at a particular work station. At present, the operator performs two operations on each production lot. Each operation requires an average of 30 minutes per production lot. The service times are exponential. The new work method would require the operator to perform three operations, each one requiring an average of 20 minutes. The production lots arrive at the work station according to a Poisson distribution with an average of 0.75 lots per hour. An important characteristic in assessing the desirability of the new work methods is the work-in-process inventory at that station. Work-in-process is analogous to the number in the system. Determine the expected percentage reduction in work-in-process inventory at the work station if the new work methods are installed.

11. A certain bank teller window experiences customer arrivals that follow a Poisson process with a mean of 0.28 customers per minute. At present, the teller can serve 0.30 customers per minute. The service times follow an exponential distribution. An efficiency expert claims that new methods could reduce the variability of the service times. If the new methods are installed, the resulting service-time distribution could be represented as a three-phase Erlang distribution with mean $1/0.30$ and variance of $1/3(0.30)^2$.

   (a) Compute the outcomes L_q, W_q, W, L, and B for the present system and for the proposed new methods.

   (b) Given the outcomes in part a, discuss the effects of a reduction in the variability in service times on the outcomes.

   (c) What considerations should bank management make before deciding on the new methods?

12. The Kramer Company has five grinding machines that break down quite frequently. The time between breakdowns for each machine is exponential with a mean of 20 hours. The present maintenance service time is also exponential with a mean of 16 hours.

   (a) Compute the expected waiting time in queue and the expected time in system for the machines.

   (b) Suppose that an improved replacement policy would result in an increase in the mean time between failures to 25 hours. This represents a 25% improvement in the time between failures. What is the percentage improvement in W_q and W?

13. Consider a three-channel single-phase queuing system. Arrivals follow a Poisson process with $\lambda = 0.80$ customers per minute. Each server's service-time distribution is exponential with $\mu = 0.40$ customers per minute.

(a) Compute the expected number in queue, the expected waiting time in queue, and the expected idleness of the servers.

(b) Suppose a salesperson from a reputable computer firm says that you can reduce the number of servers to two by increasing the mean service time per channel to 0.60 customers per minute with the firm's equipment. What effects will this have on L_q, W_q, and I? Compare to the results you got in part a. What generalizations can you make?

APPENDIX A10.1: Derivation of Erlang Density Function

Consider customers arriving at a service facility over time. Suppose that the inter-arrival time of customer i, T_i, is exponential with mean $1/k\lambda$. Then the *number* of customers arriving in the time interval $(0, t)$ has a Poisson distribution with mean $k\lambda t$. We wish to find the distribution of the time spanning k consecutive customer arrivals; this is the sum of k mutually independent, identically distributed random exponential variables: $S_k = T_1 + T_2 + \cdots + T_k$. The probability that $S_k \leq t$, $P(S_k \leq t)$, is equivalent to the probability that the number of customers arriving at the service facility in the time interval $(0, t)$ is at least k. Thus,

$$P(S_k \leq t) = F(t) = 1 - \sum_{j=0}^{k-1} \frac{(k\lambda t)^j}{j!} e^{-k\lambda t} \qquad (\lambda > 0, t > 0)$$

The density function is found by differentiating $F(t)$ with respect to t;

$$\frac{d}{dt} F(t) = f(t) = \frac{d}{dt}\left[1 - \sum_{j=0}^{k-1} \frac{(k\lambda t)^j}{j!} e^{-k\lambda t}\right]$$

$$= -\left\{\sum_{j=0}^{k-1}\left[\frac{j(k\lambda t)^{j-1}}{j!}(k\lambda)e^{-k\lambda t} - \frac{(k\lambda t)^j}{j!}(k\lambda)e^{-k\lambda t}\right]\right\}$$

$$= -(k\lambda)e^{-k\lambda t}\left\{\sum_{j=0}^{k-1}\left[\frac{j(k\lambda t)^{j-1}}{j!} - \frac{(k\lambda t)^j}{j!}\right]\right\}$$

Expanding the summation allows us to cancel most of the terms

$$f(t) = -(k\lambda)e^{-k\lambda t}\left[0 + 1 + k\lambda t + \frac{(k\lambda t)^2}{2!} + \cdots + \frac{(k\lambda t)^{k-2}}{(k-2)!} - 1 - (k\lambda t)\right.$$

$$\left. - \frac{(k\lambda t)^2}{2!} - \cdots - \frac{(k\lambda t)^{k-2}}{(k-2)!} - \frac{(k\lambda t)^{k-1}}{(k-1)!}\right]$$

or

$$f(t) = \frac{(k\lambda)e^{-k\lambda t}(k\lambda t)^{k-1}}{(k-1)!}$$

Regrouping terms we have the Erlang density function

$$f(t) = \frac{(k\lambda)^k}{(k-1)!} t^{k-1} e^{-k\lambda t} \qquad \text{for } t > 0$$

Although we have defined S_k to be the sum of the interarrival times for k successive customers, S_k could be defined to be the interarrival time for the *next* customer, where the interarrival time is assumed to be a function of k independent, identically distributed random exponential variables. This latter definition of S_k is used in this chapter.

APPENDIX A10.2: Derivation of State Probabilities for $s > 1$

Let

$\lambda \Delta t$ = probability of an arrival in Δt

$n\mu \Delta t$ = probability of a service completion in Δt when there are $n < s$ customers in the system

$s\mu \Delta t$ = probability of a service completion in Δt when there are $n > s$ customers in the system

P_n = steady-state probability that there will be n customers in the system

$n \leq s$

When $n \leq s$ we have the following equations, which must be solved for the state probabilities:

$$\mu P_1 - \lambda P_0 = 0 \qquad n = 0$$

$$\lambda P_{n-1} + (n+1)\mu P_{n+1} - (\lambda + n\mu)P_n = 0 \qquad 0 < n < s$$

Solving recursively for each state probability in terms of P_0 we obtain

$$P_1 = \frac{\lambda}{\mu} P_0 \qquad\qquad \text{State} = 0$$

$$P_2 = \frac{(\lambda + \mu)P_1 - \lambda P_0}{2\mu} \qquad \text{State} = 1$$

$$= \frac{(\lambda + \mu)\left(\dfrac{\lambda}{\mu}\right)P_0 - \lambda P_0}{2\mu}$$

$$= \left(\frac{\lambda^2}{2\mu^2} + \frac{\lambda\mu}{2\mu^2} - \frac{\lambda}{2\mu}\right)P_0$$

$$= \frac{\lambda^2 P_0}{2\mu^2} = \frac{1}{2}\left(\frac{\lambda}{\mu}\right)^2 P_0$$

$$P_3 = \frac{(\lambda + 2\mu)P_2 - \lambda P_1}{3\mu} \qquad \text{State} = 2$$

$$= \frac{\dfrac{(\lambda + 2\mu)}{2}\left(\dfrac{\lambda}{\mu}\right)^2 P_0 - \lambda\left(\dfrac{\lambda}{\mu}\right)P_0}{3\mu}$$

$$= \left(\frac{\lambda^3}{6\mu^3} + \frac{2\mu\lambda^2}{6\mu^3} - \frac{\lambda^2}{3\mu^2}\right)P_0$$

$$= \frac{1}{3!}\left(\frac{\lambda}{\mu}\right)^3 P_0$$

$$\vdots$$

Continuing in this manner, it can be seen that the probabilities will be

$$P_n = \frac{1}{n!}\left(\frac{\lambda}{\mu}\right)^n P_0 \qquad \text{for } 0 \le n \le s$$

$n > s$

The set of equations to be solved now becomes

$$\lambda P_{n-1} + s\mu P_{n+1} - (\lambda + s\mu)P_n = 0 \qquad n > s$$

Solving recursively and using our previous results we have:

$$P_{s+1} = \frac{(\lambda + s\mu)P_s - \lambda P_{s-1}}{s\mu} \qquad\qquad \text{State} = s$$

$$= \frac{\lambda + s\mu}{s\mu}\left(\frac{1}{s!}\right)\left(\frac{\lambda}{\mu}\right)^s P_0 - \left(\frac{\lambda}{s\mu}\right)\frac{1}{(s-1)!}\left(\frac{\lambda}{\mu}\right)^{s-1}P_0$$

$$= \left(\frac{\lambda^{s+1}}{s!s\mu^{s+1}} + \frac{s\mu\lambda^s}{s!s\mu^{s+1}} - \frac{\lambda^s}{s!\mu^s}\right)P_0$$

$$= \left(\frac{1}{s!s}\right)\left(\frac{\lambda}{\mu}\right)^{s+1}P_0$$

$$P_{s+2} = \frac{(\lambda + s\mu)P_{s+1} - \lambda P_s}{s\mu} \qquad\qquad \text{State} = s + 1$$

$$= \left[\frac{(\lambda + s\mu)}{s\mu}\left(\frac{1}{s!s}\right)\left(\frac{\lambda}{\mu}\right)^{s+1} - \left(\frac{\lambda}{s\mu}\right)\frac{1}{s!}\left(\frac{\lambda}{\mu}\right)^s\right]P_0$$

$$= \left[\frac{\lambda^{s+2}}{s!s^2\mu^{s+2}} + \frac{s\mu\lambda^{s+1}}{s!s\mu^{s+2}} - \frac{\lambda^{s+1}}{s!s\mu^{s+1}}\right]P_0$$

$$= \frac{1}{s!s^2}\left(\frac{\lambda}{\mu}\right)^{s+2}P_0$$

$$\vdots$$

Continued calculation would verify that the general form is

$$P_n = \frac{1}{s!s^{n-s}}\left(\frac{\lambda}{\mu}\right)^n P_0 \qquad n > s$$

It only remains to find P_0. Since

$$\sum_{n=0}^{\infty} P_n = 1$$

we have

$$\left[\sum_{n=0}^{s-1} \frac{1}{n!} \left(\frac{\lambda}{\mu}\right)^n + \sum_{n=s}^{\infty} \frac{1}{s! s^{n-s}} \left(\frac{\lambda}{\mu}\right)^n \right] P_0 = 1$$

Thus,

$$P_0 = \left[\sum_{n=0}^{s-1} \frac{1}{n!} \left(\frac{\lambda}{\mu}\right)^n + \sum_{n=s}^{\infty} \frac{1}{s! s^{n-s}} \left(\frac{\lambda}{\mu}\right)^n \right]^{-1}$$

$$= \left[\sum_{n=0}^{s-1} \frac{1}{n!} \left(\frac{\lambda}{\mu}\right)^n + \frac{1}{s!} \left(\frac{\lambda}{\mu}\right)^s \sum_{n=s}^{\infty} \left(\frac{\lambda}{s\mu}\right)^{n-s} \right]^{-1}$$

Since $\rho = \lambda/s\mu < 1$ we have the simpler expression

$$P_0 = \left[\sum_{n=0}^{s-1} \frac{1}{n!} \left(\frac{\lambda}{\mu}\right)^n + \frac{1}{s!} \left(\frac{\lambda}{\mu}\right)^s \left(\frac{1}{1-\rho}\right) \right]$$

11

SIMULATION

11.1 SIMULATION AS A TOOL FOR PREDICTING OUTCOMES

What is Simulation?
Why Use Simulation?

11.2 SIMULATION AND QUEUING

The Design of a Banking System Using Simulation
Monte Carlo Simulation
Estimating Outcomes Using Monte Carlo Simulation
Simulating a Job Shop

11.3 HEURISTIC PROBLEM SOLVING

The Mail-Processing System
Problem Statement and Objectives
The Heuristic Procedure

11.4 ESTIMATING PROBABILITY DISTRIBUTIONS WITH SIMULATION

A Capital-Budgeting Example
Simulation and the Probability Distribution of RR
Managerial Use of the Probability Distribution for RR

11.5 DESIGN OF SIMULATION EXPERIMENTS

Initial System Conditions
Sample-Size Considerations
Design Considerations

11.6 SUMMARY

References
Review Questions
Problems

The previous chapter on queuing theory introduced techniques that can be used to predict outcomes for decision problems where each outcome could be expressed as a single function of the alternative. In this chapter, we will discuss a technique useful for predicting outcomes where it is extremely difficult (if not impossible) to derive analytically a single function for each outcome of interest. The technique is called simulation.

11.1 SIMULATION AS A TOOL FOR PREDICTING OUTCOMES

Consider the Hometown Bank example of the previous chapter. We were most fortunate that the interarrival time and serivce-time probability distributions were *exponential* because we could then apply queuing theory to derive the expressions *analytically* for the system operating characteristics. As we deviate from the assumptions of exponential interarrival and service times and a first-come, first-served queue discipline, it becomes more difficult to arrive at analytical results for even the simpler problems like those we analyzed in Chapter 10. In addition, when the service-facility arrangement becomes complex, queuing theory can no longer be used to analyze the problem. Unfortunately, many practical queuing problems are complex. We need not abandon attempts at analyzing these problems, however. Simulation can be used in situations like this.

What Is Simulation?

Simulation is the act of reproducing the behavior of a system. To make this a practical approach for analyzing problems, a *descriptive model* of the system rather than the actual system itself is used. Various independent variables in the model are manipulated and the behavior of the system is recorded by the values of the dependent variables (or outcomes). For example, in a queuing analysis we may want to study the effects of changing from a three-channel, two-phase system to a four-channel, two-phase system. The model would have to contain the equations that would enable us to evaluate the system's operating characteristics, given the facility arrangement. If the operating characteristics are still not acceptable, a five-channel, two-phase system could be tried. This implies that simulation is a *trial-and-error* approach to problem solving.

Why Use Simulation?

Although simulation is a powerful technique for estimating outcomes, it requires that the analyst "try" each alternative in a trial-and-error fashion until the one that best solves the problem is found. Of course, if the "optimal" alternative is overlooked, the problem will be solved suboptimally. For this reason, the quantitative techniques for selecting alternatives in an optimal fashion would be tried first.

Many practical problems cannot be solved with the optimizing methods. Often the mathematical relationships in a model defy attempts at an optimal analytical or numerical solution because of their complexity. A trial-and-error simulation of a descriptive model may be the only way to estimate the outcomes in some cases.

Simulation models can also be used to conduct experiments without disrupting the real system. Experimenting with the actual system can be very costly. It would be unthinkable to build a 100-foot extension to a truck-loading dock just to see what effect this would have on the waiting time of semitrailer trucks. A simulation model could be used to conduct experiments such as this for a fraction of the cost of actually building the extension. In addition, the model could be used to evaluate several other alternatives that may prove superior to the 100-foot extension.

Another advantage of simulation is that estimates of the operating characteristics of the system can be generated in much less time than it would take to gather the same data from the real system. For example, a simulation model of a production job shop could be used to gather a year's operating data in a few minutes on a computer. Alternative designs can be evaluated quickly and decisions can be made on a timely basis.

This aspect of simulation, time compression, is also used in management game simulations. A descriptive model of the firm relates the decisions that managers can make to the operating characteristics of importance (such as profits, costs, market shares, etc.). Given a set of starting conditions for the firm, the managers make periodic decisions designed to improve one or more of the operating characteristics. In such an exercise, a year's time can be simulated in a few hours of "play." Management games are used to sharpen the decision-making abilities of managers and enable experimentation of new ideas without disrupting normal operation.

In this chapter we will discuss several applications of the simulation technique. Perhaps queuing problems represent the largest application area for simulation and are best suited to introduce the basis of the simulation procedure. We will also discuss some examples of *heuristic* problem-solving procedures. Heuristics can be thought of as rules or guidelines that simulate good problem-solving behavior. In addition, we will discuss the use of simulation to estimate probability distributions. The last section of the chapter will address the issue of experimental design of simulation studies.

11.2 SIMULATION AND QUEUING

In this section, we first introduce the basics of the simulation technique by manually applying it to a simple queuing problem. Following this, an example of a more complicated simulation that requires a computer will serve to demonstrate the power and usefulness of the technique in analyzing a job-shop production system.

The Design of a Banking System Using Simulation

Suppose the managers of the Hometown Bank are in the initial phases of the decision-making process regarding the drive-in window problem of Chapter 10. The problem has been stated and the objectives, performance measures, and constraints have been specified. In preparation for the model-building phase, data on customer interarrival times and service times for a single manual server have been collected. These data are summarized in Table 11.1. The sample size in each case is 1000 observations.

The data were gathered by observing the actual times (interarrival and service) in seconds and then grouping them to the nearest minute for analysis. For example, any interarrival times in the range 150–209 seconds would be counted as 3 minutes. In addition, any times recorded less than 30 seconds were grouped at zero. It was decided that this level of aggregation would not violate the sense of the problem.

Recognizing that this problem has the structure of a queuing problem, the obvious first thought would be to use queuing theory to develop a model that would predict the operating characteristics of a proposed system design. In order to use queuing theory, the empirical frequency distributions must be shown to correspond to theoretical distributions for which queuing results are available. A chi-square goodness-of-fit test can be used to test the hypothesis that the empirical data could have been generated by a certain theoretical distribution. For example, the mean customer interarrival time from the empirical distribution in Table 11.1 is 3 minutes and the mean service time is 2.4 minutes. Recall that these

Table 11.1 Empirical Frequency Distributions for Customer Interarrival and Service Times

Customer Interarrival Time, Minutes	Frequency	Service Time, Minutes	Frequency
0	150	0	0
1	240	1	400
2	120	2	250
3	190	3	170
4	80	4	10
5	0	5	70
6	100	6	100
7	0		
8	50		
9	70		
Totals	1000		1000

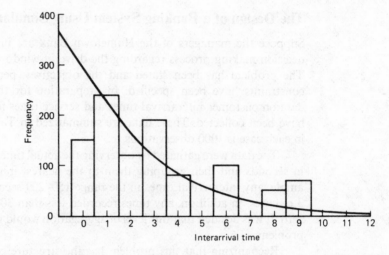

Figure 11.1 Empirical versus theoretical negative exponential interarrival distribution with $\lambda = 0.33$ and a sample of 1000.

are the same means used in the analysis of Chapter 10. This results in $\lambda = 0.33$ and $\mu = 0.42$. We might test the hypotheses that the empirical interarrival data came from an exponential distribution with $\lambda = 0.33$ and the service data came from an exponential distribution with $\mu = 0.42$.

Figures 11.1 and 11.2 show how the empirical distributions compare to the theoretical exponential distributions. The empirical distributions do not appear to correspond to the theoretical distributions, and a chi-square test would verify that these empirical distributions are not exponential. Suppose that the empirical data do not correspond to any known theoretical distribution. We must abandon our attempts at using queuing theory and turn to simulation to predict the operating characteristics of the proposed systems.

Monte Carlo Simulation

Simulating the operation of the drive-in window means that we must re-create the arrival and service of the customers according to the empirical frequency distributions and compile the data on operating characteristics as we proceed. Suppose we decided to simulate the arrival and service of 1000 customers. What would be wrong with having the first 150 customers arrive immediately, then the next 240 arrive 1 minute later, etc. (see Table 11.1)? Similarly, what would be wrong if the first 400 customers were serviced in 1 minute, the next 250 in 2 minutes, etc.? The problem with this approach is that the real drive-in window system will not operate like that. One customer may arrive at 10:00 A.M.; the next may arrive at 10:03 A.M. (3-minute interarrival time); and the next at 10:04 A.M. Similarly, the first customer may require 1 minute of service while the second may require 6 minutes. Although we are interested in generating customer arrivals and service

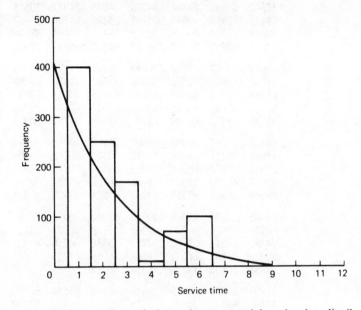

Figure 11.2 Empirical versus theoretical negative exponential service-time distribution with $\mu = 0.42$ and a sample of 1000.

according to the empirical distributions, we must do it in an unbiased way and in a manner closely approximating the way in which it will happen in the real system.

Monte Carlo simulation is a method for generating events (customer arrivals or service times) in a way that closely approximates their probability of occurrence. Random numbers are used to select the time of the next event.[1]

Recall that a number is a random number if it has the same probability of being selected as any other number. Table 11.2 contains 5-digit random numbers; thus, any number in that table has the same chance of appearing there as any other number in the table.

The events in the simulation can be generated in an unbiased way if random numbers are assigned to the events in the same proportion as their probability of occurrence. Consider Table 11.3. We would expect that simultaneous arrivals (zero interarrival time) would occur 15% of the time. If we have 100 random numbers (0 to 99) we should, assign 15 numbers (or 15% of them) to the event "zero interarrival time." Thus, the numbers 0 to 14 are assigned to that event. If we randomly choose numbers in the range 0 to 99 enough times, we would expect that 15% of the time they would fall in the range 0 to 14. Similarly, the event "interarrival time of 1 minute" should occur 24% of the time; thus, we assign the numbers 15 through 38 to that event. In total, the 100 numbers from 0 to 99 have been allocated to the events in the same proportion as the probability of their

---

[1] The term *Monte Carlo* comes from the use of random numbers to generate events and the obvious analogy to the games of chance played at the casinos of Monte Carlo.

Table 11.2 Random Numbers

10097	32533	76520	13586	34673	54876	80959	09117	39292	74945
37542	04805	64894	74296	24805	24037	20636	10402	00822	91665
08422	68953	19645	09303	23209	02560	15953	34764	35080	33606
99019	02529	09376	70715	38311	31165	88676	74397	04436	27659
12807	99970	80157	36147	64032	36653	98951	16877	12171	76833
66065	74717	34072	76850	36697	36170	65813	39885	11199	29170
31060	10805	45571	82406	35303	42614	86799	07439	23403	09732
85269	77602	02051	65692	68665	74818	73053	85247	18623	88579
63573	32135	05325	47048	90553	57548	28468	28709	83491	25624
73796	45753	03529	64778	35808	34282	60935	20344	35273	88435
98520	17767	14905	68607	22109	40558	60970	93433	50500	73998
11805	05431	39808	27732	50725	68248	29405	24201	52775	67851
83452	99634	06288	98083	13746	70078	18475	40610	68711	77817
88685	40200	86507	58401	36766	67951	90364	76493	29609	11062
99594	67348	87517	64969	91826	08928	93785	61368	23478	34113
65481	17674	17468	50950	58047	76974	73039	57186	40218	16544
80124	35635	17727	08015	45318	22374	21115	78253	14385	53763
74350	99817	77402	77214	43236	00210	45521	64237	96286	02655
69916	26803	66252	29148	36936	87203	76621	13990	94400	56418
09893	20505	14225	68514	46427	56788	96297	78822	54382	14598
91499	14523	68479	27686	46162	83554	94750	89923	37089	20048
80336	94598	26940	36858	70297	34135	53140	33340	42050	82341
44104	81949	85157	47954	32979	26575	57600	40881	22222	06413
12550	73742	11100	02040	12860	74697	96644	89439	28707	25815
63606	49329	16505	34484	40219	52563	43651	77082	07207	31790
61196	90446	26457	47774	51924	33729	65394	59593	42582	60527
15474	45266	95270	79953	59367	83848	82396	10118	33211	59466
94557	28573	67897	54387	54622	44431	91190	42592	92927	45973
42481	16213	97344	08721	16868	48767	03071	12059	25701	46670
23523	78317	73208	89837	68935	91416	26252	29663	05522	82562
04493	52494	75246	33824	45862	51025	61962	79335	65337	12472
00549	97654	64051	88159	96119	63896	54692	82391	23287	29529
35963	15307	26898	09354	33351	35462	77974	50024	90103	39333
59808	08391	45427	26842	83609	49700	13021	24892	78565	20106
46058	85236	01390	92286	77281	44077	93910	83647	70617	42941
32179	00597	87379	25241	05567	07007	86743	17157	85394	11838
69234	61406	20117	45204	15956	60000	18743	92423	97118	96338
19565	41430	01758	75379	40419	21585	66674	36806	84962	85207
45155	14938	19476	07246	43667	94543	59047	90033	20826	69541
94864	31994	36168	10851	34888	81553	01540	35456	05014	51176
98086	24826	45240	28404	44999	08896	39094	73407	35441	31880
33185	16232	41941	50949	89435	48581	88695	41994	37548	73043
80951	00406	96382	70774	20151	23387	25016	25298	94624	61171
79752	49140	71961	28296	69861	02591	74852	20539	00387	59579
18633	32537	98145	06571	31010	24674	05455	61427	77938	91936
74029	43902	77557	32270	97790	17119	52527	58021	80814	51748
54178	45611	80993	37143	05335	12969	56127	19255	36040	90324
11664	49883	52079	84827	59381	71539	09973	33440	88461	23356
48324	77928	31249	64710	02295	36870	32307	57546	15020	09994
69074	94138	87637	91976	35584	04401	10518	21615	01848	76938

Reprinted by permission of the Rand Corporation, "A Million Random Digits with 100,000 Normal Deviates." Copyright © 1955, Rand Corp., Santa Monica, CA. 90406.

Table 11.3 Random Number Assignment to Customer Interarrival Times

Event: Interarrival Time, minutes	Probability	Cumulative Probability	Random Numbers
0	0.15	0.15	00–14
1	0.24	0.39	15–38
2	0.12	0.51	39–50
3	0.19	0.70	51–69
4	0.08	0.78	70–77
5	0	0.78	—
6	0.10	0.88	78–87
7	0	0.88	—
8	0.05	0.93	88–92
9	0.07	1.00	93–99

occurrence. Note that the assignment of the random numbers follows the cumulative probability distribution of interarrival times. It is usually easier to assign the random numbers if the cumulative distribution is developed before the assignments are made.[2]

In a similar manner, the random numbers can be assigned to the customer-service times. Table 11.4 contains these assignments.

Table 11.4 Random Number Assignment to Customer Service
Times

Event: Service Time, minutes	Probability	Cumulative Probability	Random Numbers
0	0	0	—
1	0.40	0.40	00–39
2	0.25	0.65	40–64
3	0.17	0.82	65–81
4	0.01	0.83	82–82
5	0.07	0.90	83–89
6	0.10	1.00	90–99

[2] The last random number assigned to each interval is one less than the value of the cumulative probability through that event (except for the decimal point) because we started with the number zero. We could have started with one and used zero for the last interval.

Estimating Outcomes Using Monte Carlo Simulation

Suppose that the management of Hometown Bank is interested in predicting the operating characteristics of a single-channel, single- (manual) phase system during a typical operating day from 10:00 A.M. to 2:00 P.M. In particular, they would like to estimate the percentage of time that the manual server will be idle, the average customer waiting time and total time in the system, and the maximum queue length. In order to accomplish this, a table must be set up to keep track of customer arrivals and departures. Such a table, along with the results from the simulation of the first 10 customer arrivals is shown in Table 11.5.

In this simulation, we will use the first column of random numbers in Table 11.2 for the interarrival times and the second column for the service times. Since these numbers are five digits, we will use only the first two digits of each number for our random number.

The first random number is 10, which corresponds to an interarrival time of 0 minutes. This implies that the first customer arrives at the instant the drive-in window is open for business. Service can commence immediately at 10:00 A.M. The first random number in column 2 of Table 11.2 is 32, which corresponds to a service time of 1 minute. Thus, the first customer leaves the system at 10:01. The server was not idle (did not have to wait for a customer), the customer did not have to wait for service, the customer spent 1 minute in the system, and there was no queue at the time of arrival.

The second customer gets the random number 37, which means that the arrival time is 10:01. Service on the first customer ended at 10:01, so the new service can begin immediately. The next service-time random number is 04 so that service lasts 1 minute.

The third customer arrives at the same time as the second customer. Thus, the customer waits in queue until 10:02 when service can commence. The duration of service for this customer is 3 minutes, so the time of departure is 10:05. The customer arrived in the system at 10:01, the waiting time is 1 minute (column 4 minus column 3) and the time spent in the system is 4 minutes (column 9 plus column 6). At 10:01, the queue size is one (customer 3). Note that the server must wait 5 minutes for customer 4.

The simulation continues in this manner until closing time. Note that the queue builds to a size of 2 with the arrival of customer 7 because at 10:14 service has not yet begun for customer 6. Although the time period from 10:00 A.M. to 2:00 P.M. is not shown in Table 11.5, a total of 78 customers can be serviced before closing time. In addition the server will be idle 70 minutes including 4 minutes at the end of the day. The simulated time is 4 hours or 240 minutes, so we would expect that the server will be idle 29% (70/240) of the time. The average customer will wait 5.15 minutes and spend 7.41 minutes in the system. The maximum queue length to be expected is 7 for the complete simulation. Management now has some expected outcomes for the single-channel, single- (manual) phase system that can be compared to the expected outcomes for other system designs. Presumably, the outcomes for the other system alternatives would be predicted with the use of other simulation models.

Table 11.5 Queuing Simulation Work Table With the Results of Simulating the First 10 Customers

	1	2	3	4	5
Customer Number	Random Number	Interarrival Time	Clock Time	Start Service	Random Number
1	10	0	10:00	10:00	32
2	37	1	10:01	10:01	04
3	08	0	10:01	10:02	68
4	99	9	10:10	10:10	02
5	12	0	10:10	10:11	99
6	66	3	10:13	10:17	74
7	31	1	10:14	10:20	10
8	85	6	10:20	10:21	77
9	63	3	10:23	10:24	32
10	73	4	10:27	10:27	45

6	7	8	9	10	11
Service Time	End Service	Idle Time	Wait Time	Time in System	Queue at Time of Arrival
1	10:01	0	0	1	0
1	10:02	0	0	1	0
3	10:05	0	1	4	1
1	10:11	5	0	1	0
6	10:17	0	1	7	1
3	10:20	0	4	7	1
1	10:21	0	6	7	2
3	10:24	0	1	4	1
1	10:25	0	1	2	1
2	10:29	2	0	2	0

Before accepting the results of the simulation, a check should be made to determine how closely it replicates the original empirical frequency distributions. Keep in mind that we only simulated the arrival of 78 customers, which is analogous to using a sample size of 78 to estimate the operating characteristics. Table 11.6 contains a comparison of the interarrival time distributions, and Table 11.7 compares the service-time distributions.

Table 11.6 Comparison of Simulated Probabilities of the Interarrival Times and the Original Empirical Probabilities

1	2	3	4
Interarrival Time	Simulated Frequency	Probability (Column (2)/78)	Original Empirical Probability
0	17	0.22	0.15
1	16	0.20	0.24
2	7	0.09	0.12
3	14	0.18	0.19
4	5	0.06	0.08
5	0	0	0
6	10	0.13	0.10
7	0	0	0
8	2	0.03	0.05
9	7	0.09	0.07

The simulated mean interarrival time is 2.96 minutes which compares favorably with the original mean of 3.00 minutes. The individual probabilities for each event do not fare as well, however. In particular, we had a disproportionately high occurrence of simultaneous arrivals. This may have affected the results in a significant way. For example, the customer waiting-time and queue-length estimate may be inflated relative to what they should have been if the true empirical frequencies would have been obtained.

Table 11.7 Comparison of Simulated Probabilities of the Service Times and the Original Empirical Probabilities

1	2	3	4
Service Time	Simulated Frequency	Probability (Column (2)/78)	Original Empirical Probability
1	33	0.42	0.40
2	19	0.24	0.25
3	15	0.19	0.17
4	3	0.04	0.01
5	0	0	0.07
6	8	0.10	0.10

Table 11.7 shows the service time results. The simulated mean service time is 2.26 minutes per customer, whereas the empirical mean is 2.40 minutes per customer. The respective probabilities compare favorably to the empirical probabilities, except that a service time of 5 minutes was never simulated. The simulated probabilities do not exactly sum to 1 because of round-off error. The discrepancies in both the simulated interarrival and service time distributions can be rectified by taking a large sample. Sample size as well as other considerations in conducting a simulation experiment will be taken up in the last section of this chapter.

Simulating a Job Shop

One of the outstanding characteristics of the drive-in window example just analyzed is the simplicity of the system design alternatives. This enabled us to use manual simulation. Most practical queuing problems are much more complex, however, and a computer must be used to perform the simulation. Such is the case in simulating a job-shop production system.

A Classic Job Shop   Consider a production system consisting of four machine centers where jobs (production orders) arrive from outside the system on a random basis.[3] A job may require anywhere from one to five operations before it is finished, and each machine center is capable of performing more than one operation. No job can have two consecutive operations performed at the same machine center.

The job-routing patterns through the production system can be quite complex, as indicated in Figure 11.3. In the example shown there, the production order is routed from machine center 1 to 3, then to 2, and back to 3 again before being finished at machine center 4. Note that the production order enters a queue at each machine center and must await service. The length of time that the job spends in queue depends on the priority that it receives when it enters the queue. In general, a new production order may start or finish at any machine center in the system.

Two elements of this queuing system that still need to be defined are the production order (customer) interarrival time and the processing (service) time distributions. In this production system, the production schedulers have the capability of controlling the rate of input to the system. If a work-in-process inventory of 25 jobs is maintained, the system will not get overly congested and idleness at the machine centers will be within tolerable limits. Thus, with the work-in-process inventory at 25 jobs, a new production order will be released to the shop only when one is finished and leaves the system.[4] In effect, the new production order interarrival time is keyed to the service rate of the system. In this example the processing

[3] The problem description and simulation results are part of a larger study described in L.J. Krajewski, S.H. Goodman, and A. Banerjee, "Maintenance Policies and the Job Shop Scheduling Problem," Division of Research Working Paper Series, College of Administrative Science, The Ohio State University, 1976.

[4] This procedure for releasing new production orders to the shop also enables the simulation to achieve steady-state conditions in minimal time. The issue of transient simulation states will be discussed in the last section of this chapter.

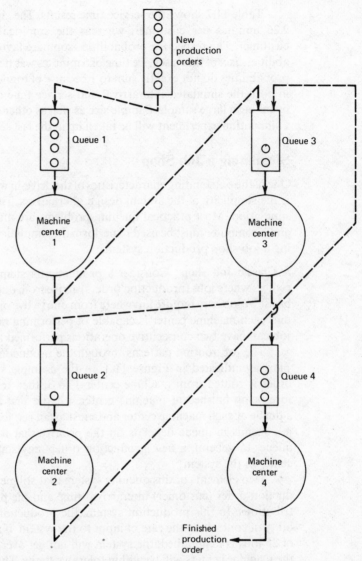

Figure 11.3 Job-shop machine center arrangement and example routing pattern for one of the production orders.

time for any operation on a production order is known to follow an exponential distribution with $\mu = 0.20$ production orders per hour.

Some Experimental Results Suppose that management wishes to select a priority rule that will be used to determine the next job to be processed at each machine center. There are three rules under consideration:

FCFS   Select the job that was the first to arrive at the machine center (first come, first served).

DDATE   Select the job with the earliest due date for completion (due date).

SPT   Select the job with the shortest processing time at the machine center (shortest processing time).

For example, if there are two jobs in queue at machine center 1 when it becomes available for processing and the operation on job 1 will take 5 hours while the operation on job 2 will take 3 hours, job 2 would be selected next if SPT is used for the priority rule.

The operating characteristics of concern are the average *flow time* per job the *average tardiness* per job, and the *average utilization* of the production system. The first two characteristics need further elaboration. The flow time of a production order is simply the time it spends in the system, from the time it enters until it leaves. Tardiness is the number of hours the job is finished after its due date. A due date D_i is assigned to each production order i as it is released to the shop in the following way:

$$D_i = 10t_i + T_i$$

where

t_i = total expected processing time for production order i

T_i = time at which production order i enters the system

The factor 10 multiplying t_i allows for the time the job may have to wait in queue. Thus, if T is the current time,

$$\text{Tardiness of job } i = \begin{cases} T - D_i & \text{if positive} \\ 0 & \text{otherwise} \end{cases}$$

Table 11.8 contains the results of simulating a job file of 1000 production orders. The same 1000 production orders are used for each priority rule. It can be readily seen that SPT is the best with respect to average flow time and utilization. DDATE does a much better job of completing the production orders by the time they are promised, however. It is interesting to note that 6.2% of the jobs are tardy for the DDATE rule compared to only 7.6% for the SPT rule. Nonetheless, production orders that require long processing times tend to remain in queue for a

Table 11.8 Simulation Results of 1000 Production Orders Processed in a Classical Job-Shop Production System

Priority Rule	Average Flow Time per Job, hours	Total Tardy Hours	Average Tardiness per Job, hours	Number of Tardy Jobs	Average Tardiness per Tardy Job, hours	Average Shop Utilization, %
FCFS	103.1	12,942	12.9	326	39.7	88
DDATE	99.4	527	5.3	62	8.5	90
SPT	82.7	24,472	24.5	76	322.0	96

long time when SPT is used, and even though only a few jobs are tardy, their tardiness is quite large. Thus, SPT is not a very good priority rule for the tardiness characteristic.

The computer simulation has provided management with the expected outcomes for each of the three alternative priority rules. It is interesting to note that no one priority rule dominates the others with respect to the operating characteristics of concern. Trade-offs must be made in order to settle on one of the alternatives. Simulation has provided information useful for assessing these trade-offs by predicting the outcomes for each alternative priority rule. Management must determine the relative importance of each operating characteristic before making a final selection of priority rule.

11.3 HEURISTIC PROBLEM SOLVING

One of the primary reasons for using simulation is the inability of analytical methods to predict outcomes and thus provide information for the selection of alternatives. Heuristics are a form of simulation because they are "rules of thumb," or guidelines, that can be used to generate a feasible alternative for the solution of a problem. In this respect, heuristics *simulate* the process that a reasonable person might follow to get a good solution to the problem. Even though heuristic problem solving involves the evaluation and eventual selection of alternatives, the resulting solution to the problem cannot be guaranteed to be optimal in general. Consequently, the heuristic procedure may be applied several times to the same problem, each time adjusting the values of certain critical independent variables and recording the resultant outcomes of interest. Thus, the decision maker may have several "solutions" to evaluate, ultimately selecting one of them to implement.

Heuristic problem-solving methods are typically used to analyze problems that can be stated in mathematical terms, but the number of feasible alternatives is very large and the use of optimizing quantitative techniques is impractical. In addition, the alternatives are usually discrete. Problems such as this are known as *combinatorial* problems. This section will describe the use of heuristics to analyze the problem of selecting tour assignments for clerks in a sectional center post office.[5]

The Mail-Processing System

Letter-sized mail arriving at a post office must pass through three general stages of processing, as shown in Figure 11.4. Most mail is processed by a mechanical processing machine called a Zip Mail Translator (ZMT). This machine, which must be operated by 20 clerks keying the address information of each letter into the machine, sorts the incoming mail to the zones within the city or the outgoing

[5] The discussion that follows parallels that found in L.P. Ritzman, L.J. Krajewski, and M.J. Showalter, "Disaggregation of Aggregate Manpower Plans." *Management Science*, Vol. 22, No. 11 (July 1976), pp. 1204–1214.

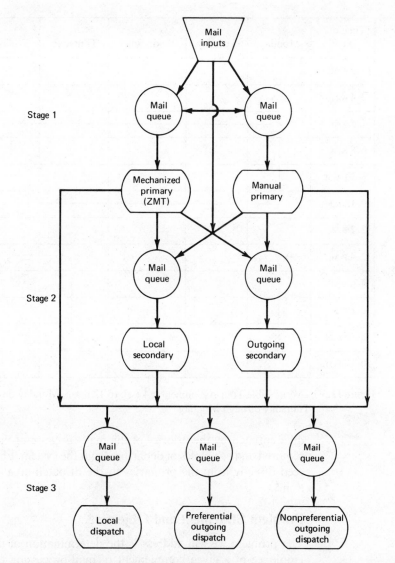

Figure 11.4 Postal processing system. Reproduced with permission from "The Disaggregation of Aggregate Manpower Plans," by L. P. Ritzman, L. J. Krajewski, and M. J. Showalter, *Management Science*, Vol. 22, No. 11 (July 1976), p. 1206, © The Institute of Management Sciences.

mail to the state of destination. Mail that cannot be machine processed is sorted at a manual primary station at a much slower pace. If the mail is coming into the city, it goes to a section called the local secondary where the mail for a particular zone is sorted according to carrier routes. Outgoing mail is further sorted by sectional center of destination in the outgoing secondary. Finally, the mail is prepared for dispatch in the last stage of processing. The outgoing dispatches are

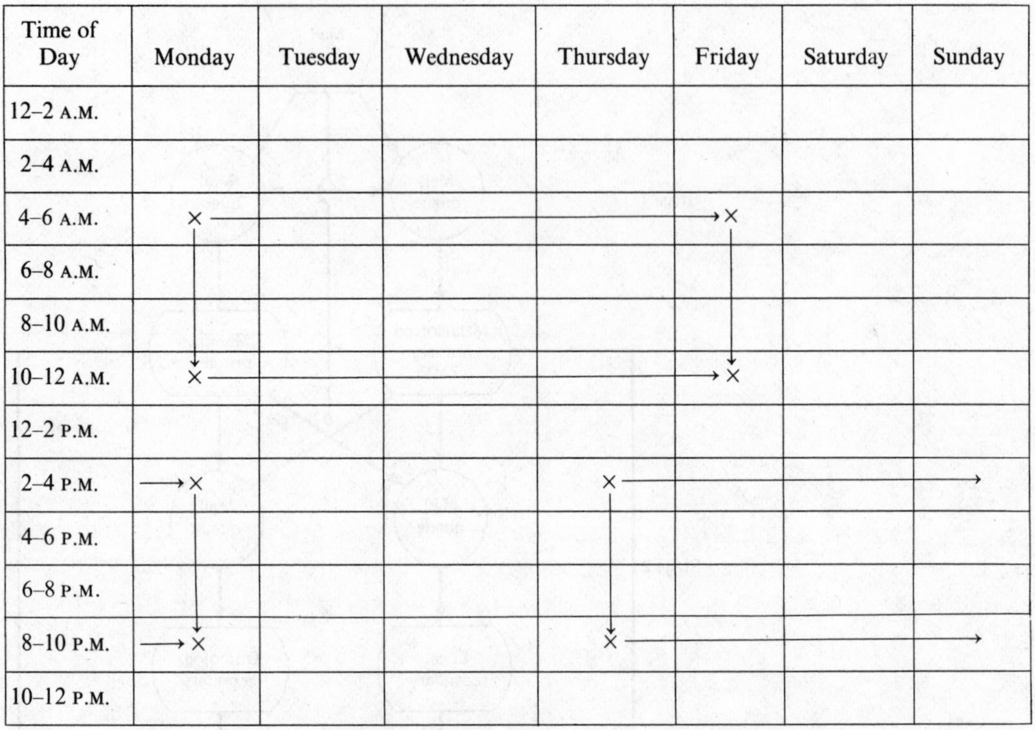

Time of Day	Monday	Tuesday	Wednesday	Thursday	Friday	Saturday	Sunday
12–2 A.M.							
2–4 A.M.							
4–6 A.M.	✕ ────────────────────────────→ ✕						
6–8 A.M.							
8–10 A.M.							
10–12 A.M.	✕ ────────────────────────────→ ✕						
12–2 P.M.							
2–4 P.M.	──→ ✕			✕ ──────────────────────────────→			
4–6 P.M.							
6–8 P.M.							
8–10 P.M.	──→ ✕			✕ ──────────────────────────────→			
10–12 P.M.							

Figure 11.5 Two Possible Tour Assignments: 4 A.M. to 12 noon, Monday through Friday, and 2 to 10 P.M., Thursday through Monday.

differentiated by the priority of the mails because of the mode of transportation required and schedules of departure from the system. Finally, some mail may proceed directly from the primaries to the dispatch area depending on its destination.[6]

Problem Statement and Objective

The problem we will address is the determination of the tours of duty for each employee of a given complement of mail-processing clerks. A tour assignment specifies the set of time periods in the week during which a clerk will be on duty as well as the specific tasks the clerk will be required to perform. Each tour consists of five consecutive 8-hour days. Figure 11.5 shows two possible tour assignments for a given work station (primary or secondary) where each day is divided into 2-hour segments. Since there are 12 starting times in any of the 7 days of the week, there are 84 possible tour assignments for any given individual at a given work station. Consequently, if there are only four possible work station assignments,

[6] The processing system described in Figure 11.4 is simplified. There may be several ZMT machines and numerous manual primary, local, and outgoing secondary stations in a sectional center office. As such, the mail flows are more complicated than that depicted.

there are 336 possible combinations of tour starting times and work station assignments for each employee.

Obviously, some alternatives will be better than others. What is "better" is determined by the objectives, and several objectives could be considered. Perhaps foremost is the objective of maximizing service to the customer. This can be accomplished by selecting tour assignments that keep the average size of the mail queues low. For a given volume of mail input, a solution that maintains low mail inventories will minimize the amount of time the mail spends in the system.

Another objective is to minimize the administrative effort associated with tour assignments. A solution that calls for 12 starting times each day will be more difficult to manage than one that calls for only 3 starting times each day.

Finally, the cost of night and Sunday assignments should be controlled. Any tour starting after 6:00 P.M. gets a night wage premium and any tour requiring Sunday work gets a Sunday wage premium. If the tour assignment solutions result in the same average mail inventory, the one with the lower night and Sunday premium hours is preferred.

The Heuristic Procedure

The purpose of the heuristic procedure is to assign a complement of employees to tour start times and work stations. The procedure begins by making total labor allocations to each of the four work stations. Given representative bihourly data for mail arrivals, mail routing, and productivities, the total number of hours of labor required at each work station per week is computed. The total employee complement is then assigned to each work station in proportion to its requirements. For example, suppose that the total complement is 500 clerks. If the manual primary must process 3 million letters during the average week and each clerk can process an average of 1000 letters per hour, then a total of 3000 hours of processing capacity is required. Suppose that the same procedure is followed to determine the capacity requirements at the other work stations. If the total number of hours required per week (including the manual primary) is 30,000 hours, then the manual primary represents 10% of the total needs. If only 500 clerks are available for processing during the week, the manual primary would get a total of 50 clerks [0.10(500)]. The other work stations would also get a number of clerks based on their percentages of the total labor requirements.

The next step is to assign tours to the employees allocated to each work station. Certain constraints, such as the maximum number of employees that can be assigned to any given station for a given time interval because of capacity limitations, are taken into account. The mail flows from the primaries to the secondaries, so assignments are made to the primaries first.

The tour assignments are made iteratively. The tour (40-hour block of time) with the largest amount of unprocessed mail is selected for the next assignment of employees. The unprocessed mail is simply the difference between the mail arrival volumes to that work station and the capacity allocated in previous assignment iterations. The number of employees assigned each time to a tour at station

i is Δ_i, the step-size. The step-size can be adjusted to affect the solution quality. The use of the unprocessed mail in determining the tour assignment is intended to achieve the primary objective of minimizing the average mail inventory. The procedure continues to assign the employees allocated to the primary station until all have been assigned.

Given the tour assignment at the primary work stations, the mail that flows into the secondary stations can be determined. After the tour assignments have been made at the secondaries, a simulation of the total processing system is conducted to compute the operating characteristics of interest, such as the average mail inventories and total night and Sunday premiums.

The heuristic procedure just described cannot guarantee an optimal solution to the problem with respect to all objectives. For example, it may yield a good solution with respect to average mail inventories, but the number of tour starting times and premium wage payments may be excessive. Each time the heuristic procedure is applied it generates an alternative (specific tour assignment) and then predicts its outcome in terms of the three objectives. The heuristic procedure could be modified to generate more alternatives and outcomes to evaluate by changing the heuristic rule used for determining the next tour assignment. For example, the rule could be biased to prefer daytime assignments to avoid the night premium hours. Or the step-size Δ_i could be decreased in an attempt to avoid employee idleness.[7] Another modification could be to limit the times during a given day at which a tour can start to a small number, such as 3, to help reduce the administrative effort.

Heuristic problem solving simulates the process a reasonable person may follow to generate a feasible alternative solution to a problem. The usefulness of a heuristic procedure, however, depends on its capability to generate more than one alternative and to predict their outcomes. A heuristically formulated alternative cannot be proved to be optimal with respect to all of the stated objectives, so it would therefore be desirable to supply the decision maker with several alternatives to evaluate. As in the example of the tour-assignment heuristic, many heuristic models have the flexibility to provide more than one alternative solution. The decision maker can then evaluate their predicted outcomes in terms of the objectives of the problem and select the alternative that maximizes utility. Heuristic models used in this way closely parallel the use of purely descriptive simulation models discussed in Section 11.2.

11.4 ESTIMATING PROBABILITY DISTRIBUTIONS WITH SIMULATION

The use of the technique of simulation is not restricted to the evaluation of alternatives with a descriptive model of the system under study. It can also be used to derive complex probability distributions that are necessary for the analysis of a

---

[7] Even though a tour has the largest unprocessed mail, a large Δ_i could assign more employees than are actually needed.

problem. Such a case arises when it is desired to determine the probability distribution of a certain outcome that is a function of several independently distributed random variables. Analytical attempts at the derivation of the probability distribution are thwarted if the outcome is a complex function of the independent variables. In this section we will examine how simulation can be used to derive a probability distribution for a relatively simple example, although the concepts are applicable for more complex situations.

A Capital Budgeting Example

A certain toy manufacturer is faced with a proposal for expanding the production of one of its best-selling model airplane kits.[8] The present production process is capable of producing 40,000 kits per year at a variable cost per kit of $3.50. The market price is $10 per kit, so the present system is able to contribute 40,000 ($10.00–$3.50) = $260,000 toward overhead and profits.

The criterion used for investment at this company is the rate of return before taxes. Based on the best estimates available, the new production system (after expansion) should be capable of producing 60,000 kits annually. The variable cost per unit of the entire system will be $2.50 per kit after the expansion. The estimated cost of the project is $1,000,000. With these data, the best *single* estimate for the annual rate of return is

$$RR = \frac{60,000\ (\$10.00-\$2.50) - \$260,000}{\$1,000,000} = 19\%$$

If the minimum acceptable rate of return for any proposed project is 17.5%, this project would appear to be acceptable.

Unfortunately, this approach completely ignores the uncertainty in the estimates for the production capability, variable costs per kit, and total project costs. Various unforeseen contingencies could cause these "most likely" estimates to be incorrect after the project has been undertaken. In particular, the rate of return could be viewed as a random variable given by the following expression:

$$RR = \frac{P(\$10 - V) - 260,000}{C}$$

where

P = actual annual production output

V = actual variable costs per kit

C = actual project cost

Since P, V, and C are random variables, management would certainly like more information about the possible returns to be expected in this kind of case. A

[8] The approach used in this section is based on the concepts presented in David B. Hertz, "Risk Analysis in Capital Investment," *Harvard Business Review* (January–February 1964), pp. 94–106.

single estimate does not supply enough information to make a good decision on the project. Monte Carlo simulation can help supply the necessary information.

Simulation and the Probability Distribution of *RR*

Let us assume that P, V, and C are independent random variables. In order to derive the probability distribution of the rate of return, data must be gathered on the various values that P, V, and C can attain. If the company has experienced many projects identical to the one in the past, frequency distributions for each random variable can be developed from historical data in a manner similar to the interarrival and service-time distributions at the Hometown Bank. Because there is no previous experience to rely on, however, this cannot be done in most cases. In these situations, we must rely on management's subjective assessments of the probabilities of various outcomes for each random variable. For example, managers of production, finance, and engineering could be asked to provide these estimates based on their experiences with other projects. At a minimum, these subjective probability distributions will collectively reflect management's uncertainty in the estimates for these random variables. Table 11.9 contains the subjective probability distributions we will use in our example.

Table 11.9 also shows the assignment of random numbers in the manner demonstrated earlier in the Hometown Bank example. Note that the single estimate for the rate of return was derived from the most likely values for each independent variable.

The procedure for deriving the distribution of the rate of return is similar to that used for simulating the Hometown Bank queuing problem. Each trial consists of drawing three *different* random numbers to determine the values of the independent variables and then computing the rate of return. For example, column

Table 11.9 Subjective Probability Distributions of the Independent Variables and the Assignment of Random Numbers

Independent Variable	Probability, %	Random Numbers
Project cost		
$800,000	30	00–29
$1,000,000	40	30–69
$1,200,000	30	70–99
Variable cost/kit		
$2.00	10	00–09
$2.50	70	10–79
$3.00	20	80–99
Production (kits)		
50,000	25	00–24
60,000	60	25–84
70,000	15	85–99

Table 11.10 Estimated Probability Distribution of the Rate of Return

Rate of Return Interval, %	Frequency	Estimated Probability, %	Theoretical Probability, %
7.5–12.49	15	15	18.00
12.5–17.49	26	26	27.25
17.5–22.49	32	32	29.40
22.5–27.49	19	19	18.45
27.5–32.49	3	3	3.30
32.5–37.49	3	3	3.15
37.5–42.49	2	2	0.45

8 of Table 11.2 can be used to get random numbers for the project cost, column 9 for the variable cost, and column 10 for the production of kits. The first trial would draw the random numbers 09, 39, and 74. This would correspond to a rate of return of

$$RR = \frac{60,000(\$10.00 - \$2.50) - \$260,000}{\$800,000} = 23.75\%$$

Continuing in this manner for 100 trials generates the distribution shown in Table 11.10[9] The difference between the estimated and theoretical probabilities is a measure of the error caused by a small sample size. More will be said about the choice of sample size in the last section of this chapter.

Managerial Use of the Probability Distribution for *RR*

The data of Table 11.10 are much more illuminating than the single estimate calculated earlier. We now have a *distribution* for the rate of return. The average rate of return using the simulated results is 19.13%, which compares favorably with the single estimate. In addition, we also estimate that there is a 59% chance that the project will yield a return on investment greater than 17.5%, the minimum acceptable return. Perhaps more important, however, is the estimate that there is a 41% chance of getting a return *less* than 17.5%. This is quite a risk, and management may not have even been aware of it had the simulation experiment not been carried out.

This type of data can be used to compare two projects. Figure 11.6 shows the estimate probability distributions of the rate of return for two *hypothetical* projects.

---

[9] The theoretical probability could be easily derived analytically because there are only 27 combinations for this simple example, but the methodology of simulation is of interest here. Nonetheless, a sample of 100 does reasonably well in estimating the theoretical probabilities.

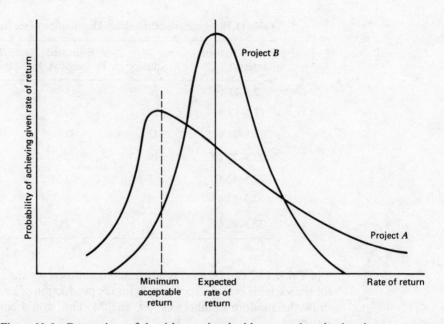

Figure 11.6 Comparison of the risk associated with two projects having the same expected rate of return.

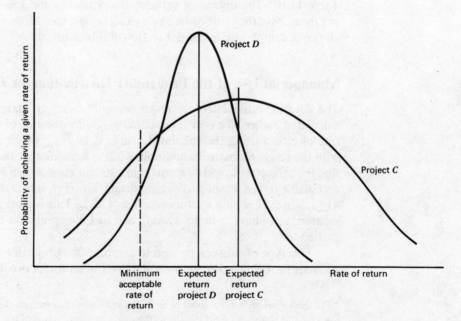

Figure 11.7 Comparison of the trade-offs in risk and rate of return for two projects.

Both projects *A* and *B* have the same expected rate of return, yet the variances of the distributions are quite different. Project *A*, with the greater variance, presents a greater risk in generating an unacceptable return on investment than project *B*. Of course, it also has a greater chance of generating a large return on investment. Given these data, management is in a better position to select the best alternative.

Figure 11.7 demonstrates the trade-offs that could be present when comparing two projects with different expected returns on investment. If only the single estimate of the rate of return is used, project *C* would be preferred to project *D*, but project *D* is less "risky" in that there is a smaller chance that it will generate a return less than the minimum acceptable return. Management must now weigh the consequences of falling below the minimum return and compare that to the benefits of getting a greater return on investment. The probability distributions of the return for each project can be used to assess the chances of success or failure and aid management in the choice of the best alternative.

11.5 DESIGN OF SIMULATION EXPERIMENTS

Conducting a simulation study using a Monte Carlo simulation model results in stochastic outcomes. These outcomes are similar to observations sampled from an ongoing system. For instance, in the Hometown Bank example, the average customer waiting time was estimated to be 5.15 minutes. This value is merely an estimate of the true mean waiting time that would result if the single-channel, single-phase system is selected. It is a function of our choice of random numbers for that particular simulation. A different set of random numbers may have resulted in a different estimate for waiting time. In effect, we used the model to generate a sample of customer arrivals, and, based on that sample, we estimated the average waiting time. This raises several questions concerning our simulation study (and simulation studies in general):

1. What effect do the initial system conditions have on the outcomes?
2. Is the sample size adequate?
3. Have all the factors that may have an impact on the outcomes been adequately controlled?

The last question can be answered in the positive if a good experimental design has been developed prior to the onset of the study. We will discuss each of these questions in the remainder of this chapter.

Initial System Conditions

The initial conditions describe the state of the system at the time we begin to observe the outcomes. Depending on the system under study, we may begin to observe the system in an *empty* condition or a *fully loaded* condition. The empty condition implies that the system is in an idle state at the start of the simulation. For example, the Hometown Bank simulation study started in the idle state. No customers were in the system at the time we began to measure waiting time, idle time, total time in system, and maximum queue length. This is the proper initial condition for systems such as the drive-in window because this is the way the system would start each day of operation. The outcomes that are measured in this way would accurately reflect the actual outcomes generated by the single-channel, single-phase system if it were put into operation.

The fully loaded condition implies that the system is in full operation at the time we start to observe the outcomes. Systems such as a job shop should be fully loaded before observing the outcomes because at the start of any day, the system will contain customers in various stages of service. To make observations when the system is empty (perhaps at the start of the simulation) would distort the estimates of the system operating characteristics.

There are two ways to load the system fully in a simulation study. One method is to allow the system to run for a while before collecting the data. The system starts in the idle state, and customer arrivals and service are simulated until the level of activity is representative of an ongoing system or, alternatively, the system is in steady state. At that time, we start to observe the system. With this method, the system passes through an initial *transient* state during which no statistics are compiled.

The other method is to load the system initially with customers in various stages of service. Although this is more difficult to do, it reduces the simulation run time considerably. In a job-shop simulation this can be accomplished by randomly specifying the first machine at which each of a specified number of jobs must begin its processing. Then the time left for processing on that machine can be determined using random numbers and a uniform distribution where the maximum remaining processing time is the standard processing time for the job on that machine. In effect, this is the procedure that was used in the job-shop simulation discussed in Section 11.2. The maximum work in process was set at 25 jobs. The system was loaded with 25 jobs and each was routed to its first machine before any observations were made.

In general, the initial system conditions have a considerable impact on the results of the simulation. These conditions depend on the nature of the system under study. Incorrectly specifying the initial conditions can result in erroneous estimates for the system operating characteristics, which, in turn, could lead to incorrect conclusions of system performance.

Sample-Size Considerations

Even though the proper initial conditions are used in a simulation study, there is no guarantee that the outcomes will be good estimators of the system operating characteristics. Another factor to consider is the sample to be taken. What constitutes a sample depends on the specific study and can be categorized in one of three ways:

1. Keep the simulated periods (or run length) constant, then take a sample of n runs.

2. Take a sample of n simulated periods (or trials). In this case, a 100-period simulation constitutes a sample size twice as large as a 50-period simulation.
3. Take a sample of n simulated transactions (customers, for example), leaving the run length free to vary.

The simulation applications we discussed earlier in this chapter used each of the above definitions of a sample. The Hometown Bank simulation is limited to a 4-hour day because of bank policy; thus, we would want to simulate a sample of n days before compiling the statistics on the system operating characteristics. Alternatively, the job-shop simulation compiles outcomes after processing 1000 jobs (transactions). In this way, we can use the same job file to compare each of the dispatching rules on an equal footing. Finally, the simulation of the return on investment involves taking a sample of n trials (periods) after which inferences are made relative to the degree of risk associated with the investment. No matter what type of sample is taken, the question still boils down to: how many observations do we need in our sample?

The answer to this question can in part by found by resorting to classic statistics. If one is willing to assume, among other things, that the observations are independent of each other, one could require that the sample size be large enough that the confidence interval constructed around the *estimator* of a population·mean will contain the *true* mean a prescribed percentage of the time.[10] Suppose that we wanted to determine the appropriate sample size for the rate-of-return simulation we discussed in Section 11.4. Let us define the following quantities:

R = Population mean rate of return we wish to estimate
$\overline{X}$ = Sample average rate of return, the estimator for R
σ = Population standard deviation
α = Percentage of the time the confidence interval will not contain the true mean [$(100\% - \alpha)$ is the *reliability* of the confidence interval]
$Z_{\alpha/2}$ = Deviate of the normal distribution that leaves $\alpha/2\%$ of the probability density in one of the tails[11]
p = Desired precision of the estimate
n = Sample size to be determined

Then the confidence interval for R with $(100\% - \alpha)$ reliability can be written as

$$R = \overline{X} \pm Z_{\alpha/2}\left(\frac{\sigma}{\sqrt{n}}\right)$$

[10] The assumption of independence is suspect in many simulation studies. In addition, one assumes that the central limit theorem applies. A more thorough discussion of sample-size determination under these assumptions can be found in Byron L. Newton, *Statistics for Business*, Chicago: Science Research Associates, 1973.

[11] The reliability expresses the probability that the confidence interval constructed will contain the true population mean. Thus Z is the number of standard deviations $(\sigma/\sqrt{n})$ one has to go from the true population mean to leave $\alpha/2\%$ in one of the tails.

This result has its foundation in the central limit theorem, which states that the distribution of *sample* means approaches a normal distribution centered at the true population mean with variance σ^2/n as the sample size n gets large. Samples greater than 30 observations are usually considered "large."

In order to determine the appropriate sample size, however, we must specify the precision we desire in the estimate $\overline{X}$. The precision p specifies one-half the width of the confidence interval. Thus, given p, we have

$$p = Z_{\alpha/2} \tag{11.1}$$

After some algebraic manipulation, we have the following equation for the sample size:

$$n = \frac{(Z_{\alpha/2})^2 \sigma^2}{p^2} \tag{11.2}$$

Unfortunately, the population variance must be estimated to make the above equation useful because the variance is unknown in almost every case. The variance can be estimated in two ways. One way is to make an estimate of the *range* that the sample rates of return will have *prior* to taking any observations. Assuming that the distribution will be *symmetric*, the range will subtend approximately 6 standard deviations as it does in the normal distribution. Thus, if r_L and r_U are the estimated lower bound and upper bound, respectively, of the range of rates of return in the population, we have

$$\hat{\sigma} = \frac{r_U - r_L}{6} \tag{11.3}$$

where $\hat{\sigma}$ is the estimate of the population standard deviation. Suppose that we make the assumption that the distribution of the population (in our case, rates of return) is symmetric. Using the data in Table 11.9, the maximum rate of return is 37.5% ($P = 70,000$, $V = \$2.00$, $C = \$800,000$) whereas the minimum rate of return is 7.50% ($P = 50,000$, $V = \$3.00$, $C = \$1,200,000$). Thus, (9.3) gives us the following estimates for the standard deviation:

$$\hat{\sigma} = \frac{37.50 - 7.50}{6} = 5$$

The sample size for a 95% confidence interval with $p = 1$ (within 1% of the population mean rate of return) is given by (11.2)

$$n = \frac{(1.96)^2 (5)^2}{(1)^2} = 96.04$$

The sample size would be rounded to the next largest integer.[12] In this case it would be 97.

---

[12] Recall that we took a sample of 100 in our example in Section 11.4. Because of the simplicity of the problem, we can compute the population mean. It turns out to be 18.24%. Our sample estimate was 19.13%, which is within 1σ of the population mean. In general, we may not be so lucky because, as we will see, the estimate of the population variance is low using this method.

The other method is to take advantage of previous studies to estimate the population variance. Sometimes other researchers have published similar studies from which an estimate of the variance can be obtained. Alternatively, a pilot study can be conducted to compute the sample variance. An arbitrary (usually small) sample is taken and the sample variance is used to estimate the population variance. In the rate of return simulation, a sample of 100 was taken and the sample standard deviation was computed, yielding $\hat{\sigma} = 6.13$. Thus, the sample size for a 95% confidence interval with $p = 1$ is

$$n = \frac{(1.96)^2(6.13)^2}{(1)^2} = 144.35$$

or 145. Note that the sample variance, as well as the sample size, is larger than the estimate for σ computed from the range because the distribution of rates of returns in this example is not symmetric. Based on this analysis, we should sample 45 more observations before proceeding with the analysis of the investment. In general, both methods of estimating σ can be used. The estimated range can be used to determine a sample size for the pilot study, and then the resulting sample variance can be used to see if more sampling should take place. Using only the estimated range could lead to erroneous estimates of the population mean.

The equation for n requires the specification of the parameters $Z_{\alpha/2}$, σ, and p. We have already seen how the estimate of σ affects the sample size. The choice of $Z_{\alpha/2}$ (or more precisely, α) also affects the sample size. We cannot ever be certain of the value of the population mean as long as we must sample. When we compare two sample means, however, the difference may be due to sampling error as opposed to a real difference in the population means. For example, the difference between the average customer waiting time for the single-channel, single-phase drive-in window design and the two-channel single-phase design may be due to an inadequate sample size or an actual difference in the waiting times. The consequences of making an incorrect inference dictate the degree of reliability one may place on the estimate of waiting time. Obviously, a mistake in favor of the two-channel design would result in a significant capital investment that would not generate the desired effects on waiting time. A reasonable level of reliability may be 95%, but in cases where the cost of making an incorrect inference is significant, a level of reliability of 99% is not out of the question. Of course, the value of $Z_{\alpha/2}$ would change from 1.96 to 2.58, increasing the sample size by a factor of 1.7. Thus, the cost of making an incorrect inference must be weighed against the cost of increasing the sample size.

The other factor that affects sample size is the precision p. Obviously, the more precision required, the larger the sample size. If p is set at 0.5 in our rate of return simulation, the required sample size for 95% reliability is

$$n = \frac{(1.96)^2(6.13)^2}{(0.5)^2} = 577.42$$

or 578. In order to be confident that the estimate of the mean rate of return we get from our sample is within 0.5 (0.5%) of the true mean rate of return from the investment 95% of the time (if we were to repeat the experiment many times) requires a sample size almost four times the size of the sample required for a precision of $p = 1$. The trade-offs in the added precision and the increase in sample size must be carefully weighed.

Design Considerations

Frequently, simulation studies involve experimenting with various factors, or independent variables, under the control of management to see what effects they may have on the outcomes. The previous discussion outlined sample-size considerations in the situation where all these factor settings have been held constant and thus it was merely a question of replication. Complex simulation models typically enable the analyst to experiment with several independent variables (decision alternatives or exogenous variables) to assess their impact on operating performance. The analyst must carefully design the experiment so that the desired information is obtained at minimal expense.

The most straightforward design is the so-called *complete factorial* design. Suppose that we wish to study a job-shop production system in which machines experience breakdowns according to a prescribed failure distribution. Three decisions must be made: the priority rule, the maximum level of work in process in the shop, and the interval of time between preventive maintenance acts. Three priority rules are under consideration: first come, first served (FCFS), earliest due date (DDATE), and shortest processing time (SPT). The two work-in-process levels to evaluate are 20 jobs and 30 jobs in the system at any time. Finally, there are three alternative preventive maintenance policies expressed in terms of the number of machine hours between preventive maintenance acts: 50, 100, and 150.

Each of the decisions is referred to as a factor in our design. Factor 1, dispatch rule, has three levels. Factor 2, work-in-process and factor 3, preventive maintenance policy, have two and three levels, respectively. Table 11.11 summarizes a complete factorial design for this experiment.

Each cell in the matrix represents one run of the simulation model. Thus, we have $3 \times 2 \times 3 = 18$ runs *without* any replication. The discussion on sample-size

Table 11.11 Complete Factorial Design for the Job-Shop Example

Priority Rule	PM = 50		PM = 100		PM = 150	
	WIP = 20	WIP = 30	WIP = 20	WIP = 30	WIP = 20	WIP = 30
FCFS						
DATE						
SPT						

determination revealed that if we are to get good estimators of the population means we need to take an adequate sample for each cell in the matrix. As it stands now we have only one observation for each combination of factor settings. If a sample of size 10 is deemed appropriate, the total number of simulation runs would be 180. The effects of the three factors (singly or in combination) can then be assessed using analysis of variance.

It can be seen that simulation experiments can require a significant number of runs. Often the number of runs can be reduced by using other designs such as the *fractional factorial* design where only a portion of the complete design is necessary to acquire the desired information. These more advanced designs are beyond the scope of this text. (See the references at the end of this chapter.) Nonetheless, it is sufficient to say that the design should be carefully planned to avoid excessive runs of the simulation model.

11.6 SUMMARY

Simulation is a tool for predicting outcomes in a decision problem involving the use of a descriptive model. Once the outcomes from a set of alternatives have been generated, the decision maker begins the task of selecting the alternative that is best with respect to all the measures of effectiveness specified for the problem. This may involve the use of alternative selection techniques such as those discussed in various chapters of this text.

A simulation model may not be the first choice for analyzing a problem. Usually, the analyst begins the model-building phase of the decision-making process by attempting to build a normative model for prescribing the best alternative. The problem may be too complex to develop such a model, which was the case in the job-shop example in this chapter that represented a complex queuing problem. Even if we gave up trying to build a model that would determine the "optimal" priority rule, it would be extremely difficult to develop an analytical model to prescribe the outcomes for each alternative priority rule in the manner we developed the functions for the outcomes in Chapter 10. Even if such a model were constructed, it is unlikely that management would accept its results because they would have difficulty in understanding how the model was developed. A simulation model is much easier to understand because it is descriptive of how the system operates. Consequently, if a simulation model is used, we are left with proposing alternatives and then predicting their outcomes, thereby providing management with useful information for the final selection of alternatives. Of course, we must remember that using simulation models involves taking samples of data to estimate the outcomes of interest. The experiment must be designed well so that proper initial system conditions are used and an adequate sample size is taken.

The concept of simulation can be used to assist in the decision-making process in a variety of ways. For example, it can be used to develop inputs to other decision models. The development of the subjective probability distribution for the rate of return discussed in this chapter is an example of this application.

Another example can be found in the area of inventory control. Consider the manager of a warehouse who must decide when to place an order to the factory for replenishment of a particular item. The order quantity is always Q units. Orders are sent to the factory when the on-hand inventory level of the item is R units, often referred to as the reorder point. In order to provide adequate service to the customers, R must be chosen with consideration for the demand during the lead time.[13] In most practical warehousing problems, both the lead time and the demand per unit of time are random variables. That is, if the lead time is measured in working days, both the lead time in days and the demand per day are subject to certain probability distributions. If we consider lead time and demand per day as independent random variables, then the technique discussed in this chapter can be used to develop the demand during lead time probability distribution. Once this distribution is determined, management can choose R in such a way that demand during the lead time will exceed R only $\alpha\%$ of the time, where α is the acceptable risk of a stock-out during the lead time. See Problems 7 and 8 at the end of this chapter for examples of the use of simulation to develop demand during lead-time distributions.

Heuristic problem solving can also be considered a simulation method. In this respect, the term simulation refers to the replication of the procedures that a reasonable person may undertake to arrive at a solution to a problem. Heuristic models simulate an alternative selection process. Consequently, the use of heuristic problem-solving methods combines descriptive models and normative models. In effect, heuristic models provide a bridge between prediction of outcomes and alternative selection in the decision-making process.

References Emshoff, J.R., and Sirson, R.L., *Design and Use of Computer Simulation Models*, New York: Macmillan, 1970.

Gordon, G., *Systems Simulation*, Englewood Cliffs, N.J.: Prentice-Hall, 1969.

Hammersley, J.M., and Handscomb, D.C., *Monte Carlo Methods*, New York: John Wiley & Sons, 1964.

Meier, R.C., Newell, W.T., and Pazer, H.L. *Simulation in Business and Economics*, Englewood Cliffs, N.J.: Prentice-Hall, 1969.

Mize, J.H., and Cox, J.G., *Essentials of Simulation*, Englewood Cliffs, N.J.: Prentice-Hall, 1968.

Naylor, T.H., Balintfy, J.L., Burdick, D.S., and Chu, K., *Computer Simulation Techniques*, New York: John Wiley & Sons, 1966.

Naylor, T.H., and Burdick, D.S., "Design of Computer Simulation Experiments for Industrial Systems," *Communications of the ACM*, Vol. 9, No. 5 (May 1966).

Naylor, T.H., Burdick, D.S., and Sasser, W.E., "Computer Simulation Experiments with Economic Systems: The Problem of Experimental Design," *American Statistical Association Journal*, Vol. 67, No. 320 (December 1967).

---

[13] The lead time is the time it takes to get a shipment from the factory once the order has been sent from the warehouse.

Naylor, T.H., and Finger, J.M., "Verification of Computer Simulation Models," *Management Science*, Vol. 14, No. 2 (October 1967).

Newell, A., and Simon, H.A., *Human Problem Solving*, Englewood Cliffs, N.J.: Prentice-Hall, 1972.

Review Questions

1. Discuss the advantages and disadvantages of using simulation to determine the number of tollbooths to have at a particular spot on an interstate highway.

2. Suppose you want to simulate the loading of semitrailer trucks at a distribution warehouse. The trucks arrive empty and must be loaded with the products ordered by the retail outlets. Loading is done manually. Specify the data you would need to do your study. How would you get the data?

3. With reference to Question 2, suppose you want to determine the best number of employees for loading the trucks. What operating characteristics would you be interested in estimating with your simulation? Why?

4. What is a random number? Why are random numbers useful in simulation studies?

5. What is a heuristic? Why is heuristic problem solving necessary in some cases?

6. The heuristic used in the postal tour assignment example discussed in Section 11.2 involved selecting the tour with the largest amount of unprocessed mail for the next assignment of employees. Specify an alternative heuristic rule that could be used to select the tour for the next assignment. What would you expect to achieve with your heuristic in light of the objectives?

7. Suppose you are the hospital administrator in charge of a large city hospital. You feel that there is a problem with the service in the emergency clinic. The clinic operates 24 hours a day and patients arrive at all hours of the day. Your concern is with the number of doctors you should have assigned to the clinic. In a simulation study of this situation, would the initial system conditions have an impact on the estimated operating characteristics? How would you determine what the initial conditions should be?

8. With respect to Question 7, what considerations would you make in determining the sample size for your study?

9. Discuss the trade-offs you would have to make in (a) increasing the reliability of the estimate, and (b) increasing the precision (make p smaller) of the estimate when determining the sample size for a simulation study. Are precision and reliability synonymous terms?

10. With respect to Question 7, set up a complete factorial design that involves two different factors where each factor has at least three levels. Make any assumptions you want regarding the problem, but make them explicit in your discussion. What outcomes (or operating characteristics) would you be interested in analyzing with your experimental design?

Problems

1. The Kwicky Kleen Company operates an automatic car-wash facility in Hometown. The manager is concerned about the long lines of cars that build up waiting for service. The service time for the system is machine paced and thus *constant*, and the manager has the opportunity to decrease the service time by increasing the speed of the conveyor that pulls the cars through the system. Of course, the quicker the pace, the lower the quality of the car wash. The manager wants to study the effects of setting the system for a 2-minute car wash. The following data on customer arrivals have been gathered:

Interarrival Time, minutes	Number of Occurrences
1	136
2	34
3	102
4	51
5	17

(a) Compute the traffic density for a service rate of 2 minutes per car.

(b) Set up this problem for hand simulation by assigning random numbers to the interarrival times and preparing a table to keep track of customer arrivals and departures.

(c) Simulate the arrival of 20 customers. The doors open at 8:00 A.M. Compute the average waiting time per customer, the average time spent in the system, the percentage of time the car wash is idle, and the maximum queue length.

(d) Based on your small simulation, would you recommend a further reduction in the service time?

2. Consider the Hometown Bank drive-in window problem and the data in Tables 11.3 and 11.4. Suppose management would like to compare the results of the simulation to that of a two-channel, single- (manual) phase system. Suppose that the second drive-in window has the same service time distribution as shown in Table 11.4.

(a) Set up a work table similar to Table 11.5. You will have to add some additional columns for the second window to keep track of service at that window. You may assume that all customers line up in one queue and are serviced at the first available window.

(b) Simulate the typical day from 10:00 A.M. to 2:00 P.M.

(c) Compare your results with those in the text. Discuss the advantages and disadvantages of the two designs.

3. Consider the Kwicky Kleen car wash facility described in Problem 1. Management would like to install a gas pump and allow discounts on the car wash depending on the amount of gas purchased. The system design would then have customers first serviced at the gas pump and then at the car wash—a single-channel, double-phase design. It is estimated that 20% of the customers

will not require gasoline. The same customer arrival distribution at the system can be used. The car wash takes a constant 2 minutes. The service time distribution at the gas pump is

Service Time, minutes	Probability, %
1	20
2	40
3	30
4	10

(a) Set up a table for keeping track of customer arrivals and service. Keep in mind that the output from the gas pump is the input to the car wash. A queue may build up in front of the car wash.

(b) Simulate the arrival and service of 20 customers. Compute the average customer waiting time, the average time in the system, the percentage of time the gas pump and the car wash are idle, and the maximum queues at each service phase.

(c) Discuss your results in light of the implications for adding another gas pump and for adjusting the speed of the car wash.

4. A certain maintenance facility is responsible for the upkeep of five machines. The machines, which fail frequently, must be repaired as soon as possible to maintain as high a productive capacity of the production system as possible. Management is concerned about the average "downtime" per machine and is considering an increase in the capacity of the maintenance facility. The following distributions have been developed from historical data:

Time Between Failures for a Given Machine, days	Probability, %
2	5
3	10
4	15
5	40
6	20
7	10

Repair Time per Machine, days	Probability, %
1	40
2	50
3	10

(a) Simulate the failure and repair of 10 machines. Begin by determining the time of the first failure for each of the 5 machines. Sequence the machines through the repair facility on a FCFS basis. If there is more than one machine waiting to be repaired, arbitrarily choose one to repair next. After a machine has been repaired, determine its next time of failure and continue until you have repaired 10. Some machines may fail twice before others have failed once.

(b) Based on your simulation of 10 failures, discuss the need for more capacity in the maintenance facility. What factors would you consider?

5. Consider Problem 4. Using the ending condition of the system you had in your simulation of 10 failures (machines waiting to be repaired) as the *initial conditions* for a new study, simulate the repair of 10 more machines. Compare your statistics on average downtime per machine, maximum queue length, and idleness for the repair facility you had at the end of the first 10 failures (Problem 4) with the total results of simulating 20 failures (and repair). Will your conclusions change? What effect do the initial conditions have in this study?

6. Consider a small machine shop that consists of three machines—A, B, and C. Although each of the machines performs different operations, it can be safely assumed that the processing-time distributions (including setups) of the three machines are identical.

Processing Time, hours	Probability, %
1	10
2	15
3	30
4	40
5	5

Customer orders for various machined parts arrive at the shop according to the following distributions:

Interarrival Time, hours	Probability, %
2	5
3	30
4	40
5	20
6	5

Routing a customer order through the shop depends on the work that has to be done to it. Two major routings exist:

Routing	% of Orders Having the Routing
A–B–C	30
A–C–B	70

The machine shop operates 24 hours a day (three shifts).

(a) All orders are processed on a FCFS basis at each machine. Assuming that the shop is empty at the start, simulate the arrival and processing of 10 customer orders. For each order, determine first its arrival time, then its routing. Each time an order is processed on a machine, determine its processing time (you will need to determine three processing times for each order). Make a chart for each machine:

Machine A

Job Number	Arrival Time	Start Service	End Service

Once a job is finished at a machine it goes to the next one on its routing. As soon as the machine is finished with a job, it takes the job with the earliest arrival time of those available (in queue) for processing. When a job is processed by the last machine on its routing, it leaves the system.

(b) Compute the average waiting time per job, the total idle time of the machines, and the maximum queue length at each machine.

(c) If you were going to perform a study to determine the best priority rule to use for this machine shop, how would you design your experiment? Include the issue of initial conditions and sample size in your discussion.

7. The manager of a warehouse is interested in designing an inventory-control system for one of the products in stock. The demand for the product comes from numerous retail outlets and orders arrive on a daily basis. The warehouse receives its stock from the factory, but the lead time (time between issuing an order for replenishment and actual receipt of the order) is not constant. The manager wants to determine the best time to release orders to the factory so that stock-outs are minimized yet inventory holding costs are at acceptable levels. Any orders from retailers not supplied on a given day

constitute lost demand. Based on a sampling study, the following data are available:

Daily Demand	Probability, %	Lead Time, days	Probability, %
1	0	1	20
2	20	2	50
3	50	3	30
4	20		
5	10		

Two alternative ordering policies have been proposed:

Policy 1: Whenever the inventory level drops below 6 units (reorder point), order 10 units (lot size).

Policy 2: Whenever the inventory level drops below 10 units, order 10 units.

(a) Simulate each of these two policies for 30 days. Assume that you have 12 units in inventory at the start of the simulations.

(b) Compare and contrast the outcomes for each of these two policies. What cost information would you want so that a final recommendation can be made? Is there another policy that might work better? Why?

8. In inventory-control problems such as the one in Problem 7, the "demand during lead time" distribution is important for determining the optimal reorder point. Based on this distribution, and given the percentage of time that the company will accept a stock-out condition, a reorder point can be specified. This may involve using simulation to determine the probability distribution of demand and lead time.

(a) Using the demand and lead-time distribution data provided in Problem 7, perform a simulation to determine the demand during lead-time distribution. Use a sample size of 100. (*Hint*: You will need more that one random number for each trial.) First sample from the lead-time distribution. If the result is 3 days, for example, sample 3 times from the daily demand distribution. Sum the daily demands to get one observation. The resulting distribution should range from 2 to 15 units demanded during the lead time.

(b) Suppose the company specifies that there be no more than a 10% probability that demand will exceed supply during the lead time. What should the reorder point be (i.e., how much stock should be on hand when an order is placed)?

9. In practical problems where simulation is used to derive a probability distribution, the theoretical distribution is too difficult to compute analytically.

The distribution in Problem 8 is simple enough to derive without simulation, however. Compare the theoretical distribution with the one simulated in Problem 8 and discuss from the standpoint of sample size.

Hint: The distribution ranges from 2 to 15 units demanded during the lead time. Assuming independence of demand, the probability that there will be a demand of 5 units is the probability of a 1-day lead time and a demand of 5 units *plus* the probability that there will be a lead time of 2 days and there is a demand of 2 on the first day and a demand of 3 on the second day or a demand of 3 on the first day and 2 on the second day. Numerically, this amounts to $0.2(0.10) + 0.5[0.20(0.50) + 0.50(0.20)] = 0.12$. Of course, the sum of the probabilities should be unity.

10. Replicate the rate of return simulation of Section 11.4. Use the data in Table 11.9 and a sample size of 50. Compare your results with those in Table 11.10. Then, using the same intervals in Table 11.10, combine your results with the frequencies in the table and compare to the theoretical probabilities. Discuss the impact of sample size on this problem.

11. Suppose that the toy manufacturer of Section 11.4 has another capital-investment proposal. The following subjective probability distributions have been obtained:

Project Cost	Probability, %
$ 800,000	50
$1,000,000	40
$1,200,000	10

Variable Cost/Kit	Probability, %
2.00	40
2.50	20
3.00	40

Production (Kits)	Probability, %
50,000	33
60,000	33
70,000	33

(a)   If the firm uses the simple rate of return, develop the probability distribution for rate of return by simulating 50 trials. Summarize the results as shown in Table 11.10. Assume a price of $10 and a contribution of $260,000.

(b)   Compare the results you get with those in Table 11.10. Discuss the advantages and disadvantages of choosing the project over the one in the example. The minimum acceptable return is still 17.5%.

12.   The manager of a check-processing department in a small bank is concerned about the amount of capacity in that department. Checks are processed on a machine called an encoder, which prints the amount of the check in magnetic ink at the bottom of each check. Each machine is available for processing only 1000 minutes per week due to the availability of clerks to run the machines and the average downtime and maintenance of the machines. The weekly volume of checks is variable and has the following probability distribution:

Weekly Volume	Probability, %
10,000	5
20,000	10
30,000	20
40,000	40
50,000	25

In addition, the clerks operating the machines have varying skills; thus, the time to process a check varies according to the distribution:

Process Time, minutes	Probability, %
0.1	40
0.2	50
0.3	10

As a prelude to a capacity analysis, the manager would like to know the probability distribution of the need for machine capacity. Following the model discussed in Section 3.3 of Chapter 3, the number of machines m is found by the following relationship:

$$m = \frac{\text{weekly requirements (minutes)}}{\text{time one machine is available per week (minutes)}}$$

Of course, the weekly requirements are uncertain.

(a)   Use simulation to determine the probability distribution for m, $f(m)$. Using a random-number table, select a weekly volume. Select another random number to determine a process time. Multiply these two values and divide by 1000 minutes to get one observation for m. Repeat for a total of 50 observations. You will get a frequency distribution ranging from 1 to 15 machines.

(b)   Compute the theoretical distribution for m, assuming weekly demand and process time are independent. Compare to your distribution in part a. What can you say about your sample size of 50 observations?

13. Consider Problem 12 and the capacity planning model in Section 3.3 of Chapter 3. Suppose that C_1, the fixed charge per machine per week, is $1000. Also, suppose that C_2, the cost penalty per week for being short the capacity of one machine, is $3000 to account for the interest lost by not depositing checks on time with the reserve bank. Using your distribution for part a of Problem 12, determine the optimal number of machines for the check-processing department.

14. A pilot run of a simulation resulted in the average waiting time per customer of 10 minutes with a sample standard deviation of 4 minutes. The sample size was 25. The purpose of the simulation is to estimate the population mean waiting time.

   (a)   If the desired reliability of the estimate is 95 % and the estimate is to be within 1 minute of the true mean, how many more observations are required?

   (b)   With the same precision as in a, if the reliability is to be 90%, how many additional observations are needed?

   (c)   If the reliability is to be 90% but the precision is to be within 0.5 minutes, how many additional observations are needed?

15. A pilot run of a simulation resulted in an average waiting time per customer of 10 minutes with a sample standard deviation of 4 minutes. In addition, the average time in the system was 15 minutes with a sample standard deviation of 6 minutes. The precision on any estimate is to be within 0.5 minutes and the reliability is to be 95 %. If the sample size of the pilot run was 25 observations, how many additional observations are required to guarantee the precision and reliability of both estimates?

12

DYNAMIC PROGRAMMING: INTRODUCTION

12.1 DYNAMIC DECISION PROBLEMS

12.2 TERMINOLOGY AND BASIC CONCEPTS

12.3 AN INVENTORY PROBLEM

Specifications and Solution of the Problem
Some Comments on the Problem Formulation and Solution

12.4 A CAPITAL-BUDGETING PROBLEM

12.5 AN EQUIPMENT-REPLACEMENT PROBLEM

Problem Formulation and Solution
An Alternative Method of Solution
Discussion

12.6 SUMMARY

References
Review Questions
Problems
Appendix 12.1   Newton's Method for Solving Equations of a
Single Variable

Our discussion to this point has not involved time as an *essential* element in the decision problem. In the terminology of economics, we have dealt only with static problems as opposed to dynamic problems. The *decision problem* has been looked at as occurring at one instant in time. To be sure, when the decision alternative is a vector—for example, $\mathbf{X} = (X_1, X_2)$—we could have X_1 stand for the action *implemented* at one point in time and X_2 for the action implemented at another. But this would not be an essential incorporation of time into the problem because both decisions would be made *simultaneously*. Only when decisions on variables must be made sequentially rather than simultaneously is a problem truly dynamic.

If the future is known with certainty, all decisions can be made at a given instant in time and we have a static problem (incidentally involving time). Therefore, uncertainty is a necessary condition for a truly dynamic decision problem. Another necessary feature is that the random events must be interspersed, in time, with the opportunities to make decisions. (If this were not the case, the random event could be treated as a single event and the problem treated as a traditional static problem.) Finally, the realizations of past random events must have an effect on subsequent decisions. These three conditions are sufficient to characterize a dynamic problem.

12.1 DYNAMIC DECISION PROBLEMS

To illustrate the essential features of a dynamic decision situation, consider an inventory-stocking problem of a large multilocation convenience-store firm. The firm must determine the optimal stocking policy for the big-selling cola drink. The demand for the drink during a 1-week period is a random variable. Each Friday the soft drink supplier appears and the store manager must decide how many cases to order. Any inventory on hand when the supplier appears can be thought of as incurring an inventory carrying cost of $\$C_I$ per case on hand. If the supply is exhausted before Friday, demand must be turned away. Lost sales are assumed to have an opportunity cost of C_u per case.

Note that the problem described in the previous paragraph has the features of a dynamic problem. The random event—demand—is interspersed with the opportunity to make a decision. Clearly, the decision at any point in time—amount to stock—depends on the outcome that results from the previous decision and the realization of the random event. Thus, if inventory at the decision point is low because of high sales or a low stocking decision from the previous Friday, this will affect the optimal decision for the Friday in question. Also, the existence of inventory carrying over from one period to the next serves to link the periods and prevent a simultaneous solution for all future periods of a planning horizon.

The method of *dynamic programming* was developed to deal with dynamic decision problems. It is essentially a computing *philosophy* and organizing method that can be applied to dynamic problems with widely varying structures. Whereas linear programming refers to the algorithms—or specific computing procedures—for solving a problem with a very special mathematical structure—a linear objective function and linear constraints—dynamic programming is an *approach* that can be applied to linear as well as nonlinear problems, concave or convex functions, or functions that are neither concave nor convex.

The approach of dynamic programming can also be used to solve problems that are not inherently dynamic. In fact, *any* decision problem can be solved using dynamic programming and, in this sense, dynamic programming is very general. But as with all general approaches, we may find that although specific problems could be solved using the general technique, frequently they are more expeditiously solved with a technique that takes advantage of the specific structure of the problem being solved.

In this chapter, we will leave out uncertainty in all discussions. By neglecting uncertainty, we will be able to illustrate more clearly the major features of the approach without overly burdensome calculations. Also, since dynamic programming, more than most approaches to decision problems, is learned by example and experience, we will introduce a significant number of problem situations in this chapter.

12.2　TERMINOLOGY AND BASIC CONCEPTS

The terminology of dynamic programming reflects its origin as a set of concepts and procedures for finding solutions to time-dependent decision problems. Models are formulated for solving *sequential* decision problems in *stages*. At each stage of solution a *policy* is developed that relates the *state* of the system to the decision variable. The decision variable then determines how the system will move from one state to another between stages. Thus the states of the system at successive stages are related by the policy function.

The solution of a dynamic programming problem involves determination of a policy function for *each stage* in the decision sequence. For example the policy function—say, $X_t = h(I_{t-1})$—relates the order quantity (the decision variable X_t) to the inventory level entering the stage (the stage variable I_{t-1}) via a function $h(\cdot)$. The successive states in stages $t - 1$ and t are then related via $I_t = I_{t-1} + X_t - d_t$ where d_t is the demand in period t.

Note that the policy function does not prescribe an unconditional decision for stage t. Instead, it prescribes the decision *conditional* on the state of the system. Intuitively one might guess the nature of the policy function for inventory problems to be such that as I_{t-1} increased X_t would decrease; that is, the policy function should prescribe that the order quantity be decreased as the inventory on hand increased.

Clearly the nature of the optimal policy function depends on the measure of effectiveness selected for the problem. Once the measure of effectiveness has been determined, the optimal policy function can be determined. Once the optimal policy function is determined it can be applied for any state that arises in the course of the decision-making process.

Given the measure of effectiveness the *principle of optimality* governs the development of the optimal policy. The principle of optimality can be stated: "An optimal policy has the property that whatever the initial state and initial decision are, the remaining decisions must constitute an optimal policy with regard to the state resulting from the first decision."[1] This *principle* guides the development of the computing procedure for determination of an optimal policy.

The usual procedure for implementing the principle of optimality is to work "backward" from the last stage—that is, first find the optimal policy for stage *n*. The policy depends only on the state of the system at stage *n* and not on the preceding states or decisions, so this stage-*n* decision problem can be solved separately from the decision problems at preceding stages. Next the optimal policy for stage *n* can be used to determine the optimal policy for stage $n - 1$. Then the optimal policy for stage $n - 1$ can be used to determine the optimal policy for $n - 2$. The solution process then proceeds "backward" in this manner with the optimal policy at any state $t = j$ being directly dependent on the optimal policy at $t = j + 1$ (and not the optimal policy at $t < j$ or $t > j + 1$). Thus the principle of optimality allows the organization of an efficient procedure for computing solutions.

The final concept is that of a *recurrence relationship*. This concept relates the cost (or profit) for stage *t* and beyond to the optimal cost for stage $t + 1$ and beyond and the cost of a policy in stage *t*. The recurrence relation stands at the heart of the solution procedure. Because the concept is complicated it will be introduced in the examples that follow.

Note that the terms and concepts discussed here are easily translated into common business usage. The concept of policy in dynamic programming has exactly the same meaning as the concept of policy used by business organizations. A policy is a rule that indicates how you are to proceed under various circumstances. For example, a policy on capital expenditures for a firm may be to let department managers make decisions so long as the project earns more than 15% and calls for less than a $2000 expenditure. If the expenditure is for more than $2000, the board of directors must consider it; if the expenditure is less than $2000, a management committee must consider it. These rules tell the department managers how they are to behave under various circumstances, which are the states.

Now let us use the concepts of stage, state, policy, the recurrence relationship, and the principle of optimality in solving some problems.

12.3 AN INVENTORY PROBLEM

Specifications and Solution of the Problem

Consider an inventory-stocking problem by a manufacturing firm in which a part is purchased to be included in the assembly of an expensive electronic hand-held calculator. The part is essential to the assembly of the calculators and if a stock-out

[1] R.E. Bellman and S.E. Dreyfus, *Applied Dynamic Programming*, Princeton: Princeton University Press, 1962, p. 15.

occurs, production will stop. Each time an order is placed on the supplier of the part, a significant expenditure in terms of order preparation, expediting, incoming inspection, and testing is incurred. This fixed cost per order is C_o. Furthermore, the item carries a price of C_p and the cost to carry inventory is kC_p per unit on hand at the end of the period. The stock-out cost per unit C_u is assumed infinite reflecting the desire of management never to run out of stock.

Demand over the next 10 weeks is known with certainty because the production schedule is established. Following the 10-week period, the item will not be produced for 6 weeks because of model changes. Therefore, the 10-week period can be considered to be the planning horizon.

Let X_t, $t = 1, \ldots, 10$ be the purchases from the supplier for each of the 10 subsequent weeks. Let d_t, $t = 1, \ldots, 10$ be the demands for the part during the subsequent weeks and let I_t, $t = 1, \ldots, 10$ be the end of period inventory. Then the total cost for the 10-week horizon could be written as

$$C(X_1, \ldots, X_{10}) = \sum_{t=1}^{10} C_o \delta(X_t) + \sum_{t=1}^{10} kC_p I_t \qquad (12.1)$$

where

$$\delta(X_t) = \begin{cases} 1 & X_t > 0 \\ 0 & X_t \leq 0 \end{cases} \qquad (12.2)$$

The problem facing the decision maker is then $\underset{\mathbf{X}}{\text{Min}}\, C(\mathbf{X})$ subject to $X_t \geq 0$, $I_t = I_{t-1} + X_t - d_t \geq 0$ for $t = 1, \ldots, 10$.

To solve the problem use the "backward" procedure. Suppose that X_1, $X_2, \ldots, X_9$ have been selected and we are about to make a decision on X_{10}. The results of the first 9 decisions are embedded in the inventory on hand—the state of the system—at the end of period 9. It is

$$I_9 = I_o + \sum_{t=1}^{9} X_t - \sum_{t=1}^{9} d_t \qquad (12.3)$$

If I_9 were known upon entering the 10th period, the problem facing the decision maker would be to select X_{10} so as to minimize the cost for the single remaining period. The cost for the 10th period depends on the entering inventory I_9 and the decision X_{10}. It is

$$g_{10}(X_{10}, I_9) = C_o \delta(X_{10}) + kC_p(I_9 + X_{10} - d_{10}) \qquad (12.4)$$

The minimum of $g_{10}(X_{10}, I_9)$ is obtained by $X_{10} = d_{10} - I_9$ if $I_9 < d_{10}$ and $X_{10} = 0$ if $I_9 \geq d_o$. Thus, the *optimal policy* for the 10th period will be

$$X_{10}(I_9) = \begin{cases} d_{10} - I_9 & I_9 < d_{10} \\ 0 & I_9 \geq d_{10} \end{cases} \qquad (12.5)$$

The cost of carrying out the optimal policy for period 10 will be

$$f_{10}(I_9) = \underset{X_{10}}{\text{Min}}\, g_{10}(X_{10}, I_9) = \begin{cases} C_o & I_9 < d_{10} \\ kC_p(I_9 - d_{10}) & I_9 \geq d_{10} \end{cases} \qquad (12.6)$$

which is a function of the inventory held when entering period 10.

Table 12.1 Optimal Policy and Cost of the Optimal Policy for Period 10

I_9	$X_{10}(I_9)$	$f_{10}(I_9)$
0	5	$2.00
1	4	2.00
2	3	2.00
3	2	2.00
4	1	2.00
5	0	.00

Even though we have barely begun to develop the solution technique for this problem, it is worthwhile to begin an example to illustrate the way in which the technique works. Let $C_o = \$2.00$, $C_p = \$10.00$, $k = 0.01$, and $(d_1, d_2, \ldots, d_{10}) = (15, 17, 20, 25, 30, 30, 30, 10, 5, 5)$. The initial inventory is $I_o = 8$.

Using these data, we can develop a table for decision making in the final period. Table 12.1 shows the optimal policy and the minimum cost for a variety of inventory levels. In the table, $X_{10}(I_9)$ is determined from (12.5) and $f_{10}(I_9)$ from (12.6).

Given that we know what to do in period 10 for *any* entering inventory, we can proceed to the problem of developing the optimal policy and cost for period 9. The cost for the *last* two periods is

$$g_9(X_9, I_8) = C_o \delta(X_9) + kC_p(I_8 + X_9 - d_9) + f_{10}(I_8 + X_9 - d_9) \quad (12.7)$$

Note that we have defined $g_9(X_9, I_8)$ as the cost for two periods and have written it as the sum of the cost in period 9 plus the *minimum* cost in period 10 if we enter that period with $I_8 + X_9 - d_9$ in inventory.

We will then define

$$f_9(I_8) = \operatorname*{Min}_{X_9} g_9(X_9, I_8) \quad (12.8)$$

as the lowest cost achievable for the last two periods if entering inventory is I_8.

The optimal policy for period 9 must be computed using (12.7). Table 12.2 shows the value of (12.7) for various values of I_8 and X_9. Consider first the case where $I_8 = 0$. The table shows that any value of X_9 less than 5 will be infeasible because inventory at the end of period 9 will be negative. Next, note that when $X_9 = 5$, a $2.00 ordering cost is incurred in period 9. Then, because demand in period 9 is 5, the ending inventory is $I_9 = 0$, with which we enter period 10. Table 12.1 then indicates that the optimal policy for period 10 with $I_9 = 0$ has a cost of $2.00. Thus, the sum of the costs for the last two periods is shown in column 6 as $4.00, which is the sum of columns 4 and 5. Now, proceeding in this manner, the

Table 12.2 Evaluation of $g_9(X_9, I_8)$ for Various Values of I_8 and I_9

1	2	3 Ending Inventory	4 Cost for Period 9	5 Optimal Cost for Period 10	6
I_8	X_9	$I_8 + X_9 - 5$	$2\delta(X_9) + 0.10(I_8 + X_9 - 5)$	$f_{10}(I_8 + X_9 - d_9)$	$g_9(X_9, I_8)$
0	0	-5	Not feasible because ending inventory is negative		
0	1	-4	Not feasible because ending inventory is negative		
0	2	-3	Not feasible because ending inventory is negative		
0	3	-2	Not feasible because ending inventory is negative		
0	4	-1	Not feasible because ending inventory is negative		
0	5	0	$2.00	$2.00	$4.00
0	6	1	2.10	2.00	4.10
0	7	2	2.20	2.00	4.20
0	8	3	2.30	2.00	4.30
0	9	4	2.40	2.00	4.40
0	10*	5	2.50	0.00	2.50
0	11	6	2.60	0.10	2.70
0	12	7	2.70	0.20	2.90
1	4	0	2.00	2.00	4.00
1	5	1	2.10	2.00	4.10
1	6	2	2.20	2.00	4.20
⋮	⋮	⋮	⋮	⋮	⋮
1	9*	5	2.50	0.00	2.50
1	10	6	2.60	0.10	2.70
⋮					
⋮					
5	0*	0	0.00	2.00	2.00
5	1	1	2.10	2.00	4.10
⋮	⋮	⋮		⋮	⋮
5	5	5	2.50	0.00	2.50
⋮	⋮	⋮		⋮	⋮

Table 12.2 (*continued*)

1	2	3 Ending Inventory $I_8 + X_9 - 5$	4 Cost for Period 9 $2\delta(X_9) + 0.10(I_8 + X_9 - 5)$	5 Optimal Cost for Period 10 $f_{10}(I_8 + X_9 - d_9)$	6
I_8	X_9				$g_9(X_9, I_8)$
6	0*	1	0.10	2.00	2.10
6	1	2	2.20	2.00	4.20
⋮	⋮	⋮	⋮	⋮	⋮
6	4	5	2.50	0.00	2.50
⋮	⋮	⋮	⋮	⋮	⋮
⋮	⋮	⋮	⋮	⋮	⋮
10	0*	5	0.50	0.00	0.50
10	1	6	2.60	0.10	2.70
10	2	7	2.70	0.20	2.90
⋮	⋮	⋮	⋮	⋮	⋮
⋮	⋮	⋮	⋮	⋮	⋮

cost for the last two periods can be evaluated for $X_9 = 6, 7, \ldots$, as shown in Table 12.2. The cost for the last two periods is minimized when $X_9 = 10$ and is denoted by an asterisk (*). This line, which is the optimal policy for $I_8 = 0$, is transferred to Table 12.3 where the cost of the optimal policy for period 9 is summarized.

Table 12.2 also contains the calculations necessary for determining the optimal policy for the cases where $I_8 = 1$, $I_8 = 5$, $I_8 = 6$, and $I_8 = 10$. For these cases, a substantial number of lines have been left out to save space. For example, with $I_8 = 1$, there is no need to consider $X_9 < 4$ because such cases would produce an infeasible solution. Furthermore, any $X_9 > 9$ would mean ordering more than was needed for the remainder of the horizon (because $d_9 + d_{10} = 10$), which cannot be optimal. Note that for $I_8 = 5, 6$, and 10, the optimal policy is to make $X_9 = 0$. A quick glance at the table yields the following intuitive description of the optimal policy: if inventory is less than the demand in period 9, order enough for the last two periods. If inventory is greater than that needed for period 9, do not order in period 9.

Table 12.3 contains the optimal policy for period 9 along with the cost of the optimal policy for the *remaining two periods*. We have not extended the table beyond $I_8 = 10$ because entering inventory greater than 10 would be extremely undesirable—there would be inventory left over at the end of the horizon. Thus, it is likely that we will not need entries in the table with $I_8 > 10$.

Table 12.3 Optimal Policy for Period 9 and the Cost of the Optimal Policy for Periods 9–10

I_8	$X_9(I_8)$	$f_9(I_8)$
0	10	$2.50
1	9	2.50
2	8	2.50
3	7	2.50
4	6	2.50
5	0	2.00
6	0	2.10
7	0	2.20
8	0	2.30
9	0	2.40
10	0	0.50

Now we can move on to determine the optimal policy for period 8 given the inventory I_7. Clearly, the cost for the last three periods is

$$g_8(X_8, I_7) = C_o \delta(X_8) + k C_p(I_7 + X_8 - d_8) + f_9(I_7 + X_8 - d_8) \quad (12.9)$$

and the optimal cost is

$$f_8(I_7) = \underset{X_8}{\text{Min}}\, g_8(X_8, I_7) \quad (12.10)$$

which is used to produce the policy contained in Table 12.4.

Instead of developing a table similar to Table 12.2 in which $g_8(X_8, I_7)$ is evaluated, we will show some example calculations and skip some of the detail. For the case $I_7 = 0$, we must evaluate $g_8(X_8, 0)$ for various values of X_8. Because $d_8 = 10$ only $X_8 \geq 10$ need be evaluated. Using (12.9) and Table 12.3 for determining $f_9(I_8)$, $g_8(10,\ 0) = 2.00 + 0 + 2.50 = 4.50$, $g_8(11,\ 0) = 2.00 + 0.10 + 2.50 = 4.60, \ldots,$ $g_8(15,\ 0) = 2.00 + 0.50 + 2.00 = 4.50, \ldots,$ $g_8(20,\ 0) = 2.00 + 1.00 + 0.50 = 3.50$. Thus, the optimal decision for $I_7 = 0$ is $X_8(0) = 20$ and $f_8(0) = 3.50$. Thus, line 1 of Table 12.4 is produced from these comparisons. Next, skip down to the line for $I_7 = 10$ and evaluate some possibilities for $X_7(10)$. Here $g_8(0,\ 10) = 0 + 0 + 2.50 = 2.50$, $g_8(1,\ 10) = 2.00 + 0.10 + 2.50 = 4.60, \ldots,$ $g_8(10, 10) = 2.00 + 1.00 + 0.50 = 3.50$ and the optimal decision is $X_8(10) = 0$ and $f_8(10) = 2.50$. Table 12.4 shows the optimal policy for period 7.

Instead of showing the detailed calculations for the remaining periods ($t = 7, 6, 5, 4, 3, 2, 1$), we will state the general formulation of the problem at any stage. The cost function is

$$g_t(X_t, I_{t-1}) = C_o \delta(X_t) + k C_p(I_{t-1} + X_t - d_t) + f_{t+1}(I_{t-1} + X_t - d_t) \quad (12.11)$$

Table 12.4 Optimal Policy for Period 8 and the
Cost of the Optimal Policy for Periods
8–10

I_7	$X_8(I_7)$	$f_8(I_9)$	I_7	$X_8(I_7)$	$f_8(I_7)$
0	20	3.50	11	0	2.60
1	19	3.50	12	0	2.70
2	18	3.50	13	0	2.80
3	17	3.50	14	0	2.90
4	16	3.50	15	0	2.50
5	15	3.50	16	0	2.70
6	14	3.50	17	0	2.90
7	13	3.50	18	0	3.10
8	12	3.50	19	0	3.30
9	11	3.50	20	0	1.50
10	0	2.50			

and

$$f_t(I_{t-1}) = \operatorname*{Min}_{X_t} g_t(X_t, I_{t-1}) \tag{12.12}$$

Substituting (12.11) into (12.12) produces the *recurrence relation*

$$f_t(I_{t-1}) = \operatorname*{Min}_{X_t} [C_o \delta(X_t) + kC_p(I_{t-1} + X_t - d_t) + f_{t+1}(I_{t-1} + X_t - d_t)]$$

Note that the function $f_t(\cdot)$ appears on the left-hand side of the relationship and $f_{t+1}(\cdot)$ appears on the right.

Tables 12.5 to 12.11 show the optimal policies for the remaining periods $(t = 7, 6, 5, 4, 3, 2, 1)$. They are computed using (12.11) and (12.12). Table 12.11 is constructed with only one line because the inventory in existence at the beginning of the horizon is known: $I_o = 8$.

Table 12.11 and its predecessors can now be used to write down the solution to the inventory problem stated at the beginning of this section. To see how the optimal solution is developed, consider first Table 12.11, which states that in period 1 it is optimal to order 24 units. This means that with demand for 15 units in period 1, there will be 17 units left over when entering period 2. Table 12.10 then indicates that the optimal policy to follow for period 2 is to order zero. Because demand in period 2 is 17, inventory would be completely depleted by the beginning of period 3. Table 12.9 then shows that 20 units should be ordered or just enough for the demand for period 3. Tables 12.8, 12.7, 12.6 then show that for periods 4, 5, and 6 exactly the amount demanded should be ordered. Finally, we would enter period 7 with zero units in inventory and the optimal policy would be to order 50

Table 12.5   Optimal Policy for Period 7 and the Cost of the Optimal Policy for Periods 7–10

I_6	$X_7(I_6)$	$f_7(I_6)$	I_6	$X_7(I_6)$	$f_7(I_6)$
0–29	$50-I_6$	$5.50	41	0	$3.70
30	0	3.50	42	0	3.90
31	0	3.60	43	0	4.10
32	0	2.70	44	0	4.30
33	0	3.90	45	0	4.00
35	0	4.10	46	0	4.30
36	0	4.30	47	0	4.60
37	0	4.50	48	0	4.90
38	0	4.70	49	0	5.20
39	0	4.90	50	0	2.50
40	0	3.50			

Table 12.6   Optimal Policy for Period 6 and the Cost of the Optimal Policy for Periods 6–10

I_5	$X_6(I_5)$	$f_6(I_5)$	I_5	$X_6(I_5)$	$f_6(I_5)$
0–29	$30-I_5$	$7.50	70	0	$7.50
30	0	5.50	71	0	7.80
31	0	5.60	⋮	⋮	⋮
32	0	5.70	74	0	8.70
⋮	⋮	⋮	75	0	8.50
59	0	8.40	76	0	8.90
60	0	6.50	⋮	⋮	⋮
61	0	6.70	79	0	10.10
⋮	⋮	⋮	80	0	7.50
69	0	8.80			

Table 12.7 Optimal Policy for Period 5 and the Cost of the Optimal Policy for Periods 5–10

I_4	$X_5(I_4)$	$f_5(I_4)$	I_4	$X_5(I_4)$	$f_5(I_4)$
0–29	$30-I_4$	$9.50	⋮	⋮	⋮
30	0	7.50	99	0	$15.70
31	0	7.60	100	0	14.50
⋮	⋮	⋮	101	0	14.90
59	0	10.40	⋮	⋮	⋮
60	0	8.50	104	0	16.10
61	0	8.70	105	0	16.00
⋮	⋮	⋮	106	0	16.50
89	9	14.30	⋮	⋮	⋮
90	0	12.50	109	0	18.00
91	0	12.80	110	0	15.50

Table 12.8 Optimal Policy for Period 4 and the Cost of the Optimal Policy for Periods 4–10

I_3	$X_4(I_3)$	$f_4(I_3)$	I_3	$X_4(I_3)$	$f_4(I_3)$
0–24	$25-I_3$	$11.50	116	0	$21.90
25	0	9.50	⋮	⋮	⋮
26	0	9.60	124	0	25.60
27	0	9.70	125	0	24.50
⋮	⋮	⋮	126	0	25.00
54	0	12.40	⋮	⋮	⋮
55	0	10.50	129	0	26.50
56	0	10.70	130	0	26.50
⋮	⋮	⋮	131	0	27.10
84	0	16.30	⋮	⋮	⋮
85	0	14.50	134	0	28.90
⋮	⋮	⋮	135	0	26.00
114	0	23.20			
115	0	21.50			

Table 12.9 Optimal Policy for Period 3 and the Cost
of the Optimal Policy for Periods 3–10

I_2	$X_3(I_2)$	$f_3(I_2)$	I_2	$X_3(I_2)$	$f_3(I_2)$
0–19	20–I_2	13.50	134	0	34.60
20	0	11.50	135	0	33.00
21	0	11.60	136	0	33.70
⋮	⋮	⋮	⋮	⋮	⋮
44	0	13.40	144	0	38.00
45	0	12.00	145	0	37.00
46	0	12.20	146	0	37.60
⋮	⋮	⋮	⋮	⋮	⋮
74	0	17.80	149	0	39.40
75	0	16.00	150	0	39.50
76	0	16.30	151	0	40.20
⋮	⋮	⋮	⋮	⋮	⋮
104	0	24.70	154	0	42.30
105	0	23.00	155	0	39.50
⋮	⋮	⋮			

units—enough to satisfy demand in periods 7, 8, 9, and 10. Table 12.12 shows the optimal solution along with the inventory for each period and the cost incurred in each period.

Some Comments on the Problem Formulation and Solution

The inventory problem we just completed may seem an ill-chosen introduction to the technique of dynamic programming because the mass of calculations required tends to obscure the simplicity of the calculating procedure. But the problem provides rich insights into the virtues and pitfalls of the use of dynamic programming in business applications.

The solution procedure we used in producing Tables 12.1 to 12.11 illustrates the concept of a *policy*—that is, $X_t(I_{t-1})$—in that each table shows the amount to order given the entering inventory level. While these tables were only vehicles to developing the optimal solution to our problem, they are intuitively compatible with the way in which businesses operate on a day-to-day basis—with rules or policies to guide action.

The policy tables also assist in further analysis. Suppose that we developed the optimal solution as described in the last section and then implemented the policy.

Table 12.10 Optimal Policy for Period 2 and the Cost of the Optimal Policy for Periods 2–10

I_1	$X_2(I_1)$	$f_2(I_1)$	I_1	$X_2(I_1)$	$f_2(I_1)$
	$17 - I_1$	\$14.50			
0–16	or				
	$37 - I_1$	14.50	121	0	\$35.00
17	0	13.50	122	0	33.50
18	0	13.60	⋮	⋮	⋮
⋮	⋮	⋮	151	0	48.00
36	0	15.40	152	0	46.50
37	0	13.50	153	0	47.30
38	0	13.60	⋮	⋮	⋮
⋮	⋮	⋮	161	0	52.40
61	0	17.30	162	0	51.50
62	0	16.50	163	0	52.50
63	0	16.80	⋮	⋮	⋮
⋮	⋮	⋮	166	0	54.30
91	0	25.20	167	0	54.50
92	0	23.50	168	0	55.30
93	0	23.90	⋮	⋮	⋮
⋮	⋮	⋮	171	0	55.70
			172	0	55.00

Also assume periods 1–7 passed without a "hitch." Then suppose that before the order was placed in period 8, a fire destroyed 4 of the units in inventory reducing the on-hand inventory to 16 units. What policy should be followed? Table 12.4 can now be used to find the *optimal* policy for periods 8, 9, and 10 given the fire loss. From it we see that 0 units should be ordered and that the cost for the last three periods will be \$2.70. Before the fire, the optimal policy called for 20 units in

Table 12.11 Optimal Policy for Period 1 and the Cost of the Optimal Policy for Periods 1–10

I_o	$X_1(I_o)$	$f_1(I_o)$
8	24	\$17.20

inventory on hand. Table 12.4 shows that the cost for the last three periods would have been \$1.50 had the fire not occurred but was \$2.70 after the fire. Thus, the result of the fire was to increase costs by \$1.20 (plus the cost of the units lost). Had 18 units been destroyed by fire, the optimal policy from Table 12.4 would be to order 18 units at an added cost of \$2.00 (\$3.50 − \$1.50).

The discussion of the revision of the plan after the fire emphasizes the meaning of the policy described in Table 12.4 (or any table) and the meaning of the principle of optimality. No matter what has happened before period 8, the *policy* given by the table is optimal for the remaining periods of the horizon. If the decision is made not to follow the optimal policy in an earlier period, the table shows what should be done to ensure that the remaining decisions will minimize the costs over the remaining period.

Let us look at one more response to a deviation from the solution expressed in Table 12.12. Suppose that for unknown reasons, 47 units were ordered for period 3 instead of 20. By how much would cost increase because of this deviation from plan? What would the optimal response be to this deviation? First note that by ordering 47 instead of 20 as called for, there would be 27 additional units in inventory at the end of period 3. Cost would increase by \$2.70 in period 3 because of this additional 27 units in inventory. Then period 4 would be entered with 27 units in inventory instead of 0. Table 12.8 shows that entering with 27 units would produce costs for periods 4–10 of \$9.70 as opposed to \$11.50, which would be the cost in the optimal plan of ordering 20 in period 3 (and ending with 0 units in inventory). Thus, the total *increase* in costs because of the deviation would be \$2.70 + \$9.70 − \$11.50 = \$0.90. Now to answer the second question. Table 12.12 shows an order of 25 in period 4; Table 12.13 shows an order of 0. Period 5 is modified slightly, and by the end of period 5 the correction is complete and the optimal policy of Table 12.12 is resumed.

We turn now from the managerial usefulness of the dynamic programming formulation to some computational aspects of it. The problem we used involved a significantly large number of calculations. There were a large number of lines to each of the tables. We cut off the length of the tables by the following reasoning: Table 12.1 for period 10 contained only 5 entries because an inventory greater than

Table 12.12 Optimal Solution for the Inventory Problem

t	1	2	3	4	5	6	7	8	9	10	Total
I_{t-1}	8	17	0	0	0	0	0	20	10	5	
$X_t(I_{t-1})$	24	0	20	25	30	30	50	0	0	0	
d_t	15	17	20	25	30	30	30	10	5	5	
I_t	17	0	0	0	0	0	20	10	5	0	
Cost for period t	\$3.70	0.00	2.00	2.00	2.00	2.00	4.00	1.00	0.50	0.00	17.20

Table 12.13 Optimal Response to Nonoptimal Order of 47 Units in Period 3

t	1	2	3	4	5	6	7	8	9	10	Total
I_{t-1}	8	17	0	27	2	0	0	20	10	5	
$X_t(I_{t-1})$	24	0	47	0	28	30	50	0	0	0	
d_t	15	17	20	25	30	30	30	10	5	5	
I_t	17	0	27	2	0	0	20	10	5	0	
Cost for period t	\$3.70	0.00	4.70	0.20	2.00	2.00	4.00	1.00	0.50	0.00	18.10

5 upon entering period 10 would mean excess inventory left over beyond the horizon and this would be nonoptimal. Similarly, we limited each table to the total demand for the remaining periods of the horizon. Thus, for example, Table 12.5, which covered periods 7–10, was limited to 51 entries ($I_6 = 0$ to $I_6 = 50$). But this simple rule could have created no end of troubles if our problem had been, say, 20 periods or if we had demands greater than those used by, say, a factor of 10 (i.e., 150, 170, 200, etc.). Consider the case where there are 20 periods. If demand had averaged 18.7 for the 20 periods as it did for the 10, this would have meant the maximum entries in a table would be 375. Demands increased by a factor of 10 would have increased the table sizes by a factor of 10.

Because of the computational burdens we have just pointed out, it is important to look for characteristics of the problem that can be exploited to reduce calculations. For example, in the inventory problem, all of the lines for each table need not have been calculated had we thought out the structure of the problem more carefully. It can be easily established that it is never optimal to enter a period with inventory and also place an order during that period. This type of behavior would increase the carrying cost and at the same time not reduce the ordering cost. This concept then leads to the conclusion that order amounts should only be for an integral number of periods of demand. That is, at the beginning of period 7, the ordering possibilities are only 30 (for one period), 40 (for two periods), 45 (for three periods), or 50 (for four periods). Thus, inventory at the *end* of period 7 would only take on values of 0, 10, 15, or 20 and Table 12.4 could be reduced to only those entries. Likewise, Table 12.5 could be reduced to entering inventories of 0, 30, 40, 45, and 50; Table 12.6 to 0, 30, 60, 70, 75, 80; and so on.

By the procedure described in the previous paragraph, the "density" of the tables could be drastically reduced with many of the intervening lines eliminated. It is also possible to reduce some of the tables further by eliminating some of the remaining bottom lines of the tables. For example, consider Table 12.7 for period 5. If we entered period 5 with 110 units in inventory we would have enough to satisfy all remaining demand. Thus, the demand for period 10 would be on hand. Those 5 units for period 10 would accumulate carrying cost for periods 5–9 that would amount to $\$0.10 \times 5 \times 5 = \$2.50$. Clearly, it would be better to order the units for

Table 12.14a Reduced Policy Table for Period 10

I_9	$X_{10}(I_9)$	$f_{10}(I_9)$
0	5	$2.00
5	0	0.00

Table 12.14b Reduced Policy Table for Period 9

I_8	$X_9(I_8)$	$f_9(I_8)$
0	10	$2.50
5	0	2.00
10	0	0.50

Table 12.14c Reduced Policy Table for Period 8

I_9	$X_8(I_7)$	$f_8(I_7)$
0	20	$3.50
10	0	2.50
15	0	2.50
20	0	1.50

Table 12.14d Reduced Policy Table for Period 7

I_6	$X_7(I_6)$	$f_7(I_6)$
0	50	$5.50
30	0	3.50
40	0	3.50
45	0	4.00
50	0	2.50

Table 12.14e Reduced Policy Table for Period 6

I_5	$X_6(I_5)$	$f_6(I_5)$
0	30	$7.50
30	0	5.50

Table 12.14f Reduced Policy Table for Period 5

I_4	$X_5(I_4)$	$f_5(I_4)$
0	30	$9.50
30	0	7.50

Table 12.14g Reduced Policy Table for Period 4

I_3	$X_4(I_3)$	$f_4(I_2)$
0	25	$11.50
25	0	9.50

Table 12.14h Reduced Policy Table for Period 3

I_2	$X_3(I_2)$	$f_3(I_2)$
0	20	$13.50
20	0	11.50

Table 12.14i Reduced Policy Table for Period 2

I_1	$X_2(I_1)$	$f_2(I_1)$
0	17 or 37	$14.50
19	0	13.50
39	0	13.50

period 10 at a later point and incur a $2.00 charge than to incur carrying costs of $2.50. Thus, we need not consider the 110 line in Table 12.7. The 105 line would amount to carrying the demand for period 9 for four periods, and therefore it would not be possible to rule out the 105 line of Table 12.7 because the carrying charge and the ordering charge would be equal. Consider the demand of 10 units for period 8 that would be carried for three periods. This would be more costly than a later order so we can rule out the $I_4 = 90$ line as well as the $I_4 = 105$ since both could be satisfied with a future order.

Using reasoning similar to that described in the preceding paragraph, the policy tables can be drastically reduced, as shown in Tables 12.14a to 12.14i. These tables could now be used to develop the optimal solution with far less computing than we originally did to find the solution.

12.4 A CAPITAL-BUDGETING PROBLEM

A firm has allocated $100,000 for capital investments during the next year and wants to maximize the net return from that budget. Table 12.15 shows the classes of available projects, the number of projects in that class, the investment required per project, and the net return that would be available per project. The problem is to select projects so that the return is maximized.

$$\text{Max}_{\mathbf{x}} \sum_{j=1}^{5} R_j X_j \tag{12.13}$$

subject to

$$\sum_{j=1}^{5} V_j X_j \leq 100,000 \tag{12.14}$$

and

$$0 \leq X_j \leq L_j \qquad j = 1, \ldots, 5 \tag{12.15}$$

Table 12.15 Available Investment Projects

Project Class	Number of Projects Available	Investment per Projects	Net Return per Project
1	14	$6,000	$300
2	10	5,000	500
3	7	12,000	1,400
4	4	25,000	2,700
5	1	60,000	10,000

where $\mathbf{X} = (X_1, X_2, X_3, X_4, X_5)$ is a vector of integers representing the number of projects of each class selected, R_j is the net return for a project of class j, V_j is the investment per project, and L_j is the number of projects available in class j.

The problem may be structured for dynamic programming solution by letting θ_K be the budget left to be allocated to project classes numbered K or greater after the first $K - 1$ classes have been allocated. Thus, θ_5 represents the resources available to be allocated to project class 5 given that classes 1–4 have been allocated; θ_4 represents the resources available to be allocated to project classes 4 and 5 given that classes 1–3 have been allocated, etc. Finally, $\theta_1 = 100,000$.

The recurrence relationships may be written as

$$f_5(\theta_5) = \underset{X_5}{\text{Max}}\ (R_5 X_5 \,|\, V_5 X_5 \leq \theta_5 \text{ and } 0 \leq X_5 \leq 1) \tag{12.16}$$

where the constraints on the allocation are written after the slash in (12.19), and

$$f_4(\theta_4) = \underset{X_4}{\text{Max}}\ (R_4 X_4 + f_5(\theta_4 - V_4 X_4) \,|\, V_4 X_4 \leq \theta_4 \text{ and } 0 \leq X_4 \leq 4) \tag{12.17}$$

$$f_3(\theta_3) = \underset{X_3}{\text{Max}}\ (R_3 X_3 + f_4(\theta_3 - V_3 X_3) \,|\, V_3 X_3 \leq \theta_3 \text{ and } 0 \leq X_3 \leq 7) \tag{12.18}$$

$$f_2(\theta_2) = \underset{X_2}{\text{Max}}\ (R_2 X_2 + f_3(\theta_2 - V_2 X_2) \,|\, V_2 X_2 \leq \theta_2 \text{ and } 0 \leq X_2 \leq 10) \tag{12.19}$$

$$f_1(\theta_1) = \underset{X_1}{\text{Max}}\ (R_1 X_1 + f_2(\theta_1 - V_1 X_1) \,|\, V_1 X_1 \leq \theta_1 \text{ and } 0 \leq X_1 \leq 14) \tag{12.20}$$

Now tables may be developed using equations (12.17) to (12.20). Table 12.16 shows the optimal policy for class 5 when all other decisions have been made. The policy is simple depending only on whether or not there is enough budget left to

Table 12.16

θ_5	$X_5(\theta_5)$	$f_5(\theta_5)$
0–59,999	0	0
60,000–100,000	1	10,000

Table 12.17

θ_4	$X_4(\theta_4)$	$f_4(\theta_4)$
0–24,999	0	0
25,000–49,999	1	2,700
50,000–59,999	2	5,400
60,000–84,999	0	10,000
85,000–100,000	1	12,700

Table 12.18

θ_3	$X_3(\theta_3)$	$f_3(\theta_3)$
0–11,999	0	0
12,000–23,999	1	1,400
24,000–24,999	2	2,800
25,000–35,999	2	2,800
36,000–47,999	3	4,200
48,000–59,999	4	5,600
60,000–71,999	0	10,000
72,000–83,999	1	11,400
84,000–96,999	2	12,800
97,000–100,000	3	14,200

include a unit of class 5. Table 12.17 represents a more elaborate calculation. Clearly, if $0 \le \theta_4 \le 24,999$, the optimal solution is $X_4 = 0$. No calculations are needed. But if $25,000 \le \theta_4 \le 49,999$, then we must evaluate the following problem:

$$\text{Max } 2,700X_4 + f_5(\theta - 25,000X_4) \qquad (12.21)$$
$$X_4$$

subject to

$$25,000X_4 \le \theta_4 \qquad (12.22)$$

$$X_4 \le 4 \qquad (12.23)$$

X_4 is an integer.

Clearly, X_4 can take on only values of 0 or 1 and each must be evaluated. For $X_4 = 0$ we have $2,700(0) + f_5[\theta - 25,000(0)] = 0 + 0 = 0$ and for $X_4 = 1$, $2,700(1) + f_5(\theta - 25,000) = 2,700 + 0 = 2,700$. Therefore, $X_4 = 1$ is the optimal decision for $25,000 \le \theta_4 \le 49,999$. If $50,000 \le \theta_4 \le 59,999$, the problem has the same structure as (12.24) to (12.26), but X_4 can take on values of 0, 1, or 2; evaluating these yields $2,700(0) + f_5(\theta - 25,000) = 0$ for $X_4 = 0$, $2,700(1) + f_5[\theta - 25,000(1)] = 2,700$ for $X_4 = 1$, and $2,700(2) + f_5[\theta - 25,000(2)] = 5,400$ for $X_4 = 2$. Therefore, the optimal policy for $50,000 \le \theta_4 \le 59,999$ is $X_4 = 2$ and $f_4(\theta_4) = 5,400$. The remaining entries in Table 12.17 are determined by a similar procedure, as are the entries in Tables 12.18, 12.19, and 12.20.

Given the tables, it is now possible to start with Table 12.20 and write down the optimal solution. From Table 12.20, $X_1 = 0$, and therefore the budget left for stages 2–5 is \$100,000. Entering Table 12.19 with $\theta_2 = \$100,000$ yields $X_2 = 0$ as the optimal solution, again leaving \$100,000 for stages 3–5. Entering Table 12.18 with $\theta_3 = \$100,000$ yields $X_3 = 3$ as the optimal solution. This means

Table 12.19

θ_2	$X_2(\theta_2)$	$f_2(\theta_2)$
0–4,999	0	0
5,000–9,999	1	500
10,000–11,999	2	1,000
12,000–16,999	0	1,400
17,000–21,999	1	1,900
22,000–24,999	2	2,400
25,000–29,999	0	2,800
30,000–34,999	1	3,300
35,000–35,999	2	3,800
36,000–40,999	0	4,200
41,000–45,999	1	4,700
46,000–47,999	2	5,200
48,000–52,999	0	5,600
53,000–57,999	1	6,100
58,000–59,999	2	6,600
60,000–64,999	0	10,000
65,000–69,999	1	10,500
70,000–71,999	2	11,000
72,000–76,999	0	11,400
77,000–81,999	1	11,900
82,000–83,999	2	12,400
84,000–88,999	0	12,800
89,000–93,999	1	13,300
94,000–96,999	2	13,800
97,000–100,000	0	14,200

Table 12.20

θ_1	$X_1(\theta_1)$	$f_1(\theta_1)$
100,000	0	14,200

that $\theta_2 = \$100,000 - \$12,000(3) = \$64,000$ is available for stages 4–5. Table 12.17 shows that $X_4 = 0$ leaving $\theta_5 = \$64,000$ and, from Table 12.16, $X_5 = 1$. The optimal solution is $(X_1, X_2, X_3, X_4, X_5) = (0, 0, 3, 0, 1)$.

The problem we solved in this section could hardly be labeled dynamic. We did, however, use the stagewise procedure described in Section 12.2 for maximizing the function. Thus, the example serves to illustrate the applicability of the dynamic programming philosophy and methodology to problems that are simultaneous as opposed to dynamic.

12.5   AN EQUIPMENT-REPLACEMENT PROBLEM

Problem Formulation and Solution

The dynamic programming problems we have analyzed to this point have involved a finite number of stages. The inventory problem in Section 12.3 involved 10 stages and 10 decision variables and the investment problem was solved as one with 5 stages. Our approach to solution could be characterized as a "backward" approach because it started with the last stage—period 10 in the inventory problem—and worked backward to the first stage. This approach would obviously provide serious computational problems and would present conceptual difficulties if the horizon were unspecified. In this section, we introduce and solve a problem with an unspecified horizon.

Suppose Ace Manufacturing Company has a machine devoted completely to stamping washers. The machine allows the company to obtain revenues of $6,000 per year and has an initial cost of $K = \$12,000$. The yearly operating costs of the machine include labor, energy, maintenance, and minor repairs and are given by

$$C(t) = \$4000 + 50t \tag{12.24}$$

with the increase in costs as the machine ages accounted for by increased maintenance and idle time. The gross profit from the machine is also a function of time given by

$$P(t) = \$6000 - C(t) = 2000 - 50t \tag{12.25}$$

If the value of money to the company is 9% per year, there is no salvage value for the machine, and there appear to be no design changes forthcoming in the foreseeable future, how long should the company keep any one machine? To answer the question, we must think in terms of a *chain* of machines. The present machine will be replaced by a new model at some future point. The new machine will, in turn, be replaced by another machine further into the future, and so on. Thus, the problem can be thought of as a dynamic programming problem with an indefinite horizon. How could the problem be solved? One approach is to *iterate* to a solution. First, assume there is a single stage to the problem. That is, the machine will not be replaced after its optimal life. We could calculate the economic life for this case and call it T_1. Next, we could assume a two-stage horizon. This would constitute a single replacement followed by retirement. The optimal life of the *first machine in this chain* could then be determined and denoted as T_2. If $T_1 = T_2$, it would be reasonable to assume that we had calculated the optimal economic life of a machine in an indefinite chain. If the two lives were not equal, we could extend the horizon one stage further calculating T_3. If $T_2 = T_3$ then we would have found the optimal life. If not, the process could be extended further until $T_{n-1} = T_n$. Then, if it could be established that the economic lives for $n + 1$, $n + 2$, etc., would not change, we would have found the optimal replacement interval. This point should be reached in a reasonable number of steps.

To see how this approach would work, form the maximum present value of gross profits for a chain of n machines

$$V_n(T_n) = \max_{T_n} \left[-K + \int_0^{T_n} P(t)e^{-it}dt + e^{-iT_n}V_{n-1}(T_{n-1}) \right] \quad (12.26)$$

where n represents the number of machines in the chain with the last (as opposed to the present) machine labeled $n = 1$. The first two terms on the right-hand side of (12.26) represent the present value of gross profits for (the first machine) machine n. The third term is the present value of profits for the other $n - 1$ machines in the chain. The factor e^{-it} is the present value of expenditures made t periods from the present when the value of money is $100i\%$.

The maximum present value (12.26) is obtained when the expression in the brackets is maximized or when[2]

$$P(T_n)e^{-iT_n} - ie^{-iT_n}V_{n-1}(T_{n-1}) = 0 \quad (12.27)$$

or, because $P(T_n) = 2000 - 50T_n$ and $i = 0.09$, we have

$$T_n = \frac{2000 - iV_{n-1}(T_{n-1})}{50} \quad (12.28)$$

as the value of T_n that maximizes present value.

Now using $K = 12,000$, $i = 0.09$, and substituting (12.25) into (12.26), we obtain

$$V_n(T_n) = -12,000 + \int_0^{T_n} (2000 - 50t)e^{-0.09t}dt + e^{-0.09T_n}V_{n-1}(T_{n-1})$$

$$= -12,000 + 2000 \int_0^{T_n} e^{-0.09t}dt - 50 \int_0^{T_n} te^{-0.09t}dt + e^{-0.09T_n}V_{n-1}(T_{n-1})$$

$$= -12,000 + \frac{2000}{0.09}(1 - e^{-0.09T_n}) - \frac{50}{(0.09)^2}[e^{-0.09T_n}(-0.09T_n - 1) + 1]$$

$$+ e^{-0.09T_n}V_{n-1}(T_{n-1})$$

$$= 4049.38 - [16,049.38 - 555.56T_n - V_{n-1}(T_{n-1})]e^{-0.09T_n} \quad (12.29)$$

---

[2] In developing (12.27) the derivative $d/dT_n[\int_0^{T_n} P(t)e^{-0.09t}dt]$ must be found. To see how this derivative is determined, let $g(t) = P(t)e^{-0.09t}$ and then, by the fundamental theorem of integral calculus, $\int_0^{T_1} g(t)dt = G(T_1) - G(0)$ where G is the antiderivative of g. Now $d/dT_n[\int_0^{T_n} g(t)dt] = d/dT_n[G(T_n) - G(0)] = g(T_n)$. Therefore, $d/dT_n[\int_0^{T_n} P(t)e^{-it}dt] = P(T_n)e^{-iT_n}$.

Now (12.28) and (12.29) can be used recursively to calculate values of T_n and $V_n(T_n)$ for various values of n. To start assume $V_0(T_0) = 0$. Clearly, this is reasonable because it is the value of a chain of 0 machines. Then with this assumption, from (12.28),

$$T_1 = \frac{2000}{50} = 40$$

and from (12.29)

$$V_1(T_1) = 4049.38 - (16{,}049.38 - 555.56(40))e^{-0.09(40)}$$

$$= 4218.05$$

Thus, when there is a single machine it should be kept 40 years and will have a present value of \$4218.05. This result can now be used to develop the life of the first machine in a two-machine chain. Letting $n = 2$ and using the results for T_1 and $V_1(T_1)$ we have

$$T_2 = \frac{2000 - 0.09(4218.05)}{50}$$

$$= 32.41$$

and

$$V_2(T_2) = 4049.38 - [16{,}049.38 - 555.56(32.41) - 4218.05]e^{-0.09(32.41)}$$

$$= 4383.42$$

These calculations show that the first machine in a two-machine chain should be kept for 32.41 years and the value of the *two machines* will be \$4383.42.

Note the dynamic programming approach to the problem. We first asked how long the second machine in the chain should be kept. By the principle of optimality this decision was not dependent on how long the first machine was kept. Next we moved back to the first machine and using the optimal policy for the second machine we were able to calculate the optimal life of the first machine.

We can now use T_2 and $V_2(T_2)$ to calculate T_3 and $V_3(T_3)$—a three-machine chain—and T_4 and $V_4(T_4)$, etc. The results of these calculations are

$$T_3 = 32.1099, \; V_3(T_3) = 4392.48$$

$$T_4 = 32.0935, \; V_4(T_4) = 4392.99$$

$$T_5 = 32.0926, \; V_5(T_5) = 4393.02$$

$$T_6 = 32.0926, \; V_6(T_6) = 4393.02$$

In a chain of six machines there is no change in the optimal life of the first machine (machine 6), so the optimal policy is to replace the machine every 32.0926 years. If the process had been continued beyond $n = 6$ we would find that the life of the first machine (T_n) would continue to be 32.0926.

An Alternative Method of Solution

The concept of dynamic programming can be used to develop an alternative solution to the equipment-replacement problem. The alternative procedure recognizes that if the chain of machines is infinite, the lives of all machines in the chain will be equal. Therefore let $T^* = T_n^* = T_{n-1}^*$ and $V^* = V_n^*(T_n^*) = V_{n-1}^*(T_{n-1}^*)$. The optimal solution T^* has the property that

$$V^* = -k + \int_0^{T^*} P(t)e^{-it}dt + e^{-iT^*}V^* \tag{12.30}$$

The interpretation of (12.30) is simple. The value V^* on the left-hand side is the value of an infinite chain of machines headed by the first (or present) machine. This value is determined at time 0. The first two terms on the right-hand side represent the present value of the first machine in the chain, while the third term represents the present value of the second and subsequent machines. The third term needs further explanation. The value of the second at time T^* is V^* because at that time it is the value of an infinite chain of machines. The factor e^{-iT^*} discounts this time $-T^*$ value to the present.

Because V^* appears on both sides of (12.30) we can solve for V^* as a function of the single variable T^*. Then using standard methods of calculus the optimal T^* can be found. First solving (12.30) for V^* yields

$$V^* = \frac{-K + \int_0^{T^*} P(t)e^{-it}dt}{1 - e^{-iT^*}} \tag{12.31}$$

To find the optimal value of T^* the derivative of (12.31) is set to zero and solved. That is, we must calculate T^* when

$$\frac{dV^*}{dT^*} = \frac{P(T^*)e^{-iT^*}}{1 - e^{-iT^*}} - \frac{ie^{-iT^*}[-K + \int_0^{T^*}P(t)e^{-it}dt]}{(1 - e^{-iT^*})^2} = 0 \tag{12.32}$$

Making use of (12.29) and (12.25), (12.32) can be written as

$$(2000 - 50T^*)(1 - e^{-0.09T^*}) - 0.09[4049.38 - (16,049.38 - 555.56T^*)e^{-0.09T^*}] = 0 \tag{12.33}$$

which can be solved by Newton's method.[3] To this end, let

$$L(T^*) = 1635.56 - 50T^* - 555.56e^{-0.09T^*}$$

which is the left-hand side of (12.33) and

$$L'(T^*) = -50 + 50e^{-0.09T^*}$$

Then, letting $T^{*(j)}$ represent the jth estimate of T^*, we have

$$T^{*(j+1)} = T^{*(j)} - \frac{L(T^{*(j)})}{L'(T^{*(j)})} \tag{12.34}$$

---

[3] For those not familiar with Newton's method, Appendix 12.1 introduces the method.

Suppose we let $T^{*(0)} = 40$, which is the solution to the single-stage chain. Then

$$T^{*(1)} = 40 - \frac{-379.6242}{-48.6338} = 32.1942$$

$$T^{*(2)} = 32.1942 - \frac{-4.8016}{-47.2419} = 32.0926$$

$$T^{*(3)} = 32.0926 - \frac{-0.0013}{-47.2166} = 32.0926$$

Therefore, in three iterations, the problem is solved.

Discussion

The equipment-replacement problem presented a distinct contrast to the two previous examples of this chapter. Whereas those examples had a fixed number of stages, the equipment-replacement problem had an indefinite number of stages. In the first two examples we were interested in the policy to be followed at every stage. In the equipment-replacement problem we were interested in finding the optimal policy for any stage in the unbounded chain of machines.

The existence of a single policy in the replacement problem resulted from the fact that all future machines were identical. Had we discussed a problem where this "stationary" feature was not present, one optimal policy holding for all stages in the indefinite future would not have been possible.

The equipment-replacement problem also exhibits another feature that was not present in the preceding two examples: the optimal solution does not depend on a *state variable*, such as inventory level upon entering the stage. Indeed, the "policy" for any stage is simply the economic life of the machine for that stage. No variable resulting from the previous stage carries over and affects the optimal solution at the subsequent stage. The dynamic programming characteristics of the problem are exhibited in the recurrence relation (12.26).

The solutions to the individual stages of the equipment-replacement problem exhibit some interesting properties. Note that with a single stage $T_1 = 40$. Then as more stages are added, the optimal life of the first machine in the chain decreases. There is an intuitive explanation to this result. For the case of a single stage, we may imagine the firm going out of business when the machine is retired. How long should it be kept in this instance? An answer might be until every last bit of profit has been wrung out of it. Note that that is exactly what is done because the machine is held for 40 years and for $T > 40$ the operating profit in that year would be negative. This leads to the question: why should, say, the first machine in a two-stage process not be kept 40 years? The answer is that eventually the machine will reach a point where its inferiority over a new model will be such that it is better to replace the machine with the new model. Replacing the machine will require an expenditure of $12,000 some years earlier than would be required if the machine were kept 40 years. Therefore, there will be an opportunity loss resulting from making the expenditure early. If, however, that loss allows a greater benefit to be made in operating efficiency, then it will be worthwhile. This is what happens.

Another aspect of the two solution procedures is significant. Using the first approach, which is the straightforward dynamic programming approach, we found that at stage 6 the policies converged. Thus we had to develop six policies before we found the policy for an indefinite horizon. This revealed some economic characteristics of the various stages that we discussed in the previous paragraph. If it had taken 25 stages to obtain convergence, we would have been unhappy with the computational aspects of the approach. On the other hand, the second approach obtained the optimal policy for an indefinite horizon without computing it for all the successive stages. In fact, through that approach, we did not know how many stages would be needed for convergence. We took advantage of a property of the optimal solution to obtain it. The first approach is to be termed *policy iteration*. The second approach is termed *value iteration*.

12.6 SUMMARY

A short introductory discussion of dynamic programming such as presented in this chapter has its disadvantages. While the examples presented may seem understandable, the first different application you try may lead to troubles. This phenomenon frequently occurs because we have discussed a *method* as opposed to a *procedure* for solving certain kinds of problems. A large number of problems can be solved as dynamic programming problems. All we have to do is succeed in formulating them as such. This is in contrast to the linear programming procedure, which works only for a very specific problem structure. Also, the linear programming procedure can be followed rather mechanically and many computer programs exist. In contrast, dynamic programming problems are, figuratively speaking, all unique, and therefore no widely used computer programs are available.

A number of concepts have been introduced in our discussion of the three main examples. Table 12.21 lists the main concepts and their realization in each of the examples. The policy statement is a function relating the *state variable* to the decision. The state variable is the inventory on hand and the budget remaining in the inventory and investment examples. The state variable could be considered not to exist or to be the stage number in the replacement problem. The stages represent time in the inventory problem, number of variables to be decided in the investment problem, and the number of machines in the chain in the replacement problem. Note that although the *recurrence relations* are mathematically different in the three examples, there is a degree of similarity between them. These concepts, as shown in Table 12.21, constitute the core of dynamic programming and will be present in any application.

We saw evidence in the inventory example that it was worthwhile to consider the structure of the problem very carefully. Our first formulation produced some large tables that we were later able to reduce considerably by applying some logic to the simplification of the computing. We also saw in the equipment-replacement

Table 12.21 The Concepts of Dynamic Programming and Their Application in the Three Examples

Concept	Inventory Example	Investment Example	Replacement Example
Policy	$X_t(I_{t-1})$	$X_i(\theta_i)$	T_n
State variable	I_{t-1}	θ_i	None (or n itself)
Stage	t; $10 - t + 1$ is the number of periods remaining	i; $5 - i + 1$ is the number of variables left to be decided	n; the number of machines in the entire chain
Number of stages	10	5	Infinite
Recurrence relation	$f_t(I_{t-1}) = \min\limits_{X_t}\left[C_0\delta(X_t) + kC_p(I_{t-1}+X_t-d_t) + f_{t+1}(I_{t-1}+X_t-d_t)\right]$	$f_i(\theta_i) = \max\limits_{X_i}\left[R_iX_i + f_{i+1}(\theta_i - V_iX_i)\right]$	$V_n(T_n) = \max\limits_{T_n}\left[-K + \int_0^{T_n}P(t)e^{-it}\,dt + e^{-iT_n}V_{n-1}(T_{n-1})\right]$

problem that the method of value iteration as opposed to policy iteration had the potential to reduce the computations considerably. These examples serve as a warning to those formulating dynamic programming problems to take time and care in the formulation so as to minimize the computations. Furthermore, they reinforce our knowledge that there are frequently unique aspects to dynamic programming problems that should be exploited.

Needless to say, there are many aspects to dynamic programming that we have not discussed in this chapter. Chapter 13 will be concerned with problems involving uncertainty and will serve to extend our understanding somewhat.

References   Bellman, R.E., *Dynamic Programming*, Princeton: Princeton University Press, 1957.

Bellman, R.E., "Equipment Replacement Policy," *Journal of the Society for Industrial and Applied Mathematics*, Vol. 3 (1955), pp. 133–136.

Bellman, R.E., and Dreyfus, S.E., *Applied Dynamic Programming*, Princeton: Princeton University Press, 1962.

Dreyfus, S.E., "A Generalized Equipment Study," *Journal of the Society for Industrial and Applied Mathematics*, Vol. 8 (1960), pp. 425–435.

Hadley, G., *Nonlinear and Dynamic Programming*, Reading, Mass.: Addison-Wesley, 1962, Ch. 10, 11.

Nemhauser, G.L., *Introduction to Dynamic Programming*, New York: John Wiley & Sons, 1966.

Peterson, E.R., "Dynamic Programming Model for the Expansion of Electric Power Systems," *Management Science*, Vol. 20 (1973), pp. 656–664.

Root, J.G., "Scheduling with Deadlines and Loss Functions on k Parallel Machines," *Management Science*, Vol. 11 (1965), pp. 460–475.

Wagner, H.M., *Principles of Operations Research*, 2nd ed., Englewood Cliffs, N.J.: Prentice-Hall, 1975, Ch. 8–11.

Wagner, H.M., and Whitin, T.M., "Dynamic Version of the Economic Lot Size Problem," *Management Science*, Vol. 5 (1958), pp. 89–96.

Review Questions

1. Distinguish between dynamic decision problems and simultaneous decision problems. Explain the roles of certainty and uncertainty in your answer.

2. Explain, in words, the meaning of the concept of a policy.

3. Explain the meaning of the terms *stage* and *state*.

4. In the inventory problem, distinguish between $g_{10}(X_{10}, I_9)$ and $f_{10}(I_9)$. How are they related? How is Table 12.2 related to Table 12.3? Explain how the line for $I_7 = 9$ is determined in Table 12.4. Explain how the line for $I_7 = 20$ is determined.

5. From the data in the inventory problem, we could compute the average monthly demand as 18.7. Then assuming demand was constant at 18.7 per month, using the cost to order as $C_o = 2.00$, and the cost to carry inventory

as $kC_p = \$0.10$ per unit per month, the lot-size model (developed in Chapter 10) yields an order quantity of $X = \sqrt{2(2)(18.7)/0.1} = 51.2$ units per order. Explain why ordering this quantity each time an order was to be placed would not be optimal.

6. Explain how the optimal policy tables of the inventory problem can be used to determine responses to changes in plans during the course of the implementation of the policy.

7. Explain why it was possible to reduce the size of the tables in the inventory problem by more refined analysis.

8. If you had renamed the project classes in Table 12.4 so that project class 5 became project class 1, project class 4 became project class 2, etc., would you have been able to reduce the computations required to solve the problem? Explain.

9. Explain the difference between value iteration and policy iteration in the context of the equipment-replacement problem.

10. Why would the optimal life of a machine in stage 1 (the last machine) be longer than the optimal life in stage 2 (the second last machine)?

Problems   1. Consider the following inventory problem. Demand for the next three months is 5, 10, and 3. Cost to carry a unit in inventory is $kC_p = \$2$, the cost to place an order is $C_o = \$2.00$, and the stockout cost is $C_\mu = \infty$.
 (a) Find the optimal policy for each month using the model of Section 12.3.
 (b) Assume that initial inventory is 0. What is the optimal solution to the problem?

2. Solve Problem 1 with $kC_p = \$0.01$ instead of $2.

3. Suppose that the cost to place an order varied between periods and was $2.00 for period 1, $4.00 for period 2, and $8.00 for period 3. With these changes solve Problem 1.

4. Suppose there is a restriction that $X_t \le 8$ for all t. Solve Problem 1 for this case.

5. Using the inventory problem of Section 12.3, what would the solution be if $C_o = 0$? Explain. What would the solution be if $kC_p = 0$ and $C_o \ne 0$? Explain.

6. Use the example of Section 12.3.
 (a) Suppose that the inventory entering a period could not exceed 10 units in the inventory problem. Develop the optimal policy for this case.
 (b) Suppose that the inventory entering a period must equal or exceed 10 units. Develop the optimal policy for this case.

7. (a) In the investment problem, suppose that a restriction $X_3 \leq 2$ is placed on the solution. Calculate the optimal investment allocation.
   (b) Calculate the optimal investment allocation if the restriction $X_4 \geq 1$ is placed on the problem.

8. Suppose that $T_1 = 20$ was a restriction placed on the replacement problem. Using the policy iteration method, calculate the optimal replacement policy for the machine.

9. Suppose that $i = 0.20$ in the replacement problem. How does the optimal policy change?

10. John Williams will inherit a fortune in 2 years. In the meantime, he must make the best of his present wealth of $100,000 and a salary of $10,000 per year. He can earn 10% on all funds he invests. His utility of consumption is

$$U = \sum_{t=1}^{2} U_t(C_t) = \sum_{t=1}^{2} (0.9)^{t-1} \ln(C_t)$$

If his salary is received at the beginning of the year along with interest earned from the previous year and then consumption occurs, find the consumption savings pattern that maximizes U. (*Hint*: The dollars available for consumption upon entering period t are $F_t = 10,000 + (F_{t-1} - C_{t-1})(1.10)$. Consumption in period 2 is $C_2 = F_2$.)

11. If Williams, from Problem 10, has no salary and the time until he inherits his fortune is 3 years, determine his consumption investment plan for the three years.

12. A mechanic must make four calls during an afternoon's work. Each call will take 20 minutes but the travel time in minutes between calls differs because of their geographic dispersion. The data are as follows:

From \ To	1	2	3	4
1	—	100	60	130
2	100	—	50	80
3	60	50	—	70
4	20	60	30	—

Assuming the mechanic is now at call 1 and it is 1:00 P.M., what time will she finish the job if she wishes to minimize the time she spends at work?

13. Solve Problem 12 if the mechanic is initially at call 4.

14. The manager of the Lac du Flambeau hardware store wants to maximize the profit obtainable from 50 feet of shelf space devoted to kitchen ware. The table below lists the profit obtainable per month per item stocked, the maximum sales, and the space required per item. How much of each item should be stocked?

Item No.	Profit per Unit	Maximum Sales	Spaces Required, feet
1473	$0.50	30	1.0
1475	1.00	20	2.0
1477	0.50	40	0.5
1478	0.80	100	1.0

15. Suppose the manufacturer of item 1477 in problem 14 redesigns its package so that the space required increases to 1.0. How would the optimal allocation change?

APPENDIX 12.1: NEWTON'S METHOD FOR SOLVING EQUATIONS OF A SINGLE VARIABLE

Suppose that we have an equation

$$L(X) = 0$$

that we wish to solve. If $L(X)$ is graphed, it may look like Figure A12.1. The solution to $L(X) = 0$ is found at $X = X_0$. To approximate X_0, assume that we have guessed a solution $X^{(0)}$. A tangent line passed through the point $(X^{(0)}, L[X^{(0)}])$ will cross the horizontal axis at the point $X^{(1)}$, which, if $L(X)$ is well behaved and $X^{(0)}$ is close to X_0, will be closer to X_0. An example is shown by the dashed line in Figure A.12.1.

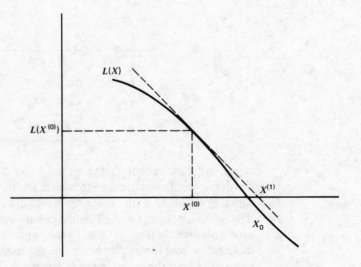

Figure A12.1 Illustration of Newton's method.

The equation of the straight line is

$$Y - L[X^{(0)}] = L'[X^{(0)}][X - X^{(0)}]$$

Now let the point where this equation crosses the horizontal axis be $(X^{(1)}, 0)$. Therefore,

$$X^{(1)} = X^{(0)} - \frac{L[X^{(0)}]}{L'[X^{(0)}]}$$

If we now repeat the entire process with $X^{(0)}$ replaced by $X^{(1)}$ we have

$$X^{(2)} = X^{(1)} - \frac{L[X^{(1)}]}{L'[X^{(1)}]}$$

which should be even closer to X_0. In general, the process may be repeated recursively with

$$X^{(j+1)} = X^{(j)} - \frac{L[X^{(j)}]}{L'[X^{(j)}]}$$

where $j = 0, 1, 2, \ldots$, with each $X^{(j)}$ being closer to X_0 than its predecessor.

When $|X^{(j+1)} - X^{(j)}| \le t$ for some small t, the process can stop. To illustrate, suppose $L(X) = X^2 - X - 6$ and we wish to find the value of $X > 0$. Suppose that the first guess is $X^{(0)} = 2.5$ and $t = 0.0001$. Then, because $L'(X) = 2X - 1$, we have

$$X^{(1)} = 2.5 - \frac{(2.5)^2 - (2.5) - 6}{2(2.5) - 1} = 3.0625$$

$$X^{(2)} = 3.0625 - \frac{(3.0625)^2 - (3.0625) - 6}{2(3.0625) - 1} = 3.0008$$

$$X^{(3)} = 3.0008 - \frac{(3.0008)^2 - (3.0008) - 6}{2(3.0008) - 1} = 3.0000$$

$$X^{(4)} = 3.0000 - \frac{(3.0000)^2 - (3.0000) - 6}{2(2.0000) - 1} = 3.0000$$

Now because $|X^{(4)} - X^{(3)}| \le t = 0.0001$, we terminate the calculation.

13

DECISIONS UNDER RISK, DYNAMIC DECISION PROBLEMS, AND DYNAMIC PROGRAMMING

13.1 STATIC-DECISION PROBLEM

An Inventory-Stocking Problem
The Value of Perfect Information
Evaluating a Forecasting System
Generalization and Discussion

13.2 DYNAMIC DECISION PROBLEMS

Building a Generating Plant
Establishing an Inventory Policy
Midwest Book Stores

13.3 SUMMARY AND DISCUSSION

References
Review Questions
Problems

In this chapter, we will expand on two topics that have been previously introduced; decisions under risk and dynamic decision problems. The former topic was introduced and briefly discussed in Chapter 2 and the latter served only as the motivating discussion for the introduction to dynamic programming in Chapter 12. A brief review of these chapters will be helpful for the discussion that follows.

This chapter is divided into two related parts. The first part discusses decisions under risk through an inventory-stocking problem. This is done in the context of static problems so that the concepts and techniques will not be obscured by the detail of the applications in which the problems arise. The second part of the chapter concentrates on the formulation and solution of certain dynamic decision problems. All problems formulated will be solvable by dynamic programming.

In the examples discussed in this chapter, the criterion will be to maximize expected profit. This assumption implies a risk-neutral decision maker and, in addition to being intuitively appropriate for all examples, relieves the burdens of calculation that would appear if risk aversion were assumed.

13.1 STATIC-DECISION PROBLEM

An Inventory-Stocking Problem

Judy's Bakery delivers bread daily to 103 stores in Milwaukee and suburbs. The deliverers for Judy's determine how many loaves to put in each store. They arrive each morning between 5:00 and 9:00 and take back any unsold loaves from the previous day and restock the shelf. Each loaf supplied costs $0.50 to produce and deliver. The bakery receives $0.65 per loaf sold. Unsold loaves are marked down to $0.20 and sold at Judy's Day Olde Store.

An improper stocking policy could cost Judy's substantial sums over a year's time, so the management contracted with a consulting firm, H.J. Granstrom, Inc., to study its stocking policy. Granstrom determined that the appropriate approach to the problem was to determine the probability distribution of demand for bread by day of the week for each store and then, given these distributions, to develop a decision rule for each store. The deliverers had been keeping detailed sales records for some time, so developing approximate probability distributions was easily accomplished and Granstrom's effort turned to developing the decision rule to be used by the deliverers in stocking.

Table 13.1 shows the probability distribution of demand for Judy's bread at Lincoln Super Foods for a Friday as determined from the deliverer's records. The data were developed from 104 Fridays representing the last two years. Before developing the distribution further, Granstrom turned to developing a decision model.

Table 13.1   Frequency Distribution of Demand for Judy's Bread at Lincoln Super Foods (Fridays)

Demand Interval	No. of Fridays	Relative Frequency
50–59	12	0.115
60–69	13	0.125
70–79	45	0.433
80–89	23	0.221
90–99	11	0.106
	104	1.000

Since the problem was a recurrent one and represented a fraction of Judy's business, expected profit was chosen as the measure of effectiveness. Profit was a function of the amount demanded and the amount stocked. Letting $\pi(d, q)$ be the profit if demand is d and quantity stocked is q, we have the expected profit as

$$E[\pi(d, q)] = \sum_{d=0}^{\infty} \pi(d, q)P(d) \tag{13.1}$$

where $P(d)$ is the probability of the demand being d. Although the consultants knew that $P(d) = 0$ for $d < 50$ as well as for $d \geq 100$, they preferred to work with an abstract model before applying it to the specific problem at hand. The limits of 0 to ∞ on the summation were convenient for analytical purposes.

Next, the consultants formulated the profit function as

$$\pi(d, q) = \begin{cases} 0.65d - 0.50q + 0.20(q - d) & \text{for } d \leq q \\ 0.15q & \text{for } d > q \end{cases} \tag{13.2}$$

The first line of (13.2) holds for the case where demand is less than or equal to the quantity stocked. In this case, $0.65d$ is the revenue from bread sales, $0.50q$ is the cost of bread, and $0.20(q - d)$ is the revenue from the sale of leftover bread at Judy's Day Olde Store. The second line holds for the case where demand exceeds stock. In this case, the entire stock is sold at a profit of \$0.65–0.50 = \$0.15 per loaf.

Using (13.2), (13.1) becomes

$$E[\pi(d, q)] = \sum_{d=0}^{q} \{0.45d - 0.30q\}P(d) + \sum_{d=q+1}^{\infty} 0.15qP(d)$$

$$= 0.45\left[\sum_{d=0}^{q} dP(d) - q\sum_{d=0}^{q} P(d)\right] + 0.15q \tag{13.3}$$

by substituting

$$\sum_{d=q+1}^{\infty} P(d) = 1 - \sum_{d=0}^{q} P(d).$$

The maximum value of $E[\pi(d, q)]$ is obtained at $q = q^*$ where $E[\pi(d, q^* - 1)]$ $\leq E[\pi(d, q^*)]$ and $E[\pi(d, q + 1)] \leq E[\pi(d, q^*)]$ are the necessary conditions for a maximum.

The first condition is equivalent to

$$\sum_{d=0}^{q^*-1} P(d) \leq \frac{0.15}{0.45} \tag{13.4}$$

The second condition implies

$$\sum_{d=0}^{q^*} P(d) \geq \frac{0.15}{0.45} \tag{13.5}$$

Therefore, combining (13.4) and (13.5), q^*, the optimal policy, must be such that

$$\sum_{d=0}^{q^*-1} P(d) \leq \frac{0.15}{0.45} \leq \sum_{d=0}^{q^*} P(d) \tag{13.6}$$

Equation 13.6 is then easy to use provided data are available. The left-hand portion of (13.6) is $P(d \leq q^* - 1)$ and the right-hand portion is $P(d \leq q^*)$. Therefore, (13.6) can be rewritten as

$$P(d \leq q^* - 1) \leq \frac{0.15}{0.45} \leq P(d \leq q^*) \tag{13.7}$$

In order to use (13.6) or (13.7) in determining the optimal stocking policy, the empirical probability distribution developed in Table 13.1 must be further refined. Figure 13.1 shows the cumulative relative frequency distribution derived from Table 13.1. The solid vertical line at 59 reaches to 0.115, which is the probability of being between 50 and 59 inclusive. The solid vertical line at 69 reaches to 0.240, which is the probability of demand being less than or equal to 69. The other solid lines are similarly interpreted. Because no data were recorded for individual demand amounts within categories and because even if such data were recorded they would tend to be erratic and not representative of the probability, the consultants chose to "smooth" the data in order to estimate probabilities for individual demands. This was done by drawing straight dashed lines between the points on the cumulative distribution on Figure 13.1. Then each demand within the category was assigned $\frac{1}{10}$ of the cumulative probability change between categories. For example, $P(50) = P(51) = \cdots = P(59) = 0.115/10 = 0.0115$ and $P(60) = P(61) = \cdots = P(69) = 0.125/10 = 0.0125$. The other probabilities were determined in a similar manner.

Table 13.2 represents a constructed probability distribution that can be used with (13.1). It should be read in the following ways. If x is between, say, 50 and 59 inclusive, the probability of demand being exactly x is 0.0115. The probability

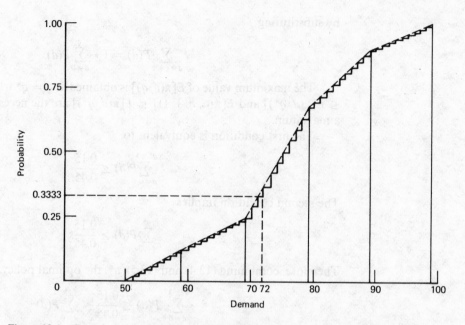

Figure 13.1 Cumulative probability distribution of demand at Lincoln Super Foods.

of demand being x or less is $0.0115(x - 49)$. For example, if $x = 53$, then $P(d = 53)$ $= 0.0115$ and $P(d \leq 53) = 0.0115(53 - 49) = 0.046$. Or if $x = 93$, then $P(d = 93)$ $= 0.0106$ and $P(d \leq 93) = 0.894 + 0.0106(93 - 89) = 0.9364$. The probabilities below $d = 50$ and above $d = 99$ are also added.

From (13.7) it is clear that we must find the value of q^* for which $P(d \leq q^* - 1)$ $\leq 0.3333 \leq P(d < q^*)$. A look at Table 13.2 reveals that q^* will be in the interval 70–79. The probability distribution in that interval is given in Table 13.3. Because

$$P(d \leq 71) = 0.3266 \leq 0.3333 \leq P(d \leq 72) = 0.3699$$

Table 13.2 Constructed Probability Distribution of Demand for Judy's Bread at Lincoln Super Foods (Fridays)

x in the Interval	$P(d = x)$	$P(d \leq x)$
0–49	0.0000	0.0000
50–59	0.0115	$0.0115(x - 49)$
60–69	0.0125	$0.115 + 0.0125(x - 59)$
70–79	0.0433	$0.240 + 0.0433(x - 69)$
80–89	0.0221	$0.673 + 0.0221(x - 79)$
90–99	0.0106	$0.894 + 0.0106(x - 89)$
100–∞	0.0000	1.0000

Table 13.3 Constructed Probability Distribution of Demand for Judy's Bread at Lincoln Super Foods (Fridays)

x	$P(d \leq x - 1)$	$P(d \leq x)$
70	0.2400	0.2833
71	0.2833	0.3266
72	0.3266	0.3699
73	0.3699	0.4132
74	0.4132	0.4565
75	0.4565	0.4998
76	0.4998	0.5431
77	0.5431	0.5864
78	0.5864	0.6297
79	0.6297	0.6730

it follows that $q^* = 72$ is the optimal stocking quantity for Lincoln Super Foods for a Friday. The optimal solution is also seen on Figure 13.1 by extending a line perpendicular to the vertical axis from 0.3333. The line intersects a vertical line from 72 on the horizontal axis.

The optimal expected cost is

$$E[\pi(d, 72)] = 0.45 \left[\sum_{d=0}^{72} dP(d) - 72 \sum_{d=0}^{72} P(d) \right] + 0.15(72)$$

$$= 0.45 \left[\sum_{d=0}^{72} dP(d) - 72(0.3699) \right] + 0.15(72)$$

$$= 0.45 \sum_{d=0}^{72} dP(d) - 1.18476$$

The term $0.45 \sum_{d=0}^{72} dP(d)$ can be evaluated from Table 13.2. It is

$$0.45 \sum_{d=0}^{72} dP(d) = 0.45[0.0115(50 + 51 + \cdots + 59) + 0.0125(60 + 61 + \cdots + 69)$$

$$+ 0.0433(70 + 71 + 72)]$$

$$= 10.598805$$

So

$$E[\pi(d, 72)] = \$9.414045$$

is the maximum expected profit that can be obtained.

The Value of Perfect Information

H.J. Granstrom, Inc., also looked at the value of perfect information for Judy's Bakery. The simple question is asked: how much more profit could be obtained if demand could be forecasted perfectly? And then, how much would Judy's be willing to pay for a perfect forecast?

The structure of costs and revenues for this problem indicates that if demand could be forecasted without error, it would be optimal to deliver exactly the amount that was forecast. Then we have, for a given Friday, $q^* = d$ where d is the demand. Then profit will be

$$\pi(d, d) = 0.15d \tag{13.8}$$

Even though demand can be forecasted perfectly in this mythical case, it is still variable and subject to the probability distribution constructed in Table 13.2. Therefore, the expected value of profit with the perfect forecast is

$$E[\pi(d, d)] = \sum_{d=0}^{\infty} \pi(d, d)P(d) = 0.15 \sum_{d=0}^{\infty} dP(d)$$

$$= 0.15[0.0115(545) + 0.0125(645) + 0.0433(745) + 0.221(845)$$

$$+ 0.0106(945)]$$

$$= \$11.29200$$

The *expected value of perfect information* (EVPI) is the difference between expected value of profit with perfect information and the expected value of profit without a forecast, or EVPI $= E[\pi(d, d)] - E[\pi(d, 72)] = 11.292000 - 9.414045 = \$1.877955$. This is the expected benefit that the managers of Judy's could obtain each Friday at Lincoln Super Foods if they could obtain a perfect forecast. It is also the maximum amount that they would pay for a perfect forecast. With this preliminary look at a single outlet on a single day and then extending this result to all days and all outlets, Judy's determined that it would be worthwhile to make some preliminary expenditures to see if accurate forecasting of bread sales could be done.

Evaluating a Forecasting System

For a fee of $10,000, J.M. Gram Co. developed a forecasting system for Judy's that showed that the sales at all outlets depended on a single factor, the weather forecast for the day. Using this information and their computers, Granstrom could forecast bread sales at the outlets that showed some improvement over no forecast at all. Table 13.4 shows the accuracy that Gram could obtain at Lincoln Super Foods. Consider Table 13.4 and the column labeled 50–59. The table shows that when the forecast is for demand between 50 and 59, that 70% of the time the actual demand will be for sales between 50 and 59 and 30% of the time demand will be between 60 and 69. Similar interpretations can be made for the other columns.

Table 13.4 Probability of Demand for Judy's Bread at Lincoln Super Foods (Fridays). Given Forecast by H.J. Granstrom, Inc.

Actual Demand			Forecast		
	50–59	60–69	70–79	80–89	90–99
50–59	0.70	0.15	—	—	—
60–69	0.30	0.70	0.15	—	—
70–79	—	0.15	0.70	0.15	—
80–89	—	—	0.15	0.70	0.30
90–99	—	—	—	0.15	0.70

Gram will only make forecasts in the categories shown, and therefore refinement of the forecast beyond the intervals shown is not possible.

J.M. Gram has informed Judy's that the cost for making forecasts for any outlet will be $7.00 per week. On a pro-rata basis, this means that Friday would be assigned a forecast cost of $1. In order to assess whether the forecasting system would be worthwhile, Judy's asked H.J. Granstrom to make an analysis of the forecasting system.

To analyze the forecasting system, Granstom used the concept of conditional probability. The probability of demand given the forecast is written as $P(d|F_i)$ and the expected cost *conditional on the forecast* is

$$E[\pi(d, q)|F_i] = 0.45\left[\sum_{d=0}^{q} dP(d|F_i) - q\sum_{d=0}^{q} P(d|F_i)\right] + 0.15q \quad (13.10)$$

Note that (13.10) differs from (13.3) only in that $P(d)$ is replaced by $P(d|F_i)$.

Because (13.10) has the same form as (13.3), the optimal value of q given F, which we will call $q^*(F_i)$, would be obtained by merely substituting $q^*(F_i)$ for q^* and $P(d|F_i)$ for $P(d)$ in (13.6) and (13.7) The comparable equations become

$$\sum_{d=0}^{q^*(F_i)-1} P(d|F_i) \leq \frac{0.15}{0.45} \leq \sum_{d=0}^{q^*(F_i)} P(d|F_i) \quad (13.11)$$

and

$$P\left[d \leq q^*(F_i) - 1|F_i\right] \leq \frac{0.15}{0.45} \leq P\left[d \leq q^*(F_i)|F_i\right] \quad (13.12)$$

Thus, an evaluation of the conditional probability distribution $P(d|F_i)$ remains before the problem can be solved.

For $F_{50} = (50–59)$ Granstrom set $P(d|F_{50}) = 0.70/10 = 0.07$ for $50 \leq d \leq 59$ and $P(d|F_{50}) = 0.30/10 = 0.03$ for $60 \leq d \leq 69$. For all other values of d, $P(d|F_{50}) = 0$. Table 13.5 shows the conditional probability distribution and

Table 13.5 Conditional Probability of Demand for Judy's Bread at Lincoln Super Foods (Fridays). Given F_{50} = (50–59)

x in the Interval	$P(d = x|F_{50})$	$P(d \leq x|F_{50})$
50–59	0.07	$0.07(x - 49)$
60–69	0.03	$0.70 + 0.03(x - 59)$

the cumulative distribution for this case. From (13.12) and Table 13.5 it is clear that the optimal solution is between 50 and 59 so Table 13.6 was developed. From it we know that $q^*(F_{50}) = 54$. Using (13.10) we find that $E[\pi(d, 54)|F] = \$7.785$. Table 13.7 shows the results of similar calculations for every forecast possibility.

It is now possible to calculate the expected profit of using the forecasting system by multiplying each value of expected cost in Table 13.7 by the probability of the corresponding forecast. The latter must be developed by use of conditional probabilities because

$$P(F_j) = \sum_L P(F_j|d_L)P(d_L) \tag{13.13}$$

where L is the set of demand intervals (50–59, 60–69, ..., 90–99).

Table 13.6 Detail of the Conditional Probability of Demand for Judy's Bread at Lincoln Super Foods (Fridays). Given F_{50} = (50–59)

x	$P(d \leq x - 1|F_{50})$	$P(d \leq x|F_{50})$
50	0.0000	0.0700
51	0.0700	0.1400
52	0.1400	0.2100
53	0.2100	0.2800
54	0.2800	0.3500
55	0.3500	0.4200
56	0.4200	0.4900
57	0.4900	0.5600
58	0.5600	0.6300
59	0.6300	0.7000

Table 13.7 Optimal Stocking Quantity and Expected Cost as a Function of Forecast for Judy's Bread at Lincoln Super Foods (Fridays)

Forecast, F_j	$q^*(F_j)$	$E\{\pi[d, q^*(F_j)|F_j]\}$
F_{50}	54	$7.78500
F_{60}	62	8.69925
F_{70}	72	10.19925
F_{80}	82	11.6995
F_{90}	90	12.75750

Table 13.8 shows the values of $P(F_j|d_L)$ derived from Table 13.4. Note the entry in the northwest corner of Table 13.8. It is derived from the formula

$$P(F_j|d_e) = \frac{P(d_e|F_j)}{\sum_i P(d_e|F_i)}.$$

Because in Table 13.4 $P(d_{50}|F_{50}) = 0.7$, $P(d_{50}|F_{60}) = 0.15$, $P(d_{50}|F_{70}) = 0$, $P(d_{50}|F_{80}) = 0$, and $P(d_{50}|F_{90}) = 0$, we have

$$P(F_{50}|d_{50}) = \frac{0.7}{0.7 + 0.15 + 0 + 0 + 0}$$

Furthermore,

$$P(F_{60}|d_{50}) = \frac{0.15}{0.7 + 0.15 + 0 + 0 + 0}$$

The remaining elements in Table 13.8 are calculated using the same approach.

Table 13.8 Probability of a Forecast Given Demand $P(F_j|d_e)$

F_j	d_{50}	d_{60}	d_{70}	d_{80}	d_{90}
F_{50}	$\dfrac{0.70}{0.70 + 0.15}$	$\dfrac{0.30}{0.30 + 0.70 + 0.15}$	0	0	0
F_{60}	$\dfrac{0.15}{0.70 + 0.15}$	$\dfrac{0.70}{0.30 + 0.70 + 0.15}$	$\dfrac{0.15}{0.15 + 0.70 + 0.15}$	0	0
F_{70}	0	$\dfrac{0.15}{0.30 + 0.70 + 0.15}$	$\dfrac{0.70}{0.15 + 0.70 + 0.15}$	$\dfrac{0.15}{0.15 + 0.70 + 0.30}$	0
F_{80}	0	0	$\dfrac{0.15}{0.15 + 0.70 + 0.15}$	$\dfrac{0.70}{0.15 + 0.70 + 0.30}$	$\dfrac{0.15}{0.15 + 0.70}$
F_{90}	0	0	0	$\dfrac{0.30}{0.15 + 0.70 + 0.30}$	$\dfrac{0.70}{0.15 + 0.70}$

Then using (13.13) along with the probabilities of demand in Table 13.8 we find that $P(F_{50}) = 0.127315$, $P(F_{60}) = 0.161331$, $P(F_{70}) = 0.348230$, $P(F_{80}) = 0.2181878$, and $P(F_{90}) = 0.144946$. As an example of the calculation, by (13.13) we have

$$P(F_{60}) = \frac{0.15}{0.70 + 0.15}(0.115) + \frac{0.70}{0.30 + 0.70 + 0.15}(0.125)$$

$$+ \frac{0.15}{0.15 + 0.70 + 0.15}(0.433) = 0.161331$$

Then, using Table 13.7, the expected value of profit is

$$\sum_j E(\pi|F_j)P(F_j) = \$7.78500(0.127315) + 8.69925(0.161331) + 10.19925(0.348230)$$

$$+ 11.6995(0.218178) + 12.75750(0.144946)$$

$$= \$10.348013$$

We previously calculated that if no forecast were made, expected profit would be \$9.414045. The difference, $\$10.348013 - \$9.414045 = \$0.933968$, is the profit due to the forecasting system. Because the cost of the forecasting system is \$1.00 per week (for the Friday forecast) H.J. Granstrom recommended that the forecasting system not be purchased unless J.M. Gram would reduce the price considerably.

Generalization and Discussion

The decision problem faced by Judy's Bakery has properties that can be generalized for application to similar problems. To see the generalization, let us define the *opportunity cost* for a given demand as the difference between the profit obtained from a clairvoyant optimal decision and the profit obtained from the actual decision made, or

$$OC(d, q) = \pi(d, d) - \pi(d, q) \tag{13.14}$$

Then, for Judy's we have

$$OC(d, q) = \begin{cases} 0.15d - 0.65d + 0.50q - 0.20(q - d) & \text{for } d \leq q \\ 0.15d - 0.15q & \text{for } d > q \end{cases}$$

$$= \begin{cases} 0.30(q - d) & \text{for } d \leq q \\ 0.15(d - q) & \text{for } d > q \end{cases} \tag{13.15}$$

The opportunity cost is then seen to be \$0.30 per unit of excess supply and \$0.15 per unit of excess demand. Note that these two numbers are easily interpreted. If demand falls short of supply and it costs \$0.50 to supply each extra unit and only \$0.20 can be recovered in the Day Olde Store, there is an opportunity loss of \$0.30 for each excess unit produced. For the case of demand exceeding supply, the opportunity cost is the lost profit or the difference between \$0.65, the selling price, and \$0.50, the cost, or \$0.15 per unit of undersupply.

In general, let

$$OC(d, q) = \begin{cases} C_o(q - d) & \text{for } d \le q \\ C_u(d - q) & \text{for } q > d \end{cases} \tag{13.16}$$

where C_u is the unit understock cost and C_o is the unit overstock cost.

Now, from (13.14) we have

$$\pi(d, q) = \pi(d, d) - OC(d, q)$$

and (13.1) becomes

$$E[\pi(d, q)] = \sum_{d=0}^{\infty} [\pi(d, d) - OC(d, q)]P(d)$$

$$= \sum_{d=0}^{\infty} \pi(d, d)P(d) - \sum_{d=0}^{\infty} OC(d, q)P(d) \tag{13.17}$$

Note that the first term on the right-hand side of the second line of (13.17) is the expected value of profit under perfect information (see (13.9)) and is independent of q. Therefore, we can maximize $E[\pi(d, q)]$ by minimizing the expected opportunity cost

$$E[OC(d, q)] = \sum_{d=0}^{\infty} OC(d, q)P(d)$$

The optimal stocking quantity q^* has two properties: $E[OC(d, q^* - 1)] \ge E[OC(d, q^*)]$ and $E[OC(d, q^* + 1)] \ge E[OC(d, q^*)]$. These conditions can now be manipulated algebraically to yield

$$\sum_{d=0}^{q^*-1} P(d) \le \frac{C_u}{C_u + C_o} \le \sum_{d=0}^{q^*} P(d) \tag{13.18}$$

as the conditions for an optimal stocking quantity. Note for the case where $C_o = \$0.30$ and $C_u = \$0.15$, (13.18) becomes (13.6).

Equation 13.18 can be used to assess the effect of price increases and cost decreases on the optimal policy for delivery to Lincoln Super Foods. Suppose that Judy's decided that the price of day-old bread must be raised to $0.40 at the Day Olde Store. Then (13.15) would become

$$OC(d, q) = \begin{cases} 0.10(q - d) & \text{for } d \le q \\ 0.15(d - q) & \text{for } d \quad q \end{cases}$$

or $C_o = \$0.10$ and $C_u = \$0.15$. Then, using (13.18), we have the optimal policy described by

$$\sum_{d=0}^{q^*-1} P(d) \le \frac{0.15}{0.25} \le \sum_{d=0}^{q^*} P(d)$$

and using Table 13.3 we find $q^* = 78$.

The two examples of the selling price at the Day Olde Store can be profitably looked at from an intuitive point of view. From Table 13.2, the median of the probability distribution is seen to be approximately 75 units. For the case of day-old price $0.20 the optimal policy is $q^* = 72$, on the "low" side of the median. For this case, $C_u/(C_o + C_u) = 0.15/0.45 = \frac{1}{3}$. When the day-old price was $0.40, the optimal policy was $q^* = 78$, on the "high" side of the median. Here $C_u/(C_o + C_u) = 0.15/0.25 = 0.60$. Note that if the resale price had been $0.35, then $C_u = \$0.15$ and the two opportunity cost parameters are the same. Therefore, $C_u/(C_o + C_u) = 0.5$ and the optimal policy should come out close to the median. Finally, one more example. If the resale price can be raised to cost—that is, $C_o = 0$—then $C_u/(C_o + C_u) = 1$ and the maximum demand 99 will be the optimal stocking quantity. Again, this is reasonable because there is no penalty for overstocking.

Equation 13.18 can be used for solution of any static inventory problem where there are constant per-unit overstock costs and understock costs. There is no need to develop a special model for applications that fall in this framework.

Another aspect of the opportunity cost formulation is worth some discussion. Suppose that q^* is derived from (13.18) and substituted into (13.17). Then, after algebraic manipulation,

$$E[OC(d, q^*)] = \sum_{d=0}^{\infty} \pi(d, d)P(d) - E[\pi(d, q^*)] = \text{EVPI} \qquad (13.19)$$

so the expected opportunity cost is the expected value of perfect information. For computational purposes, the opportunity cost approach yields all the information —the optimal solution and EVPI—that the profit approach yields but with fewer computations.

In some practical problems, it is more convenient to treat the probability distribution as continuous. Then we can write

$$E[OC(d, q)] = \int_{-\infty}^{\infty} OC(d, q)P(d)dd$$

where $P(d)$ is now the probability density function. For the case of constant over- and understock costs per unit, we have

$$E[OC(d, q)] = \int_{-\infty}^{q} C_o(q - d)P(d)dd + \int_{q}^{\infty} C_u(d - q)P(d)dd \quad (13.20)$$

To minimize $E[OC(d, q)]$ we must differentiate (13.20) with respect to q and set the derivative equal to zero.[1] Doing this produces the relationship

$$\int_{-\infty}^{q^*} P(d)dd = \frac{C_u}{C_u + C_o} \qquad (13.21a)$$

The analogy between (13.18) and (13.21a) is apparent.

---

[1] For the formula for differentiating an integral with the variable of differentiation in the limit of the integral, see footnote 2 of Chapter 12.

If $P(d)$ is normal, the solution to (13.21a) is

$$q^* = \mu + Z_\alpha \sigma \qquad (13.21b)$$

where $\alpha = C_u/(C_u + C_o)$ and Z_α is the normal deviate $(x - \mu)/\sigma$, for which the area from $-\infty$ to $(x - \mu)/\sigma$ is $\alpha = C_u/(C_u + C_o)$; μ and σ are the mean and standard deviation of $P(d)$. If $\alpha = C_u/(C_u + C_o) = 0.3333$, then $Z_\alpha \doteq -0.43$ and $q^* = \mu - 0.43\sigma$. If $P(d)$ has some other density function, the integration described in (13.21a) would have to be performed in order to evaluate q^*.

13.2   DYNAMIC DECISION PROBLEMS

Building a Generating Plant

A group of privately owned electric utilities calling themselves the Consolidated Electric Utilities Group (CEUG) must plan for a base-load generating plant to be in operation within 10 years. Preliminary studies indicate that three basic choices face the group: (1) a nuclear plant at Mohawk Bend, (2) a coal plant at Mohawk Bend, and (3) a coal plant at Crows Point. There is a great deal of uncertainty in the decision process. Public hearings will be held on CEUG's application. If the application is deemed to have insufficient analysis or if strong public opposition develops—primarily about the environmental impact—the hearings will be extended and CEUG will have to commission additional engineering studies. If the application is not approved, additional cost will be incurred to prepare a new application. Finally, if the second application is not approved, additional costs will again be incurred for the third choice.

The cost of electricity eventually produced from the plant ultimately selected will depend on the preparation costs for the hearings as well as the "bricks and mortar" to build the plant. The preparation costs are significant and extended hearings are likely to add high additional costs. The cost to produce electricity 10 years into the future is uncertain because the costs of nuclear fuel, reprocessing, and disposal (as well as the costs of coal) are uncertain and subject to various market factors as well as regulatory decisions.

Figure 13.2 is a tree diagram showing *decisions* (associated with a box) and *random events* (associated with a circle). The tree diagram illustrates the basic decision structure that the utility faces. There are three basic choices for the initial application, as shown by the three lines leading from the decision box at the left of Figure 13.2. The top branch, selection of nuclear fuel at Mohawk Bend, leads to an event circle. The two lines leading from the event circle indicate two possible random events, extended hearings designated by E and normal hearings denoted by N. The numbers below the lines denote the probabilities of the events. For nuclear fuel at Mohawk Bend the probability of extended hearings is 0.8. This reflects the fact that CEUG feels that there is growing tendency to delay nuclear applications with added issues that require extended hearings. Moving on to

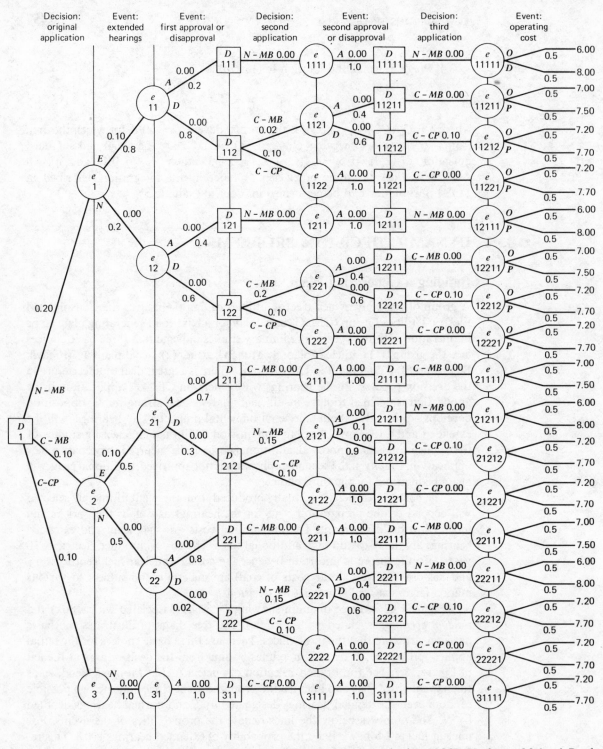

Figure 13.2 Decision tree for generating plant selection. N-MB: Nuclear at Mohawk Bend; C-MB: Coal at Mohawk Bend; C-CP: Coal at Crows Point.

event $\begin{pmatrix} e \\ 11 \end{pmatrix}$ the probability of approval is shown as 0.2. This "pessimistic" probability statement results from the fact that CEUG views nationwide experience as suggesting that if hearings are extended there is little likelihood of final approval. On the other hand, event $\begin{pmatrix} e \\ 12 \end{pmatrix}$ indices a greater likelihood of approval if extended hearings are not required. Decision $\boxed{\begin{array}{c} D \\ 111 \end{array}}$ indicates that if approval is granted, no further decisions are required. Decision $\boxed{\begin{array}{c} D \\ 112 \end{array}}$ shows the need for a choice between coal at Mohawk Bend and coal at Crows Point if nuclear fuel at Mohawk Bend is not approved. Following this decision point, another event—approval or disapproval—occurs. If, for example, coal at Mohawk Bend is not approved, the next decision is coal at Crows Point. Figure 13.2 shows that coal at Crows Point will always be acceptable.

The final event considered in the tree diagram is the actual operating cost of the plant—neglecting preparation costs. These costs represent "optimistic" and "pessimistic" operating costs of the plant. The costs of operating a nuclear plant are more uncertain than the costs of operating a coal plant.

In general, costs are associated with each decision and event. For example, a decision on the original application will result in a cost. The effect on cost per kilowatt-hour of electricity in mills is shown above the line leading from the decision box. Comparing these numbers for decision $\boxed{\begin{array}{c} D \\ 1 \end{array}}$ shows that the most expensive application is for a nuclear plant at Mohawk Bend. Coal power at Mohawk Bend and coal power at Crows Point are less expensive. The costs associated with events $\begin{pmatrix} e \\ 1 \end{pmatrix}$, $\begin{pmatrix} e \\ 2 \end{pmatrix}$, and $\begin{pmatrix} e \\ 3 \end{pmatrix}$ show that extended "nuclear hearings" are most expensive, followed by extended "coal hearings." The added cost when hearings are not extended is zero. There are no costs associated with the approval events. Also, if second decision (or third decision) is required, the added costs are for developing additional material for applications.

In general, the diagram reflects the feeling of the executives of CEUG that:

1. It will be more difficult to get approval for a nuclear plant.
2. Crows Point is the location preferred by the regulatory body. A coal plant at Crows Point will certainly be approved.
3. Once extended hearings are required on any proposal, the chances of approval are diminished.
4. The costs of operating a nuclear plant are more uncertain than the costs of operating a coal plant, but if the favorable event works out to be nuclear power, the costs of a nuclear plant will be substantially below that for coal power.

To determine the costs of a single sequence of decisions and events, it is simply a matter of adding up the costs of the entire branch. For example, the cost of nuclear fuel at Mohawk Bend, with extended hearings, approval, and the "optimistic" cost, is 0.20 + 0.10 + 6.00 = 6.30 mills per kilowatt-hour. The sequence of nuclear fuel at Mohawk Bend—extended hearings, disapproval, coal at Mohawk Bend, disapproval, coal at Crows Point, and "pessimistic" cost—costs 0.20 + 0.10 + 0.02 + 0.10 + 7.70 = 8.12 mills per kilowatt-hour.

To analyze the decision problem and pick the optimal decision, the technique of *backward induction* is used. To see how this technique works, consider the *operating cost event*. The expected cost of nuclear power at Mohawk Bend is 0.5(6.00) + 0.5(8.00) = 7.00 mills per kilowatt-hour. The expected cost of coal power at Mohawk Bend is 0.5(7.00) + 0.5(7.50) = 7.25 mills per kilowatt-hour, and the expected cost of coal power at Crows Point is 0.5(7.70) + 0.5(7.20) = 7.45 mills per kilowatt-hour. Therefore, on the eve of the operating cost event we can assign one number to the expected cost of the event. Therefore, we could replace the two branches stemming from that event circle by a single branch with the appropriate expected cost. Figure 13.3 shows this change for the first four operating event circles as an example.

Next, we can collapse back the expected cost for each decision at the third application stage. Because the decision at this stage is completely determined by the previous acts and events, we must merely add the additional costs incurred at the third decision to the expected cost for the operating cost event. Following this calculation, the right-hand portion of the diagram can be eliminated. Figure 13.4 shows an example using the first eight decision boxes in Figure 13.2. Note that

decision box $\boxed{\begin{array}{c} D \\ \hline 11212 \end{array}}$ costs 7.55 = 7.45 + 0.10 mills per kilowatt-hour.

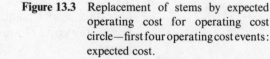

Figure 13.3 Replacement of stems by expected operating cost for operating cost circle—first four operating cost events: expected cost.

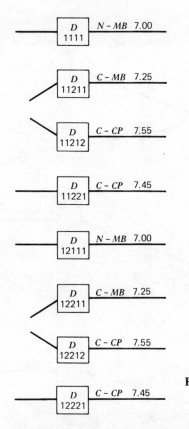

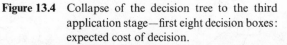

Figure 13.4 Collapse of the decision tree to the third application stage—first eight decision boxes: expected cost of decision.

The next step is to collapse the diagram back to the second approval or disapproval event stage. On the eve of the second approval or disapproval event, we can write the expected cost of $\binom{e}{1111}$ as 7.00 mills per kilowatt-hour because there is a single possible result of this random event. The expected cost of $\binom{e}{1121}$ is $0.4(7.25) + 0.6(7.55) = 7.43$, which is the weighted average of the expected costs of $\boxed{\begin{matrix}D\\11211\end{matrix}}$ and $\boxed{\begin{matrix}D\\11212\end{matrix}}$. Figure 13.5 shows an abbreviated decision tree with the expected costs for the second approval or disapproval event on the right-hand side.

The next step in the analysis of the decision tree is crucial. A contingent decision must be made at second application stage for each decision box. For $\boxed{\begin{matrix}D\\111\end{matrix}}$, no decision is necessary because the original decision has been approved, no nuclear fuel at Mohawk Bend is still the decision and its expected cost is 7.00.

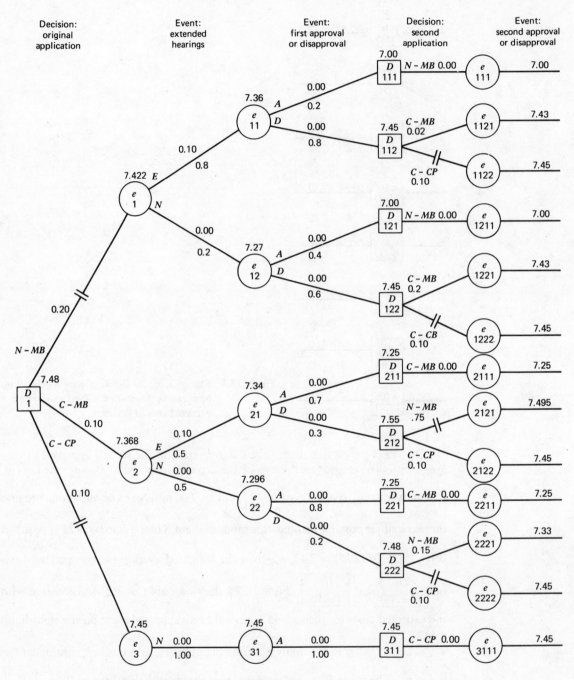

Figure 13.5 Abbreviated decision tree.

For $\boxed{\genfrac{}{}{0pt}{}{D}{112}}$, if the decision is made to go with coal at Mohawk Bend, the expected cost will be 7.43 + 0.02 = 7.45; if the decision is made to go with coal at Crows Point, the cost will be 7.45 + 0.10 = 7.55. Clearly, the optimal choice at this stage is to make the second application for a coal plant at Mohawk Bend. Thus, the decision at the second application stage involves a comparison of the expected cost for the various decisions and the selection of the least-cost alternative. In order to avoid redrawing the diagram for the remaining collapsing, we have placed a break mark for all decisions rejected and the expected cost of the selected decision over

the decision box. For example, above decision box $\boxed{\genfrac{}{}{0pt}{}{D}{111}}$, the 7.45 indicates

the expected cost for the optimal decision. Note that the decision "coal at Crows Point" is eliminated by the break mark.

The next collapse in the backward induction process is seen by examination of

$\left(\genfrac{}{}{0pt}{}{e}{11}\right)$. The expected cost on the eve of first approval or disapproval is a weighted

average of the expected values of the decision boxes $\boxed{\genfrac{}{}{0pt}{}{D}{111}}$ and $\boxed{\genfrac{}{}{0pt}{}{D}{112}}$ or 0.2(7.00)

+ 0.8(7.45) = 7.36. A similar procedure collapses the problem to the expected cost on the eve of the extended hearing discussion. At this point, we are in a position to calculate the expected cost of each of the decision alternatives. The expected cost of nuclear fuel at Mohawk Bend is 7.422 + 0.20 = 7.626, the cost of coal at Mohawk Bend is 7.368 + 0.10 = 7.468, and the cost of coal at Crows Point is 7.45 + 0.10 = 7.55. Therefore, the decision to go with coal at Mohawk Bend is made because the

The expected cost of the optimal decision is 7.468 mills per kilowatt-hour. It is interesting to compare this figure with the cost of the most favorable case for all three decisions. This can be done by referring to Figure 13.2. For nuclear fuel at Mohawk Bend the cost for the most favorable case would be 6.20 (no extended hearings, approval, and optimistic cost), for coal at Mohawk Bend the cost of the most favorable case would be 7.10, and for coal at Crows Point, 7.30. Even though the nuclear fuel at Mohawk Bend is the most favorable, it is not selected and coal at Mohawk Bend is selected. Using the expected operating cost *and* all favorable decisions, the expected costs of the three decisions would be 7.20 for nuclear fuel at Mohawk Bend, 7.35 for coal at Mohawk Bend, and 7.55 for coal at Crows Point. Again, the nuclear decision produced the lowest costs.

Nuclear power was not selected because the probability of extended hearings was greater when a nuclear decision was made. Therefore, added cost could be expected. In addition, the probabilities of having a nuclear application approved were less, and therefore there was a greater chance of having to move to the second application stage and the added costs from this reapplication.

The decision-tree analysis of the generating-plant decision illustrated the concept of a dynamic decision process. The decision tree in Table 13.5 shows the optimal original application—coal at Mohawk Bend. In addition, it also shows the second application decisions. If hearings are either extended or not extended *and* approval is given, then it is optimal to continue with coal at Mohawk Bend. But if hearings are extended and the original application is disapproved, a switch to coal at Crows Point is signaled. This is because of the very small probability of getting a nuclear plant accepted at Mohawk Bend. On the other hand, if hearings are not extended and disapproval of the original application occurs, nuclear fuel at Mohawk Bend is the appropriate decision. This result occurs because Crows Point is a relatively high-cost site and because the probability of getting a nuclear approval at Mohawk Bend is highest when the original coal hearings are not extended.

Many dynamic decision problems can be formulated and solved as decision-tree problems. A close examination of the backward-induction technique reveals that it is similar to the dynamic programming technique introduced in Chapter 12.

In the next section, we illustrate the solution of an inventory policy problem using dynamic programming.

Establishing an Inventory Policy

The James Department Store chain carries the Burmeister Wrist Alarm watch in all of its stores. The demand for the watch at the Minocqua, Wisconsin, branch of the store has the probability distribution shown at Table 13.9. The department store seeks an inventory policy that will maximize profit from dealing in the watch.

On the first working day of each month, the Burmeister representative appears at the Minocqua store with a supply of Wrist Alarms. The Minocqua store manager buys a supply for the month at a $200 cash price. The watches are sold for $220. If some watches are unsold, a carrying cost of $4 is incurred per

Table 13.9 Probability Distribution of Demand per Month for Burmeister Wrist Alarm at Minocqua

Demand Units	Probability
0	0.3
1	0.4
2	0.2
3	0.1
4 or more	0

Table 13.10 Hypothetical Policy for Buying Burmeister Wrist Alarms

I_0	$q(I_0)$
0	3
1	1
2	1
3	0
4	0

watch held in inventory. The monthly profit function is

$$\pi(d, I) = \begin{cases} 20d - 4(I - d) & d \le I \\ 20I & d > I \end{cases} \tag{13.22}$$

where d is the demand and I is the quantity in inventory following the purchase. That is,

$$I = I_0 + q(I_0) \tag{13.23}$$

where I_0 is the inventory before purchase and $q(I_0)$ is the purchase quantity.

The management of James Department Store wants to develop a policy $q(I_0)$ relating the purchase quantity to the inventory before purchase. Table 13.10 illustrates a hypothetical policy. Using it, $q(0) = 3$, $q(1) = 1$, $q(2) = 1$, $q(3) = 0$, $q(4) = 0$.

The *state* of the inventory system is defined by I_0. The expected profit of the system for the next period is a function of the state and the policy. The expected profit for the next month is

$$E[\pi(d, I)] = \sum_{d=0}^{I} (24d - 4I)P(d) + \sum_{d=I+1}^{\infty} 20IP(d) \tag{13.24}$$

Table 13.11 shows the evaluation of (13.24) for the policy shown in Table 13.10.

Table 13.11 indicates that when the system is in state $I_0 = 0$, the expected profit will be \$14.40; when it is in the state $I_0 = 1$, the expected profit will be \$16.00; etc. If the probabilities of being in each of the states were known, then the overall expected cost of the policy could be calculated.

To calculate the probabilities of being in the various states, we define P_{ij} as the probability of moving from state i to state j in a single period. (P_{ij} is clearly a function of the policy, but we will not *symbolically* note this fact so as to avoid excessive symbolism.) These *transition* probabilities can be easily calculated. For example, the probability of moving from state 0 to state 0 is the probability of getting a demand for three units (since the policy calls for inventory to be built up

Table 13.11   Expected Profit as a Function of Inventory Level Using Policy of Table 13.10

I_0	I	$E[\pi(d, I)]$
0	3	$14.40
1	2	16.00
2	3	14.40
3	3	14.40
4	4	10.40

to 3) and $P_{00} = 0.1$. The probability of moving from 1 unit in inventory to 0 units is the probability of a demand for 2 or 3 units or $P_{10} = 0.3$. The remaining transition probabilities are shown in Table 13.12.

The transition probabilities for this example are *stationary*. That is, they do not change with the passage of time. There are two reasons for this. First, the policy on which the transition probabilities depend is stationary. Second, the demand probabilities do not change as time passes.

Note also that for our example, the transition probability depends only on the inventory level (by way of the policy). That is, the transition probabilities depend only on the immediate state of the system. They do not depend on any previous state or previous demand. This property is called the *Markov* property.

The policy stated in Table 13.10 ensures that the inventory level can take on only a finite number of states. To see why this is the case, suppose the state of the system reached $I_0 = 4$. The policy indicates that $q(4) = 0$ so no new inventory would be added. Inventory would not be replenished until inventory had fallen to 2 or less. From that point on the policy calls for inventory to be built up to only 3 units. In other words, inventory will never exceed 3 again. Inventory will only take on the values 0, 1, 2, and 3. Thus, the system will be able to take on a *finite* number of states.

Table 13.12   Transition Probabilities Using Policy of Table 13.10

i \ j	0	1	2	3	4
0	0.1	0.2	0.4	0.3	0
1	0.3	0.4	0.3	0	0
2	0.1	0.2	0.4	0.3	0
3	0.1	0.2	0.4	0.3	0
4	0	0.1	0.2	0.4	0.3

The inventory level when viewed over time is a *stochastic process*. This merely means that it is characterized by a probability distribution that itself has a time dimension. Our example inventory is a special stochastic process known as a *finite-state Markov chain* because it has: (1) a finite number of states, (2) the Markov property, and (3) stationary transition probabilities. Finite-state Markov chains are one of the simplest stochastic processes to analyze.

Let us now return to the problem of determining the probabilities of being in the various states shown in Table 13.11. Suppose that the system was in the state $I_0 = 0$. Then the probabilities of being in states $I_1 = 0, I_1 = 1, I_1 = 2, I_1 = 3$ (where the subscript denotes the inventory before ordering in the next period) are 0.1, 0.2, 0.4, and 0.3, respectively. These probabilities are the first row of Table 13.12. If the system was originally in state $I_0 = 1$, the probabilities of being in $I_1 = 0, I_1 = 1, I_1 = 2, I_1 = 3$, are 0.3, 0.4, 0.3, 0, respectively, as seen from the second row of Table 13.12. Note that the probabilities of being in any state depend on the state in which the system was previously.

Now suppose we ask the question: what is the probability of being in states $I_2 = 0, I_2 = 1, I_2 = 2, I_2 = 3$ two periods hence? Suppose first that the inventory is in state $I_0 = 0$. Then if $P_{0j}^{(2)}$ is the probability of being in state $I_2 = j$ at the end of 2 periods, given that the initial state was $I_0 = 0$, we have

$$P_{0j}^{(2)} = \sum_{k=0}^{3} P_{0k} P_{kj}$$

For example, let $j = 0$. Then, using the laws of probability and Table 13.12, we have

$$P_{00}^{(2)} = P_{00}P_{00} + P_{01}P_{10} + P_{02}P_{20} + P_{03}P_{30}$$
$$= (0.1)(0.1) + (0.2)(0.3) + (0.4)(0.1) + (0.3)(0.1)$$
$$= 0.14$$

Likewise, for $j = 1$,

$$P_{01}^{(2)} = P_{00}P_{01} + P_{01}P_{11} + P_{02}P_{21} + P_{03}P_{31}$$
$$= (0.1)(0.2) + (0.2)(0.4) + (0.4)(0.2) + (0.3)(0.2)$$
$$= 0.24$$

Proceeding in a similar manner, $P_{02}^{(2)} = 0.38$ and $P_{03}^{(2)} = 0.24$.

Now the probabilities of moving from state $I_0 = 1$ to state $I_2 = j$ are given by

$$P_{1j}^{(2)} = \sum_{k=0}^{3} P_{1k} P_{kj}$$

and are $P_{10}^{(2)} = 0.18$, $P_{11}^{(2)} = 0.28$, $P_{12}^{(2)} = 0.36$, and $P_{13}^{(2)} = 0.18$. The probabilities of moving from any state to any other state in two transitions can be calculated in a similar manner. Table 13.13 shows the probabilities of being in state j after two transitions given that the initial state is i.

Table 13.3 Two-Step Transition Probabilities Using Policy of Table 13.10

i \ j	$P_{ij}^{(2)}$			
	0	1	2	3
0	0.14	0.24	0.32	0.24
1	0.18	0.28	0.36	0.18
2	0.14	0.24	0.38	0.24
3	0.14	0.24	0.38	0.24

It is also possible to determine the probability of being in state j given an initial state i after 3, 4, etc., transitions. To make the calculation for 3 transitions, we must evaluate

$$P_{ij}^{(3)} = \sum_{k=0}^{3} P_{ik}^{(2)} P_{kj}$$

for all $i = 0, 1, 2, 3$ and $j = 0, 1, 2, 3$. To determine the probability of being in state j after n transitions, we can use the relationship

$$P_{ij}^{(n)} = \sum_{k=0}^{3} P_{ik}^{(n-1)} P_{kj} \tag{13.25}$$

Table 13.14a shows the 3-step transition probabilities and 13.14b shows the 6-step transition probabilities. Note that the four rows of Table 13.14b are almost identical. Thus, the probability of being in state j after 6 transitions is nearly independent of the initial state. Let us carry the transition further to 12 steps. For this the transition probabilities are given in Table 13.14c. The columns of Table 13.14c are identical to eight decimal places (only three of which are shown). As the number of transitions increases, these probabilities will not change.

The development of Tables 13.14 illustrates an important characteristic of our problem. By the 12th transition the probability of being in state j is independent of the initial state. The probabilities shown in the columns of Table 13.14 are given the name *steady-state probabilities* or *stationary-state probabilities*. Clearly, if we would look at any point in time these would be the probabilities of being in the various states. These probabilities can then be used to calculate the expected cost of a policy.

There is another way to develop these probabilities. The probability of being in state j at the end of a period is the sum of the probabilities of being in any possible state at the beginning of the period times the probability of making a transition to state j during the period. That is,

$$P_j = \sum_i P_i P_{ij} \tag{13.26a}$$

Table 13.14a Three-Step Transition Probabilities Using Policy of Table 13.10

i \ j ($P_{ij}^{(3)}$)	0	1	2	3
0	0.148	0.248	0.376	0.228
1	0.156	0.256	0.372	0.216
2	0.148	0.248	0.376	0.228
3	0.148	0.248	0.376	0.228

Table 13.14b Six-Step Transition Probabilities Using Policy of Table 13.10

i \ j ($P_{ij}^{(6)}$)	0	1	2	3
0	0.149984	0.249984	0.375008	0.225024
1	0.150048	0.250048	0.374976	0.224928
2	0.149984	0.249984	0.375008	0.225024
3	0.149984	0.249984	0.375008	0.275024

Table 13.14c Twelve-Step Transition Probabilities Using Policy of Table 13.10

i \ j ($P_{ij}^{(12)}$)	0	1	2	3
0	0.150	0.250	0.375	0.225
1	0.150	0.250	0.375	0.225
2	0.150	0.250	0.375	0.225
3	0.150	0.250	0.375	0.225

is the probability of being in state j at the end of the period. For example,

$$P_0 = P_0 P_{00} + P_1 P_{10} + P_2 P_{20} + P_3 P_{30} + P_4 P_{40} + \cdots \tag{13.26b}$$

For the hypothetical policy, Table 13.12 can be used to determine the transition probabilities and (13.26*b*) could be written as

$$P_0 = P_0(0.1) + P_1(0.3) + P_2(0.1) + P_3(0.1) \tag{13.27}$$

In a similar fashion, we have

$$P_1 = P_0(0.2) + P_1(0.4) + P_2(0.2) + P_3(0.2) + P_4(0.1) \qquad (13.28a)$$

$$P_2 = P_0(0.4) + P_1(0.3) + P_2(0.4) + P_3(0.4) + P_4(0.2) \qquad (13.28b)$$

$$P_3 = P_0(0.3) + P_1(0) + P_2(0.3) + P_3(0.3) + P_4(0.4) \qquad (13.28c)$$

$$P_4 = P_0(0) + P_1(0) + P_2(0) + P_3(0) + P_4(0.3) \qquad (13.28d)$$

Equations (13.28) all involve P_4 but it can be seen from the transition probabilities that if the system ever arrives in states 0–3, the probability of being able to move to state 4 is zero. Therefore, in the "long run" the probability of being in state 4 is zero. Then (13.28d) can be eliminated as can all the terms involving P_4 in the remaining equation of (13.28). Doing this, note that there are four remaining equations in four unknowns—P_0, P_1, P_2, and P_3. These equations can now be rewritten as

$$\begin{aligned}
-0.9P_0 + 0.3P_1 + 0.1P_2 + 0.1P_2 &= 0 \\
0.2P_0 - 0.6P_1 + 0.2P_2 + 0.2P_3 &= 0 \\
0.4P_0 + 0.3P_1 - 0.6P_2 + 0.4P_3 &= 0 \\
0.3P_0 + \qquad\quad 0.3P_2 - 0.7P_3 &= 0
\end{aligned} \qquad (13.29)$$

Gaussian elimination can be used to solve the system (13.29). After six iterations, we have an equivalent system

$$\begin{aligned}
0P_0 &= 0 \\
-\tfrac{5}{3}P_0 + P_1 &= 0 \\
-\tfrac{5}{2}P_0 \qquad\quad + P_2 &= 0 \\
-\tfrac{3}{2}P_0 \qquad\qquad\quad + P_3 &= 0
\end{aligned} \qquad (13.30)$$

The system (13.30) has the solution

$$\begin{aligned}
P_0 &= \text{arbitrary} \\
P_1 &= \tfrac{5}{3}P_0 \\
P_2 &= \tfrac{5}{2}P_0 \\
P_3 &= \tfrac{3}{2}P_0
\end{aligned}$$

But because we know that $P_4 = 0$ we have an additional condition

$$1 = P_0 + P_1 + P_2 + P_3 \qquad (13.21)$$

and therefore

$$1 = P_0 + (\tfrac{5}{3})P_0 + (\tfrac{5}{2})P_0 + (\tfrac{3}{2})P_0 = (\tfrac{40}{6})P_0$$

or

$$P_0 = \tfrac{6}{40}, \; P_1 = \tfrac{10}{40}, \; P_2 = \tfrac{15}{40}, \; P_3 = \tfrac{9}{40} \qquad (13.32)$$

as the probabilities of being in the various states. Note that these are the probabilities given in Table 13.14c.

Given (13.32), we can calculate the expected cost of the policy using Table 13.11. It is

$$\tfrac{6}{40}(14.40) + \tfrac{10}{40}(16.00) + \tfrac{15}{40}(14.40) + \tfrac{9}{40}(14.40) = \$14.80$$

The procedure we have followed allows us to evaluate any reasonable policy. Certain policies are plainly unreasonable, however, and therefore would be ignored by a rational decision maker. The procedure would also be incapable of evaluating them. For example, consider the policy $q(I_0) = 4$ for all I_0. To see what would happen with this policy, consider the case where the demand was zero following a period that left 1 unit in inventory. This means that 5 units would be left in inventory for the next period. The policy would call for 4 more units to be ordered building inventory up to 9 units before the demand of the period. The largest demand is 3, so the probability of moving to states 0, 1, 2, 3, 4, and 5 would be zero. Now suppose demand was for 3 units during the period reducing inventory to 6 units. Then after an order of 4, the inventory on hand would be 10. Note that now the probability of moving to states 0, 1, 2, 3, 4, 5, *and* 6 would be zero. In a finite amount of time we would find that the probabilities of moving to states 7, 8, 9, etc., would become zero. In other words, there would be no *stationary probabilities* of the system being in various states. A little reflection will show that the cost of such a policy will approach infinity.

But how can we determine an optimal policy? It seems that all we have is a way of evaluating a policy once it has been determined but no rational way to determine a policy. It is possible, however, to formulate a solution procedure using the technique of dynamic programming.

Suppose we first look at the problem as a single-period problem instead of as a multiperiod problem. We could determine an optimal policy. Then using this optimal policy and the methods of dynamic programming, we could develop an optimal policy for two periods. Next, an optimal policy could be developed for a three-period horizon, then a four-period horizon, etc. The policies could then *converge*—that is, remain constant between horizons—and we will be able to show that it will not change if the horizon is extended. We will then have an optimal policy for an arbitrarily long horizon.

To start this procedure, consider the following formulation, which describes the one-period problem. Let

$$M_1[I_0, q_1(I_0)] = \sum_{d=0}^{I} (24d - 4I)P(d) + \sum_{d=I+1}^{\infty} 20IP(d) \tag{13.33}$$

subject to $I = I_0 + q(I_0)$. Then

$$M_1(I_0) = \underset{q_1(I_0)}{\text{Max}}\{M_1[I_0, q_1(I_0)]\} \tag{13.34}$$

subject to $q_1(I_0) \geq 0$. In (13.33) and (13.34), the subscript $_1$ indicates a one-period horizon.

Now, in order to find $M_1(I_0)$, (13.33) must be evaluated for all possible values of $q_1(I_0)$. For example, if $I_0 = 0$, then

$$M_1(0, 0) = \sum_{d=0}^{0} [24d - 4(0)]P(d) + \sum_{d=1}^{\infty} 20(0)P(d) = 0.00$$

$$M_1(0, 1) = \sum_{d=0}^{1} (24d - 4)P(d) + \sum_{d=2}^{\infty} 20(1)P(d) = 12.80$$

$$M_1(0, 2) = \sum_{d=0}^{2} (24d - 8)P(d) + \sum_{d=3}^{\infty} 20(2)P(d) = 16.00$$

$$M_1(0, 3) = \sum_{d=0}^{3} (24d - 12)P(d) + \sum_{d=4}^{\infty} 20(3)P(d) = 14.40$$

and from (13.34) $M_1(0) = 16.00$ and $q_1(0) = 2$. For $I_0 = 1$,

$$M_1(1, 0) = \sum_{d=0}^{1} [24d - 4(1)]P(d) + \sum_{d=2}^{\infty} 20(1)P(d) = 12.80$$

$$M_1(1, 1) = \sum_{d=0}^{2} (24d - 8)P(d) + \sum_{d=3}^{\infty} 20(2)P(d) = 16.00$$

$$M_1(1, 2) = \sum_{d=0}^{3} (24d - 12)P(d) + \sum_{d=4}^{\infty} 20(3)P(d) = 14.40$$

$$M_1(1, 3) = \sum_{d=0}^{4} (24d - 16)P(d) + \sum_{d=5}^{\infty} 20(4)P(d) = 10.40$$

and $M_1(1) = 16.00$ and $q_1(1) = 1$.

Table 13.15 shows the results of the previous two and remaining calculations for the one-period horizon case.

For the two period horizon, we have

$$M_2[I_0, q_2(I_0)] = \sum_{d=0}^{I} (24d - 4I)P(d) + \sum_{d=I+1}^{\infty} 20IP(d) + \sum_{d=0}^{\infty} M_1[(I - d)^+]P(d)$$

$$(13.35)$$

Table 13.15 Optimal Policy and Expected Profit for One-Period Horizon

I_0	$q_1(I_0)$	$M_1(I_0)$
0	2	$16.00
1	1	16.00
2	0	16.00
3	0	14.40

subject to $I = I_0 + q_2(I_0)$ and

$$M_2(I_0) = \underset{q_2(I_0)}{\text{Max}}\{M_2[I_0, q_2(I_0)]\} \qquad (13.36)$$

subject to $q_2(I_0) \geq 0$. In (13.35), we use the "upper plus" function as $X^+ = 0$ if $X \leq 0$ and $X^+ = X$ if $X > 0$.

In (13.35), the final term can be calculated using Table 13.15. For example, suppose $I_0 = 1$; then

$$M_2(1, 0) = \sum_{d=0}^{1} (24d - 4)P(d) + \sum_{d=2}^{\infty} 20P(d) + \{M_1(1)P(0)$$

$$+ M_1(0)[P(1) + P(2) + P(3)]\}$$

$$= 6.8 + 6.0 + [16.00(0.3) + 16.00(0.7)]$$

$$= 28.80$$

$$M_2(1, 1) = \sum_{d=0}^{2} (24d - 8)P(d) + \sum_{d=3}^{\infty} 20(2)P(d) + \{M_1(2)P(0)$$

$$+ M_1(1)P(1) + M_1(0)[P(2) + P(3)]\}$$

$$= 16.00 + [16.00(0.3) + 16.00(0.4) + 16.00(0.3)]$$

$$= 32.00$$

$$M_2(1, 2) = \sum_{d=0}^{3} (24d - 12)P(d) + [M_1(3)P(0) + M_1(2)P(1) + M_1(1)P(2)$$

$$+ M_1(0)P(3)]$$

$$= 14.40 + [14.40(0.3) + 16.00(0.4) + 16.00(0.2) + 16.00(0.1)]$$

$$= 29.92$$

Because profit will only fall as $q_2(1)$ is increased, no additional calculations are necessary, and clearly $M_2(1) = 32.00$ and $q_2(1) = 1$. The results of the remaining calculations are shown in Table 13.16.

Table 13.16 Optimal Policy and Expected Profit for Two-Period Horizon

I_0	$q(I_0)$	$M_2(I_0)$
0	2	$32.00
1	1	32.00
2	1	32.00
3	0	29.92

Because the policies shown in Tables 13.15 and 13.16 are identical, it would be convenient to be able to conclude that the optimal policy has been selected. Indeed, this is the case. The structure of the problem is such that a single period produces the optimal policy. Note that because inventory is replenished each period, there is no advantage in building up inventory to carry over into the next period, and the periods of an infinite horizon can be treated one at a time. More formally, note that the cost depends on I instead of I_0, and therefore the decision on $q(I_0)$ each period serves to unlink decisions.

It is interesting to use the policy of Tables 13.15 and 13.16 to determine the expected per period cost of the policy. Because Table 13.15 gives the expected cost as a function of the stage, all that remains is to determine the transition probabilities and from them the *stationary* probabilities. The transition probabilities are given in Table 13.17.

The stationary probabilities are defined by

$$P_0 = P_0(0.3) + P_1(0.3) + P_2(0.3) + P_3(0.1)$$

$$P_1 = P_0(0.4) + P_1(0.4) + P_2(0.4) + P_3(0.2)$$

$$P_2 = P_0(0.3) + P_1(0.3) + P_2(0.3) + P_3(0.4)$$

$$P_3 = P_0(0) + P_1(0) + P_2(0) + P_3(0.3)$$

and upon solving we find that $P_0 = \frac{3}{10}$, $P_1 = \frac{4}{10}$, $P_2 = \frac{3}{10}$, $P_3 = 0$. The expected cost per period is then

$$\tfrac{3}{10}(16.00) + \tfrac{4}{10}(16.00) + \tfrac{3}{10}(16.00) + 0(14.40) = \$16.00$$

Some discussion of the solution is worthwhile. Note that in the optimal solution, inventory never reaches 3 units and in all cases where demand is for 3 there will be lost sales. Why should the optimal policy prescribe the deliberate losing of some profit? A quick look at the profit function explains the result. If *an additional* unit (the third) is ordered in any period, the expected gain in profit will be $\$20P(3) = \$2$. The expected loss due to carrying excess inventory will be $\$4[1 - P(3)] = \$3.60$. Therefore, building inventory to 3 units is not worthwhile.

Analysis of the previous paragraph looks only at the results of a single period. But in our example, there is no advantage in carrying inventory over to the next

Table 13.17   Transition Probabilities Using Policy of Table 13.15

i \ j	0	1	2	3
0	0.3	0.4	0.3	0
1	0.3	0.4	0.3	0
2	0.3	0.4	0.3	0
3	0.1	0.2	0.4	0.3

period because an order can be placed without cost when the representative arrives at the beginning of the next month. This illustrates an important point. Although the Wrist Alarm case appears to require a dynamic analysis, we found that a static model gives the optimal dynamic solution. The next section describes a truly dynamic problem.

Midwest Book Stores

Midwest Book Stores is a multistore, multicity retail outlet that carries an inventory of hardcover current bestsellers, current paperbacks, and standard reference books. One of the reference books, a single-volume encylcopedia, requires an order to a specialty book dealer. Each order so placed costs $10. The book retails for $35 and has a purchase cost of $25. The cost to carry a book in inventory for a month is $5. This unusually high cost results from the fact that books held in inventory and on display are frequently damaged by browsers. The demand for the encyclopedia at one of the outlets—considered typical of the 100 retail stores around the Midwest—is given in Table 13.18. Midwest Book Stores wants to determine an ordering policy.

The profit function for the encyclopedia is

$$\pi(d, I_0, q(I_0)) = \begin{cases} 10d - 5[I_0 + q(I_0) - d] - 10\delta[q(I_0)] & d \le I_0 + q(I_0) \\ 10[I_0 + q(I_0)] - 10\delta[q(I_0)] & d > I_0 + q(I_0) \end{cases}$$

$$(13.37)$$

where

$$\delta[q(I_0)] = \begin{cases} 1 & q(I_0) > 0 \\ 0 & q(I_0) \le 0 \end{cases}$$

The dynamic programming technique will be used to establish an optimal policy. First, calculate the optimal policy for a single period. To this end define

$$M_1^*[I_0, q(I_0)] = \sum_{d=0}^{I_0+q(I_0)} \{15d - 5[(I_0 + q(I_0))]\}P(d)$$

$$+ \sum_{d=I_0+q(I_0)+1}^{\infty} 10[I_0 + q(I_0)]P(d) - 10\delta[q(I_0)] \quad (13.38)$$

Table 13.18 Probability Distribution of Demand for Single-Volume Encyclopedia

Demand	Probability
0	0.2
1	0.5
2	0.3
3 or more	0

Table 13.19 Optimal Policy and Expected Profit for a One-Period Horizon Encyclopedia Problem

I_0	$q(I_0)$	$M_1{}^*(I_0)$
0	0	\$ 0
1	0	7.00
2	0	6.50
3	0	1.50
4	0	-3.50
5	0	-8.50

and

$$M_1{}^*(I_0) = \underset{q(I_0) \geq 0}{\text{Max}} \{M_1{}^*[I_0, q(I_0)]\} \tag{13.39}$$

Now, evaluating (13.38) and (13.39) we have Table 13.19, which shows the optimal policy for a single-period horizon. Note that for every value of I_0 the optimal policy is to order zero units. This is because the cost of ordering at \$10 is very high for supplying a single period.

Next we move to a two-period horizon. The basic equations are

$$M_2{}^*[I_0, q(I_0)] = M_1{}^*[I_0, q(I_0)] + \sum_{d=0}^{\infty} M_1{}^*\{[I_0 + q(I_0) - d]^+\}P(d) \tag{13.40}$$

and

$$M_2{}^*(I_0) = \underset{q(I_0) \geq 0}{\text{Max}} \{M_2{}^*[I_0, q(I_0)]\} \tag{13.41}$$

Table 13.20 Optimal Policy and Expected Profit for a Two-Period Horizon Encyclopedia Problem

I_0	$q(I_0)$	$M_2{}^*(I_0)$
0	2	\$ 1.30
1	0	8.40
2	0	11.30
3	0	7.15
4	0	-1.50

In (13.40), the first term on the right-hand side of the equality sign is the expected profit for the first period of the horizon. The second term is the expected profit for the second period *when following the optimal policy* for the single-period horizon. Table 13.20 shows the results of evaluating (13.40) and (13.41).

Note that the policy for the two-period horizon shown in Table 13.20 is different from that for the one-period horizon in Table 13.19. This means that we must extend the analysis to three periods. In the event that we must extend it further, we will write the equations in general form as

$$M_n^*[I_0, q(I_0)] = M_1^*[I_0, q(I_0)] + \sum_{d=0}^{\infty} M_{n-1}^*[I_0 + q(I_0) - d]^+ P(d) \quad (13.42)$$

and

$$M_n^*(I_0) = \max_{q(I_0) \geq 0} \{M_n^*[I_0, q(I_0)]\} \quad (13.43)$$

The results of calculations for a three-period horizon are shown in Table 13.21.

The optimal policy for the three-period horizon is the same as the optimal policy for the two-period horizon, so there is no need to carry the analysis to a four-period horizon.

It is interesting to look at the results of this example from an intuitive point of view. If we did not have an ordering cost of $10 for this problem, the optimal policy would be to order 1 unit when inventory was zero and order no units for any other inventory level. Because demand has an average value of 1.1 units per period, this would amount to placing an order virtually every period. But when an order costs $10 it is uneconomical to order every period, so the optimal policy is to order 2 units each time an order is placed. This means that 70% of the time the 2 units will be more than demand in the period in which they are ordered and so 1 unit will be carried over to the next period. That unit will satisfy demand with a probability of 0.70, so no new order will be placed.

Table 13.21 Optimal Policy and Expected Profit for a Three-Period Horizon Encyclopedia Problem

I_0	$q(I_0)$	$M_2^*(I_0)$
0	2	$ 3.35
1	0	9.72
2	0	13.35
3	0	11.10
4	0	2.665

Table 13.22 Transition Probabilities Optimal Policy for the Encyclopedia Problem

i \ j	0	1	2
0	0.3	0.5	0.2
1	0.8	0.2	0
2	0.3	0.5	0.2

The expected per-period profit of the optimal policy can be calculated using the techniques of the last section. The transition probabilities are given in Table 13.22. Using the data of Table 13.22, the stationary probabilities are $P_0 = \frac{32}{65}$, $P_1 = \frac{25}{65}$, $P_2 = \frac{8}{65}$. The expected profit for the *next period* when following the optimal policy when $I_0 = 0$ is $-\$3.50$. This results from ordering 2 units. When $I_0 = 1$, the optimal policy is to order no units and yield a profit of $7.00. When $I_0 = 2$, the optimal policy again indicates that no units should be ordered. The expected profit for the next period is $6.50. Thus, the overall expected profit per period is

$$\tfrac{32}{65}(-3.50) + \tfrac{25}{65}(7.00) + \tfrac{8}{65}(6.50) = \$1.769$$

13.3 SUMMARY AND DISCUSSION

All business decision problems contain an element of risk. It is important to look at the techniques described in Chapters 4 through 9 as applicable to problem situations where risk is a minor factor. In these situations, ignoring risk and formulating the problem as if certainty prevailed do little injustice to the problem and produce solutions that would be very close to those that would be obtained if the risk were specifically considered. In this chapter, we devoted our attention to some techniques that are useful in solving decision problems where explicit consideration of risk was necessary.

One could argue that there are fewer difficulties in formulating a decision model under certainty than under risk. The problems we solved in this chapter contained many aspects that bear on formulating decision models under risk. We will try to highlight a few in the next few paragraphs.

In Section 13.1 the inventory stocking problem for Judy's Bakery illustrated a traditional type of static decision problem under risk. The problem was formulated using discrete probabilities. Data were not kept in as fine detail as the analysis called for, so it was necessary to make some "practical" assumptions and interpolate. This is a common requirement for dealing with decision making under risk. The approach used to solve the problem was one of many possible ways of dealing with the situation.

Table 13.23 Determination of Mean and Standard Deviation From Table 13.1

Interval	X_i Midpoint	f_i Relative Frequency	$X_i f_i$	X_i^2	$X_i^2 f_i$
50–59	54.5	0.115	6.2675	2970.25	341.57875
60–69	64.5	0.125	8.0625	4160.25	520.03125
70–79	74.5	0.433	32.2585	5550.25	2403.25825
80–89	84.5	0.221	18.6745	7140.25	1577.99525
90–99	94.5	0.106	10.0170	8930.25	946.60650
Σ		1.000	75.2800		5789.47000

$$\overline{X} = 75.28$$
$$\sigma_X^2 = 5789.47 - (75.28)^2 = 122.3916; \sigma_X = 11.063$$

Another way of dealing with the problem would be to assume a continuous distribution and use (13.21) as a "practical" approach. To see how the "practical" person might solve the problem with a continuous distribution, consider Table 13.1 where the probability distribution for demand at Lincoln Super Foods is given. By "eyeballing" the data, we might assume that demand is approximately normal with mean and standard deviation determined from Table 13.23. This would be another approximation because the normal distribution would tend to have longer "tails" and less mass in the central part of the distribution than the empirical distribution of Table 13.1. But, nevertheless, assuming normality, we have, using (13.21a),

$$q = \overline{X} + Z_{0.3333}\sigma_X \doteq 75.28 - 0.43(11.063) = 70.52$$

as the optimal solution.

There is some difference between the optimal solution from the empirical distribution and the optimal solution from the normal distribution. The difference arises because the normal distribution is not a good fit to the empirical distribution. Thus, the practical person is left with a problem of judging the relative merits of making the assumption of uniform probability within categories. This was made for the empirical distribution when it was extended to individual units, or one could assume that the normal distribution adequately describes the "real" distribution. Statistical theory can help to make this judgment. Also, other distributions could be fitted to the data. In general, much analysis could be devoted to determining the appropriate probability distribution. But these are statistical issues that cannot be discussed here. Suffice it to say that the techniques of statistical analysis are helpful, and the decision maker should be aware of the implications of statistical techniques and the quality of statistical data for decision making.

Analysis of the bakery problem also introduced the concept of the value of information. There are essentially two methods of dealing with risk. The most obvious method is to accept it and make the best of it—essentially the method of Section 13.1. But another method of dealing with risk is to seek ways to reduce it. Prior information is one way. To make an analysis of the worth of additional information is essential to many business decision problems. Dealing with both the costs and benefits of imperfect information was illustrated in Section 13.1.

Section 13.1 also dealt with two other ideas. The first was an equivalent alternative formulation to the bakery problem that allowed sensitivity analysis of the parameters. As we have tried to illustrate throughout this text, it is important for "practical" decision makers to use decision models to improve their understanding of the elements of the decision situation. We illustrated in Section 13.1 how cost parameters affect solutions. The second idea was the formulation of the problem in continuous form. This is frequently a practical necessity.

Section 13.2 illustrated a complex decision problem in the utility plant problem. It was a dynamic decision problem. It was a multistage problem involving more than one type of decision. Previous decisions affected the decision alternatives at subsequent stages as well as the choice between them. It also was a "one-time" decision sequence rather than a repetitive decision process. Furthermore, the probabilities used could only be developed through informed executive opinion as opposed to data gathering. The technique of model building centered around decisions and random events, so that isolating these key "nodes" in the decision tree constituted the essential part of model building. Through this analysis, the essential understanding of the issues in the decision problem was brought into sharp focus. The solution technique—backward induction—is just another name for dynamic programming. The tree diagram proved to be an important "graphic" in understanding the mechanics of dynamic programming.

Section 13.2 also illustrated a simple dynamic decision problem—developing an inventory policy. In this section, the basic recurrence relationships of dynamic programming under risk were developed. An important feature of the models of Section 13.2 was the transition probability. The characteristics of the demand distribution and a reasonable policy combined to ensure that the transition probabilities were unchanging. This fact, in turn, allowed us to calculate stationary probabilities of being in the various states and thereby to evaluate the expected profit of a policy. Certain policies—including those we called unreasonable—will cause transition probabilities to change as time passes. For these cases, we will be unable to calculate an expected cost and a single unchanging optimal policy. Also, when the probability distribution of demand changes from period to period, the transition probabilities will not remain constant and a single policy will not be optimal. These latter two cases could be analyzed from a decision tree format but the computations would be overwhelming. Even though the examples of Section 13.2 are special cases, they do serve as first approximations in the analysis of certain types of decision problems.

One final point is worth making at this juncture. The decision problems we discussed in this chapter had an important simplifying characteristic. At any decision point, there was only a single decision variable. No allocation decisions were present. In the next chapter we will discuss dynamic decision problems where allocation decisions are important.

References   Bellman, R.E., and Dreyfus, S.E., *Applied Dynamic Programming*, Princeton: Princeton University Press, 1962.

Derman, C., *Finite State Markovian Decision Processes*, New York: Academic Press, 1970.

Hadley, G., *Introduction to Probability and Statistical Decision Theory*, San Francisco: Holden-Day, 1967.

Hadley, G., and Whitin, T.M., *Analysis of Inventory Systems*, Englewood Cliffs, N.J.: Prentice-Hall, 1963.

Hillier, F.S., and Lieberman, G., *Introduction to Operations Research*, 2nd ed., San Francisco: Holden-Day, 1974.

Howard, R., *Dynamic Programming and Markov Processes*, Cambridge: MIT Press, 1960.

Raiffa, H., *Decision Analysis*, Reading, Mass.: Addison-Wesley, 1968.

Schlaifer, R., *Probability and Statistics for Business Decisions*, New York: McGraw-Hill, 1959.

Schlaifer, R., *Analysis of Decisions Under Uncertainty*, New York: McGraw-Hill, 1969.

Wagner, H.M., *Principles of Operations Research*, 2nd ed., Englewood Cliffs, N.J.: Prentice-Hall, 1975.

Review Questions

1. Explain, in words, the necessary conditions for maximizing profit given below Equation 13.3.

2. Show the algebra by which Equation 13.4 is derived from the first condition.

3. Explain the meaning of EVPI in words.

4. (a) Explain the meaning of Table 13.4 in words.
    (b) Explain how Table 13.8 was derived.
    (c) Explain, in words, the concept of the probability of a forecast (see Equation 13.13).

5. (a) Explain the meaning of opportunity cost as used in Equations 13.14, 13.15, and 13.16.
    (b) Explain how the relationship between understock costs and overstock costs affects the stocking decision.

6. (a) Distinguish between decision acts and random events in the decision-tree problem of Section 13.2.
    (b) Explain the technique of backward induction and collapsing the decision tree.

7. (a) Explain the concept of a policy.
   (b) Explain the meaning of transition probabilities and stationary proba-
       bilities.
   (c) Why do you need stationary probabilities?
   (d) Explain how a policy affects transition probabilities.

8. Explain the technique of convergence of policies in determining an optimal
   policy.

9. Distinguish between $M_1[I_0, q(I_0)]$ and $M_1(I_0)$.

10. Explain, in words understandable to a knowledgeable person who is un-
    trained in quantitative methods, why the wrist alarm problem can be analyzed
    as a static problem but the encyclopedia problem cannot.

Problems

1. If the cost of producing a loaf of bread increases to $0.55 and the price at
   the Day Olde Store is increased to $0.30, what will be the optimal stocking
   policy at Lincoln Super Foods? Calculate the expected cost of the new
   policy.

2. A plumbing contractor has a large service business employing 10 service
   people in a large metropolitan area. The demand per week for replacement
   of shower faucets is given in the table.

Demand	Probability
10	0.05
11	0.10
12	0.65
13	0.15
14	0.05

The contractor can get delivery of shower faucets from the supplier in one
week from the time of the order. The contractor always orders 100 faucets.
If inventory is not available, the sale will be lost and the contractor will incur
an opportunity cost of $3, which is the profit on a call. If faucets are left in
inventory for the week, a cost of $0.50 is incurred for storage. At what level
of inventory should the contractor place an order on the supplier to replenish
the stock?

3. A summer playhouse is in the process of constructing its building. The cost
   per performance—including operations, depreciation, interest, actors'
   salaries, etc.—is estimated to be $C(S) = 620 + 2S$, where S is the number of
   seats installed. The playhouse will charge $5 per seat per performance. The
   demand for seats per performance is assumed to have a uniform probability
   density function $P(d) = \frac{1}{200}$, $100 \le d \le 300$. How many seats should be
   installed? What is the expected profit for the theater per performance?

4. Suppose Table 13.4 were replaced by the following table:

Actual Demand	Forecast				
	50–59	60–69	70–79	80–89	90–99
50–59	1.00	0.10	0.10		
60–69		0.90	0.20		
70–79			0.40		
80–89			0.20	0.90	
90–99			0.10	0.10	1.00

Would it be worthwhile for Judy's to buy the forecast at $1 per forecast?

5. Using Equation 13.20 derive Equation 13.21. *Hint:* To solve this problem, make sure you use the formula

$$\frac{d}{dx}\left[\int_a^x f(t)dt\right] = f(x)$$

6. Draw a decision tree for the Midwest Book Store problem if the horizon is two periods and existing inventory I_0 is 1 unit. Include probabilities and costs. Use backward induction to solve the problem.

7. Using the decision tree of Problem 6, assume that the probability of demand for the first period is given by Table 13.18 but the probability of demand during the second period depends on the demand for the first period. If $d = 0$ for the first period, then $P(0) = 0.0$, $P(1) = 0.6$, $P(2) = 0.4$ is the distribution for period 2. If $d = 1$ for the first period, then Table 13.18 holds for the second period. If $d = 2$ for the first period, then $P(0) = 0.6$, $P(1) = 0.4$, $P(2) = 0$ for the second period.

   (a) Determine the optimal policy for period 1 and period 2 by use of backward induction.

   (b) Describe the optimal policy for the second period in words.

8. (a) If the probability of extended hearing in the CEUG example were dropped to zero for all cases, would the optimal decision remain the same as in the text? Draw the decision tree and use backward induction to solve the problem.

   (b) What probability of nuclear at Mohawk Bend being approved at $\boxed{\dfrac{e}{11}}$

   would be needed to cause the nuclear decision to be selected by CEUG?

9. M.B. Allen makes decisions on her stock investments every month. She now (time $t = 0$) holds a stock 1 in the amount of $10,000. The return over the next month is a random variable. By the end of next month (time $t = 1$) the stock could go up 10% in value with a probability of 0.7 or it could go

down 20% with a probability of 0.3. If the stock increases in value by $t = 1$, the probability of increasing 10% more by $t = 2$ is 0.8 and the probability of decreasing 20% is 0.2. If stock 1 falls in value by 10% by $t = 1$, the probability of increasing 10% from the $t = 1$ level by $t = 2$ is 0.3 and the probability of falling by 10% from the $t = 1$ level by $t = 2$ is 0.7.

Stock 2 is the other stock that Allen is considering. The probability is 0.5 that stock 2 will increase by 40% by time $t = 1$ and 0.5 that it will decline by 30%. If it increases by 40%, the probability of an additional 10% increase by $t = 2$ is 1.0. If the stock declines by 30% by $t = 1$, the probability that it will increase from its $t = 1$ value by 10% is 0.8. The probability that it will decrease by 10% from its $t = 1$ value is 0.2.

If it cost 2% of value to sell a stock and 3% of value to buy, use a decision tree to determine the strategy that Allen should follow over the next two periods if she wishes to maximize the expected value of her investment. She can sell-buy at both $t = 0$ and $t = 1$. Assume the movements of the stocks are independent.

10. Calculate transition probabilities and stationary probabilities for the demand distribution of Table 13.9 and the policy

I_0	$q(I_0)$
0	1
1	1
2	1
3	0

Calculate the expected profit of this policy using Equation 13.22.

11. Given the demand distribution of Table 13.9 and the policy of Problem 10,
    (a) Calculate the two-step transition probabilities.
    (b) Calculate the three-step transition probabilities.

12. Derive Table 13.20.

13. The profit model of Equation 13.3 relies on a special accounting system. The cost of purchase of the encyclopedia is not charged to the period if the encyclopedia is not sold. If we were to "keep the books" on a cash basis, then (13.27) would be replaced by

$$\pi[d, I_0, q(I_0)]$$

$$= \begin{cases} 35d - 25q - 5[I_0 + q(I_0) - d] - 10\delta[q(I_0)] & d \le I_0 + q(I_0) \\ 10[I_0 + q(I_0)] - 10\delta[q(I_0)] & d > I_0 + q(I_0) \end{cases}$$

Calculate the optimal policy using this cost function. Calculate the optimal expected profit.

14. Suppose Table 13.18 is replaced by

Demand	Probability
0	0.1
1	0.1
2	0.8
3 or more	0

Derive the optimal policy for the Midwest Book Store.

15. Using the cost to place an order of $10 in the Midwest Book Store problem and the cost to carry a unit in inventory of $5 and a per-period average demand of 1.1 (from Table 13.18), determine the order quantity using the lot-size model of Chapter 9. Round the result off to the nearest integer and write a policy that would most nearly describe the use of the lot-size model. Calculate the expected cost for this policy and compare it to the cost of the optimal policy of Midwest Book Store and with the cost that would be derived using the lot-size model of Chapter 9.

14
PROGRAMMING UNDER UNCERTAINTY

14.1 A TWO-STAGE PROBLEM USING DYNAMIC PROGRAMMING

Formulation and Solution of the Model
Discussion of the Solution

14.2 TWO-STAGE LINEAR PROGRAMMING

A Production Problem
Linear Programming Formulation and Solution
Model Modifications
Expected Value of Perfect Information
Generalization

14.3 CHANCE-CONSTRAINED PROGRAMMING

Problem Satement and Formulation
Equivalent Linear Program
Discussion of the Solution

14.4 SUMMARY

References
Review Questions
Problems

The decision problems presented in Chapter 13 involved a single decision variable at each stage. In this chapter, we will extend the analysis of dynamic decision problems under risk to situations where decisions on several variables must be made at each stage. With the inclusion of added decision variables comes added complexity in formulation as well as added computational burden. In fact, the computational burdens are frequently so intense that it is impractical to consider problems that consist of more than a few stages.

In some cases, multivariable, multistage programming problems under risk can be converted to equivalent linear programming problems. Solution can then follow well-known methods with little added analysis. In other cases, the problems can only be converted to nonlinear programs with their attendant extra analytical as well as computational burdens. In this chapter, we will discuss problems that can be converted to linear programs as well as touch on some problems that must be converted to nonlinear programs for solution.

14.1 A TWO-STAGE PROBLEM USING DYNAMIC PROGRAMMING

In order to understand the way in which liquidity and profitability interact in individual investment portfolios, Scientific Investment Counselors developed a simple two-stage model for investment decision making. The model contains two decision variables for each period; X_{Bt}, the dollars invested in bonds at the beginning of period t, and X_{St}, the dollars invested in savings certificates at the beginning of period t. The horizon is two periods, and maximization of expected cash at the end of two periods is the investor's objective. The investor can buy bonds at the beginning of period 1 as well as the beginning of period 2. If bonds are purchased at the beginning of period 1, both the interest and principal are not available until the end of period 2. The bonds cannot be sold. Bonds purchased at the beginning of period 2 return principal and interest at the end of period 2. Savings certificates are liquid, yielding both principal and interest at the end of each period. Interest rates on both bonds and certificates are known at the beginning of period 1. The interest rate on bonds purchased at the beginning of period 2 is viewed as a random variable that will become known before the decision is made for period 2.

Formulation and Solution of the Model

Let C_o be the cash available at the beginning of period 1. Then the cash available at the end of period 1 is

$$C_1 = C_o + r_{S1}X_{S1} - X_{B1} \tag{14.1}$$

where r_{S1} is the interest on savings certificates. This equation reflects the fact that investment in bonds does not yield a return at the end of the first period and that investment in savings certificates yields a return of both interest and principle.

At the end of period 2, the cash is

$$C_2 = C_1 + r_{S2}X_{S2} + \tilde{r}_{B2}X_{B2} + (1 + r_{B1})^2 X_{B1} \tag{14.2}$$

where r_{S2} is the known rate of interest on savings certificates during period 2, r_{B1} is the interest rate on bonds at the beginning of period 1, $\tilde{r}_{B2}$ is the interest rate on bonds at the beginning of period 2. The latter is unknown when viewed from the beginning of period 1 but becomes known at the beginning of period 2. (All interest rates are assumed to be positive.) The first three terms on the right-hand side of (14.2) represent the cash available from investments made at the beginning of period 2. To clarify, $C_1 - X_{S2} - X_{B2}$ would be the cash held and $(1 + r_{S2})X_{S2}$ and $(1 + \tilde{r}_{B2})X_{B2}$ would be the return of principal and interest on savings certificates and bonds. Then, clearly,

$$C_1 - X_{S2} - X_{B2} + (1 + r_{S2})X_{S2} + (1 + \tilde{r}_{B2})X_{B2} = C_1 + r_{S2}X_{S2} + \tilde{r}_{B2}X_{B2}.$$

The fourth term on the right-hand side of (14.2) is the return, with interest, of the investment in bonds made at the beginning of period 1.

Let us first look at the decision problem at the beginning of period 2. The problem facing the investor is given by

$$\underset{X_{B2}, X_{S2}}{\text{Max}} C_2 \tag{14.3}$$

subject to

$$X_{B2} + X_{S2} \le C_1 \tag{14.4a}$$

$$X_{B2} \qquad \le 0.6C_1 \tag{14.4b}$$

The constraint (14.4a) indicates that the investor cannot invest more than the cash available at the beginning of the period. Constraint (14.4b) is a self-imposed liquidity constraint.

The nature of the solution to (14.3), (14.4a), (14.4b) can be seen in Figure 14.1. If $\tilde{r}_{B2} < r_{S2}$, then point P_1 will be the solution. If $\tilde{r}_{B2} \ge r_{S2}$, then point P_2 will be the solution. At P_1 we have $X_{S2} = C_1$ and $X_{B2} = 0$, while at P_2, $X_{S2} = 0.4C_1$, and $X_{B2} = 0.6C_1$. If we let $C_2^*(\tilde{r}_{B2}, C_1)$ be the value of the optimal solution to (14.3) to (14.4b), then

$$C_2^*(\tilde{r}_{B2}, C_1) = \begin{cases} (1 + r_{S2})C_1 + (1 + r_{B1})^2 X_{B1} & r_{S2} > \tilde{r}_{B2} \\ (1 + 0.6\tilde{r}_{B2} + 0.4r_{S2})C_1 + (1 + r_{B1})^2 X_{B1} & r_{S2} \le \tilde{r}_{B2} \end{cases} \tag{14.5}$$

Note now that when viewed from the beginning of period 1, C_1 is a function of the decisions made in the first period and $C_2^*(\tilde{r}_{B2}, C_1)$ is a random variable. Thus, we have, as the decision problem for period 1,

$$\underset{X_{B1}, X_{S1}}{\text{Max}} E[C_2^*(\tilde{r}_{B2}, C_1)] \tag{14.6}$$

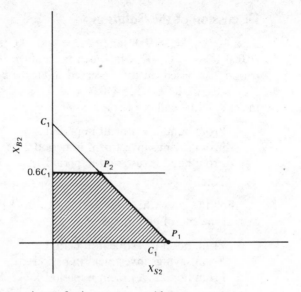

Figure 14.1 Constraint set for investment problem.

subject to

$$X_{B1} + X_{S1} \leq C_O \qquad (14.7a)$$

$$X_{B1} \qquad \leq 0.6C_O \qquad (14.7b)$$

To see how the problem would be solved, let $r_{B1} = 0.08$ and $r_{S1} = r_{S2} = 0.06$, $C_o = \$100,000$, and the probability distribution of $\tilde{r}_{B2}$ be $Pr(\tilde{r}_{B2} = 0.08) = 0.4$, $Pr(\tilde{r}_{B2} = 0.12) = 0.3$, $Pr(\tilde{r}_{B2} = 0.04) = 0.3$. Then

$$
\begin{aligned}
E[C_2{}^*(\tilde{r}_{B2}, C_1)] &= Pr(\tilde{r}_{B2} = 0.08)C_2{}^*(0.08, C_1) + Pr(\tilde{r}_{B2} = 0.12)C_2{}^*(0.12, C_1) \\
&\quad + Pr(\tilde{r}_{B2} = 0.04)C_2{}^*(0.04, C_1) \\
&= 0.4\{[1 + 0.6(0.08) + 0.4(0.06)](100,000 + 0.06X_{S1} - X_{B1}) \\
&\quad + (1.08)^2 X_{B1}\} + 0.3\{[1 + 0.6(0.12) + 0.4(0.06)] \\
&\quad \times (100,000 + 0.06X_{S1} - X_{B1}) + (1.08)^2 X_{B1}\} \\
&\quad + 0.3[(1 + 0.06)(100,000 + 0.06X_{S1} - X_{B1}) + (1.08)^2 X_{B1}] \\
&= 107,560 + 0.064536X_{S1} + 0.090800X_{B1}
\end{aligned}
$$

and (14.6), (14.7a), and (14.7b) become

$$\underset{X_{B1}, X_{S1}}{\text{Max}} \; (107,560 + 0.064536X_{S1} + 0.090800X_{B1}) \qquad (14.8)$$

subject to

$$X_{B1} + X_{S1} \leq 100,000 \qquad (14.9a)$$

$$X_{B1} \qquad \leq 60,000 \qquad (14.9b)$$

which has a solution $X_{B1} = 60,000$ and $X_{S1} = 40,000$ and the value of the objective function at the end of the second period is \$115,589.44.

Discussion of the Solution

Because $X_{B1} = \$60,000$ and $X_{S1} = \$40,000$, the cash position after period 1 is $40,000(1.06) = 42,400$, which can be confirmed by using (14.1). The solution for period 2 is based on the observed interest rate. For the case where $\tilde{r}_{B2} = 0.08$, $X_{B2} = 0.6(42,400) = \$25,440.00$ and $X_{S2} = 0.4(42,400) = \$16,960$, and therefore the cash at the end of period 2 is

From bond investment in period 2	$25,440(1.08) = \$27,475.20$
From savings investment in period 2	$16,960(1.06) = \$17,977.60$
From bond investment in period 1	$60,000(1.08)^2 = \$69,984.00$
Total	$\$115,436.80$

For the case where $\tilde{r}_{B2} = 0.12$, $X_{B2} = \$25,440$ and $X_{S2} = \$16,960$ and the cash at the end of period 2 is

From bond investment in period 2	$25,440(1.12) = \$28,492.80$
From savings investment in period 2	$16,960(1.06) = \$17,977.60$
From bond investment in period 1	$60,000(1.08)^2 = \$69,984.00$
Total	$\$116,454.40$

When $\tilde{r}_{B2} = 0.04$, the decision will be to put all cash into savings certificates in the last period. Therefore, $X_{B2} = 0$ and $X_{S2} = \$42,000$. Therefore, the cash is

From savings investment in period 2	$42,400(1.06) = \$44,944.00$
From bond investment in period 1	$60,000(1.08)^2 = \$69,984.00$
Total	$\$114,928.00$

The expected cash is

$$0.4(115,436.80) + 0.3(116,454.40) + 0.3(114,928) = \$115,589.44,$$

as noted earlier.

The solution to the problem has a definite first-stage solution (i.e., $X_{B1} = \$60,000$, $X_{S1} = \$40,000$), but the solution for period 2 is contingent on the random event. In other words, there is a policy for period 2. Note that the general procedure we used to solve this problem resembled dynamic programming. We first formulated the problem for period 2 and developed a solution policy. Then, using the policy, we developed a programming problem for period 1 that involved only first-stage variables. Second-stage variables were eliminated through use of the policy for period 2.

14.2   TWO-STAGE LINEAR PROGRAMMING

An alternative way to formulate the problem offers some advantages over the previously used method. In this section, we will introduce this procedure using our investment problem and then we will apply it to a more complicated production problem.

The approach consists of specifying three sets of second-stage variables. They are $[X_{B2}^{(1)}, X_{S2}^{(1)}]$, $[X_{B2}^{(2)}, X_{S2}^{(2)}]$, and $[X_{B2}^{(3)}, X_{S2}^{(3)}]$. The superscript is used to characterize the policy. The superscript [1] indicates the policy that will be followed when the random event $\tilde{r}_{B2} = 0.08$ is observed, [2] when $\tilde{r}_{B2} = 0.12$ is observed, and [3] when $\tilde{r}_{B2} = 0.04$ is observed. Thus, solving the problem for $X_{B1}, X_{S1}, X_{B2}^{(1)}, X_{S2}^{(1)}$, $X_{B2}^{(2)}, X_{S2}^{(2)}, X_{B2}^{(3)}, X_{S2}^{(3)}$ will produce both the first-stage solution and the *optimal* policy to follow in period 2. Formulation of the model using these variables now remains.

The objective function is the expected value of cash at the end of period 2 and is

$$E(C_2) = (1.08)^2 X_{B1} + 0.4[1.08 X_{B2}^{(1)} + 1.06 X_{S2}^{(1)}]$$
$$+ 0.3[1.12 X_{B2}^{(2)} + 1.06 X_{S2}^{(2)}]$$
$$+ 0.3[1.04 X_{B2}^{(3)} + 1.06 X_{S2}^{(3)}] \qquad (14.10)$$

The constraints are

$$X_{B1} + X_{S1} \leq 100,000 \qquad (14.11a)$$

$$X_{B1} \qquad\quad \leq 60,000 \qquad (14.11b)$$

$$X_{B1} - 0.06 X_{S1} + X_{B2}^{(1)} + X_{S2}^{(1)} \leq 100,000 \qquad (14.12a)$$

$$0.6 X_{B1} - 0.036 X_{S1} + X_{B2}^{(1)} \qquad\quad \leq 60,000 \qquad (14.12b)$$

$$X_{B1} - 0.06 X_{S1} + X_{B2}^{(2)} + X_{S2}^{(2)} \leq 100,000 \qquad (14.13a)$$

$$0.6 X_{B1} - 0.036 X_{S1} + X_{B2}^{(2)} \qquad\quad \leq 60,000 \qquad (14.13b)$$

$$X_{B1} - 0.06 X_{S1} + X_{B2}^{(3)} + X_{S2}^{(3)} \leq 100,000 \qquad (14.14a)$$

$$0.6 X_{B1} - 0.036 X_{S1} + X_{B2}^{(3)} \qquad\quad \leq 60,000 \qquad (14.14b)$$

The objective function (14.10) is the expected value of cash at the end of period 2. The first term on the right-hand side is the bond investment from period 1. The remaining three terms are the second-period investment returns.

The first set of constraints, (14.11a) and (14.11b), apply to period 1. The remaining sets apply to both the first and second periods serving as a link between the two for the various strategies. Note that X_{B1} and X_{S1} appear in all constraints. In other words, these constraints assure that period-2 *policy* is consistent with period-1 decision.

Note that (14.10) and constraints (14.11a) to (14.14b) form a linear program. Also note that the program is relatively large, consisting of 8 variables and 8 constraints. The Simplex method can be used to solve the problem yielding $X_{B1} = \$60,000$, $X_{S1} = \$40,000$, $X_{B2}^{(1)} = \$25,440$, $X_{S2}^{(1)} = \$16,960$, $X_{B2}^{(2)} = \$25,440$, $X_{S2}^{(2)} = \$16,960$, $X_{B2}^{(3)} = 0$, $X_{S2}^{(3)} = \$42,400$.

Note that the solution indicates that \$60,000 should be invested in bonds at the beginning of period 1 and \$40,000 in savings certificates. Then if the interest rate on bonds in period 2 is 0.08, $X_{B2}^{(1)} = \$25,440$ indicates that this amount should be invested in bonds in period 2; $X_{S2}^{(1)} = \$16,960$ should go into savings certificates. The same solution is prescribed for period 2 if bond interest is 0.12. But if bond interest falls to 0.04, $X_{B2}^{(3)} = 0$ and $X_{S2}^{(3)} = \$42,400$. That is, bond investment is bypassed in favor of investment in savings certificates. The solution illustrates the *policy* that is determined by the programming solution.

The formulation in (14.10) to (14.14b) appears much more cumbersome than the procedure originally developed. Indeed, if the random variable could take on, say, 10 values, there would be 11 sets of constraints (22 constraints) in the formulation of the problem. Note that we must solve an increasingly bigger problem as the number of possible realizations of the random variable increases. There is, however, an advantage to the formulation. Not only is it straightforward, but computer programs for solving linear programming problems are also readily available. The original procedure required us to recognize the solution to the second-stage problem as a function of the random variable. Fortunately, it was easy for the two constraint problems we faced. If there are more constraints at each stage, it is not always so, and therefore the "expanded" programming approach has some appeal.

A Production Problem

Falls Manufacturing Company produces screen door closers sold through a national hardware chain. The production facilities used by Falls are limited to producing 10,000 units per month on regular time along with the potential to produce any additional amount on overtime. The demand for the closers is seasonal, with sales dropping off to a very small level in August. June and July are the peak demand months. Falls produces closers in May and June and then converts its facilities to the production of various aluminum products that have a less distinct seasonal demand pattern. The June demand on Falls is known with certainty when production is planned in May. It is for 12,000 units and results from advanced orders. The July demand is uncertain in May, however; Table 14.1 shows the probability distribution of demand in July as determined by the marketing vice president for Falls. The actual demand for July will be known with certainty in time for June production.

The cost to produce one unit on regular time is $1.85, while the cost to produce a unit on overtime is $2.15. The cost to carry a unit in inventory between the two months is $0.15. All demand must be met and the company wants no unsold units

Table 14.1 Probability Distribution of July Demand — Falls Manufacturing Company

Demand	Probability
14,000	0.3
15,000	0.4
16,000	0.3

at the end of July. The problem then breaks down into the question of how much overtime should be used during the first month of production.

Linear Programming Formulation and Solution

In order to solve the problem, let

X_{R1} = amount produced on regular time during May
X_{O1} = amount produced on overtime during May
I_1 = inventory on hand at the end of May after the demand for June has been shipped
$X_{R2}^{(1)}, X_{O2}^{(1)}$ = amount produced on regular and overtime during June if demand for July is 14,000 units
$X_{R2}^{(2)}, X_{O2}^{(2)}$ = amount produced on regular and overtime during June if demand for July is 15,000 units
$X_{R2}^{(3)}, X_{O2}^{(3)}$ = amount produced on regular and overtime during June if demand for July is 16,000 units

The variables X_{R1}, X_{O1}, and I_1 will be called *first-stage* variables, while the remaining variables are called *second-stage* variables.

It is useful to specify the constraints on the solution before the objective function. The constraints associated with May production are

$$X_{R1} + X_{O1} - I_1 = 12{,}000 \qquad (14.15a)$$

and

$$X_{R1} \le 10{,}000 \qquad (14.15b)$$

Constraint (14.15a) indicates that the production $(X_{R1} + X_{O1})$ must be such that it equals or exceeds demand. In other words, some inventory can be built up—I_1 can be positive—but no shortages are allowed. Constraint (14.15b) is a capacity constraint indicating that 10,000 units can be produced on regular time. The absence of a constraint on X_{O1} indicates that any amount can be produced on overtime.

Three sets of constraints are associated with June production.

$$I_1 + X_{R2}^{(1)} + X_{O2}^{(1)} = 14{,}000, \quad I_1 + X_{R2}^{(2)} + X_{O2}^{(2)} = 15{,}000,$$
$$I_1 + X_{R2}^{(3)} + X_{O2}^{(3)} = 16{,}000 \qquad (14.16a)$$

and

$$X_{R2}^{(1)} \le 10{,}000, \ X_{R2}^{(2)} \le 10{,}000, \ X_{R2}^{(3)} \le 10{,}000 \qquad (14.16b)$$

The three constraints in (14.16a) indicate that demand in the period 2 must be exactly satisfied for any of the three demand possibilities. No inventory carryover beyond period 2 or shortages are allowed. The left-hand side of each constraint represents the inventory carried over from period 1 plus the production in period 2. The right-hand side is the demand. Constraints (14.16b) are regular time-capacity constraints.

Table 14.2 Linear Programming Formulation of the Production Problem (for Probability Distribution in Table 14.1)

$$\text{Max}[1.85X_{R1} + 2.15X_{O1} + 0.15I_1 + 0.555X_{R2}^{(1)} + 6.45X_{O2}^{(1)} + 0.740X_{R2}^{(2)} + 0.860X_{O2}^{(2)} + 0.555X_{R2}^{(3)} + 0.645X_{O2}^{(3)}]$$

subject to

$$A \begin{cases} X_{R1} + X_{O1} - I_1 & = 12{,}000 \\ X_{R1} & \leq 10{,}000 \end{cases}$$

$$B \begin{cases} I_1 + X_{R2}^{(1)} + X_{O2}^{(1)} & = 14{,}000 \\ X_{R2}^{(1)} & \leq 10{,}000 \end{cases}$$

$$C \begin{cases} I_1 \qquad\qquad + X_{R2}^{(2)} + X_{O2}^{(2)} & = 15{,}000 \\ X_{R2}^{(2)} & \leq 10{,}000 \end{cases}$$

$$D \begin{cases} I_1 \qquad\qquad + X_{R2}^{(3)} + X_{O2}^{(3)} & = 16{,}000 \\ X_{R2}^{(3)} & \leq 10{,}000 \end{cases}$$

The expected cost of a production plan is

$$
\begin{aligned}
E(C) = {}& 1.85X_{R1} + 2.15X_{O1} + 0.15I_1 \\
& + (0.3)[1.85X_{R2}^{(1)} + 2.15X_{O2}^{(1)}] \\
& + (0.4)[1.85X_{R2}^{(2)} + 2.15X_{O2}^{(2)}] \\
& + (0.3)[1.85X_{R2}^{(3)} + 2.15X_{O2}^{(3)}]
\end{aligned}
\tag{14.17}
$$

The optimal production plan may then be stated as the one that minimizes (14.17) subject to (14.15) and (14.16). This is a normal linear programming problem that may be solved by the usual methods.

Before proceeding to the solution, note the structure of the problem as seen in Table 14.2. The first two constraints, labeled A, contain only first-stage variables. The remaining sets of constraints, labeled B, C, and D, contain both first- and second-stage variables. Note that in each of these sets of constraints, the first-stage variables (only I_1 in this case) are the same. These first-stage variables are coupled with distinct second-stage variables as well as right-hand sides in each constraint set. This coupling forces first-stage decisions to be consistent with *all* second-stage decisions. Looked at from another point of view, the coupling and the three separate sets of constraints produce a strategy.

Returning now to the solution, we find the optimal solution to be $X_{R1} = 10{,}000$, $X_{O1} = 2000$, $X_{R2}^{(1)} = 10{,}000$, $X_{O2}^{(1)} = 4000$, $X_{R2}^{(2)} = 10{,}000$, $X_{O2}^{(2)} = 5000$, $X_{R2}^{(3)} = 10{,}000$, $X_{O2}^{(3)} = 6000$. The solution states that the entire regular-time capacity should be used and that overtime should be used to produce the excess demand (over 10,000 units) *in the period of the demand*.

Model Modifications

The solution to the problem is straightforward, and, indeed, we would probably have come to the same conclusion as to the optimal policy without a programming analysis. Some small changes in the parameters of the problem will reveal a much

Table 14.3 Probability Distribution of July Demand—Falls Manufacturing Company

Demand	Probability
9,000	0.2
10,000	0.2
11,000	0.6

different solution, however. If demand during June is known to be 8000 units instead of 12,000 and the probability distribution of demand remains as described in Table 14.1, we have (14.15a) replaced by

$$X_{R1} + X_{O1} - I_1 = 8000 \tag{14.18}$$

The solution is now $X_{R1} = 10,000$, $X_{O1} = 0$, $I_1 = 2000$, $X_{R2}^{(1)} = 10,000$, $X_{O2}^{(1)} = 2000$, $X_{R2}^{(2)} = 10,000$, $X_{O2}^{(2)} = 3000$, $X_{R2}^{(3)} = 10,000$, $X_2^{(3)} = 4000$. Here the procedure indicates that it is optimal to produce 10,000 units in period 1 even though the demand is for only 8000 units. The additional 2000 units are produced because, with the probability distribution of demand as given in Table 14.1, it is certain that overtime will be needed in the period 2. Therefore, any production on regular time in period 1 will be advantageous because the cost to produce and carry the unit in inventory for one period is less than the cost to produce on overtime in period 2.

To be sure, the solution just discussed could also have been easily anticipated without an elaborate model. But suppose that we changed the probability distribution for period 2 to that shown in Table 14.3. For this case, Table 14.4 shows the linear programming formulation. The solution to the problem is $X_{R1} = 9000$,

Table 14.4 Linear Programming Formulation of the Production Problem using (14.18) and Probability Distribution in Table 14.3

$$\text{Max}[1.85X_{R1} + 2.15X_{O1} + 0.15I_1 + 0.370X_{R2}^{(1)} + 0.430X_{O2}^{(1)} + 0.370X_{R2}^{(2)} + 0.438X_{O2}^{(2)} + 1.110X_{R2}^{(3)} + 1.290X_{O2}^{(3)}]$$

subject to

$$A \begin{cases} X_{R1} + X_{O1} - I_1 & = 8,000 \\ X_{R1} & \leq 10,000 \end{cases}$$

$$B \begin{cases} I_1 + X_{R2}^{(1)} + X_{O2}^{(1)} & = 9,000 \\ X_{R2}^{(1)} & \leq 10,000 \end{cases}$$

$$C \begin{cases} I_1 + X_{R2}^{(2)} + X_{O2}^{(2)} & = 10,000 \\ X_{R2}^{(2)} & \leq 10,000 \end{cases}$$

$$D \begin{cases} I_1 + X_{R2}^{(3)} + X_{O2}^{(3)} & = 11,000 \\ X_{R2}^{(3)} & \leq 10,000 \end{cases}$$

$X_{O1} = 0, I_1 = 1000, X_{R2}^{(1)} = 8000, X_{O2}^{(1)} = 0, X_{R2}^{(2)} = 9000, X_{O2}^{(2)} = 0, X_{R2}^{(3)} = 10,000,$
$X_{O2}^{(3)} = 0.$

The solution to this problem calls for a buildup of 1000 units in inventory at the end of period 1. This result occurs because of the combination of three factors: (1) the cost to carry inventory, (2) the difference between overtime and regular time costs, and (3) the probability that demand in the second stage will exceed the regular-time capacity. To see how changes in these factors could affect the solution, consider the Simplex method for finding the solution to a linear programming problem, discussed in Chapter 5. If we proceeded with the Simplex method using the model formulated in Table 14.4, we would eventually reach the tableau shown in Table 14.5.

The solution shown in Table 14.5 calls for producing what is needed in the period of demand. It calls for overtime use in period 2 if demand is for 11,000 units. Note, however, that the solution is nonoptimal because it shows that variable I_1 can be brought into the solution causing a reduction in cost. Iterating to the next tableau will produce the optimal solution, as previously stated. Rather than proceed with the iteration, it is useful to examine this tableau more carefully to see how the three factors mentioned in the previous paragraph affect the $c_j - z_j$ and hence the optimal solution.

If we let C_I be the cost to carry inventory, C_R be the cost to produce on regular time, C_o be the cost to produce on overtime, and P_1, P_2, P_3 be the probabilities of demands of 9,000, 10,000, and 11,000 for period 2, we can write

$$c_j - z_j = C_I + C_R - P_1 C_R - P_2 C_R - P_3 C_o \qquad (14.19)$$

which becomes, for our example,

$$c_j - z_j = 0.15 + 1.85 - 0.2(1.85) - 0.2(1.85) - 0.6(2.15) = -0.03$$

Now rewrite (14.19) as

$$c_j - z_j = C_I + (1 - P_1 - P_2)C_R - P_3 C_o = C_I + P_3 C_R - P_3 C_o$$

and for carrying inventory to be a profitable alternative we must have

$$C_I < P_3(C_o - C_R) \qquad (14.20)$$

Thus, if, for example, $C_I = 0.15$ and $C_o - C_R = 0.30$, we must have $P_3 > 0.5$ for it to be profitable to carry inventory. Equation 14.20 has an easy interpretation. The left-hand side is the cost to carry a unit in inventory for a period. On the right-hand side $C_o - C_R$ is the difference between regular and overtime costs to produce a unit. P_3 is the probability that demand will exceed regular-time productive capacity. So the right-hand side is the expected value of "excess" overtime costs. Thus, carrying inventory is worthwhile if the expected cost of doing so is less than the expected cost of not carrying it ("excess" overtime costs).

The formulation of the production problem as a two-stage programming problem has the advantage that we can analyze the character of the solution and,

Table 14.5 Intermediate Tableau in Simplex Solution to the Linear Programming Formulation of the Production Problem (Modified)

C_j	Basis	1.850 X_{R1}	2.150 X_{O1}	0.15 I_1	0 S_2	0.370 $X_{R2}^{(1)}$	0.430 $X_{O2}^{(1)}$	0 S_4	0.370 $X_{R2}^{(2)}$	0.430 $X_{O2}^{(2)}$	0 S_6	1.110 $X_{R2}^{(3)}$	1.290 $X_{O2}^{(3)}$	0 S_8	R	Ratio
1.850	X_{R1}	1	1	-1											8,000	00
0	S_2		-1	1	1										2,000	2,000
0.370	$X_{R2}^{(1)}$			1		1	1								9,000	9,000
0.	S_4			-1			-1	1							1,000	∞
0.370	$X_{R2}^{(2)}$			1					1	1					10,000	10,000
0	S_6			-1						-1	1				0	∞
0.290	$X_{O2}^{(3)}$			1									1	-1	1,000	1,000*
1.110	$X_{R2}^{(3)}$											1		1	10,000	∞
	z_j	0	1.850	0.180	0	0	0.370	0	0	0.370	0	0	0	-0.180	34,220	
	$c_j - z_j$	0	0.300	-0.030	0	0	0.060	0	0	0.060	0	0	0	0.180		

Pivot variable = I_1 Pivot row = Row 7

by so doing, produce valuable information for management. All of the analytical benefits of the Simplex method discussed in Chapter 12 can be used to analyze uncertainty problems formulated as two-stage programming problems.

To see how two-stage programming problems can "balloon" into large linear-programming problems, consider a problem that has n_1 first-stage variables and m_1 first-stage constraints. Suppose also that there are n_2 second-stage variables and m_2 second-stage constraints. If there are K realizations of the random event, the linear programming that would be formulated for this example would have $n_1 + n_2 K$ variables (excluding slacks) and $m_1 + m_2 K$ constraints. For the example of this section, we had $n_1 = 3, n_2 = 2, m_1 = 2, m_2 = 2, K = 3$ yielding $3 + 2(3) = 9$ variables (excluding slacks) and $2 + 2(3) = 8$ constraints. If there had been $K = 8$ realizations of the random variable—a very reasonable possibility—the number of variables would be 19 and the constraints would number 18. A problem with $n_1 = n_2 = 50$, $m_1 = m_2 = 30$, and $K = 20$ would not be an unreasonable one to formulate in a practical situation. This would yield 1050 variables and 630 constraints!

The fact that two-stage (or multistage) programming models can become very large and "messy" computing problems requires a careful look at model formulation on the part of the analyst. Because models are not reality, but convenient abstractions of reality, sound judgment requires that the analyst explore alternative formulations of decision models that may produce decisions that are "almost" as good but can be accomplished with less computing. Furthermore, the analyst should try to exploit any special structure of the problem that would help to either compute the solution or understand it better. For example, a close examination of the first example formulated in this section will reveal that demand exceeds regular-time capacity in both stages *under all realizations of the random variable.* Therefore, the optimal solution would clearly require complete utilization of regular-time capacity in all periods. This means that we know that $X_{R1} = X_{R2}^{(1)} = X_{R2}^{(2)} = X_{R2}^{(3)} = 10,000$ and these variables can be eliminated from the problem. Furthermore, we know all capacity constraints are satisfied as equalities and can be eliminated. Thus, the programming problem can be reduced to a considerable extent.

Another example of exploitation of structure was illustrated by our study of $c_j - z_j$ in the modified version of the production problem. The information derived from that analysis was useful to management and could have been obtained by solving a number of linear-programming problems with different coefficients assigned to C_I, C_R, C_o, and P_1, P_2, and P_3. But the analysis of $c_j - z_j$ eliminated the need for such time-consuming analysis.

Expected Value of Perfect Information

The concept of the expected value of perfect information (EVPI) can also be applied to problems in two-stage programming. To see how this would be calculated, consider the modified production problem of Table 14.4. With perfect information on the value of the random event beforehand, the decision maker could adapt the first-period decision accordingly. There would then be three certainty problems to solve—one for each possible second-stage demand. They would be

$$\text{Max } 1.85X_{R1} + 2.15X_{O1} + 0.15I_1 + 1.85X_{R2}^{(1)} + 2.15X_{O2}^{(1)}$$

subject to

$$
\begin{array}{llll}
X_{R1} + & X_{O1} - & I_1 & = 8{,}000 \\
X_{R1} & & & \leq 10{,}000 \\
& I_1 + & X_{R2}^{(1)} + \quad X_{O2}^{(1)} & = 9{,}000 \\
& & X_{R2}^{(1)} & \leq 10{,}000
\end{array}
$$

$$\text{Max } 1.85X_{R1} + 2.15X_{O1} + 0.15I_1 + 1.85X_{R2}^{(2)} + 2.15X_{O2}^{(2)}$$

subject to

$$
\begin{array}{llll}
X_{R1} + & X_{O1} - & I_1 & = 8{,}000 \\
X_{R1} & & & \leq 10{,}000 \\
& I_1 + & X_{R2}^{(2)} + X_{O2}^{(2)} & = 10{,}000 \\
& & X_{R2}^{(2)} & \leq 10{,}000
\end{array}
$$

and

$$\text{Max } 1.85X_{R1} + 2.15X_{O1} + 0.15I_1 + 1.85X_{R2}^{(3)} + 2.15X_{O2}^{(3)}$$

subject to

$$
\begin{array}{llll}
X_{R1} + & X_{O1} - & I_1 & = 8{,}000 \\
X_{R1} & & & \leq 10{,}000 \\
& I_1 + & X_{R2}^{(3)} + \quad X_{O2}^{(3)} & = 11{,}000 \\
& & X_{R2}^{(3)} & \leq 10{,}000
\end{array}
$$

for the three random events.

The respective solutions to the problems are $X_{R1} = 8000$, $X_{O1} = 0$, $I_1 = 0$, $X_{R2}^{(1)} = 9000$, $X_{O2}^{(1)} = 0$ with an objective function value of \$31,450; $X_{R1} = 8000$, $X_{O1} = 0$, $I_1 = 0$, $X_{R2}^{(2)} = 10{,}000$, $X_{O2}^{(2)} = 0$ with an objective function value of \$33,300; $X_{R1} = 9000$, $X_{O1} = 0$, $I_1 = 1000$, $X_{R2}^{(3)} = 10{,}000$, $X_{O2}^{(3)} = 0$ with an objective function value of \$35,330. The expected value of costs under perfect information using these solutions and the probabilities of Table 14.2 is $(0.2)(31{,}450) + 0.2(33{,}300) + 0.6(35{,}300) = \$34{,}136$. The expected cost of the optimal solution without information is \$34,190. Therefore, the expected value of perfect information is $\$34{,}190 - \$34{,}136 = \$54$.

Generalization

Our analysis of two stage programming to this point has involved uncertainty in the coefficients of the objective function—the bond-rates-in-investment example—and uncertainty in the "right-hand sides"—the demand-in-production problem.

In neither case was there uncertainty in the coefficients in the second-stage constraints. In other words, the coefficients in the second-stage constraints remained unchanged for every realization of the random variable. This is not required for two-stage programming. Indeed, we may formulate a problem with the structure

$$\text{Max} \sum_{i=1}^{n_1} \pi_i X_i + \sum_{j=1}^{K} P_j \left[\sum_{i=1}^{n_2} \pi_i^{(j)} Y_i^{(j)} \right] \tag{14.21}$$

subject to

$$\sum_{i=1}^{n_1} a_{it} X_i \le R_t \qquad t = 1, \ldots, m_1 \tag{14.22}$$

$$\sum_{i=1}^{n_1} b_{it}^{(j)} X_i + \sum_{i=1}^{n_1} d_{it}^{(j)} Y_i^{(j)} \le Q_t^{(j)} \qquad t = 1, \ldots, m_2; j = 1, \ldots, k \tag{14.23}$$

The set of first-stage constraints is denoted by the m_1 constraints comprising (14.22). The first-stage variables are labeled X_i. Constraint set (14.23) constitutes all second-stage constraints. For each realization of the random variable, there are m_2 second-stage constraints, of the form shown in (14.23). Each of these sets uses a realization of the random coefficients $b_{it}^{(j)}$ and $d_{it}^{(j)}$ as well as the random right-hand side $Q_t^{(j)}$. Each set includes the first-stage decision variables X_i and a unique set of second-stage variables $Y_i^{(j)}$. The objective function maximizes the expected value of both first- and second-stage "profits." The second term in (14.21) includes the probability P_j of event j (which is $[b_{it}^{(j)}, d_{it}^{(j)}, Q_t^{(j)}, \pi_i^{(j)}]$) occurring and the profit that will result if j occurs—$\sum_{i=1}^{n_2} \pi_i^{(j)} Y_i^{(j)}$.

14.3   CHANCE-CONSTRAINED PROGRAMMING

In some problems, it is not desirable to formulate a complete set of decision rules for the second stage of a programming problem because of the complexity of the problem and because of the very large programming problem that would develop. In this section we will look at such a problem.

Problem Statement and Formulation

Supreme Manufacturing Company produces two products using three facilities—stamping, forming, and painting departments. It keeps close control on the raw materials needed to produce its products and adjusts delivery closely to production plans so as to avoid unnecessary inventory investment. The company must determine the capacity that it will allocate to the production of each of the products. Because there are machine breakdowns, variability in productivity of the employees, and other unavoidable losses of productive time, the company treats the capacity of each department as a random variable. The fact that capacity is a random variable that can take on a continuum of possibilities and the fact that second-stage strategies are very difficult to formulate caused Supreme to reject two-stage

Table 14.6 Supreme Manufacturing Company —Profit Contributions and Productivities of Products

	Product 1	Product 2
Contribution/unit	$0.75	$1.00
Forming time/unit	2.00 Min	2.00 Min
Stamping time/unit	2.00 Min	3.00 Min
Painting time/unit	2.00 Min	2.50 Min

programming as a technique for dealing with this product-mix problem. Instead, the company chose to look at it from a chance-constrained programming point of view.

Table 14.6 gives some of the necessary technical information about profit contributions and productivities for the products. Table 14.7 shows the mean and standard deviation of capacity in minutes per day. The capacity is assumed to be *normally distributed*.

The company executives required that the product mix and amounts produced each day be picked so that any one department will have a probability of 97.5% of meeting their production requirements. The mathematical model developed by the staff of the company was

$$\text{Max } 0.75X_1 + 1.00X_2 \tag{14.24}$$

subject to

$$P_r(2.00X_1 + 2.00X_2 \leq \tilde{C}_1) \geq 0.975 \tag{14.25}$$

$$P_r(2.00X_1 + 3.00X_2 \leq \tilde{C}_2) \geq 0.975 \tag{14.26}$$

$$P_r(2.00X_1 + 2.50X_2 \leq \tilde{C}_3) \geq 0.975 \tag{14.27}$$

$$X_1 \geq 0, X_2 \geq 0$$

where $\tilde{C}_i$ is the (random variable) capacity for each department.

Table 14.7 Supreme Manufacturing Company —Department Capacities

Department	Capacity, minutes per day	
	Mean	Standard Deviation
Forming	350	40
Stamping	400	20
Painting	460	5

Equivalent Linear Program

The formulation specifies that X_1 and X_2, the production amounts of each product, should be picked so that the contribution to profit be maximized. The constraints indicate that X_1 and X_2 should be picked so that the probability of running short of capacity in any department is less than 2.5%. We might ask: can we replace the probability statement of (14.25) with an equivalent simple linear constraint? To illustrate how such a constraint might be formed, refer to Figure 14.2. Consider constraint

$$2.00X_1 + 2.00X_2 \leq E(\tilde{C}_1)$$

If the (X_1, X_2) combination eventually selected were on this line, say at point A, we would find that the capacity constraint was violated whenever the realization of $\tilde{C}_1$ was less than $E(\tilde{C}_1)$, which would happen 50% of the time. Clearly, using $E(\tilde{C}_1)$ as the right-hand side of a constraint would not accomplish the specification in (14.25). Another candidate for the equivalent constraint would be

$$2.00X_1 + 2.00X_2 \leq E(\tilde{C}_1) - 1.96\sigma_{C_1} \tag{14.28}$$

which is also shown on Figure 14.2. To test whether this is the appropriate constraint, consider point A'', which we will say could be the optimal solution. Clearly, the realization of $\tilde{C}_1$ will be greater than $E(\tilde{C}_1) - 1.96\sigma_{\tilde{C}_1}$, 97.5% of the time. Therefore, by choosing (X_1'', X_2'') we will be within the constraint 97.5% of the time. Therefore, (14.28) is the linear equivalent of (14.25).

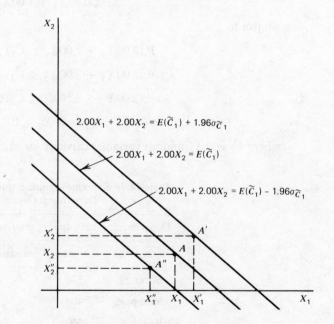

Figure 14.2 Illustration of a chance constraint.

To reinforce the understanding of the creation of the equivalent constraint, consider

$$2.00X_1 + 2.00X_2 \leq E(\tilde{C}_1) + 1.96\sigma_{\tilde{C}_1}$$

Why would it not be appropriate? Point A' in Figure 14.2 could be a solution if this constraint was used. But note that in 97.5% of the cases, the "random constraint line" would fall below the point A'. Therefore, the solution (X_1', X_2') would be infeasible 97.5% of the time.

It is now a simple matter to replace (14.24) to (14.27) by the equivalent linear model

$$\text{Max } 0.75X_1 + 1.00X_2 \tag{14.29}$$

subject to

$$2.00X_1 + 2.00X_2 \leq 350 - 1.96(40) = 271.6 \tag{14.30}$$

$$2.00X_1 + 3.00X_2 \leq 400 - 1.96(20) = 360.8 \tag{14.31}$$

$$2.00X_1 + 2.50X_2 \leq 460 - 1.96(5) \ \ = 450.2 \tag{14.32}$$

$$X_1 \geq 0, X_2 \geq 0$$

In essence, what has been done is to create a linear problem with a suitably conservative statement of capacity.

The solution to the problem is $X_1 = 46.6$ and $X_2 = 89.2$. Figure 14.3 shows the solution in graphic form. Note that the solution demands $46.6(2.90) + 89.2(2.00) = 271.6$ minutes of the forming department time. Assuming 480 minutes

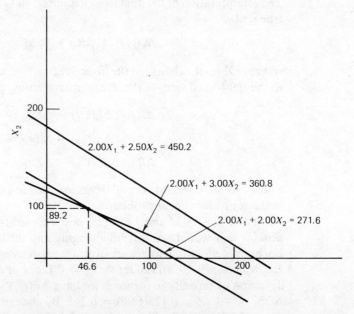

Figure 14.3 Graphic solution to the product-mix problem.

in the day, the plan calls for use of 271.6 or 56.58 % of the minutes available. The average minutes actually used will be somewhat less than 271.6 because 2.5 % of the time the plan will not be met because capacity will not allow the planned production. The stamping-department plan calls for using 360.8 minutes per day or 75.17 % of minutes available, and again 2.5 % of the time the plan will not be met because the capacity of this department will not be large enough to produce the plan. The capacity used in the painting department is $2.00(46.6) + 2.50(89.2) = 316.2$ minutes per day. The mean useful time available in painting is 450 minutes and the standard deviation is 5, so we can determine the probability of capacity falling below 316.2 minutes by finding the number of standard deviations this amount will be below the mean useful time. It is

$$\frac{316.2 - E(\tilde{C}_3)}{\sigma_{C_3}} = \frac{316.2 - 450}{5} = -26.76$$

Thus, the probability of painting capacity being short is nil.

Discussion of the Solution

It is possible to analyze the solution to the problem using the dual of the problem. The solution to the dual problem is $V_1 = 0.125$, $V_2 = 0.250$, $V_3 = 0$, where V_1 is the dual variable associated with the forming capacity, V_2 is the dual variable associated with stamping capacity, and V_3 is the dual variable associated with painting. With the dual variables, it is possible to determine the values of small changes in average capacity, variability of capacity, and probability requirements for meeting capacity. The interpretation of the dual from Chapter 5 indicated that it was approximately true that

$$\Delta \text{Obj} \doteq V_1 \Delta R_1 + V_2 \Delta R_2 + V_3 \Delta R_3 \qquad (14.33)$$

where ΔObj is the change in the objective function and $\Delta R_1, \Delta R_2, \Delta R_3$ are changes in the right-hand sides of the linear-programming problem. Clearly,

$$\Delta R_1 \doteq \Delta E(\tilde{C}_1) - \Delta Z \sigma_{\tilde{C}_1} - Z \Delta \sigma_{\tilde{C}_1}$$
$$\Delta R_2 \doteq \Delta E(\tilde{C}_2) - \Delta Z \sigma_{\tilde{C}_2} - Z \Delta \sigma_{\tilde{C}_2} \qquad (14.34)$$
$$\Delta R_3 \doteq \Delta E(\tilde{C}_3) - \Delta Z \sigma_{\tilde{C}_3} - Z \Delta \sigma_{\tilde{C}_2}$$

where Z is the standard normal deviation used in establishing the right-hand sides in the equivalent linear problem.

Equations 14.34 and 14.33 can now be used to develop an indication of the benefits that would result from changing any of the parameters of the problem. For example, for a unit increase in average capacity in forming, we have $\Delta E(C_1) = 1$, $\Delta Z = 0$, $\Delta \sigma_{\tilde{C}_1} = 0$, and $\Delta \text{Obj} = V_1 = 0.125$. For a unit decrease in the standard deviation of capacity in forming, we have $\Delta E(C_1) = 0$, $\Delta Z = 0$, $\Delta \sigma_{\tilde{C}_1} = -1$, and $\Delta \text{Obj} = +V_1 Z = 0.125(1.96) = 0.245$. By changing the probability requirement from 97.5 % to 95 %, we have $\Delta Z = -0.315$ and $\Delta \text{Obj} = 0.125(0.315)(40) = 1.575$.

We might ask one more question concerning this problem. What is the probability that at least one constraint will limit production? Painting is not a practical limitation, so we will rule it out and concentrate attention on the forming and stamping constraints. Production can be limited by one of three possible events: (1) capacity in forming is short but capacity in stamping is sufficient; (2) capacity in forming is sufficient but capacity in stamping is short; (3) capacities in both departments are short. The probabilities of these three events are $0.025 \times 0.975 = 0.024375$, $0.975 \times 0.025 = 0.024375$, and $0.025 \times 0.025 = 0.000625$, respectively, and the probability of shortage of capacity is 0.049375.

Note the results of the calculation. Production was planned so that individual departments were short of capacity 2.5 % of the time, but because of the interaction between the two capacities production would be short nearly 5 % of the time due to at least one department's shortage of capacity. The probability of shortage could then easily be calculated by one minus the probability that no (limiting) department was short of capacity—that is, $1 - (0.975)(0.975) = 0.049375$.

We can extend the idea of the previous paragraph to a larger problem. Suppose 10 *limiting* constraints were met with probability 0.975. Then the probability of at least one limiting production would be $1 - (0.975)^{10} \doteq 0.22367$. That is, production would be limited over 22 % of the time!

The discussion of the previous three paragraphs is not meant to cast aspersions on the method of chance-constrained programming; instead, it is meant to aid in understanding the implications of the chance constraints. Clearly, if there are a large number of binding constraints, each subject to an *independent* probability distribution, the probability specification for any one constraint must be very high indeed to produce a high probability of overall system reliability.

It is possible to formulate a chance-constrained programming problem in such a way that the probability statements are made about the overall realiability. For example, suppose we wanted overall system reliability to be 97.5 % for our example of this section. The chance-constrained problem could be formulated as

$$\text{Max } 0.75X_1 + 1.00X_2$$

subject to

$$P_r(2.00X_1 + 2.00X_2 \leq \tilde{C}_1)P_r(2.00X_1 + 3.00X_2 \leq \tilde{C}_2)$$
$$\times P_r(2.00X_1 + 2.50X_2 \leq \tilde{C}_3) \geq 0.975$$
$$X_1 \geq 0, X_2 \geq 0$$

This formulation is perfectly reasonable and may describe the essence of the desires of the decision maker. The certainty equivalent to the problem will be a nonlinear programming problem, however, and its solution is beyond the scope of this text.

To avoid the complications inherent in the formulation of the problem of the previous paragraph, the decision maker could use (14.24) to (14.27) with increased values of the probabilities on the right-hand sides of the constraints to accomplish a similar result.

A less technical aspect of the problem is worth discussing at this time. The formulation of the problem with probability constraints as shown in (14.25) to (14.27) requires some thoughtful interpretation. Management has decreed that the realized capacity in any one department should be insufficient no more than 2.5% of the time. Apparently, violation is a serious problem. But with the chance-constrained formulation we are given no indication of just why it is serious. Will the business fail if a violation occurs? Will it be very costly? Or will it be merely inconvenient? In other words, the situation is not modeled explicitly but is contained implicitly in the constraints on the solution.

The vagueness of the cost assumptions as they are reflected in the chance constraints presents perplexing conceptual and practical problems in interpretation of chance-constrained solutions. This is the major disadvantage in the method. But there are advantages. Chance-constrained problems do not require a set of variables for every random event nor do they require a set of constraints for every random event; therefore, a chance-constrained problem will tend to be much smaller than a comparable two-stage problem.

But chance-constrained problems have a serious drawback. If uncertainty is present in the coefficients of the constraint set, the chance-constrained problem must be replaced with an equivalent nonlinear programming problem, which is usually much more difficult to solve.

14.4 SUMMARY

This chapter has dealt with some dynamic decision problems where decisions on more than one variable must be made at a given stage. Using the investment problem, we formulated and solved a two-stage problem using a dynamic programming approach. We also illustrated how this problem could be solved by an equivalent linear program. The production problem involving the balancing of regular-time production, overtime, and inventory carrying was formulated directly as a two-stage programming problem. After solving two straightforward problems, we found the solution to a problem that was not readily apparent. We also showed how the analytical techniques of linear programming could be used to provide management with useful information on the way costs and probabilities affect the optimal solution to two-stage problems.

Two-stage programming problems increase rapidly in size—and therefore in the computing effort required—as the realizations of random events increase. This aspect of the approach is its main drawback in practical applications. Sometimes chance-constrained programming models can be formulated for dealing with dynamic decision problems. The main drawback of chance-constrained programming models is their tenuous relationship to some underlying cost models and the difficulty of interpreting the solutions of such models.

The literature on programming under uncertainty is large, growing, and in some instances esoteric. Needless to say, we have just scratched the surface in this chapter by illustrating a few formulations of decision problems that are designed to acquaint you with the possibilities and problems in this area of quantitative decision making.

References   Aghili, P., Cramer, R.H., and Thompson, H.E., "Small Bank Balance Street Management: Applying Two-Stage Programming Models," *Journal of Bank Records*, Vol. 5 (1975), pp. 246–256.

Agnew, N.W., Agnew, R.A., Rasmussen, J., and Smith, K.R., "An Application of Chance Constrained Programming to Portfolio Selection in a Casualty Insurance Firm," *Management Science*, Vol. 15 (1969), pp. B512–B520.

Bawa, V.S., "On Chance Constrained Programming Problems with Joint Constraints," *Management Science*, Vol. 19 (1973), pp. 1326–1331.

Bradley, S.P., and Crane, D.B., "A Dynamic Model for Bond Portfolio Management," *Management Science*, Vol. 19 (1972), pp. 139–151.

Charnes, A., and Cooper, W.W., "Cost Horizons and Certainty Equivalents: An Approach to Stochastic Programming of Heating Oil," *Management Science*, Vol. 4 (1958), pp. 235–263.

Charnes, A., and Cooper, W.W., "Deterministic Equivalents for Optimizing and Satisfying Under Chance Constraints," *Operations Research*, Vol. 11 (1963), pp. 18–39.

Cohen, K.J., and Thore, S., "Programming Bank Portfolios Under Uncertainty," *Journal of Bank Research*, Vol. 1 (1970), pp. 42–61.

Gunderson, H.S., Morris, J.G., and Thompson, H.E., "Stochastic Programming with Recourse: A Modification from an Applications Viewpoint," *Journal of the Operational Research Society*, Vol. 29 (1978), pp. 769–778.

Hillier, F.S., and Lieberman, G.J., *Introduction to Operations Research*, San Francisco: Holden-Day, 1967, Chapter 15.

King, W.R., "A Stochastic Personnel Assignment Model," *Operations Research*, Vol. 13 (1965), pp. 67–81.

Matthews, J.P., and Thompson, H.E., "Insurance Exposure and Investment Risks: Management and Regulatory Implications," *OMEGA*, Vol. 5 (1977), pp. 23–34.

Naslund, B., "A Model of Capital Budgeting Under Risk," *Journal of Business*, Vol. 39 (1966), pp. 257–271.

Pyle, D.H., and Turnovsky, S.J. "Risk Aversion in Chance-Constrained Portfolio Selection," *Management Science*, Vol. 18 (1971), pp. 218–225.

Resh, M., "Chance Constrained Programming of the Machine Loading Problem with Stochastic Processing Times," *Management Science*, Vol. 17 (1970), pp. 48–65.

Stancer-Minasian, I.M., and Wets, M.J., "A Research Bibliography in Stochastic Programming," *Operations Research*, Vol. 24 (1976), pp. 1078–1119.

Thompson, H.E., Matthews, J.P., and Li, B.C.L., "Insurance Exposure and Investment Risks: An Analysis Using Chance-Constrained Programming," *Operations Research*, Vol. 22 (1974), pp. 991–1007.

Van de Panne, C., and Popp, W., "Minimum-Cost Cattle Feed Under Probabilistic Protein Constraints," *Management Science*, Vol. 9 (1963), pp. 405–430.

Wagner, H.M., *Principles of Operations Research*, 2nd ed., Englewood Cliffs, N.J.: Prentice-Hall, 1975, Chapter 16.

Review Questions

1. Describe two decision problems within your knowledge and experience under the following circumstances.
   (a) More than one variable.
   (b) Multiple stages.
   (c) Significant uncertainty.

2. Explain, in words, the meaning of Equation 14.5.

3. (a) Explain how a policy (or strategy) is incorporated into the two-stage linear-programming problem.
   (b) How does the policy for the second period affect the first-period solution?

4. Using Table 14.2, explain why this two-stage problem could not be solved by dealing with just the first period and then each of the realizations for the second period separately.

5. Suppose the two-stage problem in Section 14.1 had had 5 realizations of the random event. How many variables and how many constraints would the resulting two-stage programming problem have?

6. Explain how Equation 14.20 was derived.

7. Describe a decision situation within your knowledge and experience that could be formulated as a chance-constrained programming problem.

8. (a) Explain the meaning of Equation 14.25.
   (b) Could Equation 14.25, be written in another way to mean the same thing?

9. Explain why $E(\tilde{C}_1) - 1.96\sigma_{\tilde{c}_1}$ is used on the right-hand side of the linear equivalent to Equation 14.25 instead of $E(\tilde{C}_1) + 1.96\sigma_{\tilde{c}_1}$.

10. Would the solution to the product-mix problem using chance-constrained programming change if standard deviations on all capacities were zero?

11. (a) Explain the meaning of Equations 14.33 and 14.34.
    (b) Explain why the relationships in these equations are approximate.

Problems

1. (a) Using the investment problem formulation form Section 14.1, suppose that $r_{S1} = 0.06$ and $r_{S2} = 0.09$. If all other data remain the same, find the optimal solution to the investment problem.
   (b) Show how the objective function and constraints of Equations 14.10 to 14.14*b* would change as a result of $r_{S2} = 0.09$.

2. Suppose that the investor from Section 14.1 had uncertain cash needs that would become known at the end of the first period. Suppose the needs were for $50,000 with probability 0.6 and $20,000 with probability 0.4 and that these probabilities are independent of those for bond rates. Formulate the investment problem so that these needs are considered (using the other data of Section 14.1).

3. Assume that the outcome of the random event in the problem of Section 14.1 can be forecast perfectly.

    (a) Formulate three linear-programming problems that can be used to find optimal first-period and second-period decisions for the investment problem given perfect forecasts.

    (b) Calculate the expected value of perfect information.

4. Suppose that an additional potential bond investment was added to the problem of Section 14.1. This investment has return $r_{b1} = 0.09$. The additional bond rate for the second period is perfectly correlated with the bond rate of Section 14.1—that is, $P_r(\tilde{r}_{B2} = 0.08$ and $\tilde{r}_{b2} = 0.09) = 0.4$, $P_r(\tilde{r}_{B2} = 0.12$ and $\tilde{r}_{b2} = 0.15) = 0.3$, $P_R(\tilde{r}_{B2} = 0.04$ and $\tilde{r}_{b2} = 0.01) = 0.3$.

    (a) Assuming that total bond investment cannot exceed 60% of cash, formulate the investment problem given that the investor seeks maximum expected cash at the end of the second period.

    (b) Solve the problem.

5. Using the data from Problem 4, determine the expected value of perfect information.

6. Consider the production problem posed in Table 14.4. Suppose Falls Manufacturing anticipated an increase in both regular and overtime costs during the second stage to $2.22/unit and $2.58/unit due to a labor-contract wage increase.

    (a) What would be the optimal solution to the problem?

    (b) Would the solution to the problem shown in Table 14.2 change?

7. Falls Manufacturing has added a second product to its seasonal production and will produce garden-hose holders in May and June using the same facilities as it uses to produce door closers. Each garden-hose holder requires the same amount of capacity to produce as does the door closer. The demand for garden-hose holders is 2000 for June and the July demand is for 2000 with probability 0.6 and 3000 with probability 0.4. The demand for closers and hose holders is independent. The costs to produce the hose holders on regular time and overtime are the same as the costs to produce closers, but because the holder takes more space to store, the cost to carry inventory is four times that for closers.

    (a) Using the demand for closers given in Table 14.3, formulate a two-stage linear-programming problem to solve this problem.

    (b) From the structure of the problem you have formulated, try to guess the nature of the solution.

8. National Soft Drinks is introducing a new brand of easy-mix soft drinks to be sold in supermarkets. National wants to perform a test marketing of the

product coupled with a test advertising. Following determination of the results of the test, the main advertising campaign will be developed. Top management has stated that not more than $1,000,000 can be spent on the entire advertising campaign (test and main campaign). The test and main campaign expenditures are to be divided between radio and television spots. The dollar volume of sales per dollar of expenditure on either radio or television is not known with certainty. The subjective probability distribution of $Y_i = \$$ sales/$\$$ expenditures in both radio and television has been estimated by the marketing research department to be $P_r(Y_R = 15, Y_T = 25) = 0.4$, $P_r(Y_R = 20, Y_T = 20) = 0.3$, $P_r(Y_R = 25, Y_T = 15) = 0.3$. The campaign will be conducted by first determining the test budget and the test amounts for radio and television. Then after observing the realized $\$$ sales/$\$$ expenditures for each medium, the amounts to be spent on the main campaign are to be determined. The marketing vice-president has decreed that for client relations purposes at least 20% of both the test budget and the main campaign budget must be spent on radio as well as television. Furthermore, to obtain reliability in test results, at least $100,000 has to be spent on each medium.

(a) Formulate the decision problem as a two-stage programming problem where the company seeks to maximize the total expected sales dollars to be realized with the $1,000,000 budget.

(b) Solve the problem. (*Hint*: You should be able to develop the solution without resort to the full Simplex calculation.)

9. (a) In the example of Section 14.3, suppose that the constraints could be violated 10% of the time. What would be the solution to the product-mix problem?

(b) If the constraints could be violated 1.0% of the time, what would be the solution?

10. Suppose that you wanted the probability to be 97.5% that both constraints (forming and stamping) would not be violated.

(a) Revise the model in Equations 14.24 to 14.27 to accomplish this desire.

(b) Find the solution and check to see if you have accomplished it.

11. Suppose $\tilde{C}_1$ had a probability distribution: $P_r(\tilde{C}_1 = 390) = 0.2$, $P_r(\tilde{C}_1 = 350) = 0.7$, $P_r(\tilde{C}_1 = 310) = 0.05$, $P_r(\tilde{C}_1 = 270) = 0.03$, $P_r(\tilde{C}_1 = 230) = 0.02$. Calculate the certainty equivalent.

(a) $P_r(a_{11}X_1 + a_{12}X_2 \leq \tilde{C}_1) \geq 0.90$.

(b) $P_r(a_{11}X_1 + a_{12}X_2 \leq \tilde{C}_1) \geq 0.975$.

12. Suppose that in the example of Section 14.3 the company could spend $50 per day on preventive maintenance. The $50 could increase average available capacity in forming to 370 minutes or could increase average available capacity in stamping to 410 minutes or could increase average available capacity in painting to 465 minutes. Where should the money be spent?

13. Gleeber Food Processing produces tomato juice, canned whole tomatoes, and tomato paste. Let X_1 be the pounds of tomatoes used for juice, X_2 the pounds of tomatoes used for canned whole tomatoes, and X_3 the pounds used for

tomato paste. X_4 is the pounds of the crop that Gleeber purchases and sells as fresh produce. The demand for juice, canned tomatoes, and paste is independent and normally distributed with means and standard deviations 3000 and 500, 1000 and 100, and 1000 and 200, respectively. Each pound of tomatoes converts to 0.9 pounds of juice "on the shelf" while the conversion ratio is 0.85 for canned tomatoes and 0.95 for paste. The president of Gleeber wants a probability of at least 0.90 that each type of product produced will be sold. If Gleeber purchased 10,000 pounds of tomatoes and sells juice for 85¢/pound "on the shelf," canned for 82¢/pound, paste for 77¢/pound, and can sell any amount of fresh tomatoes at 69¢/pound, how much of each should Gleeber produce?

14. Suppose that an investor can purchase three stocks A, B, and C with expected rates of return and standard deviations of $E(r_A) = 0.10$, $\sigma(r_A) = 0.04$, $E(r_B) = 0.12$, $\sigma(r_B) = 0.06$, and $E(r_C) = 0.14$, $\sigma(r_C) = 0.08$. The returns are assumed normal. The investor can also maintain the money in cash. If the investor holds \$10,000, set up a chance-constrained programming model that determines how much should be put in each stock if the investor wants to maximize the expected end-of-period wealth subject to a probability of 95% that there will be at least \$10,000 at the end of the period? Set up but do not solve. (*Hint*: The problem involves a nonlinear constraint.)

15. Show that if all of the returns in Problem 14 are perfectly positively correlated, the chance constraint becomes linear.

15

EPILOGUE: QUANTITATIVE METHODS IN CONTEXT

15.1 QUANTITATIVE ASPECTS OF THE DECISION PROCESS

Choice of Measures of Effectiveness
Integration of Quantitative Methods
An Iterative Process
Problem Complexity
Problem Size
Functional Area Interaction
Informational Aspects

15.2 PROCESSING INFORMATION FOR FINAL ALTERNATIVE SELECTION

Quantitative Model Inputs
External Inputs
Peer-Group and Superior-Group Inputs
Personal Inputs
Making a Decision

15.3 FEEDBACK AND CONTROL

Elements of Control Problems
Dynamic Programming and Control Problems
Classifying Decision Problems
The Importance of Feedback and Control

15.4 A FINAL WORD

References
Review Questions

Managerial decision making has been, and always will be, a challenge. In this day and age, when many resources can no longer be considered in abundant supply, managers must make critical decisions to ensure the efficient use of these resources and the long-term growth of their organizations. The chore is made much easier whenever the critical aspects of the decision problem can be modeled and quantified. This text has presented the quantitative methods most often used by decision makers in the decision-making process itself. In this chapter, we will review the decision-making process and discuss the role of the decision maker in this process. We will also discuss the concept of control, which monitors actual system performance and compares it to expected performance.

15.1 QUANTITATIVE ASPECTS OF THE DECISION PROCESS

Consider Figure 15.1, which depicts the quantitative methods we have presented in this text in the context of the decision-making process. In previous chapters we have applied the decision-making process to a wide variety of problems. In this section we will summarize some of the lessons we have learned as they relate to the quantitative aspects of the decision-making process.

Choice of Measures of Effectiveness

Choosing the measure of effectiveness for a decision problem may not always be straightforward. We have looked at problems where a very simple measure of effectiveness was used and other cases where this was not the case. In Chapter 1, Mr. Yef was concerned with maximizing his profit, which seemed sensible as we looked at his problem. Minimizing the cost to carry inventory in Chapter 9 also seemed like a straightforward objective. But this was not always the case. In trading off risk and return in Chapter 2 and in the investment problems of Chapters 4 and 9, we were confronted with more complicated considerations in choosing a measure of effectiveness. In such circumstances, the concept of a certainty equivalent presented in Chapter 2 can be useful.

Integration of Quantitative Methods

The quantitative analysis of a decision problem may involve more than one quantitative technique. In particular, one technique may provide data required for a model to be solved by another technique. For example, consider the Plastique Corp. distribution problem in Chapter 6. Statistical analysis was used to estimate the demand at each distribution center for type 1 pipe. In addition, linear programming was used to solve a product-mix model to determine the optimal

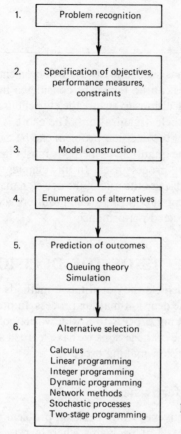

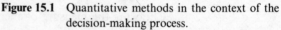

Figure 15.1 Quantitative methods in the context of the decision-making process.

product mix and thus the planned monthly output of type 1 pipe at each plant. These data were then used in a transportation model and solved using the stepping-stone (or MODI) method to find the optimum distribution pattern.

Statistical methods can also provide inputs to other models. For example, they offer a convenient way to determine probability distributions that are needed for further analysis. In Chapter 13 the probability distribution for demand for wrist alarms was a central part of the decision-making process. Indeed, any of the techniques for Step 5 in Figure 15.1 could be used to provide data for models solved by the techniques for Step 6. Queuing models and simulation models can provide useful insights to complicated problems that can be incorporated in normative models solved by other techniques.

An Iterative Process

The decision-making process depicted in Figure 15.1 is iterative. One must keep an open mind when performing the quantitative analysis. This applies in particular to Step 3, model construction. Many times data inputs are not reliable enough to allow the decision to be made from the model. This frequently happens in quantitative applications. But clearly this does not signal a failure of the methods; it merely suggests that there is more to be done before rational decision making can take place. This extra work in this case could take the form of developing a new model that is more appropriate for the decision problem at hand.

The iterative nature of the model-building process is shown in Figure 3.1 of Chapter 3. Step 3*a*, model formulation, and step 3*b*, checking for model validity, are critical steps in the successful construction of a model. No model should be applied mechanically.

Problem Complexity

Simple, orderly, and "clean" models are not the only ones that can be applied to a variety of business problems. The queuing and simulation models of Chapters 10 and 11 were what most of us would call "complex." But they are useful in applications and, indeed, may be the most widely used. It is tempting in formulating a model of an application to turn directly to simulation because the application is "complex" and a simulation model is more "realistic." We caution against this. Simulation should not be used as an escape from careful analysis. Developing and running a complex simulation model may contribute nothing to the decision maker's understanding of the problem or to the information obtained about it from the model. Simulation should be used for two purposes: (1) to get an initial intuitive feeling for a problem so that you may be in a better position to capture the essence of the problem in later model development; (2) when all analytical avenues have been exhausted and there is no other way.

The applications of quantitative methods for decision making are many. Quantitative applications are not always easy, as we have tried to demonstrate throughout this book. Experience is very important to quantitative model builders, and we have tried to provide some experience through our selection of examples and techniques for solving decision problems.

Problem Size

The decision-making process is useful to managers of all types and sizes of organizations. There may be a difference in the choice of quantitative techniques for Steps 5 and 6 of Figure 15.1. Mr. Yef's Prefinishing Corporation in Chapter 1 was a small company and the quantitative methods used were quite unsophisticated. Nonetheless, organizing the decision matrix and evaluating alternatives suggested the potential for very large benefits. In contrast to Prefinishing Corporation, Plastique Inc., in Chapter 6, was a large, complicated, multiplant organization. Here a more sophisticated technique, the transportation method of linear programming, was helpful in deciding on distribution plans. But the approach was more than helpful. It allowed a systematic processing of alternatives in search for the optimal solution. Just evaluating alternatives, willy nilly, may have landed us far from an optimal solution. In other words, the size of the problem demanded that systematic procedures be used to ensure a rational choice of alternatives.

Functional Area Interaction

Quantitative analysis often cuts across functional areas. We discussed decision problems in finance, production management, marketing, and personnel. Although the models we developed can be thought of as predominantly finance, production, marketing, or personnel models, in many cases inputs from other functional areas are necessary. For example, consider the product-mix model given by (5.72) in Chapter 5. No matter who the model was developed for (marketing or production), the production area was needed to provide the raw material and production capacities, marketing to provide the market requirements for each product group, and finance to provide the availability of working capital. Accounting could provide the data for the profit and cost parameters. Consequently, these areas must work closely together if the model is to be successful. This is why it is so important for students of management and decision making to study models from various and diverse functional areas—to understand which objectives, constraints, and decision variables are important to these various other areas and to see where interaction between the functional areas is necessary.

Informational Aspects

In essence, quantitative models enable managers to predict the outcomes of a set of feasible alternatives to a decision problem. Through the use of sensitivity analysis, systematic adjustment of critical model parameters or constraints, the decision maker is provided with a range of outcomes for a given alternative or a set of different alternatives to choose from, as the case may be. Consequently, the power of quantitative methods lies in their ability to provide the decision maker with some information relative to the decision problem at hand. Armed with all information available, including the quantitative information, the decision maker makes a final alternative selection.

15.2   PROCESSING INFORMATION FOR FINAL ALTERNATIVE SELECTION

Decision makers require information from various sources to make effective decisions. Figure 15.2, which is actually an elaboration of Step 6 in the decision process of Figure 15.1, depicts the iterative nature of various informational inputs with the decision maker when making the selection of an alternative to a decision problem. Note the feedback loop, which implies that the selection process is modified on the basis of previous performance. We will discuss this loop in the next section.

The informational inputs to the decision maker are the sources to be relied on for guidance in the decision process. In general, they help to define objectives and goals, constraints, and risks associated with the decision. Let us look more carefully at each of them.

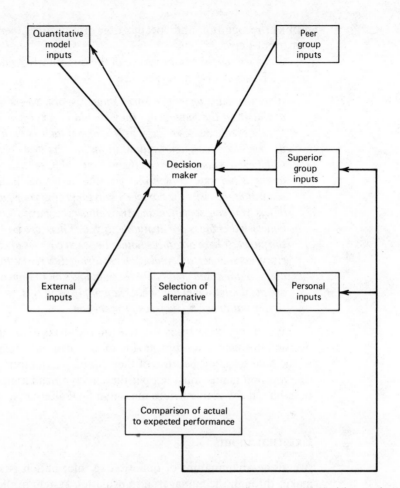

Figure 15.2   Interaction of various informational inputs with the decision maker when making final alternative selections.

Quantitative Model Inputs

Quantitative model inputs arise from the systematized decision-making process outlined in Figure 15.1:

1. Problem recognition.
2. Specification of objectives, performance measures, and constraints.
3. Model construction.
4. Enumeration of alternatives.
5. Prediction of outcomes.

Note that we have depicted a two-way flow of information between the decision maker and the quantitative analysis in Figure 15.2. This implies that the other informational inputs, as interpreted by the decision maker, help in the problem recognition and specification of objectives, performance measures, and constraint steps.

Can we gauge the importance of the quantitative model inputs to the decision maker? Drucker discusses their use:[1]

> *What the management sciences should be able to contribute are the alternatives available to the managers. They should be expected to say, "Here are four or five different courses of action. Not one of them is perfect. Each has its own risks, its own incentives, its own limitations, and its own costs . . . ." You, the manager, will have to choose between them. You will have to decide on one of them at least as the lesser evil. Which one you choose is your decision. It is your judgment regarding the risks the company can take. It is your judgment with respect to the things you can sacrifice and the things you have to insist on. But at least you know what choices are available to you. There are no "solutions" with respect to the future. There are only choices between courses of action, each imperfect, each risky, each uncertain, and each requiring different efforts and involving different costs. But nothing could help the managers more than to realize what alternatives are available to him and what they imply. And this the management scientist can supply with varying degrees of precision.*

We cannot expect quantitative analysis to provide the final solution to every decision problem. Even optimizing models can only be expected to provide *input* to the final selection because of their limiting assumptions or singular objectives. The decision maker must temper these recommendations with the other informational inputs available before making a final alternative selection.

External Inputs

A considerable amount of quantitative information is available to the decision maker through the managerial information system of the organization; however, this information should already have been incorporated into the quantitative analysis that resulted in the management science inputs. The external inputs we refer to here consist of the newspapers, magazines, and books accessible to the decision maker. These items constitute a manager's reference library. Much of this information is nonquantifiable in nature but still has an impact on the decision. For example, current periodicals contain information on pressing social problems, impending legislation, and various national economic projections. The degree of risk associated with any course of action, as perceived by the decision maker, is at least in part a function of the interpretation placed on the local and national events that may have impact on the desired results. If these risks can be quantified by the decision maker, this information can be used in the quantitative analysis. If they cannot, however, it must be used to *temper* the quantitative recommendations.

---

[1] P.F. Drucker, *Management: Tasks, Responsibilities, Practices*, New York: Harper & Row, 1973, p. 515. Copyright © 1973, Harper & Row.

Peer-Group and Superior-Group Inputs

Other managers quite often provide inputs to the decision process. The peer group consists of those managers the decision maker relates to professionally and sometimes socially. These managers may be in different functional areas of the organization and often are the sources for defining the constraints and policies that must be recognized in the decision process. Depending on how closely the manager relates to the peer group, the group may also serve to define *norms* for decision-making behavior. To the extent that peer group pressures exist in a given organization, the selection of alternatives can be affected. For example, group pressures to keep things relatively stable may urge managers to select "middle-of-the-road" alternatives instead of those that may be more risky with greater potential payoff but that require significant changes in the present environment.

The superior group consists of the managers to whom the decision maker must report. This group (or person) supplies many of the objectives and constraints for the decision process. Quite often the objectives are stated in general terms. As noted in Chapter 2, the decision maker must translate the objective into appropriate measures of effectiveness, reflecting his or her own utility function. Obviously, the input from the superior group helps to define the decision problem to be resolved.

Personal Inputs

The foundations of the inputs we have discussed so far are external to the decision maker, but the last (although not least) input to the selection process consists of the decision maker's own goals and personal beliefs. These goals are not necessarily consistent with the organizational goals as specified by the superior group. For example, a manager may have a goal of maintaining job security and, when making decisions, may resort to alternatives with low risk of failure. Although the decisions may result in some improvement, more risky alternatives with potentially greater payoffs may have been bypassed to avoid disastrous, embarrassing results.

Making a Decision

The decision maker must juggle these various inputs, evaluate them, and finally make a decision. In this text we have emphasized quantitative methods to demonstrate their advantage and limitations. The behavioral inputs to the decision process must not be overlooked, however. All of these considerations in combination affect the final choice of an alternative.

15.3 FEEDBACK AND CONTROL

Decisions have a way of becoming "undone"—that is, decision making is not a static activity; it is a dynamic process. Decisions must be monitored and corrected when the need arises. We touched on this aspect of the overall decision problem when we developed the concept of a policy in Chapters 12 and 13 and when we developed second-stage decision rules in Chapter 14. But these chapters discussed feedback and control in a specific context. Let us now turn to a more general discussion.

Elements of Control Problems

In discussing control problems mathematicians and engineers describe the situation as essentially a decision problem that requires that continual or periodic decisions be made. Hence, time is an essential feature of the problem as formulated. Other essential features are the *objective*, which may be, for example, the attainment of a certain objective by a certain point in time or a combination of an attainment and a cost (or profit) associated with the path by which the goal is attained, *equations of motion*, which merely link state variables in successive time periods, *control functions*, which are merely decision variables, and *constraints*.

Dynamic Programming and Control Problems

The dynamic programming problems we discussed can most easily be related to the concept of a control problem because dynamic programming is a solution procedure that has been applied to many control problems. Notice the types of objective functions that we formulated: minimization of inventory cost over a finite horizon, minimization of capital and operating costs of a piece of equipment over an infinite horizon, and minimization of expected cost per period for an inventory problem involving uncertainty.

What were the equations of motion? The familiar accounting linkage of inventory from one period to the next appeared in all inventory problems. In the equipment problem the equations of motion involved the deterioration of profits as time passed. In the inventory problems under uncertainty, the characteristics of the probability distribution of demand were embedded in the equations of motion. By and large, many of the important parameters of the problem appeared in the equations of motion or linkages between periods. Thus, optimal solutions are dependent on these parameters as they are felt through the equations of motion.

The control functions in our examples are the policies we determined. They are the decision rules that apply to the various periods of time. If we stop to recall the solution procedure and solutions to our examples in Chapters 12, 13, and 14, the control functions depended on time. In a finite-horizon inventory problem, the optimal policy for the first period of, say, a ten-period horizon is quite different from the optimal policy for the tenth period. A quick review of the example of Chapter 12 will reveal this fact. Some problems, such as the dynamic inventory problems in Chapter 13 that possess infinite horizons, have a single time-invariant control function or policy. But, in general, we can think of the control function as a function of time.

Why is it important to think of decision-making problems as control problems? Again, a look at our dynamic programming examples will provide some clues. The striking characteristic of these problems is that if we do not look far enough ahead in our decision making—in other words, if we look, think, and act myopically—we will most surely make suboptimal decisions. A decision at the present point in time, through the equations of motion, affects the state of the system at future points in time. And what is equally important, it affects the way in which future decisions can be used to correct any unfortunate effects of initial decisions. Therefore, present decisions are affected by future decision opportunities.

Classifying Decision Problems

Now let us try to use this framework to classify decision problems as to their control characteristics. Changes in a decision environment can be *continual* or *intermittent*. They can affect the equations of motion or they can affect the objective function. They can be *quantifiable* or *nonquantifiable*. Certainly there can be other classifications, but these will serve to illustrate our points.

Routine Decision Problems with Intermittent Environmental Changes   Certain repetitive decisions are routine, possess intermittent changes in parameters, and are relatively free of nonquantifiable elements. Peer groups and personal inputs play minor roles in these problems. In effect, the superior group has defined the problem, objectives, and constraints in such detail that the decision maker does not have any choice in these matters. The best alternative is a result of the prescribed procedures for analysis. Company policies described in a procedural handbook serve to routinize decision making at lower levels in the organization. A policy may dictate that order quantities for a certain inventory item are to be determined by use of the economic order quantities. Two managers given the same data will arrive at the same solution to the problem. There is no room for personal preferences on the part of the managers.

The control aspects of this problem are also worth discussing. Presumably, the lot-size model was selected for use because its assumptions were a reasonable representation of reality. We wish to stress two features of this situation. First, demand is assumed to be reasonably constant in the model. Second, the cost parameters are stable. Everyone knows that costs change and demand changes, but the presumptions of this model are that these changes will be only intermittent and that we need not develop elaborate control functions. Instead, when a parameter changes or when demand changes, we presume it is from one stable level to another and that we can just recalculate the model solution. The new solution will then presumably be optimal for a long period of time.

The type of control implied by the model of the previous paragraph is similar to that exercised in quality control. One assumes the policies are working adequately until there is a significant change in a parameter. Only then is the cause investigated and corrected.

Other models we developed do not require an elaborate specification of the control problem and can be solved optimally by "static" methods. Consider, for example, Judy's Bakery, discussed in Chapter 13, as well as the Minocqua Department Store dealing with wrist alarms in the same chapter. These problems were subject to probability distributions and therefore may seem, on the surface, to require a specific consideration of control problems. But the control characteristics are again simple. If the decision maker minimizes cost (or maximizes profits) each decision period by itself, the overall cost will be minimized. This results because a decision in the present period has virtually no effect on the ability to respond in future periods. Stated in terms of the example of Judy's Bakery, the delivery person will be at the store on the regular run no matter what the present decision is. The deliverer will stock the shelves with fresh bread in the future no matter what the present decision. Thus, there are no links (or equations of motion) between two successive periods. Again, only when parameters such as costs or probabilities change will it be necessary to revise optimal solutions, and this can be done by treating the problem as static. In these routinized decision situations, feedback and control play a necessary role. But the role is largely one of *monitoring* system parameters such as costs and making sure that parameters are up to date. The control aspects of the problem are ignored in determining optimal solutions.

Routine Decisions with Continual Changes   In other problems the control function plays a more important role. In the dynamic programming models of Chapter 12, the Midwest Book Stores example of Chapter 13, and the two-stage linear programming of Chapter 14, an optimal decision rule played an important role (*decision rule* is another name for the control function). It was calculated taking the dynamic nature of the problem into consideration. We might characterize problems of this sort as ones where control is exercised continually.

Nonroutine Decision Problems with Nonquantifiable Elements   Our discussion of control up to this point took the point of view that the model is fixed (although its parameters may be subject to change). We now wish to discuss the more elusive aspects of control.

As we go higher in the organization structure, the decisions are less repetitive, and the problems, which are more loosely defined, are subject to more interpretation by the decision maker. All of the inputs shown in Figure 15.2 play a greater role. For example, the Steel Company problem presented in Chapter 2 represented a situation where the overall objective, "improve the profit situation," was sufficiently vague to allow the decision maker to examine a number of novel alternatives. The resulting decision will be a function of all the inputs, quantitative as well as behavioral. The decision will require farsighted analysis, not myopia.

Another aspect of this decision distinguishes it from those we have previously discussed. Two decision makers faced with the same problem objective may arrive at different solutions. That is not to say that the logical, step-by-step quantitative analysis was completely ignored by either decision maker. It simply implies that each person is different and the emphasis placed on the various inputs varies from person to person.

The nature of these problems has important implications for control. Higher-level decisions are usually not repetitive—they are more likely "one-shot" decisions. This does not mean that no control function is necessary or that control reactions need not be considered in decision making. It merely means that in both cases—specifying a control function and considering that initial function in decision making—the decision maker will rely on less well-defined quantitative concepts.

Once a decision is made, the expected results (the predictions of outcomes) are compared to actual performance. This can be accomplished through comparison of accounting and financial reports as well as the numerous operating reports contained in the organization's information system. If actual results do not compare favorably with expected results, the control function—however ill defined it is—is applied. If the decision is "one-shot," readjustment may be costly. Furthermore, searching for the proper readjustment after such a mistake may more realistically be treated as a new decision problem than a control problem.

The deviations from expected performance may result in changes to the superior group and personal inputs to the decision process. The superior group may adjust overall objectives or constraints or place pressure on the decision maker if actual performance falls considerably below expected performance. Additionally, the decision maker's own personal goals and aspirations may be adjusted as a consequence of the resulting performance. Exceptionally good performance may encourage the decision maker to raise the level of his or her expectations, perhaps reducing aversions to risk; prior performance may result in a lowering of expectations and a more conservative outlook. Nonetheless, this information on performance returns to affect the decisions to be made in the future through the continuous-feedback process. In this way, decisions are made and revised.

It is clear that in the less-routine decisions feedback and control are essential, but they are difficult to accomplish because the situation is "fluid" with respect to just what goals and objectives are to be met.

The Importance of Feedback and Control

In this section, we have tried to emphasize the importance of thinking about the feedback and control aspects of a decision problem. It would be a mistake in discussing the context of quantitative methods to ignore the fact that one can never expect to find a never-changing, immutable solution to a business decision problem. The very nature of the environment in which business decision making takes place is change, and therefore feedback and control are an important part of the context of quantitative methods.

15.4   A FINAL WORD

Successful quantitative applications demand a proper attitude as well as an understanding of more technical matters. Although both the analyst and decision maker should understand problem identification, model building, and solution techniques, the attitudes of both are probably the most important elements of successful application. Although proper attitude is not sufficient for successful application, it is necessary. An analyst who focuses more on techniques for solution than on model formulation will not be successful. The analyst's main interest should be in providing *assistance* in decision making and not in finding methods of solution that are more elegant or marginally faster than existing methods. A decision maker who thinks that she or he can turn the analyst loose without guidance and expect to get relevant information back that can be applied directly to the problem and then forgotten will not make the best use of quantitative inputs. Instead, the interaction between the decision maker and analyst must be open, interactive, and focused on the ultimate goal of the effort: to develop and make the best use of the quantitative input to a decision problem.

References

Ackoff, R.L. *A Concept of Corporate Planning*, New York: Wiley-Interscience, 1970.

Argyris, C., "Management Information System: The Challenge to Rationality and Emotionality," *Management Science*, Vol. 17 (1971), pp. B275–B292.

Churchman, C.W., *The Systems Approach*, New York: Delacorte Press, 1968.

Hammond, J.S., "The Roles of the Manager and Management Scientist in Successful Implementation," *Sloan Management Review* (1974), pp. 1–24.

Little, J.D.C., "Models and Managers—The Concept of a Decision Calculus," *Management Science*, Vol. 16 (1970), pp. B466–B485.

Lyman, J., and Fogel, L.J., "The Human Component," in E.M. Grabbe, S. Romo, and D.E. Wooldrige, *Handbook of Automation, Computation and Control*, Vol. 3, New York: John Wiley & Sons, 1961.

Wagner, H.M., "The ABC's of OR," *Operations Research*, Vol. 19 (1971) pp. 1259–1281.

Review Questions

1. Explain the considerations that one must make in choosing an appropriate measure of effectiveness.

2. We have presented quantitative methods in the context of the decision-making process. Discuss the considerations you would make in choosing a quantitative technique for the analysis of a decision problem.

3. Suppose you are faced with a certain decision problem. Describe, in general terms, the qualities (or nature) that decision problem would have if simulation were the only logical choice of a quantitative technique for analysis.

4. Describe some situations not already mentioned in this chapter where one quantitative method is necessary to provide input for a model to be solved by another quantitative technique.

5. Discuss the iterative nature of the decision-making process.

6. A student interested in becoming a marketing manager in a large organization complained, "Why do I have to study production and finance models when I am interested in marketing? It all seems like a waste of time." Comment.

7. Models can be used to suggest optimal courses of action. They can also be used to provide information to the decision-making process. Explain the difference between optimal solutions and information.

8. Use Figure 15.2 to explain why two decision makers, each given the same quantitative inputs, may arrive at different solutions to the same problem.

9. Define the general concept of a control problem. Why can we say that dynamic programming problems can be easily related to this concept?

10. Consider the following production planning model:

$$\text{Min } Z = \sum_{t=1}^{T} (C_w W_t + C_I I_t + C_O O_t)$$

$$I_t = I_{t-1} + P_t + O_t - D_t \qquad t = 1, 2, \ldots, T$$

$$W_t = W_{t-1} + H_t - F_t \qquad t = 1, 2, \ldots, T$$

$$P_t = \alpha W_t \qquad t = 1, 2, \ldots, T$$

$$O_t \le \beta W_t \qquad t = 1, 2, \ldots, T$$

$$I_t, W_t, P_t, O_t \ge 0 \qquad t = 1, 2, \ldots, T$$

where

I_t = inventory at the end of period t
W_t = work force on hand at the start of period t
P_t = units of regular time production in period t
O_t = units of overtime production in period t
α = productivity in units/employee per period
β = maximum number of units/employee that can be produced on overtime in a period
C_w = regular wages per employee per period
C_I = inventory-carrying cost per unit per period
C_O = overtime cost per unit
T = length of planning horizon

Describe this problem in terms of a control problem. That is, identify the objective function, equations of motion, and the control function.

APPENDIX EXPONENTIAL FUNCTIONS

Exponential Functions for $|x| \leq 1$

x	e^x	e^{-x}	x	e^x	e^{-x}
0.00	1.0000	1.0000	0.29	1.3364	0.7483
0.01	1.0101	0.9900	0.30	1.3499	0.7408
0.02	1.0202	0.9802	0.31	1.3634	0.7334
0.03	1.0305	0.9705	0.32	1.3771	0.7261
0.04	1.0408	0.9608	0.33	1.3910	0.7189
0.05	1.0513	0.9512	0.34	1.4049	0.7118
0.06	1.0618	0.9418	0.35	1.4191	0.7047
0.07	1.0725	0.9324	0.36	1.4333	0.6977
0.08	1.0833	0.9231	0.37	1.4477	0.6907
0.09	1.0942	0.9139	0.38	1.4623	0.6839
0.10	1.1052	0.9048	0.39	1.4770	0.6770
0.11	1.1163	0.0958	0.40	1.4918	0.6703
0.12	1.1275	0.8869	0.41	1.5068	0.6636
0.13	1.1388	0.8781	0.42	1.5220	0.6570
0.14	1.1503	0.8693	0.43	1.5373	0.6505
0.15	1.1618	0.8607	0.44	1.5527	0.6440
0.16	1.1735	0.8521	0.45	1.5683	0.6376
01.7	1.1853	0.8437	0.46	1.5841	0.6313
0.18	1.1972	0.8353	0.47	1.6000	0.6250
0.19	1.2092	0.8269	0.48	1.6161	0.6188
0.20	1.2214	0.8187	0.49	1.6323	0.6126
0.21	1.2337	0.8106	0.50	1.6487	0.6065
0.22	1.2461	0.8025	0.51	1.6653	0.6005
0.23	1.2586	0.7945	0.52	1.6820	0.5945
0.24	1.2712	0.7866	0.53	1.6989	0.5886
0.25	1.2840	0.7788	0.54	1.7160	0.5827
0.26	1.2969	0.7710	0.55	1.7333	0.5769
0.27	1.3100	0.7634	0.56	1.7507	0.5712
0.28	1.3231	0.7558	0.57	1.7683	0.5655

x	e_x	e^{-x}	x	e^x	e^{-x}
0.58	1.7860	0.5599	0.80	2.2255	0.4493
0.59	1.8040	0.5543	0.81	2.2479	0.4448
0.60	1.8221	0.5488	0.82	2.2705	0.4404
0.61	1.8404	0.5433	0.83	2.2933	0.4360
0.62	1.8589	0.5379	0.84	2.3164	0.4317
0.63	1.8776	0.5326	0.85	2.3396	0.4274
0.64	1.8965	0.5273	0.86	2.3632	0.4232
0.65	1.9155	0.5220	0.87	2.3869	0.4189
0.66	1.9348	0.5168	0.88	2.4109	0.4148
0.67	1.9542	0.5117	0.89	2.4351	0.4107
0.68	1.9739	0.5066	0.90	2.4596	0.4066
0.69	1.9937	0.5016	0.91	2.4843	0.4025
0.70	2.0138	0.4966	0.92	2.5093	0.3985
0.71	2.0340	0.4916	0.93	2.5345	0.3945
0.72	2.0544	0.4867	0.94	2.5600	0.3906
0.73	2.0751	0.4819	0.95	2.5857	0.3867
0.74	2.0959	0.4771	0.96	2.6117	0.3829
0.75	2.1170	0.4724	0.97	2.6379	0.3791
0.76	2.1383	0.4677	0.98	2.6645	0.3753
0.77	2.1598	0.4630	0.99	2.6912	0.3716
0.78	2.1815	0.4584	1.00	2.7183	0.3679
0.79	2.2034	0.4538			

Exponential Functions for $|x + y| \leq 10$ for $0 \leq X \leq 1$[a]

y	$e^{(x+y)}$	$e^{-(x+y)}$
1	$2.7183e^x$	$0.3679e^{-x}$
2	$7.3890e^x$	$0.1353e^{-x}$
3	$20.085e^x$	$0.0498e^{-x}$
4	$54.598e^x$	$0.0183e^{-x}$
5	$148.41e^x$	$0.0067e^{-x}$
6	$403.43e^x$	$0.0025e^{-x}$
7	$1096.6e^x$	$0.0009e^{-x}$
8	$2980.9e^x$	$0.0003e^{-x}$
9	$8103.1e^x$	$0.0001e^{-x}$

[a] To find values for exponential functions greater than 1 in absolute value, use this table and the table of exponential functions for $|x| \leq 1$. For example, $e^{3.38} = 20.085\,(1.4623) = 29.370$ and $e^{-7.91} = 0.0009\,(0.4025) = 0.0004$.

Areas of a standard normal distribution

An entry in the table is the proportion under the entire curve that is between $z = 0$ and a positive value of z. Areas for negative values of z are obtained by symmetry.

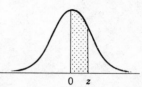

z	.00	.01	.02	.03	.04	.05	.06	.07	.08	.09
0.0	.0000	.0040	.0080	.0120	.0160	.0199	.0239	.0279	.0319	.0359
0.1	.0398	.0438	.0478	.0517	.0557	.0596	.0636	.0675	.0714	.0753
0.2	.0793	.0832	.0871	.0910	.0948	.0987	.1026	.1064	.1103	.1141
0.3	.1179	.1217	.1255	.1293	.1331	.1368	.1406	.1443	.1480	.1517
0.4	.1554	.1591	.1628	.1664	.1700	.1736	.1772	.1808	.1844	.1879
0.5	.1915	.1950	.1985	.2019	.2054	.2088	.2123	.2157	.2190	.2224
0.6	.2257	.2291	.2324	.2357	.2389	.2422	.2454	.2486	.2517	.2549
0.7	.2580	.2611	.2642	.2673	.2703	.2734	.2764	.2794	.2823	.2852
0.8	.2881	.2910	.2939	.2967	.2995	.3023	.3051	.3078	.3106	.3133
0.9	.3159	.3186	.3212	.3238	.3264	.3289	.3315	.3340	.3365	.3389
1.0	.3413	.3438	.3461	.3485	.3508	.3531	.3554	.3577	.3599	.3621
1.1	.3643	.3665	.3686	.3708	.3729	.3749	.3770	.3790	.3810	.3830
1.2	.3849	.3869	.3888	.3907	.3925	.3944	.3962	.3980	.3997	.4015
1.3	.4032	.4049	.4066	.4082	.4099	.4115	.4131	.4147	.4162	.4177
1.4	.4192	.4207	.4222	.4236	.4251	.4265	.4279	.4292	.4306	.4319
1.5	.4332	.4345	.4357	.4370	.4382	.4394	.4406	.4418	.4429	.4441
1.6	.4452	.4463	.4474	.4484	.4495	.4505	.4515	.4525	.4535	.4545
1.7	.4554	.4564	.4573	.4582	.4591	.4599	.4608	.4616	.4625	.4633
1.8	.4641	.4649	.4656	.4664	.4671	.4678	.4686	.4693	.4699	.4706
1.9	.4713	.4719	.4726	.4732	.4738	.4744	.4750	.4756	.4761	.4767
2.0	.4772	.4778	.4783	.4788	.4793	.4798	.4803	.4808	.4812	.4817
2.1	.4821	.4826	.4830	.4834	.4838	.4842	.4846	.4850	.4854	.4857
2.2	.4861	.4864	.4868	.4871	.4875	.4978	.4881	.4884	.4887	.4890
2.3	.4893	.4896	.4898	.4901	.4904	.4906	.4909	.4911	.4913	.4916
2.4	.4918	.4920	.4922	.4925	.4927	.4929	.4931	.4932	.4934	.4936
2.5	.4938	.4940	.4941	.4943	.4945	.4946	.4948	.4949	.4951	.4952
2.6	.4953	.4955	.4956	.4957	.4959	.4960	.4961	.4962	.4963	.4964
2.7	.4965	.4966	.4967	.4968	.4969	.4970	.4971	.4972	.4973	.4974
2.8	.4974	.4975	.4976	.4977	.4977	.4978	.4979	.4979	.4980	.4981
2.9	.4981	.4982	.4982	.4983	.4984	.4984	.4985	.4985	.4986	.4986
3.0	.4987	.4987	.4987	.4988	.4988	.4989	.4989	.4989	.4990	.4990
3.1	.4990	.4991	.4991	.4991	.4992	.4992	.4992	.4992	.4993	.4993
3.2	.4993	.4993	.4994	.4994	.4994	.4994	.4994	.4995	.4995	.4995
3.3	.4995	.4995	.4995	.4996	.4996	.4996	.4996	.4996	.4996	.4997

GLOSSARY

Additivity Assumption Assumption in linear programming models that the total value of the objective function for a given vector of activity levels equals the sum of the contributions of each activity level considered independent of the rest.

Alternative One possible way to resolve a decision problem.

Artificial Variable Variable that allows simple determination of a first feasible solution in a linear programming problem with lower-bound constraints or equality constraints.

Balking Customer deciding not to enter a service system at all.

Basic Variables Variables that take a nonzero value at a nondegenerate extreme point in a linear programming problem.

Big M Large number assigned to artificial variables in linear programming problems.

Binding Constraint Constraint that holds with an equality in the optimal solution.

Birth and Death Process Simple queuing process.

Branch-and-Bound Method Method for solving integer linear programming problems.

Certainty Equivalent Certain amount (CE) that would yield the same expected utility as a random variable (X); that is, $U(CE) = EU(X)$ where X is a random variable.

Chance-Constrained Programming Optimization subject to constraints expressed as probability statements.

Chain of Machines Characterization of a succession of replacements for a given machine.

Complementary Slackness Property of optimal solutions to linear programming problems that states that the product of the primal slack and dual variable equals zero, as does the product of the primal variable and dual slack.

Concave Function Function is concave over an interval (a, b) if the tangent to the function lies above the function.

Constant Entity that does not change over time and whose value is known.

Constraint Statement that rules out one or more alternatives from further consideration in a decision problem.

Conditional Probability Probability of one event given that another event has occurred.

Connected Network Network where any pair of nodes can be linked by traversing a series of branches in the network.

Convex Function Function is convex over an interval (a, b) if the tangent to the function lies below the function.

Crash Cost In a PERT network, the cost to achieve the crash time.

Crash Time In a PERT network, the minimum time duration possible for completing an activity.

Critical Path Sequence of activities that determines the total length of a project.

Cut Subset of oriented branches that contains at least one branch of every path from source node to sink node.

Cut Value Sum of the capacities of the branches in the cut.

Cutting-Plane Method   Method for solving linear programming problems when the solutions must be integer.

Degeneracy   Solution to a linear programming problem in which at least one of the basic variables takes on a zero value.

Dependent Variable   Outcome resulting from the pairing of a particular alternative and state of nature or the measure of effectiveness that combines two or more possible outcomes into one decision criterion.

Descriptive Model   Model that only describes the problem and can be used to estimate the outcomes that would be generated by a given set of alternatives.

Deterministic Model   Model involving no random variables.

Dual Problems   Equivalent of the primal problem in which the shadow prices are the decision variables.

Dynamic Model   Model that incorporates variables, constants, and parameters that may be affected by time.

Dynamic Programming   Computing philosophy and organizing method that can be applied to a wide variety of dynamic optimization problems.

Earliest Finish   In a PERT network, the earliest time each activity can finish.

Earliest Start   In a PERT network, the earliest time each activity can start.

Erlang Distribution   Distribution used to describe interarrival times in queuing problems.

EVPI   Expected value of perfect information. The difference between expected profit with perfect information and expected profit without information on the outcomes of the random variables.

Extreme Point   Those points in the feasibility region to a linear programming problem that are at the ends of boundary segments.

Feasible Region   Set of solutions to a programming problem that satisfy the constraints.

Flow Capacity of a Branch   Maximum flow in a branch of a network model.

Gaussian Elimination   Method of solving simultaneous linear equations.

Global Maximum   Largest value of function $f(X)$ over the entire domain of X.

Goal-Programming Model   Linear programming model where the objectives is to minimize the weighted deviations from prestated goals on the objectives.

Heuristic Problem Solving   Use of rules or guidelines that simulate or approximate good problem-solving behavior.

Inconsistent Constraint Set   Set of constraints in a programming problem for which no feasible region exists.

Independent Variable   Decision alternatives or the states of nature.

Interarrival Times   Time between arrivals in a queuing problem.

Isoprofit Line   Set of all points in a region that yield the same profit.

Iterative Solution Procedure   Where a number of steps are required to arrive at a final solution and partial or complete solutions are entertained at each step.

LaGrange Multiplier   Variable used in formulating a solution to nonlinear optimization problems with constraints. The counterpart of the dual variable in linear programming.

Latest Finish   In a PERT network, the latest time an activity can finish without delaying the completion of the project.

Latest Start   In a PERT network, the latest time an activity can start without delaying the completion of the project.

Linear Programming Problem   Optimization of a linear function subject to linear constraints.

Local Maximum   Function $f(X)$ taken on a local maximum of $X = X_0$ if $f(X) \leq f(X_0)$ for all X in the interval $(X_0 - \varepsilon, X_0 + \varepsilon)$ where ε is some small number.

Lot-size Model   Inventory-decision model with deterministic demand, a fixed ordering cost, and a linear cost to carry inventory.

Markov Property   Transition probabilities have the Markov property if they depend only on the immediate state of the system and not on the previous states.

Mathematical Model   Model whose relationships are expressed in mathematical terms.

Measure of Effectiveness   Indicator of the merit of each alternative in light of a number of possible states of nature in a decision problem.

Model   Abstraction of reality that maintains only the essential elements of the problem.

MODI Method   Algorithm for solving a transportation model.

Monte Carlo Simulation   Method of generating events so as to approximate their probability of occurrence closely.

Negative Exponential Distribution   Distribution of interarrival times for a Poisson process.

Network Models   Programming models that can be characterized by nodes and branches with flows in the branches.

Nonbasic Variables   Variables that take on zero values at a nondegenerate extreme point in a linear programming problem.

Noninferior Solution   Solution to a multiple-objective problem where there exists no other feasible solution that will yield an improvement in one objective without causing a degradation of at least one other objective.

Noninferior Solution-Generation Techniques   Techniques such as the "weighting method" and the "constraint method" that generate a subset of the entire set of noninferior solutions to a multiple-objective decision problem.

Nonnegativity Restrictions   Constraints in linear programming problems that ensure that all variables are nonnegative.

Normative Model   Model that selects the best alternative for a decision model.

Northwest Corner Rule   Method for determining an initial solution in a transportation model.

Operating Characteristics   Characteristics of an operating system such as queue length, customer waiting time, and server idle time.

Opportunity Cost   Difference between profit obtained from an optimal decision and profit obtained from another decision.

Oriented Branch   Branch in a network model where the flow can be in only one direction.

Parameter   Entity that varies with the particular application and must be estimated or determined by the decision maker.

Physical Model   Model that takes on the physical appearance of the object it is to portray.

Pivot Row   Row in an iteration of a linear programming problem that determines which basic variable will become nonbasic.

Pivot Variable   Nonbasic variable that will be brought into the basis in an iteration of a linear programming model.

Poisson Process   Process in which the probability that there will be n arrivals in the interval (o, t) is governed by a Poisson distribution.

Policy   Function relating the state of a system to the value of the decision variable.

Postoptimality Analysis   Analysis of how the optimal solution to a linear programming problem will change if c_j, a_{ij}, or b_i changes.

Primal Problem   Original formulation of a linear programming model.

Priority Discipline   Basis for selecting customers from the queue.

Proportionality Assumption   Assumption in linear programming models that the contribution to the objective function or the usage of any resource of any activity is proportional to the level of the activity.

Recurrence Relationship   Relationship between the cost for stage t and beyond and the optimal cost for stage $t + 1$ and beyond. Used in formulating dynamic-programming problems.

Redundant Constraint   Constraint in a programming problem that does not form part of the boundary of the feasible region.

Reneging   Customer entering the queue but leaving before being served.

Rim Conditions   Constraints in a transportation model.

Risk Neutrality   Indifference to risk described by a linear utility function.

Sampling   Statistical procedure that allows one to make inferences about a given population.

Shadow Price (dual price)   Value of a unit of the resource in a programming problem relative to the objective function. The amount the objective function will increase (or decrease) with a unit increase in the resource.

Simplex Method   Specific computing procedure for solving linear programming problems.

Single-Pass Solution Procedures   Final values of all decision variables are determined simultaneously.

Single-Server System   Queuing system with a single service facility.

Sink Node   Node with all flows oriented toward it.

Slack Time   In a PERT network, the amount of time an activity can be delayed without delaying the entire project.

Slack Variable   Variable added to $\leq$ constraint in a linear programming model to make it an equality.

Source Node   Node with all flows oriented away from it.

Stages   Sequential times at which decisions are made.

States   Description of the conditions a system can be in at a particular point in time.

States of Nature   Values of a random variable.

Static Model   A model in which the variables, constants, and parameters are unaffected by time.

Stationary Policy   Policy identical for all stages of a dynamic programming problem.

Stationary-State Probabilities   Probabilities of being in various states at an arbitrary point in time.

Stepping-Stone Method   Algorithm for solving a transportation model.

Stochastic Model   Model involving at least one random variable.

Surplus Variable   Variable added to $\geq$ constraint in a linear programming model to make it an equality.

Survey   Special form of sampling in which individuals are asked to respond to a number of questions relevant to some decision problem.

Technological Coefficients   In linear programming problems, the amount of resource i "incurred" by a unit of variable X_j.

Transition Probabilities   Probability of making a transition from one state to another state between stages.

Transportation Model   Class of LP models with a special structure such that the coefficients of the constraint set are zeros or ones.

Tree Diagram   Diagram showing the relationships between decisions and random events in a dynamic decision problem.

Utility Function   Measure of effectiveness that allows an individual to choose the bundle of goods to be consumed.

Verbal Model   Model that expresses all the functional relationships between the variable in word passages.

Vogel's Approximation Method (VAM)   Approach to determining an initial solution in a transportation model.

APPLICATION INDEX

Advertising, 243-244, 324
Automobile allocation, 208-209

Bank system design, 351-358, 373-381

Capital budgeting, 214-215, 389-393, 407-
    408, 428-432
Capital investment, 245-246
Chemical manufacturing, 164-165
Conference planning, 286-287
Consumption and investment, 441
Contract bidding, 207
Conveyor design, 280-281

Equipment replacement, 432-437

Funding mix, 102

Gasoline blending, 162
General management, 3-5

Inventory control, 61, 400, 405-406, 413-
    428, 440, 482
Investment, 508, 509

Knapsack problem, 247

Linear assignment, transportation model, 209-
    211
Logistics planning, 169, 170-189, 205,
    207-208, 243, 251-258

Machine capacity planning, 49-50, 62,
    408-409
Machine maintenance, 365, 403-404,
    510
Manufacturing, large scale, 264-273
Media-mix planning, 84-96, 134-136,
    243-244

Personnel hiring, 283-285
Plant location, 215-216, 244-245, 457-
    464
Plant sizing, 482
Portfolio selection, 62, 68-69,
    74-84, 101, 108-119, 125-
    133, 163, 483, 488-490,
    511
Pricing, 22
Printing, 21-23
Process design, 282-283
Production planning, 119-123, 141-150,
    152-155, 203-204, 205-207, 242, 285-
    286
Production routing, 103
Production scheduling, 216-218, 247, 509
Production sequencing, 21, 381-384, 404-
    405
Product mix planning, 102-103, 161,
    164-165, 244, 510
Project selection, 214-215, 246
Purchasing, 162

Sales force planning, 297-300
Shelf space allocation, 441
Shortest route problem, 250-258
Staff planning, 162
Stock and bond investment, 295-297,
    308-310, 317-319

Test marketing, 510
Tour assignment, 384-388
Traffic flow planning, 282
Transportation mode selection, 103-104
Truck loading, 363-364
Truck routing, 280

Workforce scheduling, 246-441
Work methods study, 359-360, 365

GENERAL INDEX

Ackoff, R. L., 18, 59, 524
Aghili, P., 507
Agnew, N. W., 507
Agnew, R. A., 507
Archer, S. H., 18
Argyris, C., 524
Artificial variable, 110, 120-122
  postoptimality analysis, 143, 148

Backward induction, 460, 464
Balinski, M. L., 240
Balintfy, J. L., 400
Balking, 335
Banerjee, A., 381
Basic variable, 110-111
  degeneracy, 138
  linear programming, 114
  postoptimality analysis, 143-144, 146
Basis, linear programming, 112, 114, 120-123
Batterby, A., 278
Bawa, V. S., 507
Bellman, R. E., 413, 439, 481
Beta distribution, 274
Bhat, U. N., 361
Big M method, linear programming, 121
Birth and death process, 341-344
Boundary, 304
Bradley, S. P., 507
Branch-and-bound algorithm, 228-239
  boundary, 232, 238
  branching rule, 230-232, 238
  fathoming, 232-233, 238
  initialization, 228-230, 237
  minimization problems, 239
  optimality criterion, 233, 238
Bross, I. D. J., 19
Burdick, D. S., 400

Camp, G. C., 59
Central limit theorem, 396
Certainty equivalent, 36, 296-297
Chain of replacements, 432
Chance constrained programming, 500-506
  managerial use of, 504-506
Charnes, A., 507
Chernoff, H., 38
Chu, K., 400
Churchman, C. W., 58, 59, 60, 524
Cohen, J. L., 157
Cohen, K. J., 57, 59, 507
Combinatorial problems, 384
Complementary slackness, 130
  dual, 128
  transportation model, 191
Complete factorial design, 398
Computer usage in quantitative methods:
  cutting-plane method, 227-228
  integer programs, 240
  multiple objectives, 151
  networks, 278
  simplex method, 155
  simulation, 381-384
  transportation model, 201-202
Concavity, 302, 321
Conditional probabilities, 451, 452
Confidence interval, 395-398
Constant distribution, 334, 349-350
Constraints, 7
  equality, 67, 86, 119, 311-319
  inconsistent, 78
  inequality and LaGrange multiplier, 319-320
  lower bound, 67, 86, 119
  nonnegativity, 69, 86
  redundant, 77
  upper bound, 67, 69, 86, 108, 119
Control, 17

continual or intermittent, 521-522
Convexity, 77-78, 302, 321
Cooper, R. B., 349, 361
Cooper, W. W., 507
Correlation, of rates of return, 308
Cox, D. R., 361
Cox, J. G., 400
Cramer, R. H., 507
Crane, D. B., 507
Crash cost, 269-270
Crash time, 269-270
Critical-path method (CPM), 251, 264-273
  cost-time-trade-offs, 269-273
  crash cost, 269-270
  crash time, 269-270
  dummy activity, 265
  earliest finish, 266
  latest finish, 266-267
  latest start, 266-267
  normal cost, 269-270
  normal time, 269-270
  slack, 267
Cutting-plane method, 218-228
Cutting-plane constraint, 221-224
Cycling, linear programming, 117-140
Cyert, R. M., 57, 59

Dantzig, G. B., 97, 157, 202
Decision, conditional, 412
Decision making, 5
Decision rule, 522
Decision tree problems, 457-464
  with dynamic programming, 464
Degeneracy:
  linear programming, 117, 138-140
  transportation model, 199-201
Deviational variables, goal programming,
  152-154
Domain, of a function, 300
Dreyfus, S. E., 413, 439, 481
Drucker, P. F., 518
Dual, 88, 107, 125-133
  computational advantages, 130-133
  constraints, 127
  maximization, 133
  minimization, 132
  standard form transportation model, 189-191
  surplus variable, 127-128
  tableau, 129
  theorems, 130
  see also Linear programming, 88, 107, 125-
  133
Due date, earliest, 383
  efficient set, 35
Dynamic problems, 411
Dynamic programming, 487, 520
  efficiency in calculation, 425-428
  infinite stage, 432

managerial use, 424-425
policy, 412, 413
principle of optimality, 413, 424
recurrence relations, 413
stages, 412
states, 412

Efroymson, M. A., 240
Either-or constraints, 217
Elmagrahby, S. E., 278
Emshoff, J. R., 400
Erlang distribution, 334, 349, 366-367
Equality constraints, 67, 86, 119, 311-319
  dual, 131
  postoptimality analysis, 148
Equations of matim, 520
Expected value of perfect information (EVPI),
  450, 456
  in two-stage programming, 498-499
Extreme point, linear programming, 108, 118
  multiple optima, 140
Exponential distribution, 339-341, 353
  characteristics of, 340-341
Exponential functions, 527-529

Faaland, B., 240
Feasible region, linear programming, 74-78,
  108, 135
Feasible solution, linear programming, 121-122
Feedback, 519, 523
Fiacco, A. V., 321
Finger, J. M., 401
First-come, first-served, 382
First order conditions, 321
Flow time, 383
Fogel, L. J., 524
Ford, L. R., 278
Forecasting system evaluation, 450-454
Fractional factorial design, 399
Frame, R., 38
Frank, H., 278
Friedman, M., 38
Frisch, I. T., 278
Fulkerson, D. R., 278

Gass, S. I., 97, 157, 202
Gaussian elimination, 80-81, 90-91, 109,
  115, 122, 470
Geoffrion, A. M., 240
Global maximization, 300
  and points in, 302
Glossary, 533-537
Goal programming, 107, 152-155
  goal constraints, 152
  goal definition, 152
  inferior solution, 154
  weights, 153
Gomory, R. E., 240

Good, I. J., 60
Goodman, S. H., 381
Gordon, G., 400
Graiwog, D. E., 98, 157, 202
Grayson, C. J., Jr., 19
Greenhut, M. L., 60
Gunderson, H. S., 507

Hadley, G., 98, 157, 202, 241, 321, 439, 481
Hammersley, J. M., 400
Hammond, J. S., 524
Handscomb, D. C., 400
Harrison, E. F., 19
Helmer, D., 60
Hertz, D. B., 389
Heuristics, 384-388
Hillier, F. S., 98, 157, 202, 241, 278, 361, 481, 507
Himmelblau, D., 321
Hoare, H. R., 278
Hovey, R. W., 19
Howard, R., 481
Hughes, A. J., 98, 157, 202
Huyssman, J. H. B., 60

Inflection points, 301
Information for decision making, 516, 517
Input source, 329
  arrival distribution, 332-334
  customer disposition, 334-335
  size, 330-332
Integer programming, 71, 213-239, 304
  binary variable, 216-217
  branch-and-bound method, 228-239
  contingency constraint, 215
  cutting-plane method, 218-228
  either-or constraints, 217
  feasible region, 218, 229
  heuristic methods, 240
  implicit enumeration, 228
  machine interference constraints, 217-218
  mixed-integer, 218, 239
  mutually exclusive constraints, 215
  net contribution, 225
  pivot row, 225
  pivot variable, 225
  precedence constraints, 217
  pure integer, 218-239
  round-off solutions, 213-214, 240
  zero-one, 214-218
Iso-cost line, 86
Iso-profit line, 79

Jedamus, P., 38

Kelley, J. E., 278
Khumawala, B. M., 241
King, W. R., 507
Kirkpatrick, C. A., 278
Knapsack model, 215
Kolesar, P. J., 241
Krajewski, L. J., 381

LaGrange multipliers, 312-320
  inequality constraints, 319-320
  interpretation, 313
  more than one constraint, 315-317
  theory of, 313
Lamone, R. P., 98, 157, 202
Lawler, E. L., 241
Lee, A. M., 361
Lee, S., 157
Levin, R. I., 98, 157, 202, 278
Lieberman, G. J., 98, 157, 202, 241, 278, 361, 481, 507
Linear programming, 47-48, 67-202
  advantage of, 96-97
  assumptions of, 70-71
  augmenting, 89-90
  dual, 88, 107, 125-133
  extreme point, 81-83
  functional interaction, 156-157
  general problem, 67-68
  graphical method, 67-96
  infeasible solution, 78
  initial solution, 110-111, 121-122
  initial tableau, 121
  minimization, 119-123
  stopping rule maximization problems, 116
  sensitivity analysis, 71, 91-96
  simplex method, 107-157
  slack variable, 89
  surplus variable, 89
  transportation model, 172
Little, J. D. C., 344, 524
Local maxima, 300
Lot size model, 291-295, 307-308, 311-317
  multiple items, 307-308
  sensitivity analysis, 295
Lower-bound constraints, 119
  dual, 130
  postoptimality analysis, 148
Lyman, J., 524

Machine interference constraints, 217-218
Markov chain, 467
Markov property, 466
Markowitz, H. M., 38
Marsten, R. E., 240
Matthews, J. P., 507
Max-flow min-cut theorem, 263
Maximization:
  linear functions, 67-202

strict concavity, 302
McCormick, G. P., 321
Mean-variance space, 35
Measures of effectiveness, 12, 21, 26, 47, 52, 412, 513
Measures of performance, 10
Meier, R. C., 56, 60, 400
Miller, D. W., 38, 60
Miller, R. E., 321
Mize, J. H., 400
Model, 43-51
　building process, 51-58, 515
　components of, 43-44
　descriptive, 47-48, 54, 352, 371
　deterministic, 49-50, 54
　dynamic, 48-49, 54
　formulation of, 52-56
　mathematical, 46-51
　normative, 47-48, 54
　physical, 46
　static, 48-49, 54, 352
　stochastic, 50, 54, 352
　validation of, 56-58
　verbal, 45
Model augmentation:
　dual, 127
　linear programming, 108, 120-121, 123, 134, 219
Modified-distribution method (MODI), 189-195
　compared to stepping-stone method, 194-195
Monte Carlo simulation, 372-384
Morris, J. G., 507
Morris, W. T., 19, 49, 57, 60
Morse, P. M., 348, 361
Moser, L. E., 38
Multiple objectives, 150-155
　generating techniques, 150-151
　preferences, use of, 152-155
Multiple optima, linear programming, 140-141
Mutually exclusive constraints, 215

Naslund, B., 507
Naylor, T. H., 400, 401
Negative exponential distribution, 333
Newhauser, G. L., 439
Net contribution, linear programming, 112, 122
Networks, 249-277
　activities in PERT/CPM, 264
　branch, 249
　computer, 278
　connected, 250
　CPM, 251, 264-273
　critical path, 266-269
　cut value, 263
　events in PERT/CPM, 264

flow capacity, 249, 259
　large projects, 251
　max-flow min-cut theorem, 263
　maximal flow problem, 250, 258-264
　node, 249
　PERT, 251
　shortest route problem, 250-258
　sink node, 249
　source node, 249
Newell, A., 401
Newell, W. T., 19, 56, 60, 400
Newton, B. L., 395
Newton's method, 435, 442-443
Nonbasic variable, 110, 112
　postoptimality analysis, 141-143
Noninferior solutions, 150
　objective constraints method, 151
　weighting method, 151
　trade-offs, 154
Nonnegativity restrictions, 111, 114, 120
　dual, 131
Normal cost, 269-270
Normal distribution, 530
Normal time, 269-270
Northwest corner method, transportation models, 174-177, 195

Objectives, 7, 53
Opportunity cost, 112, 127, 454
　transportation model, 177-178, 181, 192, 198
Optimal policy function, 412
Optimality criterion, linear models:
　maximization, 116
　minimization, 122
　transportation model, 187-188, 198
Outcomes, 9
Overstock costs, 456

Pazer, H. L., 56, 60, 400
Peterson, E. R., 439
Pivot element, linear programming, 114
Pivot row, linear programming, 114, 117, 122-123
　integer program, 225
Pivot variable, linear programming, 113, 117, 122-123
Poisson distribution, 332, 352-353
Poisson process, 332-333
Policy, 492
　in business organizations, 413
Policy iteration, 437
Postoptimality analysis, linear programming, 107, 141-150
　objective coefficients, 141-143
　right-hand-sides, 144-149
Prabhu, N. V., 361
Pratt, J., 36, 38

Precedence constraints, 217
Precision of estimate, 395-398
Primal constraint, 127
Primal-dual relationship, 125-127
Primal problem, linear programming, 107, 125
Primal tableau, 129
Primal variable, 127
Priority discipline, 329
Problem symptoms, 6
Program evaluation and review technique (PERT), 107-109, 251, 273-277
   activity-time estimation, 273-275
   assumptions, 275
   expected activity time, 274
   probability concepts, 275-277
   variance, 274
Pyle, D. H., 507

Queuing models, 344-350, 514
   decision making process, 351-360
   decision variables, 338
   finite input source, 350
   input source, 330-335
   multiple-channel, single phase, 346-348
   operating characteristics, 339, 344
   queue, 329
   queue constraints, 335
   service facilities, 335-338
   single-channel, single-phase, 345-346
   structure, 329-339
   unspecified service-time distribution, 348-350

Raiffa, H., 38, 481
Random number, 375, 390
Random variables, 390
Rasmussen, J., 507
Ray, T. L., 240
Reliability, 395-398
Reneging, 335
Rescher, N., 60
Resh, M., 507
Right-hand-side ranging, 144-149
Risk, 297
Risk aversion, 32, 34, 445
Risk neutrality, 34, 445
Roat, J. G., 439

Saatz, T. L., 361
Sasser, W. E., 400
Savage, L. J., 38
Schlaifer, R., 38, 481
Schuckman, A., 60
Schumacher, C. C., 19
Second derivative test for optimazation, 294, 297
Second order conditions, 321
Sensitivity analysis, linear programming, 141-150.

Service facility, 329
   arrangement, 335-337
   priority system, 337-338
   service time distribution, 337
Service system, 329
Shadow price, 88-96, 107, 125, 126
   calculation of, 88-93
   postoptimality analysis, 147, 149
   transportation model, 190
   use of, 93-96
Shortest processing time, 383
Shortest-route problem, 252-258
   linear programming formulation, 252-253
   solution method, 254-258
Short selling, 310
Simmons, D. M., 321
Simon, H. A., 19, 401
Simplex method, 107-157
   maximization, 108-119
   minimization, 119-124
   review, 123
   transportation model, 168-170
Simulation, 371-398, 514-515
   design considerations, 398-399
   estimation of probability distributions, 388-393
   initial conditions, 393-394
   Monte Carlo, 372-384
   queuing, 372-384
   random number assignment, 375-377
   reasons for use, 371-372
   sample size, 394-398
   variance estimation, 396-397
Sirson, R. L., 400
Slack variable, 108, 120, 122
   postoptimality analysis, 148
Smith, B. E., 19
Smith, K. R., 507
Smith, W. L., 361
Solution procedures, characteristics of, 54, 56
Spivey, W. A., 98, 157, 202
Stancer-Minasian, I. M., 507
Standard form, primal problem, 132
Starr, M. K., 38, 60
State probabilities, derivation, 341-344, 367-369
States of nature, 9, 43
Stationary probabilities, 471
Stationary state probabilities, 468
Stationary transition probabilities, 466, 480
Statistical analysis, 479, 514
Steady state, 342, 352, 381, 468
Stepping-stone method, 170-189
   compare to MODI, 194-195
Stochastic process, 467
Strum, J. E., 98, 157, 202
Surplus variable, 120
   postoptimality analysis, 148

Tableau format, linear programming, 110
Taha, H. A., 241
Tardiness, 383
Technical coefficient, 111, 116
 postoptimality analysis, 146, 149-150
 transportation model, 169
Teickroew, D., 322
Thompson, H. E., 507
Thore, S., 507
Thrall, R. M., 98, 157, 202
Total differential, 305
Traffic density, 344, 346
Transition probabilities, 465, 466, 468, 469, 474
Transportation model, 167-202
 complementary slackness, 191
 degeneracy, 199-201
 dual formulation, 189-191
 dual variables, 189-190
 dummy column, 197
 dummy row, 197
 general formulation, 167-168
 initial solutions, 174-180
 initial tableau, 173
 loop concept, 182-187
 maximization problems, 198-199
 MODI method, 189-195
 net contribution, 182-186, 193
 Northwest corner method, 174-177, 195
 opportunity cost, 198
 optimality criterion, 198
 pivot variable, 180-186
 properties of, 167-170
 rim conditions, 174, 195
 shadow prices, 190
 simplex method, 168-170
 stepping-stone method, 170-189
 unacceptable allocations, 197-198
 unequal supply and demands, 196-197
 Vogel's approximation method (VAM), 177-180, 195-196
Trauth, C. A., 241
Tucker, A. W., 322
Turnovsky, S. J., 507
Two-stage line on programming, 490-498

first-stage, second-stage, 491, 493, 494

Unbounded solution, linear programming, 136-138
Understock costs, 456
Unit vector, 111, 120
Upper-bound constraints, 119
 dual, 130
 postoptimality analysis, 148
"Upper plus" function, 473
Utility, 31, 295
Utility function, multiple objectives, 152

Value iteration, 437
Van de Panne, C., 508
Variable:
 artificial, 110, 120-122
 basic, 110-111, 114
 binary, 216-217
 dual, 127-128
 nonbasic, 110, 112
 pivot, 113, 117, 122-123, 225
 primal, 127
 random, 49-50
 slack, 108, 120, 122
 surplus, 120
 unbounded, 138
Vector, linear programming, 111
Vogel's approximation method (VAM), 177-180, 195-196

Wagner, H. M., 19, 98, 157, 202, 241, 278, 439, 481
Waiting time distribution, 346, 348, 356
 multiple-channel, single-phase, 348, 356
 single-channel, single-phase, 346, 356
Weingartner, H. M., 241
Wets, M. J., 507
Whitehouse, G. E., 278
Whitin, T. M., 439, 481
Wood, D. E., 241
Woolsey, R. E., 241

Yen, J. Y., 279

Zero-one variables, 216-217